WORD BIBLICAL COMMENTARY

WORD BIBLICAL COMMENTARY

VOLUME 24

Isaiah 1-33

JOHN D.W. WATTS

WORD BOOKS, PUBLISHER • WACO, TEXAS

Word Biblical Commentary
ISAIAH 1–33

Library of Congress Cataloging in Publication Data
Main entry under title:

Word biblical commentary.

Includes bibliographies.
1. Bible—Commentaries—Collected works.
BS491.2.W67 220.7′7 81–71768
ISBN 0–8499–0223–1 (vol. 24) AACR2

Printed in the United States of America

 The author's own translation of the text appears in italic type under the heading "Translation."

9 10 11 12 — 03 02 01 00 99

To
Hans Wildberger
Teacher, colleague, and "pace-setter"

Contents

Author's Preface

First, dear reader, a word to you. My often crudely literal translations of this magnificent literature are a poor way to introduce you to the polished literary art, the insightful vision, and penetrating truth of Isaiah's *Vision.* But it seems the best thing to do. I hope it opens to you the doors of understanding that it has opened to me.

Appreciation is in order for the basic books which make work of this kind possible. BDB and GKC are still indispensable foundations in lexicography and grammar. No one has yet found the way to bring newer insights of Northwest Semitic Grammar into handbook form to replace them. The excellent recent texts from which we work, *BHS,* Rahlfs and Ziegler's LXX, now with the new Jerusalem Bible's text, deserve our acclaim and thanks. To these must be added the dictionaries, atlases, histories, commentaries, and monographs that are cited.

The monumental commentary by Hans Wildberger, to whom this volume is dedicated, has summarized the critical analysis and comment of more than a century of historical critical study. I have made extensive use of its textual notes, and to a lesser degree its form-critical analyses. Because his work takes a very different literary approach to the book, much of the other excellent material in his and other commentaries has not received the notice that it should. The reader is referred to it (hopefully in an English translation soon), to Clements, and to Kaiser for help in tracking the origins and roots of the Isaianic literature which the work of the last century has traced so thoroughly. To my father, J. Wash Watts, to whom the second volume will be dedicated, must go my thanks for an introduction to the study of the Hebrew Scriptures and for the insights that all such study must look for teaching about God. And to my son, James W. Watts, my father's namesake, who has progressed to a point in his studies at which he can share in this enterprise, my thanks for his careful work in preparing the manuscript for the printer. To Professor Leslie A. Allen and President David A. Hubbard, my gratitude is recorded for their careful reading of the full manuscript and the many suggestions which improve the work in many ways.

And to students and colleagues who have shared various stages of the way toward this book, my appreciation and gratitude. Students at Fuller and Southern have endured lectures that "tried out" fledgling ideas for this work and then produced discussion and papers that have added to and corrected much of it. Those who have produced dissertations are recognized in the bibliographies and notes. I have reluctantly passed over such recognition for most others in the interest of limiting references to those that the reader can find and use. I am grateful to my colleague, J. J. Owens, for permission to use the manuscript of his *Maphteah on Isaiah* which has saved much time in finding words and forms in the lexica, and to all others who spoke encouragingly after hearing papers in SBL and IBR concerning the first steps in this project.

It has been both a surprise and an encouragement to find how many are walking parallel paths to mine in seeking a better understanding of this great book. The work of the late William Brownlee, of Avraham Gileadi, of Roy Melugin, and of W. H. Irwin is only a part of a common movement toward the attempt to establish the wholeness and meaningfulness of the book. It is a privilege to walk with them and hopefully to add a little something to what they have done.

The list of those whose support has made possible this work, the typists, family members, seminary administrations, and librarians, grows far too long to be listed individually. But they are no less important and appreciated.

Most of all, gratitude must be given to God who has granted life and health, a relatively peaceful time to work, and life-long opportunities to learn among His people. His is the center of this Vision and He imparts through it a knowledge of Himself, of His work, of His counsel, and of the immeasurable patience with which He continues through the generations, even to our own, to work out His will with peoples who are more rebellious than willing, more blind that seeing, more deaf than hearing, more self-willed than understanding. But in His determined strategy He pursues the goal of founding the new city to which the peoples of the earth may come, all who are meek and lowly of mind, to worship the Living God who teaches truth, who gives life, and who upholds justice and righteousness.

If through this work a door is opened to someone to see God in Isaiah's Vision, it will have achieved its goal.

JOHN D. W. WATTS

Louisville, Kentucky
Spring 1984

Editorial Preface

The launching of the *Word Biblical Commentary* brings to fulfillment an enterprise of several years' planning. The publishers and the members of the editorial board met in 1977 to explore the possibility of a new commentary on the books of the Bible that would incorporate several distinctive features. Prospective readers of these volumes are entitled to know what such features were intended to be; whether the aims of the commentary have been fully achieved time alone will tell.

First, we have tried to cast a wide net to include as contributors a number of scholars from around the world who not only share our aims, but are in the main engaged in the ministry of teaching in university, college, and seminary. They represent a rich diversity of denominational allegiance. The broad stance of our contributors can rightly be called evangelical, and this term is to be understood in its positive, historic sense of a commitment to scripture as divine revelation, and to the truth and power of the Christian gospel.

Then, the commentaries in our series are all commissioned and written for the purpose of inclusion in the *Word Biblical Commentary*. Unlike several of our distinguished counterparts in the field of commentary writing, there are no translated works, originally written in a non-English language. Also, our commentators were asked to prepare their own rendering of the original biblical text and to use those languages as the basis of their own comments and exegesis. What may be claimed as distinctive with this series is that it is based on the biblical languages, yet it seeks to make the technical and scholarly approach to a theological understanding of scripture understandable by—and useful to—the fledgling student, the working minister as well as to colleagues in the guild of professional scholars and teachers.

Finally, a word must be said about the format of the series. The layout in clearly defined sections has been consciously devised to assist readers at different levels. Those wishing to learn about the textual witnesses on which the translation is offered are invited to consult the section headed "Notes." If the readers' concern is with the state of modern scholarship on any given portion of scripture, then they should turn to the sections on "Bibliography" and "Form/Structure/Setting." For a clear exposition of the passage's meaning and its relevance to the ongoing biblical revelation, the "Comment" and concluding "Explanation" are designed expressly to meet that need. There is therefore something for everyone who may pick up and use these volumes.

If these aims come anywhere near realization, the intention of the editors will have been met, and the labor of our team of contributors rewarded.

General Editors: *David A. Hubbard*
Glenn W. Barker †
Old Testament: *John D. W. Watts*
New Testament: *Ralph P. Martin*

Abbreviations

Periodicals, Serials, and Reference Works

AAASH	*Acta Antiqua Academicae Scientiarum Hungaricae*
AASOR	*Annual of the American Schools of Oriental Research*
AB	Anchor Bible
AcOr	*Acta orientalia*
AfO	*Archiv für Orientforschung*
AfOBeiheft	Beihefte zür Archiv für Orientforschung
AJSL	*American Journal of Semitic Languages and Literature*
AnBib	Analecta Biblica
ANEP	*Ancient Near East in Pictures,* ed. J. B. Pritchard (Princeton: Princeton U. P., 1954)
ANET	*Ancient Near Eastern Texts,* ed. J. B. Pritchard (Princeton: Princeton U. P., 1950)
AnOr	Analecta orientalia
ANVAO	*Avhandlingar utgitt av Det Norske Videnskaps-Akademi i Oslo*
AOT	*Altorientalische Texte und Bilder,* ed. H. Gressman (Tübingen: Mohr, 1909)
APOT	*Apocrypha and Pseudepigrapha of the Old Testament,* ed. R. H. Charles (Oxford: Clarendon, 1913)
ArOr	*Archiv orientálni*
ARW	*Archiv für Religionswissenschaft*
AsSeign	*Assemblées du Seigneur*
ASTI	*Annual of the Swedish Theological Institute*
ATA	*Alttestamentliche Abhandlungen*
ATANT	Abhandlungen zur Theologie des Alten un Neuen Testaments
ATR	*Anglican Theological Review*
AuS	G. H. Dalmon, *Arbeit und Sitte in Palästina,* 1928– (reprint, Hildesheim: G. Olms, 1964)
AusBR	*Australian Biblical Review*
ÄZ	*Zeitschrift für ägyptische Sprache und Altertumskunde*
BA	*Biblical Archaeologist*
BAG	W. Bauer, W. F. Arndt, and F. W. Gingrich, *Greek-English Lexicon of the New Testament* (Chicago: Chicago U. P., 1957)
BASOR	*Bulletin of the American Schools of Oriental Research*
BAT	Die Botschaft des Alten Testaments
Bauer-Leander	H. Bauer and P. Leander, *Historische Grammatik der hebräischen Sprache des Alten Testaments* (Halle: Niemeyer, 1922; reprint, Hildesheim: Olms, 1962)
BBB	Bonner biblische Beiträge

BBC	*Broadman Bible Commentary*
BDB	F. Brown, S. R. Driver, and C. A. Briggs, *Hebrew and English Lexicon of the Old Testament* (London: Oxford U. P., 1907)
BeO	*Bibbia e oriente*
BEvT	Beiträge zur evangelischen Theologie
BFCT	Beiträge zur Förderung christlicher Theologie
BHH	*Biblisch-Historisches Handwörterbuch,* ed. B. Reicke and L. Rost, 4 vols. (Göttingen: Vandenhoeck & Ruprecht, 1962–79)
BHK	*Biblia Hebraica,* ed. R. Kittel, 3rd ed. (Stuttgart: Württ. Bibelanstalt, 1937)
BHS	*Biblia Hebraica Stuttgartensia,* ed. K. Elliger and W. Rudolph (Stuttgart: Deutsche Bibelstiftung, 1967)
Bib	*Biblica*
BibOr	Biblica et Orientalia
BibS(N)	Biblische Studien, Neukirchen, 1951–
BKAT	Biblischer Kommentar Altes Testament
BMik	*Beth Mikra*
BN	*Biblische Notizen*
BR	*Biblical Research*
BRL	K. Galling, *Biblisches Reallexikon* (Tübingen: Mohr, 1937)
Br. *Synt.*	C. Brockelmann, *Hebräische Syntax* (Neukirchen: K. Moers, 1956)
BSac	*Bibliotheca Sacra*
BSO(A)S	*Bulletin of the School of Oriental (and African) Studies*
BT	*The Bible Translator*
BTB	*Biblical Theology Bulletin*
BWANT	Beiträge zur Wissenschaft vom Alten und Neuen Testament
BZ	*Biblische Zeitschrift*
BZAW	Beihefte zur *ZAW*
CAH	*Cambridge Ancient History* (Cambridge: U. P., 1925)
CB	*Cultura biblica*
CBC	Cambridge Biblical Commentary
CBib	The Cambridge Bible
CBQ	*Catholic Biblical Quarterly*
CBQMS	*CBQ* Monograph Series
CHAL	W. L. Holladay, *Concise Hebrew and Aramaic Lexicon* (Grand Rapids: Eerdmans, 1971)
ConB	Coniectanea biblica
CQR	*Church Quarterly Review*
CTom	*Ciencia Tomista,* Salamanca
CVC	*Communio Verbum Caro*
DBSup	*Dictionaire de la Bible, Supplement*
DOTT	*Documents from Old Testament Times,* ed. D. W. Thomas (London: T. Nelson, 1958)

DTT	*Dansk teologisk tidsskrift*
EAEHL	*The Encyclopedia of Archaeological Excavations in the Holy Land,* ed. M. Avi-Yonah, 4 vols. (London: Oxford U. P., 1975)
EglT	*Église et Théologie*
EncJud	*Encyclopedia judaica*
EnsMikr	אנציקלופדיה מקראית, Jerusalem
EphMar	*Ephemerides Mariologicae*
EstBib	*Estudios Biblicos*
EstEcl	*Estudios Eclesiasticos*
ETL	*Ephemerides Theologicae Lovanienses*
ETR	*Etudes theologiques et religieuses*
EvQ	*Evangelical Quarterly*
EvT	*Evangelische Theologie*
ExpTim	*Expository Times*
FRLANT	Forschungen zur Religion und Literatur des Alten und Neuen Testaments
FuF	*Forschungen und Fortschritte*
GB	*Gesenius' Hebräisches und Aramäisches Handwörterbuch,* ed. F. P. W. Buhl (Berlin: Springer Verlag, 1915)
GKC	*Gesenius' Hebrew Grammar,* ed. E. Kautzsch; tr. A. E. Cowley; 2nd ed. (Oxford: Clarendon, 1910)
GSAT	G. von Rad, *Gesammelte Studien zum Alten Testament,* ThB 8 (Munich: Kaiser, 1958)
GTTOT	J. Simons, *The Geographical and Topographical Texts of the Old Testament* (Leiden: E. J. Brill, 1959)
HALAT	W. Baumgartner, *Hebräisches und aramäisches Lexikon zum Alten Testament,* rev. 3rd ed. of KB (Leiden: E. J. Brill, 1967)
HAT	Handbuch zum Alten Testament
HI	J. Bright, *A History of Israel,* 3rd ed. (Philadelphia: Westminster, 1981)
HKAT	Handkommentar zum Alten Testament
HSMS	Harvard Semitic Monograph Series
HTR	*Harvard Theological Review*
HUCA	*Hebrew Union College Annual*
IB	*Interpreter's Bible*
IBR	Institute for Biblical Research
ICC	International Critical Commentary
IDB	*Interpreter's Dictionary of the Bible,* ed. G. A. Buttrick, 4 vols. (Nashville: Abingdon, 1962)
IDBSup	Supplementary volume to *IDB,* ed. K. Crim (Nashville: Abingdon, 1976)
IEJ	*Israel Exploration Journal*
IER	*Irish Ecclesiastical Record*
IJH	*Israelite and Judean History,* ed. J. H. Hayes and J. M. Miller (Philadelphia: Westminster, 1977)
Int	*Interpretation*

IOTS	B. S. Childs, *Introduction to the Old Testament as Scripture* (Philadelphia: Fortress, 1979)
ISBE	*International Standard Bible Encyclopedia,* ed. G. W. Bromiley, 2 vols. (incomplete) (Grand Rapids: Eerdmans, 1979, 1982)
JAOS	*Journal of the American Oriental Society*
JBL	*Journal of Biblical Literature*
JBR	*Journal of Bible and Religion*
JCS	*Journal of Cuneiform Studies*
Jes.Erl.	K. F. R. Budde, *Jesaja's Erleben* (Gotha: L. Klotz, 1928)
JETS	*Journal of the Evangelical Theological Society*
JNES	*Journal of Near Eastern Studies*
JNWSL	*Journal of Northwest Semitic Languages*
JQR	*Jewish Quarterly Review*
JSOT	*Journal for the Study of the Old Testament*
JSOTSup	*JSOT* Supplement
JSS	*Journal of Semitic Studies*
JTS	*Journal of Theological Studies*
Joüon	P. P. Joüon, *Grammaire de l'Hebreu Biblique* (Rome: Pont. Bib. Inst., 1947)
KAT	Kommentar zum Alten Testament
KB	L. Koehler and W. Baumgartner, *Lexicon in veteris testamenti libros* (Leiden: E. J. Brill, 1951–53)
KD	*Kerygma und Dogma*
KHC	Kurzer Hand-Commentar zum Alten Testament
KS	A. Alt, *Kleine Schriften zur Geschichte des Volkes Israel,* 2 vols. (Munich: C. H. Beck'sche, 1953)
LBBC	Layman's Bible Book Commentary
LD	Lectio divina
Leš	*Lešonénu*
Löw	I. Löw, *Die Flora der Juden,* 4 vols. (Wien/Leipzig: R. Löwit, 1924–34)
LQ	*Lutheran Quarterly*
LR	*Lutherische Rundschau*
MBA	Y. Aharoni and M. Avi-Yonah, *Macmillan Bible Atlas,* 2nd ed. (New York: Macmillan, 1977)
MGWJ	*Monatschrift für Geschichte und Wissenschaft des Judentums*
MIO	*Mitteilungen des Instituts für Orientforschung*
MTZ	*Münchener theologische Zeitschrift*
Mut. Nom.	Philo, *De mutatione nominum*
NC	*La Nouvelle Clio*
NCBC	New Century Bible Commentary
NedTTs	*Nederlands theologisch tijdschrift*
NICOT	New International Commentary on the Old Testament
NorTT	*Norsk Teologisk Tidsskrift*
NThSt	*Nieuwe theologische Studien*
NRT	*Nouvelle Revue Theologique*
NTS	*New Testament Studies*

OLZ	*Orientalische Literaturzeitung*
Or	*Orientalia*
OrAnt	*Oriens antiquus*
OTFC	*Old Testament Form Criticism,* ed. J. H. Hayes (San Antonio, TX: Trinity U. P., 1974)
OTL	Old Testament Library
OTS	*Oudtestamentische Studiën*
OTT	G. von Rad, *Old Testament Theology,* tr. D. M. G. Stalker (New York: Harper, 1962–65)
OTWSAP	*Die Ou Testamentiese Werkgemeenskap in Suid-Afrika,* Pretoria
PEQ	*Palestinian Exploration Quarterly*
POS	Pretoria Oriental Series
POTT	*People of Old Testament Times,* ed. D. J. Wiseman (London: Oxford U. P., 1973)
PSB	*The Princeton Seminary Bulletin*
PW	*Pauly's Real-encyclopädie der classischen Altertumswissenschaft,* new ed., G. Wissowa (Stuttgart: J. B. Metzler, 1894–19)
RB	*Revue Biblique*
RCB	*Revista de cultura biblica*
REJ	*Revue des études juives*
ResQ	*Restoration Quarterly*
RevExp	*Review and Expositor*
*RGG*³	*Die Religion in Geschichte und Gegenwart,* ed. K. Galling, 3rd ed., 6 vols. (Tübingen: Mohr, 1957–65)
RHPR	*Revue d'histoire et de philosophie religieuses*
RHR	*Revue de l'histoire des religions*
RivB	*Rivista biblica*
RocTKan	*Roczniki Teologiczno-Kanoniczne*
RSR	*Recherches de science religieuse*
RTR	*Reformed Theological Review*
SBFLA	*Studii biblici franciscani liber annuus*
SBLMS	Society for Biblical Literature Monograph Series
SBS	Stuttgarter Bibelstudien
SBT	Studies in Biblical Theology
ScEs	*Science et esprit*
Scr	Scripture
ScrHier	Scripta Hierosolymitana
SEÅ	*Svensk exegetisk årsbok*
Sef	*Sefarad*
Sem	*Semitica*
SJT	*Scottish Journal of Theology*
SNVAO	Skrifter utgitt av Det Norske Videnskaps-Akademie i Oslo
SPCK	Society for the Propagation of Christian Knowledge
Spfdr	*The Springfielder*
ST	*Studia theologica*
STDJ	Studies on the Texts of the Desert of Judah
STU	Schweizerische theologische Umschau

StG	Studium Generale
SWJT	*Southwestern Journal of Theology*
TBC	Torch Bible Commentaries
TBT	*The Bible Today*
TD	*Theology Digest*
TDNT	*Theological Dictionary of the New Testament,* ed. G. Kittel and G. Friedrich; tr. G. W. Bromiley; 10 vols. (Grand Rapids: Eerdmans, 1964–74)
TDOT	*Theological Dictionary of the Old Testament,* ed. G. J. Botterweck and H. Ringgren; tr. D. E. Green; 4 vols. (Grand Rapids: Eerdmans, 1974–)
THAT	*Theologische Handwörterbuch zum Alten Testament,* ed. E. Jenni and C. Westermann, 2 vols. (Munich/Zürich, 1971)
ThB	Theologische Bücherei
TLZ	*Theologische Literaturzeitung*
TOTC	Tyndale Old Testament Commentaries
TQ	*Theologische Quartalschrift*
TRev	*Theologische Revue*
TRu	*Theologische Rundschau*
TSK	*Theologische Studien und Kritiken*
TTS	Trierer theologische Studien
TTZ	*Trierer theologische Zeitschrift*
TWAT	*Theologisches Wörterbuch zum Alten Testament,* ed. G. J. Botterweck and H. Ringgren, 4 vols (incomplete) (Stuttgart: Kohlhammer, 1973–)
TynBul	*Tyndale Bulletin*
TZ	*Theologische Zeitschrift*
UF	*Ugaritische Forschungen*
UUÄ	Uppsala universitetsärsskrift
VD	*Verbum domini*
VG	C. Brockelmann, *Grundriss der vergleichenden Grammatik der semitischen Sprachen,* 2 vols. (Berlin/New York: Lemcke & Buechner, 1908–15)
VT	*Vetus Testamentum*
VTSup	*VT* Supplements
WB	J. Aistleitner, *Wörterbuch der ugaritischen Sprache* (Berlin: Akademie-Verlag, 1963)
WC	Westminster Commentaries
WMANT	Wissenschaftliche Monographien zum Alten und Neuen Testament
WO	*Die Welt des Orients*
WTJ	*Westminster Theological Journal*
WZKM	*Wiener Zeitschrift für die Kunde des Morgenlandes*
ZAW	*Zeitschrift für die alttestamentliche Wissenschaft*
ZBK	Zürcher Bibelkommentare
ZDMG	*Zeitschrift der deutschen morgenländischen Gesellschaft*
ZDPV	*Zeitschrift der deutschen Palastina-Vereins*
ZKT	*Zeitschrift für katholische Theologie*

ZRGG	*Zeitschrift für Religions- und Geistesgeschichte*
ZS	*Zeitschrift für Semitistik*
ZTK	*Zeitschrift für Theologie und Kirche*
ZWT	*Zeitschrift für wissenschaftliche Theologie*

HEBREW GRAMMAR

abs	absolute	impf	imperfect
acc	accusative	impv	imperative
act	active	ind	indicative
adv acc	adverbial accusative	inf	infinitive
aor	aorist	juss	jussive
c	common	masc	masculine
consec	consecutive	niph	niphal
constr	construct	pass	passive
fem	feminine	pf	perfect
fut	future	pilp	pilpel
hiph	hiphil	pl	plural
hith	hithpael	ptcp	participle
hoph	hophal	sg	singular

TEXTUAL NOTES

'A	Aquila
Akk	Akkadian
Amor	Amorite
Arab	Arabic
Aram	Aramaic
B	MT MS, edited by Jacob ben Chayim, Venice (1524/25)
C	MT MS, Cairo Codex of the prophets
Copt	Coptic
DSS^{Isa}	Dead Sea Scroll of Isaiah = 1QIsa^{a}
Egy	Egyptian
Eth	Ethiopic
Gr.	Greek
Heb.	Hebrew
K	Kethibh
L	MT MS, Leningrad Codex
LXX	Septuagint
LXX^{A}	LXX MS, Alexandrian Codex
LXX^{B}	LXX MS, Vatican Codex
LXX^{Q}	LXX MS, Marchalian Codex
LXX^{S*}	LXX MS, Sinai Codex, original reading
LXX^{SC}	LXX MS, Sinai Codex, corrector
MT	Masoretic Text
Q	Qere
1QM	*Milhāmāh,* the War Scroll, from Qumran Cave 1
1QIsa^{a}	The St. Mark's Isaiah Scroll from Qumran Cave 1 = DSS^{Isa}
1QIsa^{b}	The Hebrew University Isaiah Scroll from Qumran Cave 1 = DSS^{Isab}
4QpIsa^{c}	*Pesher* on Isaiah from Qumran Cave 4
Syh	Syrohexaplaris
Syr	Syriac
Tg	Targum
Ug/Ugar	Ugaritic
Vg	Vulgate
Θ	Theodotian
Σ	Symmachus

Biblical and Apocryphal Books

Gen	Genesis
Exod	Exodus
Lev	Leviticus
Num	Numbers
Deut	Deuteronomy
Josh	Joshua
Judg	Judges
Ruth	Ruth
1–2 Sam	1–2 Samuel
1–2 Kgs	1–2 Kings
1–2 Chr	1–2 Chronicles
Ezra	Ezra
Neh	Nehemiah
Esth	Esther
Job	Job
Ps(s)	Psalm(s)
Prov	Proverbs
Eccl	Ecclesiastes
Cant	Canticles, Song of Solomon
Isa	Isaiah
Jer	Jeremiah
Lam	Lamentations
Ezek	Ezekiel
Dan	Daniel
Hos	Hosea
Joel	Joel
Amos	Amos
Obad	Obadiah
Jonah	Jonah
Mic	Micah
Nah	Nahum
Hab	Habakkuk
Zeph	Zephaniah
Hag	Haggai
Zech	Zechariah
Mal	Malachi
Sir	Ecclesiasticus or The Wisdom of Jesus son of Sirach
Matt	Matthew
John	John
Acts	Acts
Rom	Romans
Phil	Philippians
Heb	Hebrews
Rev	Revelation

Miscellaneous

ANE	Ancient Near East
AV	Authorized Version
B.C.	Before Christ
chap(s).	chapter(s)
cols.	columns
diss.	dissertation
Dtr	Deuteronomist
E	East
ed(s).	edition; edited by; editor(s)
esp.	especially
ET	English translation
EV(V)	English verse(s)
FS	Festschrift
hap. leg.	*hapax legomenon*
JB	*Jerusalem Bible*
JPSA	Jewish Publication Society of America Version
lit.	literally
LLS	*Los Libros Sagrados*
MS(S)	manuscript(s)
n.	note
NAB	*New American Bible*
NE	Northeast
NEB	*New English Bible*
NIV	*New International Version*
NJV	*New Jewish Version*
NT	New Testament
NW	Northwest
OT	Old Testament
p.	page
RSV	*Revised Standard Version*
S	South
tr.	translated; translator
U. P.	University Press
v(v)	verse(s)
W	West
§	section/paragraph
√	root

Introduction

The primary goal of this commentary is to present an interpretation of the Book of Isaiah. Hans Wildberger (vii) notes that it was clear to him from the beginning of his work on Isaiah that what was finally paramount was the interpretation of the book as it now exists. In spite of the invaluable worth of his commentary in summarizing and evaluating all the results of historical-critical research to date, it does not succeed in presenting an understandable interpretation of the book. He has followed the method of historical exegesis, and his work presents the tremendous results of that method. But it does not make the book come alive for the reader or student.

I think his example demonstrates that it is not possible to mix the two methods. This commentary will recognize the vast literature of research on the pre-history of the traditions and the text in the *Bibliographies,* in the *Introduction,* and, as far as the study of the text itself is concerned, in the *Notes.* Where form criticism's definitions of "genre" can be used in a literature that no longer follows their dictates, these, too, have been noted and used. But from that point on the commentary has made no effort to enter discussions of source-, form-, or redaction-criticism. For these the reader is referred to current introductions or commentaries, preeminently Wildberger's great work.

Bibliographies have been assembled to provide the reader access to literature on the passage or subject at hand. They are listed whether or not they have been used by the author or cited in this commentary. The reader will find a more complete review and evaluation of the literature in Wildberger's work.

Translations are deliberately literal to give the reader a starting point for understanding the Hebrew idiom. The metrical notation is not, and cannot be, definitive. It is intended to convey the general poetic pattern of parallelism.

Notes deal with textual variations and explain the reasons for translations. In Isaiah there are many *hapax legomena,* words that occur only once in the Bible, so that the need to explain word meanings is immense. Grammatical explanations that will help the student translator are also included.

Form/Structure/Setting sections draw on form-critical and redactional studies where applicable. They have analyzed sections to find the literary genre and to show other evidences of the shape of the compositions that may aid understanding and exposition. Throughout the discussion, the reader will find more structural analyses showing the use of an arch form than traditional outlines.

Comment sections deal with the meanings of words or of a verse or two at a time, providing information that may add to the reader's understanding. Sometimes this leads into word-studies that relate the use of a word in a verse to its use in the larger work or even in the OT as a whole. Occasionally an *Excursus* is used to give a more complete discussion of a pertinent subject.

Explanation sections attempt to pull together the insights from the earlier sections to show what a passage as a whole is about and what it means in the context of the Vision.

Because the Vision genre has been understood to be like drama, the translation is here presented in that form. The larger sections are called "acts" while the smaller ones are "scenes," which in turn contain "episodes." Suggested designations of speakers, found at the left of the translation, serve also to note the limits of the speeches.

In keeping with the reader-oriented approach, introductions to acts and scenes provide background information helpful for understanding the dialogue and the setting for the action.

I have assumed a date of completion, *ca.* 435 B.C., which is late enough to include all the historical references in the book within a present or past perspective to the "author" and which lets the text itself explicitly indicate the places where Isaiah is to be identified and heard. My aim is to keep in focus the nature of the book: a Vision that dramatically portrays God's view of history, rather than a source book from which the historian is to piece together his view of what happened during that time. I hope to recapture the grand view of God's design which the book's sweeping presentation of history through twelve generations was intended to give to a generation so badly in need of direction. By looking to the past, like a yachtsman watching his wake in the water, one can see that God's events have moved in a straight line, while succeeding generations have attempted in vain to follow a different course. The assumption is that God's course continues in a straight line established by Isaiah's messages some 300 years before, but that current leaders like those of past generations are insisting on trying to set a different course.

The book of Isaiah is explicit in pointing to datable events (chap. 7, 734 B.C.; chap. 20, 714–712 B.C.; chaps. 45–46, 540 B.C.; chap. 63, *ca.* 435 B.C.); these move forward chronologically and accurately. Chaps. 36–39 are quoted from 2 Kgs and are an exception. The superscription (1:1) provides the starting point and relates clearly to 6:1; chap. 7; 14:28; chap. 20; and chaps. 36–39—the reign of eighth-century Judean kings and the activity of Isaiah. The chronological movement (including chaps. 45–46) clearly indicates a scope broader than Isaiah's lifetime, yet the superscription for the book requires a substantial conformity to the vision and the words of Isaiah of the eighth century.

I suggest that the book provides exactly that. It establishes the essentials of that vision in 2:1–4, in 7:1–8:18 and in 20:1–6, including specific words (in addition to the quoted accounts and words in chaps. 36–39). It then traces the basic reactions of royal policy to that message through three eighth-century reigns, continuing reigns in the seventh and early sixth centuries, and in five exilic and post-exilic generations, and finally in the contemporary generation.

The book proclaims that Isaiah in the eighth century revealed Yahweh's decisions and strategy concerning Israel, Judah, and the empires. It claims that Yahweh's strategy has not varied through that period and that Isaiah's words continued to be valid in 435 B.C., i.e., that Yahweh has sent the imperial power to serve his purposes and that Israel/Judah's role must be assessed accordingly. That role (from the eighth century onward) no longer included the Davidic vision of world rule. Israel and Judah were called to a passive political acceptance of imperial rule (from Assyrian to Persian). Active attempts to reassert Davidic suzerainty had been and would be repelled by

Yahweh's authority. Israel's/Judah's positive role was to conform to Isaiah's vision (2:1–4) of Jerusalem as a pilgrimage center for all nations. The book further envisions a servant role for the Jews of the dispersion, and for Jerusalem and its inhabitants, with a role offered to other peoples (principally in Palestine) who sought Yahweh and wanted to serve him.

Yet the Vision recognizes that the generations that practiced Isaiah's vision of passive political acceptance have in fact been few (Ahaz and Manasseh) and despised, and even they showed no inclination to make Jerusalem a pure sanctuary for Yahweh's presence and their worship of him. The Vision traces a melancholy recital of rejection for Yahweh's "strategy" and of consequent failure for Israel and Judah. And it expects no change in its own day (chap. 65).

This alternative interpretation of God's relation to history (*ca.* 750–435 B.C.) merits our attention. Its witness to God's sovereign decision to "change the game plan" in the mid-eighth century, to end the charade of a divided kingdom which purported to serve his purpose and to continue his covenant, coincides with the prophetic messages of Hosea and Amos. But the book's presentation of God's plan, "his strategy" that replaced the older one, is unique, and it needs to be heard again and again. There are strong reasons for its insistence that the change of political climate in Palestine which brought the entire area under the more or less consistent imperial rule of Assyrians, Babylonians, Persians (and eventually Hellenists and Romans) was Yahweh's doing; that he intended not only to punish his people but to accomplish his own historical goals in which Israel had failed; and that he had a vital but very different continuing role for his people, a role more in keeping with their Abrahamic election than its Mosaic formulation.

WHO WAS ISAIAH?

Isaiah was a prophet who lived and worked in Jerusalem from about 750 to 700 B.C. All that is known of him is contained in a few passages of the book that bears his name.

Isaiah is said to have worked under four Judaean Kings (1:1): Uzziah, Jotham, Ahaz, and Hezekiah. A marvelous picture of the future of Jerusalem (2:1–4) and a chilling description of Babylon's fall (13:1–22) are directly attributed to him.

He and his son Shear-Yashub carried God's message to Ahaz about 734 B.C. (7:1–17). Another son bore a shatteringly symbolic name, *Maher-shalal-hash-baz* "Swift-plunder hastening-booty" (8:1–4). Isaiah was divinely commissioned to walk about Jerusalem unclothed as a walking sign of God's displeasure with Jerusalem's pro-Egyptian policies (*ca.* 714 B.C. chap. 20). And he prophesied Jerusalem's deliverance from Sennacherib's siege in 701 B.C. (chaps. 36–37 = 2 Kgs 18:13–19:37), was a witness of Hezekiah's recovery from a mortal illness (chap. 38 = 2 Kgs 20:1–11), and delivered the Lord's condemnation of Hezekiah's hospitality for Merodach-Baladan's delegation from Babylon (chap. 39 = 2 Kgs 20:12–19).

This is virtually all that the Bible knows about Isaiah, son of Amoz, unless the heroes of faith "sawed in two" (Heb 11:37) refer to a later tradition recorded in the apocryphal *The Ascension of Isaiah* (trans. by R. H. Charles, *APOT,* 155–62) that Isaiah suffered martyrdom under Manasseh.

ISAIAH THE PROPHET AND HIS SUCCESSORS

The advent of the historical study of Scripture raised questions about sources behind the canonical book of Isaiah. Against the background of assumed authorship by Isaiah, son of Amoz, in the eighth century, the concern was one of later accretions or additions to his work.

An obvious beginning lay in noting the use in chaps. 36–39 of the relevant material from 2 Kgs 18:13, 17–20:19. The differences in the two accounts are very minor. The composer of the Vision has carefully chosen the material from 2 Kings that suited his purpose. The history, of which 2 Kings is a part, continues through the destruction of Jerusalem in 587 B.C. and contains a final note on the accession of Amel-Marduk in 562 B.C. It was presumably completed soon after that and was known both in the dispersion and in Jerusalem. The composer of the Vision would have had no trouble extracting the relevant material that was useful to him.

The suggestion of J. C. Döderlein (*Esaias,* Aldorf, 1775) which was anticipated by Ibn Ezra (1100), that chaps. 40–66 must have been written in the Exile and restoration periods, has found almost unanimous acceptance among critical scholars.

Bernhard Duhm (*Das Buch Jesaja,* HAT [Tübingen: Vandenhoek and Ruprecht, 1892, 1922]) refined the theory by suggesting a third body of material, chaps. 56–66, which he understood to derive from the returned community in Palestine. Opinion on this has been less unified (cf. J. Vermeylen, *Du Prophète Isaie a l'apocalyptique* II [Paris: Gabalda, 1978] 451–54). In the first thirty-five chapters of the book, various collections and groups have been isolated, and scholars from Budde to Mowinckel and Fohrer have attempted to show how they were brought together and organized (cf. Vermeylen, 1–31).

Attempts to trace a history of prophetic tradition in the book include those of D. R. Jones, "The Tradition of the Oracles of Isaiah of Jerusalem," *ZAW* 67 (1955) 226–46; and J. H. Eaton, "The Origin of the Book of Isaiah," *VT* 9 (1959) 138–57. These see the book in terms of the gradual growth of material around a core of Isaiah tradition. J. Becker (*Isaias—Der Prophet und sein Buch* [Stuttgart: Verlag Katholisches Bibelwerk, 1968]) and H. Barth (*Israel und das Assyrerreich in den nichtjesianischen Texten des Protojesajabuches,* diss. Hamburg 1974 = *Die Jesaja Worte in der Josiazeit,* WMANT 48 [Neukirchen-Vluyn: Neukirchener Verlag, 1977]) have used redaction criticism to trace the history and form of the material. W. L. Holladay (*Isaiah: Scroll of a Prophetic Heritage* [Grand Rapids: Eerdmans, 1978]) has written a very readable summary of this view. Part of the goal in all this research was to gain an historically verifiable picture of the prophet himself. A recent new attempt is that by Gilbert Brunet (*Essai sur l'Isaïe de l'Histoire* [Paris: Picard, 1975]). He has concentrated his efforts on chaps. 7, 8, and 22. M. A. Sweeney (*Isaiah 1–4 and the Post-Exilic Understanding of the Isaianic Tradition,* diss. Claremont, 1983) continues that research.

Another part of this monumental effort has tried to gain a clear historical understanding of the nature of Israelite prophecy in the eighth and seventh centuries. Such works have supported studies of the psychology and phenomena of prophecy by Hölscher and Mowinckel.

The bibliography on these is enormous. The reader who seeks a more complete bibliography should see Wildberger (pp. 1714–38) and G. Fohrer, "Neue Literatur zur alttestamentlichen Prophetic (1961–70)," *TRu* 45 (1980) 1–39, 108–15. The *Commentary* lists the full bibliographic material only once and tries not to duplicate listings. The reader may use the *Index of Principal Authors* to find that listing.

The Role of Isaiah in the Vision

Isaiah's prophecy and prophetic ministry inspired the book and are the heart of its structure. This is acknowledged in the title (1:1) and documented by inclusion in chaps. 36–39 of the entire Isaiah narrative from 2 Kgs 18–19.

The role of Isaiah is anchored in his prophecy concerning Jerusalem's future (2:2–4), which is given a special notice in 2:1 calling attention to Isaiah's claim to this vision report. This view of the future shapes the attitude of chaps. 40–66 and culminates in a description of the fulfillment of the vision by the creative act of God (65:17–66:24).

Isaiah's active role in the reign of Ahaz is portrayed in chaps. 7–8, in which he provides hope for the monarchy even through those changing times. He retires from active ministry (8:16–18) before the scene portrays the celebration of the royal birth (chap. 9) and the picture of the future, spirit-endowed ruler, city, and nation in chaps. 11–12.

The prophet emerges from his retirement in 714 B.C. to demonstrate prophetically to the young King Hezekiah the folly of joining an Egyptian coalition of states rebelling against Assyria (chap. 20).

Another key element in the Vision concerns Babylon. The initial announcement (chap. 13) is again credited to Isaiah by the title (13:1), just as a later word from the account in 2 Kings related Isaiah to a strong word about Babylon (chap. 39).

The Vision does not again portray Isaiah's role in the events of 701 B.C. which were told in 2 Kgs 18–19 and repeated in Isa 36–39. Instead, the ideas, motifs, and thrust of those chapters dominate the composition of the entire book. The book presents Isaiah and his words (2:2–4; 7:1–8:18; chap. 13; chap. 20; and chaps. 36–39) as the core and inspiration of the Vision that has been composed around them. It is no wonder, therefore, that first-person accounts throughout the book, from chap. 6 to 50:4–9 and 61:1–3, have been heard as words from the prophet, although the Vision does not identify them as such.

WHAT IS ISAIAH?

Isaiah is a book called *The Vision of Isaiah, the Son of Amoz.* It has 66 chapters, contains all the information known about the prophet, and works it into a much larger literary complex. It bears witness to Yahweh's plan and dialogue with his people through some three centuries of their history, beginning with the decades in which Isaiah lived. Through twelve generations (one for each act), the Vision provides a divine perspective on the history of Israel and Judah through speeches by Yahweh himself and by his nonhuman representatives. It also records the responses of God's people in each generation.

Although prophetic traditions, written and oral, were incorporated into the book, there is no evidence that any part circulated as a book prior to the production of the whole. "As far as can be ascertained, only one prophecy of Isaiah existed, however scholars finally may succeed in getting from Isaiah of Jerusalem to the canonical book that bears his name" (W. S. LaSor, D. A. Hubbard, F. W. Bush, *Old Testament Survey* [Grand Rapids: Eerdmans, 1982] 378). "In light of the present shape of the book of Isaiah the question must be seriously raised if the material of Second Isaiah in fact ever circulated in Israel apart from its being connected to an earlier form of First Isaiah" (B. S. Childs, *IOTS*, 329).

Isaiah is portrayed as a prophet who looked with equanimity upon the violent political changes of his day because Yahweh was in charge and was making things work out for good. Isaiah advocated policies that accepted vassalage to Assyria for Ahaz (7:1–8) and for Hezekiah (chap. 20), in contrast to the activist politics of independence espoused by the ministers of Uzziah, Jotham, and Hezekiah. He witnessed to God's promises concerning Jerusalem (2:1–4; chaps. 36–37) and urged the kings to give God an opportunity to fulfill them without their manipulations.

Then the Vision moves well beyond the specific traditions about the prophet to portray God's plan and policies concerning Israel, Judah, and Jerusalem. It traces these through twelve generations and realistically presents Judah's post-exilic life under Persian rule as God's purposed plan for his people. It portrays God's judgment over Israel in 750–735 B.C. (chaps. 1–6) and 733–721 B.C. (chaps. 7–10), but continues to speak about Israel's destiny throughout the book to chap. 64. It pictures Jerusalem's sins in chaps. 1 and 3, but sees a vision of a future Jerusalem free of these faults and open to all peoples who seek the Lord (2:1–4; *passim* and 65:17–66:24). It traces the policies of Judean kings and governments (chaps. 7, 22, 28–33), but also describes the vision of God's plan which drew Assyria into Palestine (chaps. 18–19), and which later brought Cyrus from Persia to rebuild Jerusalem and the Temple (chaps. 45–46).

The Vision is realistic in portraying the political situation. But it also lifts realism to a higher dimension by claiming that God has a goal beyond "what is" that can be achieved if met by faith (chaps. 11–12, 19, 24–27, 41–48, 49–54, 55–59). The achievement of God's goals was frustrated in each instance by the failure of God's own people in Israel, Judah, and Jerusalem to see, hear, and believe (chaps. 7, 20–22, 30–33, 48, 50, 63–65). In the Vision the pagans, Assyria and Persia, march at God's command. Only Israel/Jerusalem is recalcitrant, rebellious, and self-willed.

The important point to notice here is Israel's refusal to heed God's call to assume a "servant role." To accept this call would have meant forgoing the claim to political independence and power which had now been delegated to the empires. But Israel was too proud and spirited for that. She had her full share of the natural human drive called "pride" which is universally applauded. God, however, does not applaud. He calls this grounds for total judgment and destruction (2:5–22). Israel and Jerusalem, "like the nations," prefer to follow human ideals so they, "like the nations," run the risk of God's wrath.

God's patience and persistence in pursuing his goals for Israel are pictured here. Through twelve generations he pleads for faith and yielding obedience, for insight and willing attentiveness. But to the very end leaders in Jerusalem prove unable or unwilling to respond to his call (65:1–16).

The structures and forms of society and religion change. It is foolish to presume that any one of these is eternal. But God's promises and the goals that they presuppose are as unchanging as God's own character. They include God's search for a people capable of blessing humanity (Abraham), a covenant people committed to the worship of God and to holy life (Moses; cf. Exodus, Numbers, Deuteronomy), a kingdom in which God is King (David; cf. 2 Sam 7; Ps 110). The Vision shows God's acts in the life of his people and in the world of the eighth to the fifth centuries to be consistent with these goals.

But the failure of the elect and the called to see God's vision, to hear God's voice, and to rise above human goals of pride, striving, and independence adds a tragic dimension to the Vision. To the bitter end a large proportion of the people cling to their version of the past as the only acceptable pattern for their present and their future. They demand that God conform to their concept of what his plans ought to be (chaps. 62–64) and thus preclude themselves from participation in God's new creation (chap. 65). The parallel to Jonah is unmistakable.

When the New Testament records that the majority of Jews of that day refused to accept Jesus as God's Son or the Cross as their oblation, it adds one more chapter to the history traced by *The Vision of Isaiah.* The Vision also had its predecessors in the books of Kings, Judges, and Numbers. One wonders at the patience of God and the stubbornness of humanity and prays "O God, be merciful to me, a sinner!"

The Book's First Audience/Readers

To ascertain who the intended audience/readers were is perforce to assign a date and place of writing as well as to have some idea of the author/composer/editor. To find these answers for the completed book it is best to look to the last acts, chaps. 60–66. There is no doubt that these are addressed to people in Jerusalem. From the first address in chap. 60 (specifically 60:14) to the picture of the newly created city, the chapters address Jerusalem.

The date is more difficult to determine. The very chronological progress of the book has brought the action to the Persian period. But specific historical references after the approach of Cyrus in chap. 46 are scarce. One exception, in 63:1–6, seems to refer to the destruction of Edom as a current or recent event, but no historical data exist to place this exactly. Yet, whereas Edom usually appears in all references to Judah's neighbors, neither Ezra nor Nehemiah mentions it. This suggests that by mid-fifth century B.C. Edom had disappeared (cf. J. R. Bartlett, "Moabites and Edomites," *POTT* 243; M. Weippert, *Edom,* diss. Tübingen, 1971; J. D. W. Watts, *Obadiah* [Grand Rapids: Eerdmans, 1969] 18) and thus indicates a date for the Vision in the third quarter of the fifth century B.C. Artaxerxes' ascension to the throne in Persia in 465 B.C. may have added another incentive for such writing in an age when every change of leadership was perceived by activist groups to be an opportune time for rebellion.

We will, therefore, assume a first audience in Jerusalem in about 435 B.C. for the *Vision of Isaiah.* But what can be known about people in Jerusalem about 435 B.C.?

K. Pauritsch (*Die Neue Gemeinde,* Jesaja 60–66, AnBib 47 [Rome: Biblical Institute Press, 1971] 24–30) has shown that the chapters address a divided congregation. Opposing parties and opinions are found throughout the book. Pro-Assyrian and pro-Egyptian parties have had roles in chaps. 1–39. The role of parties in post-exilic Palestinian life has been reported by M. Smith (*Palestinian Parties and Politics that Shaped the Old Testament* [New York: Columbia U. Press, 1971]) and P. Hanson (*The Dawn of Apocalyptic* [Philadelphia: Fortress, 1975] 79–185).

The audience/readers for the book are those gathered in Jerusalem, but it undoubtedly addresses the fragmented factions of Judaism from all parts of the Near East whose representatives may well have been in Jerusalem on pilgrimage. By 435 B.C. Judaism was just beginning to find a rallying point. There was no king. Jerusalem was still largely in ruins and the new temple had been a disappointment. Jews were scattered through the length and breadth of the Empire.

Parties and their leaders competed for attention. The elements to which they appealed included: (1) the people of the land who had stayed in (or moved into) the land or the city during the time since the Exile (Smith [107] thinks of them as basically syncretistic in religion); (2) the exiles in foreign homes and those who had returned to Palestine or Jerusalem (Smith [107] speaks of them as a "Yahweh only" group, while Hanson [209] identifies the author of Isa 60–65 and the prophetic group with these); (3) the Priests, including Levites, who were an influential and important group as Ezra's list of returnees shows (Ezra 2:36–39; Neh 7:39–42: they belonged to the Zadokite group that had staffed the pre-exilic Temple); (4) the Davidic governors (as well as the governors of neighboring districts such as Samaria, Ammon, Qeden, Dedan, etc., and their supporters; cf. F. M. Cross, "A Reconstruction of the Judean Restoration," *JBL* 94 [1975] 4–18 = *Int* 29 [1975] 187–203).

In such a setting the parties would have been active in representing every facet of Jewish concerns. The priests, the monarchists, the syncretists in Egypt (at Elephantine) and in Palestine, the apocalyptic zealots, and the wise would each have had their advocates. Regionalism as well as factions within regions would have played their parts. This is the diverse audience/readership that the Vision of Isaiah has in view. It speaks to their issues, repudiating some, advocating others, and modifying still others.

It has been customary to note a major change in the role of the prophet in the eighth century B.C. (most recently J. Holladay, "Assyrian Statecraft and the Prophets of Israel," *HTR* 63 [1970] 31). D. L. Petersen (*Late Israelite*

Prophecy, SBLMS 23 [Missoula, MT: Scholars Press, 1977] 5) points to a second major change in the sixth century B.C. in which classical Israelite prophecy was replaced by another kind of prophecy. Not only the message was different, but the medium shifted to a form of written prophecy representing groups that participated in the life and struggles of their times. The "theological streams" represented by these groups have been variously identified by four writers. O. Plöger (*Theocracy and Eschatology,* tr. S. Rudman [Richmond: John Knox, 1968]) thinks of two groups: the eschatologists and the theocratic party. M. Smith (*Palestinian Parties*) suggests that the two groups represented a syncretist group and a Yahweh-only party. O. Steck ("Das Problem theologischen Strömungen in nachexilischer Zeit," *EvT* 28 [1968] 447–48) identified four theological streams: the priestly-theocratic, wisdom, prophetic-eschatological, and Levitical-Deuteronomistic. P. Hanson (*The Dawn of Apocalyptic,* 95–96) sees a conflict between prophetic-visionary groups and the hierocracy. The Vision of Isaiah came into existence in such a sharply divided community (cf. R. R. Wilson, *Prophecy and Society in Ancient Israel* [Philadelphia: Fortress, 1980] esp. 292).

What were these issues? They involved the bedrock questions of what Judaism was and should become. They turned on the nature and role of Jerusalem, of the *Golah,* "the dispersion" in Babylon, Egypt, and elsewhere, and of the people of the land in Judah and former Israelite territories. They related to the means that would be used to achieve these goals and the unity of the Jewish people. (One should keep in mind that neither Ezra nor Nehemiah had appeared on the scene. The foundation that they laid brief decades later was not yet in place. The Vision has little use for the priestly solutions, but it affirms the central role of the Temple.)

The Vision speaks to these issues. The author may be identified in the persecuted minority addressed in 66:5–6, the humble and contrite who seek Yahweh, wait on the Lord, and tremble at his word. The opposition may be seen in 66:5b–d and heard in 62:1–12 and 63:11–64:12, as well as many other places in the book.

The author and the group he represents in 435 B.C. trace in the Vision an ancestry of faith and belief back to Isaiah, the eighth-century prophet (7:1–14), to the exilic word of 40:31, and to the post-exilic preacher of 55:1–6. They identified themselves with the prophet of chaps. 8 and 20 as well as with the exilic "servant" of chaps. 42–48, the suffering Jerusalemite "servant" of chaps. 49, 50, and 53, the called community of "servants" in 55:1–6, and with the "servant" of 61:1–4.

The Vision of Isaiah presents the following views of that group:

1) A new era under God had begun (new creation), marked by the Assyrian-Babylonian conquests which destroyed the old order and by the rise of the Persian Empire which made a new order possible.

2) Instead of the tribal confederacy or the kingdoms of the old order, God's people would rally around Zion, the city where Yahweh dwells, and they would come as pilgrims from all the earth to worship there and be taught God's word (Torah). This great testament of faith is truly a vision of the City of God. It records God's search for a people to inhabit his city.

3) Israel should recognize Persian power as God's way for her and should

oppose any move against Persia; it should say nothing that might offend Persian authorities.

4) Sacrificial worship, the demand for God's intervention, and the secret practice of pagan cults stand condemned.

The Vision avoids direct mention of the priests who are prime aspirants for power in Jerusalem. However, it eliminates other potential candidates by showing how they failed in the opportunity God provided them. They included representatives of old Israel, heirs of the house of David, the representatives of the exiles, the representatives of old Jerusalemite power, the nations around Israel, and the "new" Israelites.

The author has Yahweh address these apostates directly in chap. 65 to summarize the message of the book. The major objection to the apostates and to past history was their unwillingness to heed and follow Yahweh's will and course. Sometimes that involved obedience to law, justice, and commitment to exclusive worship, sometimes to faithful waiting (chap. 7), sometimes to readiness to march (chaps. 40–48), and sometimes to acceptance of suffering (chaps. 49–54). Contemporary leadership was still trying to shape its own destiny in terms of Messianic Zionism (chap. 62) or apocalyptic hopes based on Mosaic imperialism (63:15–64:11). Both of these repeated the errors of the past and could only expect the same judgment on these errors.

Yahweh continued to search for an attentive, responsive people, faithful to himself and obedient to his will. That people, and that people only, would share with Yahweh the right to live in joy, peace, and safety in Zion, the city of God.

The foregoing was, in essence, what its first audience would have heard from this book, all 66 chapters of it. The one who composed the response to the apostates in 65:1–16 is likely the one responsible for collecting, editing, and writing the Vision. He deserves to stand among the greatest of the prophetic writers. And we don't even know his name.

The Book's Composition: Starting Point, Materials, Goals, and Methods

The Vision displays many signs of thoughtful composition. The specific allusion to datable events moves in a straight line from the list of eighth-century kings through the approach of Cyrus and the destruction of Edom, with one exception: chaps. 36–39. The book touches virtually every important event from the eighth century to the fifth century, with one exception: the destruction of Jerusalem and the beginning of the Exile. Any attempt to reconstruct the way this book came to be formed confronts those two basic anomalies, for everything else can be fitted into a compositional pattern.

If, as suggested above, the writer/composer/editor of the book lived in the mid-fifth century B.C., the attempt to reconstruct the process must turn around him. Some of the issues and characteristics of his time and of his group have been sketched above.

One may assume, on the basis of the best of historical-literary research, that his generation was heir to literary and oral tradition (cf. W. L. Holladay, *Isaiah: Scroll of a Prophetic Heritage* [Grand Rapids: Eerdmans, 1978]). The finished writings that were generally available to it must have included what we now call the Deuteronomic History (Josh–2 Kgs) and the prophetic books of Jeremiah and Ezekiel. The first of these traced Israelite/Judaean history to the destruction of Jerusalem (587 B.C.), while the other two deal narrowly with the decades that precede and follow that event. The Vision and its audience must have had these writings in view. Many other traditions from ancient Israel and Judah would also have been current in both oral and written forms, and the author and his group would certainly have been cognizant of these. They would have included prophetic narratives of many kinds. (The Book of the Twelve includes writings contemporary with the completion of Isaiah and thus, as a book, does not belong to this heritage, although parts of it would, as tradition. Ezra was yet to bring the Pentateuch to its dominant position in Judaism, thus it, too, is not included here, though much of its contents would have been known in many circles.)

The Vision is obviously aware of the Deuteronomic History since it quotes a large portion of it (chaps. 36–39 = 2 Kgs 18:13–20:19), but it disagrees with much in the deuteronomic context. It studiously avoids the period that Jeremiah and Ezekiel record, although it takes issue with their views on worship and the political future. And it uses bits of prophetic tradition related to Isaiah that are not recorded elsewhere (chaps. 7–8 and 20). (It may use much more which our data does not allow us to identify.) It credits another portion (2:1–4) to Isaiah, which the Book of the Twelve assigns to Micah (4:1–3).

The fifth-century author and his group were attracted to the story about Isaiah in 2 Kgs 18–20. They recognized, as modern scholarship does, a discrepancy in viewpoint between the story of Isaiah and Hezekiah in 2 Kgs 18:13–20:19 and the editor's hero-worshiping eulogy of Hezekiah, his era, and his policies which preceded in 18:1–12. They lifted out the older account and made it the centerpiece of their book.

They then gathered from available prophetic traditions other materials about Isaiah (found now in Isa 7–8 and 20). They also found in prophetic traditions the vision of the new temple and the new city that fit their own dreams and what they sensed Isaiah's view had been.

They conceived the overarching concept that the course of events since the eighth century conformed to Yahweh's general purpose. He had brought the empires to do his will, and this represented a totally different strategy on God's part, introducing a new era, a new age. The breach between the ages could be likened to the Flood and the time of Noah. God had determined this by the time the Assyrians marched on Palestine in the mid-eighth century.

They were most concerned about the roles of Israel and Judah in this new age. They were convinced that God had a role for each in conformity with his commitment to them in the past. But they were equally convinced that his obligation under covenant was no longer valid and that the shape of the new roles would be radically different.

They were also concerned about the role of humankind in these changes, for they held that Yahweh is the only real God, the creator of all things and the Lord of history. They understood that man's inherent pride and ambition bring him into conflict with Yahweh's claim to authority, with predictable results (chap. 2), and that part of Israel/Jerusalem's problem lay in its determination to be proud and ambitious like the nations.

The author was close to those who produced the Book of the Twelve and used the same historical knowledge and formulas in his superscription. They also shared the artistic use of prophetic literary genre.

In this way, then, the Vision was developed in ten acts, plus a prologue and an epilogue, each representing approximate generations not unlike the ten generations from Adam to Noah in Genesis or the other uses of ten generations (cf. G. E. Mendenhall, *The Tenth Generation* [Baltimore: Johns Hopkins U. Press, 1973] 215–30). The quotation from 2 Kings fills the larger part of the sixth act assigned to the beginning of the Exile. The last act speaks directly of the author's own generation.

Whether the Vision was originally intended to be presented orally by a troup of players/speakers is difficult to determine. J. H. Eaton (*Festal Drama in Deutero-Isaiah* [London: SPCK, 1979]) has proposed that chaps. 40–66 be considered festal drama. The nature of the material makes such most fitting. The staging of drama in Greece was well advanced by this time. Perhaps the dearth of testimony to such practices in Israel can be traced to Ezra's rigid imposition of puritanlike restrictions of religious expression in Israel. The understanding of the Vision and its contemporary presentation may be considerably enhanced by using multiple speakers to speak the different parts. This commentary will follow the practice of indicating the limits of these speeches. The suggestions concerning the identity of speakers in many cases represent only the commentator's use of imagination, which the readers may do for themselves.

THE TEXT OF ISAIAH

Bibliography

(An exhaustive bibliography is found in Wildberger, pp. 1718–23.)

Masoretic Text (MT)—Hebrew

Thomas, D. Winton, ed. *Liber Jesaiae. Biblia Hebraica Stuttgartensia.* Stuttgart: Deutsche Bibelstiftung, 1967. **Goshen-Gottstein, M. H.,** ed. *The Book of Isaiah,* Part I & II. The Hebrew University Bible. Jerusalem: Magnes Press, 1975.

Septuagint: (LXX or G)—Greek

Rahlfs, A., ed. *Septuaginta* II. 9th ed. Stuttgart: Württembergische Bibelanstalt, 1935. **Ziegler, J.,** ed. *Isaias.* Septuaginta. Vetus Testamentum Graecum Auctoritate Academiae Scientiarium Gottingensis 14, 3rd ed. Göttingen: Vandenhoeck & Ruprecht, 1983.

Targum (Tg)—Aramaic

Sperber, A., ed. *The Bible in Aramaic.* III. The Latter Prophets According to Targum Jonathan. Leiden: Brill, 1962. **Stenning, J. F.,** ed. and tr., *The Targum of Isaiah.* Oxford: Clarendon Press, 1949.

Dead Sea Scrolls—Hebrew

Burrows, M., ed. *The Dead Sea Scrolls of St. Mark's Monastery.* I. *The Isaiah Manuscript and the Habakkuk Commentary.* New Haven: ASOR, 1950. Hereafter designated DSS^{Isa} = $IQIsa^{a}$. ———. *The Dead Sea Scrolls of the Hebrew University,* 1955. Designated $IQIsa^{b}$.

Vulgate (Vg)—Latin

Weber, O., ed. *Biblia Sacra iuxta vulgatem versionem* II. Stuttgart: Württembergische Bibelanstalt, 1969. For other versions the most available text is **Field, F.** *Origenis Hexaplorum quae supersunt* II. Oxford: Oxford U. P., 1875, reprinted 1964.

Isaiah is read in numerous translations in modern and ancient languages. The oldest translation is undoubtedly the Greek (G) known as the Septuagint (LXX). Early fourth century A.D. manuscripts are kept in London and the Vatican. Excellent critical editions are available.

But Isaiah was written in Hebrew. The best work of editing and transcribing Hebrew manuscripts was done by scribes called Masoretes of the ben Asher family in Tiberius (MT). A beautiful and accurate manuscript prepared by Moshe ben Asher in A.D. 1009 is kept in the Museum of Leningrad. It has been published in Kittel's *Biblia Hebraica* (*BHK*, the third edition, edited by R. Kittel himself [Stuttgart: Wurtt. Bibelanstalt, 1929]), and in the *Biblia Hebraica Stuttgartensia* (*BHS*). D. W. Thomas edited the book of Isaiah (1968). This text is used in the *Commentary.* The so-called Aleppo Codex prepared by Aaron ben Asher in the early tenth century has been published in facsimile as *The Aleppo Codex,* ed. M. H. Goshen-Gottstein (Jerusalem: Magnes Press, 1976), and *The Book of Isaiah* I & II, The Hebrew University Bible (Jerusalem: Magnes Press, 1975). The British and Foreign Bible Society's Hebrew Bible is based on another ben Asher text kept in Madrid.

The oldest Hebrew text of Isaiah is on a leather scroll found in Qumran and now kept in Jerusalem. It is thought to have been copied in about 100 B.C. and is here designated DSS^{Isa}. Important variations from MT are shown in *BHS.* A second scroll from Qumran is that of the Hebrew University. When it is cited it will be designated $IQIsa^{b}$.

The targums (Tg) are early Jewish commentaries on the Hebrew text but written in Aramaic.

The Vulgate (Vg) is the official Latin version. It has recently appeared in a new edition by O. Weber.

Other early versions are still most accessible to the student in Field's *Hexapla.*

Isaiah, then, is a book which we have in ancient manuscripts of the first century B.C. and of the fourth and tenth centuries A.D. In all these it represents one of the books of the prophets in Holy Scripture. In the Greek version it appears as the first of the major prophetic books after the minor prophets. In Hebrew it is the first of the latter prophets before the books of poetry.

Isaiah's Influence in Early Judaism and the New Testament

Isaiah's position as the first of the Prophetic books in the *Tanak* and in the Christian Bible indicates something of the esteem accorded it. The frequency with which it is mentioned in ancient literature and with which it appears among the Dead Sea Scrolls is further witness to its popularity and influence.

Josephus (*Complete Works,* tr. W. Whiston [Grand Rapids: Kregel, 1960]) follows his interest in history in quoting from historical sections of Isaiah. The Mishnah has repeated references which testify to the influence of the prophecy there. An early Christian apocalypse, *The Ascension of Isaiah,* is the only extant witness to an earlier Jewish work called *The Martyrdom of Isaiah,* which develops a legend about the death of Isaiah at the hands of Manasseh. It shows many affinities to the Qumran writings and may date from this time. Heb 11:37 seems to refer to it.

The NT quotes from some fifty-seven different passages in Isaiah. Philo and the Apostolic Fathers refer to him often. The Dead Sea Scrolls from Qumran refer to Isaiah and Deuteronomy more than any other books.

Isaiah's Influence in Judaism, Church History, and Western Literature

The Book of Isaiah has been fortunate in its translations. The renderings in Greek, Latin, English, and other languages have to a large extent conveyed a great deal of the literary excellence, the imaginative power, and theological appeal of the book.

Isaiah has been recognized as "prince of prophets." This reflects his walk with kings, but even more, the excellence of the book which bears his name.

Jews have found in Isaiah a model of the best that Judaism aspires to, in nobility of vision, faith, and life. Christians have found here a book and a person that fit the picture of faith most closely related to Jesus and the NT ideal.

Scholarly commentaries are chronicled elsewhere in this *Introduction.* They show the continuing theological interest that Isaiah has elicited.

The architecture of the world's cathedrals has repeatedly recognized Isaiah among the saints of old, worthy to stand with Moses and David as a symbolic representation of the work of God.

The Vision has left its mark on Western art through paintings like Edward Hicks's "The Peaceable Kingdom," and it has inspired poets like Lord Byron ("When the Assyrian came down like a wolf on the fold/his cohorts all shining in purple and gold") and Matthew Arnold, who arranged its chapters for his pupils to use in learning proper English style. S. Goldman (*The Book of Books, an Introduction* [New York: Harper & Bros., 1948] 8) evaluates its literary worth: "With respect to excellence of style, no page of the *Iliad,* to take one instance of many, need blush before any page of Isaiah."

Its interpretation has also been a point of controversy between Jews and Christians. Jewish interpreters have tended to object to the Christian understanding of 7:14 as a prophecy of the Virgin Birth and chap. 53 as a prophecy of a suffering Messiah (cf. S. R. Driver and A. Neubauer, *The Fifty-third Chapter of Isaiah according to the Jewish Interpreters,* 2 vols. [Oxford and London: Oxford U. Press, 1876/77]).

Isaiah has held his place among the reform prophets during the more recent interest in prophets as reformers, although Amos is famed as foremost in that respect. The modern understanding of chaps. 24–27 as belonging to apocalyptic genre has given the book the distinction of containing the first apocalyptic writings.

In all these ways Isaiah, man and book, has been honored as prince of prophets and premier prophetic book in religious and literary circles alike. E. G. Kraeling (*The Old Testament since the Reformation* [New York: Harper & Bros., 1955]) cites Isaiah fifty-four times in discussing the views of theologians and philosophers toward the OT.

The music of ancient as well as modern times has drawn from Isaiah's sonorous lines. Handel's *Messiah* takes its text from Isaiah rather than the New Testament. Countless hymns and anthems repeat its lines.

In the liturgies of Western churches, readings from Isa 7, 9, and 11 are prominent at Advent and Christmas, while chap. 53 is prominent on Good Friday. Chap. 1 is a classic text on true and false worship. Chap. 40 is a model essay for hope, while chap. 55 is a favorite for evangelistic outreach.

Isaiah in the English Bible

Isaiah has always held an honored place in the English Bible. In Protestant Bibles it is the first of the books of prophecy after the books of poetry. It is presented in the excellent translations of the AV, RSV, NIV, and many others. Its relevant messianic passages are read and sung at Christmas and Easter. Chap. 6 is a model of God's call to prophetic ministry, chap. 53 a beautiful forecast of the Crucifixion, and other passages are known for their powerful expressions of hope.

Roman Catholic Bible translations like the English JB and NAB place the book of Isaiah as the first of the prophets, which are the last group of books following the poetic books.

In Jewish Bibles like the NJV, the order of the books follows that of the Hebrew text. Isaiah is the first of the latter prophets, an honored central position in the second most influential group (next to the Pentateuch) of books of the Scriptures. It is read as a powerful warning against apostasy as well as a persuasive proclamation of hope for the people of God.

Isaiah is usually regarded by the Christian as a source of Messianic prophecies. It is important to note, however, that the prophecies in chaps. 9 and 11 are acceptably applied to Christ only when they are interpreted in the light of chaps. 51 and 53. Isaiah's Vision showed that the Davidic image was acceptable to the next age only with substantial revision that changed a triumphant king and ruling nation into a humble servant to God and on God's behalf. The second image is perfectly in keeping with the Gospel's understanding of Jesus the Christ.

But the Vision is important for many other reasons as well. It interprets God's will for an age in which his people live as a dependent minority group under the rule of pagan empires. This is the situation for the incipient Christian church, just as it was for the Jews. The Vision suggests that his people can live out their destiny under such a system without necessarily having to strive for political independence or ascendancy. The importance of this insight for the doctrine of the church is clear.

The Vision also teaches God's control of the forces of history, no matter how great and powerful they are. They, too, are and must be ultimately responsible to God. If they misunderstand their role, as Assyria did, God will bring them to heel. The rule of God over all history is real, even if it is not administered from Jerusalem according to the Davidic pattern of the Psalms.

The Vision agrees with other prophets and the Torah that God's concern for justice overrides his preference for his chosen. No doctrine of election can excuse failure to achieve justice in society.

The Vision insists on God's prerogative to do the new thing. The past is useful in discerning truth and establishing doctrine. God is (and will be) faithful to his commitments. But only God himself can determine what God must do or how he must act. He is no prisoner of the past, as people often tend to be. The NT insists on this prerogative in announcing God's work in Jesus and the new era of the church. Now the church needs to be open to God's next great move in redemption.

The Vision's fundamental picture of the one who can please God and work with him fits modern Judaism's model as well as the NT's picture. The quality of faith, the shape of hope, the patience of obedient faithfulness are still incumbent on the biblical believer.

An Annotated Chronological Bibliography of Commentaries on Isaiah (cited in the *Commentary* by author only)

For a survey of works on Isaiah, see **Young, E. J.** "Appendix II," *The Book of Isaiah* I. NICOT. Grand Rapids: Eerdmans, 1972. 487–99. ———. "The Study of Isaiah Since the Time of Joseph Addison Alexander." *Studies in Isaiah.* London: Tyndale Press, 1955. 9–101.

The church fathers wrote voluminously on Isaiah. Works are listed chronologically, with the date of the book or a date pertaining to the author in parentheses after the author's name. **Tertullianus, Q. S. F.** (d. 220). *Libros de Patientia.* Ed. J. W. Ph. Borleffs. Hagae Comitis: D. A. Daamen, 1948. ———. "Of Patience." *The Ante-Nicene Fathers.* Vol. IV. Tr. S. Thelwell. Buffalo: Christian Literature Publishing Co., 1886. **Origenes** (254). Origen's commentary in thirty books covers the first thirty chapters of Isaiah. Fields, F. *Origenis Hexaplarum quae supersunt,* II. Oxford: Oxford U. Press, 1875. Or *Patrologiae cursus completus.* Series Graeca, vol. 13. Lutetiae Parisiorum: J. P. Migne, 1864. **Cyprianus of Carthage** (258). *Opera Omnia.* 3 vols. Ed. G. Hartel. New York: Johnson Reprint Co., 1965. ———. *Writings.* Tr. R. E. Wallis. Edinburgh: T. & T. Clark, 1869–70. **Eusebius Pamphili of Caesaria** (4th cent.). *Der Jesajakommentar* (Gr.). *Eusebius Werke,* vol. IX. Ed. J. Ziegler. Berlin: Akademie Verlag, 1975. **Basilius the Great of Caesarea** (379). *Commento al profeta Isaia,* (Gr. and Ital. chaps. 1–16 only). Tr. P. Trevisan. Torino: Societa editrice internazionale, 1939. **Tyconius** (*ca.* 383) "Liber de Septem Regulis." *Patrologiae Cursus Completus.* Series Latina, vol. 18. Lutetiae Parisiorum: J. P. Migne, 1864. **Chrysostomus, J.** (407). "Hermeneia" of chaps. 1–8. *Patriologiae Cursus Completus.* Series Graeca, vol. 56. Lutetiae Parisiorum: J. P. Migne, 1864. ———. *Works.* 6 vols. Buffalo: Christian Literature Co., 1889–90. **Hieronymus (Jerome)** (410). *Commentarium in Esiam.* Libri I–XVIII. Turnholti: Brepols, 1968. **Cyrillus of Alexandria** (441). "Commentarius in Isaiam Prophetam." *Patrologiae Cursus Completus.* Series Graeca, vol. 70. Lutetiae Parisiorum: J. P. Migne, 1864. **Theodoretus of Cyrrhus** (457). "Eclogaria Interpretatio in Isaiam." *Patriologiae Cursus Completus.* Series Graeca, vol. 81. Lutetiae Parisiorum: J. P. Migne, 1864. ———. *Kommentar* *zu Jesaia.* Ed. A. Möhle. Berlin: Weidmann, 1932. ———. *The Book of Rules by Tyconius.* Tr. F. C. Burkitt. Cambridge: University Press, 1894.

The Middle Ages belong to Jewish scholars who in Europe, Spain, and North Africa wrote voluminously in Hebrew, Arabic, and Latin. Those who made the greatest contribution concerning Isaiah were: **Ibn Ezra (Abraham ben Meir)** (1090–1164). *Commentary of Ibn Ezra on Isaiah.* Heb. text. Tr. M. Friedlander. 2nd ed. New York: Feldheim, 1966. **Kimchi, David** (1160–1235). *The Commentary of David Kimchi on Isaiah.* (Heb. with introduction in Eng.) Ed. L. Finkelstein. CUOS 19. New York: Columbia U. Press, 1926; reprint, New York: AMS Press, 1966.

The Reformers returned the Church to an emphasis on the Bible including Isaiah: **Luther, Martin** (1528). *Der Prophet Jesaia,* in *D. Martin Luthers Werke.* Kritische Gesamtausgabe, vol. 25. Weimar: 1883. 87–401. ———. *Lectures on Isaiah chs. 1–39* in *Luther's Works.* Vol. 16. Ed. and tr. J. Pelikan and H. C. Oswald. St. Louis: Concordia, 1969. **Zwingli, Ulrich** (1529). *Complanationis Isaiae Prophetae.* Zürich: C. Froschauer, 1529. ———. *Aus Zwinglis Predigten zu Jesaja und Jeremia.* Ed. O. Farner. Zürich: Berichthaus, 1957. **Calvin, Jean** (1551). *Commentarii in Isaiam Prophetam* in his *Opera quae supersunt omnia.* 59 vols. in 26. Brunvigae: C. A. Schwetschke et filium, 1863–1900. ———. *Commentary on the Book of the Prophet Isaiah.* 4 vols. Tr. W. Pringle. Grand Rapids: Eerdmans, 1948.

Comments and shorter notices continue through the eighteenth century (cf. Young, I, 489–90), but commentaries, as such, are few: **Vitringa, Campegius** (1714). *Commentarius in Librum Prophetiarum Jesaiae.* 2nd ed. Basileae: J. R. im Hoff, 1732. **Döderlein, J. C.** (1775). *Esaias, ex recensione textus Hebraei.* Altorfi, 1789.

In the nineteenth century commentaries begin to blossom. Two of the earliest were: **Eichhorn, J. G.** (1819). In *Die hebräischen Propheten.* Göttingen: 1816–19. **Gesenius, W.** (1820). *Der Prophet Jesaia.* Leipzig: F. C. W. Vogel, 1829.

In the middle of the century several excellent conservative commentaries appeared: **Barnes, A.** (1840). *Notes, Critical, Explanatory and Practical on the Book of the Prophet Isaiah.* 2 vols. New and improved ed. New York: Leavitt, 1875. **Alexander, J. A.** (1846). *A Commentary on the Prophecies of Isaiah.* Rev. ed. J. Eadie. Grand Rapids: Zondervan, 1970. **Stier, E. R.** (1850). *Jesaias, Nicht Pseudo-Jesaias,* chaps. 40–66. Barmen: W. Langewiesche, 1850. **Drechsler, M.** (1845–57). *Der Prophet Jesaja.* Berlin: G. Schlawitz, 1865. **Luzzatto, S. D.** (1855). *Commentary on the Book of Isaiah* (Heb.). Tel Aviv: Davir, 1970. **Delitzsch, Franz J.** (1866). *Biblischer Commentar über den Propheten Jesaia.* Leipzig: Dörffling und Frank, 1869. ———. *Biblical Commentaries on the Prophecies of Isaiah.* Tr. J. Martin. Edinburgh: T. & T. Clark, 1910.

The last decade of the nineteenth century inaugurated the age of commentaries written under the discipline of historical criticism and of "first," "second" (and sometimes "third") Isaiah. **Cheyne, T. K.** (1880). *The Book of the Prophet Isaiah.* New York: Dodd, Mead, & Co., 5th ed. 1904. **Smith, G. A.** (1890). *The Book of Isaiah.* 2 vols. The Expositor's Bible. New York: Harper, 1928. **Duhm, B.** (1892). *Das Buch Jesaja.* HKAT 3/1. 5th ed. Göttingen: Vandenhoeck & Ruprecht, 1968. **Skinner, J.** (1896–98). *The Book of the Prophet Isaiah in the Revised Version.* CBib. Cambridge University Press, 1963. **Marti, K.** (1900). *Das Buch Jesaja.* KHC. Tübingen: J. C. B. Mohr, 1900. **Wade, G. W.** (1911). *The Book of the Prophet Isaiah with Introduction and Notes.* WC. 2nd rev. ed. London: Methuen Press, 1929.

By the end of the first decade of the twentieth century, commentators were taking the historical-critical division of the book seriously enough to write of two or three separate and distinct books. Most commentaries used different writers for the two parts. Only a few attempted to cover the whole.

Chapters 1–39:

Gray, G. B. (1912). *A Critical and Exegetical Commentary on the Book of Isaiah I–XXVI.* ICC. New York: T. & T. Clark, 1912. **Boutflower, C.** (1930). *The Book of Isaiah Chapters (I–XXXIX) In the Light of the Assyrian Monuments.* London: SPCK, 1930. **Procksch, O.** (1930). *Jesaia I.* Erste Hälfte: Kapitel 1–39. KAT IX. Leipzig: W. Scholl, 1930. **Scott, R. B. Y.** (1956). "The Book of Isaiah." *IB* 5. New York/Nashville: Abingdon Press (1956) 149–381. **Eichrodt, W.** (1960). *Der Heilige in Israel:* Jesaja 1–12. *Der Herr der Geschichte:* Jesaja 13–23, 28–39. BAT 17/1. Stuttgart: Calwer Verlag, 1960, 1967. **Kaiser, O.** (1960). *Isaiah 1–12. Isaiah 13–39.* Tr. R. A. Wilson. OTL. Philadelphia: Westminster, 1972; 2nd ed., 1983. **Wildberger, H.** (1965–82). *Jesaja 1–12. Jesaja 13–27. Jesaja 28–39.* BKAT 10. Neukirchen-Vluyn: Neukirchener Verlag, 1972, 1978, 1982. **Auvray, P.** (1972). *Isaie 1–39.* SB. Paris: J. Gabalda, 1972. **Herbert, A. S.** (1973). *The Book of the Prophet Isaiah. Chapters 1–39.* CBC. Cambridge: University Press, 1973. **Clements, R. E.** (1980). *Isaiah 1–39.* NCBC. Grand Rapids: Eerdmans, 1980.

Chapters 40–66:

Volz, P. (1932). *Jesaja II.* Zweite Hälfte: 40–66. KAT 10. Leipzig: W. Scholl, 1932. **Muilenburg, J.** (1956). "The Book of Isaiah," *IB* 5. New York/Nashville: Abingdon Press (1956) 382–773. **North, C.** (1964). *The Second Isaiah.* Oxford: Oxford U. P., 1964. **Smart, J. D.** (1965). *History and Theology in Second Isaiah.* A Commentary on Is. 35; 40–66. Philadelphia: Westminster, 1965. **Knight, G. A. F.** (1965). *Deutero-Isaiah:* A Theological Commentary on Isaiah 40–55. New York/Nashville: Abingdon, 1965. **Westermann, C.** (1966). *Isaiah 40–66.* Tr. D. M. G. Stalker. Philadelphia: Westminster, 1969. **McKenzie, J. L.** (1968). *Second Isaiah.* AB 20. Garden City, NY: Doubleday, 1968. **Elliger, K.** (1970). *Jesaja II.* (Complete through 45:7.) BKAT 11. Neukirchen-Vluyn: Neukirchener Verlag, 1978. **Bonnard, P. E.** (1972). *Le Second Isaïe, son disciple et leurs éditeurs.* SB. Paris: J. Gabalda, 1972. **Whybray, R. N.** (1975). *Isaiah 40–66.* NCBC. Grand Rapids: Eerdmans, 1975.

Only a few in this period have written on the entire book of Isaiah: **Kissane, E. J.** (1941–43). *The Book of Isaiah.* 2 vols. Rev. ed. Dublin: Browne and Nolan, 1960. **Steinmann, J.** (1949–55). *Le Prophéte Isaïe.* Paris: Cerf, 1949–55. **Fohrer, G.** (1960–64). *Das Buch Jesaja.* 3 vols. ZBK. Zürich: Zwingli Verlag, 1960–64. **Leslie, E. A.** (1963). *Isaiah.* New York: Abingdon, 1963. **Young, E. J.** (1965–72). *The Book of Isaiah.* 3 vols. NICOT. Grand Rapids: Eerdmans, 1965–72. **Kelley, P. H.** (1971). "Isaiah." *BBC.* Nashville: Broadman, 1971. 149–374. **Butler, T. C.** (1982). *Isaiah.* LBBC 10. Nashville: Broadman, 1982.

An Annotated List of Selected Books and Monographs on Isaiah

For surveys of monographs on Isaiah, see: **Fohrer, G.** "Neue Literatur zur alttestamentlichen Prophetie." *TRu* 45 (1980) 1–39, 108–15. **Wildberger, H.** 1714–38.

The annotated list that follows is given in chronological order from 1905. Monographs on Isaiah 40–66 will be noted in the second volume. Monographs on specific passages or portions are noted in the chapter bibliographies. Those mentioned elsewhere in the *Introduction* are not repeated here. **Wilke, F.** *Jesaja und Assur.* Leipzig: 1905. Reflects the growing knowledge of ancient Mesopotamia and the recognition of its relevance to Isaiah. **Budde, K.** *Jesaja's Erleben. Eine gemeinverständliche Auslegung der Denkschrift des Propheten (Kap. 6:1–9:6).* Gotha: L. Klotz, 1928. Reflects the period's interest in the personal and psychological experiences of the prophet. Continues to be a very influential interpretation of these chapters. **Behr, J. W.** *The Writings of Deutero-Isaiah and the Neo-Babylonian Royal Inscriptions.* Pretoria, South Africa: Rubinstein & Co., 1937. **Wordsworth, W. A.** *En-Roeh. The Prophecies of Isaiah the Seer.* Edinburgh: T. & T. Clark, 1939. **Allis, O. T.** *The Unity of Isaiah.* Philadelphia: Presbyterian and Reformed Pub. Co., 1950. A conservative defense of the book's unity under the authorship of Isaiah of Jerusalem. **Blank, S. H.** *Prophetic Faith in Isaiah.* New York: Harper Bro., 1958. **Fey, R.** *Amos und Jesaja.* WMANT 12. Neukirchen-Vluyn: Neukirchener Verlag, 1963. A comparison that seeks to determine characteristics of eighth-century prophecy. **Calderone, P. J.** *Dynastic Oracle and Suzerainty Treaty.* Manila: Ateneo University, 1966. **Whedbee, J. W.** *Isaiah and Wisdom.* Nashville: Abingdon, 1971. Develops the recognition of Isaiah's relation to the wise. **Vollmer, J.** *Geschichtliche Rückblicke und Motive in der Prophetie des Amos, Hosea, und Jesaja.* BZAW 119. Berlin: De Gruyter, 1971. **Lack, R.** *La Symbolique de Livre d'Isaie. Essai sur l'image literaire comme element de structuralisme.* AnBib 59. Rome: Biblical Institute Press, 1973. **Raday, Y. T.** *The Unity of Isaiah in the Light of Statistical Linguistics.* Hildesheim, 1973. Applies computer data to the issue of unity of Isaiah. **Hoffmann, H. W.** *Die Intention der Verkündigung Jesajas.* BZAW 136. Berlin: De Gruyter, 1974. **Dietrich, W.** *Jesaja und die Politik.* BEvT 74. Munich: Kaiser, 1976. **Huber, F.** *Jahwe, Juda und die anderen Völkern beim Propheten Jesaja.* BZAW 137. Berlin: De Gruyter, 1976. **Gileadi, A.** *A Holistic Structure of the Book of Isaiah.* Diss. Brigham Young University, 1981.

THIS COMMENTARY'S APPROACH TO ISAIAH

Although the present volume is limited to the first thirty-three chapters of Isaiah, the writing could begin only after study of a whole book of sixty-six chapters. It proposes to assign a date for the work that is consistent with the latest historical setting recognized in the book. It will attempt to trace the intent of those who produced this book at that time, the shape they gave it at that time, and the extent to which they brought consistency and unity to its purpose and teaching.

The issues of source criticism, form criticism, and tradition criticism which have sought to trace the prehistory of materials used in this process have been amply treated elsewhere and will not be traced in this work. We will make no effort to distinguish among literary materials which tradition has handed down to the authors (with the obvious exception of chaps. 36–39). The commentary will accept a late date for this process and for the production of the book, which will mean that our work will not conflict with the historical search for sources and origins. We will focus instead on the questions: Why were these gathered and reshaped about 435 B.C. and presented as a complete book? To whom was it presented? And what did the editors/composers/authors try to accomplish by it?

Views concerning authorship should neither enhance nor detract from confidence in the book's inspiration or revelatory value. It is not the reputation of a particular person that gives a book its sacred character. The book is accepted as being inspired, its canonical shape and position showing it to be worthy of its place in Holy Scripture.

The case for literary unity should demonstrate (1) a single purpose that shapes the book; (2) a structure that supports and communicates that purpose; and (3) movement and emphasis that develop that purpose-theme. The artistic concept which shaped and guided the formation is the best proof of unity. We believe that the treatment provided in this commentary does demonstrate these things (see the treatments of "Genre," "Structure," and "Motifs" below).

The commentary will be looking at the Vision of Isaiah as a work of literature presented to a literate people. Although it certainly is the end product of a tradition, we will contend that the process was not automatic. Tradition provided the composers of the Vision with material for their book. But they, not tradition, determined the use to which the material was put and the interpretation it received. The commentary will show that this interpretation in many instances runs counter to the conventional thought of their day and of other biblical literature dealing with those events. It may well be that the Isaiah tradition itself ran counter to the conventional concepts and was thus congenial to the writers. But they, not it, produced the final result.

A historical study of Isaiah of Jerusalem has always had a basic problem. The picture of Isaiah found in 2 Kgs 18–19 (Isa 36–39) and of his message of firm support for Jerusalem's future provides no hint of the bitter criticism of Jerusalem, of Israel, and of the nations that appears in Isa 7–8, and 20. A look at the explicit references in the Vision reveals that what it records are specific traditional reports on Isaiah the prophet (see chaps. 7–8, 20, 36–39). In addition, two passages are claimed for Isaiah by the use of superscriptions (2:1–4, chap. 13; we will argue below that the superscription in 1:1 is a title that makes no claim to authorship).

If one is to postulate an "Isaiah tradition" that claims direct relation to Isaiah of Jerusalem (*ca.* 735–700 B.C.), the foregoing is what one has to work with. Recent study of the Isaiah traditions suggests a growing body of tradition, cultivated by disciples of his "school," which continued through the next century and which provided the background for chaps. 40–66.

This commentary gladly recognizes the existence of such traditions used by the composers of the Vision as their sources. It will make no attempt to distinguish traditional literary material from original literary work of the editors. Such analysis is foreign to its purpose.

The commentary will attempt to understand and interpret the finished product. It will assume that the authors/editors/composers had full creative freedom to pick and choose from the traditional material at their disposal, that they were responsible for its arrangement and the total artistic (and theological) effect. It will be alert to find the threads of meaning, the motifs, etc., that run through the entire work and that reveal their concerns and interpretations.

The commentary will assume that the collection of materials and the artistic design of the Vision was done with the intention of speaking to people contemporary with the authors/editors/composers. In other words, the Vision of Isaiah is presented here as a conscious literary creation—not a collection of traditions that grew "like Topsy." It is not simply the end result of a process of tradition, however much it may be dependent upon knowledge and materials provided by tradition.

The Vision is focused on issues that arise at the time that it is published. Issues from history are used to illuminate and develop the themes, but they are not central to the purpose of the work. The intention of the Vision is not historical, i.e., it does not intend to define and present eighth- and sixth-century issues. Rather, it develops and presents fifth-century issues by presenting materials from eighth-, seventh-, sixth-, and fifth-century settings.

This approach will show that Isaiah is not the main speaker or character in the great Vision. That role belongs to Yahweh God. His speech begins and ends the Vision. Moreover, his speeches are presented throughout, often without benefit of prophetic messenger.

There are other surprises. Although the title speaks of an address to Judah and Jerusalem, the groups addressed throughout the book are Israel and Jerusalem. The theological significance of these names takes precedence over political implications in the title.

The Vision is a book about two ages: "the former times and the latter times." In this, the division into first and second Isaiah makes a germane point. But it is a mistake to assume that these were two different works. The "latter" assumes the "former" and the "former" looks forward to the "latter." The literary shape and structure is of one work, and it can be properly understood only in this way.

The entire work has an "end of the age—new age" quality about it. This is not only true for chaps. 24–27, which are often called "apocalyptic" for this reason, but also for chaps. 5, 10, 13, etc., where the same imagery and vocabulary for total destruction is found. The preoccupation with life and death is further found in chaps. 14, 30, etc. Yet the entire eschatological character has a "realized" quality about it. The fifth century, in which the Vision was produced, was the new age. That is what the Vision is about: a definition of the purposes of God and the assigned roles for Israel and Jerusalem in the new age.

The fragmentation of the book under analytic procedures has obscured this important understanding. The book portrays the end of an age marked by the rise of empires. There are hints in the book that the old age began with Noah, following the flood. It had been an age of cities, of the growth and movements of tribes, and of small states. The Vision implies that the campaigns of Tiglath-Pileser marked an end to that age and that Yahweh claimed credit for the decision to end it.

It further claims that the new age of empires is one in which God still exercises control of governments, calls out his people, establishes standards for conduct, and provides place and occasion for worship. Yet all of these must be radically different from what they were in the previous age. In the new age there is to be no nationhood for his people, Israel; no political authority for his city, Jerusalem; no king, and no land of their own. The key concept in the new age is "servanthood."

The Vision contends that any attempt to play the game by the old rules is doomed to failure because it presumes that God is against the system (empire) when in fact he has brought it to pass and supports it. (Daniel carries the idea forward. Whereas pre-exilic prophets announced God's judgment [control] over the little states of Palestine, Daniel deals with successive empires; and whereas Isaiah deals with Assyria and Persia, Daniel looks beyond Persia to the Hellenistic empires.)

Through the Vision, God calls on Jews to discover their place in his new order rather than harking back nostalgically to the patterns of David and Joshua. In this the book is directly in line with the message of the Twelve Prophets (esp. Joel, Zech 9–14, and Malachi), with Ezra's adaptation of the Torah in reorganizing Temple worship in Jerusalem, and with the Synagogue's interpretation of Torah, Prophets, Psalms, and Wisdom to shape the piety and faith of Judaism.

THE VISION OF ISAIAH *AS LITERATURE*

The approach adopted by this commentary owes much to the insights of the "new literary criticism" which has been extensively applied to narrative literature. It assumes that meaning from the work is to be on "this side of the text," i.e., on the reader's side.

This takes as the watershed the point at which the literary work, more or less as it is, became complete. Historical research looks into the issues related to the far slope of that watershed, tracing the process by which it came to be what it is. Literary study looks at the near slope—from the time the work is complete to the present. It tries to understand how the work has been and is meaningful to its readers or hearers. It is "reader-oriented."

Yet, reader-oriented interpretation should be as deeply planted in history as any author-oriented interpretation. The commentary will therefore identify and describe the first audience, its date, its setting, and its historical concerns. It will continue to identify the succession of historical audiences that have heard this vision to our own day.

Reader-oriented interpretation avoids subjectivity by making the text its basis and by testing its understandings against the text. The connection is made between what the text actually says and what it has been understood to say by successive audiences with their own historically conditioned capacities. As modern readers, we must be aware of the same processes at work in our reading and read in such a way as to identify with the audience implied (or anticipated) by the text itself in order to offset or correct a biased view. A survey of the ways the text has been heard and understood through the centuries adds a further dimension to current interpretation. When one looks at the book as literature, some specific issues are raised.

GENRE

The first issue is that of the specific kind, or genre, of literature before us. The prophetic books of the OT are a literary form *sui generis.* There is nothing else in literature exactly like them, although many of the smaller forms of prophetic speech are kin to those in other cultures. Among the prophetic books, Isaiah and the Book of the Twelve are different from Jeremiah and Ezekiel, but a thorough analysis of these literary differences remains to be done.

Isaiah's title calls the book a חזון "vision," a term that also occurs in the superscriptions of Obadiah and Nahum. The verb חזה "to envision" also occurs in Isaiah's title, but it is used with other genre designations in 2:1 and other books. חזה appears to be a unifying term related to the prophetic literature of Isaiah and the Twelve, which used the terms חזון "vision," דבר "word(s)," and משא "burden" for these prophetic genre. All three of the latter terms appear in superscriptions in Isaiah.

חזון must be defined by what is actually found in the literature to which it is attached. As the superscription applies to the Book of Isaiah, the content and character of the book will define "vision" as a genre.

In vision literature, the person of the prophet falls into the background. Yahweh becomes the dominant speaker, and the dominant sub-form is that of the Yahweh speech. His speeches are supported and amplified by others, but the speakers are seldom identified. They are understood to be Yahweh's aides, whether these are taken as members of his heavenly court or as prophets.

The Vision, because it consists of successive speeches by different persons (specifically some by Yahweh and some by someone else; see C. E. Crosby's forthcoming dissertation, *The "I" Speech in Isaiah 40–66,* Fuller Theological Seminary [probably in 1985]), is much more dramatic and less realistic in setting than other books. While Jeremiah usually places the prophet in a historical setting for his speech, Isaiah seldom does. The Vision is much more suited to the artificial setting of a stage. Is it conceivable that such a work was actually presented by a group of speakers, representing the characters in the drama? Before one dismisses this prospect too quickly, one should be reminded that Greek drama was reaching its height at about the time this was written.

Excursus: Drama in Israel and Early Judaism?

The student of the Hebrew Scriptures who questions the existence of drama in Israel and early Judaism receives confusing and contradictory signals from the handbooks.

There comes an almost unanimous "no!" from dictionaries and encyclopedias, which usually indicate that the earliest Hebrew drama comes from Moses Zacuto of Amsterdam in A.D. 1715. However, one article quotes Eusebius in saying that the earliest known play on a biblical theme by a Jew was on "The Exodus," by Ezekielos, an Alexandrian (so presumably in Greek), in the second century B.C.

The Encyclopedia of Jewish Knowledge (ed. Jacob de Haas [New York: Behrman, 1946] 126) quotes Josephus to the effect that Jews were opposed to dramatic representations and to all the artistic culture of the Greeks and the Romans. *The Encyclopedia Judaica* (vol. 6, p. 193) quotes several explanations: A. J. Paperna (1868) notes "the inherent contradiction between the monotheistic spirit of the Jewish religion and the dualism implicit in drama." I. Zinburg and others have stressed the objection of the sages to the ritualistic and "heretical aspects" of drama. The latter apparently refer to Christian mystery plays of the Middle Ages. J. H. Shirman (*Gilyonoth* 22 [1948] 217–67) writes: "Jewish tradition undoubtedly inhibited the development of the drama since the art of the theater was incompatible with the traditional way of life."

Bible dictionaries generally have no entry under "drama." Yet an entire *genre* of critical writing assumes that virtually all ancient cults (including Israel's) consisted of dramatic representations in some form of the basic story (or myth) on which the religion was based. The works of Mowinckel (*Psalmenstudien* I–VI [Kristiania: Dybwad, 1921–24]; *Religion and Cult,* tr. J. Sheehan [Milwaukee: Marquette Univ., 1981]; *The Psalms in Israel's Worship* I–II, tr. D. R. Ap-Thomas [Nashville: Abingdon, 1962]; and many others), of H. J. Kraus (*Worship in Israel,* tr. G. Buswell [Richmond: John Knox, 1966]; *Die Psalmen,* BKAT XV [Neukirchen-Vluyn: Neukirchener Verlag, 5th printing, 1978–79]), of the British Myth and Ritual School (cf. S. H. Hooke, ed., *Myth, Ritual and Kingship* [Oxford: Clarendon, 1958]) and the Scandinavian schools regularly assume the pervasive influence of cult drama in shaping the literature of the OT.

In addition, there have been those who found that some parts of the OT were best understood as drama. H. H. Rowley, in his typically thorough fashion, has documented the view that the Song of Songs is drama ("The Interpretation of the Song of Songs," *The Servant of the Lord,* 2d ed. [Oxford: Blackwell, 1965] 212–14, 223–42).

The *Encyclopedia Britannica* (15th ed., 10:199) summarizes the ambiguous situation: "Although there is biblical evidence in the Song of Songs and the Book of Job of Hebraic awareness of drama, Jewish religious traditions prohibited theatricals except for song, dance, and processionals."

These articles help to account for the lack of (or opposition to) drama and theater in Judaism in the Middle Ages and back into the Hellenistic period. The seat of this opposition lay in the orthodox determination to maintain its distinctive way of life, which was felt to be in peril through contact with the non-Jewish world. In medieval Europe this included Christian culture as well as pagan (or secular) populations. In the Graeco-Roman world it included the spectacles of the games, the gladiatorial contests, as well as the drama of schools. But there is nothing here to account for the lack of drama in internal Jewish festivals. Implied rejection of the dramatic form grows out of the strict rules of "traditional Judaism" (i.e., out of rabbinical or orthodox circles). These have their roots in the puritanical attitudes and restrictions of Ezra and are illustrated by the restrictions taught in the Mishnah and Talmud.

However, these were not the only forms of Judaism—not in the Hellenistic period, and certainly not in the Persian beginnings of Judaism (sixth-fifth century) or in pre-exilic Israel. There is nothing in the Torah to prohibit drama. The Mishnah also contains no such prohibition, only the restriction against contact with foreigners. Proscription of participation in foreign (i.e., Greek) drama is understandable. Even an attitude that restricts imitation of foreign forms may be fitting. But there is nothing here to prohibit specifically Hebrew forms of drama.

Thus, let the record show that the evidence against drama in Judaism applies (however appropriately) to later Judaism and is not applicable to OT times.

Drama has two faces. One is that of literature: literary drama. The other is acted theater. Although these may be separated (there is theater, even good theater, that is not literature; there is dramatic literature that is never acted), the usual practice combines the two forms, whether this be Sophocles or Shakespeare or Arthur Miller. Literary dramatic form usually presumes a developed arena where it is presented to a live audience.

Excursus: Literary Drama in the Old Testament?

Let it be noted that drama and narrative (especially narrative that contains a high degree of dialogue) are not very far apart. The OT certainly contains a great deal of such narrative.

Several pieces of OT literature have been considered possible dramatic literature. These include the Song of Songs, Job, and Jonah. Other smaller units have been thought to demonstrate a true dramatic character; for example, one might speak of the speeches of Deuteronomy as monologues.

Johannes Hempel (*Die Althebräische Literatur und ihr Hellenistisch-Jüdisches Nachleben* [Potsdam: Athenaion, 1930]) uses words like *drama* and *dramatic* to describe Canaanite ritual, which was not unknown in Israel (28), the royal songs of Jerusalem (35), prophetic speeches (61), portions of historical narrative (121), and Deutero-Isaiah (171), and notes the resistance to continual reinterpretation into drama of Hellenistic style (183). Yet he never gives a description of Israel's dramatic tradition. Explicit evidence for such is lacking. But what would such a history show, if we should construct one from the materials that we do have in comparison with what was happening in neighboring peoples?

Drama in most cultures begins with cultic observances. Israel was no different. The earliest forms were shaped by the pilgrimage sacrifices referred to in Israel's request to Pharaoh (Exod 7:16) or Melchizedek's communion meal with Abraham (Gen 14:18–21). In Canaan, much more complex forms developed in the three annual festivals which were adaptations of Canaanite festivals. The most clearly dramatic form was that of Passover (Exod 12), but highly developed royal festivals also grew in Jerusalem (1 Kgs 8; The Psalms). Each of these had dramatic elements with explanations or narrative to match. Cultic drama was bound to the specific purposes of the cult. It taught, inculcated, and purportedly brought to pass the conditions which the cult fostered. It supported the institutions and the society which the cult was designed to nourish.

The Exile brought sharp changes—a secularizing influence and a vacuum where Temple and priesthood had been. The ancient traditions could be studied at arm's length, critically, and with an eye toward a different future. Religion was no longer under the patronage of Israel's king. Persian patronage was suspect.

Prophecy, having already established a vehicle of protest and of change, now moved beyond the individual figure to literary (and dramatic) forums. Wisdom (the schools) moved in to fill the vacuum. Village festival lore moved into the center of the people's consciousness (the Festal Scrolls). Not bound to either cult or king, literature (including drama) could look critically at life and history and could ask questions beyond those allowed in the cult. The Deuteronomic History, Jeremiah, and Ezekiel belong here.

This era also produced a second wave of prophetic drama and literature to help gain perspective on the Exile. This included Isaiah and the Book of the Twelve Prophets. It brought Wisdom to the fore in Proverbs and Job, which probed the meaning of guilt and spoke of the way ahead.

A third wave belonged to Ezra and was dominated by the Pentateuch. Moses was invoked. The Torah was applied to the life of Jerusalem, the Temple, and the dispersion through the Synagogue. The age of Judaism, the scribe, and the priest had arrived. All else was pushed into a second and subordinate position.

A fourth wave sought to reverse the trend, calling on the Wisdom books of Proverbs and Job, presenting the royal story in Chronicles, and leading the people in singing the songs of Zion (the Psalms). It stormed the centers of Judaism but was pushed into a third position in authority (after the prophets). It succeeded in drawing the literature of village festivals (the Scrolls) into its orbit, but it did not shake the trend. Ezra-Nehemiah recounts the new establishment. The Torah is secure and the tradition of Jewish life which Ezra instituted would remain its flagship.

So, was there drama in ancient Israel? *Yes,* in the cult drama of the confederacy and the royal cult drama of Jerusalem, and in the village festivals throughout its history. *Probably,* in the literature whose most natural understanding is to be found in the production of oral, multi-voiced theater, in which one or more actors, a narrator, and a chorus spoke its measured lines, challenged old ideas, and suggested new ones in Jerusalem under the Persians.

In Athens, Socrates accused the theater of having destroyed his credibility, but a reforming and moralistic city put the philosopher to death instead of judging the theater. In Jerusalem, at close to the same time, Ezra was incensed at the profligacy of the city and ordered reforms that sealed the people off from surrounding cultures and effectively suppressed the thriving literary (and dramatic) movement. Some of the best of its products have survived, shorn of almost all signs of their dramatic presentation. In stodgy literary clothes they have lost some of their power and brilliance and have often been subjected to misinterpretation or to proof-text quotations which ignored their contextual intent. Nonetheless, their influence has been enormous.

The products of Athens' schools suffered similar vicissitudes although they were not deprived of their original forum. Still today Athens and Jerusalem joust for public attention. And lessons from here and yon fall on deaf ears and insensitive minds as Isaiah, Socrates, and Plato knew they would.

Drama theory has been discussed ever since Aristotle wrote his *Poetics* (fourth century B.C.). Horace (*The Art of Poetry, ca.* 24 B.C.), Sir Philip Sidney (*Apologie for Poetry,* 1595), Lope de Vega (*The New Art of Writing Plays,* 1609), and Ben Jonson (*Timber,* 1640) are only a few of those who preceded modern critics like Kenneth Burke with his dramatic theory of literature (cf. W. H. Rueckert, *Kenneth Burke and the Drama of Human Relations,* Berkeley: U. of California Press, 2nd ed. 1982).

The basic characteristics of drama have remained remarkably similar throughout history. The following have been drawn from articles in the *Encyclopedia Britannica,* 15th ed. (3:655–56; 5:980–85; 10:1091; 18:213–20, 588).

Drama mirrors life (*mimesis*), touching on themes familiar to the audience. The Vision of Isaiah does this by tracing familiar eras in Israel's history and presenting familiar personalities: Ahaz, Isaiah, and Hezekiah. The nearness of the subject to its audience, even across the time-distance of centuries, is emphasized by keeping essential issues to the fore, like the fate of Jerusalem and the identity of the true Israel. The audience may sympathize or be in awe, but it is unlikely to laugh. The Vision reveals a thread of alienation and another of empathy to God's purpose with which the audience is invited to identify.

Drama uses scenes, relating characters in a limited time-frame, and uses a chorus to interpret its meaning. Confrontation is a major device. Greek heroic drama used all these. Moreover, it typically had all its action occur within one day. In comparison, the Vision of Isaiah has a large time-frame from the mid-eighth century to the mid-fifth century, which is broken down into a chronological sequence of acts reflecting steps along that route. Some characters sustain the unity of the entire drama: Yahweh, his aides, Israel, Jerusalem. Human persons are, of course, limited to one or two of the acts or scenes. The Vision portrays a continuing confrontation between Yahweh and his people. It is tense in 1:2, and it is still strained in 66:24.

Drama uses style to signal the mode or spirit of the scene, the degree of fantasy or reality, liturgy or illusion that is to be portrayed. The Vision does this systematically. There are straightforward historical recitals in 7:1–14; 20:1–6; and chaps. 36–39. There is the continual portrayal of God as chief spokesman and actor. History is also portrayed in poetry, and utopian scenes are presented at intervals.

Drama, especially Greek drama, used a chorus to communicate the author's intention. It was a commentary on the action "to guide the moral and religious thought and emotion of the audience through the play." For Aeschylus (525–456 B.C.), Sophocles (496–406 B.C.) and Euripides (480–406 B.C.), it is said that the chorus *was* the play. Similarly, the Vision occasionally uses a chorus to respond to God.

Aristotle taught that a tragic drama should carry an audience through a catharsis of feeling. Horace (*ca.* 24 B.C.) thought it should offer pleasure. The Vision has its audience relive the change and heartbreak of three centuries of Israel's history only to place before it anew the alternatives posed by God's plan for the ages. It leads in typical Hebrew form to a renewed opportunity for faith and commitment which is seen to be offered once again despite Israel's earlier rejections.

Ideally drama should arise out of contemporary society and should deal with the very foundations of belief. The Vision does this. It rises out of issues current in fifth-century Jerusalem and traces their roots back to eighth-century Judah. It is polemical in arguing one side of the debate.

A play depends on the character of its audience to determine how it is received and what it will mean to them. Some plays tend to unify the audience; some divide it. The Vision will divide those who identify with the minority believers who follow God's lead from those who identify with the majority who reject it. In any case, the Vision leaves no doubt about God's position on the issue.

As in classic drama, the Vision subordinates characterization to plot and structures its sections to unite a particular time and place with the action that takes place.

This commentary understands the Vision to be a sort of drama in which Yahweh and his aides (Heavens and Earth, 1:2) are the principal characters. The superscription names Judah and Jerusalem as the main subjects of the Vision, but this must be revised in light of the actual contents of the book to include Israel and all of mankind.

The "horizons" of the drama are set in one dimension by historical references to eighth-century kings with the prophet Isaiah and by references to the Persian era in the latter part of the book. Another dimension includes observations and speeches from the throneroom of Heaven as Yahweh and his court view three centuries of Palestinian and Mesopotamian history. The genre of vision requires an implied "stage setting" from which Yahweh and his aides can see and relate to mundane events in Jerusalem, in Babylon, and other places.

The Vision portrays a historical era, but from a perspective that no modern historian can share. It purports to show Yahweh's view of the happenings and Yahweh's relation to these happenings. Yahweh keeps the far nations in view, even as he addresses and exhorts his people in Jerusalem or in Babylon.

SHAPE AND STRUCTURE

Bibliography

Fohrer, G. "Entstehung, Komposition, und Überlieferung von Jesaja 1–39." *Annual of the Leeds Oriental Society* 3 (1961–62) = *Studien zur alttestamentliche Prophetie (1949–65).* BZAW 99. Berlin: Töpelmann, 1967. 113–47. **Liebreich, L. J.** "The Compilation of the Book of Isaiah." *JQR* 46 (1955–56) 259–77; 47 (1956–57) 114–38. **Marshall, R. J.** "The Structure of Isaiah 1–12." *BR* 7 (1962) 19–32. **Mowinckel, S.** "Die Komposition des Jesaja-buches Kap. 1–39." *AcOr* 11 (1933) 267–92 = *Prophecy and Tradition.* Oslo: J. Dybwad, 1946. **Rendtorff, R.** "Zur komposition des buches Jesaja." *VT* 34 (1984) 295–320. **Sweeney, M. A.** *Isaiah 1–4 and the Post-Exilic Understanding of the Isaianic Tradition.* Diss., Claremont Graduate School, 1983.

A key to the structure of the Vision is found in the references to the reigns of kings in 1:1. The reigns of Uzziah and Jotham apparently overlapped in fact and are to be taken together in the Vision. Chap. 6 marks the death of Uzziah and the end of the first act. Ahaz is presented by name in chap. 7 and notice of his death appears at the end of chap. 14. Although Hezekiah is not mentioned by name in the following section, Isaiah's demonstration (chap. 20) is dated in his time and his ministers are called by name in chap. 22. Thus the generations of these three kings mark the divisions of the first quarter of the Vision.

The succeeding sections also fit into similar "generations." The fall of Tyre (chap. 23) fits the seventh-century reign of Manasseh, as does the picture of the utter destruction of "the land" (chaps. 24–27) at the height of Assyrian power. The references to Egyptian influence and to the anticipated fall of Assyria in chaps. 28–33 fit the period of Josiah/Jehoiakim.

Chaps. 34–39 are more problematical but may well be even more central for the Book (see *The Book's Composition* above).

Chaps. 40–44:23 clearly anticipate Cyrus' rise as a threat to Babylon in the last decade of the Babylonian Empire. This act develops the thought of Israel as Yahweh's servant. Chaps. 44:24–48:22 picture the Persian conquest in which Cyrus is Yahweh's servant. The servant theme is continued in chaps. 49–52:12 with a focus on Jerusalem. In 54:17 the plural "servants of Yahweh" appears for the first time, part of an act (52:13–57:21) which invites all the people of the land to join in worship and service to Yahweh. Chaps. 58–62 return to a focus on Jerusalem. Chaps. 63–66 address the "implied audience" more directly than any others. These acts may be seen as representing four stages of the Jewish experience in the Persian Empire under Cyrus, Darius, Xerxes, and Artaxerxes.

The Vision has always seemed a mystery because of the huge blank in the historical development between Sennacherib and Cyrus, between Hezekiah and Sheshbazzar. Seen in this way, however, there is no gap. The veiled references and unspoken names would have been familiar to a fifth-century audience.

THE TWELVE ACTS OF *THE VISION OF ISAIAH*

Chaps.	*Generation/ Act*	*Davidide Heirs*	*Years*	*Mesopotamian Kings*	*Years*
		PART I THE FORMER TIMES: JUDGMENT, CURSE			
1–6	First	#Uzziah/Jotham	750–735 B.C.	Tiglath Pileser III	745–727 B.C.
7–14	Second	*Ahaz	735–715 B.C.	Shalmaneser V	727–722 B.C.
				Sargon II	722–705 B.C.
15–22	Third	#Hezekiah	715–687 B.C.	Sennacherib	705–681 B.C.
23–27	Fourth	*Manasseh/Amon	687–642 B.C.	Esarhaddon	681–669 B.C.
				Ashurbanipal	669–633 B.C.
28–33	Fifth	#Josiah/ Jehoiakim	640–605 B.C.	Nabopolassar (Necho, Egypt	633–625 B.C. 609–593 B.C.)
34–39	Sixth	*Jehoiakim/ Zedekiah	605–587 B.C.	Nebuchadnezzer	605–562 B.C.
		PART II THE LATTER TIMES: SALVATION, BLESSING			
40–44:23	Seventh	Jehoiachin		Nabunaid	550–539 B.C.
44:24–48:22	Eighth	Sheshbazzar		Cyrus	539–530 B.C.
				Cambyses	530–522 B.C.
49:1–52:12	Ninth	Zerubabbel		Darius I	522–486 B.C.
52:13–57:21	Tenth	Hananiah		Xerxes I	485–465 B.C.
58–62	Eleventh	Shecaniah/Ezra/Nehemiah		Artaxerxes I	464– B.C.
63–66	Twelfth	The Age to Come			

The generations are not distinguished so much by specific years or even by the reigns of kings as by policies followed. An asterisk (*) precedes generations of vassalage. A pound sign (#) precedes generations of active rebellion or of independence. The periods represented in the seventh to twelfth generations lack hard historical data to determine how submissive the leaders were. But there is little doubt that the issue was very much alive.

The dates mark the approximate beginning and end of the period portrayed. The list of kings is neither complete nor exact, since only some of them are mentioned. The Vision makes no effort to be comprehensive or to connect the scenes into a history. Rather, it presents vignettes or illustrative scenes from each one.

PLOT

A drama normally develops a plot. So does the Vision. It portrays the continuing tension throughout these generations between Yahweh's strategy and Israel/Jerusalem's plans for themselves. The entire Vision is, in a way, an extension of Yahweh's complaint (chap. 1) against his people and his city. They have proved themselves "blind, deaf, unperceptive, unwilling, and disobedient." And they continue to be so. The Vision insists that Yahweh has not rejected his people or his city but that he has introduced a new age in history and new roles for Israel and Jerusalem to suit the new age.

The Vision is, in a sense, a tragedy, for there is no happy ending for the people. They stand rejected because of their own unyielding rebellion (chap.

65). Only individuals who are meek, yielding, and believing can enter God's newly created city (65:17–66:24). With this the Vision moves beyond tragedy to portray God's plan: the new city belongs to the believers of all peoples, but there is no room in it for national pride or ambition, whether it be of the style of Joshua (63:7–19), or David (chap. 64), or of ordinary Adamic pride.

The goal of the new city and its role is proclaimed in 2:1–4. The drama portrays the call to succeeding generations to recognize God's new order and participate in it; the drama also depicts the ways in which historically both Israel and Jerusalem refused to respond, preferring to insist that God support their own ideas of what the future should be.

CHARACTERIZATION

Ordinary character portrayal is essentially lacking in the Vision because of the many lifetimes it spans. To a limited extent, the character of Isaiah can be deduced, especially from chaps. 7–8. The characters of Ahaz and Hezekiah may also be construed from the dramatic action, while those of Manasseh and Josiah are only implied. It is interesting to note the difference between the assessment of character in the Vision for these kings and that given in the Deuteronomic History and Chronicles.

Primary characterization belongs to those who continue throughout the Vision. First among these is Yahweh. This stellar role reaches a climax in chaps. 40–48.

Israel and Jerusalem are developed as characterizations of the peoples over three centuries. The faults that led first to the destruction of the northern Kingdom and then of Jerusalem are developed at length. They turn primarily on self-will, which makes them blind to Yahweh's acts, deaf to his words, unperceptive and unknowing of his plan of action in their time. This flaw lies at the heart of the tragedy. It leaves no room for a redemptive outcome for the people as a whole.

Another characterization moves unobtrusively through these acts. It portrays אדם "mankind" who is being judged for pride and arrogant brutality. The old sins of Adam are presented here as are those of Cain or of the Tower of Babel. Israel, of course, participates in these attitudes which are condemned from the start.

Another characterization is of הארץ "the land," which seems to refer to the Palestinian/Syrian area into which Israel was brought and which David made his own. But there is none of the intrinsic beauty that Deuteronomy and Joshua see in it, nor the glory that David and Solomon brought to it. It is a sad area of total destruction and death particularly portrayed in chaps. 6 and 24. Mankind's failures and Israel's sins have left their terrible mark on the land.

STYLE AND MOTIFS

J. Muilenburg's style analysis of chaps. 40–66 (*IB* 5 [1956] 384–93) remains the best available. Analysis of chaps. 1–4 can be found in my paper "The

Formation of Isaiah Chap. 1: Its Context in Chaps. 1–4" (*SBL 1978 Seminar Papers* I [Missoula: Scholars Press, 1978] 109–20), in M. A. Sweeney's dissertation (*Isaiah 1–4*), and in B. Wiklander, *Prophecy as Literature: A Text-linguistic and Rhetorical Approach to Isaiah 2–4* (CB 22 [Malmo: Gleerup, 1984]). Unfortunately, the latter appeared too late to be used in the commentary.

The major themes of the plot are developed around central motifs. A sketch of these was given in my 1978 paper which is reproduced here.

The first motif is represented by an interesting group of words in 1:3, *know* and *understand.* The people are accused of lacking these and the verses imply in amazement that this is so. Vv 18–19 use different but related words: *reasoning together, being willing,* and *hearing* (*being obedient*). In vv 25–27, the word *turn* is used three times.

Isa 6:9–10 adds the word *see* but omits the words *be willing* and *reason together.* The appearance of the other words together (*know, understand, hear, see,* and *turn*) seemed reason enough to wonder at their appearance in chap. 1. So the concordance was used to determine appearance in other parts of Isaiah. The result is interesting. Groups of at least three of these words together appear in the following locations:

5:20–21	40:13–14, 21, 28	52:6–8, 14–15
6:9–10	41:20–23, 26, 28–29	53:1–3, 10–11
	42:16–18, 22–25	55:2–3, 5, 7, 10
28:9+	43:9–13	56:10–11
29:11–18, 21–24	44:1–2, 8–9	57:17–18
30:9–10, 15, 19–20, 30	45:2–6, 20–23	58:2–4
32:3–4	47:10–11	60:2–5, 16–18
33:13–20	48:5–8, 12–20	61:9; 63:15–17
	49:5–7, 18–26	64:3; 66:4–5, 8, 14–15, 19
37:3–9, 17–20+	50:4, 7, 10	
38:5–8	51:7	
39:1–5		

(Cf. R. L. Lambert, *A Contextual Study of YDʿ in the Book of Isaiah.* Diss., Fuller Theological Seminary, 1982.)

Even this rough list is startling, suggesting (on this point at least) a closer relation of chaps. 1 and 6 to chapters after 28 than to chapters before it.

A second motif relates to Israel/Jacob and punishment on her which appears in 1:3–7 and the following:

2:6–8	40:27	48:1
5:25	41:8–24	49:1–4
7:7–9	42:24–25	
9:8–21	43:1–7	58:1–14
17:4–11	43:22–24	59:1–19
22:3–4	43:27–28	
	45:9	63:10–13
28:1–8	46:3	65:1–7
28:9–18	47:6	

The continuation of this motif through the book is noteworthy.

A third motif relates to the purging of Jerusalem's sin and is depicted in:

1:8–17	31:4–9	50:1–3
1:21–31	32:9–20	52:3–6
3:1	33:14–24	52:7–10
4:4		52:11–12
	40:2	62:1–12
22:8–14	48:9	64:11
		65:8
29:1–10	49:8–13	66:8
30:20	49:14–21	

The fact that the Jacob/Israel and the purging of Jerusalem motifs alternate throughout the Book of Isaiah just as they do in chap. 1 is worthy of note in any analysis of the book's structure.

A fourth major motif, found in 2:2–4, is the picture of an exalted Jerusalem. The motif owes much to royal Zion traditions. It occurs in:

4:5–6	28:16	40:9–11
8:3–7	30:19	51:11–16
10:12	31:4–9	52:1–3
10:24–27	33:5	59:20
12:6	33:20–22	
14:32		60:1–14
	34:8	60:15–22
18:7	35:10	61:1–11
22:22	37:33–35	65:18–19
25:6–7	38:6	66:10–14
26:1–6		

A picture of ideal conditions often accompanies these promises of the exalted Zion.

There are also a number of secondary motifs that are important. The unique invitation of 1:18–20 has counterparts in 2:5; 24:15; 31:6; a cluster in chaps. 41–44; and strong elements in 55:1–3, 6–7. The announcements of Yahweh's exclusive exaltation and of "man's" humiliation (linked with references to idolatry) occur at intervals throughout the book.

Citing these instances is enough to demonstrate how threads of meaning, apparent in these first chapters, are a distinctive part of the book's tapestry.

THE VISION OF ISAIAH *AS THEOLOGY*

Vriezen, T. C. "Essentials of the Theology of Isaiah." *Israel's Prophetic Heritage,* ed. B. W. Anderson and W. Harrelson. New York: Harper Bros., 1962. 128–46.

The Vision identifies Yahweh as Israel's former covenant partner. But it goes on to show that the covenant has come under judgment and no longer applies, and it recognizes his continued will to deal with Israel in his new age. Emphasizing Yahweh's position as patron of Jerusalem, it teaches that he will continue to use Zion and make it his residence, the place where he will meet the peoples.

Yahweh is seen as the true God of humankind. As in Gen 1–11, he stands in judgment over human pride and ambition (cf. Isa 2:9–22 and *passim*). He also is master of life and death for all the people of the land (cf. especially chaps. 24–26).

The core of the Vision's theological message, however, is that Yahweh is the Lord of History. He calls and dismisses the nations. He determines their destinies. He divides the ages and determines the eventual courses of mankind.

When Israel in exile doubt God's ability to help them, he cites his role in creation. He contrasts his own immense capacities with the minuscule size of planets and stars, which are but dust. He reduces time by citing his control of all time. And he insists that he, the Creator, the Lord of History, and Israel's God who calls to it, are one and the same (chaps. 40–44).

Yahweh's Strategy

The Vision purports to reveal the עצה "strategy" which has determined God's actions and relationships for some three centuries prior to the writing of the drama. The Deuteronomic History, Jeremiah, and Ezekiel had focused narrowly on the Babylonian destruction of Jerusalem of 587 B.C. in trying to interpret God's will for the people in the Exile and beyond. The Vision chooses a broader arena (as does the Book of the Twelve).

The Vision says that Yahweh in mid-eighth century B.C. had already determined a strategy or plan that would make changes far greater than simply bringing about the punishment of Israel. This meant nothing less than the inauguration of a new age.

For a millennium or more, Palestine had been a land of small city-states under the fairly tolerant and benign wing of Egypt. Egypt did not lean heavily on the Palestinian states, but expected them to serve as a loose buffer against aggression from that quarter. Under this system the Canaanite and Phoenician civilizations had bloomed, David and Solomon had developed an admirable little mini-empire, and trade had flourished. Rivalries between the small states had remained within bounds, and all concerned had prospered.

In the ninth century B.C. this situation began to change. Assyrian invasions were prevented only by massive coalitions of armies from the Palestinian states. By the middle of the eighth century B.C., Assyria could no longer be withstood. At about the same time, the small Palestinian states experienced growing instability which would soon lead to their extinction. For a hundred years, to the middle of the seventh century B.C., Assyrian power worked to overcome every symbol of local autonomy. The last to fall were the Phoenician cities with their considerable commercial sea routes. At that point "the whole land" lay prostrate before the conquerors.

The Vision chronicles these events in the first four acts. It recognizes that Israel's sins as well as the pride of mankind had played a role in determining what happened. But it also says that Yahweh, who dwelled in Zion and who had been understood to administer his rule over the world from Jerusalem through its Davidic king, would no longer do so. Yahweh still dwelled in Zion and could be approached there for worship or instruction in his law. But the control of history had been transferred from David's throne to the hand of the Empire. And Assyria would be only the first in a series of empires.

The prophets, especially Isaiah, as the Vision portrays him, were given the task of revealing this change in strategy to Israel. Yahweh would not necessarily be on Israel's side in battle. Indeed, it was he who brought the Assyrians. If a king truly understood this, it behooved him to come to terms with Yahweh's chosen vessel, the emperor. Ahaz did this. Hezekiah did not. Manasseh did this. Josiah did not.

The Vision goes on to insist that this was no temporary arrangement waiting for the day when the rule would be returned to David's heir in Jerusalem. On the contrary, Israel and Jerusalem of the post-exilic period were called to come to terms with a permanent Persian hegemony. Yahweh still had important roles for Israel and Jerusalem to play in his new strategy; but they were "servant" roles, not "ruler" roles.

These ideas were rejected by most of Israel and those in Jerusalem who still dreamed of reconquering the land as Joshua did or of establishing a kingdom as David did. The Vision insists that they are out of step with God's new order and that they can only be rejected. There is nothing here to support rebellion against Persia or nationalistic aspirations at any time. God's new era makes Jerusalem a place of pilgrimage for believers from all the nations.

If Isaiah's division between the ages is taken seriously, the biblical theologian must ask whether the proper biblical division of the ages should not be "before 587 B.C." and "after 587 B.C." rather than our present B.C./A.D. formula. This would, for the Christian, put the Incarnation at the climax of the new Age rather than at the beginning of it.

YAHWEH'S PROBLEM

Yahweh's strategy assigns to the world empires the task of managing and policing the world and invites his elect, saved, and called people to be his servants in worship, witness, and mission.

God seemed to have no difficulty persuading the nations to play their part. He had the usual problem of pride, arrogance, and cruelty which regularly made a change necessary. But there was no problem in finding aspirants for the position.

God did have a problem, as the Vision sees it, in getting Israel and Jerusalem to listen, to see, to understand and agree to the new role he had for them. Even the centuries of pain, distress, and death that preceded the Exile had not stilled their thirst for power and glory, for autonomy and self-determination, and for the imagined prosperity that would go with these.

Israel's complaint is best stated in 49:1–4, while she insists in chaps. 63 and 64 that God has no right to change his plans from those that motivated Joshua and David. The scenes of covenant judgment near the beginning of the Vision (chaps. 1, 3, 5, 10, etc.) have made little impression. The unyielding determination for Israel to regain its old glory remains. That is Yahweh's problem. His frustration with a stubborn people is shown repeatedly in the book but is particularly acute in chap. 65.

The practical side of this for the author and his implied audience lies in the tendency of Judah to rebel against its overlords, only to be put down in bloody reprisals. This apparently was still true under the Persians. Half a millennium later it would still be true under the Romans.

The book of Isaiah is a major exponent of the view that the people of God be separate from the state, a spiritual gathering of those who would serve God in spirit and in truth. It teaches that God's power can more appropriately be shown in and through such a group than through national power. It teaches that God's ultimate goals are more in the sanctuary than in the palace, more in the heart than in military strength.

The Vision has been a prime support for those among Jews and among Christians, including Jesus and Paul, who held to such a view of God and his kingdom.

THE VISION
of Isaiah, son of Amoz
concerning Judah and Jerusalem
in the days of
Uzziah, Jotham, Ahaz, and Hezekiah
Kings of Judah

A Drama in Twelve Acts. Translation with Commentary.

Title (1:1)

Bibliography

Tucker, G. M. "Prophetic Superscriptions and the Growth of the Canon." *Canon and Authority,* ed. G. M. Coats and B. O. Long. Philadelphia: Fortress Press, 1977. 56–70.

Translation

[1] THE VISION OF ISAIAH[a] SON OF AMOZ
Which he envisioned concerning Judah and Jerusalem in the days of Uzziah, Jotham, Ahaz, and Hezekiah[b], *kings of Judah.*

Notes

1.a. ישעיהו "Isaiah" here and elsewhere in the text. But ישעיה in the title.

1.b. MT records variants among different passages in the forms of personal names of kings (cf. M. Noth, *Die israelitischen Personennamen,* BWANT 111/10 [Stuttgart: Kohlhammer, 1928]) while the Qumran scribes used frequent *mater lectionis* to transmit their understanding of the pronunciation.

Form/Structure/Setting

A heading of this type is common in the prophetic literature. It normally includes a designation of the nature of the book, a prophet's name, and may include the intended reading audience and a statement of the period from which it comes.

חזון "vision" is a term that describes the entire work of 66 chapters. It must mean a category of literary work like דברי "words" or משא "burden" that appear in other headings. The book contains an account of one vision (chap. 6), but the title here is much broader and its definition must be of a kind to fit the entire book.

This "vision" is arranged in acts and scenes like a play. It contains a high proportion of dialogue spoken by a number of speakers, including some in the first person plural, to be spoken like a chorus. Some of the scenes have historical settings (7:1–16), while others have an otherworldly setting in which Heavens and Earth may be addressed and God speaks (1:2–3). When references are made to historical events, they move chronologically through the Vision.

The Vision has so many of the qualities of a drama that this commentary will suggest a separation of speeches and a designation of speakers. Identification of the speaker is indicated in some places by the text. Where it is not, the commentator's choice is arbitrary. This is literary prophecy of excellent quality and great complexity.

Isaiah is not named here as the author. His name is a part of the title.

His "vision" is the subject of the book. He appears in passages where he is identified by name in 7:1–16 and in chaps. 20, 37, 38, 39. His name appears in other superscriptions in 2:1 and 13:1. First-person accounts in chaps. 6 and 8 are properly referred to him. These are the portions of the Vision that justify his name in the title. They, and the title, imply that the Vision conveys his concept.

Comment

All that is known of Isaiah son of Amoz is contained in this book. He is only mentioned elsewhere in 2 Kgs 18–20 = Isa 36–39 and in 2 Chr 32:20. One book in the Pseudepigrapha is ascribed to him.

Uzziah is called Azariah in 2 Kgs 15:1 and 2 Chr 26. The latter portion of his reign overlapped that of Jotham because of Uzziah's leprosy (2 Kgs 15:5; 2 Chr 26:19–21).

Jotham reigned sixteen years (2 Kgs 15:32–38/2 Chr 27), as did his son, Ahaz. Both Kings and Chronicles list Ahaz as one of the worst kings and blame him for bringing Tiglath-Pileser into the land. They both say the Lord brought Israel and Aram against Ahaz. The Vision sets aside chaps. 7–14 for the reign of Ahaz and clearly has a view of him and his reign different from that in Kings and Chronicles.

Hezekiah succeeded Ahaz (2 Kgs 18–20; 2 Chr 29–32). He is lauded as one of the greatest kings in both Kings and Chronicles. The Vision repeats a selection of the Kings account (chaps. 36–39). Chaps 15–21 are set in Hezekiah's reign. But the Vision also has an independent evaluation of Hezekiah and his reign.

Explanation

The Vision takes its name from the prophet. It is firmly rooted in his time, reflecting the firm belief that God began in the latter eighth century to do an epochal thing that was still in progress almost three centuries later. The Vision refers to the earlier period as "the former times" and the later as "the latter times." History, it says, will never quite be the same. Not since Noah's flood had a period and its events so divided the ages.

The Vision insists that God's own strategy (עצה) is behind it all. The coming of the empires is part of it. The scattering of Israel and the restoration of Jerusalem fit the pattern. But his people do not "know," cannot "see" or "hear," or "understand." To the very last, only a small minority are willing to take part in his "new world."

Excursus: The Chronology of Eighth-Century Reigns

Bibliography

Bright, J. "Chronological Chart: Mid-Eighth to Mid-Sixth Centuries." *HI,* 470–71. **Jepson, A.** and **Hanhart, R.** *Untersuchungen zur israelitisch-jüdischen Chronologie.*

BZAW 88, Berlin: Töpelmann, 1964. **Stiles, M.** *Synchronizing Hebrew Originals from Available Records.* 12 vols. Printed privately. 213 Siesta Drive, Aptos, CA: 1972–77. **Thiele, E. R.** *The Mysterious Numbers of the Hebrew Kings.* 3rd ed. Grand Rapids: Eerdmans, 1983. 139–92.

(The references to relative chronology of reigns in 2 Kgs 15–18 are unusually frequent, but are not clearly compatible with themselves or with external data.)

LIST OF EIGHTH-CENTURY REIGNS AND EVENTS AS RECORDED IN SCRIPTURE

Biblical Reference	*Name of King*	*Year Made King*	*Place of Reign*	*Length of Reign*
2 Kgs 15:17	Menahem	39th year of Azariah's reign	Samaria	10 years
2 Kgs 15:23	Pekahiah	50th year of Azariah's reign	Samaria	2 years
2 Kgs 15:17	Pekah	52nd year of Azariah's reign	Samaria	20 years
2 Kgs 15:29	*Tiglath-Pileser attacked Samaria and departed.*			
2 Kgs 15:30	Hoshea	20th year of Jotham's reign		
2 Kgs 15:32, 2 Chr 27:1	Jotham	2nd year of Pekah's reign	Jerusalem	16 years
2 Kgs 15:37	*Rezin and Pekah came against Judah.*			
2 Kgs 16:1	Ahaz	17th year of Pekah's reign	Jerusalem	16 years
2 Kgs 16:5–9, 2 Chr 28:1, 16, 20	*With Rezin and Pekah against Judah, Ahaz sent for Tiglath-Pileser.*			
2 Kgs 17:1	Hoshea	*12th year of Ahaz' reign	Samaria	9 years
2 Kgs 17:3	*Shalmaneser punished Hoshea.*			
2 Kgs 17:5	*Shalmaneser marched against Hoshea in the *9th year of his reign. Shalmaneser captured Samaria and departed.*			
2 Kgs 18:1	Hezekiah	*3rd year of Hoshea's reign	Jerusalem	29 years
2 Kgs 18:7	*Hezekiah rebelled against Assyria.*			
2 Kgs 18:9	*Shalmaneser besieged Samaria in Hoshea's *7th = Hezekiah's 4th year of reign.*			
2 Kgs 18:10	*Samaria is destroyed in Hoshea's *9th-Hezekiah's 6th year of reign.*			
2 Kgs 18:13	*Sennacherib attacked and laid siege to Jerusalem in Hezekiah's 14th year of reign.*			
2 Kgs 19:36–37	*Death of Sennacherib.*			
2 Kgs 21	Manasseh		Jerusalem	55 years

This list presents several problems when one is trying to arrive at absolute dates for the reigns and the events. There appear to be errors in synchronization in some of the dates, while others are factual, but the terms of reference in which they were presented were not understood by the historians. Such discrepancies relating to the synchronization of the dates for Hoshea and Hezekiah, are noted on the above list by an asterisk. Hoshea must have come to the throne at the death of Pekah when Tiglath-Pileser invaded Israel in 733 B.C., a date that can be verified by Assyrian annals. If he reigned nine years, the end of his reign would be 724–23 B.C., which accords with 2 Kgs 17:3. But Samaria fell two years later in 722–21 B.C.

Dating Hezekiah's reign has several problems, especially in its correlation with Hoshea's reign and the fall of Samaria. The key is 2 Kgs 18:13 which equates Hezekiah's fourteenth year with Sennacherib's attack on Jerusalem. It is known that Sennacherib began his reign in 705 B.C. If Hezekiah's reign began in Hoshea's 3rd year, 729 or 727 B.C., his 14th year would fall in Sargon's reign, 715 or 713 B.C. (Sargon, mentioned only once in Scripture, appears to have been virtually unknown or ignored by biblical historians.)

But if one takes 2 Kgs 18:13 at face value, knowing that Sennacherib besieged Jerusalem in 701 B.C., it follows logically that Hezekiah's reign must have begun in 715 B.C. If the other references are to be correctly synchronized, one must assume that Judean kings sometimes had overlapping reigns and that Israel was actually two kingdoms during part of this time: Ephraim/Samaria, west of Jordan; and Israel, east of Jordan. If these factors are reckoned with, the absolute dates of Assyrian conquests can be correlated with the relative dates of 2 Kgs. It will also be possible to recognize when kingdoms were subject to Assyrian vassalage and when they were not. In the accompanying chronological chart of reigns, periods of vassalage are marked with diagonal stripes. Relevant reigns in Babylon, Aram, and Egypt important for the study of Isaiah are also noted. A separate column relates the placement of chapters from the Vision of Isaiah with the reigns of the rulers included in the chart.

This arrangement depends principally on the work of M. Stiles. The customary tolerance for dates in this period of + or − one year applies.

The issue of independence or vassalage to Assyria is of major importance to the Vision. In the eighth century the kings divided over that issue as follows:

A Policy of Independence	*A Policy of Vassalage*
Pekah (Israel)	Menahem (Israel)
Rezin (Aram)	Hoshea (most of his reign)
Hezekiah 705–701 B.C.	Ahaz
Merodach Baladan (Babylon)	Hezekiah 715–706 B.C.
	700–686 B.C.
Philistine cities (intermittently)	Tyre and Sidon (usually)

Hezekiah's last years were spent in abject subjection to Assyria, and his son, Manasseh, inherited and continued this relation. He obviously had no choice in the matter. (See historical introduction, Act IV (chaps. 23–28) for more details.

Assyria's relaxation of its hand on Palestine during the last decades of its imperial existence allowed Josiah a measure of choice and freedom unknown to his predecessors. However, this was not without its problems (see the introduction to Act V, chaps. 23–33) and led to his death and to the fateful events that followed. Egypt became an active participant in Palestinian affairs during that period and for a short time exercised authority over Palestine.

Babylon inherited Assyria's mantle. By 605 B.C. it was prepared to reassert Mesopotamian dominance of the area and push Egypt out (Isa 34–39). Babylon finally brought Judah's monarchy to an end and carried out deportations scattering Jewish exiles throughout the Near East, joining the thousands of Israelites who had preceded them over more than a century (2 Kgs 25). Jehoiachin enjoyed a certain recognition as king in exile under Babylonian patronage.

CHRONOLOGICAL CHART OF REIGNS
755-700 B.C.

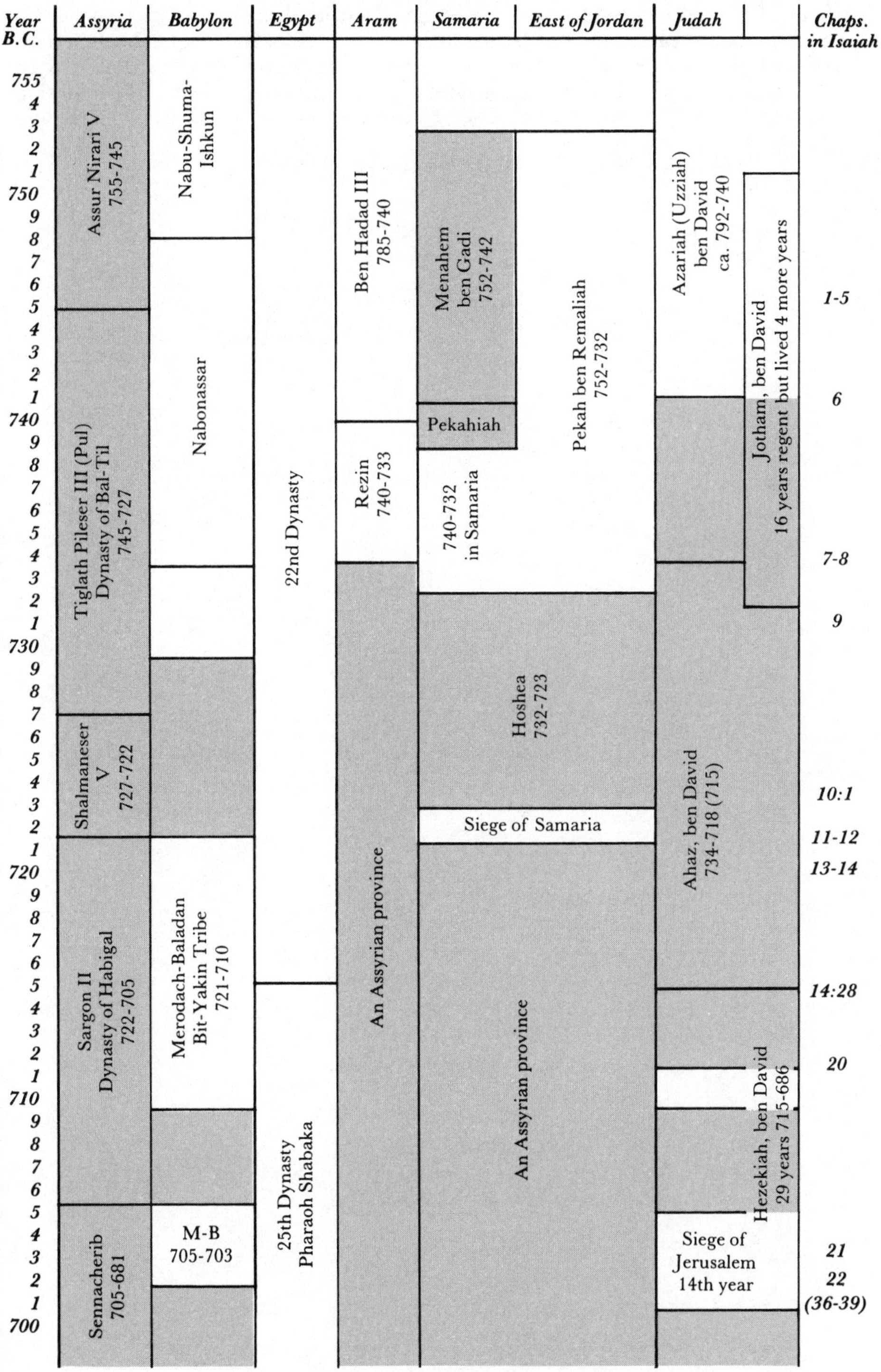

Note: Shaded areas indicate years of Assyrian sovereignty.
Unshaded areas indicate years of independence from Assyria.

In the sixth century B.C. and afterward, the issue was important to Jews. The sources record a line of leaders who counseled loyal service to the Babylonian and Persian empire. These included: Jehoiachin, Sheshbazzar, Zerubabbel (at least in the beginning), Ezra, and Nehemiah. There are indications that factions existed throughout the period who counseled rebellion at every opportunity. The following centuries record the rebellions of the Maccabees against the Seleucid rulers and the Zealots against the Romans.

The Vision takes a clear stand on the issue.

Act 1: Like a Booth in a Vineyard (Chaps. 1–6)

The First Generation: Kings Uzziah and Jotham (ca. 750–735 B.C.)

The first act serves as a prologue to the Vision just as the last act serves as an epilogue. The issues of covenant judgment introduced in chap. 1 are revealed, to be deliberately kept unresolved by chap. 6. They will remain unresolved until the final act.

The last decade of Uzziah's life provides the historical setting. The dialogue relates to conditions in Israel and Jerusalem, but the speakers act like spectators observing events rather than participating in them.

The first scene (1:2–2:4) introduces Yahweh's complaints against Israel (apparently the Kingdom of Northern Israel, although there are implications that apply to all the people in the land of Canaan) and against Jerusalem. Israel's malady is terminal. Jerusalem's ills can be healed after painful treatment.

The second scene (2:5–22) emphasizes the finality of the decision about Israel/Jacob and frames it with Yahweh's great day of retribution against all mankind. That day becomes a feature of the entire Vision.

The third scene (3:1–4:6) recapitulates the sad themes of scene 1 with documentation of the facts of the case, ending with a view of Jerusalem's hope.

Scene 4 (5:1–30) has the setting of a funeral, beginning with the "Song of the Vineyard" and continuing through the "woes" that mourn the sad fate of Israel. It notes that Yahweh's day of wrath is not yet complete.

Scene 5 (6:1–13) portrays an invitation to the heavenly throne room of Yahweh to serve as his messenger of dread tidings and as the agent of a strange mission. The speaker is not identified, but the mission defines the purpose of the Vision, as well as that of the prophet. The people's unresponsiveness is documented in each of the succeeding acts.

Historical Background

The period that followed the death of Jeroboam II (752 B.C.) in Israel was turbulent. The kingdom was apparently divided. Menahem ruled over Samaria and the territory west of the Jordan river and as a faithful vassal followed a policy of paying tribute to Assyria. Pekah ben Remaliah ruled east of the river and followed a policy of independence from Assyria. This was the age of Hosea and Amos. Their prophecies reflected the conditions of the region in that time.

Menahem was succeeded by his son, Pekahiah, who reigned a brief two years before he was assassinated. He was succeeded by Pekah, who then reigned over a kingdom uniting Samaria and Gilead for eight years. Throughout his reign, Pekah was more influenced by events in and relations to Aram (Syria) than by the more distant Assyria. Israel had competed with Aram in the area since the reign of Ahab more than a century before. Now Pekah stood with Ben Hadad III and then with Rezin who usurped the Syrian throne in 740 B.C. Pekah's policy toward Assyria undoubtedly reflected that of his northern neighbor.

Social and economic conditions in this period were greatly disturbed. The political chaos must certainly have been reflected in the breakdown of justice and righteousness that Amos and Hosea reflect.

In Judah, Azariah's (Uzziah's) longevity combined with the orderly co-regency with Jotham to provide much more stability for the tiny kingdom. They recognized the futility of resisting Assyria and paid tribute from 742 B.C. onward, in spite of their active participation in earlier military coalitions that had repelled Assyrian armies. There were no more Assyrian campaigns in Palestine during the reigns of Azariah or Jotham.

Scene 1: In the Hall of the King of Heaven and Earth (1:2—2:4)

This opening scene provides the setting and introduces the principal speakers for the Vision. Yahweh is Israel's God and covenant partner. Heavens and Earth are the original witnesses to the covenant. Israel and Jerusalem are God's partners in covenant.

Episode A: A Disappointed Father (*1:2–23*). This passage introduces a significant feature of the Vision: God's concern for Israel, as well as for Judah and Jerusalem. God is determined to end Israel's blind rebellion and to purge Jerusalem's shallow worship.

Episode B: Let Me Smelt Your Dross Like Lye (*1:24–31*). In order to purge Jerusalem, God is about to rouse himself to direct action (v 24) which is pictured in vv 24–31. This action will destroy the rebels but bring redemption with justice to the righteous. God's strategy in such direct action and his efforts to enlist the cooperation of his people make up the major theme of the Vision.

Episode C: The Mountain of Yahweh's House (*2:1–4*). This vision of Jerusalem's status and function will pervade the Vision and be fulfilled in 65:17–66:24.

Episode A: A Disappointed Father (1:2–23)

Bibliography

Begrich, J. "Der Satzstil in Fünfer. *ZS* 9 (1933/34) 204–9 (*GesStud* 162–67). **Fohrer, G.** "Jesaja 1 als Zusammenfassung der Verkündigung Jesajas." *ZAW* 74 (1962) 251–68. **Fullerton, K.** "The Rythmical Analysis of 1:10–20." *JBL* 38 (1919) 53–63. **Gitay, Y.** "Reflections on the Study of the Prophetic Discourse. The Question of Isaiah 1:2–20." *VT* 33 (1983) 207–21. **Hoffman, H. W.** *Die Intention der Verkündigung Jesajas* 82–85; 92–104. **Holladay, W. L.** "A New Suggestion for the Crux in Isaiah 1:4b." *VT* 33 (1983) 235–37. **Jensen, J.** *The Use of Torah by Isaiah. His Debate with the Wisdom Tradition.* CBQMS 3. Washington: Catholic Biblical Association, 1973. 68–84. **Jones, D. R.** "Expositions of Isaiah 1." *SJT* 17 (1964) 463–77; *SJT* 18 (1965) 457–71; *SJT* 19 (1966) 319–27. **Milgrom, J.** "Did Isaiah prophesy during the reign of Uzziah?" *VT* 14 (1964) 164–82. **Niditch, S.** "The Composition of Isaiah 1." *Bib* 61 (1980) 509–29. **Nielsen, K.** "Das Bild des Gerichts [Rib Pattern] in Jes. I–XII." *VT* 29 (1979) 309–24. **Rignell, L. G.** "Isaiah Chapter 1." *ST* 2 (1957) 140–58. **Roberts, J. J. M.** "Form, Syntax and Redaction in Isaiah 1:2–20." *PSB* 3 (1982) 293–306. **Schoneveld, J.** "Jesaia 1:18–20." *VT* 13 (1963) 342–44. **Stachowiak, L.** "Grzech Naradu Wybranego i Mozliowasc Rutunku wedlug Iz 1:2–17." *RocTKan* 24/1 (1977) 5–19. **Uchelen, N. van.** "Isaiah 1:9—Text and Context." *OTS* 21 (1981) 155–63. **Werner, W.** "Israel in der Entscheidung. Ueberlegungen zur Datierung und zur theologischen Aussage von Jes 1:4–9." *Eschatologie.* FS Engelbert Neuhäusler, ed. R. Kilian, K. Funk, P. Fassl. St. Ottilien: EOS, 1981. 59–72. **Willis, J. T.** "On the Interpretation of 1:18." *JSOT* 25 (1983) 35–54. ———. "The First Pericope in the Book of Isaiah." *VT* 34 (1984) 63–77.

Translation

Herald:	2 *Hear, Heavens!*	2+2+3
(to Heavens and Earth)	*and give ear, Earth!*	
	For Yahweh speaks!	
Yahweh:	*Children I have reared* [a] *and raised up*	3+3
(to Heavens and Earth)	*but even they have rebelled against me.*	
	3 *An ox knows its owner*	3+3
	and an ass its master's crib.	
	Israel does not know! [a]	3+3
	My people [b] *make no distinction!*	
Heavens and Earth:	4 *Woe! sinning nation!*	3+3
	People heavy with iniquity!	
	Evil-doing seed!	2+2
	Destroying children!	
	They have forsaken Yahweh!	2+3+2
	They have despised the Holy One of Israel!	
	[a] *They have slidden backward!* [a]	
(to the people of Israel)	5 *Upon what will you (pl) be beaten more?*	4+2
	Will you add rebellion?	
	Every head (is) for sores [a]	3+3
	and every stomach (is) cramped!	

	6 *From the sole of foot to the head—no sound spot!* [a]	2+2+2
	A wound or bruise, or bleeding stripe,	2+2
	they have not been closed.	2+2+3
	Nor have they been bound up.	
	And they have not been softened with oil.	
	7 *Your (pl) country is desolate;*	2+3
	Your cities burned with fire.	
	Your farmland, in your presence	2+3
	strangers are devouring it.	
Herald:	*Yea, desolation* [a] *like overthrow of strangers.*	3
(to Heavens and Earth)	8 *And the daughter of Zion is left*	2+2
	like a watchman's booth in a vineyard,	
	like a hut in a cucumber field,	2+2
	like a fortified [a] *city.*	
People of Jerusalem:	9 *If Yahweh of Hosts had not left to us a remnant*	3+3
(to Heavens and Earth)	*almost* [a] *like Sodom* [b] *we would have become,*	3+2
	Gomorrah we would resemble.	
Herald:	10 *Hear (ye) the word of Yahweh, rulers of Sodom.*	3+2
(to people of Jerusalem)	*Give ear to the Instruction of our God,*	3+2
	people of Gomorrah	
Yahweh:	11 *For what purpose (do you bring) to me*	2+2+2
	the great number of your sacrifices,	
Herald:	*says Yahweh.*	
Yahweh:	*I have had enough burnt offerings of rams*	3+2
	and the fat of fed-beasts.	
	Yea, blood of bulls and lambs [a] *and he-goats*	2+2+2
	I do not desire.	
	12 *Whenever you come to appear* [a] *before me*	2+2
	who has requested this from your hand,	3+2
	(this) trampling of my courts? [b]	
	13 *Do not bring a meaningless offering anymore.*	3+2
	It is an incense of abomination to me.	
	New moon and sabbath, calling of convocation,	2+2
	I cannot bear iniquity with solemn assembly.	2+2
	14 *Your new moons and your set seasons*	2+2
	my soul hates.	
	They are to me a burden.	3+2
	I am tired of bearing them.	
	15 *When you spread your hands [in prayer]*	2+3
	I will hide my eyes from you,	
	and also, when you multiply prayers	2+3
	I am not listening.	
	Your hands are full of blood!	3
	(Your fingers with iniquity!) [a]	+
	16 *Wash yourselves! Be pure!*	2
	Remove the evil of your doings	3+2
	from before my eyes!	
	Cease doing evil!	2+2

17 *Learn doing good!*
Seek justice! 2+2
Remedy oppression!
Bring justice to the orphan! 2+2
Plead the cause of the widow.
18 *Come now! Let us test each other,* 2+2
Herald: *says Yahweh.*
Yahweh: *If your sins are*[a] *like the scarlet robes* 3+2
like the snow they may[a] *become white.*
If they are[a] *red like crimson,* 2+2
like wool they may[a] *become.*
19 *If you become willing*[a] *and shall obey,*[a] 2+3
the good of the land you may eat
20 *but if you refuse*[a] *and shall continue obstinate*[a] 2+2
(by a) sword you may be devoured.[a]
Herald: *For the mouth of Yahweh has spoken.* 4
Heavens and Earth: 21 *How has she become a harlot?* 3
(to Yahweh) *(Zion*[a] *was) a community of faithfulness,* 3+2+3
full of justice.
Righteousness lodged in her.
But now—assassins? 2
Heavens and Earth: 22 *Your silver has become dross!* 3+3
(to Zion) *Your wine—mixed with water!*
23 *Your princes—rebelling* 2+2
and companions of thieves!
Each one a bribe-lover 3+2
and a rewards-chaser!
An orphan they never vindicate! 3+4
A widow's suit never comes before them!

Notes

2.a. MT has virtually no variants. LXX translates גדלתי "reared" with ἐγέννησα "begot," while Σ and Θ have ἐξέθρεψα "reared" and Vg *enutrivi* "brought up." LXX probably presumes ילדתי as a Hebrew original which would fit the use with "father" and "son." But the OT avoids using that verb with God as subject (except Isa 66:6 with a different meaning) and very seldom speaks of God producing offspring (exceptions: Deut 32:18; Ps 2:7). MT should be preferred.

3.a. LXX adds με, "Israel does not know me." This should be viewed as interpretation in translation. MT's concise form is better style and has a more pungent meaning.

3.b. Several MSS as well as LXX Syr Vg add "and," but it is unnecessary. The subject remains the same and parallelism is complete.

4.a-a. Omitted in LXX. A. Guillaume ("Hebrew Notes," *PEQ* 79 [1947] 40) argues for retaining the phrase. He notes a play on different meanings of words using the syllable זר: v 4 נזרו "gone, slidden," v 6 זרו "pressed out," v 7 זרים "strangers," v 8 נצורה "besieged," and v 9 שריד "remnant." Budde ("Zu Jesaja 1–5," *ZAW* 49 [1931] 21) emended to read מְאַחֲרָיו "his tarrying." G. R. Driver (*JTS* 38 [1937] 36) connects נזר with an Arabic root *zarra* meaning "express, drive back." Neither of these is a satisfactory solution. Vg (*abalienati sunt retrorsum*) and Tg (אסתחרו והוו לאחרא) appear to support MT (*BHK* to the contrary; so Wildberger). N. H. Tur-Sinai ("A Contribution to the Understanding of Isaiah I–XII," *ScrHier* 8 [1961] 155) suggests emending אחור to יחד or כאחד and translating "They have become estranged together." This makes sense, but the change is unnecessary. W. L. Holladay ("The Crux in Isaiah 1:4–6," *VT* 33 [1983] 235–37) reads נָזְרוּ אַחֵר "they have dedicated themselves to another (god)." The two words appear to exceed the metric form and the compact composition and probably should be judged a gloss (with Wildberger).

5.a. MT לחלי. G. R. Driver (*JSS* 13 [1968] 36) suggests the meaning of "sores, pustules, gangrene" from the root חלע. He also notes that לבב is from a root that suggests "something twisted." The meaning here would be "stomach" or "intestine."

6.a. H. D. Hummel ("Enclitic 'Mem,'" *JBL* 76 [1957] 105) suggests that אין־בו מתם "no sound spot" is a scribal error for אין במו תם "nothing with integrity." But אין מתם also occurs in Ps 38:4, 8. The LXX omits the phrase, but the meter requires that it remain. MT should be kept.

7.a. DSS[Isa] reads שממו עליה "they will be upset over it." Duhm, Marti, Gray, and Fohrer consider the entire line a gloss on שממה "desolate" above. S. Speier ("Zu drei Jesajastellen," *TZ* 21 [1965] 310) follows DSS[Isa], compares it to Lev 26:32, and considers it a scribal comment.

This entire stich has been challenged on numerous grounds. But the duplication of words is fitting, even necessary, within the larger composition. Both שממה and זרים "strangers" pick up words from the previous lines to connect the two speeches as is customary in this chapter (Fohrer). Wildberger notes that מהפכה "overthrow" is used in the OT without exception with "Sodom and Gommorah" (cf. Deut 29:22; Isa 13:19; Jer 49:18; 50:40; Amos 4:11) and suggests emending זרים to read סדם "Sodom." However, since the line is a deliberate connection between v 7 with which MT's reading fits and v 9 where סדם fits, the very tension in the phrase should be seen as intentional and MT's reading sustained.

8.a. נצורה has presented difficulties to translators and interpreters alike. LXX πολιορκουμένη (like Syr Tg Vg) gives the word an active meaning and seems to think of "a besieged city." A. Dillmann (*Der prophet Jesaja,* rev. R. Kittel [Leipzig: S. Hirzel, 1898]) pointed it נְצוֹרָה (niph ptcp from צור). F. X. Wutz (*BZ* 21 [1933] 11) suggested emending to read כְּעִיר בְּצִירָה and translating "like a flock on one perch." Wildberger (19) follows the emendation but translates "like a donkey-colt in a bird house." Something like this would preserve the kind of comparison of the previous line, but seems most unlikely. F. Hitzig (*Der prophet Jesaja* [Heidelberg: C. F. Winter, 1833]) and Duhm suggested a translation of "watchtower." Dillmann may have been right to reject this literally, but the tendency deserves attention. נצר means to watch or guard. Judean kings did build up fortified border cities throughout their history. Such a city would in fact be an outpost to watch or guard the border. It could be easily overrun or by-passed in an attack.

9.a. MT places the verse divider (*athnaḥ*) after כמעט "almost, little." This makes an uneven meter and an awkward sense. LXX Syr OL and Tg have divided the verse one word earlier, giving a balanced meter and a better sense (contra Wildberger).

9.b. DSS[Isa] has סודם and עומרה for MT's סדם and עמרה. Cf. the Greek Σοδομα and Γομορρα. Apparently the heavy second syllable has affected the pronunciation of the short first syllable (cf. W. Baumgartner, "Beiträge zum hebräischen Lexikon" in *Von Ugarit nach Qumran,* BZAW 77 [Berlin: Töpelmann, 1958] 29). The meaning is the same.

11.a. וכבשים "and lambs" is missing in LXX. But the meter requires the word (Procksch) and making the list full adds to the effect. It should be kept.

12.a. LXX ὀφθῆναι μοι and Syr *lᵉmeḥzâ ʾappaj* suggest the reading of one MS לִרְאוֹת, i.e., an active qal meaning "to see my face." Perhaps the change to niph "to appear before me" was intended to avoid speaking of seeing God. Whoever sees him will die (cf. Exod 23:15; 34:23; Deut 16:16; 31:11; 1 Sam 1:22; Ps 42:3).

Numerous emendations have been suggested (cf. Wildberger) to smooth out the abrupt expressions here. Even that of DSS[Isa] לרמוס "to trample" for רמס "trampling" should be thought of in this way. MT should be kept, and the abruptness attributed to conscious style.

12.b. LXX has τὴν αὐλήν μου for חצרי "courts," making a sg for MT's pl. But Wildberger notes that 2 Kgs 21:5 and 23:12 write about two courts of the Temple. Ezekiel distinguishes between an inner and outer court (8:16; 10:5).

15.a. DSS[Isa] adds אצבעותיכם בעאון "your fingers with iniquity." The addition is parallel to the previous stich and would be a metrical improvement on MT. Cf. 59:3 and Kutscher, *The Language and Linguistic Background of the Isaiah Scroll* (Leiden: Brill, 1979) 536.

18.a., 19.a., 20.a. Four conditional sentences use the impf tense in both the protasis and the apodosis. The last two add a second verb using a perfect tense with *wāw.* This sequence of tenses is the most simple form of condition in Hebrew. It may be considered ind, stating facts. Or it may be considered subjunctive, stating hypothetical situations (cf. J. Wash Watts, *A Survey of Syntax in the Hebrew Old Testament* [Grand Rapids: Eerdmans, 1964] 134). The context places these sentences early in the dialogue, thus favoring the understanding that they sketch possibilities, a view that the translation attempts to reflect.

21.a. LXX adds "Zion." The addition gives clarity to the sentence and is appropriate.

Form/Structure/Setting

Throughout the Vision of Isaiah certain passages show a marked structural resemblance to the arch in architecture, in which a wall opening is spanned by means of stone blocks assembled into an upward curve which maintains its shape and stability through mutual pressure of the separate pieces. The blocks usually have a wedge shape, with the block at the crown of the arch being called the keystone since it conveys balancing lateral pressures to the two sides of the structure. In the following example, the parallel thoughts of the verses marked A-A′, B-B′, C-C′, and D-D′ serve as the blocks of the two sides of the arch held in balance by the keystone, vv 7c–9. (Because of typographical considerations, the textual arch appears on its side, but the resemblance should be readily apparent to the reader.)

A "I reared my children—but they rebelled against me" (1:2).
  B "An ox knows—Israel does not know" (1:3).
    C "Ah! Sinful nation! Why more?" (1:4–5).
      D "Only wounds left—countryside desolate" (1:6–7b).
KEYSTONE Daughter of Zion isolated, like a city under siege—
except for the remnant left by Yahweh, would be like Sodom (1:7c–9).
      D′ Empty, useless worship (1:10–15a).
    C′ "Hands full of blood! Wash yourselves" (1:15b–17).
  B′ "Come, let us test each other" (1:18–20).
A′ "How has the faithful city become a harlot?" (1:21–23).

The formation ends here, but an overlapping structure balances vv 21–23 with vv 24–26 which follow.

Vv 2–7b speak of Israel. Vv 7c–23 describe and address Zion. Israel is spoken of as "children." Zion is viewed as a daughter. Both are badly alienated.

The passage is in the form of the beginning of a covenant lawsuit. (*OTFC* 164–66; G. E. Mendenhall, "Ancient Oriental and Biblical Law," *BA* 17/2 [1952] 26–46; H. B. Huffmon, "The Covenant Lawsuit," *JBL* 78 [1959] 285–95; J. Harvey, "Le 'Rib-pattern,' " *Bib* 43 [1962] 172–96.) Witnesses are summoned (v 2a). The chief litigant is announced (v 2b). His charges are given in brief (vv 2c–3). The accused is named (v 3c).

The witnesses are the same as those found in Deut 32 (cf. Rignell, *ST* 2 [1957] 140–58). In both Deut 32 and this passage the genre is incomplete. G. E. Wright has called this a "broken riv" ("The Lawsuit of God," *Israel's Prophetic Heritage,* FS J. Muilenburg [New York: Harper & Row, 1962], 62–67).

Vv 4–7b and 7c–9 are speeches by others than Yahweh, perhaps the witnesses already named. The change of speeches is marked by a change of subject and by repetition of a phrase (cf. Fohrer, *Studien,* 149). V 4 is a short "woe-speech" (cf. Hayes, *OTFC,* 164; C. Westermann, *Basic Forms,* 190–94; R. J. Clifford, "The use of HOY in the prophets," *CBQ* 28 [1966] 458–64; E. Gerstenberger, "The Woe-Oracles of the Prophets," *JBL* 81 [1962] 249–63; G. Wanke, "Mitteilungen הוי und אוי," *ZAW* 78 [1966] 215–18; J. G. Williams, "The Alas-Oracles," *HUCA* 38 [1967] 75–91). The meter is irregular, intentionally so. It is artfully composed (Wildberger). There is always a funereal aspect to a "woe-speech." This is no exception. The "woes" against Israel will be continued in chaps. 5 and 10 and will culminate in confirmation of total destruction decreed against her (10:25). Vv 5–7b are a chiding speech of warning instead of the more usual threat following a "woe."

The second speech (vv 7c–9) changes the subject from Israel to Zion. It is characterized by six uses of כ "like" for comparisons in parabolic style. V 9 has a chorus continue the theme.

Vv 10–17 have Yahweh speak in the style of a teacher giving instruction. He is announced by a herald who uses catchwords to join his speech to the preceding chorus. Such instruction may be given by a priest concerning proper forms of worship (Duhm, Begrich). But here the critique of worship is more than usual for a teacher (Jensen). A call for attention (v 10) and rhetorical questions (vv 11a, 12) fit the style of the wisdom teachers. The essence of the lesson is presented in a series of statements of God's attitude interspersed with imperative instructions. Vv 16–17 state the terms on which God will deal with his people. These are not negotiable.

The sequence of tenses is instructive. Imperatives dominate the "torah." Yahweh's position is stated in emphatic perfects. Zion's habits are pictured in imperfects.

Vv 18–20 are the closing appeal which defines the attitudes that would make negotiation possible. In the context of *riv,* these verses constitute what Harvey has called the fourth element (cf. *OTFC,* 166). Cultic procedures, like sacrifice, had already been eliminated from consideration.

The conditional sentences use imperfect tenses in both protasis and apodosis. They state simple indicative, more probable conditions (Watts, *Syntax,* 134, 139).

Vv 21–23 are a dirge which mourns the state of the city that was once God's pride. It begins with איכה "how," the characteristic opening for a dirge.

The perfect tense in vv 21 and 23 stresses the resultant condition. Imperfects in vv 21 and 23 contrast a characteristic condition with later characteristic results. Participles continue the characterization. V 23b–c changes to an accusation against the people or leaders of the city and prepares for the announcement of judgment to follow.

Comment

2 The Summons introduces two of the *dramatis personae.*

Heavens and *Earth* appear without the article. It is normally omitted in the vocative case (Joüon § 137*g*).

Hear, Heavens! The plural address to the heavens is maintained in MT but has become singular in some LXX MSS.

For Yahweh speaks demonstrates a reversed word order appropriate to the introduction of Yahweh as principal speaker in the Vision. The same reasoning accounts for the emphatic position of other words in the speech. The accused are presented: *children, Israel, my people.* The pronoun *they* is put before *rebelled:* "precisely these [children] have rebelled against me."

Rebelled (פשע) is a particularly appropriate word for the theology of apostasy expounded in the Vision. It fits the parent-child analogy as well as it does the king-subject pattern. It reflects the deep emotion of the problem and its effects on relationship. It shows the deliberately willed nature of the issue: the unwillingness to recognize the nature of the relationship to God as parent or king and to draw the consequences of that relation and the dependence that it implies. The entire Vision will show the effects and the results of this rebellion from the reign of Ahaz (734 B.C.) to conditions that were still current for the readers generations later.

3 *Ox and ass know.* Household animals learn and remember to whom they belong. They recognize their owners, their lords. "Ox" was used in myth to symbolize El, but that has no meaning here. One cannot think of the ass as having insight without being reminded of Balaam's patient animal (Num 22:21–30) which recognized what Balaam could not see. Only mankind rebels, refusing the most elementary recognition of the one who owns him.

Pseudo-Matthew 14 tells of the ox and the ass worshiping Jesus in Bethlehem's cradle and calls them a fulfillment of this part of Isaiah's prophecy. (Cf. E. Nielsen, "Ass and Ox in the OT," *Studia Orientalia Ioanni Pedersen dicata* [1953] 263–74; J. Ziegler, "Ochs and Esel an der Krippe," *MTZ* 3 [1952] 385–402.) The apocryphal gospel has correctly seen the meaning of the parable in Isaiah. Ox and ass are credited with recognition and discernment which men do not display.

Its masters. The plural is unusual. It could be a plural of majesty implying a superior being as in Exod 21:29; 22:10; or Job 31:39 (Wildberger). But this seems unnecessarily complex. Even if the ass has several owners, they keep him in one stall. He has only to find his way to the one place, which he does.

After the two imperative forms which introduce the speech, all the verbs are in the perfect tense. The first, *speaks,* has been translated as an emphatic present (Watts, *Syntax,* 38). The three in the second line are translated as present perfects indicating past actions with present effect (Watts, *Syntax,* 45). The tenses in v 3 are also perfects, but they speak of actions which are typical of their subjects. They are characteristic perfects (Watts, *Syntax,* 46).

4–7b Interpreters have made intensive efforts to identify the historical references in this chapter (W. T. Claassen, *JNWSL* 3 [1974] 1–18). Some have dated material to 734 B.C. making the invaders Syria and Israel, while others insist on a picture of Assyria's siege of Jerusalem in 701 B.C. (Wildberger). The pericope, like the entire chapter, evades dating and historical identification. It seems to do it deliberately. A fifth-century reader would have little concern to distinguish 734 from 701 B.C. He would also have been aware that the description had had multiple applications between the eighth century and his own time. The literary impact is far more important here than historical identification.

The addressee in vv 4–7 continues to be Israel. The distinction drawn between it and Zion in v 8 suggests the Northern Kingdom. The repeated Assyrian invasions which led to the destruction and exile of the tribes are pictured. The accusation is sustained. Israel is found guilty. The "woe speech" develops the full range of Israel's guilt with seven words to broaden the picture of rebellious (פשע) children who neither know (ידע) nor understand (בין). The words appear in three pairs with one word finally to summarize the effect. חטא and עון are the more common words for "sin" (R. Knierim, *Die Hauptbegriffe für Sünde im Alten Testament,* 2nd ed. [Gutersloh: Gerd Mohn, 1967]). They characterize the entire nation (גוי) and the people (עם). This leaves no doubt of identification. The nation is the ten-tribe Northern Kingdom which could properly be thought of as living "in sin" since the schism from the Davidic dynasty. The people are the covenant people, sealed to be God's own in covenant ceremonies from Sinai and Shechem on.

The basic idea of חטא is "to go astray, miss the mark." It means that one has missed the norm required by law, whether that be in society or in relation to God. The parallel word עון has a basic meaning of being "crooked" which leads to a life or deed that is wrong. This word suggests that the subject has an attitude that is not in line with God's will (L. Köhler, *OT Theology* [London: Lutterworth, 1957], 172–75). עון seems to always include the sense of guilt. By using the two words together Israel's position is clearly defined. They continually fail to do the right thing (note the participial meaning of continuing action). The resultant condition is one of guilt. Recent studies (Koch, Gese, Skladny) have stressed the way in which action, status, and fate are thought to interact and overlap. So here Israel's sin, guilt, and judgment are pictured together.

The second pair of words returns to the idea of children and continues to run parallel to Deut 21:18–21. זרע "seed" may be used as a synonym for "children." But here "seed" takes on a denigrating meaning. מרעים "evildoers" places them in bad company, doing bad things. While חטא and עון picture the subject as a citizen or worshiper who has failed and incurred guilt, רעה "evil" and שחת "broken" put the sinners in the ranks of criminals and outlaws. Deut 32:4 speaks of God's faithfulness contrasted with the broken (שחת) loyalty of Israel. זרע מרעים is "a seed composed of evildoers" (cf. GKC § 128*k-q*). Israel, God's children, has become his opposite.

The third pair of words stresses the distance between Yahweh and Israel, between what he stands for and what they represent. עזב "forsake" occurs some twenty-five times in Isaiah. In the first half of the Vision, it describes abandoned cities and countryside. In the second half, it is the key word in a continuing debate about God's responsibility for Israel and Zion after 587 B.C. (see *Comment* on 41:17 *passim,* esp. 54:6–7). Three times in the book עזב "abandon" is an accusation of breach of covenant in the claim that God's people have abandoned him. In 1:28 the accusation turns against the people of Jerusalem, while 65:11 uses it as one of the summary terms of judgment against those that are rejected in the new order. נאץ is a term at home in covenant literature (cf. Deut 31:20 and 32:19; also Jer 14:21). It means "to despise" in the sense of "think lightly of" or actually to ignore the covenant. The two terms "abandon" and "despise" are used in the deuteronomic literature to speak of breaking covenant and turning to other gods (Judg 2:12; 10:6, 10, 13; 1 Sam 8:8; 12:10). Israel's forsaking the covenant implies that Yahweh also abandons his covenant obligations (cf. Deut 31:19 and Jer 14:21). In Deut 31:16 "forsake" is parallel to "break my covenant," while Num 14:11 uses "despise" as the opposite of faith.

6 F. Buhl ("Zu Jesaja 1:5," *ZAW* 36 [1916] 117) cites the Annals of Tabari (III, 164) where a police officer is ordered to beat the scribe of the former mayor. Since the scribe's body appeared to be one continuous sore from the top of his head to the sole of his feet, the officer asked, "Where do you want to be beaten?" The scribe replied, "By Allah, there is no place on my body for a beating. But if you wish, then the palm of my hand."

The repugnant figure is continued. The figurative flogging has left wound over festered wound, until there seems no spot on the bruised, bleeding body where the whip can be applied. The horrible figure then turns toward an equally revolting historical reality: the ravages of war across a countryside, scarring the fields with fire and the cities with destruction.

8 *Is left.* This is the first appearance in Isaiah of a word linked to the doctrine of the remnant. It is repeated (in hiph) in v 9 with the noun *remnant.*

The watchman's booth is a familiar Near Eastern sight. The ripening fruit cannot be left unguarded against human theft or the invasion of animals or birds. The guard needs protection from the sun. So a booth of branches is made for him, elevated to enhance his field of vision. It will only last a season, but often remains long after the watchman is no longer needed.

The *fort-city* or watch-city was a fortified border town built to protect the frontiers. Solomon built these עירות נצורות as did every effective king. The direction from which danger was expected can be seen in the places where such cities are built. But these were invariably as far from the capital and the center of the nation as possible. Now the country has been overrun and Jerusalem itself is like one of those isolated watch-cities. The enemy has swept past, conquering the countryside, and leaving only the walled fortress intact.

9 The choral response accepts the evaluation of their condition, but changes the metaphor.

If not followed by the perfect tense introduces a condition-contrary-to-fact clause (Watts, *Syntax,* 136). The conditional sentence climaxes a series of comparisons. The comparison to Sodom and Gomorrah does not quite fit. *Sodom* and *Gomorrah* were ancient cities near the southern end of the Dead Sea which were reputed to have been destroyed by fire from heaven (Gen 19:24) and which lived only in memory. (Cf. *IDB,* 2:440; 4:395–97; *ISBE* 2:525.) All of the words in this group carry a potential double intention. By stressing that only this fragment is left, there is an implied accusation that God has abandoned the larger element that was destroyed or imprisoned. This negative suggestion appears in v 8. But the Vision will repeatedly stress a positive meaning of providential care which prevented complete genocide. V 9 is the first such contribution to Isaiah's doctrine of the remnant.

Intensive efforts have been made to identify the historical period to which vv 7c–9 apply (W. T. Claassen, *JNWSL* 3 [1974] 1–18). The major problems have turned on the interpretation of "an overthrow of strangers" and the description of Jerusalem's isolation or siege. The latter issue turned on the phrase כעיר נצורה, which was usually translated "like a besieged city." If the suggestion in *Notes* 8.a. is accepted, the reference is much less specific and the issue of whether this refers to an event in 734 B.C. or 701 B.C. cannot be determined by single words.

In view of the description of Israel's problems given in vv 4–7b, the period under discussion must come during one of Assyria's incursions into the land before the final fall of Samaria in 721 B.C. The language of this verse describes Jerusalem's isolation when the emperor's marauding armies were in the neighborhood. The specific horror of siege will be described later.

Assyria's incursions into west Asia began with Tiglath-Pileser's campaigns of 743 B.C. Opposition to him at that time was led by "Azriau of Yaudi" (*ANET,* 282). Bright (*HI* 270) thinks this refers to Uzziah of Judah. This would mean that Judah was involved in opposition to Assyria at a very early date. Assyria's campaigns wore down the defenses of the smaller western states so that by 738 B.C. most of them, including Damascus and Israel, were paying tribute. It is worth noting that Uzziah died about this time.

Tiglath Pileser was the founder of the Neo-Assyrian Empire. His armies fought for permanent conquest instead of simply seeking booty and prisoners, as before. He punished rebellion by transporting leaders to other areas. However, this did not prevent intrigue and struggle for power within the subject states.

Israel's history in this period reflects exactly such fluctuations, with intrigues and assassinations the order of the day (2 Kgs 15–16). Uzziah of Judah and Jeroboam of Israel may have stood together against Assyria in 750 B.C. or the years that followed. But neither unity nor stability could be found in the states by 738 B.C. Assyria made repeated incursions as punitive expeditions against Israel and Syria in the following years before Samaria's destruction in 721 B.C. In all these campaigns, Jerusalem and Judah remained isolated from the earlier coalition. War swirled so close about the city that she must have been strongly affected by it. But she survived, if only barely.

This passage has sketched the effects of this time but has deliberately avoided more specific identifications. The interpreter does well to follow suit.

11 *Sacrifice* is recorded as a part of worship from Abraham onward and is firmly anchored in the Mosaic Torah. (J. Milgrom, "Sacrifice and Offerings, OT," *IDBSup,* 763–71.) With the tendency toward centralization of worship in Jerusalem, sacrifice became increasingly important for the Temple and the city. But prophets stood in succession to Samuel (1 Sam 15:22) in insisting that sacrifice be considered secondary to obedience and faith. The Vision portrays the new Zion devoid of blood sacrifice (66:3). Yet only in that picture of the coming city is sacrifice forbidden.

The term here is שבעתי "I am satisfied, I have had enough." That which brings displeasure to God is not the sacrifice per se; the *trampling of his courts* is revolting to him. The failure to accompany sacrificial and festal worship with a lifestyle of justice and righteousness is the problem. The latter invalidates the former.

The vocabulary of worship in vv 11–16 is comprehensive. Worship occasions vary. In v 12 בוא לראות פני "come to appear before me" may describe any worship. The phrase should ordinarily have לפני "before me" for this translation. One Hebrew manuscript and Syriac reads לִרְאוֹת (qal) "to see my face." But this would be very unusual, for the OT teaches that one may not see the face of God and live. In vv 13, 14 חדש ושבת "new moon and sabbath" is one of the earliest designations for the lunar worship calendar and indicates worship at designated places at new and full moons, i.e., every fourteen days. קרא מקרא "a convened assembly" is in response to some special occasion. עצרה "solemn assembly" (v 13) is a meeting at which attendance is required. מועדים "set seasons" (v 14) are the annual festivals that are fixed in their calendar.

Worship actions include: (v 11) זבחים "sacrifices," the general word; עלות אילים "whole burnt offerings of rams"; חלב מריאים "fat of fed beasts"; דם פרים וכבשים ועתודים "blood of bulls, of lambs and he goats." This is a comprehensive list of the types of blood sacrifice. Leviticus speaks of them in terms of function, "sin offering, guilt offering," etc. But the same sacrifices are intended. מנחה (v 13) is a cereal offering; קטרת is incense; מנחת שוא "a vain offering." פרש כפים "spread your hands" (v 15a) describes prayer. תפלה (v 15b) is "prayer" in the particular sense of intercession.

The rejection of sacrificial worship is not only due to the abrogation of covenant but also belongs to the vision of the new Jerusalem (66:3–4) and is stated in much the same language. Sacrificial worship is characterized as something the people have chosen (66:3b) rather than responded to as the genuine call of God. God seeks those who will do what he requires and who seek that which delights him, those who are "willing and obedient" (v 19) and who "tremble at his word" (66:2, 5) (cf. R. D. Culver, "Isaiah 1:18—Declaration, Exclamation or Interrogation?" *JETS* 12 [1969] 133–41).

19 *Become willing and . . . obey.* The requisites of grace are the milder attitudes of submission and pliable attention: the humble willingness (אבה) simply to be God's own and do his will; the attentive listening (שמע) which heeds God's words and carefully does them. Those of God's people who do this *shall eat the good of the land.* The entire book of Deuteronomy expounds this theme.

20 *Refuse and continue obstinate.* The alternative corresponds to covenant theology (cf. Deut 27:1–28).

Explanation

The Vision of Isaiah is of a legal dispute, ריב (cf. also 3:12–15 and 5:1–7). The adversaries have been summoned in the title verse. They are Judah and Jerusalem. The witnesses have been called. Yahweh is the plaintiff; his children are in rebellion against him.

Neither the witnesses nor the readers are asked to judge them. God does that. They are called to observe and understand the ways of Israel and the ways of God.

The estranged children are first indicted for not knowing who they are or to whom they belong. "Not knowing," that is God's complaint! And, of course, action follows failure to know.

Israel is called first. This is Israel of covenant and sacred history, as well as the Northern Kingdom which claimed to perpetuate them. They have already been severely chastised. But there is no response from them or sign of repentance. That amazes the witness (vv 5–7b). The references to Israel will be continued in 2:5–9 and many times in the Vision.

Then attention is drawn to "daughter Zion," isolated and in dire straits. A chorus responds for Jerusalem (v 9). It is a pitiful and inadequate response, but it acknowledges a debt to Yahweh for his forbearance.

Yahweh takes the opportunity to address the daughter who has at least spoken a word and recognized some benefit from him. He lectures her about the inadequacy of sacrifice and prayer to deal with her problems. When one's hands are bloody, one needs to wash, clean up, and change one's way of life. It is not lack of worship, but lack of justice, that has produced the bloody hands and God's outrage.

Then Yahweh signals a willingness to negotiate. Guilt can be forgiven, former insults forgotten. But proper attitude is not negotiable in the covenant. The basic alternatives that Deuteronomy recorded for the covenant still apply. When the daughter is "willing" and attentive to the father's will, the promise of good things is still valid. But for the consistently negative and obstinate, there is no room for grace.

The witnesses wonder at the change in attitude and lifestyle that now characterizes daughter Jerusalem (v 21). They express their evaluation of the change of personality that has come over her. They do not recognize her as the fine community that once claimed Yahweh's favor (vv 22–23).

V 19 contains the distilled essence of the "knowledge" that Israel lacks (v 3). It teaches a doctrine that runs like a scarlet thread through the Vision. Ahaz will refuse it. Ephraim turns aside from it. Those called to be servants will deny it. For each of them the way of "willingness and obedience" is open, but they cannot find it in themselves to walk that way.

Paul (Rom 9:29) quotes v 9 as proof that God had not abandoned Israel. Although the Vision's primary concern at this point is to show Israel's and Jerusalem's filial sins, there is also deep concern for the future of the people of God.

Episode B:
Let Me Smelt Your Dross Like Lye (1:24–31)

Bibliography

Haymann, L. "Note on Isaiah 1:25." *JNES* 9 (1950) 217. **Hermisson, H. J.** "Zukunftserwartung und Gegenwartskritik in der Verkündigung Jesajas." *EvT* 33 (1973) 54–77. **Jones, D. R.** "Exposition of Isaiah Chapter One Verses Twenty-One to the End." *SJT* 21 (1968) 320–27. **Lack, R.** *La Symbolique,* 164–71. **Melugin, R. F.** "The Typical Versus the Unique among the Hebrew Prophets." *SBL Sem. Papers 1972,* vol. 2. Ed. Lane C. McGaughy. 331–42.

Translation

Herald:	24 *Therefore—Expression of the Lord*	1+2+2+2
	(Yahweh of Hosts), Hero of Israel!	
Yahweh:	*Woe! Let me ease myself from my adversaries!*	1+2+2
(to Zion)	*Let me avenge myself from my enemies!*	
	25 *Let me turn my hand upon you!*	3+3+3
	Let me smelt your dross like the lye!	
	Let me remove all your alloy!	
	26 *Let me return your judges as at the first*	3+2
	and your counselors as in the beginning.	
	After this you will be called	3+2+2
	City of the righteous,	
	Community of faithfulness.	
Heavens:	27 *Zion will be redeemed with justice*	3+2
	and her captivity[a] *with righteousness!*	
	28 *But a crushing*[a] *of rebels and sinners together—*	4+3
	and those forsaking Yahweh will be finished.	
Earth:	29 *For they will be undone because of their groves*	3+2
(to the people of	*which you (pl) have taken pleasure in.*	
Jerusalem)	*And you will be confounded because of the gardens*	2+2
	which you have chosen.	
	30 *For you (pl) will be like an oak*	3+2
	withered of foliage	
	and like a garden lacking water.	4
	31 *And it shall be that the strong*[a] *will become lint*	3+2
	and his product[b] *a spark.*	
	And they shall burn—the two together	3+2
	unextinguishable.	

Notes

27.a. ושביה (BDB, 995) "her captivity." LXX ἡ αἰχμαλωσία αὐτῆς (and Syr) "the captivity." *BHS* שביה (1) (BDB, 986). The emendation וישביה "her inhabitants" is interesting but unnecessary. Also ישב usually appears in a fem pl (cf. BDB, 442).

28.a. ושבר "a breaking." BDB (991) suggests a constr. But the pointing of abs is the same. Accents favor abs. LXX translates with a finite pass. verb and the two nouns as subjects as in the second stichos: καὶ συντριβήσονται οἱ ἄνομοι καὶ οἱ ἁμαρτωλοὶ ἅμα = ושברו "and they shall be broken." Vg *conteret* = ושבר, act. "and he will break" with nouns as objects. MT, though unusual, is possible and should be kept.

31.a. MT החסן "the strong" is infrequent, and as a noun is a *hapax.* DSS[Isa] החסנכם (otherwise חסן "wealth or treasure" BDB, 340) is a strange form (the article on a noun with 2 m pl pronominal suffix) "the strong of you" or "your wealth." LXX ἡ ἰσχὺς αὐτῶν "his strength" implies חסנו parallel to פעלו in the second stich. Vg follows LXX.

31.b. MT פעלו "and his product or work." DSS[Isa] ופעלכם "your works (also Syr and Tg) implies Heb ופעלו, inf constr from פעל "do or make."

The paragraph has varied from third to second pers. DSS[Isa] has chosen the second pers. LXX has turned to the third pers. MT has an impersonal reading first and a third pers for the second. MT should be sustained as the "more difficult reading." The others show signs of attempts to harmonize.

Form/Structure/Setting

The arch structure that bound vv 1–23 together has been demonstrated in the previous section. That presentation leads up to the strong "therefore" with which this section begins.

The artistic intricacy of the chapter is shown by the overlapping arches that begin in v 21 and continue through v 26 (cf. Lack, *La Symbolique,* 164–71; L. Alonso-Schökel, "Poesie hebraique," *DBSup* (1967) VII, col 47–90, particularly 59).

The first part (vv 21–23) is a speech of reproach (*Scheltwort*). V 24 begins the announcement of judgment.

A Faithful city has become a harlot (v 21a)
  B Was full of justice and righteousness (v 21b)
    C Silver has become dross (v 22)
      D Rulers have become rebels; there is no justice (v 23)
KEYSTONE Yahweh intervenes (v 24a)
      D′ I will take vengeance on my foes (v 24b)
    C′ I will purge your dross (v 25)
  B′ Let me return your judges as before (v 26a)
A′ Afterwards a community of faithfulness (v 26b)

The use of assonance and careful choice of words within the passage are worthy of careful study, as Alonso-Schökel and Lack have shown.

One may also notice the overlapping arch in vv 24–31:

A I will get relief for myself (v 24)
  B I will purge you (v 25)
    C I will restore you (v 26a)
KEYSTONE Afterwards a city of righteousness (v 26b)
    C′ Zion will be redeemed (v 27)
  B′ Rebels and sinners will die together (v 28)
A′ You will be ashamed (vv 29–31)

The lament (vv 21–23a) uses metaphors. The accusation (vv 23b–c) is direct and realistic. "Therefore" in v 24 leads into God's announcement that he will intervene directly to destroy his enemies, purify the city, and restore it. The three are bound together by the skillful weaving of the ideas of justice and righteousness in vv 21, 23, and 26 and by the ideas of change for the worse in v 21 and change back for the better in v 26 (cf. the chiastic structures demonstrated above).

The use of imperfect tenses throughout the passage is instructive, particularly in vv 27 and 28, which form a kind of summary: "Zion shall be redeemed in justice" (v 27); "Rebels (those who abandon Yahweh) will be completely destroyed" (v 28). These are continued by similar statements in imperfect in 2:2 and 3d.

Comment

24 *Therefore* is a major structural signal. This speech is the culmination of what has gone before. The elaborate introduction of Yahweh suggests the importance of the word to follow. Thus far the introductions have used simply "Yahweh" (vv 2, 10, 11, 18, 20). The speeches have contained the broader title: "Holy One of Israel" (v 4) "Yahweh of Hosts" (v 9). Here to *Yahweh of Hosts* is added *the Lord* and *Hero of Israel.*

Woe shows the dire nature of the announcement. It brings the note of a funeral dirge to God's announcement of his intentions. Six verbs follow (having seven objects) in the first person. Four are clearly marked as cohortative imperfects. They could be translated as expressing determination: "I am determined to ease myself." Or they can be expressions in which the speaker rouses himself to action. They do not ask permission to act.

The *adversaries* and *enemies* appear to be the apostate leaders of the city cited above.

25 *Turn my hand* means change from supporting to chastising.

The references to *smelt your dross* and *remove your alloy* pick up the figures of v 22.

26 *Returning your judges and your counselors* returns to the references of v 23.

After this. The Vision sees God's action as clearly dividing history into the "before" and the "after." Chaps. 40–48 speak of the "former times." 2:2 speaks of the "latter days."

Righteousness and *faithfulness* return to the references of v 21 completing the arch.

27 *Justice* and *righteousness* characterize all God's actions. The redemption of Zion will be no exception.

28 For *rebels* and *sinners* and apostates there can only await a total defeat.

29 *Groves* refer to pagan open-air places of worship. They worshiped fruitful nature and sought to participate in its bounty through fertility rites. *They* refers to the pagans. *You* (pl) is addressed to people in Jerusalem. (cf. 65:3–5).

31 *The Strong* החסן is an unusual word with implications of wealth. It implies the apparently prosperous, self-assured follower of the pagan philosophy. *This product* speaks of the results of his labor, his apparently successful attempts to build up wealth and power apart from God.

Explanation

The passage contains a crucial speech by Yahweh with echoes from two other speakers. They are addressed in large measure to the people of Jerusalem.

Having noted the sad state of the city (vv 8–23) and having invited its people and leaders to discuss a change (vv 18–20), apparently without response, the Lord determines to take unilateral action. He will act directly against his enemies in the city and outside. He will purge the city of its evils. He will restore leaders who will administer justice and rule with wisdom. Only then can the city's former character be restored.

Righteousness, faithfulness, and justice are the key qualities that the City of Yahweh must exemplify. All else is derivative and secondary. This can only come in Zion when "rebels," "sinners," and apostates are crushed and removed.

Vv 29–31 present the matter in different terms. The passage begins by noting that the "rebels," "sinners," and apostates of v 28 will "be undone" because of false worship: their addiction to the pagan pleasures and promises of the fertility worship of Baal which promised satisfaction and success to its devotees. "You" are the inhabitants of Jerusalem who have allowed themselves to participate in those rites.

The end for the pagans will also overtake the apostates who joined in their festivity. This process is pictured in the very appropriate figure of the "gardens." The dry summer has left the garden and trees dry and lifeless. In the same way the "strong" and successful pagan is like "lint," dry tinder. The produce of his thought and labor becomes "a spark" that ignites the conflagration—the dreaded fires of the dry summer which no one can extinguish. Neither the pagan nor his work survives. The Jerusalemites have deliberately chosen that kind of life and will share that end.

The central motif is "smelt away dross and remove alloys," a figure for Zion's corrupt leaders (v 23). These leaders have been urged to wash themselves and make themselves clean (v 16). They have shown themselves not willing, not obedient (v 19). Now Yahweh proposes to take over the job of cleaning out the city.

The value of the city's character, her justice and righteousness, has the figure of "silver which has become dross" (v 22). The parallel figure of watered wine is not continued. Both relate to the primary figure of the harlot. Harlotry relates to silver (her hire) and to wine (her debauchery). The figure carries double significance: corruption of the silver and corruption for silver (Lack, *La Symbolique,* 165).

The themes are carefully developed in superb poetry, but the importance of the theme is greater. A basic theme for the entire book is introduced here. Since Zion's place in God's plan is secure, the issue will turn on a people for God's city. This people will have to be pure—in righteousness, justice, and loyalty to Yahweh. All other elements—all those not "willing" and obedient—will be purged out. If they will not "wash" themselves, Yahweh will remove them. The fire which destroys God's enemies will purge the city making redemption and restoration possible.

Episode C: The Mountain of Yahweh's House (2:1–4)

Bibliography

Cannawurf, E. "Authenticity of Micah 4:1–4 (cf. to Isa 2:2–4)." *VT* 13 (1963) 26–33. **Cazelles, H.** "Qui aurait visé, a l'origine, Isaie ii 2–5." *VT* 30 (1980) 409–20.

Delcor, M. "Sion, centre universel, Is. 2:1–5." *AsSeign* 2, 5 (1969) 6–11. **Junker, H.** "Sancta Civitas Jerusalem Nova. Eine formkritische und überlieferungsgeschichtliche Studie zu Jes. 2." *Ekklesia,* FS Bp. M. Wehr. Ed. H. Gross. TTS 15. Trier: Paulinus Verlag, 1962. 17–33. **Kosmala, H.** "Form and Structure in Ancient Hebrew Poetry [includes 2:2–3]." *VT* 14 (1964) 423–45. **Martin-Achard, R.** "Israel, peuple sacerdotal." *CVC* 18 (1964) 11–28. **Pakozdy, L. M. von.** "Jes. 2:2ff.: Geschichte-Utopie-Verkündigung." *Vom Herrengeheimnis der Wahrheit.* FS H. Vogel. Berlin: de Gruyter, 1962. 416–26. **Stampfer, J.** "On Translating Biblical Poetry: Isa. chs. 1 and 2:2–4." *Judaism* 14 (1965) 501–10. **Wildberger, H.** "Die Völkerwallfahrt zum Zion: Jes. 2:1–5." *VT* 7 (1957) 62–81.

Translation

Herald: 1 *(The word which Isaiah son of Amoz envisioned*
(editor) *concerning Judah and Jerusalem)*
Prophet: 2 *And it shall be after these days* 3
(to Heavens and Earth) *that the mountain of the house of Yahweh* 2+2
will be established[a]
by the head of the mountains 2+2
and lifted up above the hills
and unto it[b] *all nations*[c] *will flow* 2+2
3 *and many peoples*[a] *will go.*
And they will say, "Come, let us ascend 3+2+3
to the mountain of Yahweh,
to the house of the God of Jacob
and he will instruct us from his ways 2+2
and we shall walk in his paths."
For from Zion Torah issues 2+2
and the word of Yahweh from Jerusalem.
4 *And he will judge between the nations* 3+3
and he will decide for many peoples.[a]
And they shall beat their weapons into ploughs 3+3
and their curved swords into pruning hooks.
Nation will not lift a sword against nation 4+3
Nor will they learn war anymore.

Notes

2.a. Syr and Mic 4:1 have a different word order and different meter. נכון "established" is placed at the beginning of the next line. The second stich of that line adds הוא "it" to gain two smooth 3+3 lines. MT should be supported here.

2.b. MT אליו "unto it." Mic 4:1 עליו "upon it."

2.c., 3.a. In Mic 4:1–2 the order of הגוים "nations" and עמים "peoples" is reversed and כל "all" is omitted.

4.a. Syr adds עד רחוק "even to a distance." Mic 4:3 also contains the additional words. As in v 2 Micah reverses "nations" and "peoples."

The use of impf tenses predominates, as in the latter sections of 1:29 and 30. So now the dominant statements in vv 2b, 3d, and 4c use impf tenses. Cons pf tenses are used to bind together the supporting clauses in vv 2–3a and v 4.

Form/Structure/Setting

V 1 has usually been understood as a superscription for a separate section, parallel to 1:1. It is superficially similar. But it is distinctly different. דבר "word" should normally be understood to refer to one speech or oracle, not a collection. The function of the verse is parallel to that of 1:24. There the long ascription "Expression of the Lord, Yahweh of Hosts, Hero of Israel" lends authenticity and force to the judgment announced in God's name. But rather than ascribing divine origin to the words, 2:1 claims them for Isaiah ben Amoz (P. Ackroyd, "A Note on Isaiah 2:1," *ZAW* 75 [1963] 320; and "Isaiah I–XII: presentation of a prophet" in *Congress Volume: Göttingen,* VTSup 29 [Leiden: E. J. Brill, 1978], 32–33, n. 44). This may be intended to counter the claim that these words belong to Micah (Mic 4:1–3). But what is more important in the book of Isaiah is the claim that this view of Zion's future without nationalistic goals actually belongs to Isaiah of eighth-century Jerusalem. It was not an invention of convenience by the post-exilic community.

Explanation

The third of these pericopes dealing with Zion puts the purging judgment into the perspective of God's purpose for Zion and brings the chapters into line with the book's full message (cf. chaps. 65–66). Zion's ultimate purpose has nothing to do with either Israel's or Judah's nationalistic dreams. Their wishes to be "nations like other nations" (1 Sam 8:5) have led to centuries of bloodshed and warfare. Nothing faintly resembling justice or righteousness has come from these.

Parties in Judaism were prepared in fifth-century Jerusalem to claim God's promises and blessing for new forms of nationalistic efforts. Some were Zionists (cf. chaps. 60–62). Some were Israelites (cf. 63:7—64:12). The purpose of the book is to deny both their claims (cf. 65:1–16) and put forward an entirely different view of Zion's destiny.

This pericope is the first clear statement: The city will be redeemed. The kingdoms will perish, but the city has an abiding place in God's future. The absolute requirements of justice and righteousness will be achieved. Thus the city will be equipped to be God's instrument. It will be ready to have his presence, to be his dwelling place.

After the purge (1:28–31), Zion reflects neither the ambitions of Joshua nor those of David. The important thing about Zion is her reputation as Yahweh's dwelling. It is *Yahweh's house,* the temple, which stands out. And that is important because he is present and active there.

Yahweh's presence in the Temple lifts its importance to supremacy. This supremacy has nothing to do with Israel or Judah, their kings or leaders. Purely because Yahweh is there, Zion attracts the nations.

Yahweh's actions are those of *torah* and word. These constitute judging and making wise. They result in turning the nations to peaceful pursuits.

It is important to note that Yahweh's purpose has been a part of Israel's revealed tradition throughout. Abraham was called to be a blessing to all the families of the earth (Gen 12:3b). Israel was called to be a "kingdom of priests" (Exod 19:6). But they had not succeeded. In Isaiah's Vision God moves to take things into his own hands. He will do what is necessary to establish the city and judge the nations. He will remove all the elements from the population that do not fit this new mode of operation.

The Vision of Isaiah pictures God's search for a people for his city. The Vision will depict successive generations of the people of God: Israelites, Judeans, Jerusalemites, and proselytes who refuse roles in Yahweh's new city and its program.

What is this new city and its program? Vv 2–4 show a city centered in Yahweh himself. The city is simply the place where he lives. His attraction for nations and peoples is so great that they "flow" uphill to the summit of the mountains to learn from "the God of Jacob" the lessons to which Israel and Judah turned deaf ears. What they learn from Yahweh will eliminate war among them. The age of peace will come.

What will be the role of God's people in this city? The rest of the book will speak to that question. Righteousness and justice have already been shown to be non-negotiable requirements. Willingness and obedience have been named as needed qualities. Faith, patience, and humility will be among the virtues taught to the servants of the King of Zion, Yahweh, the God of Israel.

This little gem seems to hang suspended between the domestic court scene in chap. 1 and the "Day of Yahweh" scene in 2:5–22. In a very real sense it expresses the condensed and controlling theme of the entire Vision. Accented by the claim that this is an authentic word from Isaiah himself (v 1), it looks to "the end" and the role of Zion in that time. Zion is portrayed as a temple city, the greatest and most popular pilgrimage city in the world. It holds this distinction because it is the place of Yahweh's dwelling. Zion will be identified with Yahweh as "the God of Jacob." He will be sought out as a teacher of individuals and as a judge who brings peace and order among nations.

This irenic picture of Zion and of Yahweh is a far cry from those of David's Jerusalem in the Psalms. There Yahweh (and the Davidic king) rules the world from Jerusalem. The rulers of the nations are forced to come there to acknowledge the sovereignty of Yahweh and the Davidic king and bring tribute. The Vision presents the immediate future in terms of turmoil and violence. Yahweh instigates and takes a primary part in it. However, this view (vv 2–4) looks at Jerusalem beyond the battles.

It is very practical and realistic. There is little here of the idealistic perfection pictured in 11:6–9 or 35:1–10. It nonetheless describes a sharp reversal of policy and goal. There is nothing here of political dominance or of nationalism. Zion's appeal will be religious and universal. The progress of the Vision will mark the steps toward this goal. They are marked especially in 4:2–6; 12:1–6; 24:21–23; 40:1–11; 49:5—54:17 (especially chaps. 52–53); and 65:17—66:24.

This beautiful picture defines the form that the restoration of the city, announced in 1:26–27, will assume. In it the first of the dominant themes of the Vision begins to take shape.

Scene 2: The Day of Yahweh (2:5–22)

Bibliography

Becker, J. *Der Prophet und sein Buch,* 46. **Bertram, G.** " 'Hochmut' und verwandte Begriffe im griechischen und hebräischen Alten Testament." *WO* 3 (1964) 32–43. **Davidson, R.** "The Interpretation of Isaiah 2:6ff." *VT* 16 (1966) 1–7. **Deist, F. E.** "Notes on the Structure of Isa. 2:2–22." *Theologia Evangelica* 10/2–3 (1977) 1–6. **Hoffman, H. W.** *Die Intention der Verkündigung Jesajas,* 107. **Lack, R.** *La Symbolique,* 38–39. **Milgrom, J.** "Did Isaiah prophesy during the reign of Uzziah?" (Excursus b: 2:10ff. and the Earthquake), *VT* 14 (1964) 178–82. **Napier, B. D.** "Isaiah and the Isaian." *VTSup* 15 (1966) 240–51. **Seybold, K.** "Die anthropologischen Beiträge aus Jesaja 2." *ZTK* 74 (1977) 401–15.

ON "THE DAY OF YAHWEH"
Cerny, L. *The Day of Yahweh and Some Relevant Problems.* Prague: U. of Karlovy, 1948. **Gelin, A.** "Jours de Yahvé et jour de Yahvé." *Lumière et Vie* 2 (1953) 39–52. **Mowinckel, S.** "Jahves Dag." *NorTT* 59 (1958) 1–56, 209–29. **Rad, G. von.** "The Origin of the Concept of the Day of Yahweh." *JSS* 4 (1959) 97–108. **Schunck, K. D.** "Strukturlinien in der Entwicklung der Vorstellung von 'Tag Jahwes.' " *VT* 14 (1964) 319–30.

ON THE PHRASE ביום ההוא:
Lefèvre, A. "L'expression 'En ce jour-là' dans le livre d'Isaie." FS A. Robert (1957) 174–79. **Munch, P. H.** "The Expression 'bajjom hahu,' is it an Eschatological terminus technicus?" *ANVAO* 2. Oslo: Hist.-Filos. Klasse, 1936. **de Vries, S.** *Yesterday, Today, and Tomorrow.* Grand Rapids: Eerdmans, 1975. Chap. 2.

Translation

A Speaker:	5 *House of Jacob,*	2+2+2
(to Israel)	*Come and let us walk*	
	in the light of Yahweh.	
	6 *For it applies* [a] *to his people*	3+2
	the House of Jacob.	
Second Speaker:	*But they are full* [b] *from the East*	3+2+3
(to the court)	*and are telling fortunes like Philistines*	
	and they do business with strangers' sons.	
Chorus:	7 *So that his land became full*	3+2+3
	of silver and gold—	
	no end to his [a] *treasures.*	
	So that his land filled with horses—	3+3
	no end to his [a] *chariots*	
	8 *So that his land became full of idols:*	3+3+3
	to the product of his hands they bowed down	
	to that which his fingers had made.	

9 *So that mankind became degraded* 2+2
and a person became humiliated.
Heavens and Earth: *Do not release them!* 2+2+2
(to the jailer) 10 *Come into the rock!*
And hide yourself in the dust!
From the face of Yahweh's dread 3+2
and from the brilliance of his majesty.[a]
Heavens: 11 *The eyes of the haughtiness of mankind* 4+3+3
shall be humbled,[a]
and exaltation of men shall be brought down
and Yahweh alone shall be exalted
in that day. 2
Earth: 12 *For there is a day belonging to Yahweh of Hosts* 4
upon everything high and raised 4
and[a] *upon everything lifted up—and it shall fall,*[a] 4
13 *and upon all the cedars of Lebanon,* 4
which are high and lifted up 2
and upon all the oaks of Bashan 4
14 *and upon all the high mountains* 4
and upon all the raised hills 4
15 *and upon every high tower* 4
and upon every impenetrable wall 4
16 *and upon all the ships of Tarshish* 4
and upon all boats[a] *of exotic lands.*[b] 4
Heavens: 17 *And the haughtiness of the human shall be brought down* 3+3+3
and the exaltation of men shall be abased
and Yahweh alone shall be exalted +3
in that day. 2
Prophet: 18 *And as for the idols—they will completely disappear.*[a] 3
Earth: 19 *And they shall go into the caves of the rocks* 3+2
and into the holes of the dust
from the face of the dread of Yahweh 3+2+3
and from the splendor of his majesty
when he rises to make the earth tremble.[a]
Heavens: 20 *In that day mankind will abandon* 2+2
his[a] *silver idols and his golden idols* 3+3+4
which he[b] *had made for himself*[b] *to worship*
for the digging of moles[c] *and bats—* 3+3+2
21 *for the going into the crevices of the rock*
and into the clefts of the crags,
from the face of the dread of Yahweh 3+2+3
and from the splendor of his majesty
when he rises to make the earth tremble.
Yahweh: 22 *Stop your (talk) about mankind,* 3+3+3
who has (only) breath in his nostrils!
For, in what[a] *(way) can he be evaluated?*

Notes

6.a. Duhm (39) thought the beginning of this section was mutilated. He judged v 5 to be a late addition. Then he read v 6 as the beginning of the new section. He accepted LXX's reading as 3rd pers but felt the need for an expressed subj and suggested emending to read: נטש יה עמו "Yah has abandoned his people." He is right in noting that the 2nd pers here is "*auffällig*" or "strange." He has followed some of the form of the LXX, but not its meaning. Ἀνῆκε means "to approach, pertain to," not "to abandon." Wildberger (92) takes a different approach. He accepts v 5 as "applicatio" for Israel which may have been added for use in worship services (77). He then makes the break between vv 5 and 6. He suggests the assumption that an original relation between vv 6 and 7 existed (92) and works on that basis in a fairly lengthy discussion of the problem, raised by the LXX, reading a 3rd pers (instead of 2nd), and by Tg using a 2nd pers pl to address the people. Syr and OL versions follow MT.

If, however, v 6a is read with v 5, as do DSS[Isa] and Tg, the next section begins with 6b. With this in mind let us take another look at the relation of MT and LXX.

The Masoretic rendering of this verse seems clear. Only the addition on the verb might draw comment: כי נטשתה עמך בית יעקב "For you have neglected your people, the house of Jacob." However, the setting in context is rough, to say the least. After the picture of the exaltation of Yahweh's house in the last days when the peoples from the nations will flow toward it, the house of Jacob is invited to join the procession and "walk in the light of Yahweh." The verb is cohortative, 1st pers pl. The tone and the address (2nd masc sg) of the following, "for you have abandoned your people, the house of Jacob," take a shocking turn. V 6 is in tune with the following verses, which reproach Israel for its sins. But one cannot avoid a sense of shock at the turn from v 5 to v 6.

It is therefore of interest to note a completely different rendering of the verb in LXX (which incidentally is not mentioned in *BHS*): ἀνῆκε γὰρ τὸν λαὸν αὐτοῦ τὸν οἶκον τοῦ Ισραηλ "for it applies to his people the house of Israel." The exchange of "his" for "your" is to read ו as ך. "Israel" for "Jacob" is a frequent variant without change of meaning. So the real difference turns on the verb ἀνῆκε "it applies" for נטשתה "you neglected." If the LXX were retranslated into Hebrew it should read something like: כי נטה את העמו. Cf. the MT: כי נטשתה עמך. The suggestion that the LXX is a witness to a superior text, while the MT records the corruption of הא into ש and the evolution of ו to ך to fit the change of pers, commends itself strongly. Or can it be a deliberate change with theological motivations? V 5 is undeniably a call to Israel (בית יעקב "house of Jacob") to go up to worship the God of Jacob at Zion. The *textus receptus* of MT negates that with the announcement that they have now been abandoned, while LXX (consistent with 2–4 and 5) confirms that the invitation is valid. This could be interpreted as an open door to Samaritans in later times.

The emended text should then read: כי נטה את־העמו בית יעקב and should be translated: "for it applies to his people, the house of Jacob." The line is then an explanation of the invitation in v 5. And the next should be translated "but" to begin the explanation of Israel's rejection of Yahweh's invitation.

6.b. An object appears to be lacking for מלאו. "Full" of what? D. W. Thomas ("A lost Hebrew word in Isa 2:6," *JTS* 13 [1962] 323–24) suggests emending מקדם "from the East" to מעקדים "enchanters." The suggestion provides a parallel to עננים: "enchanters and soothsayers like the Philistines." It is a possible rendering. MT gives a parallel to Philistines in "from the East," stressing foreign influence. MT is possible and should be kept.

7.a. ו as a sg suffix is consistently used here with verbs in the pl until the end of v 9 where the pl suffix appears. It must be judged a deliberate stylistic usage which cannot be reproduced in English.

10.a. LXX adds ὅταν ἀναστῇ θραῦσαι τὴν γῆν = בקומו לערץ הארץ "when he takes his place to make the earth tremble." The clause makes the earthquake imagery explicit. The addition adds a stich, but would otherwise fit the meter. However, MT seems sufficient as it is.

11.a. שָׁפֵל "shall be humbled" follows a plural subject. DSS[Isa] has תשפלנה (pl) which eliminates the problem. J. Huesman ("Finite Uses of the Infinitive Absolute," *Bib* 37 [1956] 287) emended to inf abs שָׁפֹל, but this does not solve the problem.

12.a-a. LXX *καὶ ἐπὶ πάντα ὑψηλὸν καὶ μετέωρον, καὶ ταπεινωθήσονται* "and upon everything exalted and lifted up, and it will be made low." This apparently adds ונבה "and exalted" and may well indicate that this originally stood here instead of (not in addition to, as LXX) ושפל "and it shall fall."

16.a. שכיות has traditionally been derived from שכה and understood as an "art object." The context calls for a parallel to אניות "ships." LXX had trouble with both תרשיש, which it translates *θαλάσσης* "sea," and with שכיות, which it translates *θέαν πλοίων* "goddess of ships." Recent studies (K. Budde, "Zu Jesaja 1–5," *ZAW* 49 [1931] 198; G. R. Driver, in *Studies in OT Prophecy,* FS T. H. Robinson, ed. H. H. Rowley [Edinburgh: T. & T. Clark, 1950], 52) suggest an Egyptian background in the word *šk.tj* meaning "ship." The same word may explain the Ug word *ṯkt* (W. F. Albright, *FS A. Bertholet,* ed. W. Baumgartner [Tübingen: Mohr, 1950], 4, n. 3; Aistleitner, *Wörterbuch* ², No. 2862).

16.b. G. R. Driver suggests that החמדה means "the desirable land" and thinks of Arabia. Hence NEB "dhows of Arabia."

18.a. MT has a discrepancy in number between subject and verb. DSS^Isa corrects it with יחלופו (pl) which is also supported by the versions.

19.a. Note the assonance of לערץ הארץ.

20.a. The afformative in אלילי כספו applies to the entire construction (cf. J. Weingreen, "The Construct-Genitive Relation in Hebrew Syntax," *VT* 4 [1954] 50–59).

20.b. There is a discrepancy of number. LXX reads עשו "they made" as a sg. It should be emended to עשה "he made."

20.c. לחפר פרות has no meaning as it stands. LXX translates *τοῖς ματαίοις* which means "useless" or "powerless" and refers to the idols. Θ has *φαρφαρωθ*, transliterating the two words as one. BDB says this is a *hapax legomenon* for "a mole" and is parallel to the next word.

22. LXX leaves this verse out altogether. Perhaps this is a recognition that it is a break in the context.

22.a. במה "in what?" Vg translates *excelsus reputatus est ipse* and seems to have read it as רמה "height," which is adopted by S. Talmon (*Textus* 4 [1964] 1270). Syr *'ajk* and Tg וכלמא השיב הוא seem to have read כמה "how much? how long?" M. Dahood ("Hebrew-Ugaritic Lexicography I," *Bib* 44 [1963] 302) proposed to vocalize this as בָּמָה and translate "animal": "Turn away from man in whose nostrils is divine breath, but who must be considered a beast." Dahood bases this on the Ug *bmt,* but Wildberger protests that this means "back," not "animal." MT's question makes sense and should be kept.

Form/Structure/Setting

The end of the previous paragraph is clearly marked. V 5 begins with a different address (Israel) and a different subject. The passage is complex. Documentation of Israel's sin and judgment digresses into a treatment of mankind's sin of pride, which Yahweh cannot tolerate.

The entire section, from v 6 through v 22, which has an arch structure, responds to the invitation to the House of Jacob in v 5 by identifying the fate of Jacob with that of mankind, and both with the Day of Yahweh.

A Come, House of Jacob—the invitation applies to his people (vv 5–6a)
  B But they are full of paganism, in which mankind (אדם) is degraded; Do not forgive them (vv 6b–9)
    C Hide in the rocks from the dread of Yahweh (v 10)
      D Arrogant mankind (אדם) will be humbled; Yahweh alone will be exalted (v 11)
KEYSTONE The Day of Yahweh shall be upon proud and lofty humanity (vv 12–16)

D′ The pride of humanity (אדם) will be humbled; Yahweh alone will be exalted (vv 17–18)
C′ Flee to the rocks from the dread of Yahweh (v 19)
B′ Humanity (אדם) will throw away idols and riches (v 20)
C′ They will flee to the rocks from the dread of Yahweh (v 21)
A′ Cease ye from humanity (אדם): for in what does he count? (v 22)

The "ye" of v 22 refers back to the speakers of v 5, commanding them to respect the ban Yahweh has placed on his people, the house of Jacob, which prevents them from joining the peoples ascending the temple mount.

The unity of the passage, as well as the identity of "the house of Jacob," has been thoroughly discussed. H. Junker (*TTS* 15 [1962] 33) defended the intimate connection of vv 2–4 with vv 6–21 on the grounds of Isaiah's view of the high and invulnerable holiness of Zion as the throne of Yahweh. The cultic reforms of Hezekiah are seen as the background of the passage in which the introduction of an Assyrian altar into the Temple by Ahaz (2 Kgs 16:10–20) was the high point of paganization of the "house of Jacob," which he understands to include Judah. Davidson (*VT* 16 [1966] 1–7) understood "the house of Jacob" to refer to the Northern Kingdom and places the time in the Syro-Ephraimite war. Kaiser in his first edition (33) understands this as a speech in the Temple during a festival occasion in which the prophet may address the people and God. In his second edition (66) he finds the entire composition belongs to the final redaction of the book.

If the search for an original setting be put aside in favor of an attempt to see the passage in its setting in the book, it may be noted:

(1) With the description of the Day of Yahweh all the major themes of the book have been touched in these two chapters. They are a most fitting prologue (or overture) for the Vision.

(2) The setting in the book favors an understanding of references in the eighth-century scenes to Israel/Jacob's being the Northern Kingdom. This commentary has so understood this chapter and 1:2–8 before it.

(3) The chronological order of the Vision suggests that everything before 6:1 be understood as belonging to the reign of Uzziah/Jotham, although more specific historical dating is not encouraged by the data provided.

Comment

6a The emendation proposed, following LXX, reverses the meaning of the first line from MT and most translations. It emphasizes Israel's role as Yahweh's people, that is, her covenant and elect status. The tension between election and conduct that required God to reject them is a theme pursued throughout the book. Indeed, Paul is still at it in Rom 5–7.

The ark of Yahweh was brought to Jerusalem as an act of "all Israel" (2 Sam 6:1–5). All Israel was accustomed to go up to Jerusalem to worship. Jeroboam had to take measures to discourage it when the northern tribes withdrew from the United Monarchy (1 Kgs 12:26–33). It is a natural assumption that the restoration of the city should make it accessible to "all Israel."

6b It is a sad commentary on two centuries of separation and the resulting religious infidelity that this was not to be. The separation had been politically and economically successful, as the wry "fullsome" comments show. But it had also been spiritually disastrous.

From the East is apparently a general statement, not intended to imply specific imports.

9 Israel's lifestyle has become indistinguishable from that of humanity in general. *Mankind* becomes the theme that will continue to the end of the chapter. The term evokes thoughts and images from Gen 1–11. Israel is judged to have relived the experiences of the "sons of Adam" and thus to share the same degradation, humiliation, and eventual judgment.

9c אל־תשא להם means literally something like "Do not lift up for them!" This has sometimes been understood as forgiveness. However, the context points more to the meaning "Do not allow them to go up in the pilgrimage!" Instead they are to prepare for the cataclysmic events to come.

V 6a has missed the important point that Zion's elevation and peaceful assessibility were to come in "the last days" after the judgment. The terrible "day" must come first.

A major motif in OT theology is here (and in vv 11–22): pride and ambition are humanity's besetting and most devastating sins. Idolatry is seen as an expression of this drive by which man seeks to exalt himself. The key word is אדם "man." The counterpoint is between words for exaltation and humiliation. In this passage (v 9) man is degraded and humbled by idolatry. The following passage (vv 11–22) views the sin in opposite terms. Idolatry is seen as a symbol of man's ambition and pride (v 18) which will be judged. For Yahweh alone can be exalted.

This, too, is a major theme for the book of Isaiah. Israel, Judah, and the inhabitants of Jerusalem cannot accept the servant role. This determination to avoid the humble prevents them from participation in God's new city.

11, 17 The entire passage relates to its context in terms that contrast the genuine and correct exaltation of Yahweh with the temporary and contemptible self-exaltation of humanity. It is a theme reflected in the building of the Tower of Babel (Gen 11) and is a recurrent theme in Isaiah. It speaks of the general day of humiliation for mankind within which Israel's special sin (vv 6–9) will be punished. Israel has not only sinned against covenant but also participates in humanity's attempt at self-exaltation against God. So one writes here of *humanity* and *men.*

12–16 This is a description of Yahweh's action against everything *high* and *exalted.* The contents are reminiscent of Ps 29 where the power of Yahweh is pictured in terms like those used in Ugarit for Ba'al (cf. 11, AB VII, 27a–41; H. L. Ginsburg, "A Phoenician Hymn in the Psalter," *Atti del xix Congr. Int.d.Oriental.* [1935] 472–76; T. H. Gaster, "Psalm 29," *JQR* 37 [1946/47] 55–65; F. M. Cross, "A Canaanite Psalm in the OT," *BASOR* 117 [1950] 19–21).

The name *Yahweh of Hosts* is fitting for the description of the day reflecting the Holy War concepts of early Israel.

The words *high, raised, lifted up,* and *exalted* describe divine characteristics which humanity has tried to appropriate to itself. This is mankind's persistent and pervasive sin, the attempt to be like God (Gen 3:5), which has prevented the achievement of a genuine humanity and led to repeated conflict with God.

The figures that follow illustrate the superlative of Israelite experience from the *cedars of Lebanon, the oaks of Bashan,* to *the ships of Tarshish.* The giant trees were wonders for the Palestinian who knew only small and warped trees on the hills. The ships were symbols of wonder for the Israelites who feared the seas.

But also included are figures of things nearer home: *mountains* and *hills, towers* and *walls.* These were symbols of pride and power in Canaan. The *tower* מגדל may be in an open field (Isa 5:2), but is more likely a fortress tower which may be a part of a wall or stand in the middle of a city (cf. Judg 9:46; E. F. Campbell/J. F. Ross, "Shechem and the Biblical Tradition," *BA* 26 [1963] 16; G. E. Wright, *Shechem* [New York: McGraw-Hill, 1964], 94, 124).

Tarshish was a distant port frequented by Phoenician ships. The term *ships of Tarshish* referred to the strong commercial ships which were used for the longest routes, flagships of the fleets.

18–21 The day of terror will lead to the end of idols which have proved useless in preventing danger. *In that day* ties the picture to the *day belonging to Yahweh* of v 12.

The passage blends the motifs of Yahweh's day with those of judgment on pride and on idols. The Day of Yahweh motif occurs in the OT from the time of Amos (5:18) when he speaks of a day which is already well known throughout the period of OT writing. It is a day on which Yahweh acts in a special way. He intervenes in the course of history.

The idea of this "day" was not yet that of a *ἡμέρα θεοῦ* or *κυρίου* which in the NT pictures the end of the world, the last judgment, and the return of Christ (*TDNT II,* 954). The idea is much more varied and flexible. Jer 46:10 speaks of "a day of vengeance" against Egypt. Ezek 30:1–9 prophesies a day of judgment against the nations. But in Ezek 7 it is a day of judgment against Israel. In Zephaniah the day brings judgment on Israel and the nations. The motif occurs also in Joel, Obad 15, and Zech 14:1 (cf. Wolff, *Joel und Amos,* BKAT XIV/2 [Neukirchen-Vluyn: Neukirchener Verlag, 1969], 38–39). But it has nothing to do with the breach of covenant (1:2–3) or Israel's status here. So the witnesses are called back to deal with the business at hand (v 22).

Milgrom notes that judgment on man's pride and grab for power runs like a scarlet thread through Isaiah's prophesies. Cf. 3:16; 13:11b; 14:11–14; 25:11b–2; 26:5; 28:1,3; 30:25; 33:18. The Day of Yahweh motif often includes ideas from the Holy War (von Rad) and some interpreters think it related to a particular festival day.

Explanation

A speaker presumes that the announcement of Zion's future destiny means that Israel is now free. But this is set straight. Israel's guilt has been proved. The jailer is instructed not to release her but that all should hide from Yahweh's awesome appearance.

Israel's materialism and paganism have caused her to lose her elect and privileged status. She reverts to the status of depraved humanity, exhibiting the characteristics of pride and arrogance that condemned the builders of Babel's tower (Gen 11), earning the reaction from God that idolators deserve. Note the irony: "all nations, many peoples" (vv 2–3), but Israel excluded with unrepentent humanity (האדם). Israel's sentence is not to be set aside. She must await Yahweh's appearance and judgment (3:13–15).

The passage is a statement of the main theme of the book (cf. 65:1–16). It shows how and why traditional Israel does not and will not participate in God's new city. The basic tension is stated in v 6. On the one side is the recognized election of "the House of Jacob." On the other is the extent to which the promised "land" has been "filled" with things that are not acceptable to Yahweh. Commerce leads to an influx of fortune-tellers and idols that would degrade any part of mankind. It is certainly intolerable for the people of God.

V 7 echoes the description of Solomon's wealth (1 Kgs 10:19–29), while v 8 summarizes consequences like those in 1 Kgs 11:4–10. The dehumanizing effect of the conditions of new wealth and the relation of greed and idolatry are nowhere stated more eloquently.

Israel's position astride the major trade routes gave her a very advantageous position for trade and commerce. It also brought her contact with the cultures, religions, and cults of the entire Near East. This was true in Solomon's time, and in Ahab's time, and also in Jeroboam's time. This passage refers to the eighth century of Jeroboam, but continued to be applicable after the fall of Samaria as the area was "filled" with people from other areas. Fifth-century Judah would have understood and seen continued application in the land that came to be that of "the Samaritans."

V 10 may be linked with v 19 in reflecting a threat of earthquake. Canaan was earthquake-prone. But a monstrous earthquake during Uzziah's reign made a particular impression on Amos (1:1; 9:1) and on Zech (14:4). Milgrom (*VT* 14 [1964] 179) suggests that Isaiah "experienced the earthquake and drew upon it for his description" here.

The passage puts the judgment of God's people into a perspective of world judgment. It is a reminder that belief in Yahweh's universal sovereignty necessarily implies that it must be revealed and justified. Wisdom's teaching concerning the need for humanity is cast within a judgment frame that is truly prophetic. But the teaching is the same. Yahweh is Lord and he is unique. He alone is ruler with the right and status of ruling. Every attempt to displace him or to appropriate his prerogatives is treason and will not be tolerated.

Scene 3: Jerusalem's Ordeal (3:1—4:6)

Attention is focused on Jerusalem. Yahweh's extreme displeasure over Jerusalem's corruption and idolatry is ameliorated by his determination eventually to redeem the city.

Episode A: Jerusalem Shall Totter (*3:1–12*). The setting in the court of Yahweh provides opportunity to discuss the worsening conditions in Jerusalem. Only in the last two lines are the people of the city addressed.

Episode B: Yahweh Stands for Judgment (*3:13–15*). When the sentence is pronounced, it falls on the elders of the people for their failure to maintain justice for the poor.

Episode C: Haughty Daughters of Zion (*3:16—4:1*). The luxury of Jerusalem's society calls for special judgment on the day of reckoning.

Episode D: Yahweh's Branch (*4:2–6*). Through and beyond judgment God has a purpose for Jerusalem's purified remnant.

Episode A: Jerusalem Shall Totter (3:1–12)

Bibliography

Bahbout, S. "Sull' interpretazione dei vv. 10–11 del cap. III di Isaia." *Annuario di Studi Ebraici.* Collegio Rabbinico Italiano 1 (1963) 23–26. **Borowski, W.** "Ciemiezcy zostana ukarani (Iz. 3:1–15)" (The oppressors will be punished), *Ruch Biblijny i Liburgiezny* 25 (1972) 242–48. **Holladay, W. L.** "Isaiah 3:10–11: an archaic Wisdom passage," *VT* 18 (1968) 481–87. **McKenzie, J. L.** "The Elders in the Old Testament." *Bib* 40 (1959) 522–40. **van der Ploeg, J.** "Les anciens dans l'Ancien Testament." *Lex tua veritas,* FS H. Junker. Ed. H. Gross & F. Musser (Trier: Paulinus Verlag, 1961), 175–91. **Shedl, C.** "Rufer des Heils in heiloser Zeit (Is. 3:1–12)." *Theologie der Gegenwart in Auswahl* 16 (1972) 92–98. **de Vaux, R.** *Ancient Israel.* 155–57. **Weil, H. M.** "Exegese d'Isaie 3:1–15." *RB* 49 (1940) 76–85. **Yalon, H.** "מקראות בישעיהו (Lectures in Isaiah) א.בלע לשון כיסוי (Is 4,6) ב.כבוד חופה. חופת כבוד." *BMik* 12.30 (1967) 3–5.

Translation

Prophet: [1] *For behold the Lord, Yahweh of Hosts* 3+2+3
(to Heavens and Earth) *is removing from Jerusalem and from Judah*
support and supply: 2+3+3
every support of bread
and every support of water;
[2] *soldier and man of war,* 3+2+2
judge and prophet,
diviner and elder;
[3] *company commander* [a] *and honorable man,* 2+2
counselor and diviner [b] *and one skilled in magic.* 3+2
Yahweh: [4] *And I will make boys their princes* 3+3
(to Heavens and Earth) *and the capricious will rule over them.*
[5] *The people will oppress each other* 2+2+2
person against person
and a person against his neighbor

	They will act boisterously: the boy against the elder	3+2
	the commoner against the gentleman.	
Prophet:	6 *If a man lay hold of his brother*	3+2
(to the court)	*in his father's house,*	
	"You have a cloak—	2+3
	be a dictator for us!	
	This ruin[a] *(be) under your hand."*	2+2
	7 *He will refuse in that day, saying,*	4
	"I cannot be a healer	3+3+2
	when there is no bread in my house	
	and no cloak.[a]	
	You cannot make[b] *me a people's dictator!"*	2+2
Heavens and Earth:	8 *For Jerusalem shall totter*	3+2
(to the court)	*and Judah shall fall*	
	because their tongue and their deed toward Yahweh	4+3
	(are) to provoke[a] *the eyes*[b] *of his glory.*	
	9 *Their favoritism*[a] *in judgment witnesses against them*	4+3
	and their sin[b] *they reveal like Sodom.*[c]	
	They do not conceal (it)!	2
	Woe to their souls!	2+3
	For they have dealt out evil to themselves.	
Chorus:	10 *Say ye:*[a] *(as for) the righteous—it will surely be good*[b]	3+3
	For they will eat the fruit of their deeds.	
	11 *Woe to a wicked one!*[a] *Evil!*	3+4
	For the dealings[b] *of his hand will return*[c] *to him.*	
Yahweh:	12 *My people—boys*[a] *(are) his taskmasters.*	3+3
(aside)	*Women*[b] *rule over him.*	
(to Jerusalem)	*My people—your directors are erring*	3+3
	and your way of life they pervert!	

Notes

3.a. The suggestion to emend חֲמִשִּׁים "fifty" to read חֲמֻשִׁים "armed" (cf. H. Graetz, "Emendations . . ." *TLZ* 19 [1894] 68; Exod 13:18; Josh 1:14; 4:12; Judg 7:11) should be rejected with Wildberger. The MT pointing fits the Assyrian military title *rab-ḫanšā.*

3.b. חכם חרשים has been understood to mean "skilled craftsmen" (cf. LXX σοφὸν ἀρχιτέκτονα and Vg *sapientem de architectis*). This has חרשים come from חרש "to engrave." Wildberger traces its root to Aram חֶרְשָׁא (Syr *ḥeršê*), meaning "magic," but suggests that it is a gloss, leaving only יועץ and חכם. The meaning is probably correct, but it need not be eliminated.

6.a. המכשלה הזאת "this ruin." LXX translates καὶ τὸ βρῶμα τὸ ἐμόν (i.e., מאכלתי "my food"). This must be a translator's misreading of his text, influenced by 3:7 and 4:1 (cf. J. Ziegler, "Untersuchungen zur Septuaginta des Buches Isaias," *ATA* 12 [1934] 136).

7.a. אין שמלה "no cloak" denies what v 6 has affirmed, that he possesses a cloak. Wildberger suggests dropping it, and the meter supports him.

7.b. תשימני "you make." LXX ἔσομαι "I will be" (אהיה). MT is the more difficult reading and to be preferred.

8.a. לַמְרוֹת "to provoke" is hiph inf with לְ. Fully written, it would be להמרות (cf. Ps 78:17 and Job 17:2).

8.b. עֲנֵי may be a defective writing of עיני "eyes" as many MSS have it, but עני is certainly older. The form seems to be an error. Suggestions for emendation include פְּנֵי "face." LXX διότι νῦν ἐταπεινώθη ἡ δόξα αὐτῶν seems to have read it as ענה "humble," a verb (cf. Dillmann;

Ziegler, *ATA* 12 [1934] 137). Wildberger considers it a corruption of עָם "people." The early MSS appear to have chosen the best course.

9.a. הכרת. ה as a preformative is rare. But this form is apparently derived from the hiph. LXX has paraphrased the meaning καὶ ἡ αἰσχύνη τοῦ προσώπου αὐτῶν "and the shame of their face." Syr and Vg (*agnitio*) understand הכיר to mean "investigate," "recognize," or "know." F. Zimmerman ("OT Passages," JBL 55 [1936] 307) suggested on the basis of Arab the meaning "deceit." The phrase הכיר פנים means "show favoritism" (Wildberger; cf. Deut 1:17; 16:19; Prov 24:23; 28:21). So the noun means "favoritism." Tg understood the text in this way: אשת מודעות אפיהון "their respecting of persons" (Stenning). The pronominal suffix refers to the entire constr phrase (cf. J. Weingreen, "The Construct-Genitive Relation," *VT* 4 [1954] 50–59).

9.b. LXX and Tg change חטאתָם "their sin" to a pl. But Isaiah consistently uses a sg (6:7; 27:9; 30:1, etc.). Cf. Wildberger.

9.c. כסודם "like Sodom." Cf. 1:9,10.

10.a. אמרו "say ye" has been widely challenged. Dillmann suggested that אַשְׁרֵי "happy" be substituted for it. This emendation is based on the LXX δήσωμεν "we declare" which seems to presuppose the verb אסר "to bind" (= אשר) which in turn was a misunderstood form of אשרי "happy." It is difficult to bring the LXX and MT into agreement, but LXX also begins with εἰπόντες "saying," which suggests MT's form (contra Ziegler, *ATA* 12 [1934] 61). The received form of MT should stand as it is.

10.b. The suggested insertion of לו "to him" is unnecessary. Cf. Wildberger.

11.a. The suggested insertion of כי "for" is unnecessary.

11.b. Procksch and Eichrodt suggested emending כי־גמול "for dealings" to כגמול "like dealings" like the LXX κατὰ τὰ ἔργα "according to the deed," but this is also not necessary (cf. Wildberger).

11.c. DSS[Isa] reads ישוב "will return" instead of MT יעשה "will do." This is a better reading. Wildberger notes that עשה "do, make" never means to do retribution, while גמול and שוב often appear together (Joel 4:4,7; Obad 15; Ps 28:4; 94:2; Lam 3:64). Cf. particularly Prov 12:14b וגמול ידי אדם ישיב לו.

12.a. נגשיו מעולל "his taskmasters a boy" is a problem because of the sg and pl forms. The early versions have various forms. The best solution is to read מעולל as a pl. עול means to be a child, although G. R. Driver (*JTS* 38 [1937] 38) suggested it meant "incline to one side, deviate from justice" like Arab *ʿâla.*

12.b. The Versions seem to have read נגשיו "his creditors or usurers." This is not necessary if עולל is read as "children" or "boys."

Form/Structure/Setting

The passage opens with כי הנה "for behold," explaining the previous verse and calling attention to the subject at hand: Yahweh's decisions and actions toward Jerusalem and Judah. The subject remains the same through v 12: Yahweh's decision to remove stable leadership from Jerusalem. V 13 clearly begins a new paragraph.

Comment

Attention is drawn back to the subject of the day: the announcement that Yahweh is removing the support of strong leadership from Jerusalem. Heavens and Earth acknowledge that the step is justified as Yahweh laments over the people and their condition.

Explanation

The judgment against Jerusalem deprives her of "support and supply." Food and water are in short supply, a basic problem of any siege or natural catastrophe. But this is expanded to speak of her leaders. Chap. 1 had placed Jerusalem's guilt on her leaders. God's peculiar gift to his people through history lay in furnishing inspired leaders. Now these will be withdrawn.

Leaders of every sort are mentioned: military champions, wise administrators, skillful counselors. Immaturity and weakness will characterize rulers. Discipline and courtesy will vanish. No one will want to lead, which is the result of apostasy and injustice. The proverb (vv 10–11) emphasizes the moral basis for the disaster. Yahweh's lament closes the section.

All society is held together by invisible bonds—common concerns that have a moral base. When these disappear the body politic disintegrates.

Judgment on a people may be passive. It does not have to come by external invasion. It may, and often does, come through internal atrophy. The passage suggests that God is responsible for it. It is his judgment on those who forget that they are all ultimately dependent on him.

Episode B: Yahweh Stands for Judgment (3:13–15)

Bibliography

Nielsen, K. "An Investigation of the Prophetic Lawsuit (Rib-Pattern)." *Yahweh as Prosecutor and Judge.* JSOTSup 9. Sheffield: U. of Sheffield, 1978. 29–32. Other literature is reviewed here.

Translation

Herald:	13 *Taking his position to contend* (*is*) *Yahweh—*	3+3
	Standing to judge peoples. [a]	
	14 *Yahweh comes in judgment*	3+3
	with the elders of my people and its princes.	
Yahweh:	*And you—you have devoured the vineyard!*	3+3
(to Leaders)	*The plunder of the poor is in your houses.*	
	15 *What* (*right*) *do you have that you crush my people?*	3+3
	And that you grind the faces of the poor?	
Herald:	*Expression of the Lord Yahweh of Hosts.*	3

Notes

13.a. Instead of עמים "peoples," LXX has τὸν λαὸν αὐτοῦ "his peoples" and Syr *le-ʿammeh.* H. D. Hummel ("Enclitic Mem," *JBL* 76 [1957] 100) suggests that the final letter is an "enclitic *Mem*" and that this should be read עמו־ם. This is a possibility. Tur-Sinai (*ScrHier* 8 [1961] 162) suggests reading it as עמם but this leaves the pronoun without antecedent. F. Hesse ("Wurzelt die prophetische Gerichtsrede im israelitischen Kult?" *ZAW* 65 [1953] 48) suggests that Isaiah is speaking like a cult prophet, introducing Yahweh as judge over the nations. Wildberger follows LXX and Syr to read עמו "his people." Judgment over the nations is the setting for judgment over Israel elsewhere (cf. Amos 1–2). MT may be followed here.

Form/Structure/Setting

The passage is framed by the formal announcement in vv 13–14 and the ascription of v 16. The importance of the words in vv 14b–15 are thus made clear.

This is the third time such a solemn introduction has preceded a statement. First, in 1:24–26, Yahweh speaks of his determination to purge Zion. In 2:1–4, Isaiah's word about Zion is formally introduced. And now there is the formal indictment of Jerusalem's elders and princes.

The speech is formulated as a prosecution speech before a court. The words ריב "contend," דין "judge," and משפט "judgment" make this clear. The judgment setting of 1:2–3 is continued.

The formulas testify to a fixed tradition for such in Israel which may have been cultivated in covenant festival celebrations (Kaiser).

Comment

14 The meaning of בער in piel (also 4:8, 5:5, 6:13) is debated. BDB translates "for destruction" while *CHAL* follows KB with "burning." The Greek translators were divided: LXX *ἐνεπυρίσατε* "you set fire" (in 5:5 *εἰς διαρπαγήν* "for plunder"); 'A *κατενεμήσασθε* "you wasted"; Σ *κατεβοσκήσατε* "you grazed upon." Modern interpreters are no different. Gray translates "departure," as do Hertzberg (*Der Erste Jesaja* [Leipzig: Schloessmann, 1936, ³1955]), Herntrich (*Jesaja 1–12,* ATD 17 [Göttingen: Vandenhoeck & Ruprecht, 1950]), Kaiser, Eichrodt, and Wildberger. Fohrer chooses "burn down." Leslie translates "devour," while Steinmann has "devastator." Procksch speaks of picking every single grape, so that the plants have been robbed and ruined.

This is called the "plunder of the poor" גזלת העני. Whatever is meant by בער, it is understood as a crime against the poor, who are seen as virtually identical with God's people. The accusations of exploiting the poor find parallels in Mic 3:2, as well as Hosea and Amos. Robbing one's neighbors is forbidden in the Law (Lev 19:13 and 5:23; cf. Ezek 18:7). Wildberger draws a parallel to Prov 22:22 and suggests an even closer background in Wisdom (cf. Amenemope, IV, 4f., 18).

15 Oppression is called *crushing* and *grinding.* No one has found stronger language. Duhm paraphrases this, "You grind the helpless, as being millstones, with your power and your legal maneuvers." The king's responsibility "to help the poor and punish the oppressor" (Ps 72:4) also belonged to the elders and princes.

Explanation

The spotlight of formal introduction and signature falls on Yahweh. His formal role as judge is announced. The accused are named: the elders and princes of his people. The members of the court would be seated. But when one spoke he would stand up (cf. L. Köhler, *Hebrew Man,* tr. P. R. Ackroyd [Nashville: Abingdon, 1956], 155). So it is in Ps 82:1 and in the frequent calls for God to stand up and exercise judgment (Pss 74:22; 82:8, etc.).

The accused are indicted on two counts. That they "devour the vineyard" means that they have exploited the agrarian economy for their own gain. No agriculture continues to prosper unless something is put back into the soil, unless care and substance are given to the plants. To fail to do so is to "devour the vineyard." The other half of the charge is that of extortion. The leaders have forced the poor to turn over their small share of the harvest to them. The second major charge is that of exploitation and oppression. The Lord identifies himself with the poor. They are "my people." He demands to know by what right the leaders treat the people in this way. The economic oppression of the eighth century was notorious. Isaiah, like Amos, spoke on the Lord's behalf against it. The speech takes the form of a rebuttal through the stress on ואתם "but you." The conditions of the times were blamed on economic or political circumstances. But God forces blame on the leaders. The role of the elder זקנים in Israel was central and ancient (cf. de Vaux, *Ancient Israel,* and McKenzie, *Bib* 40 [1959] 522–40).

The judgment speech of 1:10, 17 is continued in this accusation. The fact that the accuser is also the judge, which was possible in Israelite jurisprudence, leaves no doubt about the result. The fact that the goods of the poor were actually to be found in the homes of the elders could not be refuted.

The basis for judgment lies in the law and its place in covenant structure. The crime in God's eyes goes beyond the act against the poor. It is a breech of God's own claim on the people. The elders are judged for crime against God. (Cf. Fey, 63.)

Episode C: Haughty Daughters of Zion (3:16—4:1)

Bibliography

Branden, A. van den. "I gioielli delle donne di Gerusalemme secondo Is. 3:18–21," *BeO* 5 (1963) 87–94. **Compston, H. F. B.** "Ladies' Finery in Isaiah III 18–23," *CQR* 103 (1926/27) 316–30. **Daiches, S.** "Der Schmuch der Töchter Zions und die Tracht Istars" *OLZ* 14 (1911) 390–91. **Hoffman, H. W.** *Die Intention. . . .* **Hönig, H. W.** *Die Bekleidung des Hebräers.* Diss. Zurich (1957). **Zeron, A.** "Das Wort *niqpa,* zum Sturz der Zionstöchter (Is iii 24)." *VT* 31 (1981) 95–97.

Translation

Prophet: [16]*And then Yahweh said* 2
(to Heavens and Earth) *Because the daughters of Zion are haughty,* 4
they walk—neck extended [a] 3+2
and eyes ogling, [b]
(walking and skipping they walk 3+2
and tinkling with their feet).
[17]*The Lord* [a] *shall make bald* 2+3+3
the heads of the daughters of Zion
and Yahweh will lay bare their foreheads.

Heavens and Earth:	18 *In that day—*	2
(to the court)	*the Lord* [a] *will remove the beauty of*	3
	the anklets, the brow bands, [b] *and the crescents;*	3
	19 *the eardrops, the bracelets, and the veils;*	3
	20 *the diadems, the step-chains, and the sashes;*	3
	the vials of perfume and the charms;	3
	21 *the signet rings and the nose rings;*	3
	22 *the robes, the over-tunics, the cloaks, and the purses;*	4
	23 *the mirrors, the linens, the turbans, and the shawls.*	4
Prophet:	24 *And there shall be—*	1
	instead of sweet odor will be rottenness	4
	instead of a girdle, a rope	3
	instead of coiffured hair, baldness	4
	instead of a robe, [a] *a girding of sack-cloth.*	4
	[b] *Indeed shame instead of beauty.* [b]	4
Heavens and Earth:	25 *Your men will fall by the sword*	3+2
(to Jerusalem)	*and your strength in battle.*	
	26 *And her entrances shall lament and mourn.*	3+3
	And, having been emptied, she will (have to) sit on the ground.	
(to the court)	4:1 *And seven women will lay hold*	3+2+2
	on one man	
	in that day	
	to say: "Our (own) bread we will eat	3+2
	and our clothes we will wear.	
	Only let us be called by your name,	4+2
	taking away our reproach."	

Notes

16.a. The Q form נטוית apparently tries to put the original into a form that is acceptable to Masoretic grammar. There is no change in meaning.

16.b. The reading of some MSS ומשקרות (*shin* שׁ for *sin* שׂ) is to be judged wrong.

17.a. A number of MSS read יהוה "Yahweh" for MT אדני "Lord." DSS[Isa] places יהוה over אדני as a correction.

18.a. Many MSS have יהוה. DSS[Isa] places אדני over יהוה.

18.b. DSS[Isa] והשבישים simply substitutes one sibilant for another. The word is the same.

24.a. פְּתִיגִיל is a word not known in Hebrew. The context suggests a meaning like "embroidered girdle." Tur-Sinai ("Unverstandene Bibelworte I," *VT* 1 [1951] 307) emended it to תֻּפֵּי גִיל meaning "joyful drums." But this adds nothing to the context.

24.b-b. כי תחת יפי is lacking in LXX. Many translations have understood כי as a noun like כויה "branding" (BDB, 465). But this changes the form established in the verse. DSS[Isa] כי תחת יפי בשת is a better text, "Indeed, instead of beauty shame" (J. T. Milik, "Note sui manoscritti di ʿAin Fešḫa," *Bib* 31 [1950] 216; F. Nötscher, "Entbehrliche Hapaxlegomena in Jesaja," *VT* 1 [1951] 300). G. R. Driver (*JTS* 2 [1951] 25) takes an opposite view.

Form/Structure/Setting

The pericope is defined by its subject, the women of Jerusalem. It begins with the threat of judgment because of their pride and concludes with the humiliation of women requesting marriage at any cost to avoid the greater threats.

This is a *prophecy of disaster* (*OTFC* 159; K. Koch, *The Growth of the Biblical Tradition,* tr. S. M. Cupitt [New York: Scribner's, 1969] 192–94). It is related to the "Day of Yahweh" section by ביום ההוא "in that day." The outline describes the situation (v 16), brings the threat of judgment (vv 17–26), and describes the conditions which follow (4:1).

The entire chapter speaks of things which must be removed from Jerusalem. Because of the women's pride (v 16) the symbols of their pride must be removed (vv 17–24). The casualties of battle (v 25) and the destruction of the occupation (v 26) will leave surviving women in a humiliated and humiliating state (4:1).

Comment

16 *Because* (יען כי) introduces a causal clause. It is a stronger construction than כי and thus provides the reason for the judgment. It is typical of the prophets that they support their oracles of judgment by citing the occasion for God's anger. God does not act arbitrarily. *Daughters of Zion* occurs only here in v 16 and v 17, in 4:4, and Cant 3:11. It can hardly refer to the maidens of the capital. The description fits the dowagers of Jerusalem's society. Zion is an echo of the term "daughter of Zion" as a term for the city (1:8) with all its theological implications. Zion is the place where Yahweh dwells and reveals himself. The inhabitants of the city, including the women, must be persons fit for that privilege and responsibility. The entire book reflects God's search for a people fit to live in his city in meekness and humility.

Instead the Jerusalem women are *haughty* (cf. 2:11). They show it in their manner of walking (נטוות גרון). This is not so much the sense of "with head high" (LXX *ὑψηλῷ τραχήλῳ*) as it means "with head stretched sideways." Wildberger correctly understands it to mean that the women glance coyly to see whether their elegance is noticed or not.

17 שפח is another difficult word. BDB identifies it with ספח meaning an "eruption" or a "scab"—thus as a verb "smite with a scab." G. R. Driver ("Hebrew Notes," *VT* 1 [1951] 241) links it to Akk *suppuḫu/šuppuḫu,* meaning "to open," "to loosen" and to Arab *ʿasfaḥu,* "bald on the forehead." The Vg translated *decalvabit,* "will lay bare." פת has been translated "openings" or "secret parts." B. Stade ("Die Dreizahl," *ZAW* 26 [1906] 1930–33) suggested a relation to Akk *pūtu* "forehead," while G. R. Driver ("Linguistic and Textual Problems: Isa 1–39," *JTS* 38 [1937] 38) refers to the Akk phrase *muttutam gullubu* "to shave the hair of the forehead," a humiliating punishment in Babylon. The Vg follows this line with *Dominus crinem earum nudabit.* The verse has parallel stichoi which do not describe a disease but humiliations imposed by a conqueror.

18–23 The threat is interrupted by a catalogue of the *beauty* which the Lord will *remove* from Jerusalem. The idea of *removal* picks up the theme of "purge" from 1:16, 26, which had been continued in 3:1, applying the same word to the basic supports of the city, its leadership. It will appear again in 5:5. Now another essential obstacle to the unhindered presence and work of Yahweh is denounced. The list begins with jewelry, includes fine clothes, but also represents everything that human pride can hang on to (cf. Isa 10:2; 28:1, 4, 5). The list suggests that by this time Jerusalem was well aware of fashion in the world's capitals and was able to avail itself of its expensive luxuries (cf. Ezek 16:10–13, 17, 39; 23:26, 42). It is impossible now to gain a clear picture of the articles named (but see *ISBE*, II, 406). Fashion then as now changes rapidly and tends to name its articles in ways that defy rational definition. The list has intrigued scholars. N. W. Schroeder in 1745 wrote "Commentarius philologo-criticus de vestitu mulierum Hebraearum ad Jesai III vs. 16–24." And in 1809/10 a three-volume work by A. Th. Hartmann (*Die Hebräerin am Putztisch und als Braut* [Amsterdam: Ziegler], 203) has shown that LXX simply made a list of such articles from his own period to serve as a translation which many a translator has done in similar circumstances since then.

The term סור "remove" is used elsewhere to speak of the removal of idols (Gen 35:2; Josh 24:14, 23; Judg 10:16; 1 Sam 7:3, 4, etc.). A direct connection is drawn here between such luxury in ornament and dress and idolatry. Indeed many items listed originated in cult and in magic rituals.

24 The threat is picked up again with *and there shall be.* It contains its own list of cosmetics and ornaments. בשם is the oil of the balsam tree. It is an expensive import from Saba and Ragma (Ezek 27:22; 2 Chr 9:1) to be stored in the royal treasure house (Isa 39:2). It was used in worship (Exod 25:6) and also as a cosmetic (Esth 2:12; Cant 4:10, 14). It is to be replaced by מק, which in Ps 39:6 is the smell of a festering wound. The items that follow continue a list that contrasts the abject poverty of war-prisoners or the survivers of destroyed cities with the previous luxuries of the well-to-do.

25 The verse defines the picture of destruction by war. The second person singular addresses Jerusalem, however, not the "daughters of Zion." מתים "men" is an infrequent word (cf. also 5:13). But it is used regularly where the law of the ban is applied (Deut 2:34; 3:6) or in the traditions of the conquest of Canaan (Deut 4:27; 28:62). This stands parallel to גבורה "strength." The plural would simply mean "soldiers" or "heroes." The singular usage is unusual. Fohrer thinks it represents the generation of unmarried men, while מתים are the married men. Wildberger disagrees, considering the two virtually synonymous.

26 The address changes, but the subject remains the same. The judgment of God levels the city. פתחים means "entrances." It is used instead of the usual שערים to emphasize the destruction. There are no "gates" left, only "openings" or "entrances." אנה is lament for the dead. אבל, "to mourn," is the parallel word. The "entrances," no longer proud gates, can mourn as the land is said to mourn (Hos 4:3; Isa 24:4; 33:9; Joel 1:10) or as the fields of the shepherds do (Amos 1:2). But, as here, the walls and forts can mourn (Lam 2:5), and also the ways of Zion (Lam 1:4). נקה means "be empty." In niphal it means "be emptied." The city has been "emptied," "cleaned out," "purged" of everything of value, of everything that one could be proud of: its children, its youth, its leadership, its furniture, its gates and walls. Wildberger cites a parallel in Lam 1:1. Sitting on the ground belongs to mourning. But it also is a necessity when nothing else remains to sit on.

4:1 The precarious situation makes it especially difficult for the woman who has no man to protect her, be he father, brother, or husband. The war has significantly reduced the number of men. Of course this verse presumes the possibility of multiple wives where a married man may add other wives to his household. Polygamy was not the rule in Israel even if it was not forbidden (de Vaux, *Ancient Israel,* 24–26; W. Plautz, "Monogamie und Polygamie im Alten Testament," *ZAW* 75 [1963] 3–27). In normal times the larger household was a financial burden. According to Deut 22:29, a bride price, מהר, of fifty shekels of silver must be paid. The husband must provide food and clothes for his wives and not withhold their marital rights (Exod 21:10). The precarious and extraordinary conditions following the war mean that such rules will gladly be set aside. A bride price is out of the question. Women will even waive their rights to food and clothing, if only they can have the man's name called out over them. This does not simply mean "to bear the man's name." _____ על _____ קרא שם "call the name of _____ over _____" is a legal phrase concerning a change of ownership (K. Galling, "Die Ausrufung des Namens als Rechtsakt in Israel," *TLZ* 81 [1956] 65–70; L. Köhler, *Theology,* 15). When it was used in marriage, it confirmed the marriage contract. This would "take away her shame." חרפה meant rape as well as being childless. It meant widowhood as well as being single. To be taken into a large household meant being freed from these.

Explanation

The entire passage speaks about the women of Jerusalem as an example of the pride that makes destruction necessary and of the sad result of the judgment. The context will show that God can build his city with people in the latter condition, but not with those in the former.

Episode D:
Yahweh's Branch (4:2–6)

Bibliography

Baldwin, J. G. "*Semah* as a Technical Term in the Prophets." *VT* 14 (1964) 93–97. **Buda, J.** "*Semah Jahweh.*" *Bib* 20 (1939) 10–26. **Fohrer, G.** "Σιών." *TDNT,* VII, 292–319. **Lipinsky, E.** "De la reforme d'Esdros au regne eschatalogique de Dieu (Is. 4:3–5a)." *Bib* 51 (1970) 533–37. **Mauchline, J.** "Implicit Signs of a Persistent Belief in the Davidic Empire." *VT* 20 (1970) 287–303.

Translation

Heavens: 2 *In that day* 2+3+2
the branch of Yahweh will become
a beauty and an honor,

and the fruit of the land 2+2+2
a majesty and a glory
for the surviving remnant of Israel.[a]
Earth: 3 *And it shall be that the remainder in Zion* 3+2+3
and the separated in Jerusalem
will be called holy:
everyone written for life in Jerusalem. 4
Prophet: 4 *When the Lord*[a] *shall have washed away* 3+3
the filth of the daughters[b] *of Zion,*
he will wash from her midst the blood-guilt of Jerusalem, 4+4
with a spirit of judgment and a spirit of burning.[c]
Heavens: 5 *And Yahweh shall create*[a] 2+3+2
over all the establishment of Mount Zion
and over her assembly
a cloud by day 2+3+2
[b]*and smoke and glow of fire*
for a flame by night.
Indeed over all glory 3+3
6 [a]*it will be a canopy and a booth*
for a shade from heat by day,[b] 3+2+2
for a shelter and concealment
from thunder-shower and from rain.

Notes

2.a. DSS[Isa] adds ויהודה "and Judah." Wildberger (150) holds this to be unnecessary, which may be true. But the reason he gives is that Judah is included in Israel. On the contrary, these chapters have carefully separated Israel's fate from that of Judah and Jerusalem. If it is "unnecessary," it would be because צמח "branch" carries messianic-royal significance and thus includes Judah.

4.a. Tg has יהוה "Yahweh" for אדני "Lord," thus taking note of the unique combination of the two terms in the larger passage 3:1—4:6.

4.b. LXX *τῶν υἱῶν καὶ τῶν θυγατέρων* "of the sons and the daughters" expands the application of the passage. בנות ציון "daughters of Zion" occurs only here, in 3:16, and in Cant 3:11 (and the phrase בנות ירושלים "daughters of Jerusalem" in 1:5). Procksch and Fohrer suggest that this was originally בת ציון "daughter of Zion." Wildberger is nearer right in suggesting that 4:2–6 is a conscious continuation of 3:16.

4.c. LXX translates ברוח בער with *πνεύματι καύσεως* "spirit of burning." DSS[Isa] has סער "stormwind" instead of בער (cf. Exod 1:4; 13:11, 13; Pss 107:25; 148:8 where רוח סערה occurs). Tur Sinai (*VT* 1 [1951] 164) emends both רוח "spirit" to דּוּחַ "to purge" and משפט "judgment" to מִשְׁטָף "ablution." Wildberger suggests using the second meaning of בער "root out," "extirpate" (*CHAL,* 44) or "consume," "utterly remove" (BDB, 129).

5.a. For וברא "and he shall create" LXX translates *καὶ ἥξει* "he will come" (= ובא). The idea that Yahweh "comes" in cloud and fire occurs frequently in the OT (cf. F. Schnutenhaus, "Das Kommen und Erscheinen Gottes im Alten Testament," *ZAW* 76 [1964] 1–22). But the subject here is not a theophany, but protection. Ps 105:39 also speaks of the use of clouds and fire to protect Israel. Keep MT.

5.b.-6.b. Lacking in DSS[Isa] probably due to a scribal lapse. The last word copied is יומם "by day" and the last word of the omitted portion is also יומם.

6.a. The verse is divided at an unfortunate place, ignoring both metrical and syntactical connections. A better break point would be earlier, after לילה "by night."

Form/Structure/Setting

The passage is the third "day of the Lord" passage in the chapter, the only positive one. The other two speak of destruction. The beginning is marked by ביום ההוא "in that day." 5:1 changes style, subject, and speaker.

The structure of the passage is clearly noted in the syntax. The latter day announcement uses an imperfect verb (v 2). The two major sections are introduced with perfects with *wāw* (vv 3 and 5).

The resulting outline:

I. In that day, Yahweh's plants will flourish in Israel.
II. Jerusalem's remnant will be holy, since she will have been purged.
III. Yahweh will create a shelter and sign of his presence in Zion.

The meter of the passage supports the recognition that vv 2 and 5 belong together. Both have dominant tristich patterns, they announce the future of Israel and Zion on the great day. Vv 3–4 are in a heavy distich meter. V 3 deals with the remnant and its place in that day, while v 4 picks up the theme of 1:15 and 3:24.

The sequence of tenses is a textbook example of imperfect, perfect with *wāw,* and substantive clauses. The time view is future, set by the opening phrase.

Comment

2 The interpretation of the passage has traditionally been based on the understanding of the צמח יהוה "branch of Yahweh." LXX translated it ἐπιλάμψει ὁ θεός "God will shine forth," apparently reading צחח or צמח in the sense of Aramaic צמחא meaning "brightness" (Ziegler, *Das Buch Isaias* [Würzburg: Echter Verlag, 1948], 107; Gray). ʹΑ Σ Θ read *ανατολη κυριος* "Lord (will be) rising." Vg has *germen Domini* "sprout of the Lord," Syr *denḥeh dᵉmārjâ* "appearance or glory of the Lord." Tg translates משיחא דיהיה and understood it as a Messianic title. The Messianic interpretation of the passage continued in the Middle Ages (Kimchi) and is also represented in modern exegetes (Delitzsch; P. A. de Lagarde, *Kritische Anmerkungen zum Buche Isaias* [Göttingen: Kaestner, 1878]; E. Sellin, *Serubbabel* [Leipzig: A. Deichert, 1898]). Young also follows this interpretation (173).

The word צמח "branch" is used for the king of the time to come. Jeremiah has צמח צדיק "righteous branch" 23:5 and צמח צדקה "branch of righteousness" 33:15. Zechariah has עבדי צמח "my servant branch" 3:8 and איש צמח שמו "a man branch his name" 6:12. Wildberger notes correctly that none of these demonstrates a fixed messianic title. Jeremiah adds לדוד "to David" each time. Zechariah seems only concerned to show that Zerubbabel is a descendant of David. But here the צמח is of יהוה "Yahweh," not David. The parallel is פרי הארץ "the fruit of the land." The words in context refer to Yahweh's plans and purpose in their entirety.

The grandeur of that time is pictured in the words גאון "majesty" and תפארת "glory." צבי "beauty" is used again by Isaiah in 28:1, 4, 5. Jeremiah describes God's land as נחלת צבי (3:19) "the inheritance of beauty." Ezekiel speaks of Canaan as distinguished from the nations by its צבי (20:6, 15).

Daniel calls Israel's land ארץ־הצבי (11:16, 41) "the beautiful land" and Zion הר־צבי־קדש (11:45) "mountain of holy beauty." The word is thus characteristic of the Holy Land and here describes the future fulfillment of God's purpose for Israel in the land. כבוד has a basic meaning of "weight," "importance," and "respect." All these are things that Israel lacked in the later kingdom and in the Exile.

The Land of Israel can be called her *majesty* as well as her *beauty* (Ps 47:5[4]; Nah 2:3). The prophets spoke of Yahweh alone as Israel's גאון "majesty" (Amos 6:8; Hos 5:5; 7:10). Both words are used of Babylon as the pride and majesty of the Chaldeans (Isa 13:19). Other places call Yahweh, alone, Israel's תפארת "glory" (Isa 60:19; 63:15). That here the fruit of the land should be the subject of such praise is a contrast to the long, lean years of war and famine that Israel experienced.

The promise is for פליטת ישראל "the surviving remnant of Israel." The concern of the book for the fate of the people from the Northern Kingdom which was noted in 1:3 and 2:5 is immensely strengthened in this verse. It will be observed at various intervals throughout the book. The theology of the book certainly builds on the understanding of Israel's election as well as that of Canaan, and struggles to put it into proper perspective in light of her experiences from the eighth to the fifth centuries.

3 The concept of the remnant is expanded to include the *remainder in Zion* and the *separated portion in Jerusalem.* For them the term קדוש "holy" is applied directly, whereas the exalted phrases of v 2 are applied to the fruit of the land, not the people. For all its interest in Israel, the overriding concern of the book has to do with the people who will inhabit God's city.

This remaining group is described in v 3 as כָּל־הַכָּתוּב לַחַיִּים בִּירוּשָׁלָֽם "everyone written for life in Jerusalem." The phrase touches a theme with many variations in Scripture. Wildberger gives a current survey of possibilities. The OT speaks of a ספר חיים (Ps 69:28) "book of life," which is cited in Phil 4:3, and seven times in Acts. Dan 12:1 also speaks of a book containing the names of those to be saved. The idea is that of a book containing names of persons to remain alive. If a name is removed, he must die. But the meaning is more than simply being alive. It implies God's protection and blessing. The remnant is the group chosen to participate in the life of God's city.

4 The basis for calling Jerusalem's new people קדוש "holy" is expanded here. The necessary purge envisioned in chaps. 1 and 3 shall have already taken place. The idea of being a "holy nation" was a part of Israel's heritage (Exod 19:6). Now it could finally become reality. It was a quality necessary for living in close proximity to the Divine Presence in Zion.

This group may be called "holy" because it shall have been cleansed by the *spirit of judgment* and the *spirit of burning.* The remnant would recognize the wars and desolations of 701 and 587 B.C. in those terms. But this listing sees the work of God in both of them.

5–6 The passage closes with the pictures of divine protection over the city: *cloud* and *fire* which will be both a *canopy* and a *booth* to protect from heat and storm. The *canopy* is of cloth. The *booth* is a brush-arbor using palm branches. The contrast of God's protection with the earlier purge is marked.

Explanation

The passage, parallel to 2:2–4, completes the cycle of speeches by a view of God's goal for Mt. Zion. It speaks of the future of Israel in plant-language, but of Zion in remnant-language.

The remnant shall have been purged (cf. 1:25) of the sins pictured in chaps. 1 and 3 and may therefore be termed קדוש "holy." Zion's population will be fit for God's presence in the city.

The pictures of cloud and fire over Jerusalem are reminiscent of the priestly narrative of the presence accompanying the desert pilgrimage toward the promised land (Exod 13:21). Cf. also 1 Kgs 8:10. But this is not describing a theophany. These are created to protect Zion just as they are in Ps 105:39. The undisturbed enjoyment of God's presence is reserved for the purged remnant. God's purpose points the fifth-century Jews to potential fulfillment in their own time, if and when the basic requirements of purge from false pride and the establishment of justice are fulfilled on their part. The pre-exilic situation is not a basis for nostalgia or a wish for a return to the past.

The passage builds on the assurance in 2:2–4 of God's purpose to dwell in Zion and judge the nations from his throne there. The role of his people in the city, be it only a remnant, is secure. This passage stresses God's action to ensure the safety and permanence of the city and its people.

Scene 4: Requiem for Israel (5:1–30)

Chap. 5 comprises a new scene. The chapter has more unity than is apparent at first. The sixfold הוי or "woe" is the signal that this is a giant funeral. The opening "song" is an explanation of the tragic event. Woven into the "woe" speeches are others which tie the scene to the larger judgment scene which preceded.

Episode A: My Friend's Song for His Vineyard (*5:1–7*). The imagery of the כרם "vineyard," was anticipated in 3:14 with the charge against the elders. In 4:2, plant imagery is used in the "branch of Yahweh" and "the fruit of the land" for the surviving, purged remnant.

The funeral scene recites the events that led up to it in the song (vv 1–2), the response of the owner (vv 3–4) and of Yahweh (vv 5–6). V 7 identifies the corpses to be buried as "the house of Israel" and "men of Judah" and states the basis for judgment and death.

Episode B: Therefore My People Are Exiled (*5:8–25*). The "woes" are laments over the persons who have died, interspersed with comments about the meaning of the event. The dead are illustrative of the elements that had to be purged from the city and the country.

Episode C: Signal to a Distant Nation (*5:26–30*). The chapter that begins with a doleful song of opportunities missed and of death closes with a realistic picture of the foreign invader who serves as executioner.

Episode A:
My Friend's Song for His Vineyard (5:1–7)

Bibliography

Bentzen, A. "Zur Erlauterung von Jes. 5:1–7." *AfO* 4 (1927) 209–10. **Fang Chih-Yung, M.** "I shou hav i shen chau ti ku shih." (An Ancient Hebrew Poem) *Collectanea theol. Universitatis Fugen* 6 (1970) 541–55. **Graham, W. C.** "Notes on the Interpretation of Isaiah 5:1–14." *AJSL* 45 (1928/29) 167–78. **Junker, H.** "Die literarische Art von Is. 5:1–7." *Bib* 40 (1959) 259–66. **Kosmala, H.** "Form and Structure in Ancient Hebrew Poetry." *VT* 16 (1966) 152–80. **Loretz, O.** "Weinberglied und prophetische Deutung im Protest-Song Jes. 5:1–7." *UF* 7 (1975) 573–76. **Lys, D.** "La vigne et la double je. Exercise de style sur Esaia 5:1–7." *Studies in Prophecy.* VTSup 26. Leiden: E. J. Brill, 1974. 1–16. **Marmorstein, A.** "A Greek Lyric Poet and a Hebrew Prophet (Isaiah)." *JQR* 37 (1946/47) 169–73. **Neveu, L.** "Le chant de la vigne (Is. 5)." *AsSeign* 58 (1974) 4–10. **de Orbiso, T.** "El cantico a la viña del amado (Is. 5:1–7)." *EstEcl* 34 (1960) 715–31. **Schottroff, W.** "Das Weinberglied Jesajas, Jes. 5:1–7; Ein Beitrag zur Geschichte der Parabel." *ZAW* 82 (1970) 68–91. **Sheppard, G. T.** "More on Isaiah 5:1–7 as a Juridical Parable." *CBQ* 44 (1982) 45–47. **Whedbee, J. W.** *Isaiah and Wisdom.* 43–51. **Willis, J. T.** "The Genre of Isaiah 5:1–7." *JBL* 96 (1977) 337–62. **Yee, G. A.** "The Form Critical Study of Isaiah 5:1–7 as a Song and as a Juridical Parable." *CBQ* 43 (1981) 30–40.

Translation

Troubadour:	1 *Now let me sing for my friend*	3+3
(to the assembled	*a song of my friend for his vineyard,*	
group)	*a vineyard belonging to my friend*	3+3
	in a very fruitful hill.	
	2 *He proceeded to dig it, then to clear it (of stones)*	2+2
	then to plant it (with) choice vines.	
	Then to build a watch-tower in it	3+4
	and even a winepress he hewed out in it,	
	He waited for (it) to produce[a] *grapes,*	3+2
	but then it made stinking things.	
Owner/Husband:	3 *And now inhabitant*[a] *of Jerusalem*	3+2
(to Judeans and	*and man of Judah*	
Jerusalemites)	*judge, I pray, between me*	3+2
	and my vineyard!	
	4 *What (was there) more to do*[a] *for my vineyard*	4+3
	that I did not do with it?[b]	
	Why did I wait	2+2+2
	for (it) to produce grapes	
	but then it bore[c] *stinking things?*	
Yahweh:	5 *And now, please let me announce to you*	4+4
(to Heavens and Earth)	*What I am going to do for my vineyard!*	
	Its hedge removed—	2+2
	it shall be (open to) grazing.	

Its wall broken down— 2+2
it shall be (open to) trampling.
6 [a]*So I will make it a waste.* [a] 2+4+3
It will not be pruned, not be hoed.
It shall surely grow up (as) thorns and bushes.
And upon the clouds I will lay a command 3+3
not [b] *to rain on it.*
Prophet: 7 *For the vineyard of Yahweh of Hosts* 4+2
(to Heavens and Earth) *(is) the house of Israel.*
And the man of Judah, 2+2
the planting of his delight.
When he waited for justice, 2+2
behold bloodshed!
For righteousness, 1+2
behold a cry of distress!

Notes

The song is a self-contained unit with clearly marked beginning and end. Its unity is unchallenged (Cf. Whedbee 44–45).

2.a. G. R. Driver (*Studies in OT Prophecy,* FS T. H. Robinson [Edinburgh: T. & T. Clark, 1950], 53) suggests that עשה "produce" be understood like the parallel Arab word "to press out." Wildberger correctly thinks this unnecessary and notes the use of עשה פרי "bear fruit" in 2 Kgs 19:30.

3.a. DSS[Isa] יושבי for the sing of MT, but איש is singular like MT. Both are meant to be collective.

4.a. ל + inf constr to express necessary action (cf. Br. *Syn.*).

4.b. Several MSS have לו "to it" instead of בו "in it": LXX *αὐτῷ*, Tg להון, Syr *leh,* Vg *ei.* DSS[Isa] follows MT but also has בכרמי "in my vineyard" for לכרמי "for my vineyard" in the first stichos. Wildberger suggests that both changes are due to a copyist who failed to understand that "vineyard" is a metaphor for a woman.

4.c. DSS[Isa] וישה for MT's ויעש "and it makes." Wildberger suggests that it comes from the root נשא "bear" (cf. Ezek 17:8 נשא פרי about a vine, as well as 36:8; Ps 72:3).

6.a-a. Various interpreters have trouble with ואשיתהו "so I will make it." Perles amended it to ואשביתהו "I will cause them to return." But the main problem lies in בתה. G. R. Driver (*JTS* 38 [1937] 38) follows the Akk *batû* "destroy" and suggests the meaning "ruin" as did apparently Tg רטישין, Syr *neḥrab* and Vg *desertam.*

6.b. מן is used to negate the verb.

Form/Structure/Setting

The superb literary quality of the passage has drawn much comment. The very creative form is unique and has defied analysis which all accept. It calls itself שירת דודי "Song of my friend." It is often translated "song of my beloved." But the דוד in both word and implication is a male friend. It is a song sung by the male friend of the lover, perhaps the bridegroom. Schmidt and Fohrer think this must be the bride's song about her groom. But this hardly explains the direction the song takes. Junker (*Bib* 40 [1959] 259–66), refers to ὁ φίλος τοῦ νυμφίου (John 3:29), the intermediary who negotiates the marriage contract, the שׁוֹשְׁבִין of the rabbis. Ancient custom allowed no contact between the couple before marriage. This same intermediary must represent the groom in any complaint against the prospective bride. Wildberger suggests that the song represents this kind of intervention by the "friend" of the groom.

In that case the vineyard is symbolic of the bride in the song which in turn is a symbol for Israel as the bride of Yahweh. Bentzen (*AfO* 4 [1927] 209–10) suggests that the song was intended to be understood first as a lyric complaint presented on behalf of a bridegroom who felt that he had been cheated by his beloved. Thus v 6 should mean that the marriage will produce no children. Bentzen speaks of a double pseudonymity: the singer speaks of a friend who is really Yahweh, and of a vineyard, a bride who is really Israel.

The original genre is a complaint or, better, an accusation. The setting is that of a court of justice dealing with family matters. Fohrer notes the elements of an accusing speech: the proof that a legal relation and responsibility exist between the parties involved, the description of the fulfillment of responsibilities by the plaintiff, the accusation that the accused has failed to fulfill responsibilities, and the appeal to the court for a judgment. All these appear in vv 1–4. In v 5 the spokesman for plaintiff becomes the judge, thereby moving beyond the genre, and it becomes apparent that Yahweh is the speaker.

The poem is complex. It uses first person form in vv 1–6. Vv 1–2 are by the singer or troubadour. Vv 3–4 begin ועתה "and now" and the speaker is the owner (or husband). While vv 5–6 do not wait for the judgment by Judeans and Jerusalemites called for in v 3, v 7 implies that Yahweh himself speaks the judgment because Judah is the accused and cannot stand in judgment of themselves. There are therefore four speakers, three of whom use first person.

So the passage develops in four stages:

I. The Song of the Bridegroom's Friend vv 1–2, containing an accusation against the bride
II. The Demand for Judgment by the Husband (owner) vv 3–4
III. The Announcement of Divorce by Yahweh vv 5–6
IV. The Explanation by the Prophet, identifying Yahweh as the owner-husband, the House of Israel/Man of Judah as the accused v 7

As in the first two cycles, this one begins with a statement of judgment on בת ישראל "the house of Israel." The generation of Uzziah sealed the fate of Israel, left it defenseless before the onslaught of Assyria and its marauding neighbors. Two decades later Samaria would fall and symbolize for all history the collapse. Judeans are included in the judgment, but, significantly, neither Jerusalem nor the house of Judah is included. Their judgment is different. It is proper that Yahweh's relation to Israel is dealt with in these terms (cf. Hosea). The relation to Jerusalem is different.

Comment

1 ידיד or דוד "friend" is the bridegroom, husband, owner in this song. Wildberger (167) has shown that the word is used almost exclusively in OT for the "beloved" or "friend" of God (Deut 33:12; Jer 11:15; Pss 60:5; 108:5;

127:2). The term is used in Ugaritic and Akkadian names of gods. The perceptive hearer might well guess that this "friend" of the singer is Yahweh himself.

Song is an unlikely description for the real form and intention of the passage. This is intentional. It begins as a harmless piece of entertainment which becomes a strong accusation of the hearers.

קרן normally means a "horn." Only here in OT does it describe a piece of land. It can hardly mean a mountain peak. KB suggests "a hillside" (as does A. W. Schwarzenbach, "Die geographische Terminologie in Hebräischen des Alten Testaments" [Diss., University of Zürich, 1954], 19). Wildberger follows Budde in suggesting a horizontal figure meaning a mountain extending out from the range. *Vineyard* is a designation that brings to mind the land of Canaan, "flowing with milk and honey," a startling contrast to the desert or the fields frequented by herdsmen. The highly cultivated land, like the walled cities, represented Canaan to Israel.

2 עזק "dig" appears only here in OT. Arabic *'azaqa* means "dig up" and later Hebrew uses the word for "a most thorough working of a field" (Dalman, *AuS*, IV, 323; cf. עֲזִיקָה "ploughed ground"). Neither LXX *φραγμὸν περιέθηκα* "put around it a fence" nor Vg *saepivit* "enclose" have caught the meaning. This is the first deep breaking of the hard ground that is necessary to prepare it to receive the young and tender plants.

The next step in rocky Palestine was to *clear the ground* of stones (סקל). These were thrown in the road or piled up to form a wall. With the ground prepared, the first stage is complete with the *planting of the choice vines* (שרק), apparently ones that will produce bright red grapes (Wildberger). The term is used in names of places (Judg 16:4; Gen 36:36; 1 Chr 1:47) which were proud of their vineyards.

The owner went on to build first-class installations. He installed a *watchtower* (מגדל). Some kind of shelter for the necessary watchman was needed, usually an elevated shelter covered with palm branches like that mentioned in 1:8 (סכה or מלו). A tower is built of stone, stands higher, and is, of course, much better.

Then, as the final touch, he dug out a *wine-press* (יקב). G. E. Wright (*Biblical Archaeology* [Philadelphia: Westminster, 1958], 133) portrays a press in two parts. The upper part can be insulated with plaster or wood and is the place for trampling the grapes. A lower container collects the juice.

Having done all that can be done, the builder/owner *waited* (יקו) for the vines to produce their famous *grapes* (ענבים). They did produce. But the first fruit was a shocking disappointment. באשים is another *hapax* and unclear in meaning. LXX translates *ἀκάνθας* "thorn-plants, thistles." Vg has *labruscas* "wild vines." BDB and KB relate it to באשׁ "have a bad smell, stink." GB notes a Coptic word *bees* "unripe fruit" and conjectures with Vg "grapes with a bitter, sour taste." G. R. Driver (*Studies on OT Prophecy,* FS T. H. Robinson [Edinburgh: T. & T. Clark, 1950], 53 note 6) suggests "spoiled by anthracnosa" following 'A *σαπριας* "decayed, rotten."

3 In seven terse clauses (all but one using consecutive imperfects) the ballad is sung. The owner turns to the audience for support. The setting is in Jerusalem. The hearers are Judeans, perhaps having vineyards of their own. What went wrong? In what was the owner at fault?

ועתה "and now" (vv 3,5) marks turning points in the account (cf. H. A. Brongers, "Bemerkungen zum Gebrauch des adverbialen *we ʿattāh* im Alten Testament," *VT* 15 [1965] 289–99).

7 God expected from Israel משפט "justice" and צדקה "righteousness." The same words are used for Jerusalem in 1:21–26. They are consistent with the understanding of Yahweh throughout Scripture. The bitter fruit that resulted is described in word-play as משפח "bloodshed" and צעקה "a distress cry."

משפח is another *hapax* and, thus, not easy to interpret. LXX translates ἀνομία "lawlessness." Vg *iniquitas* "iniquity." But these general meanings are of little help. Marti, Gray, Procksch, and Wildberger suggest a root ספח (which here is rendered שפח) which can be related to the Arabic *safaḥa* "shed blood." (Cf. Koran 6:146.) KB suggests another parallel with resultant meaning of "turn aside, break the law." BDB has "bloodshed."

צעקה is the distress cry of those who suffer from political or social violence as in Gen 27:34; Exod 3:7,9; 11:6 (Wildberger). Ps 9:13 (12) says Yahweh will not forget their "cry."

Explanation

For the fourth time in the Vision, judgment on Israel (the Northern Kingdom) is described and justified (1:2–3; 2:6–8; 3:13–14). The clear tones of the indictment in each case are mixed with a question: Why have things gone so terribly wrong?

The song for a friend anticipates a wedding song for the bridegroom about his bride. But the theme turns to a vineyard. It is not unusual to describe a bride in terms of a choice vineyard (cf. Cant 8:12). One might still imagine that the vineyard speaks of a bride through v 2 with its shocking ending.

But the figure remains a vineyard. The listeners from Jerusalem and Judah have no suggestions about the problem. The owner announces his decision to dismantle the protective tower and walls and abandon all care of the plants. It will grow weeds and thistles. It will be eaten and trampled by cattle. It will even be burnt and dried for lack of rain. The owner is unmasked in this speech. He is Yahweh.

If the listeners had missed the point, he is identified in v 7. Wildberger notes the relation in old Israel to the ark which both "Yahweh of Hosts" and "House of Israel" indicate. The vineyard is also identified as Israel and the Judeans. The contrast between wine-quality grapes and "stinkers" is now spelled out: instead of justice, bloodshed; instead of righteousness, a cry. The "song" with its application opens the "woes" of chap. 5. It gives a setting for the funeral of a nation and its people who had once held such great promise as the chosen and nurtured people of God. But their fruit was a bitter disappointment which finally necessitated God's withdrawing his protection and support. Now they are mourned—but also seen as the exploiters and ravagers that they had become. The disappointing and shocking "stinking things" of the vineyard are apt symbols of Israel's fruit.

Three times (vv 2, 4, 7) the word קוה "wait" appears. God's patience is stressed. Like Nathan before David (2 Sam 12), the singer asks the hearers to first render judgment and then to accept the judgment as applicable to themselves. The figure here fits the Vision's stress on God's careful and patient planning for Israel and the world (cf. von Rad, *OTT* 2:187). Planting a vineyard takes time and patient endurance, as does the raising of a son (1:2–3) and the cultivation of a people (2:5–8). God's disappointment in the failure of the enterprise is clear in each case. The "woes" of mourning that follow are fitting and understandable.

Episode B: Therefore My People Are Exiled (5:8–25)

Bibliography

Fichtner, J. "Yahweh's Plan in der botschaft des Jesaja." *ZAW* 63 (1951) 16–33 = *Gottes Weisheit:* Gesammelte Studien zum AT. Stuttgart: Calwer Verlag (1965) 27–43. **Rad, G. von.** "Das Werk Yahwehs." *Studia Biblica et Semitica.* FS T. C. Vriezen. Wageningen: H. Veenman, 1966. 290–8.

FOR THE WOE-ORACLES:

Clifford, R. J. "The Use of HOY in the Prophets." *CBQ* 28 (1966) 458–64. **Gerstenberger, E.** "The Woe-Oracles of the Prophets." *JBL* 81 (1962) 249–65. **Janzen, W.** *Mourning Cry and Woe Oracle.* BZAW 125. New York: De Gruyter, 1972. **Kraus, H. J.** "*Hoj* als prophetische Leichenklag uber das eigene Volk im 8. Jahrhundert." *ZAW* 85 (1973) 15–46. **March, W. E.** "Basic Types of Prophetic Speech." *OTFC* 164–65. **Wanke, G.** " 'אוי' and 'הוי.' " *ZAW* 78 (1966) 215. **Westerman, C.** *Basic Forms of Prophetic Speech.* Tr. H. C. White. Philadelphia: Westminster, 1967. 139–41. **Williams, J. G.** "The Alas-oracles of the Eighth Century Prophets." *HUCA* 38 (1967) 75–91.

Translation

Mourner:	8 *Woe! for those touching house with house.*	3+3
	Field on field they joined	
	until there was no place	2+2+2
	and you had to dwell [a] *by yourselves*	
	in the open country.	
Prophet:	9 *In my hearing Yahweh of Hosts (swore)* [a]:	3
	"Many houses will become a waste,	4+4
	Great and good ones—with no tenant.	
	10 *For ten measures of vineyard*	4+3
	will produce one [a] *bath.*	
	Seed of a homer will produce an ephah."	2+2
Mourner:	11 *Woe!*	1
	Those rising early in the morning,	2+2
	they pursued strong drink.	
	Those staying back in the twilight,	2+2
	wine inflamed them.	

Prophet: 12 *And a harp and a flute,* 3+3+2
a drum and a pipe,
and wine (are in) their banquets.
But of the doing of Yahweh 2+2
they take no notice,
and the work of his hands 2+2
they do not see.
Yahweh: 13 *Therefore my people are exiled* 3+2
for lack of knowledge,
and its glory was emaciated by famine.[a] 3+3
And its multitude parched by thirst.
Heavens: 14 *Therefore Sheol has enlarged her appetite* 4+4
and has opened her mouth without limit.
And her[a] *splendor, her*[a] *growl, and her*[a] *din* 3+3
have descended with jubilation into her.[a]
Earth: 15 *Thus mankind is humbled,* 2+2+3
and a person falls.
And the eyes of the haughty are humbled.
16 *Thus Yahweh of Hosts is exalted in the judgment,* 4+4
and the Holy God is sanctified[a] *in righteousness.*
17 *And lambs graze as (in)*[a] *their pasture,* 3+4
and sojourners[b] *eat wasted hulks*[b] *of fattings.*
Mourner: 18 *Woe!* 1
Those dragging "the iniquity" 2+2+3
with the cords[a] *of nothingness,*
and sin[b] *like the cart*[c]*-ropes.*
19 *Those saying "let it hurry!"* 2+2+2
"Let his work come quickly,[a]
so that we may see!"
"Let the counsel of the Holy One of Israel 2+3+1
draw near and come,
that we may know!"
Mourners: 20 *Woe!* 1
Those saying: 1+2+2
"Good" for evil
and "evil" for good.
Those putting 1+2+2
"darkness" for light
and "light" for darkness.
Those putting 1+2+2
"bitter" for sweet
and "sweet" for bitter.
Mourner: 21 *Woe!* 1+2+3
Those wise in their own eyes.
Those prudent before their own faces.
Mourners: 22 *Woe!* 1+3+4
Heroes for drinking wine.
Men of valor for mixing liquors.

Mourner: 23 *Those justifying a criminal for a bribe.* 4+4
Who deprive the innocent[a] *of his rights.*
Heavens: 24 *Therefore,* 1+4+3
Like a tongue of fire consuming stubble,
[a]*a flame (that) makes hay*[a] *sink down.*
Their root was like rot.[b] 3+3
Their sprout rose like dust.
Prophet: *For they had rejected the instruction of Yahweh of Hosts.* 6
They had spurned the saying of the Holy One of Israel. 5
Earth: 25 *Because of this,* 2+4+4
the anger of Yahweh blazed against his people.
So his hand was extended against it and he chastized it.
Then the mountains shook, 2+2+3
so that their droppings became
like refuse in the streets.
In all this, 2+3+3
his anger did not turn.
His hand was stretched out still."

Notes

8.a. הושבתם is a hophal pf "you were made to dwell." The Versions (LXX, Vg, Tg, Syr) have given an act translation without the causative sense. MT is the better reading.

9.a. LXX adds *ἠκούσθη γάρ* = כִּי נִשְׁמַע "for he was heard" supported by Vg, Tg, and Syr. *BHS* proposes לָכֵן נִשְׁבַּע "therefore he swore." This may be implied, but MT can stand as it is.

10.a. DSS[Isa] reads אחד "one," a masc form. But the fem form is well-attested and makes no difference in meaning.

13.a. מְתֵי רָעָב "men of hunger" is a possible rendering as Wildberger has observed. But the Versions suggest a different pointing מֵתֵי רָעָב "died of hunger." Another suggestion (BDB, 607) emends to read מזי רעב "empty from hunger" (cf. Deut 32:24) which is a better parallel to the following "parched by thirst."

14.a. The fem suffixes have been challenged as not consistent with v 13. (See *Comment* on this verse). There is no textual reason to change them.

16.a. C and other MSS vocalize נִקְדַּשׁ "I sanctified," a pf, while L, the Aleppo Codex, and B have נִקְדָּשׁ "sanctifying," a ptcp.

17.a. Syr *bzdqhwn* = בְּדָבְרָם "in their pastures" for MT's "as (in) their pastures." MT should be sustained.

17.b-b. Many attempts at emendation (see Wildberger) have failed to produce an improvement on MT.

18.a. MT בחבלי "with the cords." LXX Σ (Syr) *ὡς σχοινίῳ* = כחבלי"like ropes."

18.b. LXX 'A Σ *θ* all add the article to match the first stich.

18.c. LXX *δαμάλεως* "of a heifer."

In each of these MT is to be kept. The attempts to create an absolute parallelism are fruitless. Cf. Wildberger.

19.a. יחישה has a cohortative ending (GKC § 48*c*). Syr *nsrhb mrj'* = יחיש יהוה "let Yahweh hasten" has taken the ה as an abbreviation for Yahweh. But the parallel stitch does not have Yahweh as subject. MT correctly has מעשהו "his work" as the subject.

23.a. LXX Vg are sg paralleling רשע "a criminal" in the first stich.

24.a-a. DSS[Isa] ואש לוהבת "and fire to flame." 'A Σ *θ* render חשש by *θέρμη* "heat" as does Vg *calor.* Speier ("Zu Drei Jesajastellen," *TZ* 21 [1965] 311) cites Jewish commentaries that understand חשש as "fire." But Wildberger cites Isa 33:11 as proof that it means "dry grass" (Arab *ḥašša* "dry out"), the emendations of Driver and others to the contrary.

24.b. LXX *χνοῦς* "dust" or "chaff," Hebrew מוץ.

Form/Structure/Setting

The use of הוי "woe" puts the series into the setting of a funeral, the words into a lament over the dead. This is important to translation and exegesis. These are *not* threats concerning future judgment. They recognize the present dead and their past deeds.

The "woes" continue the theme of a funeral (cf. Wanke, *ZAW* 78 [1966] 217) which was begun with the Song of the Vineyard. They mourn the announced death of the Northern Kingdom and its people and men of Judah (5:7). Clements (60) is one of the commentators who fails to note the difference between the address to "Judah and Jerusalem" of the whole book and the specific references for the eighth century which differentiate between Jerusalem's fate and that of northern Israel. He understands these words to apply to Jerusalem. The "woes" single out groups among the people who experience the punishment and travail of the invasion and exile.

The "therefore" speeches (vv 13, 14–17, 24, 25) are comments from those standing outside the ranks of mourners and thus may fittingly be ascribed to the speakers of chaps. 1–2.

In v 9 one reports hearing Yahweh's oath of judgment. (Cf. *IDB* 3:577.) The אם־לא "if not" formula presumes the full form "May Yahweh do so to me and more also" which prefaces a human's oath. God's oath presumably had a different introductory imprecation.

Comment

8 The subject of Israelite land-tenure has been widely discussed. Cf. G. von Rad, "Verheissenes Land und Jahwes Land im Hexateuch," *ZDPV* 66 (1943) 191–204 (*Ges Stud,* 87–100); A. Alt, "Der Anteil des Königtums an der sozialen Entwicklung in den Reichen Israel und Juda," *KS* III 348–72; H. Wildberger, "Israel und sein Land," *EvT* 16 (1956) 404–22; F. Horst "Das Eigentum nach dem Alten Testament," *Gottes Recht* (Munich: Kaiser Verlag, 1961), 203–21; H. Donner, "Die soziale Botschaft der Propheten im Lichte der Gesellschaftsordnung in Israel," *OrAnt* 2 (1963) 229–45; J. Dybdahl, *Village Land Tenure in Ancient Israel* (Diss., Fuller Theological Seminary, 1981).

Ancient Israel was taught that the tribe's inheritance was a sacred right which guaranteed its members land to work and fruit to harvest. 1 Kgs 21 speaks of these rights as does Lev 25:33 with its prohibition against selling these rights. When these ordinances gave way to the greed of speculators, it created a class of landless unemployed without home, livelihood, or civil rights (L. Köhler, *Hebrew Man,* Tr. P. R. Ackroyd [Nashville: Abingdon, 1956], 147). This explains *to dwell by yourself alone in the open country.*

9–10 Yahweh's judgment oath against those who violated covenant ordinances in this way calls down economic chaos on the land: vacant villages, fruitless fields. A *measure* (צמד) is the land which one span of oxen can plough in one day (*IDB* 4:838) or about 2,000 m^2. A *bath* is a liquid measure of 21–23 liters or 5½ gallons which equals an *ephah* of ⅜ to ⅔ of a bushel (*IDB* 4:834). This suggests that 6¼ acres of land would produce ⅔ of a bushel of grapes.

11–12 The *woe* identifies some of those who are dead. The exploitation of the land occasioned the economic and social chaos which preceded invasion. Amos (2:6–7; 4:6; 5:11) and Micah (2:1–2) speak of similar circumstances.

Wildberger notes the implied difference between a Canaanite fondness for wine and a general Israelite sobriety based not so much on the desert tradition of Rechabites (cf. Jer 35:6) as on wisdom's rules (Prov 20:1; 21:17; 23:20, etc.).

Morning and *twilight* are the cool times of the day when leisure can be pleasant. Musical instruments provide entertainment. (For a description of them see *IDB* 3:470–76.)

The concentration on drink and pleasure precludes any notice of פעל יהוה or מעשה ידיו "the doing of Yahweh . . . the work of his hand." Wildberger ("Jesajas Geschichtsverständnis," *Congress Volume: Bonn,* VTSup 9 [Leiden: E. J. Brill, 1963], 95) points out the unique contribution that Isaiah makes in combining these references to God's work with his plan (עצה) for history. Israel's inability to recognize these is judged her greatest failure (1:3; 6:9–10, etc.) The Vision contends that the historical events from Uzziah's reign to the post-exilic era were "God's work," that they all conform to "his plan" and thus move toward his goal for his people.

13–17 Two results of this lifestyle are noted while two other observations are drawn from it.

Yahweh's word sees *exile* as a direct result deriving ultimately from this *lack of knowledge.* Young's comment (I, 212) is fitting for the reversal of life-style which awaits this people: "By means of a pagan manner of living the nation has profaned the holy and promised land. . . . Eating and drinking had been made to serve their evil purposes; they would therefore face hunger and thirst."

14 The funeral reference is supported by the reference to large numbers of dead (*Sheol has enlarged her appetite*). The feminine reference in the second half-verse (*her splendor,* etc.) must refer to the city or the people. עם (v 13) "people" is usually masculine. But at least once it is understood as feminine (Exod 5:16 וחטאת עמך). Israel (ישראל) is usually masculine. But in 1 Sam 17:21 and 2 Sam 24:9 it is feminine. Here the best understanding is the people. Israel's best and finest are in the grave. They have gone to their death with a mistaken sense of *jubilation* and bravado.

15 This verse resumes the comment of 2:9 that *mankind* is disgraced by Israel's behavior.

16 The verse notes that the events of judgment, while they humble mankind, actually *exalt* Yahweh of Hosts. They prove the integrity of his justice and righteousness. The Holy God is *sanctified* by it. The second line repeats קדש "holy" to make the point: "the Holy God shows himself to be holy (niphal perfect, BDB, 873) in righteousness (צדקה)." The semantic spheres of "holiness" and "righteousness" are very different (cf. the theological dictionaries). The Vision insists on merging them to define Yahweh's character and to understand how his acts of "righteousness" relate to his "holy" nature.

צדקה "righteousness" in Isaiah usually refers to rewarding actions. But Wildberger is correct (contra K. Koch, "Vergeltungsdogma im Alten Testament?" *ZTK* 52 [1955] 29; G. von Rad *OTT,* 1, 395; F. Horst, "Gerechtigkeit

Gottes," *RGG*³, 11, 1404) that the breach of positive ordinances which are evidences of צדקה demands God's intervention. This, too, is צדקה "righteousness."

17 The *lambs* and *sojourners* give a sense of tranquility that belies the wasted and emptied land.

18 The use of the definite article on העון "the iniquity" and העגלה "ropes of the cart" calls for explanation. Can it be that these are references to a diabolical deity or an idol that cannot be named, whose cult, like that of India's Juggernaut, pulls its decorated cart through the streets? Or is the verse to be taken at face value to figuratively picture those who strain to further the cause of evil and tirelessly work to promote sin? Or is the phrase *the cords of nothingness* a reference to knotted cords used in magic to effect curses on enemies (cf. S. Mowinckel, *Psalmenstudien I* [Kristiania: J. Dybwad, 1921], 51; M. Jastrow, *The Religion of Babylonia and Assyria* [Boston: Ginn, 1905], 285, 288)? The woe hints at much more than it says.

19 Prophetic announcements like these in the first chapters or those of Hosea and Amos have always brought derisive rejoinders from the onlookers. The references here are very relevant to the Vision's announcement of the "work of Yahweh" and "the plan of Yahweh." They, too, are counted with the "dead" mourned in this chapter.

20 The devaluation of words is a mark of civilization's corruption and has often been a tool for false propaganda in any age. Truth, accuracy, and integrity are moral terms that are necessary ingredients of a society's health. The ones mourned include those who reversed such meanings, who "stood things on their heads."

21 חכם "wise" and נבון "prudent" are qualities expected in the greatest of men from Joseph (Gen 41:38–39) to David (1 Sam 16:18) and to the Davidic king (Isa 11:2). They are gifts from God which are recognized as needed for the good of all. For these to be used for self-aggrandizement is a perversion of values. (Cf. Prov 26:12 "Do you see a man wise in his own eyes? There is more hope for a fool than for him" (NIV); cf. 26:5, 16; 28:11.)

22 Others who present themselves as heroes prove only their "heroism" in their capacity to handle liquor.

23 Those who were available for false witness if the price were right are among the dead. The word צדיק "righteousness" occurs three times in these two lines: מצדיקי "those who justify a criminal," צדקת צדיקים "the rights of the ones in the right," or "the innocent of his rights." The Versions were having some trouble in translating this and ended with "the right of the one in the right." The verse should be contrasted with the description of God in v 16 and shows how far the standards of God are from "this people."

24 Again the mourners are interrupted by statements that interpret the relation of the characteristics cited by the mourners to the events of the times. The figure describes the awesome judgment that was like fire. But it also notes how vulnerable the people had become. They were like stubble, hay. Even their roots were dried like rot and sprouts that should have been green were dry as dust.

The second half turns from the figure to a sober appraisal: They had lost contact with the source of life and strength. By rejecting and spurning the word of God (here not the Scriptures, but the words of the prophets and the tradition taught by the priests) they had cut themselves off from his vitality and strength.

25 So God, like the vineyard owner of "the song," took action to eliminate the vines that produced only "stinking things." His upraised hand signaled the removal of the protective fences and the guard tower, the beginning of the trampling of the vineyard (5:5–6).

This refrain (25c) is repeated four times more in chaps. 9–10 (9:12, 17, 21; 10:4) while one further "woe" occurs there (10:1). The events of chap. 5 (prior to the death of Uzziah, 6:1) are continued in 9:8–10:23 (in the reign of Ahaz) until Israel and most of Judah have indeed become a "trampling place" (5:5–6).

Explanation

The fourfold woes with interspersed conclusions drawn from them continue the funeral scene over Israel and much of Judah that was begun by the Song of the Vineyard (5:1–7). They show that the generation who died and were exiled consisted of those "stinking grapes" (vv 2 and 4) who are identified by the mourners as the unscrupulous exploiters of the land (v 8); the drunkards (vv 11–12); the deceivers and scornful (vv 18–19); those who deliberately confuse the issues (v 20); the conceited (v 21); those whose heroics are only found in alcohol and who have no honor (v 22).

The entire passage supports God's decisions announced in chap. 1 and 2:6–8 and confirmed again in 10:4, 22b–23. The Assyrian invasion is only a coup de grace to the self-inflicted agonies that marked the last years of Israel.

Social crimes and degradation are symbols of their "lack of knowledge" (v 13) and their "rejection of the instruction of Yahweh of Hosts" (v 24). Ultimately this spiritual insensitivity and moral rebellion account for God's "anger" (v 25). This anger and rejection in turn account for the loss of political, social, and economic cohesion and stability that marked the last three decades of the Kingdom of Israel. This passage in the Vision precedes the announcement of the death of Uzziah (6:1) and describes conditions in the decade before 740 B.C. It will be continued ("his hand was stretched out still" 5:25) with the use of that refrain in the reign of Ahaz (9:8–10:23) for the last decade of Samaria's existence.

Episode C: Signal to a Distant Nation (5:26–30)

Translation

Heavens: 26 *When he raised a signal to distant nations* [a] 4+4+4
and whistled for him from the ends of the earth,
behold, with swift haste, he came.

Earth: 27 *None weary, none stumbling in it,* 2+3
not drowsy nor asleep, 2+2
waist band not loose, 4+4
sandal-thong not torn,
28 *whose arrows (were) sharp,* 3+3
all his bows (were) bent.
His horses' hoofs 2+2+2
were thought (to be) like flint.[a]
His wheels like the very wind.
29 *He had a growl like a lion,* 3+2
a roar[a] *like a young lion.*
He growled and seized prey. 3+3
He escaped! (There was) no deliverer.
Heavens: 30 *He growled over it* 2+2+2
in that day
like the sea's growl.
When he looked to the land 2+3+3
behold: darkness,[a] *a distress*
and light (became) darkness in her spray.

Notes

26.a. The first reference is גוים "nations" while the second and third, לו "to him" and יבוא "he comes," are sg. A suggested emendation follows Jer 5:15, dividing the letters differently to read לְגוֹי מִמֶּרְחָק "to a nation from afar."

28.a. DSS[Isa] כצגר "like rock." Cf. LXX *στερεά πέτρα* "solid rock." MT may be pointed כַּצֹּר to make it conform. G. R. Driver (*JTS* 45 [1944] 13; and *Studies in Prophecy,* FS T. H. Robinson [Edinburgh: T. & T. Clark, 1950], 55) suggested the צר meant "a meteor." Tur-Sinai ("A Contribution to the Understanding of Isaiah I–XII," *Studies in the Bible,* ed. C. Rabin, ScrHier 8 [Jerusalem: Magnes Press, 1961] 168) suggests reading כַּצִּנּוֹר instead of כצר meaning "God's lightning." MT or the emended pointing should be kept.

29.a. Q יִשְׁאַג; K וְשָׁאַג. *BHS* has the consonants of K and the vowels of Q. If the verbs in the second line are a clue it should be וְיִשְׁאַג. The meaning is not materially different.

30.a. MT has accent marks over the first חשך "darkness" and over ואור "and light" requiring a reading "and behold darkness; distress and light; darkness in her clouds." *BHS* suggests one accent, *zakef katon,* over צר "distress," permitting a division like the translation.

Form/Structure/Setting

At regular intervals the Vision reminds its readers (hearers) of God's "work" in the period. 3:1 identified his removal of responsible leaders in Jerusalem.

Here "his anger" takes concrete form in an invader, "a distant nation from the end of the earth." The nation will be identified in chap. 7 as Assyria. The description of Assyrian military discipline and tactics is accurate. The notice of King Uzziah's death in 6:1 suggests that a time before that is intended here. Tiglath-Pileser III was already known in Palestine. Menahem and possibly Uzziah were involved in stopping his invasion of the West in 738 B.C.

V 26 identifies Yahweh as the initiator of the invasion. Vv 27–29 is a graphic poetic description of the army. V 30 returns to Yahweh as subject in documenting the dark fate ahead.

Crenshaw has listed this section as a "Liturgy of Wasted Opportunity" (*OTFC*, 262). This may fit the frame of vv 25 and 30, but hardly does justice to the strong military description of vv 27–29.

Comment

26 The verse pictures a concrete event in terms of God's direct intervention in the historical process. The subject of נשא "raise" is understood to be Yahweh. His visual and audible signals direct the foreign armies.

נס is a flag or ensign to which the troops may rally or reorient themselves (11:10; 18:3). The Assyrians carried elaborate symbols on poles, as their inscriptions show. These may be placed on raised ground with high visibility (13:2; 30:17). The emphasis here is on God's participation and direction. The armies respond promptly and with alacrity.

"The enemy from afar" is a theme that fits the historical reality of that period, but it is also a theme that continues in prophecy (cf. Jer. 4:16; 5:15). The *distant nation* and *from the ends of the earth* are parallel phrases in much of Hebrew poetry (cf. Deut 28:49; Ps 72:8; Zech 9:10; Sir 44:21).

The great distance is matched by the speed with which the army responds. The Assyrians prided themselves on their maneuverability and quickness.

27–28 The physical condition of the troops is excellent in spite of the forced-marches over great distances. Their equipment is in excellent condition and chosen for the kind of warfare that is needed. The arrow-points, made of horn, bone, flint, bronze, or iron, are sharpened and ready. The bow, when not in use, would have the string fastened on only one end. Before use the bow must be bent, דרך, implying that a foot is placed on it to bend it so that the other end of the string may be attached. The bows are ready for combat. The condition of horses and wagons/chariots is excellent, belying the reported distance they have traveled.

29 The picture closes with an analogy to a lion. The words used are לביא "lion" and כפיר "young lion." Lions were still known in Palestine and made a great impact at least on the imagination of Palestinians. In addition to these words two others, אריה and ליש, were used. *IDB* (3:136–37) recognizes אריה as the common word, while others are poetic designations. KB distinguishes לביא the Asiatic lion from Persia from the African lion אריה. כפיר is a young lion old enough to hunt alone. The metaphor emphasizes the terror inspired by the determined successes of the army.

30 In a manner familiar from chap. 1, the metaphorical theme is continued with a very different meaning. The "growl" of the lion/enemy became the growl of Yahweh, the Divine Warrior, whose appearance on that fearful day brings gloom to all.

Explanation

The Vision contends that God's strategy controls and directs historical events. His signals start the army's advance. His movements keep the action moving or bring it to an end. His upraised hand signals his continued displeasure with Israel (v 25). He will not protect her. He has disavowed her. It is the counterpart of the vineyard owner's removal of fences and guard tower in v 5. In v 26 he raises a banner and sounds a signal for invading armies. (Similar actions occur in 13:2; 30:17.) Such a signal may have a positive purpose (cf. 11:10, 12; 18:3). God's judgment is more than a word. Actions follow. In all of them God is in control.

Neither Yahweh nor the invading enemy is named in this section (vv 26–30). But the implication is clear. What is here implicit will be made explicit in 7:17. The light of God's countenance is denied Israel in this time; 2:6 had already confirmed that. No amount of optimism can conceal it. The theme is confirmed in the vision of chap. 6 and continued in 9:7(8)—10:20 after a section dealing with Jerusalem (7:1–9:6[7]).

Scene 5: In God's Courtroom (6:1–13)

Bibliography

Cazelles, H. "La vocation d'Isaie (ch 6) et les rites royaux." *Homenaje a Juan Prado.* Madrid: Consejo Superior de Investigaciones Cientificios, 1975. 89–108. **Engnell, I.** *The Call of Isaiah.* UUÄ 11/4. Uppsala: Lundequistska, 1949. **Evans, C. A.** "The Text of Isaiah 6:9–10." *ZAW* 94 (1982) 415. ———. *Isaiah 6:9–10 in Early Jewish and Christian Interpretation.* Diss., Claremont, 1983. **Jenni, E.** "Jesajas Berufung in der neueren Forschung." *TZ* 15 (1959) 321–39. **Knierim, R.** "The Vocation of Isaiah." *VT* 18 (1968) 47–68. **Liebreich, L. J.** "The Position of Chapter Six in the Book of Isaiah." *HUCA* 25 (1954) 37–40. **Metzger, W.** "Der Horizont der Gnade in der Berufungsvision Jesajas." *ZAW* 93 (1981) 281–84. **Milgrom, J.** "Did Isaiah Prophesy during the Reign of Uzziah?" *VT* 14 (1964) 164–82. **Montagnini, F.** "La vocazione di Isaia." *BeO* 6 (1964) 163–72. **Müller, H. P.** "Glauben und Bleiben. Zur Denkschrift Jesajas 6:1—8:16." VTSup 26. Leiden: E. J. Brill, 1974. 25–54. **Steck, O. H.** "Bemerkungen zu Jesaja 6." *BZ* 16 (1972) 188–206. **Steinmetz, D. C.** "John Calvin on Isaiah 6: A Problem in the History of Exegesis." *Int* 36 (1982) 156–70. **Tsevat, M.** "ישעיהו (Isa 6)." *FS Z. Shazar.* Ed. B. A. Luria. Jerusalem: Kirjath Sepher, 1973. 161–72. **Whitley, C. F.** "The Call and Mission of Isaiah." *JNES* 18 (1959) 38–48. **Zeron A.** "Die Anmassung des Königs Usia im Lichte von Jesajas Berufung: zu 2 Chr. 26:16–22 und Jes. 6:1ff." *TZ* 33 (1977) 65–68.

PROPHETIC CALL NARRATIVES:

Crabtree, T. T. "The Prophet's Call—A Dialogue with God." *SWJT* 4 (1961) 33–35. **Habel, N.** "The Form and Significance of Call Narratives." *ZAW* 77 (1965) 297–323. **Tidwell, N. L. A.** "*wāʾōmār* (Zech 3:5) and the Genre of Zechariah's Fourth Vision." *JBL* 94 (1975) 343–55.

THE TEXT OF 6:13:

Ahlstrom, G. W. "Isaiah VI 13." *JSS* 19 (1974) 169–72. **Brownlee, W. H.** "The Text of Isaiah 6:13 in the Light of DSIa." *VT* 1 (1951) 296–98. **Hvidberg, F.** "The Masseba and the Holy Seed." *NorTT* 56 (1955) 97–99. **Iwry, S.** "Massebah and Bamah in 1Q Isaiah A 6:13." *JBL* 76 (1957) 225–32. **Sawyer, J.** "The Qumran Reading of Isaiah 6:13." *ASTI* 3 (1964) 111–13.

Translation

Prophet:	1 *(It was) in the year of King Uzziah's death*	4+2
	that [a] *I saw my Lord:* [b]	
	sitting on a throne,	2+2
	high and raised,	
	his robes [c] *filling the hall;*	3
	2 *seraphim standing above him:* [a]	4
	six wings—	2+3
	six wings [b] *to each.*	
	With two he covered [c] *his face.*	3+3+2
	With two he covered [c] *his feet.*	
	With two he flew. [c]	
	3 *And one called* [a] *to another and said:* [a]	4
	"Holy! Holy! Holy! [b]	3+2
	Yahweh of Hosts!	
	The fullness [c] *of all the earth (is) his glory!"*	4
	4 *The foundations* [a] *of the threshold shook*	3+2+3
	from the sound of the calling	
	as [b] *the hall began to be filled with smoke.*	
	5 *So I said: "Woe is me,*	2+2
	that [a] *I was silent,* [b]	
	that [a] *I (am) a man of unclean lips,*	5
	and I dwell in the midst of people of unclean lips,	4+2
	that my eyes have seen the King, Yahweh of Hosts!"	4+2
	6 *Then one of the seraphim flew to me.*	4+2+4
	In his hand (was) a smooth stone [a]	
	[b] *he had taken with tongs from on the altar.*	
	7 *Then he made it touch my lips and said*	3+4
	"Behold this has touched your lips!	
	Your guilt has departed!	2+2
	Your sin has been atoned!"	
	8 *Then I heard the voice of my Lord* [a] *saying:*	4
	"Whom shall I send?	2+3
	Who will go for us?" [b]	
	So I said: "Here I am! Send me!"	3
	9 *Then he said: "Go!*	2+3
	and you shall say to this people:	
	'Listen constantly! [a] *But do not understand!*	2+2
	Look regularly! [a] *But do not know!'*	2+2

10 [a]*Dull the heart of this people!* 3+2+2
Make its ears heavy
and shut its eyes, [a]
lest it see with its eyes, 3+2
hear with its ears,
and its heart [b] *understand* 3+2
and it may turn and will have healing."
11 *Then I said: "How long, my Lord?"* 3
Then he said: 1
"Until there be desolation: 4
Cities without inhabitant, 3+3+3
buildings without a person,
and the fields are ruined [a]*—a desolation."*
12 *When* [a] *Yahweh shall have removed humankind* 3+4
and the abandoned area [b] *in the land's core (shall*
have become) great,
13 *if (perchance there be) yet in it a tenth-part,* 3+3
if it turn, will it be for burning? [a]
Yahweh: *Like the terebinth or like the oak of an asherah,* [b] 3+3+3
cast down, [c] *(becomes) a monument of a high-*
place [d]*—*
the seed of the holy [e] *(will be) its monument.*

Notes

1.a. DSS^{Isa} omits ו but the use of *waw* consecutive after a temporal phrase is sound Masoretic grammar (Br. *Synt.* § 123).

1.b. Many MSS read יהוה "Yahweh" for אדני "Lord." Wildberger thinks a tendency to substitute אדני for יהוה can be found in many places in Isaiah. However, note the distinctive use of אדני by Amos in vision texts combined with יהוה (7:1, 2, 4, 5; 8:1, 3, 11; 9:5, 8) and alone (7:3; 9:1). The use of אדני appears to have a special intention in these visions.

1.c. LXX *καὶ πλήρης ὁ οἶκος τῆς δόξης αὐτοῦ* "The house (was) full of his glory" avoids reference to ושוליו "his train" or "skirts" (BDB, 1062). This is usually seen as the tendency of the LXX translator to correct what he considers flagrant anthropomorphism. It can hardly be considered witness to a different original text. The LXX translator had a special love for *δόξα* (cf. L. H. Brockington, "The Greek Translator of Isaiah and His Interest in ΔΟΞΑ," *VT* I (1951) 23–32). שוליו means "lower extremities," i.e., from waist to feet. They were undoubtedly thought of as clothed or covered by a robe except the feet (G. R. Driver, *NE Studies,* FS W. F. Albright [Baltimore: Johns Hopkins, 1971], 90).

2.a. LXX *κύκλῳ αὐτοῦ* "around him" for ממעל לו "from above him." The translator appears to object to the seraphim standing above the Lord. But MT is consistent. See יעופף "he flew" at the end of the verse. They are pictured as flying above the throne.

2.b. DSS^{Isa} does not repeat שש כנפים "six wings," probably due to haplography. Repetition emphasizes the distributive expression (Br. *Synt.* § 87).

2.c. Each of these imperfects speaks of characteristic or customary action (Watts, *Syntax,* 60).

3.a-a. DSS^{Isa} reads וקראים "and they were calling" for וקרא "and one called" and omits ואמר "and said." MT sustains the line of verbs in sg and is correct. DSS^{Isa} clearly thinks of several seraphim. MT might be understood to think of only two. (Cf. Engnell, *Call of Isaiah,* 34 and 246.)

3.b. DSS^{Isa} has קדוש "holy" only two times which has occasioned a debate (cf. N. Walker, "Origin of the Thrice-Holy," *NTS* 5 (1958/59) 132–33; "Disagion Versus Trisagion," *NTS* 7 (1960/61) 170–71; B. M. Leiser, "The Trisagion," *NTS* 6 (1959/60) 261–63; D. Flusser, *Immanuel*

3 (1973) 37–43). Wildberger correctly notes that the thrice-holy formula is consistent with liturgical usage in Ps 99; Jer 7:4; 22:29; Ezek 21:32.

3.c. LXX πλήρης "fullness" appears to have translated מלאה (i.e., an abs fem form rather than MT's masc constr). Vg follows LXX with *plena,* Tg מליא, Syr *dᵉmaljâ* which are all in line with Pss 33:5; 72:19; 104:24. But Wildberger has correctly noted Ps 24:1 ארץ ומלואה and Deut 33:16; Pss 50:12; 89:12. The Vision uses מלא "fullness" in 8:8 and 31:4. LXX makes כל־הארץ "all the earth" the subject. MT makes מלא כל־הארץ the subject (cf. Br. *Synt.* § 14).

4.a. אמה usually refers to the "forearm" (*CHAL,* 19) or a "cubit" measure (BDB, 52). אמות הספים has been variously translated here (Cf. R. B. Y. Scott, "the Hebrew Cubit." *JBL* 77 [1958] 205–14). LXX ὑπέρθυρον refers to the upper part of the door. But the term here applies to the entire door structure, hence "foundations of the threshhold" (Leslie; Engnell, *The Call of Isaiah*).

4.b. The use of impf and an inverted word order suggests a circumstantial clause.

5. The translation of this verse turns on the meaning of כי (3x) and נדמיתי.

5.a. כי may mean "because," or "that," or an emphatic particle "indeed" or "but," or "if, or when." LXX translates 2x with ὅτι and once with καί. The second כי clearly introduces a reason clause. The first and third are not so bound.

5.b. נדמיתי is usually translated "I am undone" or something similar (cf. BDB, 198). LXX κατανένυγμαι "I am stupefied" or "stunned." Syr *tawîr ʾnâ* "I am overthrown." But 'A Σ θ have εσιωπησα, aorist "I am silent," and Vg *tacui.* Jewish exegesis agrees and relates this to Isaiah's silence relating to Uzziah's wrongs (2 Chr 26:16–22); Tg הבית "I have transgressed" (Stenning). The meaning "be silent" has now been adopted very widely (cf. L. Köhler, *Kleine Lichter* [Zürich: Zwingli-Verlag, 1945], 32–34; Jenni, *TZ* 15 [1959] 322; Eichrodt, Fohrer, Kaiser, and Wildberger. Cf. *CHAL,* 72).

6.a. רצפה apparently means "a smooth stone" used for paving or used as a heated stone for cooking (BDB, 954). LXX translates ἄνθραξ "glowing charcoal," apparently depending on Lev 16:12. But there the Heb is גחלי. MT is to be preferred (contra Wildberger and *CHAL*).

6.b. Word order and tense structure indicate that the last clause is circumstantial (cf. Engnell, *Call of Isaiah;* Wildberger).

8.a. Many MSS read יהוה "Yahweh." See notes to v 1.

8.b. MT לנו "for us." LXX πρὸς τὸν λαὸν τοῦτον "for this people" appears to have been drawn in from v 9 (לעם הזה) although some suggest LXX read an original לגוי "for a nation" for MT's לנו.

9.a. The inf abs following its cognate finite verb indicates continuation of the action (cf. GKC § 113*r*).

10.a-a. LXX reads ἐπαχύνθη γὰρ ἡ καρδία τοῦ λαοῦ τούτου καὶ τοῖς ὠσὶν αὐτῶν βαρέως ἤκουσαν καὶ τοὺς ὀφθαλμοὺς αὐτῶν ἐκάμμυσαν "for the heart of this people became dull and their ears heard with disgust (lit., heavily) and their eyes closed," i.e., instead of the prophet's receiving an order to dull the hearts, the people have made themselves stubborn and unwilling. The theological problem the MT presents is eliminated by the change (cf. Wildberger).

10.b. DSS[Isa] בלבבו "with its heart" to conform with the other nouns. The Versions appear to follow the same pattern (cf. Eichrodt). However, MT makes sense and is the "hard reading."

11.a. LXX reads καὶ ἡ γῆ καταλειφθήσεται ἔρημος "and the ground will be left desolate," apparently seeing תשאר "are left" instead of MT תשאה "are ruined." The appearance of שאו "desolation" in the previous line has caused some commentators to favor the LXX here.

12.a. The *wāw* continues the question. A pf tense in the protasis of a conditional clause describes a condition taken for granted (Watts, *Syntax,* 134).

12.b. עזובה (BDB, 737) "desolation." *CHAL* 269 identifies it as a pass. ptcp fem from עזב "abandon." It also occurs as a proper name. LXX translates the verse: καὶ μετὰ ταῦτα μακρυνεῖ ὁ θεὸς τοὺς ἀνθρώπους καὶ οἱ καταλειφθέντες πληθυνθήσονται ἐπὶ τῆς γῆς "and by this God will remove mankind and those left in the land will be multiplied." Engnell, (*Call of Isaiah,* 14) suggests that by this the harsh word of judgment has been reinterpreted to indicate salvation.

13.a. בער in the piel stem may mean to burn or to destroy (BDB, 129). *CHAL* (44) has a second meaning "graze, ruin, sweep away." Wildberger holds that Isa 3:14 and 5:5 have shown that the word means "grazed over" as when goats have eaten every blade and twig to the point that nothing is left. Hertzberg, Kaiser, and Budde ("Schranken, die Jesajas prophetischer Botschaft zu setzen sind." *ZAW* 41 [1923] 167) agree. KB, Eichrodt, and Fohrer contend for the meaning "burn" as with fire.

13.b. MT אשר "which." Iwry (*JBL* 76 [1957] 230) accepts the next three changes in DSS^{Isa} and emends here to read אשרה turning the relative particle into a noun "Asherah." This restores the meter and continues DSS^{Isa}'s trend in giving meaning to an otherwise obscure passage. Iwry's other emendations are unnecessary.

13.c. MT בשלכת "in falling," a preposition with an obscure noun (BDB, 1021). DSS^{Isa} משלכת by the change of one letter becomes a hoph ptcp "being cast down." LXX ὅταν ἐκπέσῃ "when it falls" seems to support MT in form. But it adds ἀπὸ τῆς θήκης αὐτῆς "from its funeral vault," thus supporting the broader implications of DSS^{Isa}. Read with DSS^{Isa}.

13.d. MT בם "in them." DSS^{Isa} במה "high place." One hundred MSS read בה "in her." Vg reads *quae expandit ramos suos* "which spread its branches."

13.e. MT קדש "holy," an adjective. DSS^{Isa} הקדוש "the holy ones."

The translation has adopted the reading of DSS^{Isa} and Iwry's emendation, judging them to make good sense of an otherwise obscure passage (see *Comment*).

Form/Structure/Setting

The chapter begins a new scene marked by a monologue, first-person narrative, and a chronological notice. The next chapter changes to a third-person account.

Chap. 6 has unity and movement. Wildberger (234) calls it a "kerygmatic unity." It is composed of five parts: (1) vv 1–4: the Hall of the Lord, Heavenly King; (2) vv 5–7: the purging of the prophet's sin; (3) vv 8–10: the task for "this people"; (4) v 11: how long?; (5) vv 12–13: if some survive and return, what of them? Each builds on what precedes and moves the thoughts along.

The combination of the parts is unique. The nearest parallel is the account of Micaiah's prophecy (1 Kgs 22) which also involves kings of Israel and Judah and which also deals with the fate of Israel's king. That passage also deals with prophecy which manipulates the one God intends to execute.

The chapter has often been named a "call narrative" (H. Graf Reventlow, *Das Amt der Propheten bei Amos,* FRLANT 80, Göttingen: Vandenhoeck & Ruprecht, 1962) and interpreters wonder why it does not come at the beginning of the book as in Ezekiel (chap. 1). The chapter is *not* a "call narrative" (cf. Koch, *The Prophets* I [Philadelphia: Fortress, 1983] 113). Its position in the book (cf. M. M. Kaplan, "Isaiah 6:1–11," *JBL* 45 [1926] 251–59; Y. Kaufmann, *Toledot ha-Emunah ha-Yisraelit* [Tel-Aviv: DVIR Co., 1947] III, 206–7; J. Milgrom, *VT* 14 [1964] 164–82; C. P. Caspari, *Commentar til de tolv foste Capitler af Propheten Jesaja* [Christiania: P. T. Malling, 1867] 240–45; S. Mowinckel, *Profeten Jesaja* [Oslo: Aschehoug, 1925], 16–20; I. P. Seierstad, *Die Offenbarungserlebnisse der Propheten Amos, Jesaja, und Jeremia,* SNVAO 2 [Oslo: Norske Videnskaps-Akademie, 1946] 43; note Wildberger's remark (240): שלח "send" is never used of a "call"—always of a particular task and message) marks the *end* of the Uzziah section as the opening words clearly indicate. Its purpose is to show that the nature of God's actions toward Israel and Judah which had emerged in Uzziah's reign would remain the same until a complete destruction would come (i.e., over Samaria in 721 B.C.). The time clause "in the year of Uzziah's death" points backward, making this a closing scene. There is no indication that this is the prophet's first vision or first prophetic experience.

Three features need discussion before a detailed analysis is presented.

A First-Person Speech

Accounts of prophetic vision are often told in the first person. Micaiah's vision (1 Kgs 22:17, 19–23) is a case in point. Amos's visions (Amos 7:1–9) are of the same type (cf. J. D. W. Watts, *Vision and Prophecy in Amos* [Leiden: E. J. Brill; Grand Rapids: Eerdmans, 1958] 28). Zechariah's visions (Zech 1:8—6:8) follow this pattern. Ezekiel's visions are also told in the first person, as are Jeremiah's. A number of these speeches do not use the prophet's name in the immediate context.

First-person speeches are frequent in Isaiah. The majority present Yahweh speaking for himself. Some are choral passages using the first person plural. Some are indirect quotations of Israel (like 40:27b). Some have Israel as a speaker (49:1–4). Some follow a narrative about Isaiah and are naturally to be understood as his speech (8:1–4; 8:5–8; 8:11–18). But there are also first-person speeches by unidentified speakers like 5:1–6; 21:2—22:4; 24:1; 25:1. Unidentified speakers appear in 49:5–6; 50:4–9, and 61:1–3a with basic messages on the theme of the book, while others speak in opposition, as in 61:10–11; 62:1–5, 6–7; 63:7.

The form fits the dramatic character of the book. It should be a warning against too hasty identification of either the genre, its meaning, or the identity of the speaker. Traditionally the speaker has been identified with Isaiah whose name is called in the following chapters. But if Isaiah is the subject of the Vision rather than its author (see *Introduction*), one must note that he has not so far been introduced in person (only in the superscriptions of 1:1 and 2:1). Thus the unsuspecting readers/hearers have no way to identify this speaker. In afterthought they may wonder if the mysterious and anonymous speaker was indeed identical with Isaiah the prophet who appears in the following scene.

An Authenticating Vision

The chapter has often been understood as an account of Isaiah's call to be a prophet. W. Zimmerli, in his commentary on Ezekiel (BKAT 13 [Neukirchen-Vluyn: Neukirchener Verlag, 1968] 16–21 = Hermeneia, tr R. E. Clements [Philadelphia: Fortress Press, 1979] 97–100), has distinguished two types of narratives related to a call. One type is found in the stories of Moses, Gideon, Saul, and Jeremiah. In it reluctance and excuses must be overcome. "Do not be afraid" is a recurrent phrase (cf. Isa 7:4).

In a second type Zimmerli found that a vision played a much greater role. The account in 1 Kgs 22:19 begins ראיתי את יהוה "I saw Yahweh." In Isa 6 it begins ואראה "I saw." The person is drawn into the midst of the Divine Council and observes the glory of the King. He, like the serving spirits about the King, is prepared to do the King's will (cf. Ps 103:20–21). He becomes a part of God's plan and his work. The telling of the vision authenticates him as God's genuine messenger. Zimmerli goes on to draw a parallel with Paul's vision (Acts 9:3–6; 22:6–11; 26:12–18).

F. Horst ("Die Visionsschilderungen der alttestamentlichen Propheten," *EvT* 20 [1960] 198) has summarized well: "In all these cases in which the prophet is allowed to be present through visionary experience during discussions or decisions in the throneroom of God, and thus know the 'knowledge of God,' and thus know the 'knowledge of the Almighty' . . . he is claimed and empowered to make an unusual and overwhelming proclamation—unusual in its shocking harshness or in its great expectation." Horst is right. Yet the biblical precedents are broader. Isa 6 stands in a tradition in which God reveals (and in some measure defends) his decisions to bring judgment.

God's appearance to Noah (Gen 6:11–21) simply notes the conditions, warns of disaster to come, and instructs him to build the ark. God acts to save the righteous from the disaster.

God's appearance to Abraham (Gen 18) reveals the impending judgment of Sodom and Gomorrah (vv 17–21). He cites the complaints against the cities (v 20). Then he enters into dialogue with Abraham on the theme: "Will you sweep away the righteous with the wicked?" which culminates in the admission that he will not, if there are at least ten righteous. The question is not finally answered, but its relative validity is recognized.

Moses' meeting with God on Sinai to discuss the covenant (Exod 32) is interrupted by the incident of the golden calf (vv 5–14). God tells Moses what has happened (vv 7–8) and announces his decision to destroy them (vv 9–10). Moses objects and intercedes for the people (vv 11–13). God agrees to postpone judgment (v 14).

Samuel's meeting with God comes after a "man of God" had announced God's rejection of the house of Eli (1 Sam 2:27–36). The boy Samuel hears God's voice in the night (3:4–10). The Lord tells him of the coming judgment against Eli and his family (vv 11–14). No dialogue follows.

THE HEAVENLY COUNCIL

The setting in the Hall of the Heavenly Council appears in several OT passages (notably 1 Kgs 22:17–23; Job 1:6–12; 2:1–6; Zech 3:1–5). These may well be related to the prophetic claim to have "stood before Yahweh" and "shared his council" (סוד). The subject has been discussed widely (see the lengthy discussion of the tradition in Wildberger 234–38 and E. C. Kingsbury, "The Prophets and the Council of Yahweh," *JBL* 83 [1964] 279–86). Wildberger (237) notes that the pictures of Isaiah and Ezekiel are carried over into the Vision of the Seer of Patmos (Rev 4 and 5). (Cf. H. P. Müller "Formgeschichtliche Untersuchungen zu Apc. 4f," Diss. Heidelberg, 1963.)

Discussion concerning the genre of this chapter continues to be lively (cf. recent articles by Tidwell and Steck with full bibliographies). A consensus is forming that the chapter is a unique combination of forms. The frame of the chapter is composed of a heavenly throneroom scene (vv 1–2) which in turn is a subcategory of narratives of meetings with God (theophanies, if you will). As in 1 Kgs 22:19; Job 1:6 and 2:1; and Zech 1:8; 3:1; and 6:1–3, the scene is described in detail. The names and descriptions of the King's servants vary. But they are always there. The reader of the Book of Isaiah will find the scene familiar. No such description is found in chaps. 1–5. But Yahweh is central in every scene while speakers mill around his room in much the same way they do here.

A second element (vv 3–4) describes the speech in the room. There is no discussion leading to a decision. This decision has already been made (cf. Knierim, *VT* 18 [1968] 58). The discussion and the decision have already been described in chap. 1. The seraphs support the decision with a chorus of praises for the holiness and glory of God.

A third element has the cry of woe reflect the narrator's response. Tidwell (*JBL* 94 [1975] 343–55) sees this as a parallel to the protests of the "call narratives." But v 7 takes the cry to be a confession of sin which is promptly purged. The call for a messenger and the commission are elements in other descriptions like 1 Kgs 22:2 or 22 and Job 1:12 and 2:6–7. Only in Isaiah is any other than one of the heavenly court sent on such a mission. The commission is not directed so much toward a message as toward a task. This is parallel to 2 Kgs 19:20; Job 1:12 and 2:6. It is a very unusual assignment for a divine messenger. In this, too, it is parallel to the other accounts.

The narrator intervenes for the third time—after his "woe" cry (v 5) and his volunteer's cry (v 8b). But this is different. It contains a tone of protest like that of Abraham's questions (Gen 18:23–25) or of Moses (Exod 32:11–19) or of Amos (7:2 and 5). This is an element from another genre altogether. The question elicits a confirmation of the judgment decision (cf. Steck, *BZ* 16 [1972] 195).

The narrator persists with his question (see *Notes*) probing the fate of the surviving and returning remnant in the land. The parallel to Gen 18:23–25 is very close. It tests the continuing effect of the ban on future generations.

The chapter has drawn upon several types of theophanic narratives to create a unique literary piece which has inner consistency and contextual integrity.

Vv 12–13 have often been judged extraneous to the core of the chapter. This may be defended if the chapter is seen as an eighth-century composition only. Within the larger unity of the fifth-century Vision (see *Introduction*), the verses continue the logical development to answer the inevitable "audience" question: How does that affect us?

Comment

1a *The year of King Uzziah's death.* The co-regencies of Judean kings in this period make the precise date difficult to determine. Bright (*HI*) places it in 742 B.C. Donner puts it in 736 B.C. (*IJH,* 395). In the Vision of Isaiah it marks the close of events portrayed in chaps. 1–5 in which God's fateful decision was made to destroy Israel and send its people in exile.

I saw my Lord. The Vision presents the speaker without identification. It is usually presumed that Isaiah the prophet speaks here. The assumption is based on the view that Isaiah wrote the book (or at least this part) or that the succeeding narrative and autobiographical sections (7:1—8:18) form a unity with this (Duhm calls it a *Denkschrift* "memoir") and are to be dated from the eighth century. If the Vision is seen essentially as a fifth-century composition and as a unity, this may be questioned. If the reader is intended to read these as Isaiah's words, why is he not introduced at the beginning? Also the unidentified first-person speech must be studied in light of other such speeches in Isaiah (such as 5:1–6; 21:3–4, 10; 22:4; 49:1–6; 50:4–9; 61:3; 62:1–6). One does well to reserve judgment on the issue.

Whether the account is spoken by the historical prophet or by (on behalf of) the literary prophet, its purpose is clear. It is a claim for divine authority in the task at hand. It claims to place this work with other reports from those who "stood before the Lord," who saw God and lived.

1b The throneroom description is the first and only one in the entire Vision. It may well serve to give the background for all the rest of the scenes where God is the center of discussion and drama (such as chaps. 1–5 and 40–59).

God is clearly the Heavenly King, exalted on his throne. His glorious presence dominates the scene as *his robes fill* the room. ההיכל "the hall" may refer to the Temple in Jerusalem or the great heavenly hall. The word cannot settle the question, but the context favors a heavenly setting.

2 The *seraphs* minister to God's every need. Such throneroom scenes regularly describe the heavenly "host" but use different words. Gen 3:24 calls them "cherubs." They are often referred to as "messengers" 2 Kgs 22:21 calls them "spirits." Job 1:6 calls them "sons of God" and identifies one as השטן "the adversary." Ezekiel's vision (1:5–21) sees them integrated into God's portable throne. These six-winged creatures (*IDB* 1:131) occur only here in the OT. They, like the cherubs, reflect ancient Near Eastern ideas. In the Bible they are a part of descriptions of what are more generally called "angels."

Only two wings are used to fly. Two more cover his eyes in deference to God's glory. The remaining two cover his feet. Perhaps "feet" are here euphemisms for the genital areas as in Exod 4:25 and Isa 7:20. Kaiser relates this to the very ancient experience of relating sexuality and guilt-feeling. One may also note a prevailing oriental custom that forbids showing the soles of the feet in polite society.

3 The threefold *sanctus* praises the Lord for the revelation of his essential being. God is by definition "holy." But he reveals his "holiness" by his decisions and his acts. (Cf. H. Ringgren, *The Prophetical Conception of Holiness,* UUA 12 [Uppsala: Lundequistska, 1948], 19.) The praise is directed to him as *Yahweh of Hosts.* This is the cult name used in the Jerusalem Temple. *Yahweh* had been used with worship around the ark from the beginning of Israel's existence. Exod 3:14 and 6:2 tell of the revelation of the name to Moses. But the seraphs claim *his glory* to be *the fullness* of the entire earth. The *holiness* of God seems opposite to physical nature. Procksch noted that קדוש "holy" denotes God's innermost nature, while כבודו "his glory" describes the appearance of his being. God is known through his work.

4–5 The praise would be fitting at any time, but the dating of the passage suggests a timely meaning here as does the shaking of the threshhold and the smoke of incense. It suggests approval of God's decision to destroy Israel and to purge Jerusalem that was reached in chaps. 1–5 (cf. Knierim's thesis of a decision already made, *VT* 18 [1968] 47–68). Wildberger correctly notes that the "woe" recognizes that the very existence of the speaker is threatened. A funeral cry may already be spoken over him.

נדמיתי has often been translated "I am lost." This fits the context. But the word properly means "be silent." (Zeron, *TZ* 33 [1977] 65–68, relates the silence to Uzziah's leprosy.) The prophet is constrained to join the praise, but dares not. His own nature ("unclean lips") as well as that of his people does not allow him to speak in the assembly. It is astonishing enough that he has been allowed to see *the King, Yahweh of Hosts* and still be alive. Hebrew tradition held that to be impossible (Exod 24:10). The prophet's protest parallels those of Moses and Jeremiah (Tidwell).

6–7 A seraph performs the purging rite that gives the prophet his right to speak. It parallels the sacrifices which were needed to enter the Temple.

8 With the decision fixed, the Lord calls for a messenger to put it into effect (cf. 1 Kgs 22:20). The usual messenger would be one of the heavenly host, called a spirit, or a messenger (angel), or in one case the adversary. Here the prophet volunteers to go at God's command. This is unique to call narratives, but is normal in heavenly-throneroom descriptions.

9–10 *Go! and you shall say to this people.* God accepts the offer and sends the volunteer. *This people* picks up the references in 1:3; 2:6; 3:12, 15; 5:13, 25. It will be continued exactly in 8:6 and 11. The references appear without exception to refer to Israel. It is a correct term to use for the covenant people.

Hearing-seeing-understanding-knowing. The words are part of a motif that runs through the length of the Vision from 1:3 through 42:16–20. The usual accusation is that Israel *is* "blind" and "deaf." The LXX reflects this understanding of these verses as well: "You shall indeed hear, but not understand . . . the heart of this people became dull." The messenger's task is to testify to an existing tradition which prevents repentance.

The MT, however, sees the messenger playing an active part in hardening and dulling so that repentance will not take place, now that the decision to destroy has been taken. This parallels the spirit's task in 1 Kgs 22:20–23. It is even closer to the "hardening of Pharaoh's heart" (Exod 8:11, 28 [15, 32]; 9:7, 34). Wildberger is right in saying that this is not a one-sided action. That Israel's heart is "hard" and that Yahweh has made it so must be spoken in dialectical balance. The message remains the same: There is no turning back. The decision has been made and will be carried out. The commission addresses the question of prophetic success or effectiveness. As evangelists to bring the nations to repentance, the eighth-century prophets, indeed the great seventh-century prophets, were remarkably unsuccessful. This commission insists that this was not their task.

The closing line in a backhanded way provides a lucid description of revelation's normal purpose: Seeing and hearing (the vision and word of God) should lead to understanding (of their perverted and evil ways) which should cause rational beings to change and be healed. שוב "turn" is the usual word for repentance (cf. H. W. Wolff, "Das Thema 'umkehr' in der alttestamentlichen Propheten," *Gesammelte Studien Zum Alten Testament,* ThB 22 [München: Kaiser, 1964] 139; and G. Saner, "Die Umkehrforderung in der Verkündigung Jesajas," *Wort-Gebot-Glaube,* FS W. Eichrodt, ATANT 59 [Zürich: Zwingli-Verlag, 1970] 279–84). The issue is much more prominent in Jeremiah than it is here.

11 The prophet asks for more precise definition. *How long, my Lord?* The judgment is an effective curse or ban on Israel in which Yahweh has "abandoned his people" (2:6) and is "hiding his face from the house of Jacob" (8:17). The inevitable question is whether this is temporary or permanent. Is it a chastisement which is intended to eventually bring about the turning and "healing"? Or does this exclude Israel forever?

The answer is equivocal. It speaks of a total destruction of cities, houses, and fields. This may be understood to include social and political institutions that leave the land of Israel vacant and abandoned. But it does not answer the question about the people or about the possible future rehabilitation of the land. These are relevant questions to post-exilic readers or hearers.

12–13 The prophet's second question (see *Notes* and *Translation*) asks for clarification, assumes the fulfillment of God's judgment, but also (it is hoped) assumes the survival of a tiny remnant. It then poses the question of the future: Will the ban apply to all future generations? Will they too be banned from repentance and summarily condemned to "burn"? The word שׁוב "turn" or "return" carries a double meaning in this context. It may mean "repent," but may also mean "return." The latter would specifically apply to the exiles who return to Palestine.

The question has certainly raised a fundamental issue. Can the future remnant (the post-exilic *Golah* "exile community") hope to return to the land and faith of their forebearers and thus reclaim their inheritance in blessing? Or will they forever be under the "ban"?

This answer also is equivocal. The good news is the parable of the trees. When the hardwoods are cut down, they play a continuing role as funeral monuments in the burial grounds of the worship areas; that is, the remnant will continue to have a significant role.

The seed of the holy (see *Notes*) joins the use of the term in 4:3 and eschews the returning exiles' use of "holy ones" to refer to themselves as God's remnant. But the concluding *its monument* suggests for them a role they would not enjoy. They would be a continuing reminder of the nation that was now dead and of the reason why it was destroyed. The final verse of the Vision (66:24) suggests the same gruesome role.

Explanation

Vv 1–4 give us a formal description of the stage setting for most of the Vision. It functions for the Vision of Isaiah in the same way that Rev 4 and 5:8–14 do for the Apocalypse of John. The Lord, Yahweh of Hosts, is the center around whom all else moves. Seraphs serve him and act as his messengers, as the spirits do in 1 Kgs 22:21 and Zech 6:5. Gathered around are the "host of Heaven" in 1 Kgs 22:19. In Job 1:6 the "sons of God" gathered on a certain day. (Cf. the elaborate descriptions of Rev 4 and 5:8–14, etc.)

It also marks an historical milestone with the death of Uzziah. This first historical reference in the Vision implies that chaps. 1–5 belong in Uzziah's lifetime. Chaps. 7–8 will expand this historical identification.

The chapter is intended to authenticate the entire Vision. This is true whether one identifies the spokesman as the historical prophet or the "literary" prophet. It supports the claim that he "stood before Yahweh" in his council. It recognizes the uniqueness and strangeness of God's acts toward

Israel in this period (cf. 28:21). Its claim to integrity is only that it reflects what God actually said and did. It supports the message of these chapters that the Lord decided in the eighth century to destroy Israel (cf. 7:8b, 10:22b–23). Every effort to minimize the judgment is turned back. A basic faith that salvation lies beyond judgment (Jenni, *TZ* 15 [1959] 339), while not totally denied, is not allowed to come to the fore. The message is doom.

Having arrived at the decision, God commissions the prophet to aid in carrying it out. The prophet's two questions only strengthen the gravity and the long-term effect of the judgment. The future role of a "remnant" is narrowly defined in terms that are not hopeful. The Vision will support this view by a picture of post-exilic Israel as recalcitrant and unwilling (40:12—49:4) and of a community in Jerusalem that insists on forcing God to return to ancient forms (chaps. 62–64). Such peoples are only funeral monuments, reminders of the ill-fated history of Israel during the divided kingdom (6:13).

Act II: The Gently Flowing Waters (Chaps. 7–14)

The Second Generation: The Age of King Ahaz (ca. 750–735 B.C.)

Chaps. 7–14 are designated as the era of Ahaz by the mention of his name in 7:1 and the notice of his death in 14:28. This act of the drama takes place for the most part in periods of crisis during his reign. The primary issue deals with the question of Jerusalem's and the dynasty's survival during the critical period when Israel was losing both. Scenes 1, 3, and 4 end with a strong affirmation that the throne/city is secure (9:5–6; 12:1–6; 14:32).

Scene 1, "Of Sons and Signs" (7:1–9:6[7]), tells of the Syro-Ephraimite war (734 B.C.) and the Assyrian intervention.

Scene 2, "A Word against Jacob" (9:7[8]–10:23), describes the siege and fall of Samaria to the Assyrians (724–721 B.C.).

In scene 3, "Do Not Fear, You Jerusalemites" (10:24–12:6), Yahweh guarantees Zion's future (720 B.C.). Scene 4, "Burden: Babylon" (13:1–14:32), concerns the temporarily successful revolt against the oppressor.

The scenes balance Isaiah's call for reliance on Yahweh alone in speeches that remind one of the judgment that has been determined and contrasting speeches that are idealistically optimistic.

Throughout, the pressure of Assyrian expansion makes itself felt. While the promise of Assyrian invasion relieves pressure on Jerusalem in Scene 1, the coming of the armies reduces Israel and Aram to the status of provinces in Scene 2. Scene 3 looks hopefully to the possibility that tiny Judah may survive with a modicum of self-government as her neighbors are being subjugated.

The major political changes that Yahweh is accomplishing through the Assyrian have begun to take shape. Judgment falls on an entire past age in which Israel has had its existence. Small nations collapse before the imperial might. Yet Yahweh has preserved Jerusalem as he promised (2:1–4). With change—God-willed change—all about, some things remain firm. Jerusalem as the place where people can go to worship Yahweh is still in place.

The conditions for the survival of Jerusalem, of Judah, and of the Davidic house are exemplified in Ahaz. The Assyrian, not the Davidic king, has been called to political rule. Ahaz understood the political realities. He was called to adapt himself to the changing times. He submits to be Assyria's loyal vassal. But in this he is also called to remain true in faith to Yahweh and his purposes. He is not perfect in these respects, as the account in 2 Kings makes clear. But his conduct is such that his son can be crowned king in Jerusalem with great ceremony and high hope (Scene 3). Jeroboam's throne and Ben-Hadad's throne had not survived. Ahaz was able to pass on his royal status to Hezekiah after a reign in relative peace.

Scene 4 pronounces Yahweh's judgment on the active rebellion of Merodach-Baladan in Babylon. This is not God's will for this age, and not an example for Israel to follow.

Excursus: Types of Political Organization

Political and military power was exercised and experienced at several levels in the ANE. The highest was that of the Big Power (Empire). At this level Egypt, Assyria, Babylonia, Persia—and later, the Hellenistic empires and Rome—worked. They all established forms of administration to keep contact with and control over their dominions.

There were other powers who roamed the lands taking booty and exacting temporary tribute only, occasionally having one of their number stay on as king of a city or a region. The Hittites, Mittani, and Midianites fit this picture.

Then there were the smaller states who functioned as mini-empires when they were strong, or who banded with (or struggled against) similar states. Judah, Israel, Aram, Moab, Edom, the Philistines, and Phoenicia were such units.

And throughout the period there were the cities that preceded the states in existence and importance and usually continued to exist with various states or after the states were gone. Babylon, Damascus, Tyre, and Jerusalem were some of these.

Israel had first existed as a people made up of loosely related tribes. As such they had displaced most of the small city-states of the Canaanites. Then came the United Kingdom, followed by the divided Kingdoms, north and south.

The Vision of Isaiah spans the period when the major empires reassert themselves. The small kingdoms are doomed. One after another they are conquered and reorganized as Assyrian districts. By the time of Tiglath-Pileser III (740–727 B.C.), only the Phoenicians, a reduced Israel, Judah, the Philistines, Ammon, Moab, and Edom remained. Hamath, Damascus, Dor, Megiddo, and Gilead were already incorporated into the Assyrian system. Under Sargon II (722–705 B.C.) Samaria and Ashdod were added to that group. The other small states were vassals paying tribute. These included Jerusalem, the Philistine cities, Tyre, Edom, and Moab.

Isaiah's Vision is fully aware of these things. Aram and Israel maneuver in preparation to meet the Assyrians in chap. 7, but not after that. Aram was subdued and deported in 734 B.C. and Israel and Ashdod in 721 B.C. The list of the nations (chaps. 13–23) includes those areas still somewhat autonomous, but threatened by Assyrian power. Tyre (chap. 23) was attacked in 701 B.C., as were the cities of the west, including Ashkelon and Lachish and Jerusalem. Only Jerusalem escaped destruction. Ammon, Moab, and Edom paid tribute.

Esarhaddon invaded Egypt in 669 B.C. When his son Asshurbanipal put down an insurrection there two years later the Empire had unchallenged control from Egypt to the Persian Gulf and Elam. During the eighth to seventh centuries Assyria had had considerable trouble with rebellions in Babylon (chaps. 13–14 and 21) with Elam (21:2) and with the Medes (21:2 and 13:17).

The setting of chaps. 1–39 fits the eighth to seventh centuries, so there is no reason to look elsewhere for it. If the editorial composition came after the exile, the editor's perception of the events is clear and accurate. Only those states or cities are included which were autonomous enough still to be participating in intrigue against Assyria: Babylon (13:17–22; Israel is already in exile, cf. 14:1–3),

Babylon (14:4–23), Assyria (14:24–25), Philistines (14:29–32), Moab (15:1–16:14), Damascus (with Israel, 17:1–3), Egypt (19:1–20:6), Desert by the Sea (Babylon, 21:1–10), Dumah (Edom, 21:11–12), Arabia (21:13–16), Valley of Vision (Jerusalem, 22:1–25), and Tyre (23:1–18).

HISTORICAL BACKGROUND: JUDAH UNDER ASSYRIA (CA. 750–700 B.C.)

Bibliography

Aharoni, Y. & Avi-Yonah, M. *MBA* maps no. 135, 138, 146, 147, 148, 149, 150, 151, 153, 154, 157. **Bright, J.** *A History of Israel.* 249–87. **McKay, J.** *Religion in Judah under the Assyrians: 732–609.* SBT² 26. Naperville: Allenson, 1973. **Saggs, H. W. F.** "The Assyrians." *POTT* 156–78. **Thiele, E. R.** *The Mysterious Numbers of the Hebrew Kings.* Chicago: University of Chicago Press, 1951. 55–166.

That the Assyrian period is important in Old Testament history is largely due to Isaiah 1–39. Of course Amos, Hosea, and Micah play a role. But Isaiah is the one that insists that this period is the turning point, the fateful "point of no return" in the history of Israel and Judah. The composer/editor of the Vision linked the Assyrian eighth century with the Persian sixth–fifth centuries, largely ignoring the periods before and between.

The Neo-Assyrian period parallels much of Israel's history (930–612 B.C.) The militaristic regimes carried out "countless military campaigns in which the king, to do honor to the god Asshur, personally commanded the army and dedicated captives to Asshur" (*IDBSup,* 75). The area between the Tigris and Euphrates was conquered before Shalmaneser III (858–824 B.C.) came to the throne. His attempts to move westward brought the first contacts with Israel. Ahab was an ally in the battle of Qarqar (853 B.C.) which turned back invading Assyrian armies. Jehu paid tribute in 841 B.C. Adad-nirari III (810–783 B.C.) collected tribute from Joash in 806 B.C.

A half-century later Tiglath-Pileser III (745–727 B.C.) began a century of imperial authority. He assumed the title "King of Babylon" and extended Assyrian authority to the Mediterranean. He readopted the policy of relocating entire populations to discourage ethnic solidarity and will to independence.

Shalmaneser V ruled briefly (727–722 B.C.). He was followed by Sargon II (722–705 B.C.), whose family ruled Assyria to its end a century later. His military exploits extended from Ashdod on the West to Iran on the East.

Sennacherib (705–681 B.C.) marked a trend toward less military activity and more building, culture and administration. Ironically, he is known for his destruction of Babylon.

INVASIONS AND EXPEDITIONS IN PALESTINE

742 B.C. (listed by some as 738 B.C.) Invasions of northern Aram led to an indecisive battle which involved Menahem of Israel and Azriyau of Yaudi, probably Azariah (Uzziah) of Judah. (H. Tadmor, "Azriyau of Yaudi," *Studies in the Bible.* ScrHier 8 [Jerusalem: Magnes, 1961] 232–71.) Cf. 2 Kgs 15:19–

20 and 2 Chr 26:6–15. Judah joined Israel as a tributary vassal of Assyria (2 Kgs 16:7).

734 B.C. Tiglath-Pileser responded to rebellion involving Gaza with a campaign down the coast taking Gaza and stationing a garrison on the Egyptian border (*MBA* 147).

733 B.C. The following year the campaign followed an inland route that stripped Israel of its northern tier of defenses and established Assyrian provinces there (*MBA* 148). Hoshea came to the throne and saved Samaria by the payment of massive tribute.

732 B.C. A punitive expedition destroyed Damascus and continued South to Ashtaroth forming these into Assyrian provinces.

724–722 B.C. Shalmaneser V laid siege to Samaria in response to revolt inspired by Egypt. The city fell in 721 B.C. Both Shalmaneser and his successor Sargon II claimed the victory.

720 B.C. Sargon was back a year later quelling revolt in Ashdod and Gaza. Israelites were also involved. So he began massive deportations of the population to Assyria and Media. Judah submitted to Assyria again which saved it from a similar fate. Samaria and Ashdod were added to the list of Assyrian provinces.

713–12 B.C. Sargon returned to put down a revolt in Ashdod inspired by the Egyptian delta kings (cf. Isa 20). Judah, Moab, and Edom submitted again, paying heavy tribute.

701 B.C. Sennacherib had spent four years establishing his authority in other regions after the death of Sargon II before he sent his armies against Tyre, Ashkelon, and Ekron. From his headquarters at Lachish he directed a siege of Jerusalem. His deputy commander was Rabshakeh. He captured forty-six cities of Judah (chaps. 36–37; cf. Isa 10:28–32 and Mic 1:10–16). Hezekiah's offer of tribute was refused. When Rabshakeh returned to Lachish, the king was gone. The siege was not renewed and Jerusalem escaped, although, of course, it was a chastened vassal nonetheless. In this condition it survived for more than a century longer.

Assyria and the Last Years of Israel

The death of Jeroboam II (753 B.C.) brought a period of instability in Israel which the state would not survive. His son, Zechariah, was murdered, to be replaced by a usurper. Menahem ruled for ten years (752–742 B.C.) to be succeeded first by Pekahiah (2 yrs, 742–740 B.C.) and then by Pekah (739–732 B.C.), who murdered him to take the throne. The first two were apparently compliant vassals of Assyria. But Pekah became the center of intrigue and rebellion with Rezin of Aram and the Philistines. Together they tried to re-establish the coalition which had often withstood earlier attacks from without.

To make the coalition viable they needed the participation of Judah. Ahaz had established a policy of conciliation toward Assyria and could not be moved (cf. Isa 7). So the conspirators invaded Judah in an attempt to put a certain son of Tabeel on the throne to change the policy. Their campaign brought great misery to Judah (*MBA* 144). Rezin set Edom free who then invaded

Judah (2 Kgs 16:6; 2 Chr 28:17). People from Philistia occupied cities of the Negeb and the Shephelah (2 Chr 28:18).

Tiglath-Pileser's response to Ahaz's plea for help was to bring an effective end to Israel's national existence well before the celebrated siege of Samaria. In 734, 733, and 732 B.C. he campaigned in the area, reducing Galilee and Damascus to the status of border provinces of Assyria. The territory still left to Israel was minuscule (*MBA* 148). The rebellious king was killed and Hoshea (732–722 B.C.) whose policies were more to Assyria's liking was installed as king after paying a heavy tribute.

After the death of Tiglath-Pileser, Hoshea was tempted by Egyptian intrigue. In 724 B.C. his capital was under siege. By 721 B.C., the city was captured and destroyed. By late 720 B.C., the first of the inhabitants were on their way to an exile that would never end in Assyria near the Habur River and in Media. The territory of Israel was partitioned into four Assyrian districts: Samaria (including the former district of Dor), Megiddo, Gilead, and Karnaim.

ASSYRIA AND JUDAH

Azariah (Uzziah) of Judah paid tribute to Tiglath-Pileser in 742 B.C. Despite the pressure of his neighbors in 734 B.C., Ahaz was a faithful vassal. This, plus tribute, earned respite for Judah when Aram, Israel, and Philistia were reduced to provinces of the Empire. This was not without cost, however. The three neighbors inflicted considerable damage by attacks in 734 before the Assyrians arrived (cf. *MBA* 144 and 145).

In 720 B.C. a further rebellion in the area brought Sargon back only a year after the fall of Samaria. He conquered Gaza and Raphia. An Egyptian expeditionary force was beaten back. Judah escaped by submission and tribute (cf. *MBA,* 149).

In 713–712 B.C. the Assyrians were back to put down a rebellion in Ashdod which was supported by the delta kings of Egypt (Isa 20). Assyrian inscriptions claim Judah was involved, but quickly surrendered. Ashdod became an Assyrian province. Hezekiah (715–686 B.C.) had come to the throne two years before. Judah's response indicated the change in the kingdom's diplomatic stance that he brought in. He was no longer willing to be simply a submissive vassal, but 712 B.C. was not yet the time for genuine resistance.

In 705 B.C. Sennacherib came to the throne and for four years was fully occupied in other parts of the realm. Hezekiah seized the opportunity to arm his kingdom to make a stand (*MBA* 152). He reorganized the nation and began extensive building of fortifications (2 Chr 32:28–30). He strengthened the fortifications of the capital and pushed the building of aqueducts and pools to increase water supplies (2 Kgs 20:20; 2 Chr 32:30; Isa 22:8–11). He fortified and prepared the cities of Judah for attack (1 Chr 4:38–41).

The conspiracy involved Ashkelon, Ekron, Babylon, and Egypt (2 Kgs 20:12–19; Isa 30:1–5; 31:1–3). Hezekiah received in chains the former king of Ekron, who had refused to join the allies. He reconquered extensive territory from the Philistines and Edom when they refused to join the revolt (*MBA,* 152).

Sennacherib's response came in 701 B.C. after he had retaken Babylon. After going down the coast, defeating Tyre and Ekron (*MBA* 153, 154), he launched a campaign against Judah from his camp in Lachish. His inscriptions claimed capture of forty-six cities in Judah. Hezekiah's offer of tribute was refused. Assyrian threats to the city were not carried out (cf. 2 Kgs 19:36 = Isa 37:37), although the immediate reason for his withdrawal remains a mystery.

Excursus: The Ahaz Era

The decade before Ahaz came to the throne was already clouded for the Levant by Assyrian ambitions. The sense of doom is portrayed in chaps. 1–5 although Assyria is not named. (See also the prophecies of Amos and Hosea for that period and 2 Kgs 15:17–36.)

Ahaz's reign covers not quite two decades (ca. 734–718[15] B.C., give or take a year or so on either end). In the Vision it is portrayed in chaps. 7–14. The decades were crucial and testing times for the Palestinian states. Old power centers which had brokered political and military events and privileges for almost a century and a half, since Omri and Ahab had fought with Ben Hadad to divide the pie of power and land, were systematically subjugated or destroyed by expanding Assyrian power. Proud, rebellious states were invaded and crushed by the armies of Tiglath Pileser in 733, 732, and 728 B.C., of Shalmaneser in 724–722 B.C. and of Sargon II in 722–718 B.C.

At the beginning of Ahaz's reign, Aram and Israel carried the flag of resistance. But in the course of his reign they and others were destroyed, deported, and assimilated. At the end of the reign Babylon's wily king Merodach Baladan was the standard bearer of rebellion.

Through these difficult times Judah/Jerusalem *survived* with its own king and that modicum of autonomy that is accorded to a loyal vassal. With her were some Philistine cities, Edom, Moab, and the city of Tyre. And, of course, there was Egypt to the south.

The Second Act of the Vision portrays that era, Zion's survival, and Israel's fall, all within God's plan for Assyria. The themes of Israel's destiny and that of Zion within the overarching strategy of God are carried forward from Act One. It introduces the Assyrian by name and takes up issues relating to the continuance of the House of David. It also begins to deal with the issue of rebellion against a God-sent Assyria in the case of Aram, Israel and then of Babylon.

Scene 1:
Of Sons and Signs (7:1—9:6[7])

(Cf. **Brodie, L.** "The Children and the Prince: the Structure, Nature, and Date of Isaiah 6–12." *BTB* [1979] 27–31.)

The setting is Jerusalem. The time begins with the threat of the Syro-Ephraimite war (734 B.C.) to the birth of the child announced in 7:14. Following a narrative account of the setting (7:1–2), the scene is presented in nine episodes.

In *Episode A, "Keep Calm and Steady"* (*7:3–9*), the prophet brings a word from God to the new king in his time of crisis. His advice is: be calm, remain steady, and do nothing. In *Episode B, "Within Three Years"* (*7:10–16*), Ahaz makes a shaky start by refusing the offer of a sign. But Isaiah assures him that he will have a son and that this son will succeed him on the throne in Jerusalem. *Episode C, "Critical Times—the Assyrian"* (*7:17–25*), makes an announcement: God is bringing the Assyrian to Palestine to inaugurate a new age for Judah and her dynasty. The Assyrian's coming will end the alliance of Aram and Israel. *Episode D, "Swift Plunder, Hastening Booty"* (*8:1–4*), describes the Assyrian crisis that is rushing down on Israel and Judah. *Episode E, "Waters of Shiloah Refused"* (*8:5–10*), tells that Israel's refusal to accept gradual processes has led to violent measures and strange alliances. No hope remains for the survival of the state. *Episode F, "Yahweh Is Your Fear"* (*8:11–15*), discusses the problem inherent in having God present among the people and in their capital. They depend upon his presence for security while also trying to act autonomously. *Episode G* is titled *"Sealing the Prophet's Testimony"* (*8:16–18*). The prophet determines to withdraw from public life, but his very existence and that of his children will be continuing reminders of the truth that has been spoken in God's name. *Episode H, "To Instruction and to Testimony"* (*8:19–22*), carries a warning not to be misled by the occult and bizarre. Only genuine revelation, instruction and testimony, should be heeded. *Episode I, "To Us a Son is Born"* (*8:23–9:6* [*9:1–7*]), heralds a glorious event in Jerusalem. In the gloomy times of Assyrian wars which destroy Israel and Aram, the promised sign of 7:14, the birth of an heir for David's throne, is fulfilled.

The scene portrays the essential problem of the House of David (and of Israel, for that matter): their stability depends upon "God being with them." This in turn demands from them a high quality of piety and faithfulness to Yahweh. Thus God's holy presence (*Immanuel*) is a "stone of stumbling" for both houses. The scene continues to recognize that "God is hiding his face from Israel." But it closes on cheerful hope generated by the birth of a royal heir.

7:1—9:6[7] is a virtual tapestry of interwoven motifs. The entire section deals with "sons" and "signs." "Sons" appear in 7:1, 3, 6, 14; 8:3–4, 18; 9:5–6[6–7]. "Signs" and symbols are found in the name of Isaiah's son (7:3), the reference to the other kings as "smoldering firebrands" (7:4), and 7:8–9a, 10, 14; 8:1–4, 18, 19, 23; 9:5–6[6–7]. In addition, the descriptions of the Assyrian as a barber (7:20), the gentle water contrasted with the floods (8:6–8) and "the stone of stumbling" (8:14) may be mentioned as signs.

The section forms an arch whose keystone returns to the subject of "the day." The sounds of battle break through with the brave assertion that the "plans" of the nations will not stand up (8:9–10). The "plan" in 7:6 proposes a coup d'etat which would place a usurper on Jerusalem's throne. The entire section deals with that theme, ending with the assurance that the legitimate heir will succeed to the throne in due time.

Other theme-threads may be traced: *Immanuel* "God with us": 7:14; 8:8, 10; 9:5–6[6–7]; test/try: 7:12–13; conspiracy: 8:12; stone of stumbling: 8:14; Yahweh as warrior: 7:17; 8:7, 10, 23; 9:2, 4, 6b [3, 5, 7b]; plans: 7:6; 8:10; 9:6[7].

The arch may be plotted as follows:

A God sends Isaiah and his *son* to confront the *son* of Jotham about the *son* of Tabeel (7:1–6)

B A *sign* for Ahaz: "It will not happen . . . if you do not believe you shall not be confirmed" (7:7–9)

C The Lord's *sign:* a virgin and a son, Immanuel; the Lord is sending the king of Assyria (7:10–25)

D A *son—sign* of approaching disaster for Aram and Israel (8:1–4)

E This people—the wrong sign. O *Immanuel!* Assyria—a flood over Israel and Judah (8:5–8)

KEYSTONE Do your worst, nations; *Immanuel* (God with us) (8:9–10)

E′ *God in your midst*—a stone of stumbling for Israel and Judah (8:11–15)

D′ Isaiah and his *sons/signs* wait/hope for the Lord (8:16–18)

C′ Warning of false signs; to the Law and the Testimony; God humbles and *he* exalts (8:19–22)

B′ Light will come; God will act, as at Midian (8:23–9:4 [9:1–5])

A′ God's action, God's gift, God's presence, God's *sign;* to us a *son*—Wonder-Counselor, God-Warrior (9:5–6 [6–7])

The Setting (7:1–2)

Bibliography

Brunet. *Essai,* 101–39. **Dietrich, W.** *Jesaja und die Politik.* Munich: 1976. **Wurthwein, W.** "Jesaja 7:1–9," *Wort und Existenz.* Göttingen: Vandenhoeck & Ruprecht, 1970. 127–43.

ON THE REIGN OF AHAZ:

Bright, J. *A History of Israel,* 2nd ed. 252–57. **Donner, H.** "The Syro-Ephraimite War and the end of Israel." *IJH.* 420–34. **Pritchard, J.** "Tiglath Pileser—Annals." *ANET.* 282–84. **Thompson, M. E. W.** *Situation and Theology: OT Interpretations of the Syro-Ephraimite War.* Sheffield: The Almond Press, 1982. 22–24.

Translation

Narrator: [1] *In the days of Ahaz son of Jotham, son of Uzziah, king of Judah, Rezin,* [a] *king of Aram, went up with Pekah, the son of Remaliah,* [b] *king of Israel, (against) Jerusalem to fight against it.* [c] *But he* [d] *was not able to overcome it.* [2] *When it was announced to the house of David, "Aram has rested* [a] *upon Ephraim," his heart trembled with the heart of his people like the trembling of the trees of the forest before the wind.*

Notes

1.a. רְצִין means something like "a spring." But the LXX has Ραασσων and Assyrian sources suggest a reading of רְצוֹן or רַצְיָן meaning "well-pleasing" (cf. Landsberger, *Sam'al* [Ankara:

Türkischen Historischen, 1948] 66n. 169; W. von Soden, *Das akkadische Syllabar,* AnOr 27 [Roma: Pont. Bib. Inst., 1948] 108; M. Noth, *Die israelitschen Personennamen,* BWANT 46 [Stuttgart: Kohlhammer, 1928] 224.)

1.b. MT רמליהו. DSS[Isa] רומליה and in vv 5 and 9, but in v 4 רמליה. LXX Ρομελιου in 1, 5, and 9. Cf. *BASOR* 189 (1968) 42.

1.c. למלחמה עליה has often been judged a dittography for להלחם עליה But 2 Kgs 16:5 also contains both verbs. It should be kept as it is in MT.

1.d. 2 Kgs 16:5 is pl. But the singular meaning is clear and accurate. Rezin was the driving force in the campaign (H. M. Orlinsky, "St. Mark's Isaiah Scroll, IV," *JQR* 43 [1952–53] 331–33).

2.a. נחה has usually been translated "rest," "light upon." But this has brought suggestions for correction (cf. G. R. Driver, *JTS* 34 [1933] 377; KB נחה II "support"; O. Eissfeldt, *FS L. Köhler* STU 20 [Bern: Büchler, 1950] 23–26, "make a contract with"). These fit the translations, LXX συνεφώνησεν and Syr *ʾestᵉwî* "to conspire together." Wildberger (265) suggests that the use of על does not fit this meaning. He correctly notes that Judah's panic must have been caused by more than an agreement. It could be understood if an Aramean army was already encamped in Israel. נוח should be understood here in the sense of "occupied," "overrun" as it is in v 19 and Exod 10:14; 2 Sam 17:12, 21:10.

Form/Structure/Setting

These verses are the first direct historical narrative in The Vision. The change in syntax to the use of imperfects with *wáw*-consecutive in the 3rd person marks the change. The Vision's intention to deal with historical situations and realities is thus clearly marked. However, the reader should note that this kind of historical reference in the book is much rarer than ordinarily recognized. Note the parallel references in 2 Kgs 16:5–9 and the full account in 2 Chr 28:5–21. The evaluations of Ahaz's reign are significantly different.

Kings is brief with v 5 quoted in Isaiah. This is preceded by the negative evaluation of Ahaz by the editor. But the account of Israel's and Aram's invasion is without rancor or criticism. The new altar that Ahaz built on the model of an Aramean altar is described in vv 10–18. Other changes in the temple were made "in deference to the King of Assyria" (NIV) מפני מלך אשור. His deference to the King of Assyria is noted, but not criticized.

2 Chr 28:5–21 is much more critical of Ahaz. It describes in much greater detail his humiliation by the armies of his neighbors (vv 5–15). At the same time the Chronicler writes appreciatively of the leaders and people of Israel (vv 9–15). He implies that Ahaz summoned help from Assyria because of the raids by Edomites and the Philistines.

The evaluation of Ahaz in the three stories is significantly different and requires an explanation. Isaiah's account is clearly dependent on 2 Kgs or the same sources which Kings used.

Comment

1 בִּימֵי אָחָז בֶּן־יוֹתָם "in the days of Ahaz son of Jotham." The chronology of this reign is notoriously difficult to fix (cf. discussion of chronology in the Introduction). Bright dates Ahaz's reign 735–15 B.C. while Aharoni (*MBA*) dates it 742–26 B.C. Thiele uses the years 735–16 B.C. while Jepsen has 741–25 B.C. The problems lie in the conflicting testimony of Kings and Chronicles. We will use Bright's dating adjusted to Stiles's chart above since that fits the Vision's plan best. It is highly likely that Ahaz's reign overlapped Jotham's years, as Jotham had acted as regent during his father's years.

Most of this verse is identical to 2 Kgs 16:5 and undoubtedly depends on that account. However, the attempt to form a perfect correlation is useless (Wildberger).

Rezin was king of Aram from 740–733 B.C. He is listed among kings paying tribute to Tiglath-Pileser III early in his reign. But by 735 B.C. he is leader of a plot to overthrow Assyrian suzerainty.

Pekah, son of Remaliah, came to power in Samaria in 740 B.C. by murdering Pekahiah, son of Menahem (2 Kgs 15:25). He is credited with reigning twenty years, but a reconstructed chronology must make this five or six years. He was soon caught up in Rezin's scheme. He and the Philistines were Rezin's unquestioning followers.

2 Chr 28:5–7 records Rezin's invasion of Judah (*MBA,* 144). He attacked through Moab, freeing the Edomites, and continuing on to Elath and Ezion-geber on the Gulf of Akaba. The Edomites then turned on Judah (2 Kgs 16:6; 2 Chr 28:17). The Philistines used the opportunity to take cities in the Negeb and Shephelah of Judah (2 Chr 28:18).

Rezin's coalition then turned to take Jerusalem, joined by Pekah. But the fortified city was too much for them. Their momentum came to a halt.

2 וַיֻּגַּד "when it was announced" The consecutive picks up from וַיְהִי "and it proceeded to be" at the beginning of v 1 and sets the scene near the beginning of the invasion. Ahaz has just been informed of the alliance between Aram and Israel. He is understandably alarmed.

Explanation

These verses introduce Act II, indicating its setting in the reign of Ahaz. Ahaz succeeded Jotham in 734 B.C. He inherited a difficult situation. Assyria under Tiglath-Pileser III (745–727 B.C.) moved vigorously to establish its authority over its neighbors including Babylon, Urartu, and Media. In 743 B.C. he began a series of campaigns westward into Palestine. His first campaign was stopped by a coalition led by a certain "Azriau of Yaudi," who may have been Uzziah of Judah. But the results were not permanent. By 738 B.C. Israel and the other north Palestinian and Aramean states were paying tribute to Assyria.

Israel had experienced one political crisis after another since Jeroboam II died in 753 B.C. Finally Menahem (752–42 B.C.) took control. He apparently bought a period of respite by paying heavy tribute to Tiglath-Pileser (2 Kgs 15:19). His son reigned scarcely a year before being assassinated by an army officer, Pekah ben Remaliah, who assumed the throne (740–32). His determination to throw off the Assyrian yoke may have inspired the coup d'état as it did his prompt alignment with Rezin of Damascus, some Philistines, and perhaps some Edomites to form a coalition against Assyria. Passages in Hosea and Amos describe that period.

This coalition tried to force Judah to join them. Up to this time Judah had apparently escaped subjection to Assyria and the payment of tribute which weighed so heavily on Israel (2 Kgs 15:19 and the Assyrian inscription,

ANET, 283). Ahaz had abandoned the militaristic policy of Uzziah to accept Assyria's larger rule. This military pressure was a difficult beginning for the young king's reign. But he refused to join with the conspiracy.

Assyria's attention was concentrated elsewhere in those years, so Aram and Israel felt secure on their northern borders. They launched an extended campaign against Judah (cf. *MBA*, 144). Rezin marched down the eastern side of Jordan, stripping Judah of its dependencies in Ammon, Moab, and Edom. Pekah joined an Aramean force in a siege of Jerusalem to force a change of rulers and a more militaristic and nationalistic policy. These moves encouraged Edomites to rise up against their Judean neighbors and take back towns in southern Judah (2 Kgs 16:6; 2 Chr 28:17). The Philistines used the opportunity to seize a piece of Judah on their border (cf. *MBA*, 145) as 2 Chr 28:18 records.

The situation was serious. Ahaz followed protocol as a loyal vassal of the Assyrians. He apparently sent word of his plight and expected them to fulfill their pledge to help him.

V 1 describes the stalemate in the campaign. V 2 gives the specific setting for Isaiah's meeting with Ahaz: early in the war, when he had just received word that a Syrian army was encamped on Israelite soil. Succeeding events proved that he had good reason for anxiety.

Episode A: Keep Calm and Steady (7:3–9)

Bibliography

Barr, J. "Did Isaiah Know about Hebrew 'Root Meanings'?" *ExpTim* 75 (1964) 242. **Blank, S. H.** "Traces of Prophetic Agony in Isaiah." *HUCA* 27 (1956) 81–92. **Bouzon, E.** "A Mesagem Triologico do Immanuel." *Rev. Ecl. Brasileria* 32 (1972) 826–41. **Day, J.** "Shear-jashub (Isaiah VII 3) and the Remnant of Wrath (Ps 76:11)." *VT* 31 (1981) 76–78. **Fichtner, J.** "Zu Jes. 7:5–9." *ZAW* 56 (1938) 176. **Höffken, P.** "Notizen zum Textcharakter von Jes. 7:1–17." *TZ* 36 (1980) 321–37. **Keller, C. A.** "Das quietistische Element in der Botschaft des Jesaja." *TZ* 11 (1955) 81–97. **Lescow, T.** "Jesajas Denkschrift aus der Zeit des syrisch-ephraimitischen Kriege." *ZAW* 85 (1973) 315–31. **Saebo, M.** "Formgeschichtliche Erwagungen zu Jes. 7:3–9." *ST* 14 (1960) 54–69. **Steck, O. H.** "Rettung und Verstockung: Exegetische Bemerkung zu Jes. 7:3–9." *EvT* 33 (1973) 77–90. **Wagner, N. E.** "Note on Isaiah 7:4." *VT* 8 (1958) 438. **Wolff, H. W.** *Frieden ohne Ende. Eine Auslegung von Jes. 7:1–7 und 9:1–6.* BibS(N) 35. Neukirchen: Neukirchener Verlag, 1962. ———. *Immanuel. Das Zeichen, dem widersprochen wird.* BibS(N) 23. Neukirchen: Neukirchener Verlag, 1959.

ON THE "REMNANT" IN ISAIAH:

Brunet, G. *Essai*, 123–39. **Hasel, G. F.** *The Remnant.* Berrien Springs, MI: Andrews U. P., 1972. **Müller, W. E.** *Die Vorstellung von Rest im Alten Testament.* Leipzig: 1939. **Stegemann, U.** "Der Restgedanke bei Isaias." *BZ* 13 (1969) 161–86.

Translation

Herald: 3 *Then* [a] *Yahweh said to Isaiah:*
Yahweh: *Go out now to meet Ahaz,* 3+4
You and Shear-yashub, your son,
to the end of the conduit of the upper pool, 4+3
to the highway of the Washermen's Field.
4 *And you shall say to him:*
"Take hold of yourself and be calm. Do not be afraid. 3
As for your heart, do not soften (it) 2+3+2
because of two stumps.
these smoking [a] *firebrands,*
[b] *because of the burning anger* [c] *of Rezin* 3+3
and Aram and the son of Remaliah. [b]
5 *Because Aram has counseled evil against you* 5+2
[a] *(with) Ephraim and the son of Remaliah* [a]*:*
6 *'Let us go up against Judah, terrorize* [a] *her and* 3+2
split it open for ourselves.
And let us set up a king in its midst: 3+3
the son of Tabeel.' " [b]
Herald: 7 *Thus says the Lord* [a] *Yahweh:*
Yahweh: *It will not stand! It will not happen!* 4
Heavens: 8 *For the head* [a] *of Aram is Damascus.* 4+3
And the head [a] *of Damascus is Rezin.*
Earth: [b] *Within sixty-five years* 4+3
Ephraim will be too shattered to be a people. [b]
Heavens: 9 *The head of Ephraim is Samaria* 3+3
and the head of Samaria is the son of Remaliah.
Earth: *If you (pl) will not believe,* 3+3
certainly [a] *you (pl) cannot be confirmed!* [b]

Notes

3.a. The *wāw* consecutive places the narrative in the setting and time just described.

4.a. DSS[Isa] העושנים, a ptcp, for MT העשנים, an adjective. The DSS[Isa] form is also found in Exod 20:18.

4.b-b. LXX *ὅταν γαρ ὀργὴ τοῦ θυμοῦ μου γένηται, πάλιν ἰάσομαι* "in case I restore again the offspring (from the punishment) of the fury of my anger." MT is to be preferred. It explains "smoking firebrands."

4.c. MT בחרי "because of the burning"; Syr *men ḥemtâ* "from the burning." DSS[Isa] בחורי. Wagner (*VT* 8 [1958] 438) suggests DSS is constr ptcp, but Wildberger correctly finds it only an orthographic variant.

5.a-a. LXX omits. The words may well be a gloss. It correctly interprets the previous line.

6.a. In place of ונקיצנה "and let us terrorize her" Gesenius suggested ונציקנה "and let us oppress her." Lagarde (*Sem* 1 [1978] 14) suggested וְנִתְּצֶנָּה "and want to burn it." Driver (*JSS* 13 [1968] 39) follows LXX *συλλαλήσαντες* and the Arab *qāḍa* translating "let us negotiate with him." Orlinsky ("Heb. and Gr. texts of Job 14:12." *JQR* 28 [1937/38] 65–68) assumes a root קוץ II (= Arab *qāṣa*) meaning "tear apart" which Speier ("*Unesiqennah:* Isa 7:6a." *JBL* 72 [1953] xiv) applies to Isa 7:6. The form may come from קיץ and mean "let us awaken her," i.e. make her see the error of her ways and change her mind.

6.b. MT טָבְאַל means "Good-for-nothing." But the original may well have intended טָבְאֵל "God is good" as LXX Ταβεηλ suggests. Ezra 4:7 records such a name and Zech 6:10, 14 has a parallel טוֹבִיָּה. The form of the name is Aramaic. Albright (*BASOR* 140 [1955] 34–35) cites a text which indicates that *Bêt Ṭāb'el* was a strip of land north of Gilead. The intendent was undoubtedly someone who would be friendly to Aram and its policies.

7.a. LXX reads *κύριος σαβαωθ* "Lord of hosts" for MT אדני יהוה "Lord Yahweh."

8.a. ראש "head" has appeared wrong to some commentators. M. Scott ("Isaiah 7:8." *ExpTim* 38 [1926/27] 525–26) suggested emending to ידוש "will tread upon" or "will thresh." E. Baumann ("Zwei Einzelbemerkungen." *ZAW* 21 [1901] 268–70) suggests that it is a play on words which can mean "capital," but also "poison" (cf. BDB, II, 912). Wildberger correctly notes the possibility that the double meaning was not lost on Hebrew listeners. The form and meaning "head" will, of course, be sustained.

8.b-b. has often been thought to be a secondary addition. It changes the time reference to the rather distant future, but the prediction is not easily related to an event 65 years hence. The next verse follows directly on the first line of v 8. However, the line is firmly anchored in LXX's text tradition.

9.a. כי "certainly," an emphatic particle. Cf. GKC 159*ee*.

9.b. For MT תאמנו "confirmed," LXX has *συνῆτε*, Vg *intelligetis* which would translate תָּבִינוּ "you will (not) understand." The reading of the translations makes sense, picking up the theme of chap. 6. However, the word play in Hebrew is too artistic and meaningful to be put aside.

Form/Structure/Setting

The limits of the little episode are marked by the narrative imperfect in v 3 which begins the episode within the larger narrative. A similar imperfect with *wāw* consecutive begins v 10 marking a new unit.

The episode is a clear unit. It narrates God's instructions to Isaiah and Isaiah's word given in obedience to the instruction. It fits the genre of prophetic narrative with several characteristics: (a) the imperative to go (v 3); (b) the mission to be fulfilled (vv 3–6); (c) the "word" of Yahweh (v 7); (d) an explanatory expansion (vv 8–9a); (e) an exhortation to faith (v 9b). The "word" in v 3 is introduced by the formula "thus says the Lord Yahweh." Cf. Westermann, *Basic Forms,* 100; Hayes, *OTFC,* 154–55.

The use of the prophetic narrative at this point in the Vision gives the work its first specific historical foundation. By naming the prophet, his son, and the king; giving the exact location of the meeting; and by describing the historical circumstances, the earthly historical setting is unequivocally presented. God's decisions communicated to "heavens and earth" in chap. 1 and experienced in the heavenly king's court by the prophet in chap. 6 are communicated to historical earthly rulers to influence political decisions at a very specific time.

Comment

3 This is the first appearance of the prophet by name, except in the superscriptions, 1:1 and 2:1. Isaiah receives divine instruction to confront Ahaz with a personal message from Yahweh in the classic tradition of prophetic narrative in the OT.

"A Remnant Shall Return" is the name of Isaiah's son. The practice of naming a child as a prophetic symbol is also documented in Hos 1:6, 9 and

Isa 8:3. He is already old enough to accompany his father and is a witness to Isaiah's participation in prophecy for some time. The name may be viewed positively or negatively: "*only* a remnant shall return" or "*at least* a remnant shall return." It may assure a physical return from battle or captivity, or it may be understood to imply "repentance" as in "turning to God." The theme is important in the Vision of Isaiah. It appeared in 6:12–13. It will appear again in 10:20–23 and is a fundamental presupposition for chaps. 40–66. Tiglath-Pileser had re-established the practice of mass deportation. 2 Kgs 15:29 records a deportation from Israel while Pekah was still king which must have taken place within two years of this incident.

The reason for the chosen place is not given. *The highway of the Washermen's Field* is the same place mentioned in 36:2/2 Kgs 18:17 outside the walls where the Assyrian officer stood to shout his message to the city. It may be that Isaiah is sent to a place where his confrontation would not be as public as it would have been in the court. Apparently the King is inspecting the construction of the water works.

There is no agreement on the location. The *upper pool* may be located near the spring of Gihon in the Kidron Valley east of the northern part of the city. An aqueduct carried water from it to a pool inside the south wall. This is probably the aqueduct mentioned in 7:3. This refers to the southern end of that aqueduct at a point apparently outside the wall. (See the *Excursus* on pools and reservoirs of Jerusalem in chap. 22).

The place is called שׂדה כובס "a field (for) washing" (cf. G. Brunet, "Le Terrain aux Foulons," *RB* 71 [1964] 230–39) or in a older English parlance "a fullers' field."

Excursus: The Ancient Craft of Washing Clothes

Fulling, or washing, in the ancient world was a special craft with learned skills and special equipment (J. R. Forbes, *Studies in Ancient Technology,* IV [Leiden: E. J. Brill, 1956], 87). There are ancient references to fullers and laundrymen. By Hellenistic times there were guilds of fullers in Syria, Egypt, and North Africa. In the Sudan and in India today there are places outside cities with holes in the ground where men work on a variety of textiles and animal skins. They work in that place because it has a source of clean water and avoids polluting city water. Their used water contains some still active catalysts used in the work (Brunet, 231).

Ancient Egyptians used several "detergents" like natron (natural soap), potash, soapwort (*Saponaria officinalis*), asphodel, and other alkaline plants. They knew that these agents absorbed grease and removed dirt. They also used "fuller's earth"—a natural, fine, hydrated aluminum silicate, the *creta fullonica* mentioned by Pliny (Nat. Hist. XVI. 146).

The OT refers to such detergents in Jer 2:22, Mal 3:2, Job 9:30 and Isa 1:25. The Hebrews also used depressions in rocks as washing tubs like the Homeric Greeks (*Iliad* VI 86). Excavations in the Kidron Valley south of Jerusalem found such depressions near the spring En-Rogel which Vincent called "the fullers' workplace" (R. Weill, *La Cité de David* II, 118, quoted in L. H. Vincent, *Jerusalem de l'Ancien Testament* [Paris: Librairie Lecoffre, J. Gabalda, 1959], 290–91).

(I am indebted to my student Daniel Bodi for the basis of this material.)

3 (cont'd) עין רגל "En-Rogel" probably comes from רגל "foot" and "to tread." It may well be traced to a place where fullers worked the cloth or leather with their feet.

The building of the *conduit of the upper pool* was undoubtedly part of military preparations to maintain supplies of water for the siege that was expected. (Cf. *Comment,* chap. 22.) The king's presence there reflected his concern for the city's military posture at that critical juncture.

4 The message is one of encouragement, of support for the king and his policy. He had resisted the pressure of his northern neighbors to join them in rebellion against their common liege-lord, Assyria.

Donner (*IJH,* 419) has described Assyrian policy relating to neighboring lands which included three stages. First, they established a dependent (or "vassal") relation by showing Assyrian military power. This meant that the nation cooperated with Assyria and made periodic "gifts" of tribute or taxes to Assyria for the protection which she provided for the state. Second, on suspicion of conspiracy Assyria intervened to remove the disloyal vassal and install a new king who could be counted on to be dependent on Assyria and therefore loyal to it. This was often accompanied by a sharp reduction in territory with the remainder becoming an Assyrian province. Third, upon suspected disloyalty further military intervention followed effecting "liquidation of political independence . . . and establishment of an Assyrian province with an Assyrian governor."

Syria, Israel and Judah were already in the first stage of vassalage due to Assyria's invasion in 742 and 738 B.C. when all three paid tribute. Soon afterward Pekah led a successful rebellion against Menahem's son (Assyria's vassal) in a revolt probably inspired and supported by Rezin, King of Aram. This set the stage for their attempt to organize a movement among the Palestinian states to expell the Assyrians from the region. They tried to force Ahaz to join them in the revolt. 2 Kgs 16:6 says that Rezin's forces captured Elath on the Gulf of Akabah and turned the region over to the Edomites who had been subject to Judah. 2 Chr 28:5–15 tells of much larger military operations with disastrous defeats in the field for Ahaz.

It is at this point that the two kings approach Jerusalem with plans for a coup d'état which would replace Ahaz with a king more amenable to their plans. It is plain that Ahaz maintained a policy of loyalty to Assyria, while his enemies tried to force his participation in a rebellion against Assyria. God's message through Isaiah urges him to remain firm in this resolve. Assyria needed no invitation from Ahaz, although he would have been well within his rights as a vassal to demand that Assyria protect him. The Vision of Isaiah nowhere blames Ahaz for the Assyrian invasion or even implies his participation in the matter, although he will definitely be affected by the military operations that follow (cf. 7:17—8:8). The kings are called *smoking firebrands* implying that there is more smoke than fire in their conspiracy.

5–6 Isaiah is informed of the detailed purpose of the invasion. This includes the name of the person they hope to make king, *the son of Tabeel,* who is otherwise unknown.

7–9a The specific message of encouragement is simply: *it will not happen.* The kings will not succeed. Ahaz need have no fear in resisting his neighbor's forces and policies. They are no stronger than the particular persons who lead them and inhabit their capitals. When these are replaced, the countries will be no threat to Ahaz.

The message is often seen as an attempt to dissuade Ahaz from calling for the Assyrians. This interpretation comes from the words of 2 Kings and 2 Chronicles which accuse Ahaz of asking the Assyrian for help. But there is no reference to this possibility in Isaiah. Here the issue is: shall Ahaz give in to Rezin's planned conspiracy to cooperate against Assyria or remain firm in his policy of cooperation with the Assyrian? Isaiah's word urges him not to fear the invaders. The conspiracy will not succeed. They will not survive.

9b The familiar words need comment at several points. Whereas the address in v 4 was singular, here it is plural. Perhaps *you* includes the court and the government that makes the policy. Perhaps, it only is used in deference to royalty. Or perhaps, it is a general maxim that applies to everyone.

The second comment must note the word-play in Hebrew. The same verb, אמן *ʾamen* meaning "to be firm," appears twice in different forms. Another form of the word אמונה means "faith" or "faithfulness." A very literal translation would be: "If you (pl) do not firm up, you (pl) will not be confirmed." The issue before the king suggested that his throne was endangered. He has only been king for a short time and might well fear that he did not yet have things fully under control. The prophet calls for the king to "pull himself together," to strengthen his faith, as a necessary condition to being confirmed in office by the Lord and by his people.

Explanation

Yahweh sent Isaiah to Ahaz with a message to encourage him to continue his policy of refusing to join Aram and Israel in rebellion against their Assyrian liege-lord. This policy was undoubtedly unpopular with the militaristic super-patriots of the realm. The attack by Aram's armies had already broken Judah's authority over Edom and threatened Jerusalem itself. The Arameans and Israelites could hardly expect to storm the walls of Jerusalem. But they did hope to force Ahaz to abdicate, making way for a ruler more amenable to collaborations in their resistance to Assyria. Isaiah shows that Yahweh supports Ahaz and his policy of peaceful acceptance of Assyrian hegemony. This is the meaning of the entire Vision. Since Yahweh's decisions, made in the reign of Uzziah (cf. 1:2—2:4), the Davidic king is no longer destined to be Yahweh's means of ruling the nations. Ahaz's policy is the realistic application of this insight.

The prophet's message is concise and to the point: "Be calm. Do not be afraid." This encouragement from the Lord indicated approval and support from God. The second part brought the content: "It will not come to pass!" Their plan will not succeed. "Within sixty-five years Ephraim will no longer be a people" expresses the applied judgment of chap. 1, which is all the more reason for Ahaz to keep his distance from their adventures.

The explanation of vv 8a and 9a implies that only the policies of the current kings in Damascus and Samaria dictate the actions of these countries. When they are removed the threat will vanish. This is given in a riddle using "head" as the key. The double meaning of this word of "head" or "poison" may explain its use here.

V 9b brings a word of encouragement in one of the most meaningful couplets in Scripture. The verbs shift to second person masculine plural address, although the king has been addressed in the singular. The words are meant for the entire government, the king and his advisors. The key verb is from the root אמן (our word "amen"), so familiar from liturgical usage. The first usage is causative with the meaning "make yourself firm," i.e., "believe." The second is pointed as a passive by the Masoretes, meaning "you will be confirmed." The sentence is a classic example of a simple conditional sentence. (Cf. Watts, *Syntax,* 134.) An entire doctrine of the role of faith is in this verse.

LXX has emended the second verb to συνῆτε which keeps an active sense and means "understand." It has the sentence speak to the relation of faith to understanding. The translation is suggestive and meaningful—especially in the light of 6:9–10. However, it can hardly be original.

Excursus: The Risk of Faith

Bibliography

Buber, M. *Zwei Glaubensweisen. Two Types of Faith.* Tr. N. P. Goldhawk. London: Routledge and Paul, 1951. 27–29. **Wildberger, H.** " 'Glauben' im AT." *ZTK* 65 (1968) 129–59. ———. " 'Glauben'. Erwagungen zu האמין." VTSup 16 Leiden: E. J. Brill, 1967. 372–86.

This passage pictures the exercise of faith as a risk; without risk—no reward. When David gives his charge to Solomon (1 Kgs 2:4), he couches the promise in terms conditioned on Solomon's walking "before (God) faithfully" (NIV). באמת may also be translated "in truth." It is from the same root אמן which is prominent in 9b. When Ahijah presents God's challenge for Jeroboam to be king over ten tribes, it is again couched in conditions of obedience. If they will be fulfilled God will build for Jeroboam בית־נאמן "a sure house" (1 Kgs 11:38). At this point Isaiah's message is nearer to the Deuteronomist's understanding of God's promises than to the usual Jerusalemite terms which view the throne as נכון "established" by God forever.

The young king is clearly uncertain and frightened, as well he might be. He is reminded of God's faithfulness and of God's assurance. But in v 9b he is reminded that he has a task to fulfill, like that outlined for Solomon and Jeroboam, before he can be confirmed on his throne. V 10a offers Yahweh's sign. This is his "risk." He tests Ahaz through the offer, just as he tested Abraham (Gen 22:1). When Abraham obeyed the bizarre command, he clearly tested God in return. Every encounter in faith consists of a mutual testing. God's actions toward his people is a test and a risk (cf. Deut 4:34). God's blessings and providential acts are "tests" (Exod 15:25; 20:20; Deut 8:2). Test and countertest are the very stuff of personal encounter and growth in faith.

But this encounter can go wrong. Deut 6:16 speaks of a bitter experience at Massah when Israel "tested" God and warns against "testing" God. Apparently the right encounter begins with God's initiative, with God's offer of a test. In

Isaiah, this is the case. God offers a sign (v 11). This will clearly become a "test" both of Ahaz's faith and of God's faithfulness. There is a risk. But without risk there is no reward.

Episode B: The Sign: "Within Three Years" (7:10–16)

Bibliography

Buchanen, G. W. "The Old Testament Meaning of the Knowledge of Good and Evil." *JBL* 75 (1956) 114–20. **Coppens, J.** "Un nouvel essai d'interpretation d'Is. 7:14–17." *Salmanticensis* 23 (1976) 85–88. **Feuillet, A.** "Le signe propose a Achaz el l'Emmanuel (Isaie 7:10–25)." *Revue des Sciences Religieuses* 30 (1940) 129–51. **Fohrer, G.** "Zu Jes. 7:14 im Zusammenhang von Jes. 7:10–22." *ZAW* 68 (1956) 54–56. **Jensen, J.** "The Age of Immanuel." *CBQ* 41 (1979) 220–39. **Kida, T.** "Immanuel-yogen (Immanuel Prophecy—A Study of Is. 7:1–16)." *FS I. Takayanagi,* ed. by N. Tajima. Tokyo: Sobunsha, 1967. 275–93. **Kissane, E. J.** "Butter and Honey Shall He Eat (Isaiah 7:15)." *Orientalia et Biblica Louvaniensia* 1 (1957) 169–73. **Kosmala, H.** "Form and Structure in Ancient Hebrew Poetry." *VT* 14 (1964) 423–45. **Lindblom, J.** *A Study on the Immanuel Section in Isaiah* (Is 7:1—9:6). Studien utgiv. au. Kungl. Humanistika Vetenskapssamfunde i Lund 4. Lund: Gleerup, 1957–58. **McKane, W.** "Interpretation of Isaiah 7:14–25." *VT* 17 (1967) 208–19. **McNamara, M.** "The Emmanuel Prophecy and its Context." *Scr* 14 (1962) 118–25; 15 (1963) 19–23. **Olmo Lete, G. del.** "La profecia del Emmanuel (Is. 7:10–17). Estado actual de la interpretacion." *EphMar* 22 (1972) 357–85. **Rice, G.** "The Interpretation of Isaiah 7:15–17." *JBL* 96 (1977) 363–69. **Scullion, J. J.** "Approach to the Understanding of Isaiah 7:10–17." *JBL* 87 (1968) 288–300. **Steck, O. H.** "Beiträge zum Verständnis von Jesaja 7:10–17 und 8:1–4." **Wolf, H. M.** "A Solution to the Immanuel Prophecy in Is. 7:14—8:22." *JBL* 91 (1972) 449–56.

Translation

Herald: 10 *Then Yahweh* [a] *spoke again to Ahaz:*
Yahweh: 11 *Ask for yourself a sign from Yahweh your God, making it deep as Sheol* [a] *or raising it to a height!*
Herald: 12 *Then Ahaz said:*
Ahaz: *I shall not ask, for I shall not test Yahweh.*
Herald: 13 *Then he said:*
Prophet: *Hear ye now, House of David!* 3+4+4
Is (it) too small (for) you (pl)—the wearying of humans
that you also weary my God?
14 *Therefore my Lord himself will give you (pl) a sign.*
Behold, the woman [a] *shall conceive* 3+2+4
and bearing a son—
she shall call [b] *his name Immanuel.*
15 *Curdled milk and honey will he eat until he knows to refuse the evil and to choose the good.* 16 *For before*

the lad knows refusing the evil and choosing the good, the ground will be forsaken by those of whom you are standing in dread, by the presence of her two kings.

Notes

10.a. Tg ישעיהו "Isaiah." The change makes sense, but the unanimous testimony of MT and Versions demands respect.

11.a. 'A Σ Θ *εις αδην* "to Hades." LXX *εἰς βάθος* "to depth." MT reads שְׁאָלָה "please ask it." The Versions read another vowel שְׁאֹלָה meaning "Sheol" with a ה directive. The reading is universally recognized since it fits the contrast with "heights" to follow.

14.a. LXX *ἡ παρθένος* "the virgin." 'A Σ Θ *ἡ νεᾶνις* "the young woman." The article of MT is attested in all MSS.

14.b. DSS[Isa] and LXX[S] have a 2 m pl *καλέσετε* "you will call." But other versions including LXX support MT.

Form/Structure/Setting

The passage begins like the last one with a narrative imperfect which both relates it to the context of vv 1–2 and vv 3–9 yet also sets it off. It is a second episode. This has the genre of a sign narrative. In biblical stories it is usual for a sign to be offered without being requested (cf. 1 Sam 10:7, 9; 1 Sam 2:34). Hezekiah is given such a sign (Isa 37:30 = 2 Kgs 19:29). So, giving the sign without having Ahaz request it is not out of character.

The pericope has two parts: first the dialogue about the sign (vv 10–13) and then the actual sign itself. The sign supports the prophecy of vv 7–8. The Hebrew particles structure the sign passage. לכן "therefore" (v 14) begins the speech, relating it to the earlier offer of a sign. The sign itself is presented with הנה "behold" (v 14). The explanation is introduced with כי "for" (v 16).

Comment

10 The narrative expressly indicates a second word and a second occasion. The purpose continues that of the previous episode. Ahaz is being encouraged to remain firm in his policy of loyalty to Assyria and resistance to Aram and Israel.

11 A *sign* (אות) is frequently offered by a prophet so that someone may know that God is fulfilling the promises he has made. Samuel offers signs to Saul that will confirm God's choice and endowment as king (1 Sam 10:7, 9). Eli is given to see that the death of his sons will be a sign that God has brought judgment on him (1 Sam 2:34).

12 So God offers Ahaz such a confirmation that these events are all part of his will. But the use of such aids to faith have always been controversial. Some consider a religion built on such to be a counterfeit of true faith. It could be a means of "testing" or "trying" (נסה) God. Israel is accused of such in Exod 17:2, 7; Num 14:22; Deut 6:16; Pss 78:18, 41, 56; 95:9; 106:14.

(This root is closely kin to נסס "be conspicuous" from which the noun נס "flag" or "ensign" comes which appears in Isa 5:26; 11:12, 18:3.)

13 Ahaz had been addressed in the singular (vv 10–12). When the formal address turns to "O House of David" (v 13) the plural is used. The appellation gives the entire passage royal (i.e., Messianic) significance. It relates to the destiny of the Davidic House in Jerusalem. The Vision has not until this point dealt with the role of the Davidic ruler in the new order. Judgment on Jerusalem's ruling classes had not been explicitly applied to the king in chap. 1 or chap. 3. The prophet's mission to the king has indicated God's approval of Ahaz's action and offers support for his policies.

The word לאה "to weary," "to wear out," is used here about the king. It is a key word in Isaiah. In 1:14, Yahweh is "weary" of Jerusalem's vain worship. Wildberger notes that the word belongs to the vocabulary of the ריב "argument," as Mic 6:3 and Job 4:2, 5 show. It means that someone has had enough of his opponent's argument. He will accept no more. LXX however, has translated this by ἀγῶνα παρέχειν "occasion strife." This adds a nuance to the meaning of "weary."

In what sense has Ahaz "wearied" or "occasioned strife" for men? This meeting occurs early in his reign. He has inherited a crisis for which he is not to blame. Undoubtedly, many of his subjects expected from him a vigorous new policy to rescue the country from its difficulties. This has not happened. He has neither rallied his country to a vigorous counter-offensive, nor launched a diplomatic move to join his foes in rebellion against Assyria. It is understandable that this had "wearied" many and "occasioned strife" among his subjects.

Isaiah's role was to strengthen his resolve to continue his present policy of neutrality and appeasement toward Assyria. But Ahaz did not make it easy. There is no evidence that Ahaz is a man of faith. He distanced himself from the religious confirmation which would have strengthened his hand. Isaiah's word for Ahaz is "wearying" (לאה). Both Kings and Chronicles find stronger condemnation for the king. But at this stage he is young, inexperienced, and indecisive.

14–16 The "sign" is revealed anyway. A *young woman* who is apparently present or contemporary, but not yet married (i.e., a virgin) will in due course bear a child and call his name *Immanuel* meaning God-(is)-With-Us. By the time the child is old enough to make decisions, the land of the two opposing kings will be devastated. The sign is simple. It has to do with a period by which time the present crisis will no longer be acute or relevant. This is parallel to the statement in v 8b but indicates a much shorter period. The shorter period accords with history. Tiglath-Pileser's reactions to Rezin and the son of Remaliah came in 733 B.C. when he reduced most of Israel to the status of an Assyrian province.

Explanation

Yahweh commissions Isaiah with a further mission to Ahaz. He is authorized to offer Ahaz a sign (אות) to bolster his faith and direct his decision. The story develops along two lines. The first shows that Ahaz is incapable of serious spiritual interaction with God or his prophet. His policy is to avoid religious or spiritual contact because it might lead him to a cultic or religious mistake. Perhaps he is thinking of his grandfather's mistake when he tried to exercise priestly office in the Temple (2 Chr 26:16). He knows just enough to know that approaching the Lord risks being accused of manipulating him. He knows the laws about not "testing" (נסה) God and quotes them as a reason to avoid "inquiring" of Yahweh.

Isaiah refuses to see it that way. He warns the king about "wearying" (לאה) God with his empty excuses. The records show that within his reign Ahaz actually designed and built an altar of Damascene style specifically to "inquire before." He also was very active in rearranging the Temple and its worship. The editors of Kings judge his motivation to have been political and pagan (cf. 2 Kgs 16:10–18). The accumulation of testimony is that Ahaz was religious enough, but that his real gods were idols. The word and picture are typical for the book of Isaiah. The Vision portrays God as vocal and active—but his people at every stage as unresponsive, unwilling, disobedient. "Wearying" fits the picture very well for Israel as well as for Ahaz.

The mass of bibliographic references alone which deal with 7:14 make it necessary to deal with the verse in a special section. This is done in a series of excursuses, each with a selected bibliography. The limits of space prevent a full review of the research.

Excursus: The ʿAlmah *(7:14)*

Bibliography

Brunet, G. *Essai,* 35–100. **Coppens, J.** "La Prophetie de la *ʿAlmah.*" *ETL* 28 (1952) 648–78. **Delling, G.** "Παρθένος," *TDNT* V (1954) 826–37. **Fahlgren, K. H.** "*ha ʿalma.* En undersokning till Jes. 7." *SEÄ* 4 (1939) 13–24. **Gordon, C. H.** "*ʿAlmah* in Isaiah 7:14." *JBR* 21 (1953) 106. **Kipper, B.** "O Problema da *ʿAlmah* nos Estudos Recentes." *RCB* 7/25s (1963) 80–92; N. S. 1 (1964) 180–95. **Lattey, C.** "The Term *ʿAlmah* in Is. 7:14." *CBQ* 9 (1947) 89–95. **Myers, A. E.** "Use of *ʿalmah* in the Old Testament." *LQ* 7 (1955) 137–40. **Owens, J. J.** "The Meaning of *ʿalmah* in the Old Testament." *RevExp* 50 (1953) 56–60. **Rehm, M.** "Das Wort *ʿalmah* in Is. 7:14." *BZ* 8 (1964) 89–101. **Steinmueller, J. F.** "Etymology and Biblical Usage of *ʿAlmah.*" *CBQ* 2 (1940) 28–43. **Vendrame, C.** "Sentido Coletivo da *ʿAlmah* (Is. 7:14)." *RCB* 7/24 (1963) 10–16.

Two questions must be asked. First what does עלמה mean? The Greek translators staked out the possible meanings: LXX ἡ παρθένος, followed by Vg *virgo* "the virgin." Other Greek versions translate η νεανις "the young woman." Both are possible translations of the word. The definite article is important. Not just anyone, but "the" or "that" virgin or young woman is meant.

OT usage is instructive. Gen 24:43 speaks of an unmarried young woman, apparently eligible for marriage. Exod 2:8 refers to Miriam, the baby Moses' sister. Ps 68:26 (25) in the plural speaks of tambourine players in the Temple. Brunet (*Essai,*

41–2) notes the relation to the plural used in the superscription of Ps 46:1 and in 1 Chr 15:20 with the apparent meaning "for sopranos or women's voices."

Cant 1:3 and 6:8 use עלמה to speak of the beloved; Prov 30:19 "the way of a man with an עלמה" is followed in the next verse with "the way of the adulterous woman." This leads Brunet (*Essai,* 49) to conclude that עלמה has dishonorable meanings as well as the honorable references to Miriam and Rebecca. This dishonorable reference is connected in Proverbs and in a related word עלומים in Isa 54:4 to sterility.

This word study suggests that עלמה had two different and contrasting semantic implications which provide an invitation to *double entendre.* The one implies the spotless candidate for marriage. The other implies a type of available sexual partner not condoned by Yahwistic norms or the Law. The common meaning signifies one who is sexually mature. It is difficult to find a word in English that is capable of the same range of meaning. "Virgin" is too narrow, while "young woman" is too broad.

The second question is: to whom does the prophet refer? Interpreters continue to differ in answering. The traditional answer of the Christian community points to Mary, the mother of Jesus (cf. *Excursus: Isa 7:14 and the Virgin Birth*). But the context in its primary meaning requires a sign that will be fulfilled in the immediate future ("before the boy knows . . . the land will be laid waste," v 16).

In seeking an answer it is important to determine the nature of the sign. Is it a positive promise of blessing? Or does it reflect Isaiah's impatience with Ahaz and have the same ironic or sarcastic tone which appears in the following oracles? The answer probably depends upon which of the two meanings of עלמה is understood to be operative here.

The answers which interpreters have given to this question are legion. Wildberger (290–91) and Brunet (*Essai,* 55–100) have made exhaustive surveys of these opinions. These range from the view that "the virgin" is identified with Mary, mother of Jesus, to the one that "the virgin" is the cult figure of the bride in the ritual sacred marriage, a cult prostitute, chosen to fill the role with all its mythological overtones. Other views which tend toward "the marriageable young woman" identify her as the young queen or a consort of the king, the prophet's wife, an unidentified young woman in the crowd, or a collective sense of all those who will be brides in this year. In these, the meaning of the prophecy turns on the time span until the child is born and on the mood of the times reflected in the choice of names.

Wildberger (291) is surely right when he says, "If we have difficulty in solving the mystery of the עלמה, that does not mean that the prophecy was a riddle for those who heard the prophecy (or originally read the book). It is not characteristic of prophetic oracles that they cannot be understood." M. Buber (*Glaube der Propheten* [Zurich: Manesse Verlag, 1950], 201) noted that the עלמה had to be someone known to the king. Steinmann (90) identifies her as a princess who has just entered the household of Ahaz, possibly Abia, the daughter of Zechariah, a friend of the prophet (cf. 2 Kgs 18:2), who would become the mother of Hezekiah.

It is entirely possible in large royal households that the mother would give the child its name. Some have objected that Hezekiah must have been older by this time for him to assume the throne when he did. But the chronologies of this period are very uncertain, so no sure statement can be made. The view that the child to be born is a royal heir, and that his mother belongs to the king's household does justice to the evidence, fits the context, and provides the potential of messianic intention that is needed.

Excursus: Immanuel (*7:14*)

Bibliography

Blank, S. H. "Immanuel and Which Isaiah?" *JNES* 13 (1954) 83–98. **Brunet, G.** *Essai.* 3–34. **Ginsberg, H. L.** "Immanuel (Is. 7:14)." *EncJud* 8 (1971) 1293–95. **Gottwald, N. K.** "Immanuel as the Prophet's Son." *VT* 8 (1958) 36–47. **Hammershaimb, E.** "Immanuelstegnet (Jes. 7:10ff)." *DTT* 8 (1945) 223–44. ———. "The Immanuel Sign." *ST* 3 (1949) 124–42. **Hindson, E. E.** "Isaiah's Immanuel." *Grace Journal* 10/3 (1969) 3–15. **Jones, B. E.** "Immanuel: A Historical and Critical Study." Diss., University of Wales, Aberystwyth, 1966/67. **Kilian, R.** *Die Verheissung Immanuels, Jes. 7:14.* SBS 35. Stuttgart: Kath. Bibelwerk, 1968. Cf. G. Fohrer, *ZAW* 81 (1969) 277; M. Rehm, *TRev* 67 (1971) 173. ———. "Prolegomena zur Auslegung der Immanuelverheissung." *Forschung zur Bibel* 2 (1972) 207–15. **Lattey, C.** "The Emmanuel Prophecy: Is. 7:14." *CBQ* 8 (1946) 369–76. ———. "Various Interpretations of Isaiah 7:14." *CBQ* 9 (1947) 147–54. **Liver, J.** "עמנואל" *EnsMikr* 6 (1971) 292–95. **Lust, J.** "Immanuel Figure: a charismatic judge-leader (Is. 10:10–17)." *ETL* 47 (1971) 464–70. **Moriarty, F. L.** "The Immanuel Prophecies." *CBQ* 19 (1957) 226–33. **Price, C. P.** "Immanuel: God with us (Is. 7:14)." *Christianity and Crisis* 23 (1963) 222–23. **Reese, J. M.** "The Gifts of Immanuel." *TBT* 27 (1966) 1880–85. **Rignell, L. G.** "Das Immanuelszeichen; Eine Gesichtspunkte zu Jes. 7." *ST* 11 (1957) 99–119. **Stamm, J. J.** "Die Immanuel-Perikope. Eine Nachlese." *TZ* 30 (1974) 11–22. ———. "Die Immanuel-Perikope im Lichte neuerer Veroffentlichungen." *ZDMG,* Supp. 1 (1969) 281–90. ———. "Die Immanuel Weissagung, ein Gesprach mit E. Hammershaimb." *VT* 4 (1954) 20–33. ———. "Die Immanuel Weissagung und die Eschatologie des Jesaja." *TZ* 16 (1960) 439–55. ———. "Neuere Arbeiten zum Immanuel-Problem." *ZAW* 68 (1956) 44–53. ———. "La Propheties d'Immanuel." *RHPR* 23 (1943) 1–26. **Testa, E.** "L'Emmanuele e la santa Sion." *SBFLA* 25 (1975) 171–92. **Vischer, W.** *Die Immanuel-Botschaft im Rahmen des königlichen Zionfestes.* Zollikon-Zürich: Evangelische Verlag, 1955. Cf. R. Tournay, *RB* 64 (1957) 124; J. Hempel. *ZAW* 68 (1956) 284. ———. "La prophetie d'Emmanuel et la fete royale." *ETR* 29 (1954) 3:55–97. **Wolff, H. W.** *Immanuel. Das Zeichen, dem widersprochen wird.* BibS (N) 23. Neukirchen: Neukirchener Verlag, 1959. **Zimmermann, F.** "Immanuel Prophecy." *JQR* 52 (1961) 154–59.

The very size of the bibliography indicates how intense has been the discussion about this name. עִמָּנוּ אֵל is a statement with two elements: "God—with us." Hebrew sentences may be formed with no expressed verb. There is always an ambiguity about such statements, because the hearer or reader must supply the verb form in both its time and its mood. Therefore, the context is of vital importance. The words appear twice more in the larger context. In 8:8 the threatening context suggests a translation: "May God (be) with us." In 8:10 the defiant context requires the meaning "For God (is) with us." The issues involved in the cry are dealt with in 8:12–15.

Names that express faith in God's nearness are known in many languages of the ANE. Ps 46:8, 12 contains the assuring word "Yahweh of Hosts is with us," while the reassurances given leaders in holy war were similar: Deut 20:4; Judg 6:12

Wildberger (293) notes that Isaiah usually uses יהוה "Yahweh," while here אל "God" is used. This may indicate that a well-known formula is being employed.

Vischer (*Die Immanuel-Botschaft,* 22) refers to 2 Sam 23:5 where David speaks of his house being secure עם־אל "with God."

Mowinckel (*Psalmenstudien* 2 [Kristiania: Dybwad 1921], 306, n. 1) assumes that עמנו אל was an ancient cultic cry. Vischer calls it a choral shout in the liturgy of the royal Zion festival. (See the commentary on 8:10.)

Wildberger (293) is correct in seeking a meaning for the name in connection with the prophecy of vv 4–9 and thus with the traditions of the Davidic dynasty. God promised to be "with" the sons of David in a special way (2 Sam 7:9; 1 Kgs 1:37; Ps 89:22, 25; and 1 Kgs 11:38). If the verse is understood within this larger context which concentrates on the Davidic tradition and succession, surely Wildberger is right. Immanuel will be the King's son and the עלמה is Ahaz's wife.

Excursus: Isaiah 7:14 in Context

Bibliography

Carreira das Neves, J. "Is. 7:14: da Exegese a Hermeneutica." *Theologica* (Braga) 4, 4 (1969) 399–414. ———. "Isaias 7:14 no Texto Massoretico e no Texto Grego. A obra de Joachim Becker." *Didaskalia* 2 (1972) 79–112. **Coppens, J.** "L'interpretation d'Is. 7:14 a la lumiere des etudes les plus recentes" (bibliogr.), *Lex Tua Veritas.* Fs. H. Junker. Trier: Paulinus Verlag, 1961. 31–45. **Criado, R.** "El valor de *laken* (Vg "propter") en Is. 7:14." Contribucion al estudio del Emmanuel, *Estudios Ecclesiasticos* 34 (1960) 741–51. **Dequeker, L.** "Isaie 7:14: *wqrʾt smw ʿmnw ʾl.*" *VT* 12 (1962) 331–35. **Hartmann, K. C.** "More about the RSV and Isaiah 7:14." *LQ* 7 (1955) 344–47. **Hindson, E. E.** "Development of the Interpretation of Isaiah 7:14. A Tribute to E. J. Young." *Grace Journal* 10 (1969) 19–25. **Koehler, L.** "Zum Verständnis von Jes. 7:14." *ZAW* 67 (1955) 48–50. **Lacheman, E. R.** "A propos of Isaiah 7:14" *JBR* 22 (1954) 43. **Lescow, T.** "Das Geburtsmotiv in den messianischen Weissagungen bei Jesaja und Micha (Is. 7:14, 9:11, Micha 5:1–3)." *ZAW* 79 (1967) 172–207. **Lohfink, N.** "On Interpreting the Old Testament (Is. 7:14)." *TD* 15 (1967) 228–29 (from *Stimmen der Zeit* 176 (1966) 98–112). **Mejia, J.** "Contribucion a la exegesis de un texto dificil." *EstBib* 24 (1965) 107–21. **Messerschmidt, H.** "Se, jomfruen skal undfange og fode en son (Is. 7:14 . . .)." *Lumen* 6 (1962) 160–69. **Moody, D.** "Isaiah 7:14 in the Revised Standard Version." *RevExp* 50 (1953) 61–68. **Motyer, J. A.** "Content and Context in the Interpretation of Isaiah 7:14." *TynBul* 21 (1970) 118–25. **Porubsan, S.** "The Word *ʾot* in Isaiah 7:14." *CBQ* 22 (1960) 144–59. **Salvoni, F.** "La profezia Isiana sulla 'Vergine' partoriente (Is. 7:14)." *Ricerche Bibliche e Religose* 1 (1966) 19–40. **Surburg, R. F.** "Interpretation of Isaiah 7:14." *Spdfr* 38 (1974) 110–18. **Sutcliffe, E. F.** "The Emmanuel Prophecy of Is. 7:14." *Estudios Ecclesiasticos* 34 (1960) 737–65.

What then is the meaning of the verse and the sign? לכן "therefore" relates to v 13 in which God shows his impatience with Ahaz's timidity and vacillation. So the Lord himself will give them, the House of David, a sign. The position of the royal house and its succession (vv 4–9) is established.

The announcement is of a birth. The Queen (העלמה) is either pregnant or soon will be. She will bear a son, potential heir to all the promises to David. She will name him Immanuel. The sign is specifically a birth (the assurance of an heir to the throne) and a name (the assurance of God's faithfulness to his promise to be "with" the sons of David).

The announcement is continued with the description of the child's well-being in v 15 and the explanation in v 16 which comes full circle to relate the whole to the events of vv 1–2 and the prophecy "It will not happen!" of vv 4–9.

Excursus: Isaiah 7:14 as Messianic Prophecy

Bibliography

Berg, W. "Die Identität der 'jungen Frau' in Jes 7:14, 16." *BibNot* 13 (1980) 7–13. **Creager, H. L.** "Immanuel Passage as Messianic Prophecy." *LQ* 7 (1955) 339–43. **Rehm, M.** *Der königliche Messias im Lichte der Immanuel-weissagung des Buches Jesaja.* Eichstädter Studien 1. Kevelaer: Butzon & B, 1968. Cf. B. S. Childs, *JBL* 88 (1969) 365; G. Fohrer, *ZAW* 81 (1968) 428; J. Bright, *Int* 20 (1970) 389; P. A. H. deBoer, *VT* 20 (1970) 381; G. M. Landes, *CBQ* 32 (1970) 300; D. R. Jones, *JTS* 22 (1971) 559. **Rice, G.** "The Interpretation of Isaiah 7:15–17." *JBL* 96 (1977) 363–69. **Savoca, G. M.** "L'Emmanuele al centro della storia, segno di salvezze e di rovina." *Palestro del Clero* 33 (1954) 753–61. **Sancho-Gili, J.** "Sobre el sentido mesianico de Is. 7:14. Interpretaciones biblicas y magisteriales." *CB* 27 (1970) 67–89. **Willis, J. T.** "The Meaning of Isaiah 7:14 and its Application in Matthew 1:23." *ResQ* 21 (1978) 1–18. **Young, E. J.** "The Immanuel Prophecy. Isa 7:14." *Studies in Isaiah.* Grand Rapids: Eerdmans, 1954. 143–98. (Reprinted from *Westminster Theological Journal.*)

Did the sign have "messianic relevance" as it was originally announced? The passage turns on a threat to the throne and to the "son of David" who occupies it. The prophecy: "It will not happen" announces that the threat is empty and that the throne will remain secure. V 9b speaks of being "confirmed" and surely refers to confirmation in his position on the throne. So now the sign deals with the same issue. Whatever deals with the Davidic promise of the throne to his heirs must have relevance to "Messiah."

The entire setting shows a positive attitude toward the House of David. העלמה must be someone in sight to whom Isaiah points. The most likely women to have been present with the King would have been the Queen and her escort. If this is true, the son that is to be born would be the heir apparent to the throne, i.e., the Anointed One.

In this sense, at least, the passage is "messianic." It related to the fulfillment of God's promises to David and his dynasty. It warns Ahaz that it is in the interest of the throne and his succession to allow his troubles to pass without escalating them by rash acts. In this way he can pass on to his son an independent, even if poor and ravished, kingdom.

It is significant that all the passages that explicitly deal with messianic themes related to the Davidic dynasty occur in the Ahaz section of the Vision (7:1–16; 9:5–6 [6–7]; and 11:1–5, 10).

The survival of the royal house of Judah in the day when Tiglath-Pileser unleashed his armies in Palestine is nothing short of miraculous. That the very king who eschewed military might and the attempt to save his kingdom from Rezin and the son of Remaliah by force would outlive both of them and place his son on the throne of the still-intact little kingdom was indeed a miracle. What would have been seen as impossible by human measures was well within the power of God who delighted to exalt the meek and lowly but was at pains to humble the proud and ambitious (2:11–18). The sign implied all of this for the Davidic dynasty under Ahaz.

Excursus: Isaiah 7:14 and the Virgin Birth of Jesus

Bibliography

Abschlag, W. "Jungfrau oder Junge Frau? Zu Is. 7:14," *Anzeiger für die kath. Geistlichkeit* 83 (1974) 200. **Beecher, W. J.** "The Prophecy of the Virgin Mother," *Classical*

Evangelical Essays in OT Interpretation, ed. W. C. Kaiser. Grand Rapids: Baker, 1973. 1979–85. **Brennan, J. P.** "Virgin and Child in Is. 7:14." *TBT* 1 (1964) 968–74. **Feinberg, C. L.** "The Virgin Birth in the Old Testament and Is. 7:14." *BSac* 119 (1962) 251–58. **Haag, H.** "Is. 7:14 als attest. Grundstelle der Lehre von virginitas Mariae." *Mariologische Studien* 4. Essen: Driewer, 1969. 137–43. **Kilian, R.** "Die Geburt des Immanuel aus der Jungfrau, Jes. 7:14." *Zum Thema Jungfrauengeburt.* Stuttgart: Kath. Bibelwerk 1970. 9–35. **Kruse, H.** "Alma Redemptoris Mater. Eine Auslegung der Immanuel-Weissagung Is. 7:14." *TTZ* 74 (1965) 15–36. **Loss, N. M.** "Ecce Virgo concipiet. Reflexoes sobre a Relacao entre Sinai e Significacao em Is. 7:14–16." *Actualidades Biblicas,* aos cuidados de S. Voigt e o. Petropolis: 1971. 309–20. **Mueller, W.** "Virgin Shall Conceive." *EvQ* 32 (1960) 203–7. **Prado, J.** "La Madre del Emmanuel: Is. 7:14 (Reseña del estado de las cuestiones)." *Sef* 2 (1961) 85–114. **Stuhlmueller, C.** "The Mother of the Immanuel." *Marian Studies* 12 (1961) 165–204. **Vella, G.** "Is. 7:14 e il parto verginale del Messia." *Atti della Settimana Biblica* 18 (1964) 85–93.

No record exists of special attention given to 7:14 in pre-Christian Judaism. The ambiguity inherent in the word העלמה is reflected in the divergence of Greek translations. LXX translates *ἡ παρθένος* "the virgin." 'A, Σ, and Θ use *η νεανις* "the young woman." But no record exists of any debate on these issues in pre-Christian times.

Matthew (1:22–23) finds in the LXX rendition of 7:14 a coincidental convergence of this sentence in Scripture with the events he is recounting and interprets it as prophecy and fulfillment. He quotes the LXX almost verbatim, with only the variation *καλέσουσιν* "they will call" for *καλέσεις* "you (sg) will call." The translation *ἡ παρθένος* "the virgin" suits Matthew's intention perfectly. If one supposes a divine intention in this connection, part of God's work was done through the Greek translator. The translation of the other Greek Versions, while accurate enough in context, does not serve Matthew's purpose. Only a part of the prophecy was literally fulfilled. The Incarnate Son is named by divine command "Jesus," not Immanuel. And no effort is made to relate his childhood to fulfillment of the prophecy concerning Rezin and Pekah. With Matthew the verse took on heightened significance and importance, becoming a central issue in Jewish-Christian polemic about Messiah and Jesus.

Christological interpretation focused on the words "a virgin shall conceive" and the child's name, Immanuel. Both were used to develop the doctrine of the incarnation. The divinity of Jesus was expressed in the name and the Virgin Birth became the classical means of explaining "how" the incarnation took place.

Several things contributed to connecting Isa 7:14 with the gospel events. The messianic hope burned particularly bright in the Jewish community of the first century. Distance in time separated them from the issues of the eighth-century prophecy and the fifth-century book. Another factor lay in the special relevance which the Vision of Isaiah had for the Jewish and Christian communities of the first century. It provided the "world view" of God's plan for that period which supported the synagogue and Temple. Its teaching of God's plan for that age was very congenial to the Gospel and the church in details (such as Messianic teachings) as well as the general direction (antipathy to sacrifice and monarchy). Jesus' and the church's understandings of the Messiah are directly in line with that of the Vision, although the book does not develop such a view or program.

A second factor facilitated the use of Isa 7:14 in Matthew. A hermeneutical method was in general use which allowed verses to be separated from their contexts. Verses or individual words were understood to have esoteric meanings whose significance could be revealed to an inspired teacher or writer. Thus the entire Scripture was viewed as a prophecy intended to interpret the moment in which the reader lived. Verses were abstracted from both the historical and literary setting in which they originally appeared. They were then identified with an event or a doctrine which was altogether extraneous to the original context or intention. This kind of interpretation presumes a view of inspiration and of history in which God moves in all ages mysteriously to plant his secrets so that later ages may put the puzzle together and thus reveal his purposes and the direction of his intention.

In the case of 7:14 the relation to christology was secret no longer. The verse continued to play an important role in Christian teaching and preaching. However, there were those who protested its translation in the way that this interpretation demanded. Aquila, Symmachus, and Theodotian translated העלמה by ἡ νεᾶνις "the young woman" in their translations of the Old Testament (cf. J. Ziegler, *Septuaginta* xiv *Isaias* [1939], 147). Justin Martyr met the objection of Trypho (*Dialogue with Trypho,* 67) that the passage should be translated ἰδοὺ ἡ νεᾶνις ἐν γαστρὶ λήψεται καὶ τέξεται υἱόν "Behold! The young woman shall conceive and bear a son." (Cf. E. J. Young, *Studies in Isaiah,* 144.)

However, the line of Christian interpretation of 7:14 in accordance with Matthew continued through the Fathers (both Greek and Latin), the Reformers, and on to current conservative scholars such as E. J. Young. It presumes a christological interpretation of the Old Testament. העלמה is to be translated "the virgin" and is a prediction of Mary, the Mother of Jesus. Equally, Immanuel is the name for Jesus.

This kind of interpretation is subject to the criticism that it ignores the rightful demands of contextual and historical exegesis which call for a meaning related to the end of the Syro-Ephraimite War in terms of v 16. Christological implications may more profitably be discussed in the commentary on Matthew than in the one on Isaiah.

But a consideration of christological significance must also note the way the Vision calls to a faith that serves rather than conquers, that is humble rather than triumphal, and that accepts suffering rather than seeking vengeance. This is supported by the demonstration that God is thoroughly capable of achieving his goals by miraculous means (2:2–4; 9:1–6 [2–7]; 11:1–16; 35:1–10; 65:17—66:24) as well as by the manipulation of historical forces (7:17; 10:5–11; 13:1–5; 24:1–3; 45:1–7; 63:1–6). Thus the announcement of God's sign to Ahaz in his hour of despair is a fitting reference to illuminate the birth of a lowly infant in stable straw whom God had destined to save the world not by force of arms but by meek acceptance of humiliation and death. That God chooses to accomplish his primary goals in such ways is the message of Isaiah as it is of the Gospels.

Episode C: Yahweh Is Bringing Critical Times— the Assyrian Era (7:17–25)

Bibliography

Childs, B. S. *Isaiah and the Assyrian Crisis.* SBT 2nd ser. 3. Naperville, IL: Allenson, 1967. **McKane, W.** "The Interpretation of Isaiah VII 14–25." *VT* 17 (1967) 208–19.

Translation

Isaiah: (to Ahaz)	17 *Yahweh* [a] *will bring upon you (sg) and upon your people and upon your father's house times such as have not come since the day Ephraim revolted against Judah:* [b] *(that is, he will bring) the king of Assyria.* [b]	
An Oracle:	18 *It shall be in that day:*	3
	Yahweh will whistle for the fly	3+4
	which (is) at the source of the rivers [a] *of Egypt,*	
	And to the bee	1+3
	which (is) in the land of Assyria.	
	19 *They shall come—all of them shall settle*	3
	in the valleys of precipices, [a]	2
	and in the clefts of rocks	2
	and in all the thorn bushes [b]	2
	and in all the watering places. [c]	2
An Oracle:	20 *In that day,*	2
	The Lord will shave with a razor	3+3+2
	that is hired beyond the river,	
	the King of Assyria.	
	The head, the pubic hair, [a]	3+3
	And also the beard it will remove.	
An Oracle:	21 *And it shall be in that day:*	3
	A person will keep alive a calf and two goats.	2+2+2
	22 *And it shall be that*	1
	from the amount of milk produced	3+2
	[a] *he will eat curds.*	
	For [a] *curds and honey will be the food*	4+4
	of everyone left in the heart of the land.	
An Oracle:	23 *And it shall be in that day:*	3
	Every place which has	3+3
	a thousand vines (worth) a thousand (pieces) of silver	4
	will become thorns and briers.	3
	24 *One will (only) go there with bow and arrow*	4+4
	for all the land will become thorns and briers.	
	25 *And all the mountains*	2+3
	which should be for cultivation with a hoe,	
	no one will go there	3+3
	(for) fear of briers and thorns.	
	They will become open range for cattle	3+2
	and pastorage for sheep.	

Notes

17.a. LXX ὁ θεός "God." DSS[Isa] has ו before יביא, LXX has ἀλλα ἐπάξει. These would require a translation "But Yahweh will bring." MT's direct statement is to be preferred. It begins a new pericope.

17.b-b. The phrase is often thought to be a gloss, and it does seem to be tacked on. However, it cannot be eliminated without dropping vv 18–28, which depend upon it for meaning. Its abrupt appearance may well be for dramatic effect and emphasis.

18.a. יאר is a translated Egyptian word (*jtr*[*w*] or *jrw*). In forty-nine of fifty-three cases in the OT it means the Nile River. The pl refers to "the arms of the Nile" in its upper stages.

19.a. בתות is of uncertain meaning (cf. also 5:6). LXX χώρα "country." Vg *vallis* "valley." From Arab, בתת may mean "cut off." Hence the assumed meaning: "precipice."

19.b. נעצוץ "thorn bush." Löw (II 416) identifies this as *Alhagi Camelorum Fisch,* but it has also been called *Zizyphus spina Christi* or "Christ's thorn" (cf. Wildberger, 301).

19.c. נהלל is a *hap. leg.* BDB derives it from נהל and translates "watering place." Dalman (*AuS* II 323) suggests another kind of thorny bush, the *Prospis Stephanica* which grows only three feet high as against some fifteen feet for the Christ's thorn.

20.a. Lit., "the hair of the feet," a euphemism. Cf. Exod 4:25.

22.a-a. Missing in LXX.

Form/Structure/Setting

The announcement of crisis (v 17) is followed by four independent oracles of doom relating to Assyria. Each pictures the catastrophe of "that day." "In that day" (ביום ההוא) is a fixed prophetic formula introducing an oracle concerning the coming judgment. (See the discussion on chap. 2.) It often is related to "the Day of Yahweh" and is an eschatological formula. Here the oracles are related to an historical event: the invasion of the Assyrians. That event is seen as Yahweh's action against the king, his dynasty, and his people. But it is lifted to a new dimension by that. It is *a* day of Yahweh's wrath and judgment.

7:17	Announcement: The Lord will bring Assyria against Judah
18–19	1st "in that Day" oracle
20	2nd "in that Day" oracle
21–22	3rd "in that Day" oracle
23–25	4th "in that Day" oracle

Comment

17 The announcement contains three important elements. First, the source of the event is *Yahweh.* In the announcement Ahaz is not blamed (as he is in 2 Kgs 16:7–9; 2 Chr 28:16–26). Rather this is portrayed as part of God's plan guaranteeing the suppression of Aram and Israel (v 7). Second, the events are significant for the young king himself (who will have to carefully balance his vassal status in order to survive), for his people (the people of Judah and Jerusalem who have suffered greatly in the Syro-Ephraimite war and must now adjust to being permanently dependent on the Assyrian), and for the Davidic dynasty (which will need to adjust its theological and liturgical base to accommodate itself to the new realities). Third, the announcement suggests that the Assyrian crisis will be more decisive and bring more change for Jerusalem/Judah than any event since Jeroboam led the civil war that divided the kingdom after Solomon's death.

This is a key verse for understanding the Vision. It calls for fifth-century Jews to recognize the Assyrian invasions of the eighth century (not 587 B.C.) as the watershed in God's history. (Cf. Donner, *IJH,* 416: "an empire of a completely new type, an incomparable power structure which determined the destinies of the ANE for almost half a millennium.") God created that watershed. Its results were his planned intention. Ahaz had to learn to live with that. Jews of the fifth century also had to adjust their thinking to God's reality.

The King of Assyria puts a name on what has until now been a mysterious, unnamed force (cf. 5:26–30). Hosea had named Assyria in prophecies of fifteen to twenty years before this (cf. Hos 7:11; 8:9; 9:3; 10:6; 11:12) while Amos had cited Assyrian victories at Calneh, Hamath, and Gath (6:2). God's use of the Assyrian will be discussed in 10:5–16 and 24–26; assurance of an end to the Assyrian's dominance will come in 14:24–25.

18 The mention of Egypt as well as Assyria takes the meaning beyond the immediate Assyrian invasion. V 17 speaks particularly of a new and different era. V 18 defines it as one characterized by big-power conflict in which Judah will continually be involved (cf. Budde and Fohrer). In some sense this has always been true (cf. Hos 9:3, 6; Jer 2:36). But Assyria pushes the frontier to the river of Egypt in Isaiah's lifetime and in the next century actually conquers Egypt for a short period. Many battles between the two will be fought here. Hezekiah becomes an active participant in the struggle (cf. chaps. 29–33).

The Egyptian *fly* from the sources of the Nile may refer to the Ethiopian pharaoh Pi (730–716 B.C.) who founded the twenty-fifth Dynasty and fought a battle with Assyria on Palestinian soil about 720 or 714 B.C. (cf. chap. 20; *MBA,* 149). Why he is called a fly is not clear. Upper Egypt has the hieroglyphic sign of a wasp.

Apparently, Assyria's mountains were famous for their bees. *Whistling* for the bees is described in about A.D. 440 by Cyrillus of Alexandria (Migne, *Patrologia,* Series Graeca 70 [1864] 209) as the means by which the bee-keeper drives the bees out of their hives to the fields and brings them back again. Ovid and Homer described bee-culture in detail. The picture is that of wild bees (cf. Deut 32:13; Ps 81:17 [16], etc.). The figure for war was used in Deut 1:44 and Ps 118:12. So the figure fits for the warring Assyrian armies.

20 *Shaving* may mark the end of a Nazarite's vow (Num 6:5). But it also was applied to prisoners and slaves. It was a mark of dishonor. It was a sign of being insulted and despised. *The river* is the Euphrates. The mercenary troops are hired by Assyria.

21–22 The verses picture a reduction of the standard of living to a minimal nourishment of a herder culture. This is a reduction from the city life of commerce that Judah has known.

23–25 The verses picture a loss of horticulture. The once carefully terraced slopes of vineyards and flat fields of grain will be lost to the wild. *Thorns,* weeds, and *briers* have gained control of land once carefully and fruitfully cultivated. Now only the herders take their cattle, sheep, and goats there. War's devastation will remove all signs of culture and prosperity that once made Canaan a "land of milk and honey."

Explanation

Having called Ahaz to turn his attention away from Aram and Ephraim, Isaiah points to Assyria. The Assyrian is coming. He is being sent by Yahweh.

And his coming will precipitate the greatest crisis that the people of Judah and the Davidic dynasty have experienced since the division of the Kingdom two hundred years before under Rehoboam. So the Assyrian crisis is seen as a personal problem for Ahaz, a constitutional problem for Judah, and an issue of survival for the dynasty. It must be seen as a turning point in history.

The reference to Ephraim's defection in 930 B.C. puts the announcement in perspective. The kingdom had received God's blessing reluctantly (1 Sam 12), but it was confirmed on a new basis to David (2 Sam 7). But Jeroboam's rebellion tore the fabric of the kingdom's unity as successor to the confederacy and the kingdoms had been living on borrowed time ever since. They had failed to be reunited and now God was moving to terminate an era and the form of his people's existence as an independent political unit. The Assyrian is the means to be used to bring about this change. This theme will control the book's message from chap. 7 through chap. 39.

As Isaiah speaks, Judah has already been devastated by the raids of Rezin and Pekah. Now he announces that Assyria will come and its presence will postpone restoration of the land for a long time. Assyria's presence will be ubiquitous and pervasive (vv 18–19). It will strip the land (v 20). It will reduce the standard of living to a survival limit (vv 21–22). And it will cause the land to lie fallow, uncultivated, and barren (vv 23–25).

The chapter has called attention away from the petty internecine quarrels and battles among the little states of the ANE which had dominated virtually all of Israel's history from its separation from Judah to this time. A new reality was emerging on a much larger scale. Their history would be dominated from this point on by the great empires. They were genuinely unusual "days": a watershed in history.

The prophetic announcement stresses that this is God's doing. The king and the people are urged to look for God's intention and direction in the troubled times to come. Ahaz, whatever his faults, by his more passive acceptance of his vassal's status under Assyria, fit this pattern. Hezekiah in his zeal to put things right for God through reform and rebellion was doomed from the beginning. He was blind to the signals from Heaven that the Lord was not in it.

The Vision of Isaiah is much closer to wisdom's verdict: "there is a time for everything . . . a time to plant and a time to uproot" (Eccl 3:1–2). It suggests a divine historical chronology: a time to rise up and a time to remain still, a time to repent, a time to reform, and a time to be quiet and listen to the challenge of God. It suggests that God's will for his people cannot be achieved by simply "going by the book," not by imitating Joshua or David, or Solomon or Jehoshaphat. One must look and listen, know and understand, to catch the change of signals that come from God.

The program that called for God's people in his land (even in its adapted monarchical form) had failed by the middle of the eighth century. What remained was to clean up the details and launch a new program. Hezekiah, Josiah, and all who like them insisted on "playing David and Joshua" simply got in the way and hindered God's reform. The Vision suggests that God proposed to use the empires in the revised program: first, Assyria in demolishing the old; then Persia (Cyrus) in building the new.

The Vision sees a continuing but different role for "Israel/Jacob" as God's Servant in the new age. But Israel feels she is too old to change jobs and change roles. She feels it is unfair for God to expect her to fit into a new plan of organization. He ought to adapt his plan to her old role. The Vision also sees a central role for Zion, but also a vastly different one. No longer a symbol of rule and power, she is a place of pilgrimage, known for God's presence there. Her experience makes her a fitting "Suffering Servant" to demonstrate God's new plan. But she, too, resists having her role redefined.

The announcement that the Lord will bring Assyria against Judah (v 17) is addressed to Ahaz (sg). The future is announced as the worst crisis for his people and for his dynasty since the division of the kingdom at the death of Solomon. The crisis is being deliberately brought on by Yahweh. When the king of Assyria appears Ahaz should understand this as God's doing.

The announcement is supported by a series of oracles beginning "in that Day":

Vv 18 and 19. The Lord will summon "flies" from Egypt and bees from Assyria—figures for the hordes that will invade the land.

V 20. The Lord will shave the head, legs, and beard, using a foreign hired razor, i.e., the king of Assyria.

Vv 21–22. Each person (will be lucky to have) a cow and two goats to give milk, for curds and milk will be the staple of food.

Vv 23–25. Fine vineyards will be untended and overrun.

The first point is that *Yahweh is bringing* a period of disaster on Judah more terrible than any since the division of the kingdom. The coming of the Assyrian will not bring relief from military pressures or support for the dynasty, as Ahaz hoped. It will be a period of pure disaster and destruction. Yahweh's action will be directed against Ahaz, personally. His indecision, lack of faith and faithful worship were responsible for the situation. It will also be directed against his dynasty, his father's house. A Davidide will never again (possibly with the exception of Josiah's brief reign) rule an independent political state. Although the kingdom continues it will always be only a vassal kingdom, paying tribute, enduring subordination. It will also be against the king's people. The people are always those who suffer in war. But this people shared responsibility with Ahaz and they must also share the judgment.

The first oracle envisions armies summoned from central Africa and from the upper Euphrates swarming over the Judean hills and valleys. The Assyrian Empire was *not* a new element in international relations when Isaiah faced Ahaz in 734 B.C. Shalmanezer III was stopped in westward conquest in 853 B.C. at Qarqar in Syria by a coalition of armies which included Omri of Israel.

But the next serious moves toward the conquest of West-Asia were undertaken by Tiglath-Pileser III (745–27 B.C.). Jeroboam II had died in 746 B.C. In 743 B.C. Tiglath-Pileser met a coalition of armies in northern Syria (cf. Pritchard, *ANET,* 282–83) which included Azriau of Yaudi, possibly Azariah (Uzziah of Judah). (But see Donner, *IJH,* 424, and N. Na'aman, "Sennacherib's 'Letter to God' on His Campaign to Judah," *BASOR* 214 (1974) 25–29.) The battle must have been indecisive, but Assyria continued its pressure. Uzziah died in 740 B.C. By 738 B.C. most of the states of northern Palestine and Syria, including Israel, were paying regular tribute to Assyria. The prophecy in 5:26–30 concerning Assyria's coming against Israel probably refers to that period.

By 734 B.C. Menahem (745–738 B.C.), who had paid tribute to Assyria, is no longer king of Israel. New rulers were fostering rebellion, as the previous paragraphs have demonstrated.

The prophetic word now deals with the coming of the Assyrians. One needed no prophet to know that Assyrian armies would appear in due time to deal with the insurrection. The prophecy distinctively interprets the Assyrian's coming.

Episode D: Swift-Plunder, Hastening-Booty (8:1–4)

Bibliography

Anderson, R. T. "Was Isaiah a Scribe?" *JBL* 79 (1960) 57–58. **Buchanen, G. W.** "The Old Testament Meaning of the Knowledge of Good and Evil." *JBL* 75 (1956) 114–20. **Rignell, L. G.** " 'Das Orakel' *Maher-salal Has-bas.*" *ST* 10 (1956) 40–52.

Translation

Isaiah: [1] *Then Yahweh said to me, "Take for yourself a large tablet* [a] *and write* [b] *on it with a stylus* [c] *of disaster* [c] *'To* [d] *Swift-Plunder, Hastening-Booty.' "* [d] [2] *So I took witnesses* [a] *for myself, faithful witnesses, Uriah, the priest, and Zechariah, son of Jeberechiah.* [b] [3] *When I approached the prophetess,* [a] *she conceived and bore a son. For Yahweh said to me, "Call his name Swift-Plunder, Hastening-Booty,* [4] *for before the lad knows how to say 'my father, my mother,' one will carry away the wealth of Damascus and the plunder of Samaria before the king of Assyria."*

Notes

1.a. גליון גדול. The Versions all agree in rendering גדול "large," but they vary in translating גליון: LXX *τόμον καινοῦ* "new volume"; 'A *διφθερωμα* "tanned hide"; Σ *τευχος* "book"; Θ *κεφαλιδα* "chapter"; Tg לות "tablet"; Vg *librum* "book." Galling uses the only other appearance of the word in 3:23 to suggest that it means a piece of cloth, perhaps of papyrus. He thinks of a family record to support a claim to land. Wildberger has correctly rejected the suggestion. Isaiah's purpose is to gain the attention of the city, not to keep a family record. Driver in *Semitic Writing* (2nd ed. [London: Oxford U.P., 1954] 80, 229) suggests a large placard. In *JSS* 13 (1968) 40, he describes a wooden board covered with wax which was found in Nineveh. This would fit the description here very well. (Cf. also D. Leibel, *Beth Mikra* 15 [1963] 50–55.)

1.b. It is unusual for the narrative to tell of prophets "writing." It is likely that this activity was the exclusive prerogative and skill of scribes. Jeremiah uses an emanuensis in Baruch. But of all the prophets Isaiah is the one most likely to have known that art. (Cf. R. T. Anderson, *JBL* 79 [1960] 57–58.)

1.c. חֶרֶט אֱנוֹשׁ. MT presents the words to mean "a man's stylus." This is a strange usage and has occasioned much discussion. It is common to translate "an ordinary stylus" and refer to similar usages in Exod 32:16 מכתב אלהים "God's writing," or Deut 3:11 and 2 Sam 7:14 where אמת־איש and שבט אנושים are rendered "a usual elle" and "an ordinary rod." But Wildberger notes that both of these are in contrast to God's judgment. That is not the case here. Other commentators (Procksch, Fohrer, and others) have suggested a form of writing known to the common man. But the word here is "stylus," not "writing." Another direction in the search for meaning suggests a different vocalization: אָנוּשׁ. H. Gressmann (*Der Messias*, FRLANT 43 [Göttingen: Vandenhoeck & Ruprecht, 1929] 239, n1) suggested translating this as "a hard stylus." K. Galling ("Ein Stück judäischen Bodenrechts in Jesaja 8," *ZDPV* 56 [1933] 209–18) noted that אָנוּשׁ means "incurable" (Qal pass ptcp √אנשׁ) and suggested it means "a writing that cannot be erased." But Wildberger again comments that חרט means a "stylus," not a "writing." F. Talmage ("חרט אנוש in Isaiah 8:1," *HTR* 60 [1967] 465–68) draws on Akk *enēšu* and Arab *ʾanuṯa,* both of which mean "to be weak" to explain אָנוּשׁ as a broad, soft pen which should make the writing more legible. Wildberger uses the emendation in its literal meaning, "a stylus of sickness" and cites 1QM 12:3 בחרט חיים "a stylus of life" as the linguistic opposite. The stylus that writes disaster may well be the intention of the phrase. (Cf. also D. Leibel, *BMik* 15 (1963) 50–55).

1.d-d. Translations of the name have varied. The two verbs, מהר and חשׁ, may be understood as imperatives, as perfects, or as participles. מהר has also been read as a foreign term for a soldier (A. Jirku, "Zu 'Eilebeute' in Jes 8:1–3," *TLZ* 75 [1950] 118; S. Morenz, "Eilebeute," *TLZ* 74 [1949] 697–99; Aistleitner, *WB* § 1532; A. F. Rainey, "The Military Personnel of Ugarit," *JNES* 24 [1965] 17–27; A. R. Schulmann, "*Mhr* and *Mskb,* Two Egyptian Military Titles of Semitic Origin," *ÄZ* 93 [1966] 123–32; A. F. Rainey, "The soldier-scribe," *JNES* 26 [1967] 58–60). They would translate "Soldier of Booty, Hastening to Plunder." H. Torczyner (*MGWJ* 74 [1930] 257) suggested reading both verbs as perfects and pointing מַהֵר as מִהֵר. If the verbs are to be understood as participles then מַהֵר is a short form of מְמַהֵר (cf. GKC §525 and Zeph 1:14). E. Vogt ("Einige Hebräische Wortbedeutungen," *Bib* 48 [1967] 57–74) notes that מהר is often used as an adverb, "quick," "soon," "immediately" and suggests that the verb נשׂא in v 4 is to be understood here. The use of participles is clearly the best with the translation: "Swift-Plunder, Hastening-Booty."

2.a. וְאָעִידָה seems to indicate a jussive meaning, "So let me take witnesses." LXX reads *καὶ μάρτυράς μοι ποίησον* "make a witness for me" (2 sg aor act impv). Tg has ואַסְהֵיד; Syr has *washed lî sāhdê.* These have led many to suggest emending the word to read וְהָעִידָה—an impv meaning "take witnesses." But Wildberger is surely right in taking the lesser emendation וָאָעִידָה following the Vg reading *et adhibui* which brings the verb into parallel with that in v 3. The verse is narrative: "And so I took witnesses."

2.b. יברכיהו "Jeberechiah." LXX reads *βαραχιου* which would require ברכיהו "Berechiah." Yet MT is to be preferred. LXX is probably comparing it with names in Zech 1:1 and 1:7.

3.a. הַנְּבִיאָה "the prophetess" is used of Miriam (Exod 15:20) and Deborah (Judg 4:4). It appears for Huldah (2 Kgs 22:14; 2 Chr 34:22) and Noadiah (Neh 6:14). But this last is the only instance referring to a prophet's wife. There is no record that she was an active prophet in her own right. Here, by conceiving the child of the ominous name, she is a direct participant in God's revelation and deserves the title. (Cf. A. Jepsen, "Die Nebiah in Jes 8:3," *ZAW* 72 [1960] 267–80; E. Vogt, "Einige Hebräische Wortbedeutungen," *Bib* 48 [1967] 57–74; Z. Falk, *BMik* 14 [1969] 28–36.)

Form/Structure/Setting

The pericope is first person narrative of the type called prophetic autobiography. The passage is composed of two parts, vv 1–2 and vv 3–4. The first half tells of instruction received from God to write on a large board the words למהר שלל חש בז "To 'Swift Plunder Hastening Booty.' " The second tells of the birth of a son who is given this name and of the meaning the name carries. Although the explanation is directly related to the son, it explains the entire passage. The pericope is actually a unit. The writing is dedicated to מהר שלל חש בז. The story implies that the succeeding steps are directly related to that: taking witnesses, producing a son with this name, and explaining the entire process.

The three narrative imperfects use all the possible implications of the form ואעידה "so I took witnesses" (cf. note 2.a.) to describe a normal sequence of resulting action following the imperative of v 1. ואקרב "when I approached" and ותלד "and she bore" continue the sequence of events with the conception and birth. But the next verb ויאמר does not indicate a new step but summarizes the entire sequence with a reference to the imperative beginning and is best translated "for Yahweh said." (Cf. Watts, *Syntax,* 127.)

There is no need to translate the second verb as a pluperfect as Duhm, Marti, Rignell, and Kaiser do: "and I had approached." Isaiah must have known the meaning of the name from the beginning (contra Vriezen, VTSup 1 [1953] 209, n. 2) and he must have understood the name on the board to be that for the son yet to come (so also Vogt and Wildberger). The people knew Isaiah's stand on current policy. They will also have understood the general direction indicated by the announcement on the board even before the birth occasioned repetition and emphasis of it.

The passage is a unity from prior announcement to the explanation.

The pericope uses the formulas of narratives of symbolic actions: v 1 קַח־לְךָ גִּלָּיוֹן גָּדוֹל "take for yourself a large tablet," cf. Hos 1:2; Ezek 4:1; 4:9; 5:1; 1 Kgs 11:31; Jer 13:4; 25:15; 36:2, 28; 43:9; Zech 11:15. The closest parallel is undoubtedly Ezek 37:16. (Cf. Hayes, *OTFC,* 172.)

The outline of such a report should contain the command to perform the act, the report of its performance, and a statement of its meaning. This account reports a command to write, a statement of compliance with an expansion concerning witnesses, then it reports two further actions which continue the symbolic act: the conception, birth, and naming of a son. It then closes with the usual explanation.

Comment

1 The exact meaning of גליון remains uncertain (cf. n. 1.a. above). Such tablets may have been shaped of wood, clay, or leather. Ezekiel speaks of עץ (37:16) in a similar situation, but he seems to mean a carved stick rather than a tablet (cf. Zimmerli, *Ezekiel*). But in 4:1, Ezekiel scratches letters on a tile. It is also unclear where the tablet was to be shown or on what occasion. Wildberger has noted that Hab 2:2 records the practice a century later in Jerusalem of displaying prophecies in easily read letters.

The name is preceded by לְ like that on seals which indicate the owner. But this does not quite fit here. GKC § 119*u* speaks of a meaning like "in relation to" or "of" in the sense of "concerning." This is more likely. (Cf. S. Moscati, *L'epigrafia Ebraica Antica* [Rome: Pontifical Biblical Institute, 1951] 85–89 for a discussion of לְ on jug handles.)

The name Maher-shalal-hash-baz is not a usual name in the OT or the ANE. Noth (*Personennamen,* 9) speaks of it as a product of literary creativity. Yet P. Humbert ("*Mahēr Šalāl Ḥāš Baz,*" *ZAW* 50 [1932] 90–92) and S. Morenz ("Eilebeute," *TLZ* 74 [1949] 697–99) have noted an Egyptian name, *ʾis ḥʾḳ,* which appears in the documents of the Eighteenth Dynasty. The name is, grammatically, composed of two imperatives: "Hurry! Plunder!" The Egyptian military usage may well have been known in Jerusalem in that time (cf. H. Wildberger, "Die Thronnamen des Messias," *TZ* 16 [1960] 314–32). Thus there may well have been known parallels. The applied meaning, however, comes from contemporary history. שלל "plunder" and בזז "booty" occur as a word-pair also in Deut 2:35; 3:7; 20:14; Isa 10:6; Ezek 29:19; 38:12f. The second pair, מהר "swift" and חוש "hastening" are also parallel forms. The repetition enhances both the certainty and the nearness of the events.

2 The practice of taking witnesses is regulated by law (Deut 17:6; 19:15). Two are required. They are called "faithful witnesses." It was important that they be trusted by the public as well as by Isaiah. 2 Kgs 16:10–16 tells of a priest named Uriah who, at the command of King Ahaz, had a new altar built in the Temple. He was apparently the chief priest. If Zechariah is the man mentioned in 2 Kgs 18:2/2 Chr 29:1 as the father-in-law of King Ahaz and grandfather of Hezekiah, the witnesses are drawn from the highest levels of Jerusalem's leadership. Both men's names include "Yahweh." Uriah probably means "Yahweh is Light" (cf. Isa 10:17 and Ps 27:1; Noth, *Personennamen,* 168). Zechariah means "Yahweh has remembered" (cf. Ps 74:2, 18; Lam 3:19; 5:1). Jeberekiah means "May Yahweh bless" (cf. Ps 67:6–7; Ps 115:12–15). Wildberger comments that the names fit Isaiah's times and demonstrate how well the leaders of his day represent the piety of the Psalms.

The reason for witnesses undoubtedly lay in confirming the date of the prophecy. Months, even years would pass before its completion. The political situation would have changed drastically. The written words and the sworn witnesses alone could confirm that and when he had prophesied it.

3 After the sign was written Isaiah approached his wife. "Draw near" (קרב) is used often to describe sexual relations (Gen 20:4; Lev 18:6, 14, 19; 20:16; Deut 22:14; Ezek 18:6). Although Yahweh's specific instructions applied only to the message to be written on the board, the narrative's structure leads the reader to understand that the entire process followed God's instructions and served his purpose.

נביאה "prophetess" must refer to Isaiah's wife. Wildberger is right (contra Duhm and Procksch) that the title does not simply mean "a prophet's wife." Rather it is understood that she, like Hulda (2 Kgs 22:14) served as a prophet in the Temple as well as participating in the sign by birthing a son (cf. the discussion and literature in Wildberger 318). The entire episode and its narration confirm Isaiah's message.

4 The reason for the strange and meaningful name begins with the same words as in 7:16 כי בטרם ידע הנער "for before the lad shall know." But the specific ability is different "to say 'my father,' 'my mother.' " A child can do this at a younger age than one could expect him to turn away from evil and do good.

Then the actual intent of the inscription meant: the booty is to be taken from Damascus and Samaria. The plunderer is the king of Assyria. לפני מלך אשור "before the king of Assyria" pictures a parade of triumph before the king's throne (cf. Pritchard, *ANET,* 274; Pritchard, *ANEP,* I, fig. 100a–b). The prediction was fulfilled. In 733 B.C. Tiglath-Pileser III of Assyria invaded Israel (*MBA,* 147). He reported, "Bit-Ḫumria (=Israel) with all its inhabitants and its goods, I led to Assyria. They overthrew their king Paqaḫa (=Pekah), and I crowned Ausi (=Hoshea) king over them" (*ANET,* 284). Israel's territories were made Assyrian provinces (cf. *MBA,* 148; 2 Kgs 15:29; Isa 9:1) except for a very small area in the highlands of Ephraim. In 732 B.C. Tiglath-Pileser III of Assyria conquered Damascus. That event brought to a close a two hundred-year period in which the Aramean kingdom played a leading role.

Explanation

Chap. 7 has brought the shocking announcement (early in 734 B.C.) that God is bringing the Assyrian army against the land and that his coming will bring very hard times. The prediction put this at some time into the future. In the meantime Judah's patience wears thin as Aram and Israel press their attacks through that year and into the next.

The opening episode in chap. 8 speaks to that issue. God through Isaiah promises a speedy military action. The first public showing with the witnesses may well have followed the meeting with Ahaz (chap. 7) by only a few weeks (i.e., early in 734 B.C.). The birth of the child and the full explanation came late in that year, emphasizing that military relief was hastening to lift the siege. The Assyrian campaign against Israel came in 733 B.C. (i.e., within two years). This timing fits the prediction exactly. Assyria's campaigns have indeed made "swift plunder and hastening booty" against Judah's foes.

This episode continues the series of chap. 7 introduced by the announcement in 7:2 of the alliance between Aram and Israel. Isaiah (and apparently Ahaz) is still convinced that Assyria is the major issue for Judah to face.

This episode is set between the time of that announcement (*ca.* 735–34 B.C.) and Assyria's invasion of Israel (733 B.C.). It narrates events concerning the better part of a year. Assyria's retaliation against Aram and Israel is anticipated. Isaiah speaks after the birth of his son, recounting his earlier prophecy before the child was conceived, reiterating and explaining the message. Retribution on Judah's neighbors is imminent.

The time between the writing and the birth has been critical for Judah. Rezin and Pekah have invaded Judah (*MBA,* 144). Rezin's forces drove down the east bank of Jordan freeing the Edomites from Judean dominance and continuing as far south as Elath (2 Kgs 16:6/2 Chr 28:17). Another force, joined by Pekah's army, surrounded Jerusalem, wreaking havoc on the countryside (2 Kgs 16:5). The freed Edomites attacked the southern cities (2 Kgs 16:6b/2 Chr 28:17) and the Philistines used the occasion to raid border towns (2 Chr 28:18). 2 Kings and 2 Chronicles record a plea from Ahaz to Tiglath-Pileser for help. Both of them pass judgment on Ahaz for unfaithfulness to Yahweh (2 Kgs 16:3–4, 5–10; 2 Chr 28:1–4, 22–26). He is accused of cultic changes in the temple and of pagan practices. He is also accused of appealing to Tiglath-Pileser for help, a political mistake. It is important to note that the Vision of Isaiah takes a very different stance in this section (chaps. 7–13).

While Kings and Chronicles view Judah's weakness as due to the unfaithfulness of the kings like Ahaz and Manasseh, Isaiah sees a turning point in

God's intention for Judah in Uzziah's time which makes Ahaz's policies more compatible with his will than those of Hezekiah. The times (and God's will for his people in them) demanded an acceptance of the Assyrians as God's chosen rulers. Ahaz, for all his religious infidelity to Yahwistic traditions, fitted that time. Hezekiah, with his burning religious and political zeal, did not. That is the point of the Vision with its implied message for fifth-century Jews: Persia's hegemony is Yahweh's will. Accept it! Live with it! Find the will of God for you within it.

This pericope (8:1–4) is an example of Isaiah's ministry in supporting Ahaz's policy of not squandering his dwindling military force to counteract armies which are about to be annihilated anyway. It is a difficult time for Judah. But Isaiah calls upon her and her king to recognize the "signs of the times," to see God's great scheme, and to make their decisions and policies in light of it.

The time has passed when a David could in the name of Yahweh take things in his own hands and police the area. Now the Assyrian is God's policeman and Judah is being prepared to be the "servant people" dedicated to worship and teaching at the Lord's temple as the peoples of the world flow to it. But it would take two centuries more to reach that point and God would twice replace the appointed imperial power. The punitive action against the neighboring outlaws, Aram and Israel, is imminent. So says the Lord through Isaiah's sign. Hang on!

Episode E: Waters of Shiloah Refused (8:5–10)

Bibliography

Budde, K. "Zu Jesaja 8:19–10." *JBL* 49 (1930) 423–28. **Driver, G. R.** "Isa 1–39: Problems." *JSS* 13 (1968) 36–57. **Fullerton, K.** "The Interpretation of Isaiah 8:5–10." *JBL* 43 (1924) 253–89. **Honeyman, A. M.** "Traces of an Early Diakritic Sign in Isa 8:6b." *JBL* 63 (1944) 45–50. **Klein, H.** "Freude an Rezin." *VT* 30 (1980) 229–34. **Lutz, H. M.** *Jahwe, Jerusalem, und die Völker.* WMANT 27 Neukirchen-Vluyn: Neukirchener Verlag, 1968. 40–47. **Rehm, M.** See reference in Excursus on 7:14 as Messianic Prophecy. **Saebø, M.** "Zur Traditionsgeschichte von Jesaja 8:9–10." *ZAW* 76 (1964) 132–44. **Schmidt, H.** "Jesaja 8:9–10," *Stromata,* Festgabe des Akademisch-Theologischen Vereins Zu Giessen, tr. v. G. Bertran (1930) 3–10. **Schroeder, O.** "ומשוש eine Glosse zu רצון." *ZAW* 32 (1912) 301–02. **Wolverton, W. I.** "Judgment in Advent: Isaiah 8:5–15." *ATR* 37 (1955) 284–91.

Translation

Isaiah: 5 *Then Yahweh spoke to me yet again:* 6 *"Because this people has refused the waters of Shiloah which flow gently: a joy* [a] *to Rezin and Remaliah's son,*
7 *therefore behold my Lord* (*is*) *bringing up over them the waters of the River* 3+2
strong and many,

the King of Assyria 2+2
and all his glory.
And it shall rise over all its channels, 3+3+2
and it shall go over all its banks.
8 *And it shall fly into Judah.*
It shall overflow and pass by, 2+2
unto the neck it will reach.[a]
And there shall be a stretching of its wings, 3+3
filling the breadth of your[b] *land."*
Chorus: *God, be with us! (Immanuel)* 2
9 *Make an uproar, you peoples, and be broken!* 3+4
and give ear all you lands afar!
Gird yourselves and be broken! 2+2
Gird yourselves and be broken!
10 *Counsel counsel! Nothing will come of it!* 2+1
Speak a word! It will not stand! 2+2
For God is with us (Immanuel). 3

Notes

6.a. ומשוש את־רצין "and a joy to Rezin" is a syntactically awkward phrase. Hitzig and Giesebrecht (*Die Berufsbegabung der Alttestamentlichen Propheten* [Göttingen: Vandenhoeck & Ruprecht, 1897]) suggested omitting את־רצין ובן־רמליהו "to Rezin and Remaliah's son" and changing משוש to מסוס (cf. 10:18) meaning "the gently flowing and running water." But Wildberger (321) has correctly called this impossible because the water of Shiloah is a picture of Yahweh's protection for Jerusalem which cannot be described as running away. The suggestions to omit רצין "Rezin" (Schroeder) or to amend משוש to משה "pull out (of the water)" (Honeyman) must also be rejected. Wildberger would change it to מָסוֹס and אֵת to לפני to mean "but melts before the pride of Rezin." With all this, it seems better to work with the received text, awkward as it is. But the vowel pointing must be מָשׂוֹשׂ—an abs before the preposition.

8.a. LXX appears to have another text *καὶ ἀφελεῖ ἀπὸ τῆς Ἰουδαίας ἄνθρωπον ὅς δυνήσεται κεφαλὴν ἆραι ἤ δυνατὸν συντέλεσασθαί τι* "and he will cut off from Judah a man who will be able to raise a head or complete something mighty." Other Versions follow MT.

8.b. The 2nd pers seems strange and appears to make the passage address Immanuel. In spite of this unclear address, it should be kept. However, עמנו אל "God with us/Immanuel" should be read with the following line. See *Explanation.*

Form/Structure/Setting

The prophet relates an oracle received from Yahweh in vv 5–8. The first lines (vv 5, 6, 7a) are prose. The rest of the oracle is preserved in tight parallel lines of poetry. The prophet is the speaker throughout as he relates what God has said to him in indirect quotation.

The speech is a threat. V 6 gives the reason. V 7a–b announces the act of God. V 7c–8b interprets the results of God's action. V 8c adds a comment which changes the metaphor and is only loosely related to the preceding lines. The last stichos of v 8 belongs with the following lines. Its first person plural indicates the beginning of the choral speech which continues through v 10. It opens and closes with עמנו אל, Immanuel.

The passage fits the genre of the "challenge to battle" (Saebø, *ZAW* 76 [1964] 132–44; R. Bach, *Die Aufforderung zur Flucht und zum Kampf im alttestamentlichen Prophetenspruch,* WMANT 9 [Neukirchen: Neukirchener Verlag, 1962]).

Parallel forms are found in Jer 46:3–6, 9 and Joel 3:9–12. Overtones of the belief that Jerusalem will be kept unharmed may be noted like those in Pss 46, 47, 76 (cf. Kaiser). Immanuel has a parallel in Ps 46:8, 12 יהוה צבאות עמנו "Yahweh of Hosts (is) with us." Here elements of holy war thought are mixed with those of Davidic kingship and Zion's sanctity (cf. Wildberger).

Comment

6 העם הזה "this people." The term continues to echo the covenant identification (cf. 1:3b), the people without understanding who are destined to destruction and exile (6:9, 10). The earlier passages speak of the whole people, but particularly the claims of the Northern Kingdom to represent them all. Note the reference is directly to the Kingdom of Israel (contra Young).

הַשִּׁלֹחַ "Shiloah" is a noun from the common root שלח, to send. Cf. Akkad *šalḫu* "watering pipe" and *šiliḫtu* "water course." The verb in piel means to "send water" (Ps 104:10; Ezek 31:4). A parallel word is הַשֶּׁלַח (Neh 3:15), which means an aqueduct or conduit for water. מֵי הַשִּׁלֹחַ occurs only here in the OT. It is unlikely that the reference is to the tunnel of Shiloah, first built by Hezekiah (2 Kgs 20:20; 2 Chr 32:30). The "waters of the Shiloah" are those diverted from the spring of Sihon southward from the east of the city (M. Burrows, *ZAW* 70 [1958] 226). The waters of the aqueduct flow softly and gently. Isaiah uses the "waters of the Shiloah which flow gently" to characterize the policy of Ahaz (cf. 7:1–9) which accepts the necessity of loyalty to Assyria as being in the will of God for that time. The spirit of rebellion has no time for the slow processes to work, but demands action now.

מָשׂוֹשׂ, "a joy" to Rezin. Israel's willingness to participate in Rezin's uprising was undoubtedly a "joy" to him and his puppet ruler in Samaria.

7 מי הנהר "the waters of the River" contrasts with "the waters of Shiloah." The simple metaphors relate irrigation ditches with rushing river water. But "the river" inevitably also implies the Euphrates and the nations beyond. This contrasts with the policy of Jerusalem's "waters of Shiloah" which have counseled quiet acceptance of Assyria's sovereignty. Rebellion and refusal to pay taxes will bring the flood-waters of the King of Assyria. "Glory" is a synonym for "might" or "power."

8 עמנו אל Immanuel is the name of the child who is a sign (7:14). It means simply "God—with us." It may imply an indicative "God is with us" like the name of the child or the clause in 8:10c. Or it may be an imperative "God be with us," as here.

9–10 The conviction of these verses is that events follow the determined will of God. He has promised that Jerusalem will survive. No effort of the enemy—even the swirling waters of the Assyrian—can change that. Judah's villages may suffer, but God's city will survive.

Explanation

The prophecy (v 6) clearly relates to the alternatives which "this people" (Israel) faced. Instead of following a policy of peaceful coexistence with the growing power of Assyria ("the waters of Shiloah which flow gently"), it chose to follow the reckless adventure of rebellion and coercion advocated by Rezin and Pekah. Behind the Lord's reaction lies the growing understanding in the Vision that he has raised up Assyria to rule the world. To resist Assyria is to resist Yahweh. So now it is the Lord himself who brings the Assyrian against Israel. This final rebellion seals the doom already envisioned in 1:1–7 and 2:6–8. Also, here as in 1:8ff, Judah is caught up in the resultant flood. Israel and Aram were buffers against the Assyrian threat. When they are gone Judah is a border state and bears the brunt of Assyrian power.

The prophecy implies that Judah should learn from Israel's mistake. The policy Ahaz has followed is like "the waters of Shiloah," avoiding offense to Assyria. Despite the coming repercussions of Israel's adventures, Isaiah in the name of Yahweh encourages Ahaz to continue this policy.

The description of the dangers for Judah elicits a response from the chorus. The threat to Judah is a threat to Zion where Yahweh is present in the Temple. The shock that the chorus feels is expressed in terms like that used in the Temple liturgies which claim the real presence of Yahweh in the Holy City and believe that no powers on earth can overcome it.

Vv 9–10 echo the theme of 1:24–27; 2:2–4; 4:2–6. It will continue in passages such as chaps. 13, 24, to the end of the Vision in chap. 63 and 66. The events, tumultuous as they are, are in God's control. His purpose and his promise remain secure. He has promised his presence for Zion. Nothing will overcome that. The key to the passage is the appeal to God's promise. So long as God is present, the city is secure (cf. Ezek 10–11 where God removes his presence from the city before it is destroyed).

Episode F: Yahweh Is Your Fear (8:11–15)

Bibliography

Driver, G. R. "Two Misunderstood Passages of the O.T." *JTS* 6 (1955) 82–84. **Ford, J. M.** "Jewel of Discernment; a study of stone symbolism." *BZ* 11 (1967) 109–16. **Häusserman, F.** *Wortempfang und Symbol in der alttestamentlichen Prophetie.* BZAW 58. Giessen: Töpelmann, 1932. **Lohfink, N.** "Isaiah 8:12–14." *BZ* 7 (1963) 98–104. **Rignell, L. G.** "Das Orakel 'Maher-salal Hasbas.' " *ST* 10 (1956) 40–52. **Stahlin, G.** "Skandalon" BFCT II 24 (1930). **Wolverton, W. I.** "Judgment in Advent." *ATR* 37 (1955) 284–91.

Translation

Prophet: 11 *For thus Yahweh said to me, as* [a] *though someone took* [b] *(me) by the hand so that he might turn me away* [c] *from walking in the way of this people,*

Yahweh: 12 *Do (pl) not call "a conspiracy"* [a] *everything that this people calls "a conspiracy." What it fears, you need not fear nor* [b] *dread.*

Prophet: [13] *You may call Yahweh of Hosts "a conspirator"!* [a] 2+2
He is your (pl) fear! 2+2
He is your (pl) dread! [b]
[14] *He shall become a conspiracy* [a] 2+2
and a stone of stumbling;
a rock of offense 2+3
for the two houses of Israel; [b]
a trap and a snare 2+2
for the inhabitant [c] *of Jerusalem.*
[15] *Many shall be offended* [a] *because of them* 3+2+2
and shall fall and be broken
and shall be snared and taken captive.

Notes

11.a. *BHK*[3] reads בחזקת "in . . .". *BHS* reads with L, C, DSS[Isa] and other MSS כחזקת "as . . . ."

11.b. חזקת "take" is an inf constr here. Cf. Bauer-Leander § 43*g*.

11.c. MT points וְיִסְּרֵנִי as impf from יסר "to teach." But this does not fit the context. Gesenius (*Kommentar,* I, 132, n. 2) suggested reading it as וְיְסִרֵנִי from סור "to turn away." This is supported by Σ *και απεστησε με*, Syr *nasṭeni,* and DSS[Isa] ויסירני, and is to be preferred.

12.a. Although the introduction implies a word for the prophet alone, the oracle is in the 2nd pers pl. It is obviously addressed to a group. The words of v 12 are repeated in v 13, with one variation: קשר in v 12 parallels תקדישו "you call holy" in v 13. It appears that one of these has been changed. Wildberger is right in holding that both should be קשר. The translation of this word is debated. The root means to "tie in a knot." LXX translates here with *σκληρόν* "stubborn." G. R. Driver (*JTS* 6 [1955] 82) translates as "knotty affair," "difficulty." Lindblom (*The Immanuel Section*) and Kaiser follow suit. Wildberger, however, correctly notes that the noun קשר in other places in the OT regularly means "conspiracy."

12.b. Tg makes the line a complete parallel as if MT read: . . . ואת־מערצו לא "and what it dreads, you need not dread" (cf. *BHS*). But this is not necessary. Hebrew parallelism is seldom complete.

13.a. For the change of תקדישו to תקשירו, cf. n. 12.a. above.

13.b. MT is a ptcp. A change of one vowel makes מַעֲרַצְכֶם "dread," a noun parallel to מוראכם "fear" as Duhm, Buhl (*Jesaja,* 2nd ed. [Copenhagen: Gyldendal, 1912]) suggested. Cf. also ʹA *θροησις*, Σ Θ *κραταιωμα*, Vg *terror vester.*

14.a. מקדש "considered holy" continues the problem of תקדישו in v 13. It is not a good parallel to אבן נגף "stone of stumbling" and צור מכשול "rock of offense." Wolverton (*ATR* 37 [1955] 288) translates "taboo-place." LXX translates *ἁγίασμα* "holy place" but puts a negative before the following parallels. Tg has פורען "recompense." Others omit or have מוקש "snare." Driver (83) suggests מקשיר be translated "cause of difficulty." Wildberger (335) is preferable, reading מקשר "conspiracy."

14.b. LXX reads *ὁ δε οἶκος Ἰακώβ* for לשני בתי ישראל. It is unusual for MT to speak of "two houses of Israel," especially parallel to יושב ירושלם "inhabitant of Jerusalem." But there is no compelling reason to change it.

14.c. Many MSS as well as LXX OL Σ read a plural יושבי "inhabitants" for MT's singular יושב.

15.a. Many commentators (including Duhm and Leslie) suggest omitting the beginning of v 15. But Wildberger correctly sees that כשל "offend" is necessary to pick up the מכשול "offense" of v 14.

Form/Structure/Setting

The passage is addressed to a group of intimates. Perhaps these are the "disciples" mentioned in the next pericope. They are cautioned against the general panic of "the times." "This people" is often identified as those of Jerusalem. But in chap. 9 it is used of Israel and the occurrences in 8:6 can also best be understood of Israel. Here, too, it must describe Israel's attitude toward Assyrian sovereignty and Judah's reluctance to join in the rebellion. So Yahweh instructs the prophet and his group concerning their position in that troubled time.

The pericope is marked in the beginning by the particle כי "for" which connects it to the last verse of the chorus. The end in v 15 closes the discussion of choices and turns to other matters. The passage is introduced by a prophetic first person narrative in prose (v 11). It reports a warning oracle from Yahweh (v 12) and continues with an expansion of the oracle by the prophet in the form of a commentary.

Vv 12–15 are a threatening oracle. V 11 is an introduction marking it as a word from the Lord. It is a "hard saying" and thus needs the legitimizing formula.

(Note the word play in קשר, תקשיר, and מקשר; ירא and מורא; העריץ and מערץ; מכשול and כשל; מוקש and נוקש. Also note the alliteration between מורא, מוקש, and נוקש; between מערץ, מקשר, מכשול, and מוקש; and between ונלכדו, ונוקשו, ונשברו, and ונפלו.)

Comment

11 The usual prophetic formula to report a word from God is expanded with a note about the manner and intention of the word (cf. Ezek 1:3d and 8:1d). העם הזה "this people" resumes the reference of v 6 and must refer to the Kingdom of Israel. *The way of this people* refers to their determination to join in rebellion against Assyria. Isaiah is being taught that Yahweh has brought the Assyrian to power. To oppose Assyria at this stage is to oppose God.

12 קשר "conspiracy" is a word of ambiguous intent here. The verse calls for critical and independent thinking from the prophet and the people of Jerusalem. This is an emotional epithet being used to urge Jerusalem to back Israel and Aram in their rebellion. Policy which is born of panic is not sound. Israel's fear of Aram or of Assyria need not be the motive for Jerusalem's decisions.

13 The focus of Jerusalem's attention should be on Yahweh—not on the "scare propaganda" of Israel. *A conspirator* (see the textual note on this) is a reminder that Yahweh is the activator in history—not the Assyrian.

14 The idea of *conspiracy* is developed in this verse. The events of those dark decades are incomprehensible to Israelites or Jerusalemites. No easy theological clichés will explain them. The parallel terms, *stone of stumbling* and *offense, trap* and *snare,* develop the implicit idea of *conspiracy.*

Explanation

This warning, which shows just how confusing the times were for believer and prophet alike, picks up the theme of 6:9–13. It was a natural reaction for Judah and Israel to stand together against the foreign invader. It would have been natural for the Davidic heir from Zion to lead the allies in the name of Yahweh as his grandfather had done. It would have been natural for Yahweh to defend "his land" against attack as in the time of the Judges. But the entire Vision of Isaiah has stressed that these were not usual times. Yahweh was doing something different. The people are called to look to him and wait for his word. He, in judgment, had already decided to turn Israel over to its enemies to be destroyed (1:1–7) and to have Judah "purged" with only Jerusalem surviving (1:8–2:4). Yahweh himself had called the Assyrian to do these things (7:17–8:8). All this was difficult to comprehend or to accept. But to resist it was futile.

What was difficult in the situation lay in the decisions and actions of God—not in the rise of Assyria. If one wants to find fault, do not blame Assyria, question God. Yahweh himself is "the conspiracy." His decisions are the stone of stumbling and the snare. If people are "trapped," broken, and "taken captive," it is because they cannot accept and relate to God's judgments and directions for this age and the age to come. It is a "knee-jerk" reaction for one to defend himself. But if this means fighting against God, it is a very unwise reaction. This message applied to Jerusalem in the eighth century. But it was equally applicable to Jews trying to adjust to the changed situation of the sixth or fifth centuries. It can equally apply to Jews facing the claims of Christ in the first century A.D..

Episode G: Sealing the Prophet's Testimony (8:16–18)

Bibliography

Boehmer, J. B. " 'Jahwes Lehrlinge' im Buch Jesaja." *ARW* 33 (1936) 171–75. **Driver, G. R.** "Hebrew Notes on Prophets and Proverbs." *JTS* 41 (1940) 162–75. ———. "Isaianic Problems." *FS W. Eilers.* Wiesbaden: Harrassowitz, 1967. 43–57. **Ginsburg, H. L.** "An Unrecognized Allusion to Kings Pekah and Hoshea of Israel." *Eretz Israel* 5 (1958) 61–65. **Guillaume, A.** "Paronomasia in the Old Testament." *JSS* 9 (1964) 282–90. **Rost, L.** "Gruppenbildungen im Alten Testament." *TLZ* 80 (1955) 1–8. **Skehan, P. W.** "Some Textual Problems in Isaiah." *CBQ* 22 (1960) 47–55. **Whitley, C. F.** "The Language of Exegesis of Isaiah 8:16–23." *ZAW* 90 (1978) 28–43.

Translation

Prophet: 16 *Binding* [a] *of testimony* [b]*—sealing of instruction with my disciples* [c] *(will be there)*; 17 *and I will wait for Yahweh who is hiding his face from the house of Jacob and I will hope for him.* 18 *Behold I and the children which Yahweh has given to me (became) signs and symbols in Israel from Yahweh of Hosts who dwells in Mount Zion.*

Notes

16.a. צור "binding" may be impv or inf abs. Its counterpart חתום "sealing" is pointed as an impv sg. If both verbs are understood as impv, the speaker must be Yahweh and the למדים are his disciples (as Boehmer, *ARW* 33 [1936] 171–75, suggests). V 17 then introduces a new speaker. Following Wildberger (342) and Watts (*Translation,* 19), the reading as an inf abs is preferred (with the pointing change [cf. BHK]). Thus the speaker is the prophet throughout vv 16–18.

16.b. תעודה "testimony." Ginsburg's emendation (*Eretz Israel* 5 [1958] 62), based on the old Aram *ʿddw* "soothsayer," is unnecessary. LXX has a totally different understanding of the line.

16.c. LXX renders בלמדי as *τοῦ μὴ μαθεῖν* (מִלְּמֹד) "of those who do not learn." Syr connects it to the following sentence. Neither change is justified. Tur Sinai ("Isaiah I–XII," *Studies in the Bible,* ScrHier 8 [Jerusalem: Magnes, 1961] 175) emends to למדיה "her strings" following למדים in the Mishna.

Form/Structure/Setting

Lindblom (*The Immanuel Section,* 46) has called the genre a "prophetic confession" to be compared with the words of Jeremiah and the lamentations among the Psalms. The verses are written in prose. The scene in which Isaiah the prophet and his son have been introduced by name in 7:3 and in which he speaks in the first person (8:1–3; 8:4–8; 8:11–15) is brought to climax in the prophet's withdrawal with his sons. However, the scene which makes so much of signs and sons continues on these themes through 9:6[7].

Comment

16 The words are clipped and abrupt. Each deserves a comment. תעודה "testimony" is a rare form found only here, v 20, and Ruth 4:7. The basic meaning of the root is "to give testimony," "to be a witness." The hiphil form means "to warn." Wildberger correctly notes how fitting the use is for the speaker of the covenant festival who confronts the people with the word about the will of God.

תורה "instruction" also fits the teaching activity of the prophet. It also fitly describes the priestly teaching of tradition and thus the Torah of Moses, the Pentateuch.

The meaning of בלמדי "with my disciples" has occasioned wide discussion along with the *binding* and *sealing.* The first undoubtedly implies that Isaiah has built up a circle of supporters who hang on his words. Wildberger's warning not to suppose a formal "school of prophets" like that of Elisha (1 Kgs 20:35; 2 Kgs 2:3, 5, 7, 15; 4:1–38) or a king of "spiritual Israel" within the nation is appropriate (cf. L. Rost, *TLZ* 80 [1955] 4). Some interpreters (Duhm; J. Mauchline, *Isaiah 1–39,* TBC [London: SCM, 1962]) have understood this to mean Isaiah committed to them a written scroll. But there is no further evidence of this. Others translate *with my disciples* meaning "in their presence" (Dillmann, Kaiser). Others have taken it to mean "through my disciples," "with their help" (Hitzig; H. Ewald, *Commentary on the prophets of the OT,* tr. J. F. Smith [London: Williams & Norgate, 1875/1881]). Fohrer would eliminate the word *my disciples* altogether.

A figurative intention is more meaningful as Gray, Procksch, Leslie, and Wildberger have noted. O. Eissfeldt (*Der Beutel der Lebendigen* [Leipzig: Akademie der Wissenschaften, 1960] 26) suggests that the figure is that of tying up a purse. As one preserves something precious in a purse, so Isaiah deposits his treasure of warnings and teachings with his disciples. The word appears again in 50:4 and 54:13 of those who are taught and led of God.

17 Isaiah anticipates a longer period of time before his words are fulfilled. His attitude of *waiting* is expanded to include *hope.* קוה is a word on the lips of the suppliant in the Psalms of Lament (Pss 25:2, 5, 21; 27:14; 130:5); "I will hope in Yahweh." חכה "wait," though found in Ps 33:20 and Ps 106:13 (not Laments), also fits the context in Hab 2:3 and Zeph 3:8. Wildberger (" 'Glauben' im Alten Testament," *ZTK* 65 [1968] 137–38) has noted their near relation to האמין "believe" of 7:9b. (Cf. C. Westermann, "Das Hoffen im Alten Testament," *Gesammelte Studien,* ThB 24 [München: Kaiser, 1964] 219–65.)

Hiding his face is also a theme of Psalm Laments (Pss 10:11; 13:2; 44:25[24] and others). Thanksgiving Psalms look back on a time when God "hid his face" (Pss 30:8[7]; 22:25[24]). Isaiah does not hope for a return of a personal relationship, but for the fulfillment of God's word. When God's face shines over his people, his grace is abundantly in evidence. If it is hidden, they are left to the frightful sense of being lost and abandoned (Pss 104:29; 143:7; Deut 32:20; Jer 33:5; Mic 3:4). This often means being left to power of the enemy (Ezek 39:23). The historical period here is that of Pekah's and Hoshea's reigns in Israel with the Assyrian incursions of 732 and 724–21 B.C. which marked the end of the Northern Kingdom.

House of Jacob refers to the Northern Kingdom as it and similar references do throughout this section. The distinction made here between "Jacob" and "Judah" or "Jerusalem" has been lost on most interpreters, who have failed to note the oscillation between the two themes which began in chap. 1 and which continues especially through chap. 12. The distinction is important in the Vision, not only because of the different fates of the two nations in the eighth century, but also because of the identification of Jacob/Israel with the Jewish dispersion in chaps. 40–48 as distinct from the inhabitants of Jerusalem in chaps. 49–54.

18 This section (7:1–9:7) is filled with references to *signs* and *symbols,* many of which consist of children and their names (see C. Keller, "Das Wort OTH," [Diss., Basel, 1946]). This verse reinforces the earlier references. Their very presence in Jerusalem was a reminder of Yahweh's presence and intentions during the "silent years" that follow.

In Israel—from Yahweh of Hosts who dwells in Mt. Zion. The juxtaposition is not accidental. The period is crucial for the relation of Israel and Jerusalem. The war posed critical questions concerning Yahweh's position. Will he support Israel with its traditions of election or Jerusalem with its claim of favors for David? The question raised by Jeroboam's rebellion two centuries before has come to a head. Isaiah's intervention (7:1–9) and the Immanuel sign (7:10–16) provided one answer. His second son's birth (8:1–4) and the following oracle (8:5–8) provide a second. They remain as signs of Yahweh's decision that dooms the Northern Kingdom and confirms his support of Jerusalem and its king.

Wildberger notes Isaiah's qualified support of Zion traditions. Zion is "the city of God, most holy of the dwellings of the Highest" (Pss 46:5[4]; 48:2, 4[3]; 78:3; 84:2[1]; 87:1–3). When David brought the Ark to Jerusalem and installed it in a permanent resting place (Ps 132:5–13), it symbolized Yahweh's taking residence in the city (see Pss 74:2; 135:21; and A. Kuschke, "Die Lagervorstellung der priestlichen Erzählung," *ZAW* 63 [1951] 84–86; G. Fohrer, "Σιών, Ἰηρουσαλημ, . . ." *TDNT* 7:307–19; W. Schmidt, "מִשְׁכָּן," *ZAW* 75 [1963] 91–92). In exilic and post-exilic prophets from Ezekiel to Joel it was a very important concept, as it is here in Isaiah (2:3; 56:7; 57:13; 65:11, 25; 66:20). See T. C. Vriezen, "Essentials of the Theology of Isaiah," *Israel's Prophetic Heritage,* FS J. Muilenberg (New York: Harper & Brothers, 1962), 128–31.

Explanation

Isaiah's brief appearance which began in 7:1 is brought to an end by his own act and decision. The Vision records his next activity in the year that Ahaz died. In the meantime Assyria's invasions of 732 and 724–21 B.C. will have brought the Northern Kingdom to an end. Only the submissive policies of Ahaz will have spared Judah a similar fate.

Isaiah speaks of "testimony" and "instruction," descriptions of the word of God which has been revealed. He speaks of "binding" and "sealing": recording and preserving through a difficult time for a time of better hearing and understanding. It is committed to his "disciples" who have listened and learned the precious words.

The times are dark because Yahweh is "hiding his face" from the Northern Kingdom. The decision about their fate has already been reached (10:22b) and God does not entertain further entreaty on their behalf. The prophet sets an example of the proper attitude for the believer in such a time. He will "wait for Yahweh" and he will "hope for him," expecting a day when his countenance will turn toward his people, when his spirit will once again move among them. In the meantime he is aware that he and his children with their meaningful names are signs and symbols reminding Judah and Jerusalem that God has spoken, warned and encouraged them before and during those dark hours. For Yahweh of Hosts, God of history and of judgment continues to make his home on Zion's ridge.

Episode H: To Instruction and to Testimony (8:19–22)

Bibliography

Carroll, R. P. "Translation and Attribution in Isaiah 8:19ff." *BT* 31 (1980) 126–34. **Hoffner, H. A., Jr.** "Second Millennium Antecedents to the Hebrew ʾÔ*B*." *JBL* 86

(1967) 385–401. **Jepsen, K.** "Call and Frustration: A New Understanding of Isaiah VIII 21–22." *VT* 32 (1982) 145–57. **Müller, H. P.** "Das Wort von den Totengeistern Jes. 8:19ff." *WO* 8 (1975) 65–76. **Schmidtke, F.** "Träume, Orakel und Totengeister als Kunder der Zukunft in Israel und Babylonien." *BZ* 11 (1967) 240–46. **Schwarz, G.** "Zugunsten der Lebenden an die Toten?" *ZAW* 86 (1974) 218–20.

Translation

Protester (derisively):	19 *If they say to you,*	3+3+2
	"Seek out the fathers and the diviners,	
	who chirp and mutter!	
	Should not a people	2+2
	seek out its God?	
	On behalf of the living,	2+2
	(seek out) the dead?"	
	20 *To Instruction and to Testimony!* [a]	2
Second Voice:	*If not—* [b]	2+3+3
	they speak like this word	
	which has no thing to prevent disaster. [c]	
Third Voice:	21 *If someone* [a] *pass by her,* [b]	2+2
	hard-pressed and hungry, [c]	
	when he is hungry	1+2+1
	he will rage. [d]	
	He will curse by his king and by his God	3+2
	and turn his face upward.	
Fourth Voice:	22 *But let them look at the land.* [a]	2+3
	Behold, distress and darkness,	
	gloom of anguish,	2+2
	and being thrust into darkness. [b]	

Notes

20.a. תורה "instruction" and תעודה "testimony" are translated in terms of 8th-century meaning. By late post-exilic times, after Ezra's reform, they would have been understood as "Law" and "Revelation" (Wildberger).

20.b. This translation takes the opening two pairs of words as short and abrupt phrases to be read alone. MT's accentuation fully supports this for the first pair and partly supports the second break.

20.c. LXX δῶρα and Syr *šuḥda* suggest שחד, meaning "give a bribe," instead of שחר "be black." Driver (JTS 41 [1940]162; and "Isaianic Problems," *FS W. Eilers* [Wiesbaden: Harrassowitz, 1967], 45) refers to the use of שחר in Isa 47:11 and KB's translation "magic" as well as the Syr *šḥr* (pael) and Arabic *s̱ḥr* meaning "tame," or "force." He suggests that שחר be translated "magic" or "power to overcome (disaster)." Perhaps δῶρα "gift" was also understood as the gift to perform magic or to prophesy.

21.a. The subject is unnamed.

21.b. Rignell (*ST* 10 [1957] 49) suggests translating בה "as a result of it." *BHK* and *BHS* suggest emending to בארץ "in (the) land," which may catch the intended meaning. But emendation is unnecessary.

21.c. Guillaume (*JSS* 9 [1964] 289) translates רעב "frightened, weak, cowardly" following the Arabic *raʿib.* Wildberger (355) rightly responds that Hebrew does not have this word and that repetition here is a matter of style, not tautology.

21.d. DSS^{Isa} has יתקצף, an impf instead of MT's perf with *wāw.* E. Y. Kutscher (*The Language and Linguistic Background of the Isaiah Scroll,* STDJ 6 [Leiden: E. J. Brill, 1974]) has shown that consecutive perfects were in decline in Qumran literature.

22.a. DSS[Isa] adds the definite article הארץ "the land."

22.b. Wildberger (355) notes that אפלה מנדח may mean "(he is) pushed into the darkness." LXX reads *σκότος ὥστε μὴ βλέπειν* "darkness so that (there is) no seeing" which would imply Hebrew אפלה מֵרְאוֹת and is not close to MT. Gray noted long ago a similar vocabulary in Amos 5:20 (ואפל ולא־נֹגַהּ) and suggested emending מנדח to read מִנֹּגַהּ (see *BHS*) meaning "from shining, or brightness." (Cf. Jer 23:12.)

Form/Structure/Setting

The first question must settle the limits of the passage and its place in the book. Wildberger (343) has noted that v 19 is certainly not a continuation of the previous verses, but he has failed to draw the obvious consequences. With Isaiah and his family withdrawn from the scene (v 17), responses to his word and work are in order. For the first time in the Vision the opposition has a voice. The people who have been characterized as unknowing, deaf, and blind can now speak out. Most of chaps. 9–12 will express their response.

The end of this first transitional section is more difficult to mark. The different choices in the Hebrew and the Versions show this. Even in the Hebrew, B has divided v 23, putting the second part in chap. 9—a division which Wildberger has adopted (355). LXX follows the same division. The English versions put all of v 23 into the ninth chapter. V 23 responds directly to v 22 using the same word, which ties the closing verse to the introductory section. But the verse also moves to the theme of hope and confirmation which will characterize the next six verses. It is a true bridge between the passages.

Recognition of the dramatic dialogue in the section enables us to follow the abrupt changes without resorting to emendations which those who have read the passage otherwise have felt necessary. The dialogue reflects the skeptical responses of Israel's hearers who prefer the more comfortable assurances of traditional forms.

The Hebrew presents word plays in עבר and רעב and alliteration which cannot be reflected in translation: קלל/חתקצף, מעלה/מלכו, מעוף/מנדח, צוקה/צרה. Also the similar vowel sounds of אֲפֵלָה/חֲשֵׁכָה and the dark closing words מעוף, צוקה, and נדח (cf. Wildberger, 357).

Comment

19 *Seek out the fathers:* a reference to the cult of the dead and the practice of receiving oracles from the spirits of those who had gone before. Spiritualist mediums flourished throughout the ANE. (Cf. the experience of Saul with the medium from Endor in 1 Sam 28:7–20.)

Diviners who chirp and mutter: a derisive reference to practices of necromancy such as were common in the area. Israel's prophets were undoubtedly put on a level with Canaanite fortune-tellers by the unbelieving.

The dead is again a reference to the cult of the dead. Ancient saints are sought out to help the living.

The ANE (including Israel) was as inclined to fortune tellers as any other people and time. Mosaic legislation forbids such (Deut 18:10–11). But the context suggests that this is directed at Isaiah. As a prophet, he brings a "word from the Lord" which is unmediated. This speech implies that he is no better than the diviners and the spiritualists.

20 The first response ends with a call to turn their attention to תורה "instruction" and תעודה "testimony." *Torah* or *Instruction* or *Law* was the area of the priests. The people sought their instruction on forms of worship and on the interpretation of tradition. In post-exilic times it would be understood as "law"—indeed as "law-book." The reference here is to the official priestly teaching based on legal precedent. Tradition attributes its source to Moses.

תעודה "testimony" is as unusual as *torah* is familiar. This form appears here, in 8:16, and in Ruth 4:7 only. In Ruth the reference is to the symbolic removal of a sandal: "this was a תעודה in Israel." Earlier in that verse, the words הגאולה "the redemption" and התמורה "the exchange" are parallel in form and setting with התעודה, meaning the means of recording a transaction. Isa 8:2 makes extraordinary use of this word in another form: אעידה עדים נאמנים "I called reliable witnesses to witness" the Maher-shalal-hash-baz prophecy. In v 16 Isaiah instructs that the "witness" and the "torah" should be bound up among his disciples. He considers his message to be vital for the instruction and life of his people.

In v 20, *testimony* refers to the other leg on which authority rested: royal tradition and theory. Tradition traced this to David. It included the recited account of God's revelation to Nathan (2 Sam 7) and other teachings about the monarchy and Jerusalem. Together *Instruction* and *Testimony* included all the authority of official traditions. This is opposed to a prophet who claims to be God's spokesman.

21–22 Vv 20b–21 warn of the potential result from such words of warning, leading to panic and chaos. V 22 calls attention to the reality already abroad in the land.

Explanation

This is a transition episode between the great Isaiah scenes and the traditional expressions of comfort that come in chap. 9. When the dialogue in the section is recognized, the abrupt changes of person and viewpoint that have disturbed interpreters in the past can be appreciated and understood.

In derisive comments the crowd characterizes their view of a prophet who purports to have a word direct from God. Except for Ahaz's reply to Isaiah in 7:12, this is the first time representatives of people who are "unknowing, deaf, and blind" have a chance to speak.

The genre of the larger section is that which pits prophet against prophet (cf. S. de Vries, *Prophet against Prophet* [Grand Rapids: Eerdmans, 1979]; J. L. Crenshaw, *Prophetic Conflict* [New York: De Gruyter, 1971]). Elijah's conflict with the Ba'al prophets (1 Kgs 18) was an extreme form. Micaiah's conflict with Yahweh prophets (1 Kgs 22) is more typical, while Jeremiah's disagreement with Hananiah (Jer 28) shows the issue at its height. Note: the other prophets are *not* speaking false doctrine in any of these incidents (except

Elijah's). They quote from sound traditional (i.e., scriptural) sources. It is in the application to the present that they differ. They meet a purported "Word from the Lord" through an inspired prophet with a word from Scripture (tradition).

Two times in the Vision the people find a voice, in 8:19—12:6 and in chaps. 60–63.

Isaiah and his children have withdrawn. The crowd presses forward, making fun of the prophet's words. They seize on Isaiah's claim to having received a word from Yahweh. They jeer at his boast that he and his children are signs and symbols.

The first speech mocks Isaiah, identifying him with the heathen spiritualists and fortune-tellers, ecstatic mutterers and omen-readers. It ends by calling people to return to real law and real testimony—not that claimed by Isaiah's private interpretation (v 16). The second speaker notes the lack of a bright message of hope such as the traditional interpreters of law and testimony customarily brought. The gloomy message of doom from Isaiah is clear. A third voice expresses his fears of the kind of reaction such a word will bring. A fourth finds reality which matches the gloomy word.

The debate between the classical prophets and the populace is brought into full focus. The traditional prophets, the priests, the monarchists, and many others surge forward to denounce the lone figure of Isaiah. Here is the evidence that God was right. They in Jerusalem were blind and deaf, stiff-necked and stubborn, unwilling to listen and turn.

The rest of this scene will develop the opposition, quoting traditional Zionist liturgies including promises concerning David and Jerusalem. The post-exilic audience knows that the house of David lost what was left of its sovereign powers in the humiliations suffered by Hezekiah (chaps. 36–39), the servility of Manassah, and the disastrous reigns of the puppet kings Jehoiakim, Jehoiachin, and Zedekiah.

Jerusalem was stripped of its defenses by Samaria and Aram in 734 B.C. (chap. 7), by Assyria in 714 and 701 B.C. (chaps. 20 and 36–37), and finally by the Babylonians in 598 and 587 B.C. The latter is ignored in the Vision except the flashback references in chaps. 10 and 49–54. But it must have been very much on the mind of the audience.

The arguments of assured political and military success by Zionists and monarchists were echoed by contemporary monarchists who urged Judah to rebel against Persia. The eighth-century message from Isaiah carried a fifth-century relevance—and was probably as unpopular as its original.

Episode I:
To Us a Son Is Born (8:23—9:6 [9:1–7])

Bibliography

Alonso-Schökel, L. "Dos poemas a la paz." *EstBib* 18 (1959) 149–69. **Alt, A.** "Jesaja 8:23–9:6. Befreiungsnacht und Krönungstag." *FS A. Bertholet.* Ed. W. Baumgartner.

Tübingen: J. C. B. Mohr, 1950. 29–49 = *KS* II 206–25. **Bentzen, A.** *King and Messiah.* 2nd ed. Oxford: Blackwell, 1970. **Coppens, J.** "Le roi idéal d'Is. IX 5–6 et XI 1–5, est-il une figure messianique?" *Memorial A. Gelin,* 1961. 85–108, Bibliography. ———. "Le messianisme royal." *NRT* 90 (1968), in six parts; = *Le messianisme royal. LD* 54. Paris: Editions du Cerf, 1968. 77–82, 491–96. **Crook, M. B.** "A Suggested Occasion for Isaiah 9:2–7 and 11:1–9." *JBL* 68 (1949) 213–24. ———. "Did Amos and Micah know Isaiah 9:2–7 and 11:1–9?" *JBL* 73 (1954) 144–51. **Driver, G. R.** "Isaianic Problems." *FS W. Eilers.* Wiesbaden: Harrassowitz, 1967. 46–49. **Emerton, J. A.** "Some Linguistic and Historical Problems in Isaiah VIII 23." *JSS* 14 (1969) 151–75. (Bibliography). **Grelot, P.** "L'interpretation d'Isaïe IX 5 dans le Targoum des prophètes." *De la Torah au Messie.* FS H. Cazelles, 1981. Ed. M. Carrez et al. 535–43. **Gressmann, H.** *Der messias.* FRLANT 43. Göttingen: Vandenhoeck & Ruprecht, 1929. **Harrelson, W.** "Nonroyal Motifs in the Royal Eschatology." *Israel's Prophetic Heritage.* FS J. Muilenburg. New York: Harper & Row, 1962. 149–53. **Lindblom, J.** *A Study of the Immanuel Section in Isaiah. Isa vii 1—ix 6.* Lund: Gleerup, 1958. **Mowinckel, S.** "Urmensch und 'Königsideology,' " *ST* 2 (1948) 71–89. ———. *He That Cometh.* Tr. G. W. Anderson. Oxford: Blackwell, 1956. 102–10. **Müller, H. P.** "Uns ist ein Kind geboren . . ." *EvT* 21 (1961) 408–19. **Olivier, J. P. J.** "The Day of Midian and Isaiah 9:3b." *JNWSL* 9 (1981) 143–49. **Rad, G. von** "Das judäische Königsritual." *TLZ* 72 (1947) 211–16 (also in *GesStud* 205–13). **Ringgren, H.** "König und Messias." *ZAW* 64 (1952) 120–47. ———. *The Messiah in the Old Testament.* SBT 18. Chicago: A. R. Allenson, 1956. **Scharbert, J.** *Heilsmittler im Alten Testament und im Alten Orient.* Freiburg: Herbert, 1964. ———. *Der Messias im Alten Testament und im Judentum: Die religiöse und theologische Bedeutung des Alten Testaments.* 1967. **Schmidt, W. H.** "Die Ohnmacht des Messias." *KD* 15 (1969) 18–34. **Schunk, K. D.** "Der fünfte Thronname des Messias." *VT* 23 (1973) 108–10. **Seybold, K.** *Das davidische Königtum im Zeugnis der Propheten.* FRLANT 107. Göttingen: Vandenhoeck & Ruprecht, 1972. 82. **Thompson, M. E. W.** "Isaiah's Ideal King." *JSOT* 24 (1982) 79–88. **Vermeylen, J.** *Du prophète Isaïe à l'apocalyptique.* 2 vols. Paris: J. Gabalda, 1977. **Vollmer, J.** "Zur Sprache von Jesaja 9:1–6." *ZAW* 80 (1968) 343–50. **Wildberger, H.** "Die Thronnamen des Messias. Jes. 9:5b." *TZ* 16 (1960) 314–32. **Zimmerli, W.** "Vier oder fünf Thronnamen des messianischen Herschers in Jes. IX 5b.6." *VT* 22 (1972) 249–52. **Zorell, F.** "Vaticinium messianicum Isaiae 9:1–6 Hebr. = 9:2–7 Vulg." *Bib* 2 (1921) 215–18.

Translation

The Official: 23[1]* *But no gloom* [a] 3+3
for her who had such anguish!
An Aide: *As the first time* [b] *brings contempt* 3+2+2
to the land [c] *of Zebulun*
and to the land [d] *of Naphtali,*
The later [b] *brings honor* 2
to the Way of the Sea, 2+2+2
Trans-Jordan,
Galilee of the Nations.
Chorus: 1[2] *The people walking in the dark* 3+3
see a great light.
Residents in the land of shadow [a]*—* 3+3
light shines on them.
First Bystander: 2[3] *You multiply the rejoicing* [a] 2+2
you magnify the joy.

They rejoice before you 2+2
like rejoicing[b] *in harvest,*
just as they exult 2+2
when spoil is divided.
Second Bystander: 3[4] *If*[a] *the yoke of his burden,*[b] 3+3+3
the staff[c] *of his shoulder,*
the rod of his oppressor
You smash, like the day of Midian.[d] 3
Third Bystander: 4[5] *If*[a] *every boot of trampling in tumult*[b] 3+3
and garment rolled[c] *in bloody deeds*
becomes for burning 2+2
food for fire,
Chorus: 5[6] *If*[a] *a child* 2+2+3
is born to us,[b]
a son is given to us,
Official: *When*[c] *the administration*[d] *comes to be* 2+2
on his shoulders,
Aide: *When one begins to proclaim*[e] *his name* 2
Chorus: [f] *Wonder Counselor* 2
God-Hero 2
Father of Future 2
Prince of Peace,[f] 2
Official: 6[7] *To the increase*[a] *of rule* 2+2
(offering a toast) *and to peace (may there be) no end*
upon the throne of David 3+2
and upon his kingdom.
Aide: *To establish it* 2+1
and to confirm it
with justice and with righteousness 1+1
from now and to the age. 1+2
Chorus: *May the Zeal of Yahweh of Hosts* 3+2
do this!

Notes

*There is a discrepancy between MT and LXX (and thus all modern translations) in the numbering of verses. Thus MT 8:23 = Eng. 9:1, MT 9:1 = Eng. 9:2, etc. The numbers below follow MT.

23.a. Vg translates *et non poterit avolare de angustia sua* "and is not able to fly because of his anguish." This takes מועף as a form of עוף in the lexicon, meaning "to fly," but fails to note the connection with the word in v. 22.

23.b. The subject of the verbs is not named. Budde (*Jes. Erl.*, 99) thought הראשון "the first" stood for Tiglath-Pileser and was subject of the first verb, while a later oppressor was represented by האחרון "the later." But surely God is the subject here, although it is not necessary to add יהוה "Yahweh" (as Kaiser and Alt do) to the text.

23.c. DSS[Isa] reads ארץ "land" for ארצה "to the land." MT is hardly an Aramaism (Kaiser) but rather an old acc or locative as L. G. Rignell (*ST* 10 [1956] 51) and Emerton (*JSS* 14[1969] 152) have noted. See GKC § 90*f*.

23.d. DSS[Isa] reads והארץ instead of וארצה. MT is consistent and correct.

9:1.a. צַלְמָוֶת was understood by the Versions to be composed of צל "shadow" and מות "death": G ἐν χώρᾳ καὶ σκιᾷ θανάτου (which is followed by Matt 4:16 and Luke 1:79), Tg

טולי מותא, Syr *ṭelālê mawtâ,* Vg *umbra mortis.* But modern study has established the root to be צלם "be dark" and the proper vocalization to be צַלְמוּת (D. W. Thomas, "צַלְמָוֶת in the OT," *JSS* 7 [1962] 191–200).

2.a. הגוי לא "the nation not." MT's accent suggests that לא "not" should be read with the second stich "you do not magnify joy." Yet there has been a persistent attempt to divide the line after לא. Rignell (*ST* 10 [1956] 33) reads "Thou has made the not-a-people great" (cf. H. W. Wolff, *Frieden ohne Ende,* 22). Some MSS, Qere, Tg, and Syr read הגוי לו "the nation that belongs to him." Wildberger follows the conjecture that a false division of the words has occurred in transmission and suggests reading הַגִּילָה "the rejoicing" for הגוי לא. The emendation fits the meaning, temper, and meter, and it commends itself here.

2.b. שִׂמְחַת "rejoicing" is a constr form followed by a preposition. S. Rin ("ֵי as an absolute plural ending." *BZ* 5 [1961] 255–58) suggests that this is an old abs ending. But see GKC § 130*a*(1). The form is unusual, but not impossible.

3.a. Read כִּי as a conditional particle. Cf. GKC § 159*l* and Watts, *Syntax,* 135.

3.b. For the form סֻבֳּלוֹ consult GKC § 93*q.*

3.c. Wildberger supports earlier suggestions to change the vowel pointing of מַטֵּה "staff" to מוֹטָה "pole" (cf. 58:6, 9). The change seems unnecessary. The parallel is close enough for the purpose here.

3.d. LXX Μαδιαμ; DSS[Isa] מדים. The Greek appears to have been the normal pronunciation for Midian. (Cf. Philo, *Mut. Nom.,* 110). DSS[Isa] follows the Greek.

4.a. Read as a conditional particle.

4.b. LXX δόλῳ "deceit" or "treachery," supported by Tg, seems to have read this as בְּרֶשַׁע. Tur-Sinai (*ScrHier,* 8) changed the vowels. But Wildberger is correct to reject it.

4.c. Syr *mepalpal* "spotted" has left Zorell (*Bib* 2 [1921] 217) and Procksch to emend מגוללה "rolled" to מְגֹאָלָה "defiled, polluted." MT makes sense and should be sustained.

5.a. Read as a conditional particle.

5.b. The alliteration in ילד ידל לנו is worth notice.

5.c. Note the decisive change of tense. The perfects that have characterized the verses since 8:23 give way to consec imperfects and finally to inf in v 6. The translation reads the consec imperfects as subordinate introductory clauses. The weight of the "toast" to the King falls on the verbless substantive clause beginning v 6.

5.d. משרה is hap. leg. LXX translated ἡ ἀρχὴ "rule." BDB, 976, posits an otherwise unknown root שרה to support this meaning. Gray related it to שרר "to rule," the noun שׂר "a prince" and Akk *šarru* "king" and suggested that it should be pointed מְשֻׂרָה/מְשָׂרָה. DSS[Isa] משורה has still another pronunciation (cf. F. Nötscher, "Entbehrliche Hapaxlegomena in Jes," *VT* 1 [1951] 302 and G. R. Driver, *VT* 2 [1952] 357).

5.e. ויקרא "then he will call" has no named subject which has caused problems in translation and interpretation. DSS[Isa] וקרא changes the tense to a cons pf. Others have used a pass to convey the meaning: LXX καλεῖται, Syr *ʾetqerî,* Vg *vocabitur.* If MT is translated with an impersonal subject, it makes sense, fits the tense pattern, and should be kept.

5.f-f. The Versions were at a loss to translate these titles which by that time were understood as names for Messiah. DSS[Isa] follows MT except for adding the article before "peace." LXX reads: Μεγάλης βουλῆς ἄγγελος. ἐγὼ γὰρ ἄξω εἰρήνην ἐπὶ τοὺς ἄρχοντας, εἰρήνην καὶ ὑγίειαν αὐτῷ "Messenger of mighty counsel; for I will keep peace over the rulers, (bring) peace and health to them." Ἀ Σ Θ follow MT more closely than LXX does. None of these, however, renders אל as "God," but some MSS add to LXX θαυμαστος συμβουλος θεος ισχυρος "a wonder of a counselor, mighty God," probably influenced by Origin's *Hexapla* (cf. Ziegler). Tg reads מפלי עיעא אלהא גינירא קיים עלמיא משיחא דשלמא יסגי עלנא ביומוהו "Wonderful counselor, mighty God who lives forever, the Messiah in whose days peace will be great over us." Vg *Admirabilis, consiliarius, Deus, fortis, pater future saeculie, princeps pacis* "Wonderful, counselor, God, mighty, father of coming ages, prince of peace" has found six names, reading the first four separately and only joining the last two pairs of words (cf. Zorell, *Bib* 2 [1921] 218).

6.a. לםרבה "to increase." The final *mem* within the word is strange. Many MSS as well as DSS[Isa] and Qere replace it with the usual מ. LXX μεγάλη ἡ ἀρχὴ αὐτοῦ, followed by the other Versions, has led to suggestions for emendations: that לם be understood as dittography and dropped, leaving רבה "the rule is great." Other suggestions were to read לְמוֹ רַבָּה or לוֹ מְרֻבָּה "to him is great (rule)." Alt (*FS A. Bertholet,* 219) thought of the customary Egyptian number five for throne names. He suggested the לםרבה is a fragment of a fifth name such as מרבה

המשרה "one who enlarges the realm." Wildberger (365 and 394) has taken this suggestion, emended the text in comparison with the Versions (assuming dittography "fore and aft") reading רב המשרה and translating *in (seiner) Herrshaft gross* "great in his rule." These arguments are cogent and draw the name into close connection with the preceding line. However, MT has seen the phrase in close parallel to the following lines in which three more times key words begin with לְ. As parallels to לשלום "to peace," להכין "to establish," and לסעדה "to confirm it," the more traditional reading and translation (with MT) should prevail. (See the discussion under *Form/Structure/Setting.*)

Form/Structure/Setting

The structure and unity of the passage are shown by its syntax and arrangement. It moves with freedom, no slave of metrical structures, shaping its own forms and meanings. It can suspend parallelism (v 5) for five single statements of two words each, then resume parallelism with pairs of prepositional phrases. It is capable of putting three pairs of words opposite a single pair in vv 23 and 3.

The whole is dominated by the particle כִּי which in vv 23, 3, 4, 5 introduced the speeches. To understand its meaning and significance for the passage is to open the door to its treasures. The dominant position of perfect verbs (in vv 23, 1, 2, 3, 5a) is instructive—always in inverted order with substantives first. The strange appearance of a perfect with *wāw* in v 4c breaks the pattern, as does the imperfect in v 2c, while the consecutive imperfects in v 5b and c are important. The passage closes with an imperfect.

What is one to do with all this? It is no ordinary prosaic, or even poetic style. First, let us deal with the כִּי particles. They may be strong assertatives—either negative or positive. Apparently the first (v 23) is such and is rendered "but." The sentence is an objection to the previous one, negating it word for word—but with no verb. The next line softens the contradiction by ascribing them to two different "times" and uses inverted word order and perfect tenses to achieve the effect. The verbs are strong but the syntax leaves them suspended and timeless, like the substantive statement which introduced them. The first strophe has halted the confused lament with the assertion that the future can be made good, just as the past has been bad. The contrast is between "contempt" and "honor."

9:1: The two lines are balanced in meter. They support the theme. The present times of trouble are presented by participles, while hope is expressed in perfect verbs like the first strophe. The contrast is now between "light" and "dark."

9:2: The pattern is broken. Inverted order is abandoned, as are also the impersonal verbs. Second person singular "you" is addressed. This is often taken to be God. It is more likely that the broken pattern indicates a different speaker who addresses the one who has just spoken either in v 23 or v 1.

9:3: This is the first of three passages beginning with כִּי. In each the meaning is different. The statements do not contradict the previous line. Rather, they state contingencies that must be met for the announcement to be true. This first one poses the issue of the presence of a powerful oppressor who has subjugated the land. If the speaker, like Gideon, can smash that power—the apodosis is understood but not uttered. The inverted order poses the three fold emphasis on that oppressor before the verb of deliverance.

9:4: The second contingency is a reminder of the forces of violence and chaos that stand in the way of a solution. These, too, must be destroyed. The verse is only half-spoken: the first part has no verb—stopping abruptly—while the second has a perfect with *wāw* which normally requires an antecedent. It is as though the lines are to be stammered out, being distorted in delivery. But the meaning is clear. Years of war cannot be put aside in a night. All the weapons and uniforms (not to mention psychic scars) must be eradicated. Is that possible?

9:5: The third contingency takes a more direct suggestion. It is spoken in chorus and takes its *we* from the "great light" of v 1. They hear this in terms that suggest the hope that one of the line of David may seize the chance apparent in the fall of Samaria to reunite the kingdoms and inaugurate a second era of peace and prosperity like that of David and Solomon.

The idea, improbable as it is under the Assyrian (or Persian), evokes a nostalgic burst of patriotic fervor—a reminder of what enthronement hymns sound like. Then the section closes on the prayerful invocation of the Zeal of Yahweh.

Comment

23[1] The laments of the doomsayers of 8:19–22 are interrupted by a claim of hope. The speech denies that *gloom* and *anguish* are the inevitable results of the events. While recognizing the bitterness of the moment, it reminds them of a hope based on God's intervention. Election is viewed as a guarantee of his eventual redemption.

The perfect verbs begin a series that extends through the first line of 9:5. Note that they are used here both for "the first" as well as "the later" time. They are independent of a time context. We have tried to show this by translating with present time throughout (Watts, *Syntax,* 46).

The *first time* for the lands of Zebulun and Naphtali is not easy to identify. *Zebulun* was located in south Galilee astride the valley east of Carmel that is drained by the river Kishon. But its significance as a tribe had been diminishing since the days of the Judges. Solomon's districts have the territory absorbed into that of Asher (1 Kgs 4:16). Whatever of its territory was not seized in Tiglath-Pileser's drive down the coast in 734 B.C. was taken the following year in the invasion of Naphtali. The Province of Dor was established for the coastal region from Carmel south to Joppa (MBA, 148).

Naphtali was the northernmost territory of the Kingdom of Israel, occupying the northwest of the lake of Galilee on up to the southern slopes of Mount Hermon. It had also not been significant since the period of the Judges, although Solomon did have a district named Naphtali. The *first time* could appropriately refer to a time beginning before the monarchy. But it is also possible that this reference is simply figurative for the area of the Northern Kingdom that was occupied by Assyria in 732 B.C. The Assyrian campaign of 733 B.C. drove across the heart of its territory (*MBA,* 147), attacked its major cities, and reduced it to a province under an Assyrian governor (2 Kgs 15:29). The same campaign subdued Gilead and it, too, was made an Assyrian province (*Annals of Tiglath Pileser III*). Some of its leaders were taken into exile (1 Chr 5:6).

A. Alt's (*FS A. Bertholet*) suggestion to add a line listing parallel terms such as the Valley of Sharon and the Mountain of Gilead is appropriate as a comment on the geography even if it is judged unnecessary for the strophic structure of the passage.

Being *brought into contempt* apparently refers to these invasions and the subsequent oppression under a foreign ruler. Both verbs in this verse lack an explicit subject. Two possibilities are likely. One is that Yahweh is the subject. Some commentaries suggest that he should be put into the text. This would fit, especially if the second persons of the verbs in 9:3–4 also are addressed to him. Another possibility is that the subject is "the first time" and "the later" (Budde, *Jes. Erl.*, 99; Wildberger). We have chosen this second course. The emphasis is on the hope that a later time can bring a reversal of fortunes for the stricken area. But the subject's ambiguity is deliberate and is intended to let the hearer or reader make the choice.

The *Way of the Sea, Trans-Jordan,* and *Galilee of the Nations* appear to be Hebrew names for the districts the Assyrians called Dor, Megiddo, and Gilead (cf. *MBA,* 148). The fate of this region was separated from that of Samaria as early as the eighth century. Matthew quotes the verses to support the account of Jesus' ministry in that region (Matt 4:15–16).

In content the message is simply an appeal to hope that the future has got to be better, and that the future will rectify the bad times of the past. The announcement proclaims that the new political realities (i.e., redistricting and renaming territory) need not prevent a new period of glory and honor. (Note: the announcement is not given as a word from the Lord or supported in any way.)

1[2] A pro-Israelite group in the crowd picks up the note just sounded. There is *light* at the end of the tunnel for Israel.

2[3] A bystander challenges the first speaker, asking what in his speech there is to be happy about. And he scornfully derides the gullible crowd who act as though a great victory has been won just by saying so.

3–6[4–7] Three characteristics of that great future salvation are each introduced with כִּי, which may have various meanings. "If" has seemed most suitable here.

3[4] The first emphasizes freedom from foreign domination. It believes this is possible because God has led Israel to victory in impossible situations like the one Gideon successfully faced (Judg 7): *The Day of Midian.*

4[5] The second portrays the end of Holy War against the enemy when all the booty, including the war-boots and military uniforms, had to be burned.

5–6[6–7] The third is voiced by monarchists in the crowd who see in the prophecy of future light the restoration of power and glory to the House of David. The future of a new heir to the throne can be full of hope that all the promise of the age of the United Kingdom when David and Solomon ruled can now be restored and fulfilled. This passage is one of the most beautiful and expressive passages in the OT reflecting high monarchical tradition and ideology. The ideas and phrases may well echo those used in enthronement ceremonies. (Cf. *Excursus,* "Messiah Son of David," below.)

The episode ends with the murmured response of the crowd: *May the Zeal of Yahweh of Hosts do this.* This effectively represents the theologically inclusive faith that united the divergent elements in the crowd. Those who supported the position of northern Israel (8:22–23[8:22–9:1]), those with a general faith that God would certainly make things right (9:1–2[2–3]), the rebellious zealots (v 3[4]), the Holy War enthusiasts who said "Let God fight the battles" (v 4[5]), and the monarchists who saw hope in a revival of the House of David and the birth of a new David (vv 5–6[6–7])—all these could intone the prayer for God's zeal to save them.

Explanation

This passage has often been understood as promise. Yet the analysis above does not support this for its original setting. It is not spoken by the prophet or in the name of God. It is an attempt to assemble from the resources of faith and doctrine words to bolster hope. Yet the chorus knows that only a miracle can bring the light, restore the joy, or reestablish the power and authority of David's reign. That is why they sigh, "May the Zeal of Yahweh of Hosts do this!" Of course, nothing is impossible with God.

The speaker tries to change the mood of doom and gloom that dominated the previous response (8:19–22) to Isaiah's speeches. The anguish of God's people need not be forever. History belongs to God. He can turn things around. But the speaker carefully avoids being too specific about it. The perfect tenses in the passage give a timeless appearance. This directly contradicts the message of Isaiah in 6:11–21, in 7:8, and in 8:7. It turns against the announced plan of God in 2:6–9 and implies an easy grace for the apostasy spoken of in 1:2–8.

The theme is picked up in 9:1[2] with an eagerness that reflects the great need of the people to believe. The dark moment will pass. There is hope.

The second person singular of the verbs at the beginning of v 2[3] and the end of v 3[4] have usually been understood to refer to God. But this need not be necessary if the passage has a dialogical character. They may refer to the previous speaker and the sudden shift of mood which his speech has made in the people. V 3[4] is saying that any true change will need to destroy the oppressor in the land and that this would require a miraculous deliverance like that of Gideon. V 4[5] continues the sceptical mood noting that a total disarmament will be required to achieve this goal. But the crowd now breaks into a chant which speaks the royal hopes for an heir to the throne of David in whom all of the promises to David will be fulfilled in terms of 2 Sam 7:12–14 and royal Psalms like Pss 2, 72, and 89. The destruction of the government in Samaria opens the door to such a dream, if the foreign oppressor can be dealt with.

The episode draws to a climax with the speeches toasting the idea of such a "messianic" hope and closes with the fervent prayer that the Zeal of Yahweh of Hosts may do this. The invocation of the old battle name for God recognizes that this is only possible with the kind of miraculous intervention that brought Israel through the Reed Sea, brought down the walls of Jericho, and devastated the Midianite hosts before Gideon.

This hope is a legitimate part of Israel's heritage. It is not, however, a part of Isaiah's word for Israel or Judah in the eighth century or of the

Vision of Isaiah for Jerusalem in the fifth century. The traditionalists opposed the prophet in those days, as they opposed Jesus and John the Baptist in their day. The issue is not that God is unable to fulfill his promises or that God is unfaithful to them. It *is* that Israel has eliminated itself from God's agenda. He is now in the process of judging and cleansing, so that his goals for his people can be achieved.

Two places in the Vision allow for the opposition to be heard. The first is here in 8:19—9:6[7] and in the dialogue from 10:3–12:6. The second is in chaps. 60–64. The sharpest contrast to the Isaiah message is in 8:23—9:6[7] and in 62:1–12, 63:11b—64:12. These passages have many things in common, especially their presumption. They presume upon God's miraculous power and intervention (like Satan's temptations to Jesus, "cast yourself down," "make the stones to bread," in Matt 4:3, 6).

The chorus here represents a kind of "government in exile" in Jerusalem and appears to represent a party that actively campaigns for Israel to be reunited to Judah under a Davidic king. The collapse of the government in Samaria (probably that of Pekah in 733/732 B.C.) offers an opportunity for the dreams to be realized and for a return of the united monarchy. So now they break into a throne song of the Davidic royalty, claiming it applies "to us." "His kingdom" (v 6[7]) refers to the united reign which they fervently hope will be established and confirmed. (See *Excursus* below "Throne Names for Messiah," for further details on this passage.)

This is heady stuff for the frustrated group of exiles from Israel in Jerusalem and for the inhabitants of the city. They recognize the practical impossibility of accomplishing this ideal, but shout approval of a politically popular theme: "May the Zeal of Yahweh of Hosts do this!" It would take a miracle. But it would also require God's approval. The next episode deals with that issue.

This episode is united in replying to Isaiah's message of gloom. Parallel to the refutation of Israel's fate given in 8:22–23 [9:1], it poses a more general prophecy of light, prosperity, and joy awaiting them after this time of distress (9:1–2[2–3]). There is no sense of guilt or of need for spiritual or moral change, only a firm belief in the good future God has in store for his people.

The responses may accurately reflect the popular elements of eighth-century Jerusalem. But they also found echoes in fifth-century Jerusalem. By then the oppressor was the Persian rather than the Assyrian. For both groups the thrust of Isaiah's message was equally obnoxious.

Traditional Christian interpreters have correctly noted that 9:5–6[6–7] is part and parcel of royal liturgy and used it as a messianic text. It is then to be associated with the Royal Psalms. This is achieved by lifting the verses out of context and changing the genre of the larger work to match. This is legitimate. The Vision apparently quotes from other contexts. But it is important to keep in mind that this is not the function or meaning of the verses in this context.

The prophetic task lay in interpreting the fall and destruction of the kingdom and in preparing the people to live as God's people without king or royal dominion. The Vision follows in the path of Jeremiah and Ezekiel in this regard and will later reinterpret royal motifs to fit that situation. One should note that in the sense that Jesus was understood to be the Messiah, these motifs of kingship and dominion had to be radically reinterpreted to fit the crucified carpenter's son. In this the NT follows the path laid out in the Vision of Isaiah. Christian interpretation has found the appropriate place for the original meanings to be applied to Christ's second coming to reign in glory.

Excursus: Messiah, Son of David

Bibliography

Becker, J. *Messianic Expectation in the Old Testament,* tr. D. E. Green. Philadelphia: Fortress, 1980. **Coppens, J.** *Le messianisme royal.* LD 54. Paris: Editions du Cerf, 1968. Reprinted from *NRT* 90 (1968) 30–49, 225–51, 479–512, 622–50, 834–63, 936–75. **LaSor, W. S.** "The Messiah: An Evangelical Christian View." *Evangelicals and Jews in Conversation on Scripture, Theology, and History.* Ed. M. Tannenbaum, M. R. Wilson, and A. J. Rodin. Grand Rapids: Eerdmans, 1973. 76–95. **McKenzie, J. L.** "Royal Messianism." *CBQ* 19 (1957) 25–52. **Motyer, J. A.** "Messiah." *IDB* 3:987–94. **Ringgren, H.** *The Messiah in the Old Testament.* SBT 18. Chicago: A. R. Allenson, 1956.

Christian exegesis of the OT is keenly aware of the elements which the NT understands to be fulfilled in Jesus. Foremost among these are the royal aspects of Messiah. Jesus is understood to be *the Son of David,* heir to divine promise of an everlasting and universal throne.

This understanding of Messiah is founded on 2 Sam 7:11b–16 and on the royal Psalms (including Pss 2, 45, and 110). These proclaim a very high view of the king and the kingdom, in which God is directly involved with both. Among the OT passages which present such a view, none ranks higher than Isa 9:5–6[6–7] or 11:1–5. The first lists throne names for the Davidic king of Zion (see below), while the second announces, or prays for, the spirit of the Lord to so fill him that he achieves the highest aims of the kingdom.

What the OT, including Isaiah, can only record as promises and ideals that contrast starkly with human reality, the NT invites the Christian to see fulfilled in Jesus Christ, Son of David and Divine King of Heaven and Earth.

Excursus: Throne Names of Messiah

Bibliography

Fohrer, G. "υἱός κτλ." *TDNT* VIII, 349–52. **McClellan, W. H.** "El Gibbor." *CBQ* 6 (1944) 276–88. **Olmo Lete, G. del.** "Los titulos mesianicos de Is. 9:5." *EstBib* 24 (1965) 239–43. **Rehm, M.** *Der Königliche Messias im Licht der Immannuel-Weissagungen des Buches Jesaja.* Eichstätter Studien 1. Kevelaer: Butzon und Bercker, 1968. 145–66. **Snaith, N. H.** "The Interpretation of El Gibbor in Isaiah ix. 5." *ExpTim* 52 (1940/41) 36–37. **Wildberger, H.** "Die Thronnamen des Messias, Jes. 9:5b." *TZ* 16 (1960) 314–32.

Whether this passage is understood to relate to the birth of a royal heir or to his coronation (see Wildberger, *Jesaja,* 377, for a review), these names certainly and succinctly present the most elaborate statement of Jerusalem's view of its God-given sovereign, the Son of David. Ps 2 and 2 Sam 7:14 prepare the reader for the view that the king will be understood to be God's son. But passages such as this are a strong reminder of the seriousness with which ancient Israel and early Judaism thought of the Davidic Kingdom as an expression, indeed the earthly expression, of the Kingdom of God.

Scene 2: A Word against Jacob (9:7[8]—10:23)

Episode A: A Prophetic Interpretation of History (*9:7[8]—10:4*). The scene begins with the sharp reminder that the Lord has already spoken a word of judgment against Israel.

Episode B: Assyrian, Rod of My Anger (*10:5–19*). The scene continues with an interpretation of Assyria's role in this era.

Episode C: Only a Remnant (*10:20–23*). The scene ends with the confirmation that this judgment is total and certain.

The speeches of the scene form an arch. Note the balance of its themes. The capstone of the arch (10:12) is of a completely different genre and meaning from all the rest.

A A word against Jacob; the people know (9:7–12[8–13])
B The people have not turned; the Lord will cut off (9:13–17[14–18])
C The wrath of Yahweh will scorch the land (9:18–20[19–21]) (10:1–4: A "woe" outside the structure)
D Assyrian, rod of my anger (10:5–6)
E But he does not intend it so (10:7–11)
KEYSTONE After work is finished on Jerusalem and Judah, Yahweh will punish the Assyrian (10:12)
E′ The Assyrian's prideful attitude (10:13–14)
D′ Does the axe raise itself against the woodsman? (10:15–16)
C′ The light of Israel will become a fire (10:17–19)
B′ In that day a remnant will rely on Yahweh (10:20–21)
A′ The Lord will carry out the decreed destruction upon the whole land (10:22–23)

Episode A: A Prophetic Interpretation of History (9:7[8]—10:4)

Bibliography

Donner, H. *Israel unter den Völker.* VTSup 11. Leiden: E. J. Brill, 1964. 64–75. **Goshen-Gottstein, N. H.** "Hebrew Syntax and the History of the Bible Text. A Pesher in the MT of Isaiah." *Textus* 8 (1973) 100–106. **Honeyman, A. M.** "Unnoticed Euphemism in Isaiah 9:19–20?" *VT* 1 (1951) 221–23. **Ockinga, B. S.** *"rās wĕzānāb kippah wĕʾagmōn* in Isa 9:13 and 9:15." *BN* 10 (1979) 31–34. **Thomas, D. W.** "A Note on the Meaning of *jada* in Hosea 9:9 and Isaiah 9:8." *JTS* 41 (1940) 43–44. **Vollmer, J.** *Rückblicke,* 130–44. **Wallenstein, M.** "Unnoticed Euphemism in Isaiah 9:19–20?" *VT* 3 (1952) 179–80.

Translation

Heavens:	7[8] *A word,* [a]	1
	the Lord [b] *sent* [c] *against Jacob,*	3+2
	fell in Israel.	
Earth:	8[9] *The people, all of them, acknowledged* [a] *(it):*	3+3+3
	Ephraim and the inhabitants of Samaria	
	[b] *with arrogance and stout heart.* [b]	
Ephraim:	9[10] *If bricks fall,*	2+2
	let's build with hewn stones!	
	If sycamores are cut down,	2+2
	let's exchange [a] *(for) cedars!*	
Heavens:	10[11] *Then* [a] *Yahweh exalted Rezin's adversaries* [b] *against him and armed his enemies.*	
Earth:	11[12] *With Aram before* [a] *and the Philistines behind, they proceeded to devour Israel with open mouth.*	
Heavens:	*With all this, his anger has not turned.*	4+3
	His hand (is) stretched out still!	
Earth:	12[13] *The people have not turned toward the one who strikes them.*	4+4
	Yahweh of Hosts [a] *they have not sought.*	
Heavens:	13[14] *Then Yahweh* [a] *cut off from Israel* [a] *head and tail,*	3+2
	Palm branch and swamp-reed in one day,	2+2
	14[15] *Elder and respected man, (he is the head).*	3+2
	Prophet and teacher of lies [a] *(he is the tail).*	3+2
Earth:	15[16] *So the leaders of this people became "misleaders"*	4+2
	and their followers (were) confused. [a]	
Heavens:	16[17] *Because of this*	1
	the Lord [a] *cannot rejoice over their choice youth.*	3+3
	Their orphans and widows he cannot comfort.	
Earth:	*For everyone of them is profane and an evildoer.*	4+4
	Every mouth speaks foolishness.	
Heavens:	*With all this, his anger has not turned.*	4+3
	His hand (is) stretched out still.	
Earth:	17[18] *For wickedness burns like a fire.*	4+3
	It devours briers and thorns	
	when it burns in the forest thickets,	3+3
	when it rolls up [a]*—a column of smoke.*	
Heavens:	18[19] *When Yahweh of Hosts overflows,*	3+2
	a country is burned up. [a]	
Earth:	*So the people become like fuel for fire.*	4+4
	They have no compassion for each other.	

Heavens: 19[20] *Then one carves on the right, but is hungry.* 4+4+4
Another eats on the left, but is not satisfied.
They each devour the flesh of his neighbor: [a]
Earth: 20[21] *Manasseh on Ephraim* 2+2+3
and Ephraim on Manasseh.
Together on Judah.
Heavens: *With all this, his anger has not turned.* 4+3
His hand (is) stretched out still.
Mourners: 10:1 *Woe—(you who are) decreeing* [a] *meaningless*
decrees, [b] 1+3+3
who write [c] *burdensome writs* [d]
2 *to turn the needy from judgment* [a] 3+4
Yahweh: *and to tear away justice (due) the poor of my*
people.
To let widows be their spoil 3+2
and (let them) plunder [b] *orphans.* [c]
Earth: 3 *What can you (pl) do for the day of reckoning?* [a] 4+3
Or for devastation [b] *that will come from afar?*
Upon whom can you depend for help? 3+3
And where [c] *can you leave your glory*
4 [a] *Unless one crouch beneath prisoners* [a] 4+3
or that they fall beneath the slain?
Heavens: *In all this, his anger has not turned.* 4+3
His hand is stretched out still.

Notes

7.a. LXX *θάνατον* has read דָבָר "word" as דֶבֶר "plague" which has often been translated with *θάνατος* "death." (Cf. Exod 5:3; 9:3; 15; Lev 26:25; Num 14:12; Deut 28:21.)

7.b. DSS[Isa] יהוה "Yahweh" instead of MT אדני "Lord." Wildberger follows DSS[Isa]. MT is adequate and should be kept.

7.c. The time viewpoint of the passage is determined at this point. The pf and the inverted order here are different from those in 8:23—9:6. The inversion is for emphasis: "a word" names the theme of the scene. The verb describes in pf tense a past action which remains valid in the present (Watts, *Syntax,* 35–36). The "word" is pictured in chap. 1, emphasized in 2:6–8, 7:7–9, and 8:1–3. So the time viewpoint must be past-present throughout the passage and tenses are translated accordingly.

8.a. ידע "know" has been understood by some to mean "be subdued." Cf. D. W. Thomas (*JTS* 41 [1940] 43) and G. R. Driver, *JTS* 41 [1940] 162. The use of ידע in Isaiah is significant and the problem of knowing and understanding is so important that it is doubtful that a variation could be expected. Further, the sense of "know" is vital to this passage. The pf with *wāw* indicated a concomitant fact with the first verb (Watts, *Syntax,* 47–54). God's sending his "word," its "falling" on Jacob, and the people's "knowing" of it are central to the meaning of the passage. Yet here the verb introduces the quotation and needs something more than "know." "Acknowledge" serves both purposes.

8.b-b. Interpreters have found this needs emendation (cf. Wildberger). It is abrupt and concise, but the sense is sound.

9.a. LXX adds *καὶ οἰκοδομήσομεν ἑαυτοῖς πύργον* "and let us build for ourselves a tower" like Gen. 11:3–4. There has also been much discussion of חלף. G. R. Driver (*JTS* 34 [1933] 381) uses Syr and Arab parallels for a meaning "to cut down." F. Wutz (*BZ* 21 [1933] 18) suggests "to fell." The ordinary meaning given by BDB, "exchange," "cause to succeed" or by KB, "to substitute for," is satisfactory here.

10.a. The cons impf tense shows God's next move. This (and the one in v 13) with the pf in v 7 form the skeleton of the entire passage.

10.b. Wildberger pontificates "צרי רצין cannot be right" and notes manuscript changes and recent attempts to emend the text. But why not? The words mean "Rezin's enemies." Rezin has been Samaria's patron. Chaps. 7 and 8 have announced Assyria's invasion of Aram. The phrase makes good sense. LXX had trouble with the text and tried to turn צרי רצין into על הר ציון "Mount Zion." However, MT makes good and fitting sense as it stands. It also reflects the play on sounds and letters that is typical of the Vision.

11.a. קדם means "in front." אחור means "behind." Because one cites direction as though facing the sunrise, קדם becomes "East," אחור "West." This fits Israel's position with Aram to the east and Philistia to the West.

12.a. צבאות "Hosts" is lacking in LXX. Σ Θ and Origen's *Hexapla* support MT. However, את before יהוה is unusual. It is used to avoid misunderstanding in the inverted stich.

13.a-a. The suggestion that יהוה מישראל "Yahweh from Israel" is an addition (Wildberger, Duhm, Fohrer, Kaiser) has missed the polarity of these two which dominates the entire passage, making repetition important.

14.a. מורה "teacher" in MT appears in opposition to נביא "prophet." However, three LXX MSS (41, 106, 233) and Cyrill read *καὶ διδάσκοντα* which would make this stich have two parts reading "and false teachers." However, this is the easier reading and not well attested.

15.a. מבלעים "confused." There are two roots בלע "to swallow" and בלע "confound" (BDB, 118). בלע I appears in 28:4, בלע II piel in 3:12, niph in 28:7. The parallel to מתעים "those who cause to err, wander about" (BDB, 1073) suggests the second root.

16.a. A number of emendations have grown up around a misunderstanding of the text (cf. Wildberger). If one eliminates אדוני "Lord" the parallel seems forced. MT makes sense and should be kept.

17.a. ויתאבכו "when it rolls up" is a *hap. leg.* (BDB, 5). It has usually been related to Akk *abāku* "to bring or carry away" or to Hebrew הפך "turn."

18.a. נעתם is another *hap. leg.* LXX *συγκέκαυται* "was burnt," "consumed," Tg חרובה "is destroyed," Syr *zāʿat* "is shaken," Vg *conturbata est* "is distracted, confused." KB does not translate, but suggests emending it to נִתְעָה "led astray." Others follow LXX and Tg to emend to נִצְּתָה "be burned" (Cheyne, Procksch, Donner). W. L. Moran ("*ʿtm* in Isa 9:18." *CBQ* 12 [1950] 153–54) sees the word as third pers pl from נוע with enclitic *mēm.* Kaiser and H. D. Hummel agree (*JBL* 76 [1957] 94) "at the wrath of Yahweh the earth reeled." Wildberger considers LXX to be about right, judging from the parallel.

19.a. MT's "The flesh of his own arm" does not make good sense. The Alexandrian group of LXX adds *τοῦ ἀδελφοῦ* "of his brother." Tg has קריביה which in Hebrew is רֵעוֹ (Wildberger), eliminating one letter: "his neighbor" instead of "his arm."

10:1.a. DSS^{Isa} חוקקים "decreeing" without the article. However, MT is valid.

1.b. חִקְקֵי "decrees" is derived from חק by BDB, 349. Joüon § 96*Ap* derives it from חָקַק (cf. also GKC § 93*bb*). DSS^{Isa} reads חוקקי (cf. G. R. Driver, "Hebrew Scrolls," *JTS* 2 [1951] 21). The pointing חִקְקֵי is also found in Judg 5:15. L. Köhler, "Bermerkungen zur tiberischen Masora," *HUCA* 23 (1950/51) 155, suggested the double use of ק might be an ancient form of writing. Wildberger (1979) suggests the alternative pronunciation of חק is chosen to make alliteration with הקקים clearer.

1.c. Tg וכתב "write" for ומכתבים "writers." A pl constr form with enclitic ם (cf. H. L. Ginsberg, "Some emendations in Isaiah," *JBL* 69 [1950] 54; H. D. Hummel, "Enclitic *Mem,*" *JBL* 76 [1957] 94 and Kaiser) is the probable explanation: ומכתבי־ם "the writers of."

1.d. כִּתֵּבוּ "writs" is the only use of כתב in piel. It demonstrates the thoroughness of the lawmakers and also completes the alliteration with מכתבי "write." The clause is construed as a contact relative clause, i.e., without a relative particle.

2.a. מִדִּין has caused comment. Some take it as a noun. Others refuse that possibility (Luzzato). Ginsberg (*JBL* 69 [1950] 54) and Kaiser suggest another enclitic *mēm.* However, MT has pointed it as a preposition מן "from" before דין "judgment." The construction is different from תטה משפט "pervert justice" in Deut 16:19; 24:17; 27:19.

2.b. The use of an impf to continue the action of an impf construction is also unusual. Cf. Joüon § 124*g.*

2.c. The use of את with an indefinite object is unusual. Cf. Joüon § 125*h.*

3.a. פקדה is translated by Delitzsch "penal visitation."

3.b. שואה. BDB, 996 suggests the root שאה meaning "devastation." Wildberger (179) insists on שוא "emptiness or vanity." The distinction is unimportant here.

3.c. ואנה is the particle אנ "where" with ה directive.

4.a-a. The text here presents problems. כרע "crouch" lacks a subject. It is sg while its parallel is pl, etc. This has led to many suggested emendations. P. de Lagarde (*Symmicta* 1 [1877] 105) suggested בֵּלְתִּי כֹּרַעַת הַת אֹסִיר "Belthis is sinking, Osiris is broken." This required no change in consonantal text and has been used by Steinmann, Eichrodt, Leslie, and Fohrer. K. Budde ("Zu Jesaja 1–5," *ZAW* 50 [1932] 69) objected that Osiris is never mentioned in the OT. Neither is Beltis, which must mean Isis beside Osiris. H. Zimmern (*Oriental Studies,* FS P. Haupt [Baltimore: Johns Hopkins, 1926], 281–92) suggests that Beltis refers to Sarpanitu, the city-god of Babylon. The Versions leave out the second half of the line, but that is no help. Gray suggests reading לְבִלְתִּי כְּרֹעַ (or מִבִּלְתִּי) "to avoid crouching under (?) prisoners and falling under the slain." C. J. Labuschagne ("Ugaritic *blt* and *biltî* in Isa 10:4," VT 14 [1964] 99) reads בֶּלֶת יִכְרַע "No, he will crouch" (cf. Ugar *blt* meaning "no" or "yet"). Wildberger (180) suggests letting בלתי stand alone as "nothing (remains)" and make כרע an inf abs כָּרֹעַ "one must bow down." He also insists that תחת אסיר does not mean "among prisoners" but "at the place of prisoners" (cf. Exod 16:29; 2 Sam 7:10; 1 Chr 17:9).

Form/Structure/Setting

Repetition of the refrain, "In all this his anger has not turned, His hand is still outstretched" in 9:11b[12b], 16d[17d], 20b[21b]; 10:4b demonstrates the unity of the passage as well as the strophes of the poetic unit. The refrain also appears in 5:25 which has led Wildberger (207) and others to try to rearrange the book. 10:1–4 do in fact resume the "woe" forms, but the relationships are complex. Note that 10:5 begins with "woe" but has no refrain.

The entire scene is formed about the Word which the Lord has spoken. Israel's response (or lack of response to it) is reflected in the first two strophes. The last two record no such response. Israel is too far gone. In the last strophe the funeral tone of the lament takes charge. Israel is presumed dead.

The strophes recite God's actions and then allow commentary on the reactions of God and Israel. It is as though the speakers are spectators for this play within a play. The reader learns of it through their reports.

Intro.	vv 7–9	God's "word"—Israel's response.
I.	vv 10–12	Against Rezin—they are against Israel.
		God's punishment continues—Israel has not turned.
II.	vv 13–17	Against the leaders—they become tyrants.
		God's punishment continues—wickedness burns on.
III.	vv 18–20	Overflowing anger—internal strife
		God's punishment continues.
IV.	vv 1–4	*Woe*—God's punishment continues.

The entire scene resumes the viewpoint of chaps. 1–5. There is no resistence to God here like that shown in 7:1—9:6[7]. The dialogue shows the detached observation of heavenly observers, the reintroduction of the personae that we came to know in 1:2 as Heavens and Earth. 10:1 reintroduces the company of mourners that appear in chap. 5. This woe-oracle returns to the form of the series in 5:8–24 and is often considered misplaced. (See *Comment* to that section.)

The insertion of the seventh "woe" here revives the theme and mood of chap. 5. The positive and hopeful notes of 8:23—9:6 (9:1–7) and of 10: 5–19 change nothing in the necessity for God to respond to Israel's flagrant sins.

Comment

7[8] *A word* is used here in the sense of "a message." But it is also much more, like a verdict from a court, a decision by a business on a contract. It reports a decision and determines a future. This *word* involved *Jacob/Israel,* the elect people, the two hundred-year-old nation that laid claim to that promise with its capital in Samaria, the rival and sometime enemy of Judah/Jerusalem. Yahweh's complaint in 1:2–3 was about Israel. The announcement in 2:6–8 was about Israel. The song of the vineyard applied to Israel (5:7). The "woes" of chap. 5 applied to Israel. Isaiah's vision and "this people" in God's words were about Israel (6:9–10). Isaiah's word to Ahaz was about Israel (7:7–9). His prophecy of "Maher-Shalal-Hash-Baz" (8:1–3) was about Israel. Indeed, *a word* had gone out from Yahweh against Jacob.

8[9] "All the people know" is one translation. There is no way for the people to ignore the obvious disaster. Yet they choose not to recognize its deeper meaning. *Arrogance and a stout heart* are those nemeses of mankind that invite God's retribution (cf. 2:11–17).

9[10] The determination to "tough it out" is bravado. In some times and against some adversaries it would have been admirable. Against Assyria's determination to root out potential rebellion and re-structure the government of the entire region, it was fool-hardy. In face of God's announcement that covenant would not be renewed, it was spiritually reprobate.

10[11] The Son of Remaliah was Rezin's puppet. Rezin effectively controlled Samaria. Thus God's first action is against Rezin. With his enemies in power in Damascus, Israel had hostile regimes "before and behind" even before the Assyrian arrived.

11–12 [12–13] God's "no" sign was still showing. *Anger* is not to be seen in terms of uncontrolled emotion. It reflects God's stimulus to provoke a response that he can deal with. But they do not respond to God. They only respond (inadequately) to the threatening situation (v 9[10] above).

13–16[14–17] The second round of encounter has Yahweh remove effective leadership from Israel. A second action has the remaining leaders confuse their followers. God cannot bless this situation.

16b[17b] The refrain observes that the "no" of God continues to apply.

17[18] Israel's response is pictured as "wickedness that burns like fire."

18[19] The third round of the encounter speaks of God's judgment as a counter-fire that singes the land and turns the people into highly combustible material. The figure changes, becomes more personal. The extreme situation leaves no room for compassion and mutual aid.

19–20[20–21] The people turn on each other in an orgy of self-destruction. The proud boast of self-reliant rebuilding (v 9) forgotten, the inner fabric of social and political relationship succumbs to chaotic violence. Yet

God's "no," his decision to abandon (2:6), his hidden face (8:17) continue in force. This time no reference to Israel's response is made.

10:1–4 Mourners take the hint and pick up a lament. The helplessness of ineffective crisis government is pictured. The "misleaders' " (v 15) show of decrees and executive orders only increases injustice, but brings no order to those chaotic times. The state is dead, the mourners chant, and the leaders have no option but to share its fate. The final comment notes that *God's anger has not changed.* Israel's fate, as a nation, is sealed.

Explanation

The scene acts to stem the tide of patriotic euphoria that had broken out in Jerusalem in the previous scene. The optimism that saw only opportunity, glory, and light beyond the crisis tended to be blind to the dire implications inherent in the approach of the Assyrian. They, and the audience, are called back to the grim implications of God's decision to end the covenant relation with Israel (which was something of a farce anyway on the part of the Northern Kingdom).

But the issue of Israel—election and God's intentions for his people—will be back. It cannot so easily be disposed of.

10:1–4 respond to the dark picture of Israel's condition, lamenting the bad leadership which had precipitated its current state. Oppressive laws against the weak and helpless for the hope of ill-gotten gain have weakened the fabric of society. It cannot withstand the external pressures. The exploiters will suffer like all others. Thus they experience God's anger which was aroused by their deeds.

Episode B: Assyrian, Rod of My Anger (10:5–19)

Bibliography

Childs, B. S. *Isaiah and the Assyrian Crisis.* SBT 2/3. Naperville, IL.: Allenson, 1967. 39–90, especially. **Fohrer, G.** "Wandlungen Jesajas." *FS W. Eilers.* Wiesbaden: Harrassowitz, 1967. 67–70. **Fullerton, K.** "The Problem of Isaiah, Chapter 10." *AJSL* 34 (1917/18) 170–84. **Sander, O.** "Leib-Seele-Dualismus im Alten Testament." *ZAW* 77 (1965) 329–32. **Schildenberger, J.** "Das 'Wehe' uber den stolzen Weltherrscher Assur." *Sein und Sendung* 30 (1965) 483–89. **Skehan, P. W.** "A Note on Isaiah 10:11b–12a." *CBQ* 14 (1952) 236. **Tadmor, H.** "The Campaigns of Sargon II of Assur." *JCS* 12 (1958) 22–40; 77–100.

ON THE TEXT:

Driver, G. R. "Isaiah 1–39: textual and linguistic problems." *JSS* 13 (1968) 36–57. **Robertson, E.** "Some obscure passages in Isaiah." *AJSL* 49 (1932–33) 320–22. **Schwarz, G.** ". . . das Licht Israels? Eine Emendation (Isa 10:17a)." *ZAW* 82 (1970) 447–48.

Translation

Mourner:	5 *Woe—*	1
Yahweh:	*Assyria!*	1
	Rod of my anger!	2+2+2
	[a] *Staff of my wrath,*	
	It is in their hand! [a]	
	6 *I send him against a godless nation.*	3+3
	I command him against the people of my wrath.	
	To take spoil!	2+2
	To seize prey!	
	To make it [a] *a trampling ground,*	2+2
	like the mire of the streets!	
Heavens:	7 *But what about him?*	1
	He does not think that way.	2+3
	His heart does not feel like that.	
	On the contrary—	1
	His mind is on destruction	2+2+2
	On slaughtering nations	
	Not a few. [a]	
Earth:	8 *He says:*	2+4
	"Are each [a] *of my vassals not kings?*	
	9 *Is not Calno* [a] *like Carchemish?*	3+3+3
	Or Hamath like Arpad? [b]	
	Or Samaria like Damascus?	
	10 *Just as my hand finds* (*its way*)	3+2+3
	to the idolatrous Kingdoms	
	whose idols surpass Jerusalem's and Samaria's,	
	11 *as I do to Samaria and her idols*	3+2
	shall I not do to Jerusalem and to her images?"	2+2
Heavens:	12 *It will be*	1
	when the Lord will finish all his work	4+3
	against Mount Zion and against Jerusalem—	
Yahweh:	*I will punish* [a] *the fruit of the King of Assyria's expanded mind*	4+3
	and the glorification of his elevated eyes.	
Heavens:	13 *Because he says:*	2
	"I act by the strength of my hand.	3+3+3
	For I decide by my wisdom	
	When I change people's boundaries.	
	I plunder [a] *their treasures* [b]	2+3
	When I knock down inhabitants like a bull. [c]	
	14 *Then my hand searches as in a net*	3+2
	for the people's wealth.	
	Like gathering abandoned eggs	3+4
	I myself gather the whole earth.	
	And no wing flutters,	4+3
	nor does any mouth open or chirp."	

Earth: 15 *Does the ax exalt itself* 2+2
over the one cutting with it?
Or the saw magnify itself 2+1
over the one using it?
As (if) a rod were to wave its bearers 3+3
As (if) a staff were to lift (the one who is) not wood.[a]
Heavens: 16 *Therefore—* 1
The Lord,[a] *Yahweh of Hosts, will send* 4+2
leanness against his fat ones.
Earth: *Under his glory* 2+2+2
he will kindle a kindling
like a kindling of fire.
17 *And the Light of Israel*[a] *will become a fire* 4+2
and his Holiness a flame.
It will burn and devour 2+2+2
his thorns[b] *and his briers*
in one day,
18 [a] *With the glory of his forests and his acreage.* 3
Heavens: *Body and Soul it will consume*[a] 3+3
and he shall be like a sick man wasting away.[b]
Earth: 19 *What is left of the trees*[a] *of his forest* 3+2+2
will be so few
that a child can count them.

Notes

5.a-a. The second half of the line is a problem, complicated by MT's *makeph.* Various attempts at emendation have been made (cf. Wildberger) but none is satisfactory.

The problem pair of words is הוא בידם. By itself this means "he (is) in their hand." Joined to מטה "staff" it may be rendered "which (is) in their hand." However, it divides two words which the parallelism suggests should be in constr relation.

It is best understood as a gloss note added by a scribe, to ameliorate the theological problem of ascribing full identification of the Assyrian as God's instrument. Instead, it suggests, God's instrument was "in their hand." G. Driver (*JTS* 34 [1933] 383) suggested transposing the phrase to achieve the same effect: ומטא זעמי הוא בידם "And the rod of my wrath—it is in their hand."

6.a. K לשימו "to make it," but Q לשומו "to make it." Masoretic Hebrew knows both forms. The difference is meaningless.

7.a. Tg translates לא מעט "not a few" with לא בחיס "without protection" (cf. S. Speier, "Zu drei Jesajastellen," *TZ* 21 [1965] 312 and Hab 1:17b).

8.a. M. D. Goldman (*AusBR* 1 [1951] 63) shows that יחדו means not only "together" but also "alone, separately."

9.a. כַּלְנוֹ "Calno" is usually pronounced "Calneh." See LXX, Amos 6:2, and the cuneiform inscriptions.

9.b. אַרְפַּד "Arpad" is usually written with *kametz.*

12.a. LXX *ἐπάξει* "he will bring (punishment)." Many suggest changing MT to third person.

13.a. שושתי is apparently a variant writing for שוסיתי as several MSS preserve it: piel pf 1 sg שסה (cf. GKC § 6k) is שסיתי "I plunder." The context calls for an active verb.

13.b. Q ועתודותיהם "their he-goats," meaning their leaders. K ועתידתיהם "their supplies." Parallelism is better served by K.

13.c. The Versions vary the reading: LXX *καὶ σείσω πόλεις κατοικουμένας* "and I will shake inhabited cities"; Tg בתקוף ית יתבי כרכין תקיפין ואחיתית "and I subdued with force inhabitants of strong cities." MT suits the basic form, meter, and sense as well as any.

15.a. לא־עץ "not wood" has appeared cumbersome to some interpreters. E. Robertson (*AJSL* 49 [1932/33] 319) suggests emending to ל(ו)חֵץ "oppressor." MT should be sustained with Wildberger.

16.a. האדון "the Lord" is missing in some MSS. LXX only has it once where האדון יהוה "the Lord Yahweh" would require it twice. But MT is good meter in a tri-stich line and should be kept. (Contra G. R. Driver, *JSS* 13 [1968] 41.)

17.a. אור־ישראל "Light of Israel" may also be a name for God. Cf. Pss 27:1 and 36:10.

17.b. שִׁיתוֹ "his thorns" appears only in the first part of Isaiah (cf. 5:6). The form with suffix would ordinarily be שֵׁיתוֹ. Wildberger suggests the alternative pronunciation is given to match וּשְׁמִירוֹ "and his briers."

18.a-a. MT has only one verb: יְכַלֶּה "it will consume." LXX has two verbs ἀποσβεσθήσεται "will be extinguished" and καταφάγεται "it will consume."Wildberger suggests changing וכרמלו "his cultivated land" to a verb form. Driver (*JSS* 13 [1968] 42) joins Σ αναλωθήσεται, Vg *consumetur* and *BHS* in suggesting a pass reading יְכֻלֶּה. However, MT may well be kept as it is.

18.b. כמסס נסס is a *hap. leg.* נסס has been compared to Syr *nassîs* or *nᵉsîs* "sick." T. Nöldeke (*Mandäische Grammatik* 1875 [=1944] XXX and *ZDMG* 40 [1886] 729, n. 2) pointed to Gr νόσος "sickness." G. R. Driver (*JTS* 34 [1933] 375; *JSS* 13 [1968] 42) refers it to Akk *nasâsu* I "sway to and fro," II "wave (of hair), shake," while Wildberger prefers to derive it from נס "signal" ("As if a flag-bearer falls"). Cf. Robertson, *AJSL* 49 (1932–33) 320–22.

19.a. Wildberger has properly rejected the suggestion of BHK עצי. MT is to be kept.

Form/Structure/Setting

A formal similarity ties this new section to the last episode: the use of "woe." But the subject and orientation turn from Israel to Assyria. The episode comes to grips with the anomaly that God is using the enemy—is claiming to own and control the enemy—against his own people. The problems God faces in doing so are portrayed from the viewpoint of those who believe that God has a special relationship with Jerusalem.

The passage has one theme: Assyria, God's chosen instrument. But the disparity in character and intention between God and his instrument tests the unity of the passage.

Yahweh speaks twice on the issue. In vv 5–6 he announces the Assyrian's commission. In v 12b he promises to punish the Assyrian king's ambition. The rest of the section reacts to these announcements. The Assyrian is not actually present, but he is quoted at such length that his presence is "felt" (vv 8–11, 13–14). The indignation of the players at the appointment (vv 7 and 15) is supported by these quotations, and mollified by the expanded assurance of God's judgment of the Assyrian (vv 16–17).

The composition is a literary masterpiece in which the choice and balance of the vocabulary and grammar, not to mention the sounds of the words, work together to achieve the effect intended. It is one of the strongest literary pieces in the entire Vision.

It begins as though it would continue the "woes" that precede. But the Yahweh-word breaks in to turn attention to the active perpetrator of the violence instead of its victim. The speech begins with strong phrases—no verbs (v 5). It continues (v 6) with inverted sentences—prepositional phrases up-front—and imperfect tenses. It closes with three infinitives to emphasize the intent of the appointment. The use of cognate verb-object combinations adds strength to the speech.

5–7 The objection turns to the subject, the Assyrian, by using "but as for him." Vv 5–6 have spoken of God's intention. The response is concerned about the Assyrian's intentions. Again, inverted word order brings emphasis and passion to the words (v 7a) while the decisive statement is made with infinitives—no finite verbs (v 7b)—matching the Lord's words in v 6b. The rhetorical question of v 7a–d marks the sharpness of the dialogical exchange.

8–11 The quoted speeches (vv 8–11 and 13–14) are modeled on those of Rab-shekah (2 Kgs 18:19–25, 28–35; 19:10–13; Isa 36:4–10, 13–20; 37:10–13). However, the literary function differs. In the narrative, the speeches fit naturally into the psychological warfare of the siege. They are intended to intimidate—to prepare for negotiation. Here they are plucked out of context to illustrate the Assyrian's attitude and character.

The opening lines (vv 8–9) are strong, assertive statements without verbs. The comparison that follows is deliberately insulting and denigrating in likening the idolatrous nations to Samaria and Jerusalem. The verbs in (vv 10 and 11a) "my hand finds" "as I do" are in the perfect tense, while that in 11b, "shall I not do," returns to the imperfect like v 7a. Again the use of rhetorical question (11b) strengthens the speech.

The taunt against nations easily slips into a blasphemy of their gods (cf. Wildberger). Childs (*Isaiah and the Assyrian Crisis,* 88) has traced a historical tradition in Israel that began with Goliath and David (1 Sam 17:43) and moved beyond to the references in Ezekiel and finally to Daniel.

The speeches have clear parallels in 36:4–10, 13–20; 37:10–13, 24–25. The latter setting is that of siege and the preparation for negotiation. But here the setting is more general. While those in chaps. 36 and 37 belong to the genre of battle taunts like that of Goliath, these in chap. 10 are like the words of Babylon's leaders in Gen 11:3–4, of Babylon's king in Isa 14:13–14, of Tyre in Ezek 27:3 and 28:2, of Egypt in Jer 46:8, or of Edom in Obad 3.

12 The announcement by and on behalf of Yahweh contrasts with the boasts of the Assyrians.

15 The parable of the ax and the workman has a flavor of the wisdom schools. The use of metaphor, the question, and comparison make the point.

16 לכן "therefore" corresponds to כי "because" in v 13 and introduces the announcement of Yahweh's punishment of Assyria which is elaborated in two forms. The first decrees a wasting illness to replace his plump good health (16a and 18bc). The second announces a seering fire that will destroy his forests (vv 16b–18a and 19).

Comment

5 Three words dominate the verse.

Assyria is already familiar from the announcement in 7:17 and the following speeches. (Cf. 7:18, 20; 8:4, 7.) Even the idea that God is sending the King of Assyria has been stated there. *Anger* (אפי) and *wrath* is also familiar. The Vision began by explaining Yahweh's displeasure in chap. 1 and by citing the day of retribution in chap. 2. The great funeral scene in chap. 5 has the repeated refrain: "his anger is not turned away" (5:25b) which is picked up again in 9:17c, 21c, and 10:4. This passage is, in a sense, an explanation of that repeated phrase.

In their hand. That God's work should be placed in the power and authority of the Assyrian raises a serious issue of faith. The dilemma was posed in the shocked question of the prophet in 6:11 "How long?" It is implicit in Ahaz' refusal to put Yahweh to the test (7:12). It is there in the admonition concerning "conspiracy" in 8:12, in the rock that causes men to stumble in 8:14. (Note the emphatic use of first person in vv 5–6, 12b, with the counterpoint in the first person from the Assyrian in vv 8–11, 13–14).

שׁבט "rod" can refer to a ruler's scepter as it does in Gen 49:10; Num 24:17; Judg 5:14; Isa 9:3[4]; 11:4; 14:5; and Amos 1:5, 8. Or it may refer to the disciplinarian rod of punishment as in Job 9:34 and 21:9 where God's discipline is shown. Cf. also Prov 13:24, etc.; 2 Sam 7:14; 23:21; Isa 14:29. מטה "staff" may also refer to a scepter as it does in Jer 48:17; Ezek 19:11–14; Ps 110:2, but not to an educator's tool. It is more a magician's wand (cf. Exod 7:12). Aaron and Moses use such (Exod 4:2–4; 7:9–20; 17:5) and it is once called מטה האלהים "the staff of God" (Exod 17:9). It becomes מטה־עז "the staff of power" (Jer 48:17; Ezek 19:11; Ps 110:2). Together, the words indicate that God's royal authority and awesome power have been delegated to the Assyrian—expressions of God's anger and his wrath.

6 The verse precludes the obvious objection that Israel is elect, the children of Abraham. Not so—they are that no longer. They are *a godless nation* or a profane nation. The use of גוי "nation" is deliberate. (Cf. 1:2b–4; 2:6–8.)

They are a people of God's wrath. This implies not only rejection but active measures toward extermination. That is the role of the Assyrian.

7 Attention is drawn to the character and intention of the instrument. His interest is in violence and slaughter for its own sake—to build up his own image, to expand his ego.

8 שׂרים "vassals" and מלכים "kings" apparently recognize the distinction in Akkadian between *malku* or *maliku* which refers to the king of a city and *šarru* the king of a country. The Assyrians allowed the defeated city-kings to keep their titles.

9 He recites his victories over the great city-states of Syria. As independent powers in an earlier time, they were a barrier to aggression from the north or east. *Calno* (apparently the same as כַּלְנֵה "Calneh" in Amos 6:2) is to be located in northern Syria. Opinions differ on the likely location. It fell to Tiglath-Pileser in 738 B.C. *Carchemish* was a city on the Euphrates near the boundary between modern Turkey and Syria. It was known in the early second millennium and its history touched that of Egypt in the fifteenth century and that of the Hittites in the fourteenth. The city was sacked by the Assyrians repeatedly in the ninth and eighth centuries. Tiglath-Pileser III received tribute from it. In 717 B.C. Sargon finally destroyed the city and deported its inhabitants (*ISBE* 1:616).

Hamath lies well to the south on the Orontes river in Syria. It was an important independent city. David collaborated with its king. It was subdued by Assyria in 738 B.C. and a brief uprising was totally put down in 720 B.C. *Arpad* is always paired with Hamath (cf. 36:19 and 37:1); they are mentioned as cities destroyed by Tiglath-Pileser III (*ISBE* 1:298). It was located about twenty-five miles north of modern Aleppo.

Samaria was the city built by Omri to be the capital of Israel. It had come under pressure from Tiglath-Pileser as early as the reign of Menahem (745–738 B.C.) (2 Kgs 15:19–20). In 733 B.C. Tiglath-Pileser invaded the land (2 Kgs 15:29), Pekah was murdered, and the Assyrian put Hoshea on the throne and imposed tribute. When Tiglath-Pileser died (727 B.C.) Hoshea rebelled. Shalmaneser threw him in prison and besieged the city, finally subdued by his successor Sargon II in 722 B.C.

Damascus was the capital of Aram and one of the oldest cities in the world. In 732 B.C. Tiglath-Pileser conquered Damascus and its territory. He made it an Assyrian province with an Assyrian governor.

Jerusalem apparently paid tribute to Assyria under Uzziah, Jotham, and Ahaz. But there is no record of a specific threat during this period. Under Hezekiah the threats became serious (cf. chaps. 20 and 36–37).

10 In worldly terms the Assyrian recognized the role of religion in each of the countries he captured. Undoubtedly, from his point of view, the idols of northern Syria were much better known and more respected than the religion of Samaria and Jerusalem.

11 The speech indicates a threat to Samaria (i.e., prior to 722 B.C.) and an extended threat to Jerusalem. This is exactly the situation envisioned by 8:7–8. The battle threat becomes blasphemy in this setting (cf. Childs, *Isaiah and the Assyrian Crisis,* 88) and is answered accordingly.

12 Throughout this section the Vision has recognized the unity of the Assyrian's task. First the destruction of Samaria, including exile of its people, followed by the chastising purification of Jerusalem. Only after this is complete will Yahweh turn his attention to the Assyrian.

The masterful, artistic use of language appears throughout the section; e.g., פרי "fruit" and תפארת "glorification" show assonance.

13 The king's second poem of self-praise supplies the evidence to support Yahweh's judgment of him. The king should possess physical power and wise counsel to make plans (cf. פלא יועץ "a wonder counselor" and אל גבור "God-Hero" in 9:5[6]). These the king claims.

14 The changing of boundaries was a fixed part of Assyrian imperial practice along with the exchange of peoples. He is proud of his ability to extort tribute and raise funds for his campaigns and the empire. He finds it as easy as taking eggs from under a nesting hen. No complaint is raised. No resistence dares raise its head.

15 It is not the violence or the destruction to which protest is directed. It is only that he claims full credit, putting himself in the place of God.

16–19 The statement of judgment picks up its theme from v 12. The announcement uses Yahweh's full title, as it was used in Holy War of old. As in the old Holy War themes, the application of power is indirect. A wasting disease appropriately attacks the result of rich living in Assyrian subjects. A fire will destroy the similar signs of a rich land—his forests.

Explanation

God is not reacting in the events of that time. His decision and action activate the scene. Assyria is his agent. The Assyrian invasions are identified as God's work to accomplish his destructive judgment. But the protest is raised: the Assyrian does not know that. His drives and ambition are totally selfish. How can one identify God's work in one so ungodly? God will judge the Assyrian in time. One thing at a time. The limitations that time imposes are accepted, even as they apply to the work of God. With this passage a major thesis of the Vision has been fully stated and defended. God uses the pagan empires to further his purpose. (Cf. Cyrus in chaps. 45–46.) This is a change from the Kingdom of God theology of the United Monarchy and the Psalms. There God ruled the world through the Davidic king in Jerusalem. In Isaiah a part of that rule is delegated to the empires and Israel's role is radically redefined.

The basic issue of faith as it relates to history is faced directly in this scene. The fact of Assyria's ascendancy, power, and tyranny in the latter eighth century is unchallenged. The question probes the deeper explanation of the factors which made that possible. Yahweh claims that Assyria belongs to him: "Rod of my anger! Staff of my wrath!" He claims authority over him: "I send him! I command him!" He accepts responsibility for the King's excesses: "I will punish him!" But the speakers insist that another view be heard. The Assyrian proclaims his own autonomy, integrity, and credit: "My vassals;" "my hand;" "I do." He will not share credit or responsibility: "I acted by the strength of my hand. I decided by my wisdom!" He wants full recognition and credit for his acts: "I changed people's boundaries. I plundered their treasures. I knocked down inhabitants. I myself gather the whole earth."

God's commitment that "the arrogance of man will be brought low—Yahweh alone will be exalted" (2:17) is challenged by the very one that he has chosen and used to do his work of judgment. The doctrine that God works through human agency faces this dilemma. When God strengthens and guides someone to accomplish God's will he runs the risk of convincing the person of his own importance and ability which complicates his usefulness to God or at that point makes him the object of God's judgment.

The stark presentation of the problem here (and in chap. 2, chap. 14, and chap. 27) forms a background to the argument for the "servant" role which could help Israel and Jerusalem break this vicious cycle.

R. Kittel (*Geschichte des Volkes Israel* II, 6th ed. [Stuttgart: Kohlhammer, 1925] 386, n. 1) characterizes this as "one of the strongest of Isaiah's speeches and at the same time the first attempt to enunciate a philosophy of history in grand style which is built on the law of a moral world-order in history. World history is world judgment."

Episode C: Only a Remnant (10:20–23)

Bibliography

Binns, L. E. "Midianite Elements in Hebrew Religion." *JTS* 31 (1930) 337–54. **Stegemann, U.** "Der Restgedanks bei Isaias." *BZ* 13 (1969) 161–86.

Translation

Heavens:	20 *And it shall be in that day:*	1+2
	no longer will	3+2+3
	the remnant of Israel	
	and refugees of the house of Jacob	
	rely on their oppressors	2+2
	but will rely on Yahweh,	
	the Holy One of Israel,	2+1
	in a truth.[a]	
Chorus of Israelites:	21 *A remnant will return!*	2+2+2
	A remnant of Jacob!	
	To the Mighty God!	
Heavens:	22 *Even if there are*	2+2+2
	(of)your people, Israel,	
	(a number) like the sand of the sea,	
	(only) a remnant of it[a] *will return.*	3
Earth:	*Annihilation has been determined!*	2+2
	Righteous (anger) is overflowing!	
	23 *Indeed, what the Lord,*[a] *Yahweh of Hosts,*	3+3+3
	is doing in the land	
	is a completed and fixed decree.[b]	

Notes

20.a. באמת "in truth" has been found to be superfluous by Procksch and H. Schmidt (*Die grossen Propheten,* 2nd ed. [Göttingen: Vandenhoeck & Ruprecht, 1923]). Wildberger correctly holds that its position intentionally emphasizes its point. LXX τῇ ἀληθείᾳ "to the truth" uses a dative case without preposition, which patently changes the meaning. Cf. further H. Wildberger, "אמן," *THAT,* I, col. 201.

22.a. בו "in it." G. R. Driver (*JSS* 13 [1968] 42) and *BHS* suggest that it be read with the following phrase. Wildberger correctly insists on a partitive meaning: "In Israel—only a few can agree to repent."

23.a. אדני "Lord" is standard in Isaiah (see 3:17; 6:8; 7:14; 8:7; 9:7–16). LXX has only ὁ θεός for the entire long title. Most of the other Greek versions have κυριος.

23.b. כלה ונחרצה, lit., "completion and a fixed thing" are probably to be understood as hendiadys, i.e., two words which together express one idea.

Form/Structure/Setting

The scene returns to an "earthly" setting. Traditional words of hope are offered, interrupted by heavenly reminders of God's true intentions. The episode is joined to the one before by the formula "and it shall be in that day" and by the play on the word "remnant." In v 19 it referred to trees that survived conflict and exploitation, but touches off a discussion of the remnant of Israel in vv 20–22. The consecutive of the perfect verb "and it shall be" continues the thought of ישלח "he will send" in v 16. The arrangement of vv 20–22 is dialectical with different voices and ideas engaged. This entire chapter has looked at the predicament of Northern Israel as refugees and friends in Jerusalem might see it and Heavens and Earth might observe it.

Comment

Vv 20–23 expressly speak of Israel/Jacob, i.e., Northern Israel, while vv 24–27 speak to Jerusalem. Commentators have often created confusion by ignoring this distinction.

The time, "that day," refers to the Assyrian invasion which has dominated chaps. 8–10. That is the incursions from 733 to 721 B.C.

20 The verse assumes the dispersion of the people of Northern Israel (cf. 11:11, 16; 2 Kgs 17:6) and refers directly to them. It assumes two prior attitudes among the people. Both relate to the word שען "lean on." The word appears in a religious context in Mic 3:11 which condemns the corruption among leaders, priests, and prophets who piously "lean on Yahweh," saying, "Is not Yahweh in our midst? Nothing can happen to us." In 30:12 the word is parallel to בטח "trust" and describes those who reject God's word and then "depend on deceit and oppression." In 31:1 it again is parallel to "trust" and speaks of those who "rely" on horses and Egypt. So the term is current in a religious context to mean a frivolous reliance on God to get them through regardless of their behavior. It was also current in referring to political reliance on arms, alliances, or authoritarian methods.

מכהו "their oppressors" is literally "those striking it." This could well apply to Pekah's puppet relationship to the Rezin of Aram who defeated Israel in 736 B.C. and supported Pekah's coup d'etat. (Cf. Bright, *HI,* 271–72). Or it could apply to Hoshea's ascending the throne in 732 under Assyria's sponsorship after the Assyria campaign of 733 (cf. 2 Kgs 15:25—16:9, especially vv 25–29, 37; 16:5–9). The bootlicking attitude is contrasted with a genuine dependence on Yahweh which makes for a genuinely independent political attitude.

The Vision emphasizes Isaiah's view that *faith* and the *confirmation* related to it (אמונה /אמן; cf. Wildberger, "אמן," *THAT,* I, cols. 202–4), that בטח *trust* and שען *dependence* on Yahweh, which are genuine, are essentials of life under God.

The reference to *leaning on their oppressors* is a reminder of 9:12[13], which accused the people of Israel of failure to return to Yahweh when he punished them. The word המכהו "the one striking them" is the same. Because "lean on Yahweh" had a negative religious connotation the באמת "in truth" is particularly appropriate and necessary. שאר "remnant" is taken here to imply that a small group of those left over as exiles will finally exercise genuine faith in Yahweh, in contrast to the picture in 9:7[8]—10:4.

21 The chorus picks up the hint of hopeful content and they understand it in their own way. They begin by chanting the name of Isaiah's son שאר ישוב "A Remnant Will Return." The words are packed with connotations and meaning, some of which are ambiguous and self-contradictory. It is just the kind of thing that makes a good slogan. These are several meanings that elements of the crowd could have understood from the slogan.

שאר can mean the pitiful remainder of a decimated people or army which survives a battle or a war. But it also apparently had a technical (perhaps cultic) meaning of the authentic and integral core of the people who were the genuinely elect, the genuine Israel. The rest of the nation depended on this core and assumed that they all would be saved, or would prosper because of it. They are "the pious remnant," the "righteous remnant," the "faithful remnant." Many would have felt that this second meaning cancelled out the first. (Cf. G. F. Hasel, "Remnant," *IDBSup,* 730–36.)

ישׁוב "will return" is equally ambiguous. It means simply "to turn" or "to return." It can mean to physically come back, as from exile, or it can refer to a change of mind or policy. It may become "repent" when related to God. The doctrine of repentance becomes widespread from Jeremiah onward (cf. J. Milgrom, "Repentance in the Old Testament," *IDBSup,* 736–38).

The slogan is applied and narrowed in the second line: "A remnant of Jacob." It is applied specifically to Northern Israel as v 20 had done.

The third line adds another ambiguous expression: אל גבור "God, the heroic warrior." However, the same title is applied in 9:5[6] as one of the throne names of the heir to David's throne. The hint that the misfortunes of the Northern Kingdom might open the door to a reunited Kingdom under Jerusalem and its king is not alone in these pages (cf. comments on 9:5–6[6–7] and 11:12–14).

22–23 The verses are a reminder of the context. God's decree for the political destruction of Israel has been fixed. It will not change. The Lord himself is at work to accomplish it in the land. No pious platitudes will change that fact. Thus שׁאר "remnant" is to be taken literally, as it was for the trees of Lebanon in v 19. The surviving fragment of the population will be frightfully small. There is nothing glorious about it from this viewpoint.

This reminder of God's consistent policy toward Israel in this period continues the line of announcements from 1:2–4; 2:6; 3:13–15; 5:13, 24, 25; 6:11–13; 7:8; 8:2, 5–7; 9:7–21, especially 14. The view of the Vision is that God's unalterable decision to end Israel's political existence as a nation had been made as early as Uzziah's time.

Scene 3:
Do Not Fear, You Jerusalemites (10:24—12:6)

The scene is marked by a clear change of subject, picking up the anomalous subject of 10:12 to become the dominant theme and address.

Again an arch structure may be perceived to shape the scene.

A Very soon my anger will be against the Assyrians (10:24–25)
  B The Lord will lash them in the way of Egypt (10:26–27)
    C He marches on Zion and waves at Jerusalem (10:26–27c)
      D The Lord is cutting trees in Lebanon (10:33–34)
        E The shoot from Jesse's root (11:1)
          F The Spirit of Yahweh rests on him (11:2)
            G The fear of Yahweh—his delight (11:3a)
KEYSTONE Yahweh's righteousness and justice (11:3b–4)

G′ Righteousness his belt (11:5–8)
F′ Knowledge of Yahweh in all the earth (11:9)
E′ The Root of Jesse, a banner to the nations (11:10)
D′ The Lord to recover refugees and restore the United Kingdom (11:11–14)
C′ Yahweh will dry up the sea (11:15–16)
B′ You will sing in that day (12:1–2)
A′ And you will drink from the well of salvation (12:3–6)

Three layers may be distinguished in the arch. The outer layers AB and A′B′ are directly addressed to God's people in Zion. CDE and C′D′E′ are about Yahweh's work of salvation, with E and E′ mentioning the king indirectly but explicitly. F and F′ speak about God's spiritual gifts and the knowledge of Yahweh. G and G′ speak of righteous judgment through the fear of Yahweh. The keystone speaks of Yahweh's just rule.

Interpreters have had trouble marking the divisions here. But the chiastic chart helps to clarify the situation.

Episode A: Yahweh's Anger against Assyria (*10:24–27c*). Vv 24–25 begin with לכן "therefore," a strong connective with a previous assertion, which in this case must be the keystone of the previous chiastic order, 10:12. Vv 26–27c expand on this, again using the full name of God and an "in that day" construction in 27a–c.

Episode B: The March of Conquest (*10:27d–32*), is a masterful poetic construction—unconnected syntactically—a theophanic vision inserted into the developing scene to prepare for the climactic announcement to follow.

Episode C: The Forester before Jerusalem (*10:33–34*), interprets the theophany but, more important, introduces the speeches that follow in chaps. 11 and 12. J. G. Herder (*The Spirit of Hebrew Poetry* [1782], tr. J. Marsh [Naperville; IL: Aleph Press, 1971], 294) noted this separation between vv 32 and 33. A. Bruno (*Jesaja, eine rythmische und textkritische Untersuchung* [Stockholm: Almquist & Wiksell, 1953]) and Kaiser have followed his lead. Wildberger has not recognized the syntactical connections. V 33 begins with הנה "behold." The subject is the Lord Yahweh. The announcement: as a master forester he is trimming and thinning the forests (cf. 10:17–19). Lebanon (read Assyrian power on the northern border) will fall (v 34).

The results are pictured in a series of picture passages (motifs), each beginning with a verb in perfect tense with *wāw:*

Episode D: A Shoot from the Stump of Jesse (*11:1–10*): A shoot from Jesse will thrive (vv 1–5). The people will not hurt; the earth will be full of the knowledge of Yahweh (vv 6–9). In that day the nations will rally to David's heir (v 10).

Episode E: Yahweh's Second Deliverance (*11:11–16*): In that day Yahweh will reach out to recover the scattered people.

Episode F: Hymns for "That Day" (*12:1–6*). In that day the King will sing to Yahweh (vv 1–2). In that day the people of Jerusalem will give thanks (vv 3–6).

The complete mosaic pictures the achievement of God's and Jerusalem's goals: stable continuance of the Davidic dynasty, peace with knowledge of

Yahweh, leadership over neighboring peoples, return of exiles, and unity in the Kingdom. These will all be achieved when Yahweh "cuts down the trees" (10:33–34), sends his Spirit on the King (11:2), judges in righteousness (11:4–5), and acts to bring back the exiles (11:11–12). The emphasis throughout is on Yahweh's initiative and Yahweh's action. Jerusalem, the King, and the exiles are to be either "receptive" or "reactive" only. Then they can sing (chap. 12).

Yahweh has brought the Assyrian (7:17) as a judgment on Israel and Aram. Israel continued rebellious (9:7[8]—10:4) and was destroyed (10:22–23). But his promise to purge Jerusalem (1:24–26) so that it can be his dwelling (2:1–4) is being carried out. An heir is promised to Ahaz (7:14) and is born amid rejoicing (9:6[7]).

Yahweh promises that the Assyrian will be punished when he has finished his work with Zion and Jerusalem (10:12). This is fulfilled: "See, he is lopping off branches" (10:12). A promise of a successor, (Hezekiah) blessed and successful (11:1–4), and of wonderful peace (11:5–9) seems within reach. The destruction of Samaria is past without Jerusalem being drawn into the rebellion. This is reason for hope (11:11–16) and for rejoicing (chap. 12).

It is also reason for a reassessment of the Vision's view of the reign of Ahaz. For all his timidness in response to a call for bold faith (7:10–13), Ahaz did obey the command to be calm and not give in to Rezin (7:4–6). He calmly maintained his status as an Assyrian vassal through the following rebellions and invasions. Although his kingdom did not go unscathed, he, his throne, and his kingdom survived. That in itself is the reason for the optimism of this scene. With God being the activist, Jerusalem's (and Israel's) role was a passive one. This Ahaz accepted and he was rewarded.

(A fifth-century reader/hearer could hardly help drawing a parallel to the reign of Manasseh. He also was a loyal Assyrian vassal through-out his reign. His policies also drew the ire of patriots within his realm and among the historians. However, he, too, saved Jerusalem from invasion or plundering. He, too, preserved his kingdom and his throne for his son and grandson.)

Episode A: Yahweh's Anger against Assyria (10:24–27c)

Bibliography

Binns, L. E. "Midianite Elements in Hebrew Religion." *JTS* 31 (1930) 337–54.

Translation

Herald: 24 *Therefore—thus says the* [a]*Lord, Yahweh of Hosts*[a] 1+4
"Do not be afraid
my people dwelling in Zion, 1+3+1
because of Assyria

when he strikes with the rod 2+3+2
when he lifts his staff against you
[b]*in the Way of Egypt.*[b]
25 *For in a very short while* 3+2+3
indignation will be finished,
and my anger, (will be intent) on their destruction."[a]
26 *Yahweh of Hosts*[a] *will lay bare a whip against him,* 2+2+1
like the one that struck Midian 2+2+3
by the rock of Oreb
or his staff across the sea,
and he will raise it in the Way of Egypt.[b] 3
27 *And it shall be in that day* 1+2
his burden will move from your shoulder 2+2
and his yoke be broken from your neck.[a] 1+2

Notes

24.a-a. LXX translates *κύριος σαβαωθ* "Lord of Hosts." Since it usually translates יהוה with *κύριὸς*, it has omitted the אדוני "Lord."

24.b-b. בדרך would be literally translated "in the way of." LXX reads *τοῦ ἰδεῖν ὁδὸν Αἰγύπτου* "of knowing the entrance of Egypt." In v 26, LXX paraphrases the same phrase *εἰς τὴν ὁδόν* which means "before the entrance" but then continues *τὴν κατ' Αἴγυπτον* "the one by (or in the manner of) Egypt." The meaning "in the manner of Egypt" is documented in BDB, 203 and still used by Wildberger, among others. However, the phrase also has good geographical connotation referring to the coast highway to Egypt where important battles were fought in this period. Also the interest in the Red Sea in 11:15 favors a geographical connotation for the phrase here and in v 26.

25.a. על־תבליתם has caused considerable discussion; cf. Wildberger. Some MSS read תכליתם, deriving the word from כלה, which appeared earlier in the verse. But DSS[Isa] supports MT. LXX reads *ἐπὶ τὴν βουλήν αὐτῶν* "upon his purpose." This has virtually transliterated בלי for *βουλήν*. But MT may best be understood as a noun coming from בלה with the meaning "destruction" (BDB, 115).

26.a. LXX omits צבאות "Hosts" but there seems to be no reason to drop it in the Hebrew.

26.b. See n. 24.b.

27.a. *BHS* reflects current views (cf. discussion under 10:27d–33) that the verse should be divided after חבל "be broken" instead of with MT before it. The last stich should be joined to the following poetic lines. This and the meter of v 27b–c should make חבל the verb for the second stich parallel to יסור in the first. W. R. Smith (*Journal of Philology* 13 [1885] 62) suggested reading יחבל and setting the *athnaḥ* on its last syllable. LXX translates *καὶ καταφθαρήσεται* which supports the meaning, if not the division.

Form/Structure/Setting

The episode (vv 24–27) is set off by לכן "therefore" as v 16 was above. It relates the following announcement to the fact of God's decree which affects כל הארץ "the whole land." It is introduced formally by כה־אמר אדני יהוה צבאות "Thus says the Lord Yahweh of Hosts." It designates what follows as a "Yahweh word." It also gives emphasis to the formal title of God, like v 16, in sending a destruction on the whole land; and v 33 on lopping off limbs of power.

The passage is addressed to עמי "my people" but to that part ישב ציון "who inhabit Zion." The message is short: "Do not be afraid because of Assyria." This shows it to be a "salvation oracle" (J. Begrich, "Das priesterliche Heilsorakel," *ZAW* 52 [1934] 81–92 = *Gesammelte Studien zum Alten Testament,* ThB 21 [München: Kaiser, 1964], 217–31). The admonition has a fixed place in ancient Holy War tradition (cf. N. Gottwald, "War, Holy," *IDBSup,* 942–44; G. von Rad, *Der Heilige Krieg im Alten Israel* [Zürich: Zwingli Verlag, 1951], 70). It was used in 7:4 in the message to Ahaz. It is a fixed part of the Lord's message in chaps. 35:4; 40:9; 41:10, 13 f.; 43:1, 5, etc.

The imperative is followed by consecutive perfects in vv 25, 26a, d which form the backbone of the oracle. The outline is:

"Do not fear because of Assyria in the Way of Egypt" (v 24)
Indignation will be finished (v 25)
Yahweh will lay bare a whip against him (v 26a)
He will raise it in the Way of Egypt (v 26d)

Until now, Jerusalem's involvement has been largely peripheral, but there is a sense that she will be involved (cf. 8:8, 14). The idea that Israel's problems might open doors for reunion are hinted at in 8:23—9:6[9:1–7], though the Lord through the Assyrian has business with Jerusalem after that with Israel (v 12). But now he turns directly to the Jerusalemites as they have been reminded that Israel's fate is sealed and that it involved "all the land"—and as they fearfully watch the march of Assyrian armies along the coastal plain toward Egypt.

Comment

24 The strong and encouraging oracle is addressed to the people *in Zion.* In contrast to those in Northern Israel they have no need to fear the Assyrians. *Smiting, rods* and their synonyms dominate the passage. In keeping with the tone in chaps. 9–10, the passage seeks to show how Yahweh's violent acts through the Assyrian are to be distinguished from the Assyrian's own acts, and how both are to be distinguished from God's punishment of the Assyrian when the first tasks are complete (cf. 10:12, 16).

בדרך מצרים "in the way of Egypt" may be understood to refer to the oppression before the Exodus. But the most natural designation is to take it geographically to refer to territory along the *sea* on the way to Egypt as דרך הים "way of the sea" in 8:23[9:1] refers to the district of Dor or Sharon.

In this time (733 B.C.) Tiglath-Pileser's campaign reached as far south as the Brook of Egypt (cf. Annals of Tiglath-Pileser). He paused at Aijalon and Gaza on the borders of Judah. He then left a garrison on the Egyptian border (*MBA,* 147). This posed a direct threat to Judah, not least because it interfered with the major trade route to Egypt.

25 The Assyrian role is definitely related to the period of God's anger, the day of wrath (cf. 5:25 and 26; 6:11–13). When this time and this task (cf. 10:12 and 10:23) are finished, things will change.

אפי על־תבליתם "my anger on their destruction" needs some explanation.

The first part of the line כלה זעם is impersonal: "indignation shall be complete." The second brings in two personal pronouns: *my* anger on *their* destruction. The preposition appears to be best understood as indicating intention. *My* is God speaking. *Their* must refer to Israel alone (vv 22b and 23). God's anger is directed to their destruction.

26 The instrument of God's retribution against Assyria is compared to the great victory of Gideon over the Midianites (Judg 8:25). The location must have been near the Jordan River, but is otherwise unknown. The *whip* of Gideon was neither arms nor armies, but was like the *staff over the sea* (Exod 14:15–16).

It is important to note that ונשאו "and he shall raise it" continues the line of consecutive perfects from ועורר "and he will lay bare." It brings attention back to the main thought concerning Yahweh and the Assyrians.

בדרך מצרים "on the way to Egypt" locates the scene of God's action to relieve Jerusalem of the Assyrian's presence as the same as that mentioned in v 24. When this actually happened is not sure, but it is clear that Tiglath Pileser and succeeding kings were unable to maintain their presence on the border. And so they were unable to continue to assess levies or taxes on the caravan trade that passed through.

27 With this *burden* and this *yoke,* i.e., the military presence on the Egyptian highway, removed, Zion's prosperity is assured.

Episode B: The March of Conquest (10:27d–32)

Bibliography

Albright, W. F. "The Assyrian March on Jerusalem, Isa. X 28–32." *AASOR* 4 (1924) 134–40. **Christensen, D. L.** "The March of Conquest in Isaiah X 27c–34." *VT* 26 (1966) 395–99. **Donner, H.** "Der Feind aus dem Norden." *ZDPV* 84 (1968) 46–54. **Federlin, L.** "A propos d'Isaie X 29–31." *RB* 3 (1906) 266–73.

Translation

Heavens:	27d [a]*He has ascended from Pene-Yeshemon.* [a]	3
	28 *He has come upon Aiath.*	2+2+3
	He has passed through Migron.	
	By Michmash [a] *he stores his baggage.* [b]	
Earth:	29 *They* [a] *have crossed the pass.*	2+3
	At Geba they have made [b] *their lodging.*	
	Rama is terrified.	2+3
	Gibeah of Saul has fled.	
Heavens:	30 *Shriek,* [a] *daughter of Gallim.*	2+2
	Pay attention, Laishah.	2+2
	Answer her, [b] *Anathoth.*	

[31] *Madmenah is a fugitive.* 2+3
Inhabitants of Gebim have sought refuge.
Earth: [32] *Until* [a] *today* 2+2
to stand [b] *at Nob.*
He waves his hand [c] 2+2+2
to make Zion large, [d]
the Hill of Jerusalem [e]

Notes

27d.a-a. The stich has been the subject of many attempts to point it in a way that is suitable to its context. MT treats it as a continuation of v 27, points על as a parallel to וְעֻלּוֹ "his yoke" earlier in the line and שמן the Assyrian's "opulence" in v 16, and puts the *athnaḥ* before וחבל: "and a yoke shall be broken because of fat." LXX reads *δαταφθαρήσεται ὁ ζυγὸς ἀπὸ τῶν ὤμων ὑμῶν* "the yoke will be broken from your shoulder."

Modern interpreters have judged the MT to have wrongly divided the verse. The indication of parallelism and meter lead them to include וחבל "be broken" in the previous stich (see above). This leaves על מפני־שמן to parallel the following lines: בא על עית, etc. The meter is right. The lack of article fits. This would make of על a verb, some form of עלה "to ascend," "go up" and of שמן a place name, as in all the lines that follow. Suggestions have been many and free: W. R. Smith (*Journal of Philology* 13 [1885] 62): עלה מצפן שדד "The Destroyer arises from the North." Duhm: עלה מפני רמן "He has come up from Pene Rimmon." Albright (*AASOR* 4 [1924] 134–40): וחבל לעלם בנשמתי "And be destroyed forever in my wrath." Procksch, followed by Kaiser, Fohrer, Wildberger, reads שֹׁמְרוֹן "Samaria" for שמן. Christensen (*VT* 26 [1966] 395–99): מפני ישמן "from Pene-Yeshemon," pointing to the established usage of shared consonants. This view has the advantage of requiring no change in the consonantal text and of fitting the setting of the passage.

28.a. MT מכמשׂ "Michmash" was written מכמשׁ in B and the same variation occurs in 1 Sam 13:2, 5, 11, 16. Ezra 2:27 and Neh 7:31 write מכמס supporting MT's pronunciation.

28.b. H. Donner (*Israel unter den Völkern,* VTSup 11[Leiden: E. J. Brill, 1964]) translates למכמש with the first stich "he passed over from Migron to Michmash" and the remaining words "he gathered his war-materials." But Wildberger is correct to support MT in the division.

29.a. DSS[Isa] LXX Syr Vg Tg read a sg here (G. R. Driver, *JTS* 38 [1937] 39). The change of person makes sense and accords with the dynamic style of the passage. MT should be kept.

29.b. מלון לנו, lit., "a lodging for us" or, reading as a pf 3 c pl לנו, a cognate of מלון, "they made their lodging." (Cf. Josh 4:3.) GKC 73*d* =Judg 19:13.

30.a. צהלי "cry shrilly," BDB, 843. קולך "your voice" an adv acc. BDB, 876, "make your voice shrill."

30.b. MT עֲנִיָּה "poor" = "Anathoth is poor." LXX ἐπακούσεται "hearken to" is repeated with Anathoth after use with Laishah. Syr *waᶜᵉnī* has led to the suggested change in pointing: עֲנִיהָ "answer her" which is widely accepted. A verb here parallels the previous two stichs.

32.a. עוד may indicate continuance "still," or addition "again," or "besides" BDB, 728–29. Note use of כי־עוד in v 25, "for yet a very little while" referring to the end of God's anger. So עוד היום seems to mark that point "Again (or still) today."

32.b. לעמד "to take a stand," an inf with no previous verb to depend upon. The subject has again returned to the approaching one. The place name has a preposition like those in v 28. The inf may depend on the previous verbs in v 28 "he came up, came, and passed over" in order "to again stand on Nob today." (GKC § 114*g*.) This makes it mark the purpose of the march from the Jordan.

32.c. ינפף ידו "he waves his hand." The understanding of this context as referring to the Assyrian has caused translators to interpret this as brandishing a fist. But the words simply mean "to wave his hand." The impf tense and normal word order mark an ordinary sentence.

32.d. K הר בית "mountain of the house of" creates some difficulties. Q followed by virtually all the Versions reads בת־ציון "daughter of Zion," a parallel to "the hill of Jerusalem." But the real problem lies in the combination with הר, reading "the mountain of the daughter of Zion." The only other usage of הר and בת is in Isa 16:1. Another solution would read them as one word: הִרְבִּיתְ/הִרְבִּיתָ (hiph pf 2 m or f) or הַרְבּוֹת (qal inf constr; cf. 2 Sam 14:11, GKC § 75*ff*) from רבה "to make to grow" or "increase." This change makes the section lead directly into the sense and mood of chap. 11 with which it is joined by *waw* consecutives. (See 11:1.)

32.e. K ירושלם Q ירושלים documents a frequent disagreement in textual sources about the pronunciation of the city's name. Q insists it is "Yerushalayim." K continues "Yerushalem."

Form/Structure/Setting

The poem has similarities to 63:1–6 and fits the tradition of Yahweh's march (cf. Judg 5:4–5; Ps 68:8–9, etc.). The passage is marked in the beginning by a sudden change of subject and setting. As v 26 has the Lord for subject, the Assyrian as the object, and the Way of Egypt for the setting, vv 27d–32 have an unnamed subject approaching Jerusalem from the East and North. (The passage continues with the identification of the Lord in vv 33–34 as the Divine Forester. It then continues with a chain of consecutive plurals through chaps. 11 and 12.)

Christensen (VT 26 [1966] 396) has identified the poem in 27d–32 as a liturgy from the "Ritual Conquest" tradition. This would fit here as a prelude to the Lord's appearance and its interpretation in the old theophanic traditions of God who comes from Paran or Sinai.

A major question turns on the intent of the march. It has usually been understood as malevolent—the approaching "destroyer." The words have been translated accordingly. But there is evidence to the contrary. The immediate context (10:24–27 and 11:1 ff.) is positive to Jerusalem. Although there is awesome terror in the villages, appropriate to the approach of the Almighty God, there is nothing in the words that dictate terror for Jerusalem. V 10:24 had commanded the opposite (contra Christensen and others).

(Recent treatments that view this as the approach of an Assyrian force may be found in Wildberger and H. Donner, *Israel unter den Völkern,* VTSup 11 [Leiden: E. J. Brill, 1964], 30–38 and *ZDPV* 84 [1968] 46–54.)

Delitzsch writes, "Seen aesthetically, the description belongs among the most splendidly picturesque that human poetry has ever produced. . . . Through v 32a the speech moves in quick stormy steps, then it becomes hesitant as if shaking for fear."

Wildberger notes the rich use of alliteration: מעברה עברו, עלה, על עית, לנו
מלון, נדדה מדמנה, בנף נפף, הרמה הרדה, עלי קולך בת גלים, עניהו ענתות
and the use of dark o-vowels (cf. L. Alonso-Schökel, "Is 10, 28–32: Análisis estilístico," *Bib* 40 [1959] 223) to depict the dark and awesome movements of suspense. This is one of the things lost in translation, although Duhm made a valiant effort to recapture it in German: "sie *pass*iren (sic) den *Pass, Geba* gibt Her*b*erge uns, *er*regt ist Ha*r*ama . . . *M*admena *m*acht sich davon, *an*tworte ihr *An*athoth!"

The recognition of the form or genre as a theophany is supported by the use of בא "come" (v 28) and לעמד "to stand," "to take a stand" (v 32). It also is supported by the formula of identification הנה "behold" in v 33. The theophanic vision must be seen beginning in 10:24 with "do not fear."

The problem with the Assyrian lies "on the way to Egypt," i.e., southwest of Jerusalem on the coastal highway some distance away. The Lord will deal with that problem in that place in his own time (v 25–26) and at that time Jerusalem will be free (v 27a–b). In the meantime, attention is called to the theophanic scene of an approach from the other side, according to the ancient cultic forms (vv 27c–32). He stands at the ancient cultic site of Nob and gestures toward Jerusalem.

Comment

The passage is dominated by place names which are easily identifiable as towns and villages only a few miles north and east of Jerusalem. But exact location is much less certain, cf. Wildberger. MBA, 154 traces the movement from Aiath to Michmash to Geba and on to Nob which is just across the valley from Jerusalem. The individual places deserve comment.

27d *Pene-Yeshemon.* Christensen (VT 26 [1966] 399) has identified this as a location near Gilgal. The word means "facing the wasteland or wilderness." It appears in Num 21:20 and 23:28 "where it refers to the end-point of the wilderness wandering." In 1 Sam 23:19, 24 and 26:1, 3 it applies to a wilderness territory on the Dead Sea north of Ziph.

Christensen locates the passage as having come from a Gilgal tradition of monarchical times which re-enacted the march of conquest of Josh 8 over Ai. With Jerusalem as the goal, the processional symbolized the move of the Ark from Gilgal to Jerusalem. It established in the cultic ritual that Yahweh who sits over the cherubim in Zion's temple was identical with Yahweh Sabaoth who comes from Sinai, who led Israel in the conquest of Canaan. The path leads sharply up from the river floor to the towns on the mountain ridge.

28 *Aiath* is the Ai of Josh 7 and 8. Neh 11:31 shows the Aramaic name "Ajja." (*GTTOT* § 1588 #2.) From here the route turns south. *Migron* lies some few miles south of Aiath. This is the area of the narrative in 1 Sam 14:2 ff. (Cf. *GTTOT* § 1588 #3.) *Michmash* lies a little to one side. The change of tense implies a subsidary clause like "while he stores his gear at Michmash." (Cf. *GTTOT* § 1021.)

29 The Pass from Migron to Geba appears also in 1 Sam 13:23. (*GTTOT* § 674.) *Geba* is the next stop on the road only a couple of miles southeast of Migron. This marks the end of the first stage of the journey. The names that follow are not on the line of march, but close enough to be afraid of forraging soldiers.

31 *Madmenah* and *Gebim* are unknown. They do not occur otherwise in Scripture, unless Madmenah is referred to in Isa 25:10. They would both be near Jerusalem. They mean "place of doing" and "the pits" which might indicate the garbage dumps of the city. (*GTTOT* § 1588 #11, 12 and § 1261.)

32 *Nob* (cf. 1 Sam 21:2; 22:9, 11, 19) had been a temple city and was called a "city of priests" (1 Sam 21:1 and 22:19). Perhaps 2 Sam 15:32 refers to Nob: "the height where God was worshiped." *GTTOT* § 96 suggests a location "on the ridge east and north-east of 'Jerusalem,' " which includes the Mount of Olives. From this vantage point he could look across at Jerusalem.

In ancient ritual the gesture of waving the hand may have indicated his claim to the city. In this setting it indicates his pleasure, his decision concerning the city. In chap. 36 a conquering general stands at another vantage point to negotiate the surrender of the city. But the awesome one here approaching the city does not negotiate. His imperious gesture seals the fate of the city. The gesture is not threatening—on the contrary, the one who has it in his power to utterly destroy indicates his will for the city to prosper. The gesture continues the message of vv 24–25 to the city. It need not fear. God will first deal with his enemies and then turn his attention to Zion when his anger is past.

The ravages of the war with Samaria and Aram of 736–34 B.C. and the backlash of Assyrian invasions of Israel and Philistia in 734–32, 728, and 723–21 B.C. had left the city, as it had the country, stripped of virtually all economic assets and probably reduced in population. The divine gesture indicates his pleasure that Zion "grow large."

Explanation

The great divine drama unfolds in the majestic words of the text. A major message of Scripture is that God comes in majesty and power. Christians observe this in Epiphany, which celebrates the coming of Christ. Israel celebrated God's coming in a number of ways. One pervading theme pictured him coming from Mount Sinai or from Paran. Another recited the conquest narrative of God's leading Israel into Canaan as in the book of Joshua. Here the great description of awesome approach along the road of conquest turns toward Jerusalem, rather than continuing as in Joshua to the conquest of Judah and Ephraim. It supports the word of encouragement and hope of v 24 and prepares for the identification of Yahweh who like a great forester chooses which trees shall be cut and which shall be allowed to grow.

Excursus: The Divine Forester

The vision presents God in various roles such as the Gardener in chaps. 5 and 17. One such motif has him in the role of the great forester who manages the planting of the world. He manages the forests, deciding which trees are to be cut, which pruned, and which allowed to grow; which areas are to be cut for grazing or planting and which are to be cultivated for the great trees. He commands the greatest and mightiest of the trees. If he says they are to be cut, they are cut.

The motif moves into a dominant position in the middle of the section 9:8—11:16. (Perhaps the picture of God's use of the Assyrian in 7:18–25 should fall under this picture.) God's decision to destroy northern Israel is pictured as felling trees (9:9b[10b]), as cutting off palm branch and reed (9:13[14]), as burning off underbrush (9:17–18[18–19]). The figures of the axe and the woodman (10:15) are most appropriate in this motif. The burn-off of underbrush reappears in 10:17–19. It all fits the picture of the decreed destruction of the whole land (10:23).

The peak of its use comes in 10:32—11:1. The Lord's march through Israel arrives at Nob. The unmoving hand signal of 9:16[17]; 9:20[21]; and 10:4 changes. He waves his hand toward Zion (10:32).

His signal before Zion is for her to grow and expand (10:32). So a shoot can now spring up from the stump of Jesse and a branch will bear fruit (11:1). The Forester's management can bring peace and prosperity to the primeval forest (11:6–8). The Root of Jesse becomes God's signal to the nations. With that the forester motif ends for this section.

Episode C: The Forester before Jerusalem (10:33–34)

Bibliography

Cf. *Bibliography* for 10:27d–32.

Translation

Herald:	33 *Behold—*	1+3+3
	The Lord [a] *Yahweh of Hosts*	
	designating [b] *beauty* [c] *with awesome* [d] *(skill),*	
	(as) the tops of the heights are being cut down	3+2
	and exalted ones are laid low.	
	34 *He strikes* [a] *forest thickets with the iron*	4+3
	(as) the Lebanese (forest) falls by a majestic (blow).	

Notes

33.a. האדון "the Lord." The use of this form, sg abs with article, occurs only three times outside Isaiah (Exod 23:17; 34:23; Mal 3:1) and but five times in Isaiah, two in this chapter (1:24; 3:1; 10:16, 33; 19:4). Exod 23:17 has "the Lord, Yahweh," Exod 34:23 "the face of the Lord Yahweh, God of Israel." Isaiah is consistent: "The Lord, Yahweh of Hosts." Mal 3:1 has simply "the Lord." Of course the form אדני occurs many times with and without the other titles.

33.b. מסעף "designating" The verb occurs only here. BDB (703) judges the root to mean "cleave," "divide." Nouns formed on it mean "clefts" as in rocks or "branches" as in fruit trees in Isa 17:6; 27:10; Ezek 31:6, 8. A second root produces a *hap. leg.* adjective in Ps 119:113 which BDB (704) calls "divided, half-hearted." The usual translation "lopping-off" goes beyond the evidence. "To divide" or "to branch out" with causative meaning from the piel stem demands something more like "separating between two alternatives"—in the case of the forester, "deciding which trees shall be felled and which remain." Hence the term "designating." The ptcp follows הנה "behold" and characterizes the one being pointed out.

33.c. K פארה Q פוארה is a *hap. leg.* which BDB (802) calls "boughs," a collective noun. The root פאר means to "beautify," "glorify." Derivations mean "a head-dress," "beauty," "glory" and something to do with trees, perhaps a "bough." The famous mountain's name is similar: פארן *Paran.* It is wiser to remain with the general meaning "a beauty."

33.d. מערצה "an awesome thing," another *hap. leg.,* derives from a root meaning "cause to tremble" (BDB, 791–92). It means something "awe-inspiring."

34.a. וְנִקַּף is usually thought to be piel pf 3 m sg with *wāw* cons. This should give a pass meaning. Wildberger makes "the forest thickets" its subject. But the controlling noun "thickets" is pl. NIV notes this and continues the sg subject of the previous verse, but forces an act meaning on this verb. There are apparently two verbs נקף BDB, 668–69. The first means "strike off" and has usually been understood here. The second means "go around," "make the circuit" (cf. Isa 29:1; 15:8), but apparently does not occur in piel or niph which MT's pointing requires. It should be read as piel pf 3 m sg "he strikes." The second meaning, however, remains attractive if one may emend to וַיַּקֵּף hiph impf 3 m sg.

Form/Structure/Setting

The verses break the awesome march theophany by identifying the marcher and describing his profession and the result of his mission. They should be set off from the theophany as G. E. Wright (*The Book of Isaiah* [Richmond: John Knox Press, 1964], 49) noted. הנה "behold" announces the identification and sets it off. The full title "the Lord Yahweh of Hosts" indicates the importance of the announcement following its use in 10:16, 23, 24, and 26. It is followed by a participle describing action in process. This will set the stage for six pericope statements, each beginning with verbs (perfect + *wāw*) which link them to this action. (A similar הנה, participle and verbs [perfect + *wāw*] will begin the great final theophany of the Vision [65:17—66:24]).

The presence and the gesture are then interpreted in 10:33—12:6. "Behold" identifies the gesturing figure as "The Lord, Yahweh of Hosts," surely a title of considerable significance in view of the Assyrian on the coastal plains opposite. It is Yahweh who "designs a beautiful (thing) with awesome (skill)." The destructive loss of powerful forces and great nations, like the cutting of trees in the forest to clear the way for one majestic and beautiful one to flourish, opens a door for God's chosen city and dynasty. The description of the theophany drops the figure of the forester, but the importance of the hand signal (which picks up the note of 9:11[12], 20[21]; 10:4) is continued by 11:10, 12. The grammatical structure continues the הנה with participles in v 33 and begins a series of consecutive perfects in v 34 that continues through 12:4, twenty-four times in all. For the significance of this syntactical device, cf. Watts, *Syntax,* 113–17. The basic structure is shown by the consecutive perfects with Yahweh as subject in v 34 (ונקף "he strikes") and 11:11 ("it shall be that the Lord will stretch out his hand a second time") and 11:15 ("and Yahweh shall dry up").

Comment

33 The verse identifies the Lord as the one at work here. The title *Yahweh of Hosts* fits the theophanic description of his ascent to Zion from the Jordan. It connects the description to God's ancient relation to Israel and to Jerusalem. It presents that work as מסעף "cleaning," "separating," "branching." He distinguishes between the things to be cut down and those to be pruned and nurtured. The particular work here relates to a פארה "a thing of glory and beauty" like a person's turban headdress. The heart of God's action is not destruction; it looks beyond that to glorious nourishment of his beautiful thing. The work has a breathtaking, *awe-inspiring* quality about it (במערצה). The three words are infrequently used and have been much misunderstood.

The sentence interprets the hand-signal toward Jerusalem in v 32. The Vision has pictured an unflinching and unbending signal in the still outstretched hand of God from chap. 5:25 through 10:4 which signaled his unchanged determination of destruction toward the Northern Kingdom. This one foresees the day, very near, when the signal toward Jerusalem will change, calling for growth and nurture of the thing of beauty that it is and can be.

The verse continues in circumstantial clauses to describe the work of destruction against the high and mighty as well as the underbrush. It continues the themes of 2:12–18 and 10:18–19 [17–19]. The Divine Forester goes about his work with neither fear nor favor. The רמי הקומה "tops of the heights" are the highest parts of tall trees, as are the הגבהים "exalted ones." They are cut and lowered.

34 The סבכי היער "forest thickets" refers to thick underbrush that must be cleared to allow the fine trees to grow. הלבנון "the Lebanon" refers, not to a country as today, but to a region on the slopes of Mount Hermon to the north of Israel. It was renowned for the magnificent gigantic trees which grew there.

יד "hand" and עוד "yet or still" occur frequently and together in chaps. 8–12. They are significant. יד "hand" refers to deeds and signals. עוד "still" "yet" indicates continuance and continuity. יד "hand" is used to show God's signals—like the thumbs up or down of the Roman arena. This begins in 1:25 "I will turn my hand against you." It is continued in that series of refrains "his hand is upraised" (5:25; 9:11[12], 16[17], 20[21]; 10:4). It figures in the Lord's actions toward Zion (10:32; 11:11, 15). It is used throughout the book, as it was undoubtedly a common term in Hebrew speech.

עוד "still" is used in loose conjunction with a number of these. It characterizes a series of statements about Israel's continuing rebellion against the Lord and his continuing anger toward them. While 1:5 asks "Why will you be smitten still more?" 2:4 reverses the point "not teach war anymore." Five times the refrain goes "his hand is stretched out [indicating continued anger] still" (5:25; 9:11[12], 16[17], 20[21]; 10:4). Again a reversal in 10:20: "no longer rely on." Then twice it is used for Zion as it urges patience in the continuing process in which judgment on Israel must precede God's favor to Judah: 10:25 "yet a very little while" and 10:32 literally "*yet the day to stand on Nob.*" The effect is to stress the continuity of Israel's attitude and God's decree of judgment on Israel on the one side (1—10:23) with the continuity of God's elective providence for Zion on the other (10:24—12:6).

Explanation

The verses break the dramatic spell of the liturgical recital. The awesome figure is identified as the Lord, Yahweh of Hosts. In line with references in chaps. 9 and 10 he is pictured as an Imperial Forester who has authority to cultivate the imperial forests. Trees were highly valued and rulers claimed exclusive rights. Forest lands, like those of the Lebanon on the slopes of Mount Hermon, were admired. The Bible often uses the oak and the cedar as figures for strong personalities. God decides which trees are cut down. He exercises his authority of decision over the greatest and the mightiest.

But the key message lies in 33b, a verse that has baffled translator and interpreter alike because it is composed of three rare Hebrew words. As a result it has usually been translated to accord with a presumed context of threat to Jerusalem. As shown above, v 32 is not a threat, only a signal. Vv 24 and 11:1–9 are positive words. So the words need to be examined again (cf. *Comment,* v 33).

The verse shows Yahweh as the Forester whose pruning, thinning, and burning of underbrush are all part of a larger plan—"designating beauty." This plan and this beauty has Jerusalem as its focus and center. The Forester's decision allows this part of his area to grow, to increase (v 32), in order to become a thing of "beauty" (v 33b). It will allow an old stump "to sprout" (11:1) and the sprout to become glorious.

Episode D: A Shoot from the Stump of Jesse (11:1–10)

Bibliography

Alonso-Schökel, L. "Dos Poemas a la Paz." *EstBib* 18 (1959) 149–69. **Barrois, G.** "Critical Exegesis and Traditional Hermeneutics: A Methodological Inquiry on the Basis of the Book of Isaiah" (includes 11:1–19). *St. Vladimir's Theological Quarterly* 16 (1972) 107–27. **Bodenheimer, F. S.** *Animal and Man in Bible Lands.* Leiden: E. J. Brill, 1960. **Childs, B. S.** *Myth and Reality in the Old Testament.* London: SCM, 1960. 65–69. **Crook, M. B.** "A Suggested Occasion for Isaiah 9:2–7 and 11:1–9." *JBL* 68 (1949) 213–24. **Delord, R.** "Les Charismes De L'ancienne Alliance Commandment: La Paix Du Mond Nouveau, Esaie 11:1–10." *ETR* 52:4 (1977) 555–56. **Freedman, D. N.** "Is Justice Blind?" (Isaiah 11:3f) *Bib* 52 no. 4 (1971) 536. **Gross, H.** *Die Idee des ewigen und allgemeinen Weltfriedens im Alten Orient und im Alten Testament.* TTS 7. Trier: Paulinus-Verlag, 1967. **Harrelson, W.** "Nonroyal Motifs in the Royal Eschatology" (includes 11:1–9). *Israel's Prophetic Heritage,* FSJ. Muilenburg. New York: Harper and Brothers, 1962. 147–65. **Hermisson, H. J.** "Zukunftserwartung und Gegenwartskritik in der Verkundigung Jesajas." *EvT* 33 (1973) 54–77. **Kock, R.** "Der Gottesgeist und der Messias." *Bib* 27 (1946) 241–68. **Lange, F.** "Exegetische Problems zu Jes. 11." *LR* 23 (1975) 115–27. **Montagnini, F.** "Le roi-Messie attendu, Is 11:1–10." *AsSeign* 2,6 (1969) 6–12. **Rehm, M.** *Der königliche Messias im Lichte der Immanuel-weissagung des Buches Jesaja.* Eichstätten Studien 1. Kevelaer: Butzon u. Bercker, 1968. 185–234. **Schmid, H. H.** *Shalom: Frieden im Alten Orient und im Alten Testament.* SBS 51. Stuttgart: KBW Verlag, 1971. **Schmidt, W. H.** "Die Ohnmacht des Messias. Zur Überlieferungsgeschichte der messianischen Weissagungen im AT." *KD* 15 (1969) 18–34. **Stamm, J. J. and Bietenhard, H.** *Der Weltfriede im Alten und Neuen Testament.* Zürich: Zwingli Verlag, 1959. **Wildberger, H.** "Die Völkerwallfahrt zum Zion, Jes. 11:1–5." *VT* 7 (1957) 62–81.

Translation

Chorus: [1] *And a shoot shall go out from the stump of Jesse.* 4+3
A Branch from his roots will bear fruit. [a]
[2] *And the Spirit of Yahweh shall rest on him:* 4+3
a spirit of wisdom and understanding,

	a spirit of counsel and heroism,	3+4
	a spirit of knowledge, and fear, of Yahweh.	
Interlocutor:	3 [a]*His delight (will be) in the fear of Yahweh:*[a]	3+4+4
	[b]*who does not judge by what his eyes see,*	
	nor make a decision by what his ears hear.	
	4 *When he judges poor people with righteousness,*	3+4
	or when he gives fair decisions to the afflicted[a] *of the land,*	
	or when he smites a land[b] *with the rod of his mouth,*	4+4
	with the breath of his lips he kills the wicked.	
Chorus:	5 *And it shall be, (when)*	1
	righteousness (is) the girdle[a] *of his loins*	3+3
	and faithfulness (is) the belt[a] *of his waist,*	
	6 *wolf will feed with lamb,*	4+4
	leopard will rest with goat,	
	calf, lion and yearling[a] *together,*	4+4
	with a little child leading them.	
	7 *Cow and bear feed*[a] *together—*	3+3+4
	together their young relax.	
	A lion will eat straw like an ox.	
	8 *A nursing child will fondle the hole of the cobra.*	4+3+3
	On the viper's young[a]	
	the weaned child will put[b] *his hand.*	
Yahweh:	9 *They will do no harm—*	2+2+3
	they will not destroy	
	in all the mount of my holiness!	
Spokesman:	*For the earth shall have become full*[a]	3+3+3
	of the knowledge[b] *of Yahweh*	
	as waters (are) coverings for the sea.[c]	
Monarchist:	10 *And it shall be in that day:*	3
	the root of Jesse,	2+2+2
	who is standing	
	as a signal to the peoples,	
	to him nations will come seeking,	3+3
	and his resting place will be glory.	

Notes

1.a. יפרה "will bear fruit" is not a close parallel to ויצא "will go out" in the first half. LXX translated ἀναβήσεται, Tg יתרבי, Syr *nafra'*, Vg *ascendet* which suggests that they read יפרח "will spring up." Wildberger follows the Versions. However, MT makes sense and should be followed.

3.a-a. Versions and commentaries have had trouble with this stich which repeats יראת יהוה "fear of Yahweh." LXX adds ἐμπλήσει αὐτόν "will fill him," Tg ויקרביניה "will approach him," Syr *w^eednaḥ* "and he shines," Vg *et replebit eum* "and fill him." Others have tried emendations (cf. G. Beer, "Jes. 11,1–8," *ZAW* 18 [1898] 345; G. R. Driver, "Abbreviations in the MT," *Textus* I [1960] 129). Wildberger and others judge it dittography of the previous line. It should be read as a choral refrain which echoes the previous line.

3.b. The ו before לא is omitted by most Versions.

4.a. לְעַנְוֵי "to the poor, afflicted," BDB, 776. Σ reads πτωχους "beggars," while LXX reads ταπεινούς "humble, depressed" ones. *BHS* suggests לְעֲנְיֵי "for the humble." MT makes sense and the change gains little. However, one may compare the parallel terms in 10:2.

4.b. ארץ "land," "earth" has been thought a repetition from the previous line. Some recommend reading עָרִץ "a terrorist," "ruthless one" as a parallel to רשע "wicked." Yet the Versions support MT.

5.a. אזור "girdle" occurs twice, which has forced translators to seek substitutes to avoid repetition (G. R. Driver, *JTS* 38 [1937] 39). Vg translates *cingulum* and *cinctorium:* similar but not synonomous words. Wildberger emends the second to חֲגוֹר "belt." None of these is a compelling substitute for MT.

6.a. LXX βοσκηθήσονται "will be tended in pasture" has apparently combined מריא "yearling" and יחדו "together" to get this meaning. Vg has a similar form. Each of the parallel lines has two subjects. ומריא "and a fatling, yearling" gives this one three. Wildberger suggests reading יִמְרְאוּ "will fatten" or "become fat." This verb is not found in biblical Heb but does appear in middle-Hebrew and is supported by Ug.

7.a. MT תִּרְעֶינָה "will feed" has been challenged. De Lagarde suggested reading תִּתְרָעֶינָה matching the reflexive hithp with the יחדו "together" of the previous line (cf. LXX ἅμα = יחדו). But this may be simply understood and MT left as it is.

8.a. MT מאורת, a *hap. leg.* 1 MS reads מאירת a ptcp fem sg constr (cf. M. Dietrich, *Neue palästinisch punktierte Bibelfragmente* [Leiden: E. J. Brill, 1968], 52). LXX τρώγλη, OL *cubile,* Tg חור, Syr *ḥôrâ,* Vg *caverna* seem to have in mind מְעָרָה "hole" or מְעוֹנָה "dwelling," or "camp." F. Perles ("Übersehenes Akkad. Sprachgut," *JSOR* 9 [1925] 126) related the form to Akkad *mûru* "young." Wildberger follows Perles.

8.b. ידו הדה has often been translated "stretch out his hand." הדה is another *hap. leg.* Its meaning is unknown. BDB uses Arab and Aram parallels to get its meaning. J. Reider ("Etymological Studies," *VT* 2 [1952] 115) suggests combining the two words into one יְדַהְדֵּה which he translates, according to the Arab *dahdah,* as "throw stones" or "play pebbles." Wildberger correctly put this aside as too daring.

9.a. DSS[Isa] תמלאה changes the pf to impf, which may be supported by Tg ארי תתקלי and Syr *d^{e}tetm^{e}le'* (cf. S. Talmon, "Textual Transmission," *Textus* 4 [1964] 117). Wildberger recognizes the possibility, but chooses to stay with MT, translating "will have become full."

9.b. דֵּעָה "knowing" is an inf constr (BDB, 393) which explains the following acc.

9.c. לים מכסים, lit., "for the sea, a covering." Joüon § 125k explains the לְ as an acc particle and the lack of an article otherwise, § 138f. However, the simple and literal meaning makes sense as it is.

Form/Structure/Setting

The choral speech begins with a verb (pf + *wāw*). This continues the chain from 10:34 and is carried through the chapter and into chap. 12. They all depend on the participial announcement of God's act in 10:33. The "lopping off" of branches in northern Palestine reduces the power of the Assyrian Empire in that area (10:33b).

The genre of the literature is to be found in the poems that deal with royal ideology in the Psalms and in some prophets. Yet there are also distinctive elements unique to this composition. Parallels may be found in Mic 5:2–5a and Ps 72:2, 4, 13. Wildberger (439) sees vv 1–5 as an "oracle" of a future king, while Ps 72 sings of a current monarch.

An outline must recognize that the passage contains the central elements of the arch structure that begins in 10:24 and continues through 12:6 (see the *Introduction* to Scene 3):

E The shoot from Jesse's root (11:1)
  F The Spirit of Yahweh rests on him (11:2)
    G The fear of Yahweh—his delight (11:3a)

KEYSTONE Yahweh's righteousness and justice (11:3b–4)
G′ Righteousness and justice his girdle (11:5–8)
F′ Knowledge of Yahweh in all the earth (11:9)
E′ The Root of Jesse, a banner to the nations (11:10)

5–9 The section is set off and related to the preceding by והיה "and it shall be." But it does not add "in that day" showing that the section relates to the immediately preceding description of "the Branch."

10 A new ביום ההוא "in that day" sets off this third section relating to "the Branch." It is separate in grammar and in theme. It claims that the Davidic King *is* the "signal to the peoples" which the Vision has announced in 5:26; 7:18; 10:32 and will announce in 13:2, etc.

There is an interplay throughout this passage between Davidic themes and emphatic recognition of Yahweh's direct gifts and action. While David's scion appears in vv 1 and 10, the emphasis is on Yahweh's spirit (v 2), the fear of Yahweh (v 3), and the knowledge of Yahweh (vv 6–9). Vv 4 and 5 are not clearly directed and may be understood to apply to Yahweh or to the king. The ambiguity is deliberate. Davidic ideology was structured to think in terms of God's work through the king. This passage deftly keeps attention on God's work. The paragraph is carried along by perfect with *wāw* in vv 1, 2, 5, and 10. Vv 3 and 9 clearly interrupt this pattern. V 4 uses perfects with *wāw* to relate the thought to v 5. The meter of the entire section is heavy with bicolons and tricolons using 3 and 4 accents. Vv 9–10 continue with tricolons but lighten them to two and three accents.

The genre of royal psalms has been subtly reshaped. The explicit position of the king is minimized (only in 11:1 and 10 directly). The passage, in tune with the larger context of 10:24–34 and 11:11–16, keeps its attention on the work of Yahweh. Its centerpiece in 11:3b–4 picks up the work of Yahweh from 10:33–34 in picturing his righteous judgment. He is the subject of these verbs, not the king. In addition, the surrounding sections shift the emphasis from the king to Yahweh's endowments which are necessary for peace, prosperity, and success: his Spirit (v 2), his "fear" (v 3b), his righteousness and justice (v 5), and his "knowledge" (v 9). The king does have a role, but as in 9:6 [7] the composition carefully subordinates it to the wider view of God's work and makes it contingent on the Spirit, fear, righteousness, and knowledge of Yahweh which are the essential elements for the fulfillment of God's purpose for his people and the world.

The genre of description of "the peaceable kingdom" is virtually unique to Isaiah (cf. chap. 35 and 65:17–25). It is used in contrast to the violent pictures of Yahweh's warfare in the Vision to convey the sense of Yahweh's goals toward which his strategy with the nations and with Israel are moving.

Comment

1 ויצא "and . . . will go out." The verb form (perfect + *wāw*) does not set the time as future (see Watts, *Syntax,* 47–54; contra Wildberger), but relates the passage to the controlling sentence (10:33) and the great mosaic of pictures that follow. הנה "behold" and the participle in 10:33 portray an act of God which is already apparent. Thus this passage begins to picture the possibilities that derive from that act. יצא "come out" can refer to being born (Gen 35:11) or to his appearance as king (Zech 5:5). Gen 17:6 uses it for his genealogy. The same verb appears in Mic 5:1[2].

The prophecy reaches behind David to *Jesse* (as Mic 5:1[2] reaches behind Jerusalem to Bethlehem). גזע "stump" is descriptive of a broken, cut-off dynasty. It takes up the figure of the Master Forester from 10:33–34 with the trimming and thinning of the forest describing the troubled times of Ahaz's reign. It realistically recognizes the severely reduced status of the throne, a reduction by the division of the kingdom (cf. 7:17) and more recently by the vassal status of Ahaz and the reduced area controlled by Judah. A "*stump*" indeed!

The *shoot* (חטר) or the *branch* (נצר) does not spring from fresh new ground (a new dynasty) but from the old stump or roots. Jesse's descendants will take on new life. Job 14:7 uses the same words to picture the revival of an apparently dead tree. The term *shoot* is used only here in this meaning, while נצר "branch" appears only here in royal Davidic literature. In 14:19 it refers to the dead king of Babylon and in 60:21 to the returned people of Jerusalem. Dan 11:7 designates a royal heir by it. The "Branch of Yahweh" in 4:2 uses a different word.

G. Widengren (*The King and the Tree of Life,* UUÄ [Uppsala: Lundequistska bokhandeln, 1951] 50) has drawn on ANE parallels to suggest a relation between kingship and the tree of life. The verse (with v 10) continues the concern shown in Act 2 with the survival of the Davidic dynasty (cf. 7:1–14; 9:5–6 [6–7]).

2 In contrast with the usual royal passages, the king is not named again, nor is he the subject of a verb, until v 10. Instead, the passage turns to the gifts, attributes, and acts of God which make survival and revival possible. The first is *the spirit of Yahweh.* This is a feature not found in the parallels from other books. It is a factor apparent throughout Isaiah's vision (cf. 4:4; 32:15–20; 34:16; 40:7, 13; 42:1; 44:3; 47:16; 48:16; 59:19,21; 61:1,3). Although the term is unusual in other Davidic passages, it is not unknown in Psalms that speak of the king's needs. Ps 51:12 [10] pleads for a "firm spirit" and v 14 (12) for a "willing spirit." V 13 [11] prays for God not to remove his "holy spirit." V 19 [17] recognizes God's demand for a "broken spirit" (cf. Isa 57:15; 66:2). See also Pss 104:30; 106:33; 139:7; 143:10. There is, then, a strand in the Psalms like Isaiah. But it is not shown to have been original to Davidic genres.

Perhaps there is a return here to the charismatic nature of kingship (1 Sam 10:6, 10; 11:6; 16:13, 14; 19:9) which had been replaced by the dynastic principle of Davidic promise (2 Sam 7:14). This teaches that God's spirit speaks and acts through his Anointed One. Anointing (1 Sam 12:13) is intended to impart the gift of the spirit.

The spirit of Yahweh gives the king the skills needed to reign. They are listed in three pairs. *Wisdom and understanding* are standard qualities required in the king (G. von Rad, *Wisdom in Israel* [Nashville: Abingdon, 1972] 28, 36). The Assyrian king claimed them for himself (10:13). They are demonstrated in David (2 Sam 14:17) and Solomon (1 Kgs 3: 5, 6). *Wisdom* is the quality which enables the king to make good judgments. *Understanding* is the deeper intellectual insight into events and persons that is required to establish policy.

עצה וגבורה "counsel and heroism" are the second pair. Prov 8:14 lists them among the "fruits" of the spirit of Yahweh. Note also the throne names in Isa 9:5[6] "Wonder Counselor, God-Hero." *Counsel* includes the formation of strategy, the planning of battle and policies for the kingdom (2 Kgs 18:20; Isa 36:5). The king is commander-in-chief of the armies and leads in battle (1 Kgs 15:23; 16:5,27; 22:46[45]). Wildberger cites Prov 8:14 to show that these also have civil usage, a peaceful application.

דעת ויראת יהוה "knowledge and fear of Yahweh." Both words relate to Yahweh. They are basic terms for Yahwistic faith. The spirit will inspire the king to a powerful life of faith and worship. The *knowledge of Yahweh* has a very special place in the Vision. Lack of knowledge was grave sin (1:3). The major picture of the new age was one in which "the knowledge of Yahweh will cover the earth" (11:9). *Knowledge* refers to a true understanding and relation to God and his will.

Fear of Yahweh depicts the basic awe and submission of the king to the Holy God who, in mystery beyond understanding, can only be worshiped. The spirit of Yahweh makes these possible.

3 *The fear of Yahweh* is a complex phrase. The complexity begins with the old question of whether it is a subjective or objective genetive. Does the "fear" come from Yahweh or is it directed toward Yahweh? Hebrew does not distinguish the two. Probably, overtones of both should be heard in the phrase. The phrase echoes v 2 and implies that the Spirit's work in the king brings genuine devotion, a real *delight,* to his worship and service, or that such devotion is the Spirit's *delight.*

Vv 3 and 4 lack an expressed subject. Conjunctions join the sentences, but the antecedents of pronouns and verb—subjects is not defined. The echo nature of 3a makes the king the likely antecedent. But the others are open. The usual answer is the king or the "messianic king."

The theme of these verses is unbiased justice and rule. They are characteristics that belong to Yahweh and should also belong to the king. The chiastic outline above and the failure to return to the king as subject after v 1 suggest that it is Yahweh who is the understood subject. The translation has shown this by making it a relative clause. Righteousness and justice are elementary requirements of divine justice and of royal rule (Ps 72).

4 Yahweh's commitment to justice for the *poor* is paramount. No regime that fails on this point can claim to be the work of Yahweh. God's own participation in judgment makes this a possibility.

Yahweh's power is expressed here through *the rod of his mouth* and *the breath of his lips.* The naked power of the Forester lopping off branches is no longer necessary. Genuine authority can be exercised by decree (*the rod of his mouth*) and execution of the guilty criminal can be effected by orderly judicial process (*the breath* [*or spirit*] *of his lips*).

5 *Righteousness* and *faithfulness* were basic characteristics required of a good king and expected from God. The question—whose loins? whose waist?—is the same as in v 3. The ambiguity is undoubtedly deliberate. Yahweh, his Spirit, and the king are properly indistinguishable when the fear and knowledge of Yahweh permeate the realm. The reality of these things in the experience of the people are prerequisites to the order of peace that follows.

6–8 The picture of pastoral tranquility depends on the custom of having a boy (or girl) who serves as the village herder for domestic animals gather the sheep, the goats, and the calves to lead (or drive) them out to pasture in the morning and bring them back at night. After feeding they lie down in the pastures, seeking any shade available from the eastern heat. Biblical stories like that of David (1 Sam 17:34–37) reflect the hazards of that occupation that are banned under these conditions. The innocence of the *child-herder,* the *suckling,* and the *toddler* accent a world without harm or danger.

9 "My holy mountain" (RSV) is literally *the mount of my holiness* and is a fixed part of Zion's traditions. But here it parallels *the earth* and implies the totality of God's redeemed and re-created world. The *knowledge of Yahweh* imparted by his Spirit has made it possible for all the world to be as God's own sanctuary with no need for separations and barriers. *The knowledge of Yahweh* (cf. v 2 above) implies such a relationship and commitment to Yahweh and his ways that fellowship with him is possible and easy and that the fulfillment of his pleasure is presumed in all. The translation *the earth* rather than "the land" is justified by the parallel of *the sea.*

10 *To him nations will seek.* The verse first identifies the function of the Davidide ruler, a function which the divided monarchy had virtually nullified in practice. It then asserts that this function will be fulfilled and glory restored to the dynasty.

Explanation

The passage is one element of the larger "vision" that began with the call not to fear the Assyrian 10:24, gathered momentum in the theophanic approach of God to Zion (10:27d–32), and was given definition and direction in the call to "Behold the Lord—designing a beautiful thing." The passage is connected to this by its beginning with consecutive perfect ויצא "and it shall go out." A clear and unifying theme is that of the Branch from Jesse's roots. This passage (with 9:5–6[6–7]) is from the stock of literature belonging to the lore of the Davidic monarchy. Parallels can be found in Pss 2, 21, 45, 72, 110; 2 Sam 7; 1 Kgs 2–3; Chronicles, and in some other prophets like Mic 5:2–6.

The announcement that the Davidic monarchy in that time (i.e., Ahaz's reign, eighth century) is a centerpiece of God's design of "a beautiful" thing (v 1) is followed by the promise that God's Spirit on him will guarantee the spiritual characteristics needed in a king (v 2), while the qualities of insight (3b–c), fairness for all his subjects (v 4a–b), and powerful authority (v 4cd) will follow.

It presumes the connection of the king to the two-hundred-year-old dynasty and its ideals including divine choice, promise, and sustenance (2 Sam 7). It equally presumes God's (and therefore, the king's) priorities of justice for the poor and helpless.

The beginning recognition of fulfilled requirements for a reign of righteousness and faithfulness (v 5) is followed by a picture of a return to Eden's tranquility and innocence that is unique in its force and power (vv 6–9b). It is closed by an explanation that these conditions flow from the universal presence of "the knowledge of Yahweh" (v 9c–d).

The poetic power of the picture continues the superlative beauty of vv 2–3. The pictures of the Davidic king resemble oriental ideals for kingship (Wildberger, 457–62, cites parallels). The king needs wisdom for justice and for peace. This peace is often presented as applying to the natural as well as the social and political world. Yet these pictures are unique in the OT, except for the parallels in chap. 35. They are also consistent with the Divine Gardener and Divine Forester motifs which show God's concern for nature's welfare blending with his rule of peoples and nations. The "knowledge of Yahweh" (v 9) neatly closes the circle by recalling the spirit-imbued "knowledge and fear" of Yahweh (v 2). We may also remember that the Vision sees Israel's fatal flaw in lack of this knowledge (1:3 and passim).

The nature of the passage requires discussion. Wildberger joins a long line of interpreters in calling this "a promise." Yet it is not put in a Yahweh "thus says the Lord" speech. The element of promise is very close, however, in the admonition of 10:23–24 and the clear promise that Yahweh "in yet a little while" will whip the Assyrians (10:25–26). Also in the call to recognize Yahweh's theophany and the attendant designation of Zion as a beautiful thing to be spared and nurtured (10:32–33). But this, too, was qualified by the עוד היום "until today."

The context calls for a near fulfillment. The Assyrian threats in 734–32, 728, and 724–21 B.C. finally destroyed Samaria and Northern Israel. Ahaz is on the throne. This section assures the continuation of the Davidic dynasty beyond the Assyrian crisis. This was fulfilled: Hezekiah (and, a century later, Josiah) was yet to occupy the throne.

The thrust of the passage, however, does not emphasize the role of the king. Consistent with the Vision's perspective, God's role stands out. The passage (vv 1–10) begins and ends with confirmation of the dynasty's renewal (v 1) and its established status (v 10). But the emphasis is on three facets of God's support and blessing. First is the "spirit of Yahweh" (v 2) which provides the wisdom necessary for rule. The second is the "fear of Yahweh" (v 2c and 3a) which makes possible the administration of justice (v 4a) and the authority to rule (v 4b). The third is "the knowledge of Yahweh" (v 2d) and (v 9) which assures the reign of peace. These are not royal achievements. They are facets of Yahweh's evident presence in Jerusalem. When a king rules by "the Spirit of Yahweh," in the "fear of Yahweh," and with the intent of spreading "the knowledge of Yahweh," the ethos of Davidic kingship is at work. Unfortunately, the opposite is also true. When kings rule by the guidelines of their own ambition and power, God's purposes are thwarted and judgment awaits.

The Vision was read (perhaps heard) by a people 250 years removed from the scene. They were well aware of the story recounted in 2 Kgs 18:2–5. While they share the thrill inherent in this scene, they know Hezekiah's weakness, Manasseh's shame, and Zedekiah's final debacle. They are prepared for the shift in mid-chapter (v 11) in which Yahweh alone assumes responsibility for returning the exiles. Yet there is also inherent here a deeper promise which reaches beyond the historical and literary context. It rests on the classic understanding that David and his sons, like Abraham and his children, were chosen with a destiny that God will not deny himself.

The Vision of Isaiah is keenly aware of the potential for faith and hope in this promise. It is also aware of the irreparable harm that repeated and ill-chosen royal revolts against imperial power had brought to Judah under Hezekiah, Josiah, Jehoiakim, and Zedekiah, not to mention the plots against the Persians that are only hinted at in our sources. Therefore it is important to note that these exuberant Messianic passages are scarce in the Vision. The tendency of the Vision is to lead readers to see God's purposes which can be fulfilled in ways other than political and military authority and power. Yet for this moment in time, even under the pressure of Assyria's yoke (10:27), assurance was valid: "Do not fear the Assyrians!" The throne would survive the crisis, the throne of Yahweh's anointed, David's son.

The classic view of Zion's king understood that natural order as much as social and political order depended on him (A. R. Johnson, *Sacral Kingship in Ancient Israel,* 2nd ed. [Cardiff: U. of Wales Press, 1967] 58). The effective reign of God's anointed brought justice to the people and peace (שלום in the sense of wholeness and health) to all of God's creation. The conditions for this are noted in beginning and end: a king whose entire being is clothed by righteousness and faithfulness to his God, his calling, and his subjects, and one whose "knowledge and fear of Yahweh" are spread to cover the whole earth. Thus the chosen king has effectively fulfilled his destiny as "Prince of Peace" (9:5[6]).

The scene in vv 6–8 is a village with simple huts, mud floors, and human beings and animals in crowded association. The same may be found in large areas of the world today. The people eke out an existence in sharp and often bitter conflict with a hostile nature. Predators prey on the domestic stock. Snakes keep the rats under control, but pose a constant threat, especially to the children who live on the mud floor for lack of furniture. (India loses hundreds of children to snakebite annually.) Such villages were (and are) the economic backbones of their societies. The cities could not exist without them. A society and regime that brought peace and prosperity to the villages was successful beyond belief. But they were most vulnerable to the ravages of war, famine, and drought.

When "righteousness, faithfulness, and the knowledge of Yahweh" control the palace, such a scene is possible. Under God even predators are tamed (obviously otherwise well-fed) and the reptiles are no threat.

The picture is one most people have long since despaired of seeing. Jerusalem in 725 B.C. (in 475 B.C. or A.D. 1985) despaired. No king was found who fulfilled these conditions. And no world was found to allow the "knowledge of Yahweh" such room. The Vision wrestles with these issues further in the next paragraphs and in its later chapters.

The claim is put forward (v 10) that the king should be the rallying point of the nations, i.e., that his "glory" will be in military leadership. This accords with monarchic theory. God will rule the nations through the Davidic king.

It also accords with historical precedent from David through Jehoshaphat to Uzziah. History also records some great disasters. The Vision and its audience (readership) are well aware of Hezekiah's ambitious coalition that rose against Assyria some twenty years later (cf. chaps. 36–39) and will contain arguments that sought to restrain Josiah (chaps. 28–33).

The view of the Vision does not generally support this position for the monarchy of the eighth and fifth centuries. A corrective will appear in vv 11–16 and the criticisms of Jerusalem's leadership in chaps. 1, 3, 7, 20, 22, 28–33 will surely also include the kings involved. This verse, like vv 1–9, reflects the glorious heritage of Davidic tradition which is significant in its own right. The Vision gives it its due, but recognizes the significant problems which the application of monarchist assurance brought for Judah's policies in the eighth century and for Hebrew Jerusalem in the fifth century. They posed similar problems for Jesus and early Christians, as they do for Jews and Christians today who seriously seek to know how God intends to work in history. The Vision's contributions to these issues are found in chaps. 6–8 and again in chaps. 49–54 and 65–66.

These verses remain among the most beautiful examples of monarchic ritual and poetry in Messianic literature. They shine as a luminous light. The problems come from the generations, including our own, that "do not know, do not understand," who have "eyes but do not see, ears but do not hear," with whom God has to work to reach these goals.

Episode E:
Yahweh's Second Deliverance (11:11–16)

Bibliography

Erlandsson, S. "Jes. 11:10–16 och dess historiska bakgrund." *SEA* 36 (1971) 24–44. **Luria, B. Z.** "The Prophecy in Isa 11:11–16 on the Gathering of the Exiles." (Heb.) *BMik* 26 (1981) 108–14. **Vajda, G.** "Fragments d'un commentaire judeo-arabe sur le livre d'isaie (Isaie 11:10—13:14)." *VT* 13 (1963) 208–24. **Vollmer, J.** *Geschichtliche Rückblicke.* 172–73.

Translation

Heavens: 11 *And it shall be in that day* 3
the Lord [a] *will lift* [b] *his hand again* 4+3
to acquire the remnant of his people
which is left from Assyria and (lower) Egypt 4+3
from Pathros, from Cush, and from Elam,
from Shinar and from Hamath [c] 2+2
and from the islands of the sea. [d]

Earth: 12 *And he shall raise a banner for the nations* 3+3
and gather the banished [a] *of Israel.*
And the dispersed of Judah he will assemble 3+3
from the four quarters of the earth.
Heavens: 13 *Ephraim's jealousy shall turn aside.* 3+3
Judah's enmities [a] *will be cut off.*
Ephraim will no longer be jealous of Judah, 3+3
and Judah will no longer vex Ephraim.
14 *And they will fly on the shoulder* [a] *of the Philistines*
westward. 4+4
Together they will plunder the easterners.
Edom and Moab (will be) the extension [b] *of their power,* 4+3
and the Ammonites their lackeys. [c]
Earth: 15 *And Yahweh shall dry up* [a] 2+2+2
the tongue
of the Sea of Egypt.
And he shall wave his hand 2+2+2
over the River
with the violence of his wind. [b]
Heavens: *When he breaks (it) into seven streams* 3+2
one will cross with his sandals (on).
16 *And there shall be a highway* 2+2+3
for the remnant of his people
who are left from Assyria,
as there was for Israel 3+2+2
in the day they came up
from the land of Egypt.

Notes

11.a. Many MSS read יהוה "Yahweh."

11.b. MT שֵׁנִית "a second time" is redundant with יוסיף "again." LXX δεῖξαι "to show," "declare," "announce." *BHS* suggests שְׁנוֹת which is suggested by Arab *sanija* "be high." But no use of this verb in Heb is known. H. Fitzgerald ("Hebrew yd = 'love' and 'beloved,' " *CBQ* 29 [1967] 369) suggests that יד means "love": "He will move to double his love." But the best suggestion is to compare with 49:22 and read שְׂאֵת qal inf constr from נשׂא "to lift up."

11.c. מחמת "from Hamath." Hamath is a city in Syria. There is no record of Jewish exiles being there. Numerous emendations have been suggested. But Wildberger's comment, that it should be seen to represent all of Syria and left as it is, prevails.

11.d. מאיי הים "islands of the sea" is missing in LXX, although the Hexapla inserts it again.

12.a. נדחי "banished" is usually thought a niph ptcp m pl constr נדח, the *daghesh forte* in ד has fallen out over the vocal *shewa* (GKC § 20m).

13.a. צֹרְרֵי "enmities" has received considerable attention. Some seek an abstract parallel to קנאת (P. Joüon, *Bib* 10 [1929] 195: צָרֲרֵי—an abstract pl meaning "enmity"; Procksch reads MT as an abstract pl without change). But the pl verb that follows is reason enough to reject both.

14.a. בְכָתֵף "on the shoulder" MT points as an abs form. In this form one must translate "The Philistines fly on the shoulder to the East." The context calls for another subject. General attempts at emendation have been made (F. Wutz, *BZ* 18 [1929] 27). *BHS* follows the Vg *humeros Philisthiim* to a constr pointing כֶּתֶף "the shoulder of the Philistines." (Cf. BDB, 509.)

14.b. מִשְׁלוֹח "extension" L and BHS, but many editions including *BHK* follow correct Masoretic grammar מִשְׁלוֹחַ.

14.c. MT משמעתם lit., "the ones who listen to them," i.e., obediently.

15.a. MT וְהֶחֱרִים "and he will dry up" is pointed as hiph pf 3 m sg from חרם "to ban, exterminate," BDB, 355. LXX καὶ ἐρημώσει "and he will lay waste" followed by Tg ויביש, Syr *wᵉraḥreb,* Vg *desolabit* implies והחריב "and he will make desolate." H. J. Stoebe (*TZ* 18 [1962] 399) and *BHS* argue for MT. G. R. Driver ("Vocabulary of the OT," *JTS* 32 [1931] 251) points to the Akk root *harâmu* "to cut off." Wildberger properly follows the Versions.

15.b. Wildberger notes that בעים רוחו has no satisfactory explanation. LXX πνεύματι βιαίω "to a violent spirit"; Tg במימר נביוהי "by the word of his prophets"; Syr *bᵉʾuḥdānâ dᵉrûḥeh* "with the power of his wind"; Vg *in fortitudine spiritus sui* "in the strength of his spirit." *BDB,* 744 lists עְיָם as dubious, possibly "glow." J. Reider ("Contributions to the Scriptural Text," *HUCA* 24 [1952/53] 83) supports a connection with Arab *ġāma* "plagued by a burning thirst" and translates "with the violence of his wind." H. Beers ("Hebrew Textual Notes," *AJSL* 34 [1917] 132–33) suggests בעים is an adverb from the root בעה (cf. 30:13; 64:1) meaning "beyond the normal, energetic, strong, powerful." Hummel ("Enclitic *mem,*" *JBL* 76 [1957] 94) calls it an inf abs from בעה followed by enclitic *mem* to be translated "boiling of water." Tur-Sinai ("Isaiah I–XII," *Studies in the Bible,* ScrHier 8 [Jerusalem: Magnes, 1961] 188) relates it to Akk *ûmu* and sees in it a Heb word meaning "storm." There is no convincing suggestion here. Keep MT, but translate like the Versions (cf. Wildberger).

Form/Structure/Setting

The entire passage is controlled by the opening verse which sets it "in that day" and which announces God's purpose to "acquire" his people from distant places. The first part (vv 12–14) announces God's signal to the nations to gather the dispersed of Israel and Judah. The result is the unification of the kingdom and the reestablishment of its sovereignty over its neighbors, i.e., the return to the conditions of the United Kingdom which David established.

The second part (vv 15–16) pictures God's direct intervention to remove the natural barriers to return. His power parallels the crossing of the Red Sea when Israel left Egypt under Moses. The result is a highway for the return. In the larger chiastic structure these balance 10:33–34 and 10:27c–32 (cf. Introduction to Scene 3).

Comment

11 *In that day* picks up the relation to the event announced in 10:33. *And it shall be* falls in line with the verbs plus *wāw* that have marked aspects of that event and its concomitant effects from 10:34 to this point.

Again concedes the failure of earlier efforts, whether those be understood as the Exodus or the restoration of the "Branch" (i.e., Hezekiah). It announces a further effort. The rescue concentrates on the שְׁאָר עמו "the remnant of his people," the fragments of the elect, the children of Abraham. This has been used in the Vision to refer to the exiles from Northern Israel.

קנה "to acquire" is noteworthy. The noun קנה "owner" appears in 1:3 "an ass knows its owner." Eve said, "With the help of God I have acquired a son" (Gen 4:1). The verb appears in Gen 14:19,22 and Deut 32:6 as a parallel to "create." It is used in Exod 15:16 and Ps 74:2 of God's redemption of his people. With overtones of redemption and creation, God will act to bring back the exiles in a way parallel to the Exodus, a way that is like his creation of a people for himself.

The verse documents the places from which they will be rescued. *Assyrian* captivity is recorded in 2 Kgs 15:29 in 733 B.C. 2 Kgs 17:6 (18:11) tells of deportation during the siege of Samaria (724–721 B.C.) to Halah on the Habor River. *Egypt* is lower Egypt, which had groups of Israelites from Solomon's time on. *Pathros* is Upper Egypt from Aswan southward. *Cush* is still further up the Nile into the Sudan (cf. Gen. 10:6,8). *Elam* lies east of Mesopotamia. *Shinar* is in the Euphrates delta (*MBA,* 15; see Gen 10:10.) *Hamath* is closer to home in Syria (Gen 10:15), while the *islands* turn to the Mediterranean and the Aegean. Perhaps the list anticipates the "four quarters" (lit., "wings") of v 12. Thus great diagonals are drawn from Assyria (northeast) to Cush (extreme south) and from Elam (due east) to the islands (west and northwest). Cf. the list of places in Obad v 20.

12 *Raise a banner* interprets the movement of Yahweh's hand in v 11. נס "banner" occurs in 5:26 and 13:2. In each instance Yahweh raises the banner as a signal to the *nations.* Yahweh's use of the nations to accomplish his will is patent throughout. In other passages the nations' task is one of war and destruction, but here the task is one of gathering and assembling Israelites and Judeans from distant places. The *four quarters* are literally "wings" and are defined in the previous verse.

13 The tensions and wars between *Ephraim* and *Judah* have dominated their history since the time of Jeroboam's split from Rehoboam. This must be overcome for God's purposes with the kingdom to be achieved.

14 When unity is achieved, the reestablishment of sovereignty over the former subject peoples is possible.

15 לשון ים מצרים "the tongue of the Sea of Egypt." The term has no parallel in the OT but apparently refers to the upper end of the Gulf of Suez which is referred to simply as הים "the Sea" Exod 14:2,9; 15:4,8,22; Isa 51:10; 63:11 and as the ים־סוף "the Reed Sea" Exod 13:18; Num 14:25; Deut 1:40, etc.

הניף ידו "wave his hand," picks up the chain of references to God's hand-signals that began in 5:25. Here, like 10:32, the hand is not rigid, but moving. However, the purpose is not to signal troops, but to bring the עים רוחו "power of his Spirit/Wind" into play. The parallel to Moses' outstretched arm and staff and the mighty East wind (Exod 14:21) is unmistakable.

הנהר "the River" usually refers to the Euphrates. The return of captives from Assyria is being seen as a parallel to Israel's exodus from Egypt—a theme that reappears in the Vision. The *seven streams* is not interpreted here. In this setting it shows the silt building up to a point that the stream has seven channels so small one does not need to remove his sandals in crossing.

16 סלה "highway" means an artificially built up road, not simply a "path" or a "way." The Vision returns to this in 19:23; 35:8; 49:11; 62:10. The Persians are known to have developed an extensive network of such roads (cf. A. T. Olmstead, *History of the Persian Empire* [Chicago: U. of Chicago, 1948] 299–301) which were forerunners of the famous Roman roads. The parallel to the Exodus moves beyond the facts in suggesting that a similar highway existed for Israel's flight from Egypt. This parallel extends throughout the Vision (cf. W. Zimmerli, "Der 'neue Exodus,' " *FS W. Vischer* [1960]

216–27 = *Gottes Offenbarung* ThB 19 [München: Kaiser, 1963] 192–204; B. W. Anderson, "Exodus Typology in Second Isaiah," *Israel's Prophetic Heritage*, FS J. Muilenburg [New York: Harper & Brothers, 1962] 177–95).

Explanation

The passage from vv 11–16 is united by the single theme of Yahweh's gathering the scattered exiles of his people (vv 11 and 15). The signal with his hand occurs three times (vv 11, 12, 15). The major concerns are with those in Assyria (vv 11 and 15) while two middle sections are concerned that both Israel and Judah be involved (vv 12 and 13–14). In v 11 two lines are drawn. One from north (Assyria) to south (Cush), a second from east (Elam) to west (Islands of the Sea). This parallels the four "wings" of the earth (v 12).

References to the Remnant are careful to include both Israel and Judah (v 12) in accordance with practice throughout the Vision. The references to Egypt pick up the more likely area for Judean dispersion. People from Israel were in Egypt as early as Solomon's day when Jeroboam fled there (1 Kgs 11:40). Some suspect that Solomon furnished mercenaries in exchange for chariots so that the military settlements which are documented for cities on the Nile in the sixth century may well have been there much earlier. The exile to Assyria began at least as early as 721 B.C. (2 Kgs 17:6) but possibly earlier in 733 B.C. (2 Kgs 16:9) as one of the Assyrian documents claims.

Vv 13–14, predicting a reunited kingdom, return to a theme hinted at before (cf. *Comment* on 9:5[6]). The theme is still very pertinent to the growing rift between Jerusalem and Samaria in the fifth century.

Vv 15–16 emphasize the axis from Assyria through Egypt that crosses Canaan. God's return of his people from both directions miraculously removes the natural barriers, the gulf and the river, by the power of his Spirit, or wind.

The description then falls back on historical comparison with the journey from Egypt rather than maintaining the future picture of movement from both directions.

Episode F: Hymns for "That Day" (12:1–6)

Bibliography

Alonso-Schökel, L. "De duabus methodis pericopam explicandi." *VD* 34 (1956) 154–60. **Craigie, P. C.** "Psalm *XXIX* in the Hebrew Poetic Tradition." *VT* 22 (1972) 143–51. **Crüsemann, F.** *Studien zur Formgeschichte vom Hymnus and Danklied in Israel.* WMANT 32. Neukirchen-Vluyn: Neukirchener Verlag, 1969. 227. **Gottlieb, H.** "Jesaja, Kapitel 12." *DTT* 37 (1974) 29–32. **Loewenstamm, S. E.** "The Lord is my Strength and my Glory." *VT* 19 (1969) 464–70.

Translation

Herald:	1 *And you (sg) shall say in that day:*	
Zion:	*I will raise my hands* [a] *to you, Yahweh.*	2
	Indeed you have been angry with me.	3
	[b] *May your anger turn*	2+1
	that you may comfort me. [b]	
	2 *Behold God* [a] *(is) my salvation.*	3+3
	I shall trust and I shall not live in fear.	
	Because Yah [b] *Yahweh (is) my power and my strength,* [c]	3+2+3
	he becomes my salvation.	
Herald:	3 *And you (pl) shall draw water with rejoicing*	3+2
	from the wells of salvation.	
	4 *And you (pl) shall say on that day:*	3
Chorus:	*Lift up your hands* [a] *to Yahweh,*	2+2
	call on his name.	
	Make known his acts among the nations.	3
	Bring to remembrance:	1+3
	that his name has been exalted.	
	5 *Sing of Yahweh*	2+3
	for he has done a majestic thing,	
	making this known [a]	2+2
	in all the earth.	
	6 *Shrill out and sing,*	2+2
	inhabitant [a] *of Zion,*	
	for great in your midst (is)	3+2
	the Holy One of Israel!	

Notes

1.a. MT אוֹדְךָ "I will praise you." DSS[Isa] דה. .א has two letters missing, but shows no 2nd pers suffix. A hiph form from ידה could produce א(הו)דה or the hith א(תו)דה (cf. Dan 9:4). Both mean "let me give thanks" or "praise" by using a verb root which suggests lifting the hands as a gesture. MT may also have this meaning and is translated "let me lift my hands to you." For the relation to "hands" symbolism in these chapters cf. the *Form* section. כי may here be a strong assertive particle "indeed."

1.b-b. MT's two juss verbs are unexpected in a psalm of thanksgiving (cf. Wildberger, 477). LXX *διότι ὠργίσθης μοι καὶ ἀπεστρεψας τὸν θυμόν σου καὶ ἠλέησάς με* "because you were angry with me, and you turned back your wrath and were gracious to me" (also Syr *wʾhpkt rwgzk wbjʾtnj;* Vg *conversus est furor tuus, et consolatus es me*) reads the Hebrew as cons imperfects which restore the normal form of a thanksgiving psalm. Wildberger correctly rejects moves to make the text conform, which might rob the text of its own integrity. Gunkel (H. Gunkel & J. Begrich, *Einleitung in die Psalmen* [Göttingen: Vandenhoeck & Ruprecht, 1933] 275) notes that a thanksgiving psalm may include supplication.

2.a. Syr inserts על "upon the God of my salvation," DSS[Isa] reads אל אל "toward the God of my salvation" or a double אל "God" as a parallel to יה יהוה "Yah Yahweh" in the next line. But MT is sound. We read the stich as a substantive sentence without a verb.

2.b. יה is often omitted with LXX and Vg (cf. *BHS*). The exact parallels in Exod 15:2 and Ps 118:14 are gounds for keeping it. Wildberger follows R. M. Spence ("Yah, Yahve," *ExpTim* 11 [1899–1900] 94) in omitting יהוה "Yahweh" on grounds of dittography for the following ויהי "he becomes." Both may be kept to sustain the emphasis.

2.c. זמרת יה is an unusual formula (also in Exod 15:2; Ps 118:14). DSS[Isa] זמרתיה makes the *yodh* a suffix "my" but then writes the ה above the line (cf. S. Talmon, "Double Readings," *VT* 4 [1954] 206; "Double Readings in MT," *Textus* 1 [1960] 163, n. 47). G. R. Driver ("Hebrew Scrolls," *JTS* 2 [1951] 25) notes that in both other instances some MSS also read זמרתי. Perhaps the MT has lost a *yodh* in liturgical use (cf. Wildberger, 478; O. Lehman, "Biblical Textual Tradition," *JNES* 26 [1967] 98; and Loewenstamm *VT* 19 [1969] 465). זמרה has usually been translated "song" (BDB, 274). But studies (J. Zolli, "Note esegetiche," *Giornale della Societa Asiatica Italiana* 3 [1935] 290–92; KB 111 have sought its meaning in Arab *ḏamara* "drive" and *ḏimr(un)* "strong" and Amor *zmr* "protect." Also studies in personal names like זמרי (Noth, *Personennamen,* 176) have turned to the meaning "strength" or "might" (contra Loewenstamm, 465).

4.a. Cf. 1.a. above.

5.a. K מידעת pual ptcp "something made known," "a monument." Q מודעת hoph ptcp "something caused to be made known." LXX ἀναγγείλατε impv "announce it" suggests a Heb הוֹדִיעוּ. Tg and Syr have participles like MT. DSS[Isa] מודעות ptcp pl. MT should be sustained in either K or Q forms.

6.a. Fem to indicate a collective sense (cf. Joüon, § 134c).

Form/Structure/Setting

ואמרת "and you shall say" continues the line of consecutive plurals that began in 10:34 and 11:1. They each and all hark back to the הנה "behold" of 10:33 with the following participle. Yet they are not a chain in which each link depends on the one before. Each responds to the theophany in 10:27d–32 (cf. Watts, *Syntax,* 47–54).

This is emphasized by the conscious use of אודך "I raise my hands to you" (v 1) and הודו "lift up your hands" (v 4) to respond to the ינפף ידו "he waves his hand" (10:32). A beautiful dramatic effect is created. Throughout 5:1—10:23 Yahweh's hand has remained unyieldingly "outstretched"—a signal that the battle is to continue. In 10:32 he waves his hand toward Jerusalem. In 11:11 he reaches out his hand toward the exiles. And now in response, worshipers extend their hands toward him.

There are two distinct parts. In the first, the Herald instructs the city (vv 1–2) and uses the singular (cf. Crüsemann, *Studien,* 50–55). In the second, instruction is directed to its inhabitants (plural). It gives a promise (v 3) which completes the admonition of 10:24 not to fear the Assyrian. Then it instructs them in the proper liturgical response for "that day." The setting is unusual for liturgy. The events to which the hymns should respond are viewed as yet to occur (cf. 10:24 and the repeated use of "in that day"). Yet the normal liturgical forms respond to events as or after they happen.

The tenses reflect this unusual quality. In v 1 אָנַפְתָּ "you are angry" is perfect, reflecting the existing situation. The song of thanksgiving, which the introductory אוֹדְךָ "I raise my hands to you" seems to begin, usually is followed by an explanation in perfect tenses throughout. But here the tenses in the second part turn to jussives יָשֹׁב and תְּנַחֲמֵנִי "may it turn" and "may you comfort me." The strict form is broken, but the change fits the context here beautifully.

Comment

1 *You* is masculine singular and apparently refers to Zion. אוֹדְךָ "I will confess you" is built on the verb ידה which is apparently derived from יד "hand." In the causative hiphil stem it means something like "throw up (or out) the hands" as one might do in prayer, pleading, or worship. It comes to have the meaning "praise" or "confess." It is hardly accidental that the hymn which responds to a scene in which God's hand and that of the Assyrian have been so important should begin with the same phoneme.

God's *anger* is a direct reference to 10:25. The destruction of Samaria seems inevitable. The appearance of Yahweh as of old to defend his city (10:27d–32) gives rise to the hope that Jerusalem, by a miracle, will survive. The call to give thanks and praise is based on an admonition (10:24), a promise (10:25, 26–27), and the recall of the great theophanic vision (10:27d–32).

On the basis of this vision, faith saw the Mighty God approaching his land and his city like a great Forester (10:33–34) and sang out beside the old promises of history in God's hands and of God's own king and the peace he brings (11:1–10) a newer promise that scattered exiles will be returned (11:11–16). Now the hymns respond to the great theophany, daring to hope for an end very soon to God's period of anger.

2 The city confesses its reliance on *Yahweh-God* for its hope and its future.

4 הודו is from the root ידה (as in v 1), either hiphil perfect 3rd person plural or hiphil imperative second person plural. In this context the latter is called for: *lift your hands.*

5 גאות "a majestic thing" is from גאה "to be high." In contrast to human attempts to make themselves great or rise to heights, Yahweh's acts to redeem Zion and return Israel are inherently "high" and praiseworthy.

Explanation

The song is highly nuanced with the tenses conveying the hints of meaning. Words that usually are clear-cut imperatives and indicatives of hymnic praise in other settings are in v 1 tentative, pleading, wanting to believe, testing the water. A single male is addressed and told that these will be his thoughts "in that day." He begins his worship: "I will raise my hands to you, Yahweh."

The theme that dominated chaps. 5 and 9–10 was Yahweh's wrath toward Israel. It now asserts itself in the song "You have been angry." The perfect tense in the conditional clause indicates a condition taken for granted (Watts, *Syntax,* 134). The worshiper knows that this condition does occur. His prayer in jussive tenses applies to that: "May your anger turn that you may comfort me!"

The prayer turns to confession of faith (v 2):

> Behold, God is my salvation
> I shall trust and I shall not live in fear.
> Because Yah Yahweh is my power and my strength,
> he becomes my salvation.

The theme here is *salvation.* The prayer has no hope but in God, in Yahweh. The tentative approach of v 1 moves to greater confidence and ardor in v 2.

This is the opportunity promised for "that day" beyond the *Dies Irae.* But to whom? Who is addressed? Is this the heir of David? The song is like

Psalmic laments of an individual. Is this addressed to Ahaz or his heir? The address in v 3 turns to a group (priests, men of the city). They are promised that they will "draw water with rejoicing from the wells of salvation." What are these "wells of salvation"? Are they not the sources of blessing existing in the house of David and in Zion, the salvation that is confirmed in the king's prayer in v 2?

So now the people share again in God's blessings through the "anointed one" of the stock of Jesse. They are called to join in the worship, praise, and testimony of that event (vv 4–5). They will give again the joyful cries of worship in Zion to lift the hands to Yahweh, exalt his name, make remembrance of his acts before all the nations. The women of the city are exhorted to join their shrill voices to the cacophony of praise (v 6).

The reason for all of this is summarized: "For great in your midst is the Holy One of Israel." The Holy, Awesome, Divine Warrior who approached the city in 10:27–32 has again taken up his residence there and is to be worshiped and praised accordingly. The possibility that the Davidic monarchy may again function as conceived under David and Solomon is allowed to bloom in these chapters. The monarchy united and flourishing: that is the picture and the dream portrayed in this act.

These positive statements concerning the future of the Davidic house and the throne in Jerusalem are the last of their kind in the Vision. Only in Act V (chaps. 28–33) will tentative hints of such occur again. There is hope in the Vision for the future of Israel and Jerusalem. But the Davidic dynasty is not included.

Scene 4: Burden: Babylon (13:1—14:32)

Bibliography

Erlandsson, S. *The Burden of Babylon: A Study of Isaiah 13:2—14:23.* ConB, OT 4. Lund: Gleerup, 1970.

Form/Structure/Setting

The outer limits of the scene are marked by the superscription in 13:1 and by the reference to the death of Ahaz in the heading of the last speech (14:28). The latter marks the end of the act, which deals with the reign of Ahaz.

The first three episodes belong most obviously under the theme burden of Babylon, while the two closing episodes interpret the plans of Yahweh and speak doom for the Philistines. The last is dated in the year of Ahaz's death. The titles and extent are as follows:

Episode A, The Burden of Babylon (13:2–22a)

Episode B, Babylon's Fate/Jacob's Hope (13:22b—14:7)
Episode C, Taunt over a Fallen Tyrant (14:8–21)
Episode D, Three Statements of Yahweh's Plans (14:22–27)
Episode E, Burden over the Philistines (14:28–32)

The theme returns to the keystone statement of the previous scene (11:5a). The larger structure is composed around a keystone in 14:4b–7 on the same theme. The following outline demonstrates the unity of the scene's arch structure.

A A call to arms (13:2–3)
 B The noise of coming battle that will destroy the whole land (13:4–5)
  C The fear of the Day of the Lord (13:6–8)
   D The events of the Day of the Lord (13:9–16)
    E Yahweh stirring up Medes to destroy Babylon (13:17–22)
     F Yahweh will have compassion on Jacob (14:1–2)
      G You (m sg) will taunt the king of Babylon (14:3–41)
KEYSTONE Yahweh has broken the scepter of rulers (14:4b–7)
      G′ You (m sg) will taunt the fallen tyrant (14:8–20a)
     F′ Curse on the tyrant's family (14:20b–21)
    E′ Yahweh will destroy Babylon (14:22–23)
   D′ Yahweh's plan to destroy Assyria himself (14:24–25)
  C′ Yahweh's plan for the whole world (14:26–27)
 B′ Yahweh will destroy the Philistines (14:28–31)
A′ Jerusalem's establishment by Yahweh's order (14:32)

Introduction

This scene continues the positive tone of the previous scene (10:24—12:6), although fragments of the scene could leave an opposite impression. But the dominating keystone (14:1–21) picks up the theme of 11:11–16 and the positive tone is echoed in 14:24–25 and 32b.

There is also a sense of crisis in Scene 3. Scenes 1 and 2 centered in the crises Ahaz faced in 734 and 724–21 B.C. The crisis in Scene 4 is defined at the end (14:32). Envoys (probably from the Philistine cities) demand an answer to their invitation for Jerusalem to join them in rebellion against Assyria. At the very end of the reign of Ahaz (*ca.* 720–18 B.C.) Sargon II, despite his success in completing Shalmaneser's siege of Samaria, was experiencing difficulty in establishing his authority in other parts of the empire. Babylon had been seized by the Chaldean Yakin tribe under Merodach-Baladan. Sargon was not able to retake Babylon for a decade or eliminate the threat from Merodach-Baladan during his lifetime.

The Philistines saw Babylon as proof that the Assyrians were vulnerable. They began to organize the Palestine states in rebellion. This provoked a punitive campaign from Sargon in 720 B.C. (*MBA,* 149) with battles at Gaza and Raphia. The Egyptians were part of the force defeated at Raphia. Apparently Samaria was again involved. This led to the massive deportations to regions near Nineveh on the Habur River and to cities in Media (2 Kgs 17:6).

Babylon's success posed a tempting example for nationalists in Judah. Ahaz had continued his policy of loyal vassalage, maintaining neutrality during these conflicts. The Vision sees this to be in accordance with Yahweh's strategy. Yahweh himself will dispose of the Assyrian in his own time (14:24–25). Not ready to change his mind on the issue (vv 26–27), he guarantees Zion's security (vv 29–30). That Yahweh will not tolerate the ambitious kings or nations who frustrate his plans to use the Assyrian is clear. The prohibition applies to Babylon (13:17–22; 14:22–23) and to the Philistines (14:29–30). Jerusalem is warned against a "do-it-yourself" scheme for redemption. The scene continues the "Day of Yahweh" descriptions that mark his initiatives to bring an end to the "old age" and to inaugurate the "new age."

Excursus: Babylon and the King of Babylon in the Vision of Isaiah

Bibliography

Brinkman, J. A. *A Political History of Post-Kassite Babylonia.* AnOr 43. Rome: Pontifical Biblical Institute, 1948. ———. "Merodach Baladan II." *Studies Presented to A. Leo Oppenheim.* Chicago: The Oriental Institute of the University of Chicago, 1964. 6–53. **Buccellati, G.** "Enthronement of the King." Ibid., 54–61. **Lambert, W. G.** "The Babylonians and Chaldaeans." *POTT* 179–96. **Suggs, J. F. W.** *The Greatness that was Babylon.* London: Sedgwick and Jackson, 1962. **Smith, S.** "The Supremacy of Assyria." *CAH,* I 39–62.

The City

The players on the stage of ancient history included peoples or tribes (like Aramaeans and Hebrews) and cities. The former provided the dynamic of ever-replenished manpower and social pressure to fuel the wars and struggles of the time. The latter provided what stability and meaning the period possessed. Kings ruled over cities and peoples or groups of peoples. But rule was fluid and seldom permanent. Dynasties relating to tribes or cities were more durable.

Only in the resurgent Assyrian Empire under Tiglath Pileser III (745–27 B.C.) did a change appear. He and his successors instituted mass deportations as a deliberate attempt to break up the unity of peoples and assimilate them into the larger unity. The policies were only partially successful. They never managed to impose an imperial peace on the empire, nor did the Neo-Babylonian empire which followed them. Only Cyrus and the great Persian Empire (539–331 B.C.) began to organize and administer the larger political force in a way that brought increased stability.

Some cities antedated the arrival of the new peoples and survived the political changes of these millennia. Jerusalem was (and is) such a city. Babylon, Damascus, and Tyre were also such cities. They each play a role in Isaiah's Vision. But Jerusalem and Babylon are the central protagonists. In this large central portion of the Vision, Babylon's fate and history play an important role.

The symbolic role goes well beyond the historic reality. The Assyrian Empire is the major threat and oppressor of the eighth century. But neither Nineveh nor Assur figure in the Vision. The Persian Empire moves to the fore in the sixth and fifth centuries, but none of her cities appears. Only Babylon, which, of course, was used by both (and which at times opposed both), is presented here.

The name "Babylon" conjures up for the Israelite and the reader of Scripture memories of the Tower of Babel (Gen 11:1–9). The story is consistent with the city's claim to a prestigious antiquity. The name means "The Gate of God." Its influence through the centuries had a religious base.

The great Hammurabi used Babylon as his capital in the eighteenth century B.C. Other rulers over Mesopotamia treasured the right to "seize the hands of Bel" in the annual Babylonian enthronement ceremonies which gave them a legitimacy in the eyes of the citizens that nothing else could effect. The Assyrian rulers from Tiglath-Pileser III to Sennacherib did this. Of course Nabopolassar and Nebuchadnezzer II did this. And the Persians, from Cyrus to Xerxes, did this. Most of these added the title "King of Babylon" to their names and other titles.

So the city had special meaning for that time in relation to political religion and in relation to monarchy in theory and practice. The Vision features the role of Babylon in full awareness of the significance it carried in the eighth, as well as in the sixth–fifth centuries.

Babylon: 740–687 B.C.

The Assyrian Tiglath-Pileser III strengthened the realm and moved to establish his authority in lower Mesopotamia and in the western states. So he was concerned simultaneously with affairs in Babylon and in Israel-Judah in the seventh decade of the century. He had himself crowned King of Babylon, "taking the hand of Bel," in the ancient cultural and cultic center in 728 and 727 B.C., claiming authority thereby over the major religious centers and over the Aramaean tribes of the area. His son, Shalmaneser V, continued the dual monarchy during the five years of his reign (726–22 B.C.).

Sargon II was unable to establish sovereignty over Babylon. Merodach-Baladan, a powerful prince of the Aramean tribe Bit Yakin that occupied an area on the Persian Gulf, seized power over Babylon with the help of the four other Aramean (Chaldean) tribes and the neighboring Elamite king. He held the throne for twelve years. In two campaigns in 710 and 709 B.C. Sargon II invaded the south. When Merodach-Baladan heard of initial Assyrian successes he fled Babylon and retired to a town on the Elamite frontier. Sargon II was crowned king of Babylon in 709 B.C. In a later battle at his tribal capital of Deir-Yakin Merodach-Baladan was beaten again, but escaped capture. Many of the Bit Yakin tribe were deported.

Merodach-Baladan appeared again when Sennacherib assumed the throne. This was probably 704 B.C. Merodach-Baladan pushed aside Marduk-Zakirsume II who reigned in Babylon for one month. Sennacherib moved rapidly against the usurper and ousted him within nine months. Again Merodach-Baladan fled. Sennacherib installed Bel-ibni on Babylon's throne. It is remarkable that Merodach could have gained such wide support so quickly. He was undoubtedly a master diplomat, however bad a soldier. 2 Kgs 20 and Isa 39 are witness to his efforts. Apparently he attempted to coordinate uprisings in Babylon and Palestine, but was forced to rush his plans for Babylon when another stepped in before him.

In 700 B.C. Sennacherib campaigned again in Babylonia, putting his son Assur-nadin-sumi on the throne and carrying out a punitive campaign against Bit Yakin territory. Again Merodach-Baladan escaped. This was the last to be heard of him. But Sennacherib's troubles with Babylon continued. After the murder of Assur-nadin-sumi in 689 B.C., he sacked the city, destroying its fortifications and great buildings. The statue of Marduk was taken to Assyria and Sennacherib assumed the title of king.

The references to Babylon in Isa 13–39 are apparently all intended to refer to this period. But much more happened to that city before the rise of Cyrus (539 B.C.; Isa 45) and the predicted humiliation in Isa chaps. 46 and 47. It had been the capital for the Neo-Babylonian empire under Nabopolassar (625–605) and Nebuchadnezzer II (605–562). It had tasted again the sweet fruits of power for a few short years only to let it slip away before opening its doors to the Persian emperor. He, like those before him, "took the hands of Bel" and became King of Babylon.

By the time the Vision was written, three more Persian emperors had included that title in their own. Babylon continued to be a rebellious problem for its rulers. Xerxes was forced to put down a rebellion about 480 B.C. The city was severely punished. Fortifications were demolished, temples destroyed, the golden statue of Marduk was melted down, confiscated land was given to Persians. Babylonia was incorporated into the Persian administration. Xerxes and succeeding kings omitted Babylon from their titulature.

The references to Babylon in the Vision are, therefore, intended to be understood as follows:

13:17–22 and 14:22–23: Under Ahaz *ca.* 720 B.C. after the revolt under Merodach-Baladan.
21:9: Under Hezekiah *ca.* 710 B.C.
23:13: Under Hezekiah after 710 (or 689) B.C.
Chaps. 45–48: 540 B.C. prior to Cyrus' conquest.

(The King of Babylon in 14:4a for whom the taunting poem set in the reign of Ahaz was deemed appropriate must have been Merodach-Baladan.)

The destructions or falls of Babylon which are predicted in the Vision were fulfilled:

13:19–22 and 14:22–23 in *ca.* 710 B.C. by Sargon.
21:9 and 23:13 in *ca.* 710 B.C. by Sargon or 703 B.C. by Sennacherib.

(Possibly, Sennacherib's thorough destruction of 689 B.C. is intended, but that seems unlikely in the dramatic frame of the Vision.) Chaps. 46–47 show the capitulation of the city to Cyrus in 539 B.C. (Perhaps there are overtones of the destruction of the city by Xerxes in 480 B.C.)

Long passages on Babylon serve as a kind of "enclosure" around a large central section or sections of the book. The "Burden" in chap. 13 includes a description of world judgment and an oracle against Babylon promising defeat and destruction. Chap. 14 begins with hope for Israel and continues (vv 4b–21) with a powerful taunt to be sung over the king of Babylon. The chapter then has a closing oracle against Babylon (vv 22–23) before a reconfirmation of God's purpose to remove the Assyrian from his land (vv 24–27).

The last passages about Babylon appear in 44:28—48:20. Cyrus is identified as Yahweh's appointed servant to return Israel and rebuild the Temple (44:28—45:7) but Babylon is not mentioned. 46:1–2 announce the humiliation and captivity of Babylon's gods, while chap. 47 is a major taunting song against "daughter Babylon." 48:14 announces that Yahweh's purposes will be fulfilled through his chosen one and calls on Israelites to leave Babylon (v 20). Between these are notices of Babylon's misfortunes in 21:1–10; 23:13, and of her continued intrigues and conspiracies in chap. 39.

Yahweh's plan (14:26) includes the work of the Assyrian as "rod of his anger" (7:17–25; 10:5–6) and the Persian Cyrus as the shepherd-servant to restore Israel to Canaan (44:28—45:13). But Babylon is the supreme example of those who seek to thwart his purpose. Yahweh does *not* support the rebellions against Assyria. Ahaz is warned against involvement either in the intrigue of Pekah and Rezin or in alliance with Assyria to overcome them. Yahweh himself will deal with Assyria in his own good time (10:5–19; 14:24–27). In the meantime his "burdens" lie heavy upon the rebels (chaps. 13–23).

Babylon also illustrates the pride of humanity (13:11b) that must find judgment under Yahweh (2:11–17). In this she is like the Assyrian (10:5–34). These motifs are found in 13:19; 14:11–15; 47:5.

The entire section (chaps. 13–48) is a defense of the divine strategy (14:24) that Isaiah had announced, i.e., that God was sending the Assyrian to do his will in punishing the nations and to bring about a change to a new order. He had counseled a passive attitude, a "waiting on the Lord." Israel (and the other subject nations) were restless, repeatedly conspiring revolt. But it could not succeed. God was not in it.

By the fifth century B.C. God had "finished all his work against Mount Zion and Jerusalem" (10:12). He had also "punished the Assyrian" and removed him from Canaan. And he was ready to fulfill his own strategy to bring back the exiles and rebuild Jerusalem (chap. 44–45). The entire Vision is an exposition of that strategy, of Israel's and Judah's resistence to it, and of the continued necessity of judgment in carrying it out.

To the reading or hearing audience, about 435 B.C., these echoes of Babylon's involvement with Jerusalem's fate in the eighth century and the sixth century were filtered through their knowledge of the destruction of Babylon in 480 B.C. by Xerxes. They could not help but view it as another fulfillment of God's curse of chaps. 13–14. This also sharpened the point of the Vision's warning to Jerusalem against active rebellion (cf. Vermeylen, I, 288).

The Superscription (13:1)

Bibliography

de Boer, P. A. H. "An Inquiry into the Meaning of the Term משא." *OTS* 5 (1948) 197–214. **Gehman, H. S.** "The 'Burden' of the Prophets." *JQR* 31 (1940/41) 107–21. **Scott, R. B. Y.** "The Meaning of *massa*ʾ as an Oracle Title." *JBL* 67 (1948) v.

Translation

1 *The Burden*[a] *of Babylon*
which Isaiah the son of Amoz envisioned.

Notes

1.a. משא is not easily translated or understood. The Versions vary: LXX translates *ῥῆμα* "speech," "prophecy" or *ὅρασις* "vision" or *ὅραμα* "vision" (cf. Ziegler, 96). ʼA always uses *αρμα* "vision." Σ and Θ use *λημμα,* an obscure word which in the Similitudes of Hermes means "gain" (cf. BAG, 474). Vg translates *onus* "burden."

Form/Structure/Setting

The genre of superscriptions is treated in the commentary on 1:1. משא is used in superscriptions in Nah 1:1, Hab 1:1, Zech 9:1; 12:1; and Mal 1:1 as parallels to דבר "word" and חזון "vision."

Gehman (*JQR* 31 [1940/41] 120–21) thinks of משׂא as an oracle or prophetic speech, especially a severe prophecy to be laid on an individual or a nation. Scott (*JBL* 67 [1948] v) identifies it as a threatening oracle accompanied by lifting the hand as a gesture for an oath or curse. It is a "grim vision" or a "harsh oracle." חזה "envisioned," may indicate a scene witnessed in the Divine Council (D. G. Reid, "The Burden of Babylon: A Study of Isaiah 13," Fuller Theological Seminary, 1979).

The role of the superscription has frequently been understood as indicating a major division in the book (most recently Wildberger, 506). It is seen as a heading for a collection of oracles which were ultimately incorporated into the book. However, in 2:1 the commentary has shown that the superscription had a different function. Here, too, it signals a change of form and claims Isaianic responsibility for the prophecy against Babylon (cf. chap. 39), as 2:1 did for the prophecy about Jerusalem and chaps. 7–8 did for the admonitions to Ahaz. This commentary sees the notices of the death of kings in 6:1; 14:28; and 38:1–8 as the more important divisions in the Vision.

The superscription applies to all of chaps. 13–14. The chiastic analysis has shown the unity of their contents and structure (contra Erlandsson, *The Burden of Babylon* [Lund: Gleerup, 1970]).

Comment

משׂא "burden" appears to derive from the root נשׂא "to raise" or "carry." The noun may mean "a burden" or "a heavy speech." The passages in Isaiah where it occurs fit the meaning "a threat of doom" (14:28; 15:1; 17:1; 19:1; 21:1, 11, 13; 22:1; 23:1). Each of these names the city or country which is the target of the threat.

Wildberger suggests that the term משׂא derives from נשׂא קול "lift the voice" (cf. Num 14:1; Isa 3:7; 42:2; Job 21:12). 2 Kgs 9:25 "he raised over him this משׂא" in the sense of a speech. Lam 2:14 speaks of empty משׂאות which have lead the daughter of Zion astray. Jer 23:33 makes a word play on the meanings "speech" and "burden."

Scott suggests that one relate משׂא to נשׂא יד "raise a hand" as a signal. This parallels נטה יד "stretch out a hand" and נשׂא נס "raise a banner," phrases which occur repeatedly in these chapters of Isaiah.

נשׂא, the root of משׂא, is used with נס "banner" in 5:26; 11:12; 13:2. These are signals for armies to gather and march. In 49:22 Yahweh raises his hand to signal the nations, while ארים נסי in the same verse uses a synonym of נשׂא with God's banner. The same combination of רום and נס occurs in 63:10. In 10:32 Yahweh waves his hand toward Zion (נפך ידו).

The pervasive term in chaps. 5–14 is "stretch out his hand." In 5:25 Yahweh's anger against his people, Israel, causes him to "stretch out his hand against them" ויט ידו עליו and the note ועוד ידו נטויה "his hand is stretched out still" is repeated like a refrain in 9:11[12], 16[17], 20[21]; 10:4. In 14:27 the words occur again: וידו הנטויה "(It is) his hand that is stretched out." The hand signals parallel verbal ordinances and commands: "The Lord has sent a word" (9:7[8]) and "Yahweh spoke to me with a strong hand" (8:11).

Thus, in Isaiah, especially chaps. 5–23, the interaction of hand signals and words "raised" by Yahweh in threat, warning, or judgment is pervasive. This makes it likely that משא in Isaiah means that which Yahweh signals (by hand or word) against someone or some group. This usually involves bringing other forces to fulfill God's intention or strategy (עצה). It may also signal God's ban, the removal of this protection from someone or some group.

"Babylon." The name of the fabled city occurs here for the first time in the Vision. The scene speaks of many other things, but the references to Babylon (13:19; 14:22) and to Babylon's king (14:4) catch the ear and earn the headline. Its appearance is surprising. It is the only city or country in this part of the Vision which is not directly involved in the events of eighth-century Palestine. Its role may be explained by the suggestive influence of chap. 39.

Episode A: Burden: Babylon (13:2–22a)

Bibliography

Alonso-Schökel, L. "Traducción de textos poéticos hebreos I (Isa 13)." *CB* 17 (1960) 170–76. **Bach, R.** *Die Aufforderungen zur Flucht und zum Kampf im alttestamentlichen Prophetenspruch.* WMANT 9. Neukirchen: Neukirchener Verlag, 1962. **Budde, K.** "Jesaja 13." *Abhandlungen zur semitischen Religionskunde und Sprachwissenschaft.* FS W. W. v Baudissin. Giessen: A. Töpelmann, 1918. 55–70. **Fensham, F. C.** "Common Trends in Curses of the Near-Eastern Treaties and *kudurru*-Inscriptions compared with Maledictions of Amos and Isaiah." *ZAW* 75 (1963) 155–75. **Grimme, H.** "Ein übersehenes Orakel gegen Assur (Isaias 13)." *TQ* 85 (1903) 1–11. **Hillers, D. R.** "Convention in Hebrew literature; the reaction to bad news (Includes Isa 13:7–8, 21:3–4)." *ZAW* 77 (1965) 86–90. ———. *Treaty-Curses and the Old Testament Prophets.* BibOr 16. Rome: Pontifical Biblical Institute, 1964. **Miller, P. D.** "The Divine Council and the Prophetic Call to War." *VT* 18 (1968) 100–107. **Reid, D. G.** "The Burden of Babylon: A Study of Isaiah 13." Research paper, Fuller Theol. Seminary, 1979. **Schwarz, G.** "Jesaja 13:7–8a, eine Emendation." *ZAW* 89 (1977) 119.

Translation

Yahweh: 2 *Upon a bare* [a] *mountain,* 3+2+3
raise (pl) a banner!
Raise the voice to them!
Wave a hand 2+3
[b] *that they enter the gates of nobles.* [b]
3 *I myself give command to my dedicated (holy, sanctified) ones.* 3+4+2
Also I call my heroes to my wrath [a]
those rejoicing in my sovereignty.

First Speaker:	4 *A sound of tumult in the mountains*	3+3
	like many people.	
	A sound of uproar (from) kingdoms [a]	3+2
	nations gathering.	
Second Speaker:	*Yahweh of Hosts*	2+3
	mustering an attack force (for) battle.	
	5 *Coming from a distant land,*	3+2
	from the end of the heavens, [a]	
	Yahweh and instruments of his indignation [b]	3+2
	to destroy the whole land.	
Third Speaker:	6 *Wail ye!*	1+4+3
	For the day of Yahweh (is) near.	
	It comes like destruction from Shaddai. [a]	
	7 *Therefore, all hands* [a] *are feeble*	4+4+1
	and every mortal heart [b] *is faint*	
	8 *and they are confounded.* [a]	
	Pangs and anguish seize them.	3+2
	Like a travailing woman [b] *they writhe.*	
	Each at his neighbor [b] *stares aghast.*	3+3
	[b] *Their faces* [c] *are faces aflame.*	
First Speaker:	9 *Behold the day of Yahweh (is) coming,*	3+4
	cruel, overflowing, burning anger,	
	to make the earth a desolation,	3+3
	its sinners to be destroyed from it.	
	10 *For the stars of the heavens and their constellations* [a]	4+3
	do not give light. [b]	
	The sun is dark in its rising	3+4
	and the moon does not produce [c] *its light.*	
Yahweh:	11 *And I shall visit upon the world (its)* [a] *evil*	3+2
	and upon the wicked their sins,	
	and I shall stop the arrogance of the proud	3+3
	and the haughtiness of the terrible I will lay low.	
	12 *I will make a mortal rarer than pure gold* [a]	3+3
	and a human than pure gold of Ophir.	
	13 *Because of this I will make the heavens tremble* [a]	3+3
	and the earth will shake in its place.	
Second Speaker: (echo)	*In the overflowing wrath of Yahweh of Hosts,*	3+3
	in the day of his burning anger.	
Third Speaker:	14 *And it will be that*	1
	like a hunted gazelle,	2+3
	and like a sheep which no one herds,	
	they will turn each to his own people	3+3
	and each to his own land they will flee.	
	15 *Everyone captured* [a] *is stabbed*	3+4
	and every one caught falls by a sword.	
	16 *Their babies are dashed in pieces before their eyes.*	3+2+2
	Their houses are plundered	
	and their wives raped. [a]	

Yahweh:	17 *Behold me stirring the Medes against them* *whom silver does not buy* *nor gold entice.*	4+4+4
	18 *Bows of youths are dashed in pieces.* [a] *They will not show mercy to the fruit of the womb,* *upon children their eyes will not look with compassion.*	3+4+4
First Speaker:	19 *And Babylon, jewel of kingdoms,* *the glory of Chaldean pride, will become*	4+3
	like God's overthrow *(of) Sodom and Gomorrah.*	2+2
Second Speaker:	20 *It will never be inhabited again,* *it will not be dwelt in generation to generation.*	3+4
	No Arab [a] *will camp* [b] *there* *and no shepherd will rest* [c] *his flocks there.*	4+4
	21 *Desert creatures* [a] *will rest there* *and jackels* [b] *will fill their houses.*	3+3
	Owl will dwell there *and wild goats will run around there.*	4+3
	22 *Hyenas* [a] *will echo in its palaces* [b] *and jackels* [c] *in its temples of pleasure.*	3+3

Notes

2.a. נִשְׁפֶּה niph ptcp from שפה "make smooth," "sweep bare," BDB, 1045. LXX πεδινοῦ "on a plain" implies standing alone on otherwise level ground. But LXX apparently reads שפלה (cf. 32:19). The Versions have more trouble with the word: 'A has γνοφωδους "misty," "gloomy"; Vg *caliginosum,* meaning about the same. Σ ομαλου and Syr "smooth," "even."

2.b-b. DSS[Isa] יבוא is sg. 'A = MT. LXX ἀνοίξατε is an impv making "the nobles" the subject. Vg, Syr also make נדיבים the subject: "the attackers will enter the gates." MT is to be sustained.

3.a. LXX πληρῶσαι τὸν θυμόν μου "to fulfill my wrath" is a paraphrase which has caught the meaning as Dillmann, Gesenius, and others have noted.

4.a. LXX φωνὴ βασιλέων "sound of kings." Vg also has *regum* "kings" instead of *regnorum* "kingdoms." Later LXX MSS have βασιλειῶν "kingdoms." Erlandsson (*The Burden of Babylon,* 19) suggests the ממלכות may have had both meanings as Phoenician inscriptions would indicate. DSS[Isa] and Syr support MT.

5.a. LXX adds θεμελίου "foundation of" to imply that they did not come from heaven itself. Cf. J. Ziegler, *Untersuchangen zur Septuaginta des Buches Isaias* (Altestamentl, Abhandlungen 12/3. Münster in Westfalen, 1934).

5.b. LXX οἱ ὁπλομάχοι αὐτοῦ "his armed men."

6.a. MT כשד משדי (cf. also Joel 1:15) is a play on words that sound alike. The Versions did not see the humor in them. שד is used in 16:4 and 22:4 with similar meaning: "devastation" from war. שדי is a name for God in Genesis and Job, but here is apparently related to the root שדד and means "Devastator" (cf. Erlandsson, *The Burden of Babylon,* 20 and Gray).

7.a. MT ידים is dual, lit., "every pair of hands."

7.b. LXX translates "heart" with ψυχή "soul" in the accustomed fashion.

8.a. *BHS* places ונבהלו "and they are confounded" on a line with v 7 separating it from צירים in v 8. Vg does the same. Syr begins v 8 after ונבהלו. LXX πρέσβεις "elders," "ambassadors" translates צירים (BDB, II, 851) as the subject for "are confounded." However, the parallel with חבל "anguish" suggests the ציר should be translated with BDB, 852 IV, as "pang." ונבהלו simply remains outside the metric lines.

8.b. LXX separates the verbs with *καί* "and."

8.c. LXX reads פָּנוּ "for the turn" instead of MT פני "faces of," making it a verb parallel to those in the previous stichs.

10.a. כסיל in the singular appears in Amos 5:8; Job 9:9; 38:31 meaning "Orion." The usual suggestion for the pl is "constellations."

10.b. יהלו "shine," "give light" (BDB, I, 237). DSS[Isa] יאירו has the same meaning using a cognate of אורם that follows.

10.c. Many MSS correctly add the *mappiq:* יַגִּיהַּ.

11.a. *BHS* suggests reading רעתה "its evil" parallel to "their sins" in the next stich. Wildberger argues against it that the wicked are responsible for their sins but the world תבל is not.

12.a. MT פז "pure gold" BDB, 808; LXX *τὸ χρυσίον τὸ ἄπυρον* "unrefined gold." KB translates "chrysolite," a green mineral, but this suggestion has been rejected by Wildberger and G. Gerleman (comment on Cant 5:11 in *Ruth/Hoheslied,* BKAT 18 [Neukirchen-Vluyn: Neukirchener Verlag, 1965], 173).

13.a. MT ארגיז "I will cause to tremble" is parallel to a verb in the third pers in the stich. LXX *θυμωθήσεται* third pass pl "be enraged" appears to translate יִרְגְּזוּ "tremble." However, the first pers expostulations by Yahweh are not infrequent in Isaiah (cf. 10:12). MT should be sustained. LXX smooths the variant with the pass verb.

15.a. MT הנמצא lit., "the one who is found." Wildberger translates "is met or encountered" citing Ugar *mẓa* (Aistleitner, *WB* # 1649). See E. Jenni's discussion in *THAT,* I, 922.

16.a. K תשגלנה "raped" is changed in Q to תשכבנה "lie down." The meaning is the same but avoids the "unclean" expression שׁגל. Cf. R. Gordis, *The Biblical Text in the Making* (Philadelphia: Dropsie, 1937), 30.

18.a. "Young bowmen dash in pieces" is a literal translation, but does not seem to make sense. "Bowmen" do not "dash in pieces." LXX *τοξεύματα νεανισκῶν συντρίψουσι* "bows of young men break in pieces" reading קַשְּׁתוֹת a constr for קְשָׁתוֹת an abs and a pass verb, perhaps pual instead of piel. Syr *ḳeštātā daʿlajme nettabrān* supports this. E. J. Young and Erlandsson (*Burden of Babylon*) defend MT by referring to a parallel (W. G. Lambert, "Three Unpublished Fragments of the Tukulti-Ninurta Epic," *AfO* 18 [1957/58] 40) *[giš]kakku [d]ašur tiba dapna mušharmiṭa šalamda iddi* "the weapon of Assur, it threw down as corpses the aggressors, the fierce, the destroyer." Wildberger notes that *kakku* is a staff or club which is properly understood as "breaking things in pieces." This is not true of a bow. The translation above follows LXX.

20.a. The reference is not ethnic but speaks of the life-style of the nomad.

20.b. יַהֵל BDB, 14 verbal denominative from אהל "he will pitch his tent." Cf. also KB and GKC § 68k. This is supported by the Versions contra Hitzig who read it a hiph from נהל "to lead to water."

20.c. LXX *ἀναπαύσονται* "abide," "dwell"; Tg ישרון "dwell"; Vg *requiescent* "rest," "respose." Wildberger says DSS[Isa] has put a י over the ב, but a careful reading shows that it is either a ו (as Burrows transcribed it) or a decorative feature like so many on that page. MT's hiph reading is sustained.

21.a. The animals are difficult to identify. ציים BDB, 850 "desert dweller," "crier," "yelper"; cf. 23:13, 34:14. Wildberger translates "demons," but does not support his translation. NEB translates "marmots."

21.b. אחים, a *hapax legomenon.* BDB, 28 "jackel." Some translate as "owl."

22.a. איים means something like "hyena." LXX *ὀνοκένταυροι* "apes."

22.b. MT אלמנותיו "its widows." Syr, Tg, Vg translate "palaces," suggesting a Heb ארמנות.

22.c. תנים are other creatures, perhaps jackals.

Form/Structure/Setting

Reid's prosodic analysis has shown that the chapter is composed of fifteen units. When speakers are assigned to these, they may be grouped in twelve speeches.

Yahweh, vv 2–3	2 bicola + 1 tricola, all interrelated
1st speaker, v 4a–b	2 bicola, interrelated
2nd speaker, vv 4c–5	3 bicola, interrelated
3rd speaker, vv 6–8	1 tri-cola + 2 bicola + 1 tricola; interrelated
1st speaker, vv 9–10	4 bicola
Yahweh, vv 11–13a	3 bicola, interrelated, + 1 bicola
2nd speaker (echo), v 13b	1 bicola
3rd speaker, vv 14–16	2 bicola, interrelated, + 1 bicola and 1 tricola, interrelated
Yahweh, vv 17–18	2 tricola, interrelated
1st speaker, v 19	2 bicola
2nd speaker, vv 20–22a	2 bicola + 3 bicola; interrelated
3rd speaker, v 22b	1 bicola

When seen in chiastic parallel to 14:22–32, the outline should be (see outline of scene above):

A	13:2–3	A call to arms	A′	14:32	Jerusalem is established
B	13:4–5	The noise of battle will destroy the whole land	B′	14:28–31	Yahweh will destroy the Philistines
C	13:6–8	Day of Yahweh	C′	14:26–27	Yahweh's plan for the whole world
D	13:9–16	Day of Yahweh	D′	14:24–25	Yahweh's plan to destroy Assyria
E	13:17–22	Yahweh stirs up the Medes against Babylon	E′	14:22–23	The Lord will destroy Babylon

The chapter is a complex, carefully balanced composition which builds dramatically from theophanic views of the Divine Warrior preparing for battle (vv 2–16) to an explanation of the events in historical terms. Yahweh is acting to subdue and destroy Babylon by subverting her traditional allies, the Medes, against her.

The dramatic format sets the scene in the Heavenly Council. The speakers may well include Heavens and Earth (cf. 1:2) among the members of the court. Neither Israel nor Jerusalem is addressed in this chapter nor is any direct reference made to them. Both will appear in chap. 14, the center and second leg of the chiastic arch.

The smaller units are composed in familiar genre. The "Call to Arms" (vv 2–3) is a familiar form in Divine Warrior literature (cf. 5:26–30 and parallels cited in Miller, *VT* 18 [1968] 100–101). The dramatic presentation of the sights and sounds of mobilization (vv 4–5) fits the same category. Two "Day of Yahweh" passages follow which are to be seen in the genre of 2:10–11, 12–18, 19–21; 22:5; 24:1–3, 21–23.

Vv 6–8 follow the genre "Summons to a People's Lament." H. W. Wolff described the form ("Der Aufruf zur Volksklage," *ZAW* 76 [1964] 55 and *Joel/Amos*. BKAT 16/2 [Neukirchen-Vluyn: Neukirchener Verlag, 1964] 23–24), which has parallels in 14:31; 23:1, 6, 14; Jer 4:8; 25:34; 49:3; Ezek 21:12; Joel 1:5, 11, 13; Zech 1:11. It may be accompanied by fasting (cf. Joel 1:14; 2:15). The genre usually consists of three parts: an imperative beginning (הילילו "Wail ye"), the name of those summoned, if not already clear from the context, and a clause beginning with כי to list the occasion for the summons from the first part. The second element is missing here. The reason for the call is the threat posed by the approaching Day of Yahweh.

The announcement of God's action against Babylon, which calls the nation by name (13:17–22), is parallel to the similar word against Assyria (10:12) and that against Edom (34:5–7). The curse on the city (vv 20–22) is parallel to that on Edom (34:8–15). On the form of curses against cities and nations compare Fensham (*ZAW* 75 [1963] 155–75) and Hillers (*Treaty Curses*). The Vision will later note the fulfillment of the curse on Babylon (21:9) as it also does the fulfillment of the curse on Edom (63:1–3).

Comment

2 The call to arms of dedicated and loyal troops is ordered by Yahweh. Messengers are sent out to gather the armies for the battle. They are not identified, referred to only as להם "to them." Whether these are earthly or heavenly armies is not defined.

The gates of nobles: נדיבים "nobles" reflects the Song of Deborah (Judg 5:2, 9) where another form of the root describes "volunteers" for battle (cf. Wildberger, 512). The *gates* may well be the entrance to the camp. By entering, the *nobles* swear allegiance and participation in the campaign. The messengers are to call out the noble volunteers by *raising a banner,* by calling loudly, and by *waving a hand.* The *raising of a banner* appears in 5:26 and 11:10. It marks the meeting place or the direction of march.

3 צוה "command" may also be a technical term for mobilizing an army (cf. E. A. Speiser, *BASOR* 149 (1958) 21; J. Scharbert, *BZ* 4 [1960] 212).

No names are given for those who are called out. The ancient pattern of Holy War would have mentioned the tribes of Israel (Judg 5). Here only descriptive titles are given: מקדשי is literally "My hallowed ones" (cf. Josh 3:5; Jer 51:27; Joel 4:9). To participate in "holy war," soldiers were required to prepare themselves with rituals of holiness (Deut 23:10–15; 1 Sam 21:5; 2 Sam 11:11; F. Stolz, *Jahwes und Israels Kriege,* ATANT 60 [Zürich: Theologische Verlag, 1972] 25, 140).

The second title is גבורי "my heroes." While in Ps 103:20 they may be called "heroes of power, doing my word," they are here "heroes for my wrath" as the Assyrians were "rods of God's anger" (10:5). The third title is עליזי גאותי "ones rejoicing in my sovereignty," i.e., those who delight to be in his service. The theme of volunteerism appears again. There is still no hint to identify more closely the troops being summoned.

4a–b A speech reports the voices of mobilization. The sounds are those common to the gathering of armies.

4c–5 A second speaker identifies the sounds with Yahweh's call of vv 2–3. The armies are identified as those from kingdoms in *distant lands* and *from the end of the heavens.* War that is carried out by the heavenly host supporting earthly armies is conceivable within the frame of Holy War. They combine as *instruments of his indignation* (כלי זעמו) to *destroy the whole land.* The phrase echoes 10:23. *Destruction* is rendered with a different word (however, cf. 10:27). But *the whole land* is the same. Whether this refers to a limited geographical area (Palestine in 10:23; the lower Euphrates in 13:5) or to the whole world must remain open. Perhaps the ambiguity is deliberate. All the descriptions of the "Day of Yahweh" in Isaiah imply a universal application as well as a specific target area (cf. Miller, *VT* 18 [1968] 100).

6–8 A third response to Yahweh's mobilization is more emotional: a call to *wail* in mourning because of the expected terror of Yahweh's day. Wolff has shown that the summons reacts to a threat by causing such an outcry that God may be influenced to change the order. In the dramatic scene the genre reinforces the impression of the awesome and terrible prospect.

כשד משדי "like destruction from the Destroyer." *The Destroyer* is the Divine name, *Shaddai,* which is common as אל שדי "El Shaddai" in the patriarchal section of Genesis and in Job. The usage here in v 6 would support an understanding of שדי which derives it from the root שדד "to destroy." Discussion of the meaning of the name has been extensive (L. R. Bailey, "Israelite 'EL SADDAY and Amorite BEL SADE," *JBL* 87 [1968] 434–38; M. Weippert, "Erwagungen zur Etymologie des Gottesnamens Saddaj," *ZDMG* 3 [1961] 42–62 and *ZDPV* 82 [1966] 305, n. 172). These suggest that the Akkadian word *šadû* "mountain" may explain the term. The god Enlil is called *šadû rabû.* The understanding of ancient translators varied. LXX translates with *ϑεός* "God." Vg translates with *Dominus* "Lord" (G. Bertram, "Die Wiedergabe von *shadad* und *shaddaj* im Griechischen," *WO* II [1954–59] 502–13; and "IKANOS in den griechischen Ubersetzungen des AT's als Wiedergabe von *shaddaj,*" *ZAW* 70 [1958] 20–31). In Job LXX translates *παντοκράτωρ* "overpowering ones," which includes the idea "Omnipotent One," a word usually reserved to translate צבאות "of Hosts." 'A and Σ use *ἱκανός* "the sufficient," "self-sufficient," which builds on the rabbinic suggestion that שדי is formed from שֶׁ + דַּי meaning "he who is himself sufficient." Gen 49:25 relates the name to שדים "breasts" (cf. M. A. Canney, "Shaddai," *ExpTim* 34 [1922/23] 332; F. Stolz, *Structuren und Figuren im Kult von Jerusalem,* BZAW 118 [Berlin: De Gruyter, 1970] 158). Ancient interpreters were not of one mind about the meaning of שדי despite their agreement concerning the importance of the ideas related to it.

Vv 7–8 portray the panic and impotence of the victims. The theme is common in descriptions of Holy War when Yahweh goes ahead of the armies terrifying the enemy.

9–16 These speeches pick up the themes of vv 2–5 from which vv 6–8 turned aside. The mobilization of an "attack force" (v 4) is pointedly (הנה "behold") related to the larger cosmic events of Yahweh's day, as in v 17 it will point to the historic stirring of Median warriors.

בָּא is a form which may be an active participle or a perfect. Wildberger (516) insists that it is a prophetic perfect, citing Zimmerli on Ezek 7:12 (*Ezekiel,* BKAT 13/1 [Neukirchen-Vluyn: Neukirchener Verlag, 1969] 167). However, the comparison is poor. In Ezek 7:12 בא is the first word of the verse as a finite verb should be. Here it is introduced by הנה "behold," which in Isaiah is usually followed by a participle and it is placed after its subject as a participle usually is. It is a participle emphasizing the dramatic event that is unfolding in their very sight.

The many words for "wrath" are emphatic. הארץ "the earth" may point to the world or to a particular land. The setting seems to lean toward a universal meaning. The destruction of its "sinners" through judgment picks up a theme from the Flood (Gen 6:13). Cosmic upheaval accompanies the Day of Yahweh (cf. Amos 5:18, 20; 8:9; Zeph 1:15; Jer 4:23; Ezek 32:7; Joel 2:10, 3:4[2:31]). It is the end of an age that is described, however, not the end of the cosmos, as such.

Like 2:12–17 it is arrogance in man that is the particular target of divine retributions. Yahweh himself speaks the order (vv 11–13).

אוקיר "I will make rare" (v 12) is a rare word probably chosen in alliteration to אופיר "Ophir" (cf. Alonso-Schökel, "El juego fonetico oqir-opir," *Estudios de Poetica Hebrea* [Barcelona: J. Flors, 1963] 408; I. Eitan, "A Contribution to Isaiah Exegesis," *HUCA* 12 [1937] 61). *Ophir* has been thought to be southwest Arabia, northeast Africa, or even northwest India, but the concept "gold from Ophir" was a real part of ancient Near Eastern commerce. KB thinks כתם "pure gold" is a Nubian word.

Vv 14–15 describe the horrible consequences as vv 7–8 had done before. *Each to his own people* presumes a population that has migrated to the great cities in search of jobs or buyers for goods or as mercenaries. They return to their villages in times of trouble. It may also picture exiles from other countries who have been deported to the region.

V 16 שגל means "sexual intercourse" (cf. Deut 28:30). Wildberger aptly notes: "The offensive word was consciously chosen by the author, just as it is consciously replaced by the Massoretes."

17–18 As the macabre scene resulting from the cosmic quake passes, the finger points to historical movement. Yahweh calls attention to stirrings among the feared Medes for which he claims responsibility.

Excursus: The Medes

Bibliography

Widengren, G. "The Persians." POTT, 313–16.

The Medes are attested as an ancient people in Gen 10:2. They inhabited the high country of northwestern Iran between the Elburz Mountains, the Salt Desert, Persia, and the lowlands of Mesopotamia. Their capital was Ecbatana. No written records have survived. Elam lay to the south and Assyria directly east.

In the eighth century Assyria had to deal with the Medes repeatedly, as indeed Shalmanezer III had done in the ninth. Tiglath-Pileser III (745–27 B.C.), Sargon II (722–705 B.C.), and Sennacherib (705–681 B.C.) campaigned against them repeatedly.

From Sargon's time for about three-quarters of a century, Media was subject to Assyria (*IDB* 3:319). Some Israelites were deported to "cities of the Medes" (2 Kgs 17:6; 18:11).

Media would normally have been separated from Babylon by Elam, which was Babylon's ally against Assyria (*IDB* 2:70). Isa 21:2 speaks of both Elam and Media as attackers of Babylon. This implies a situation when Media and Elam support Assyria's campaign against Babylon. Such a situation could well account for Merodach-Baladan's defeat *ca.* 710 B.C.

Media, allied with Persia, is much better known in the OT for the empire of the sixth and fifth centuries, and for the occupation of Babylon in 539 B.C. But there is no reason to look beyond the eighth century for the intended setting of chap. 13.

The threat posed by the Medes is obvious. For independence Babylon had to rely on Elamite support. A threat of Elamite military invasion of Babylon would neutralize that support. Since Media was subject to Assyria throughout this period, it takes little imagination to see how the plans were effectively laid to bring Babylon back under Assyrian power. Wildberger (520) sees the Medes as the "dedicated ones" of v 3 whom Yahweh has "called." Yet the chapter has set the isolated event of Media's move against Babylon (vv 17–19) in the larger frame of Yahweh's Day with its cosmic and historical aspects. The Medes may well be seen as only one aspect of the broader picture. Within that broader setting, attention is focused on stirrings among one people, the Medes. God will use them as Isaiah views his using the Assyrians and Cyrus. They are impervious to bribes. Their famous bow and arrow will overcome all.

19 The target of their agitation is finally named (only in the superscription v 1 has it appeared so far): *Babylon, jewel of kingdoms, glory of Chaldean pride.* The *Chaldeans* were a group of tribes in the lower delta of the twin rivers below the most southerly Babylonian cities (*IDB,* 1:550). They are called כשדים in Ezra and Daniel, but the *Kaldai* in cuneiform writings. About 722 B.C. the Chaldean leader of the Bit Yakin tribe, Marduk-apla-iddina (called Merodach-Baladan in Hebrew), conquered Babylon, making it his capital. A century later they would recapture the city and establish the neo-Babylonia empire of Nebuchadnezzer. For a people of village tribesmen, the legendary city was indeed their *pride* and *glory.*

The comparison with *Sodom* and *Gomorrah* (cf. Gen 19:23–29) matches the fabled glory of the city by the symbols of divine destruction above all others (cf. D. R. Hillers, *Treaty Curses,* 74–76). Jerusalemites referred to Sodom and Gomorrah in 1:9 to describe a fate they had narrowly escaped. The description goes beyond military plunder to set the stage for the curse of permanent devastation (vv 20–22b) that follows.

20–22a The depopulated city is a virtual ghost-town. The ruins are empty. The cries of desert animals hint at ghosts and demons in the eerie place. *Arab* probably speaks of a nomad wanderer.

V 22b brings the chapter full circle. קרוב "near" and לבוא "to come" resume the very words of v 6 concerning the Day of Yahweh. Both are protrayed as announced for the near future.

Explanation

The heavenly court is abuzz with excitement. Intensive mobilization of military forces is underway. Yahweh, the Heavenly King, has given the order to mobilize for a massive action. Its goal is destruction of the whole world. Mourning is in order, for Yahweh's day of reckoning is at hand. Everyone will quail before it.

The extent of the day's action is again defined. It will desolate the earth (v 9b). It will destroy its sinners. Its cosmic dimensions involve the stars, the sun, and the moon. Evil, iniquity, and the wicked will be punished. The arrogant will be humbled. The earth will have its population drastically reduced. To this end the cosmic upheaval that serves Yahweh's overflowing wrath will be a time of terrible chaos and of violence.

In this way the punishment of Babylon is put into the perspective of the Vision which sees the events affecting Israel and its neighbors from the eighth century to the fifth as facets of "the great and terrible day of Yahweh" which ends the old age and inaugurates the new age. (See the Commentary on 2:5–22 above.) That Babylon should head the list of nations under judgment in the eighth century in chaps. 13–23 comes as a surprise. The suggestion that this must be Assyria is met in 14:25 with the assurance that in all good time her turn would come. In the meantime Assyria is God's tool, not his enemy. Babylon's significance for Israel in all times was great (see *Excursus: Babylon and the King of Babylon*). At the end of Ahaz' reign its meaning was unique. The Bit Yakin tribe seized control of the city and their chief was proclaimed king. He was to occupy the throne for some twelve years.

At this time Babylon was the prime symbol of successful revolt against Assyrian sovereignty, while Samaria stood out for the Judeans as the symbol of failure. God's promise of action against Babylon supports the Assyrian claim to loyal submission by all her vassals. Assyria is still "the rod of Yahweh's anger" and has his support. Rebellion by any of the small nations would be futile and, worse, it would be rebellion against God.

God's weapons for battle are more than the direct intervention of the heavenly armies summoned in vv 2–3. The Medes are summoned from the east to do his bidding. This will effectively remove Merodach-Baladan's support from Elam and his neighboring tribes. Babylon, whose very name conjures memories of glory and majesty, will become a symbol of destruction like Sodom and Gomorrah.

Episode B: Babylon's Fate—Jacob's Hope (13:22b—14:7)

Bibliography

Alonso-Schökel, A. "Traducción de textos poéticos hebreos II (Isa 14)." *CB* 17 (1960) 257–65. **Erlandsson, S.** "Burden of Babylon; a study of Isaiah 13:2—14:23." *Spfdr* 38 (1974) 1–12. **Heintz, J. G.** "Aux origines d'une expression biblique: umusu qerbu, in ARM X/6,8." *VT* 21 (1971) 528–40. **Orlinsky, G. M.** "*Madhebah* in Isa 14:4." *VT* 7 (1957) 202–3.

Translation

First Speaker: [22b] *And her time (is) near to come,* 3+3
her days will not be prolonged.

	1 *But Yahweh will have compassion on Jacob*	4+3+2
	and again elect Israel	
	and give them rest on their own ground.	
Second Speaker:	*The sojourner will join himself to them.*	3+3
	They will cleave to the house of Jacob.	
	2 *Peoples will take them*	2+2
	and bring them to their place.	
	And the house of Jacob will divide among themselves	3+2+2
	Yahweh's land	
	for slaves and maidservants (to work).	
Third Speaker:	*They will be taking their captives captive.*	3+2
	They shall rule over their oppressors.	
First Speaker: (to	3 *And it shall be:*	1
Israel)	*In the day of Yahweh's giving you (m sg) rest*	4+2+4
	from your trouble and your turmoil	
	and from the hard labor done by you,	
	4 *You will raise this taunt*	3+2
	over the King of Babylon,	
	when you say:	1
	"How oppressing has ceased!	2+2
	Arrogance [a] *has ceased!*	
	5 *Yahweh has shattered*	2+2+2
	the staff of the evil ones,	
	the rod of rulers.	
	6 *In anger it was striking peoples—*	3+3
	blows without let-up—	
	In wrath it was pursuing nations—	3+3
	pursuit [a] *with restraint.*	
	7 *All the land is at rest, is quiet.*	4+2
	They break into joyful song."	

Notes

4.a. MT מַדְהֵבָה "arrogance" is unknown in Hebrew (cf. BDB, 551). DSS[Isa] מרהבה supports the conjectures of scholars (BDB, 923) although there is no parallel for the form in the OT. Wildberger (533) suggests pointing it as a hiph, or piel ptcp and reading it as masc as LXX ἐπισπουδαστής "oppressor" and Syr *mḥpṭn*ʾ do. The issue has been discussed at length (cf. F. Nötscher, "Entbehrliche Hapaxlegomena in Jes," *VT* 1 [1950] 300; G. R. Driver, "Hebrew Scrolls," *JTS* 2 [1951] 25; M. D. Goldman, *AusBR* 1 (1951) 10; M. Dahood, "Hebrew-Ugaritic Lexicography," *Bib* 48 [1967] 432). DSS[Isa] and *BHS* support a reading with ר and also a fem. The best rendering is to read מרהבה a hiph ptcp fem "arrogance," while the implication of oppressive tax-gathering is likely.

6.a. MT מֻרְדָּף hoph ptcp "one caused to be pursued" or "persecution" (BDB, 923). A parallel to רֹדֶה in the first stich would make one expect an act meaning. LXX has apparently skipped the word. Syr reads *weradef* (an act form) and Vg *persequentum* which suggest reading a piel ptcp מְרַדֵּף "pursuit" or "pursuing" (so *BHS*).

Form/Structure/Setting

The passage is set off by the change in mood and content on both sides. It consists of three parts. The first, 13:22b—14:2, contrasts Babylon's fate with Israel's hope. The contrast is balanced on the other leg of the chiasmus with 14:20b–21 which stresses the hopeless future for the Babylonian ruler's family. The second part is 14:3–4b, which announces the מָשָׁל "poem" which heightens the contrast still further. The third part includes vv 4b–7. It precedes the מָשָׁל and says nothing specifically about the King of Babylon. It is an extended exclamation of joy and relief that "Yahweh has shattered . . . the rod of rulers." This is the center of the chiasmus. The subject of the poem is Yahweh, as in most of the units comprising the two-chapter scene. The meter sets it off from the *qinah* lines in 3+2 that will follow.

Comment

13:22b—14:1 The statements concerning Babylon's fate and Israel's hope are related by the two words קרוב "near" and עוד "yet." *Her time* and *her days* refer to the events of the end of Babylon just predicted. The OT teaches that everything has its own time (Eccl 3:1–8; G. Von Rad, *Wisdom in Israel* [Nashville: Abingdon, 1972]). Babylon's fate cannot be rushed. One must wait for it (cf. Heintz, VT 21 [1971] 535–40). Babylon's time, like the Day of Yahweh (13:6), is near and calls for "wailing" and distress.

Israel's hope is contrasted to Babylon's hopelessness. It is to come *again.* It continues the promising tone of 11:11–16 in contrast to the heavy sentence of judgment portrayed in Scene 2 (9:7[8]—10:23). This hopeful passage concerns Israel, not Jerusalem. It is cast in the thoughts and vocabulary that are usual to Israel's hope.

The Vision places the speech in the last years of the reign of Ahaz. Samaria had fallen. Babylon had successfully thrown off the Assyrian yoke. But stirrings of rebellion in Palestine were being brutally suppressed by Sargon. Major exchanges of populations were under way (2 Kgs 17:6b, 24). Israel, or what is left of it, is warned not to follow Babylon's example, but to wait for Yahweh's redemption.

The speech reiterates the major elements of Israel's ancient faith and hope. It was Yahweh's רחם "compassion" on Jacob that motivated the Exodus (Exod 34:6; Deut 4:31; Joel 2:13; Jonah 4:2; Ps 78:38). Quell calls it "the strongest word for love that biblical language has" ("Jesaja 14:1–23," *FS F. Baumgärtel* [Erlangen: Universitätsbund, 1959] 140). The root is derived from רֶחֶם "womb" and describes the almost instinctive inclination of a mother to her child, so dependent on her, yet incapable of offering anything in return (Wildberger, 525). The term is used again in 49:10 and 54:8, 10. The statement draws upon other instances when God declares his continued compassion—even in moments when Israel is apostate, such as after the Golden Calf incident (Exod 34:6). It is appropriate as a restatement of God's commitment even after the edict of "total destruction" (10:23).

The speech is developed further with an assurance that Yahweh will *choose* (or *elect*) *Israel again.* The עוד "again" is needed in the context where such election has been set aside to allow judgment to do its work (chap. 10). The doctrine of election stood in jeopardy from the time Israel was no longer unified (i.e., the beginning of the divided kingdom). Destruction of Samaria and deportation of its people from their own land made it even less tenable.

Eventually, Jerusalem and Judah would follow suit. All this made exilic Israel and Jerusalem struggle to find a foundation for their faith (cf. H. Wildberger, "Die Neuinterpretation des Erwahlungsglaubens Israel in der Krise der Exilszeit," *Wort, Gebot, Glaube,* FS W. Eichrodt [Zürich: Zwingli Verlag, 1970] 307–24).

The assurance is given that *Yahweh will choose Israel again.* The promise to Abraham will again apply. Chaps. 41–48 will pick up the application of this theme to the exilic diaspora, not that the statement that follows concerning the "land" will be different in those chapters. The meaning of this speech about *the house of Jacob* must be seen in the Vision in the context of those which begin in 1:1–7; 2:5–9, and continue throughout the book. The debate about Israel's position and future in God's plan ranges throughout the book.

This speech continues by tying election to Israel's place in Canaan: והניחם על־אדמתם Yahweh "will give them rest on their own ground" (cf. Deut 3:20; 12:9; Jer 27:11; Ezek 37:14). This statement will become questionable in later parts of the book as it did in Judaism. Can election be proved only on possession and prosperity in the Holy Land? The speech foresees such economic prosperity and earned esteem that wandering peoples will volunteer to serve them.

2 The ideas are expanded to include an escort of the peoples returning Israel *to their place* (cf. 60:4–12 applied to Jerusalem, 61:4–7 and 66:19–21 applied to pilgrimages to Jerusalem's temple). The passage envisions a reversal of roles from their present miserable condition of subservient captivity. Jacob will "yet" be respected and served again. It reinforces the appeal of these chapters to "wait on Yahweh" rather than attempt to follow Babylon's example of violent rebellion.

3–4a *In the day* refers to the fulfillment of the words of vv 1–2. הניח "giving rest" is a term taken from Israel's old traditions. In some it meant to settle down in Canaan after long years of wandering (Deut 3:20; Josh 1:3). In others it referred to peace from surrounding foes (Deut 12:10; 25:19; Josh 23:1) (cf. Wildberger, 538; G. von Rad, "Es ist noch eine Ruhe vorhanden dem Volke Gottes," *Gesammelte Studien* [München: C. Kaiser, 1958] 101–108).

But this setting speaks of rest from *trouble, turmoil,* and *hard labor.* עבדה "labor" means the slave labor imposed by an oppressive government or conqueror. The parallel in Israel's tradition is that of slavery in Egypt. Chap. 40 will pick up that theme again.

4–7 The verses portray a time to come for Israel, like that of chap. 11 for Jerusalem. Then Israel will say, as Jerusalem will say (chap. 12), the things that follow. ונשׂאת המשׁל הזה "you (masc sing) will raise this taunt." מָשָׁל means to "compare." The noun is used for a parable, a synonym, or a proverb. But it can also be used for the ironic or taunting comparison of a taunting song. משׁל appears in Num 21:27 and in Isa 28:14 for those who are taunting. The actual taunting song begins in v 8. The form of the משׁל is dealt with in that section.

Over the King of Babylon. Most readers expect a taunt over Assyria. That is the nation that is causing Israel's pain and slavery in the eighth century. Others would hold to the meaning of slave-master and point to the Neo-Babylonian empire of Nebuchadnezzer. But the artistic and dramatic impact is all the more effective because of the surprise, consistent as it is with the thrust of chap. 13.

The King of Babylon here is the wily, stubborn, and arrogant Merodach-Baladan, who was still a thorn in Assyria's side in 703 B.C. when he sent his delegation to Hezekiah (chap. 39). In the setting of this scene, however, he has just taken Babylon and stands at the height of his prestige and power. Vv 3–4 look beyond his fall to a time when his prowess will be well on the way to oblivion in the ruins of his city, but when Yahweh's *rest* for his people will have only begun.

Vv 4–7 precede the taunting song proper. They say nothing about the King of Babylon. Their theme, instead, speaks of the coming *rest* (v 7). אֵיךְ "how" is an element taken from funeral poems (cf. 2 Sam 1:19, 25, 27), but is used here in rejoicing over an end to tyranny rather than grief over a hero. In these verses (4–7) it is not the person of the tyrant, but the condition of tyranny whose end is celebrated. Thus, appropriately, the impersonal מַרְהֵבָה "arrogance" determines the translation of נֹגֵשׂ "oppressing" (rather than "oppressor") and the word שׁבת "ceased" is used rather than the usual נפל "fallen."

The poem celebrates Yahweh's victory in *shattering the rod of rulers* and bringing *rest* and *quiet* that provokes *joyful song.* It is the key element in the chiastic structure of chaps. 13–14 (see the chart that begins the commentary on the chapters). As such it draws together the themes of the entire section. Oppression has ceased because Yahweh himself has broken the power of rulers. *All the land is at rest* because of Yahweh's intervention. The implication is clear—not because of rebellions by Babylon, by Egypt, by Philistia, or any others.

Explanation

The passage imparts a sense of God's control of all things which will be ordered in their own time. God assured Jerusalem (10:12) that he himself would deal with the Assyrian when the assigned task was complete. Now here he refers to Babylon's assigned "time"—yet to come, but sure to come—and calls Israel's attention to the goals God has set for her that are "yet" to come to pass—but also sure. These are goals that provide for "rest," "quiet," and "singing." They are goals, fixed in God's own strategy for the world (vv 24–27), which will come only through his direct intervention when his victory is complete.

Episode C: Taunt over a Fallen Tyrant (14:8–21)

Bibliography

Alonso-Schökel, A. "Traducción de textos poéticos hebreos II (Isa 14)." *CB* 17 (1960) 257–65. **Carmignac, J.** "Six passages d'Isaie eclaires par Qumran." *Bibel und Qumran,* ed. S. Wagner. B-Ost: Evang. Haupt. Bibelgesellschaft, 1968. **Clifford, R. J.** *The Cosmic Mountain in Canaan and the Old Testament.* Harvard University Monographs 4. Cambridge, Mass: Harvard U.P., 1972. 160–68. **Cobb, W. H.** "The Ode in Isaiah xiv." *JBL* 15 (1896) 18–35. **Craigie, P. C.** "Helel, Athtar, and Phaethon (Isa 14:12–15)." *ZAW* 85 (1973) 223–25. **Dupont-Sommer, A.** "Note exégétique sur *Isaïe* 14:16–21." *RHR* 134 (1948) 72–80. **Gorman, F. H.** "A Study of Isaiah 14:4b–23." Research paper, Fuller Theol. Seminary, 1979. **Grelot, P.** "Sur la vocalisation de הילל (Is. 14:12)." *VT* 6 (1956) 303–4. **Hudson, J. T.** "Isaiah xiv. 19." *ExpTim* 40 (1928/29) 93. **Jahnow, H.** *Das hebräische Leichenlied.* BZAW 36. Giessen: Töpelmann, 1923. 239–53. **Keown, G.** *A History of the Interpretation of Isaiah 14:12–15.* Diss., Southern Baptist Theological Seminary, 1979. Diss Ab 40 (1979/80). **Köhler, L.** "Isaiah xiv. 19." *ExpTim* 40 (1928/29) 236 and 41 (1929/30) 142. **van Leeuwen, R. C.** "Isa 14:12 *ḥôlēš ʿal goyim* and Gilgamesh XI.6." *JBL* 99 (1980) 173–84. **Lohmann, P.** *Die anonymen Prophetien gegen Babel aus der Zeit des Exils.* Diss., Rostock, 1910. ———. "Jes 14:19." *ZAW* 33 (1913) 253–56. **McKay, J. W.** "Helel and the Dawn-Goddess. A Re-examination of the myth in Isa 14:12–25." *VT* 20 (1970) 450–64. **Prinslov, W. S.** "Isaiah 14:12–15. Humiliation, Hubris, Humiliation." *ZAW* 93 (1981) 432–38. **Quell, G.** "Jesaja 14:1–23." *FS F. Baumgärtel.* Erlanger Forschungen A 10. Erlangen: Universitätsbund, 1959. 131–57. **Stolz, F.** "Die Bäume des Gottesgartens auf dem Libanon." *ZAW* 84 (1972) 141–56. **Vandenburgh, F. A.** "The Ode on the King of Babylon, Isaiah XIV, 4b–21." *AJSL* 29 (1912/13) 111–25.

Translation

Court Singer: 8 *Even the juniper trees* [a] *rejoice because of you,* 4+2
the cedars of Lebanon:
"Since you have lain down 2+2+2
the woodcutter comes no more
against us!"
9 *Sheol below is stirred up because of you,* 4+2
to meet your arrival.
Waking ghosts because of you, 3+3
all "the rams" [a] *of the earth.*
Rousing [b] *from their thrones* 2+3
all the kings of the nations.
10 *They all respond* 2+2
and say to you:
"Even you— 2+2+2
you have weakened [a] *as we (did).*
You have been made like ourselves."
11 *Your pomp is lowered to Sheol,* 3+2
a groan of your disgrace: [a]
Beneath you a couch [b] *of maggots,* 3+2
your covers [c] *(are) worms.*
12 *How you have fallen from heaven,* 3+2
O Shining One, [a] *Son of Dawn!*
You have been cut down to earth, 2+3
you plunderer [b] *of nations!*
13 *But you: you had said in your heart* 3+2
"I will ascend to heaven,

above the divine stars [a] 3+2
I will raise my throne.
I will sit in the Mountain Assembly [b] 3+2
in the farthest North.
14 *I will rise over the backs* [a] *of clouds.* 3+2
I will be like the Most High."
15 *How you are brought down to Sheol,* 3+2
to the deepest pit!
16 *Onlookers stare at you.* 3+2
They think about you:
"Is this the man 2+2+2
who terrorized the earth?
Who shook the kingdoms?
17 *Who made the world like a desert* 3+2+3
and laid waste its [a] *cities?*
Who did not release [b] *his prisoners to their homes?"*
18 *All the kings of the nations—yes all of them* [a]*—* 3+2+2
lie down in glory,
each in his own house. [b]
19 *But you! You are thrown out of your tomb* [a] 3+2
like an abhorred, aborted fetus! [b]
(Like) dead men's clothes 2+2
of those stabbed by a sword.
(Like) those who fall to the stones of a pit. 3+2
Like a corpse (that is) trampled.
20 *You cannot be united with them in burial* 3+2+2
for you have destroyed your own land,
killed your own people.
First Speaker: *Never again will anyone recall* 3+2
(such a) race of scoundrels. [a]
Second Speaker: 21 *Prepare a place of execution for his sons* 3+2
because of the guilt of their fathers! [a]
So that they cannot rise and possess the earth 3+3
and fill the world's surface with their cities!

Notes

8.a. KB defines ברוש as the "Phoenician juniper," *iuniperus phoenicea* L. (cf. Löw, III, 33–38).

9.a. עתודי "bucks" refers to the rams or bucks of the flock. Wildberger (534) calls attention to Zech 10:3 where the word is paired with "shepherds." The metaphorical relation of shepherd (the great king) and the heads of the flock (his vassal kings) is appropriate here.

9.b. הֵקִים is pointed as hiph pf. However, its parallel עוֹרֵר is poel inf abs, which suggests the parallel pointing as hiph inf abs הָקֵים "raising up."

10.a. חלית is usually derived from חלה "be sick" or "weak" (BDB, 317). G. R. Driver (*JSS* 13 [1968] 43) suggests the Ug root *ẖly* "was alone" and the Arab *ẖalâ* "was vacant," "disengaged."

11.a. MT נבליך "your harps" appears in DSS[Isa] as נבלתך, which could mean either "your disgrace" or "your corpse" (BDB, 615).

11.b. MT יֻצַּע. BDB (426) calls this a hoph impf (cf. GKC § 193–94). Delitzsch (309) thought it a pual pf 3rd m sg (like יֻלַּד in 9:5) "be laid," "spread." Parallelism to מכסיך "your covers" leads one to expect a noun form and suggest the *BHS* pointing יָצֻעַ or יָצוּעַ (Duhm and Jahnow, *Leichenlied*) or יָצוּעַ (Marti) meaning "couch."

11.c. Some MSS and DSS[Isa] read a sg מכסך "cover." LXX καὶ τὸ κατακάλυμμά σου "and his covering." *BHK* simply offers an alternative reading where MT knows two forms.

12.a MT הילל (BDB, 237) "shining one" (cf. Grelot, *VT* 6 [1956] 303). KB, *BHS,* Vandenburgh (*AJSL* 29 [1912/13] 118) would change the pronunciation to הֵילֵל following Arab *hilālun* "new moon." LXX translates ἑωσφόρος "Morning-star," Vg *lucifer.*

12.b. MT חוֹלֵשׁ (BDB, 325) qal ptcp act "weaken," "prostrating" usually appears with acc. The use of על "over" is strange. LXX ὁ ἀποστέλλων πρὸς πάντα τὰ ἔθνη "the one sending forth to all the nations" suggests that he read כל for על (cf. McKay, *VT* 20 [1970] 453, n. 4). H. Guillaume ("The Use of חלש." *JTS* 14 [1963] 91) compares Arab *ḫalasa* to suggest the meaning "to plunder" for חלש.

13.a. MT אל "God" is the first of two words for God (cf. עליון in v 14) which are also known for separate gods in the Canaanite pantheon. D. W. Thomas ("A Consideration of Some Unusual Ways of Expressing the Superlative in Hebrew," *VT* 3 [1953] 209–24) suggested that it only meant a superlative (cf. Fohrer, "the highest star"). M. Dahood ("Punic *hkkbm ʾl* and Isa 14:13," *Or* 34 [1965] 170–72) has demonstrated the close connection of El to the stars (cf. Job 22:12; Ps 147:4; Isa 40:26).

13.b. הר־מועד "the mount of assembly" means "the mountain where the gods assemble." Apparently the phrase is so common that "gods" could be left out (cf. Ugar *pḫr mʿd,* Akk *puḫur ilī*).

14.a. במתי "high places" (BDB, 119). However DSS[Isa] בומתי suggests the word comes from במת "backs" (*CHAL,* 42 and *HALAT,* 131).

17.a. תבל "world" is fem. Therefore the Eth version has a fem suf ועריה instead of MT ועריו. LXX καὶ τὰς πόλεις (followed by Syr, Arab) suggests reading a pl ועריםו.

17.b. MT פתח "open." LXX ἔλυσε and Syr *sᵉraʾ* "set free." Wildberger (535) suggests an emendation for the last word of v 17 and the first of 18: instead of ביתה כל "their homes all" read בת הכלא "the house which he keeps locked."

18.a. DSS[Isa], LXX, Syr omit כלם "all of them."

18.b. Wildberger suggests that איש בביתו "each in his house" is a gloss. The repetition of "house" suggests an echo-like gloss or a deliberate emphatic play on the house of prisoners and the tombs of the kings.

19.a. MT מקברך "from your grave." LXX ἐν τοῖς ὄρεσιν "in the mountains." Vg *de sepulchro tuo* "from his tomb." Wildberger (535) reads as *mem privativum* meaning "without your tomb." The text does not require the meaning "thrown out of your tomb," but may be read "thrown out without a tomb."

19.b. MT נצר "sprout." LXX ὡς νεκρὸς ἐβδελυγμένος "as a loathsome dead one." Σ εκτρωμα "an abortion," "aborted fetus," which in Heb would be נֵפֶל. 'A ιχωρ and Jerome's *sanies* mean "fluid from a running wound" (KB). Wildberger (536) follows the emendation first suggested by Schwally ("Miscellen," *ZAW* 11 [1891] 257) to read נפל "aborted fetus." It makes a good parallel to כפגר מובס "like a trampled corpse" at the end of the verse. Erlandsson (*Burden of Babylon,* 37) cites the Vg *stirps* and Syr which both mean "shoot" to support MT. He understands it as a "wild vine, which is felled and left useless" (18:5, 6). Schwally's emendation offers the best solution.

20.a. מרעים "wicked ones" breaks the direct reference to the king by the pl. LXX σπέρμα πονηρόν and Syr *zarʿā bîšāʾ* are sg. Marti understood the phrase to be related to 1:4. Wildberger (536) interprets both instances to mean "a race composed of evil doers" rather than "descendant of evil doers."

21.a. MT אבותם "their father." LXX τοῦ πατρός σου "his father." M. Dahood ("Hebrew-Ugaritic Lexicography I." *Bib* 44 [1963] 291) calls the Heb a pl *excellentiae.* Rinaldi (*BeO* 10 [1968] 24) translates עון אבותם as "fathers' guilt."

Form/Structure/Setting

The משל or taunt, proper, is found in vv 8–20a. It is a common style and content which could have been sung by any of Israel's neighbors about any aspiring world-conqueror. This is in sharp contrast to the Yahweh-centered content and form of vv 4b–7. The taunt is also characterized by its direct address to the fallen and disgraced tyrant.

Lohmann (*Prophetien gegen Babel*) and Jahnow (*Leichenlied*) recognized the basic elements of the funeral song like those of David's lament over Saul and Jonathan (2 Sam 1:19–27), "How the mighty are fallen!" The taunting song parodies that cry in vv 12 and 15 to portray the tyrant's plunge from his pretentious heights to his unlamented disgrace. Other elements of the lament are reversed in the taunt.

The term משל "parable" (v 4) normally describes a proverb or story which draws a comparison. This describes the poem well. A normal element in a lament contrasts the "once" with the "now." The Vision has already done this effectively in describing Jerusalem's change (1:21–23). (Because the taunt is understood to be appropriate at a future time [14:3–4a] the "once" of the taunt is the real "now" of the scene in which it occurs.) The taunt ridicules the pretensions of divine status and power which the tyrant affected with the bitter reality of his overthrow and assassination (vv 11–15). His ambitions are compared to the gods (vv 13–14a). His end is compared unfavorably with that of kings (vv 18–19a). His abandoned corpse is likened to those which all-too-often are simply "thrown away" (v 19b–d). The frame of the poem contrasts his condition in life with that in death.

Comparative passages may be found in 37:22–29 and in Ezek 19:1–4; 27:2–10, 25b–36; 28:12–19. Funeral songs are sung after the event and use the perfect tense. This is equally true here. The poem consists of four parts: Vv 8–10, the response of the trees and the kings in Sheol; vv 11–14, "How you have fallen!"; vv 16–17, thoughts of onlookers; and vv 18–20a, a contrast to the usual royal funeral. Two responses to the poem are included in this section of comments because they refer to the king of Babylon. But they are separate speeches. V 20b is a proverb. V 21 is an order for the execution of his sons.

Comment

8 Mesopotamian kings regularly took working parties to the forests of *Lebanon* to cut timber to build their palaces and public buildings. Such timber is unavailable in Mesopotamia as in Palestine. See the account of Nebuchadnezzer (*ANET*, 307). (For other Mesopotamian references, *ANET*, 275, 291; for Ugarit see *ANET*, 134; for Egypt see *ANET*, 27b, 240b, 243.) The fall or weakening of a monarch or empire brought welcome respite to Lebanon's forests.

F. Stolz (*ZAW* 84 [1972] 141–56) and R. J. Clifford (*Cosmic Mountain*) have drawn on texts such as *ANET*, 307 and OT passages such as Ezek 31 and Isa 14 to depict a divine garden on Lebanon's mountains which God planted. The Vision and Ezekiel have used that for serious theological reflection (Wildberger, 546). Thus the verse continues the depiction of Yahweh as the Forester of 10:33–34 and of 10:15–19.

9–11 If one follows the view of Stolz, the verses portray the fall into the underworld, the nether regions of the dead, of the intruder into Yahweh's garden. (Note the parallel to banishment from Eden for the offense of tampering with Yahweh's trees.) שאול "Sheol" without an article, as usual, is the underworld, the place of the dead (cf. *IDB,* a–d, 787–88). The etymology of the word has been explained variously. W. F. Albright (*Oriental Studies,* FS P. Haupt [Baltimore: Johns Hopkins U.P., 1926] 143–54) and W. Baumgartner ("Zur Etymologie von *scheʾol,*" *TZ* 2 [1946] 233) used the Akkadian *suʾaru,* the dwelling place of Tammuz in the underworld, to explain it. L. Köhler ("Scheʾol," *TZ* 2 [1946] 71–74; *KB*) derived it from שאה and compared it with Arabic *sûʾ* and *sûʾa* "catastrophe." Others have sought to derive it from a root שול like Arabic *safala,* meaning "be low," or from שאל "to ask" as a place where one must answer for one's deeds. E. Devaud ("Gefilde der Binsen," *Sphinx* 13 [1910] 120) sought to derive it from the Egyptian *sḫ.t—ȝrw* which is a description of life beyond this one. LXX has translated sixty-one of the sixty-five appearances of שאול with ᾅδης "Hades" showing that the two concepts are very close (cf. Wildberger, 548). Vg uses *infernum* or *inferi.* W. Zimmerli's section on the realm of the dead (*Ezekiel,* BKAT 12/2 [Neukirchen-Vluyn: Neukirchener Verlag, 1969] 784) is very useful here.

The inhabitants of Sheol are the רפאים "ghosts." They are the "dead" מתים who are in Sheol (26:14; Ps 88:11[10]) or in אבדון "Abaddon" (Ps 88:12[11]). The origin of the term is complicated by use of the word to describe a race of giants in very ancient Palestine (cf. Gen 15:20; Deut 3:11) which lead LXX to translate the word γιγαντες and Vg *gigantes* "giants." The Ugaritic texts have added a new complication. They use *rpum* for seven mythical beings. J. Gray ("The Rephaim," *PEQ* 79 [1949] 127–39) considers the Ugaritic *rpum* to be an ancient royal family who were later considered able to guarantee fertility as members of the followers of Baal. Wildberger's judicious advice (549) is sound. The three uses of רפאים (in Ugarit, for giants, and for the dead) should be considered separately until we learn a better way to relate them. He adds that *rpum* may be related to Heb רפא "to heal," while רפאים in the sense of inhabitants of the underworld may come from רפה "to sleep." The latter meaning certainly fits the context of v 10.

The realm of the dead is normally still and silent. But the fall of the tyrant *stirs* it, especially the area reserved for the former great ones of the earth, who *rouse* themselves to greet the newcomer. They even speak (or sing) in chorus: *You have been made like ourselves,* weak, silent, and helpless.

12–15 *The Fall of Helel.* As v 8 seems to pick up themes of an ancient myth of God's forest in Lebanon, so this section seems to be based on another such myth. A suggested summary of the story would be: *Helel son of Schachar* was a great hero who determined to make himself the equal of a god, *El Elyon.* His ambition was to raise himself above the clouds, above all *the stars of god,* to the very *mountain in the farthest north* where gods gather and there to reign as king over the universe, including the gods. But the conclusion of this ill-advised ambition was his precipitous *fall into Sheol,* perhaps after a battle with El Elyon himself. It is generally thought that this must have come from a culture outside Israel, but as yet no such myth has been found in Canaan or among other peoples. The taunt in vv 12–15 has "historicized the motif and poetically related it to the fallen tyrant" (cf. A. Ohler, *Mythologische Elemente im Alten Testament* [Düsseldorf: Patmos Verlag, 1969], 175–77).

The passage begins with the usual Qina opening: איך "How!" But the next phrase *from heaven* sets this one apart from ordinary mortals. This is further demonstrated by the comparison with *Helel son of Schachar.* הילל "Helel" is unknown in the OT. LXX translates the entire name ἑωσφόρος ὁ πρωὶ ἀνατέλλων "Eosphoros (Morning Star), who makes the morning rise"; Vg, *Lucifer, qui mane oriebaris* "Lucifer, you who made the morning rise."

שחר "Shachar" is known as a god's name. In the OT Ps 139:9 speaks of his "wings"; Job 3:9; 41:18 "his eyelashes" or "rays." Other references (Cant 6:10; Pss 57:9; 108:3; 110:3) show personalized poetic views of the dawn that may reflect such an idea. Phoenician theophoric names carry the name ברשחר, שחרבעל as does 1 Chr 7:10 אחישחר *Ahishahar* "my brother is Shahar" (cf. R. de Vaux, "Le Textes de Ras Shamra et l'Ancien Testament," *RB* 46 [1937] 547, n. 3). A Ugaritic text ("Shahar and Shalem") portrays El's fathering Shachar and also his birth by one of El's wives. He is seen as parallel to Shalem, the god of Twilight. In Ugarit, Shahar is also found in personal names (cf. Stolz, *ZAW* 84 [1972] 182, n. 10).

הילל "Helel" is much more difficult to trace (cf. McKay, *VT* 20 [1970] 450–64; Craigie, *ZAW* 85 [1973] 223–25). Arabic *hilâlun* "New Moon" has led many to translate it as "New Moon" (GB, KB, *BHS*). N. A. Koenig thought of it as the waning moon. Others would change שׁ to שׂ, because in other semitic languages שחר means the moongod, called "Newmoon, son of (old) moon." Wildberger calls both nonsense when applied to "the son of dawn." He points to the Hebrew root הלל "to shine" (BDB, 237) and relates it to Akkadian usage to show that it is an epithet for a god, rather than a name. Grelot ("Isaie XIV 12–15 et son arriere-plan mythologique," *RHR* 149 [1956] 18–49) and McKay have picked up Duhm's suggestion (1922) of a connection with the Greek myth of Phaethon (Φαέθων). The name was used for one of the horses that pulled the chariot of Eos (*Odyssey,* 23/245). The name in other places may refer to the sun or to the son of Helios since it, like הלל, means "shining." Hesiod (*Theogonia,* 986) calls Phaethon the son of Eos, the star Venus. In *Theogonia,* 378, Hesiod reports that Eos gave birth to the morningstar ἑωσφόρος, also called φωσφόρος or Lucifer. Grelot concludes that Helel son of Shahar is the same divinity known as Phaethon, son of Eos. The other Phaethon, son of Helios and Klymene, was reported in his ambitious daring to have tried to drive his father's chariot, the sun, with its horses of fire, through the clouds. This exceeded his abilities so that Zeus was forced to intervene to prevent a universal catastrophe. By a lightning bolt he made him crash to earth (McKay; Grelot, *RHR* 149 [1956] 30–32). If this story were transferred to the other Phaethon, the parallel to Isa 14:12–15 would be apparent. McKay pursues a similar suggestion. But Wildberger (552) and Craigie have warned against using the Greek parallels. Too many differences appear between the Greek and Canaanite mythologies. Craigie supports Albright (*Archaelogy and the Religion of Israel* [Baltimore: Johns Hopkins U.P., 1942] 84, 86) and Oldenburg ("Above the Stars of El: El in Ancient Arabic Religion," *ZAW* 82 [1970] 199) in noting that *ʿAṯtar* had the epithet "the Luminous" (J. Gray, *The Legacy of Canaan,* 2nd ed. [Leiden: E. J. Brill, 1965] 66). Thus the Canaanite background is more credible than the Greek.

Whatever the myth might have said, the text in Isaiah tells of a tyrant king who is overcome, not by the resistance of a god, but by his own ambition to be as high as a god, to *ascend to heaven,* to reign *above the stars,* to sit in *the mountain assembly,* and to be *like the Most High.* Three locations for *the Most High* or *Elyon* are given. In Canaanite mythology El's dwelling was above the stars, in heaven. The OT speaks of אל השמעים "El of the Heavens" (Ps 136:26; Lam 3:41). In Jerusalem God is commonly understood to dwell in heaven and look down on earth (Isa 18:4; Ps 14:2).

The Mountain Assembly is located *in the farthest north.* It appears in this context as a synonym to *heavens.* The same combination occurs in Greek thought (E. Oberhummer, PW 18/1 [1939] 277–79). The idea of a mountain assembly for the gods was widespread in the area. It was regularly understood to be "in the farthest north" whether this be spoken in Mesopotamia, in Canaan, or in Greece. Ps 48:3[2] likens Zion, Yahweh's holy mountain, to צפון "the North."

V 14 speaks of עליון "Most High." This was an epithet for El (cf. Gen 14:18–22) in Jerusalem from earliest times. It was widely used in Canaanite stories. It is particularly suitable in the poem for the parallelism אעלה "I will rise" לעליון "to the Most High." He is also called the Lord of Heaven. He is the highest, the ruler of all. Wildberger (555) properly notes that the OT knows nothing of attempts to dethrone Yahweh, but often the wish of men and tyrants "to be like (דמה) God" (cf. the fourfold use of the word in Ezek 31). If it was common for funeral songs to praise the "incomparable" person who had died, the taunt satirically points to his wish to be "comparable" to divinity.

Yet his ambitions (v 15) led to being *brought down* (not up) *to Sheol* (not heaven), *to the deepest pit* (not the farthest north). The same word ירכתי has been rendered "deepest" and "farthest." This is the basic message of the taunt: "You have died and gone to Sheol." בור "pit" is actually a cistern (an underground room) and is regularly used, parallel to Sheol, to describe the place of the dead (cf. N. J. Tromp, *Primitive Conceptions of Death and the Nether World in the Old Testament,* BibOr 21 [Rome: Pontifical Biblical Institute, 1969] 166).

16–20a The observations of those who view the corpse reflect their astonishment and horror. The body has not been buried, but abandoned like garbage (v 19). He shares the fate of the dead among the poorest people: like the *aborted fetus,* like *the clothes of one stabbed* in a brawl, one killed in a *fall,* one *trampled* by a mob or on a battle-field, he is simply dumped in a pit and left to the birds and animals.

It is hard to believe that this man once ruled the world with tyrannical cruelty and absolute power. But now he is contrasted to kings who rule through orderly processes and are buried with honors (v 18). But this tyrant is in disgrace because he is perceived to have "fouled his own nest," *destroyed his own land,* and *killed his own people.*

20b–c The tyrant has no hope for the future—not even in memory.

21 The verse may also be spoken over his corpse. It puts into effect the curse of 20b–c by ordering the execution of his sons. But a massive change must be noted: vv 8–20 speak of the results of ambition, a kind of fateful, deserved end. But here people are urged to take matters into their own hands. It was often near eastern practice to execute the family of a fallen ruler (cf. 1 Kgs 15:28–30; 2 Kgs 10:17). *The fathers* suggests that guilt belongs to the dynasty, not simply the man. But the idea is broader (cf. Exod 20:5; 34:7).

The second half of the verse bases the execution on prevention. *So they cannot possess* and build *cities.* It was common practice among Assyrians and Persians (and later Greeks and Romans) to maintain control of conquered lands by building their own fortresses and administrative cities there. They guaranteed their fame and protected their borders in this way. Such cities must have been both feared and hated by the older populations.

Explanation

This powerful poem which is proposed as appropriate for Israel to sing when the king of Babylon is dead must be seen for what it is and is not. It is not specifically Israelite or Yahwistic in content or theology. It is not specifically tailored for the king of Babylon. It is a masterful poem to be sung over a tyrant who has fallen victim to his ambition and pride. Its picture of death and the realm of the dead was common to the ANE. Israel, for lack of a specific doctrine of its own, shared it, even if without enthusiasm or conviction. The apparent reflection of a "Lucifer myth" in v 12 is just that. It is a simile to picture the fall and disgrace of the tyrant.

The poem has meaning in the Vision and in Scripture only in its context as a poetic embellishment of the promises of vv 1–7, the warnings implied by the judgment on Babylon and its king (vv 20a–23), and the assurance of God's control of history (vv 24–27). The fragile and temporary nature of tyrannical power is the theme. It speaks to the human tendency to idolize momentary power, forgetting how fleeting its terror and its glitter can be, forgetting that history's mills "grind slow but wondrous fine." Death is the great leveler. This is a universal truth that requires neither revelatory explanation nor theological reflection—only dramatic reminder. Those who depend on the power of an individual, contrary to the lasting social structures and contracts, will not survive his death. This bit of common wisdom also needs only to be spoken to be found true. When the poem has been used in apocryphal and Christian circles to picture the fall of an angelic Satan, the reference must be to the shadowy mythical background of the poem rather than to the poem itself. It is significant that the account of the fall of Satan (Rev 12) makes no reference to Isa 14.

Episode D: Three Statements of Yahweh's Plans (14:22–27)

Bibliography

Bailey, L. R. "Isaiah 14:24–27." *Int* 36 (1982) 171–76. **Childs, B. S.** *Isaiah and the Assyrian Crisis.* SBT 3 Second series. Naperville, IL: Allenson, 1967. 38–39. **Donner, H.**

Israel unter den Völkern. VTSup 11. Leiden: E. J. Brill, 1964. 145–46. **Eareckson, V. O.** "The Originality of Isa 14:27." *VT* 20 (1970) 490–91.

Translation

Yahweh: 22 *And I shall rise against them.* 2+3
Herald: *Oracle of Yahweh of Hosts.*
Yahweh: *And I shall cut off for Babylon* 2+2+2
name and (surviving) remnant,[a]
offspring and descendant.
Herald: *Oracle of Yahweh.* 2
Yahweh: 23 *And I shall establish her to (become) a possession of* 3+2+3
porcupines and pools of water
and I shall sweep it with the broom of destruction.
Herald: *Oracle of Yahweh of Hosts.* 3
24 *Yahweh of Hosts has sworn:*[a] 4
Yahweh: *Just as I thought (it),* 2+2
so it came to be.[b]
Just as I planned (it), 2+2
will it be established:[b]
25 *to shatter Assyria in my land.* 3+3
On my mountains I shall trample him.
Herald: *And his yoke will depart from them.*[a] 3+4
His burden[b] *will leave its*[a] *shoulder.*
First Speaker: 26 *This is the strategy* 2+2
that is planned for the whole earth.
This is the hand 2+2
that is stretched out over all the nations.
Second Speaker: 27 *For Yahweh of Hosts has planned (it).* 4+2
Who can thwart (it)?
His hand (is) the one stretched out.[a] 2+2
Who can turn it back?

Notes

22.a. MT ושאר "and remnant." Syr *šeʾer* "flesh" (cf. *BHK*). Wildberger (536) interprets as "blood relative." DSS[Isa] ושארית is a variant on MT. In 2 Sam 14:7 שם "name" and שארית occur together (cf. H. Wildberger, "שאר," *THAT*, II, 844–55).

24.a. For אם־לא in an oath see Joüon § 165c; Watts, *Syntax,* 148–49.

24.b. היתה and תקום are fem, translate as neuter (cf. Joüon § 152c). The change of tense is remarkable. DSS[Isa] uses impf in both (תהיה for MT's היתה). LXX translates *ἔσται* and *μενεῖ* both fut ind. Donner (145) translates היתה as pres pf: "has happened," and תקום as fut "it shall come to pass." The first refers to Assyria's rise to power, the second to God's judgment over its arrogant pride.

25.a. LXX reads *ὤμων* for שכמו, a pl "their" for MT's sg "his," as do OL, Syh, Syr, Tg, Vg, Eth, and Arab. Wildberger (565) notes that this is an almost verbatim quote from 10:25b and that congruence in suffixes would probably not be required. DSS[Isa] has מעליכמה (2 m pl) and שכמכה (2 m s) using second person instead of third (like 10:25) but also moving from pl to sg. Perhaps "them" refers to the mountains, while "its" refers to the land.

25.b. MT סבלו "his burden." LXX *τὸ κῦδος αὐτῶν* "their fame." H. S. Gehman ("Errors of Transmission in the LXX," *VT* 3 [1953] 399) suggests that *κῦδος* is an internal Greek corruption of *κῆδος* "their trouble." Σ and Θ translate literally *βασταγμα* "suffering."

27.a. MT הנטויה "(is) the one outstretched." LXX lacks the article (cf. M. Lambert, *REJ* 50 [1905] 261) as does the similar construction in chaps. 5 and 10. However, the emphasis on "Yahweh's hand" and question of "who can withdraw it" justify keeping it. See also the use of the article in v 26.

Form/Structure/Setting

Three short passages make up this section. Vv 22–23 are a quote from Yahweh himself which emphasizes the oracular form of the words by three uses of the formula "Oracle of Yahweh," twice using the formal title "Yahweh of Hosts." The oracles emphasize Yahweh's determination to destroy Babylon. They balance the words in 13:17–22.

The second passage (vv 24–25) is cast as an oath spoken by Yahweh of Hosts that Assyria will, in time, be eliminated from Palestine. It begins with an assurance that Yahweh's plans and his fulfillment are congruent and may be trusted. It closes with an echo of his promise in 10:27. This passage parallels the "Day of the Yahweh" passage in 13:9–16. Yahweh's oath is a form used frequently in prophetic oracles. The closing couplet of v 25b is almost an echo, a reminder of the promise spoken in 10:27.

The third passage (vv 26–27) is the strongest claim for Yahweh's strategy in a book in which the idea occurs repeatedly. It parallels the first "Day of Yahweh" passage in 13:6–8. The question-and-answer style leans on wisdom's style (see Eareckson, *VT* 20 [1970] 490–91; and Childs, *Assyrian Crisis* 128, 136). It is spoken in the third person in a kind of concluding summary (see 17:14b and 28:29) which Childs sees as drawn from wisdom's pedagogical concern (187). The combination of direct quotation from God with prophetic reflection is common in prophetic books (H. Wildberger, *Jahwewort und prophetischer Rede bei Jeremia,* Diss., Univ. of Zurich, 1942). Most such reflection has explanatory, causal, or adversative content. But this passage strengthens and confirms what precedes (Wildberger, ibid. 102).

Comment

22 Like 13:1 and 14:19–22 the object of God's wrath is again *Babylon* itself, not simply her king and dynasty. The verse fulfills and strengthens the curse of 13:19–22. Interpreters (most recently Wildberger, 560) have suggested that Babylon is here much more than the Chaldean capital, but represents the contemporary "super power" (as it does in Rev 18:10, 12). Undoubtedly, overtones of the broader symbolism are here (cf. *Excursus* above, "Babylon and the King of Babylon").

The destruction is to be total. *Name* includes its reputation, fame, and value. A *remnant,* though it be a very small one, may hope for restoration. Babylon will have none. No *offspring or descendant* emphasizes the absolute destruction of the city as a people.

23 The city as a geographical location, a place of human habitation will be equally destroyed, covered with swamps, peopled by wild animals. *Sweep* and *broom* have the same root in Hebrew and occur only here. The root may be derived from טיט which means "mud," "dirt," "slime," a fitting connection with the pools of water and mud that have occupied the low-lying areas of a city no longer protected by dikes and levees.

24 The oath formula stresses Yahweh's firm consistency and faithfulness. The two distich lines speak of the ways that thought (plan) and action (fulfillment) go together with God. The *thought* of having Assyria serve as his agent in change and punishment has, by this time, actually been largely accomplished. The campaigns of 733–32 and 724–21 B.C. had demonstrated that, as had the deportation of Israelites in 720 and 718 B.C. The second distich calls for recognition of Yahweh's *plan* to limit the period and extent of Assyria's power (10:12) and trust that *the plan will* (in due time) *be established.*

25a The intention to destroy Assyria in Canaan, God's land, is spelled out.

25b This is a comment on the assuring oath: that the Assyrian hegemony will end for *them,* the mountains of Palestine, and for *it,* the land which Yahweh claimed as particularly his own.

26–27 The third of the three statements speaks of Yahweh's *plan* (see *Excursus* below, "Yahweh's Strategy"). The *strategy* that is planned is the one which the entire Vision reveals and discusses. It includes the judgment on his people and the purification of his city (chaps. 1–5). It covers the role of the Assyrian and judgment on those who oppose this role. It will be shown in later chapters to span the time to the Exile and the Persian period. But the verses stress again the impossibility of successfully opposing God. Only God himself can end the punishment, can call off the Assyrians, can turn back the judgment. Rebellion or resistance is futile.

Explanation

The three statements are all intimately related to Yahweh, his intentions, and his might. The first two are direct quotes as oracle or oath. The third is a proclamation of his strategy and power. The destruction of Babylon for its rebellion and the certain end of Assyrian power over Canaan are fixed in God's plan, assured by his authority and sovereignty.

In Act II Israel's sin and resistance to God has led to her destruction (733 and 721 B.C.) and to her deportation (720 and 718 B.C.). The neutral stance of Ahaz has made it possible for his dynasty to continue and for Jerusalem to survive. Undoubtedly, these points were not missed by the early readers of the Vision. Nor should they be missed by the modern reader.

Excursus: Yahweh's Strategy

Bibliography

DeBoer, P. A. H. "The Counselor." *Wisdom in Israel and the ANE.* VTSup 3. Leiden: E. J. Brill, 1955. 5. **Fichtner, J.** "Jahwes Plan in der Botschaft des Jesaja." *ZAW* 63 (1951) 16–33. Reprinted in *Gottes Weisheit.* Gesammelte Studien zum A. T. Arbeiten zur Theologie 2/3. Stuttgart: Calwer Verlag, 1965. 27–43. **Vriezen, T.** "Essentials of the Theology of Isaiah." *Israel's Prophetic Heritage.* FS J. Muilenburg.

Ed. B. W. Anderson and W. Harrelson. New York: Harper & Bros, 1962. 128–46, esp. 142–46. **Wildberger, H.** "Jesajas Verstandnis der Geschichte." *Congress Volume: Bonn.* VTSup 9. Leiden: E. J. Brill, 1963. 83–117.

עצה/יעץ can be used in the sense of advice given (cf. de Boer in *Wisdom*) like that of Ahithophel to Absalom (2 Sam 15–17) or of the elders to Rehoboam (1 Kgs 12:6–28). The words are used in Isa 40–48 to deny Yahweh's need for such a counselor (40:13, 14; 41:28; 44:26; 45:21; 47:13). A similar meaning can be found in chaps. 1–39. Beyond that, there is throughout the Vision of Isaiah an argument that Yahweh has a plan (a strategy) which he is following, which is being fulfilled, and which Israel should recognize and accept. Three times this is explicitly expounded. Each of these uses עצה/יעץ to define the strategy: 14:24–27 speak of the Assyrian; 19:12–17 relate to the defeat of Egypt and Tyre; 46:10–11 speak of the role of Cyrus. The Assyrian conquests (and fall) and the Persian rise to power under Cyrus are the historical pillars of Yahweh's strategy in Isaiah's Vision. But it is Zion and Israel that are called to play the key roles in the plan. How it can be that Assyria and Persia possess the political might and authority while Israel and Zion are called to be the more important elements in the age to come—that is the theme of the entire Vision.

The idea of God's control over events is common in the prophets or even in the OT. The use of עצה to describe God's plan occurs elsewhere (cf. Fichtner, *Gottes Weisheit,* 28–29). Yet apparently Isaiah is the classic and perhaps the first book (and prophet) to speak of Yahweh's plan on so universal a scale (Fichtner, 28; M. Schmidt, *Prophet und Tempel* [Zürich: Evangelischen Verlag, 1948], 19–54).

This conviction expresses a basic prophetic axiom. "It is the mark of all genuine prophetic proclamation that they see and interpret the present in relation to the past and the approaching march of time, that they, more or less clearly follow and extend the lines, which for the eyes of the prophets become visible from the origins of the people with its God through the now into the immediately immanent to come. God stands in the center of his view of history as the one who is acting. He has a goal in what he does. He is following a plan. Knowledge of these facts stands basically behind the entire prophetic message of the Old Testament" (Fichtner, 27). Vriezen describes it: "He (Isaiah) sees his time in the light of the living God" (*Israel's Prophetic Heritage,* 131). "For Isaiah all sins are rooted in failure to recognize God (his work and his plan), failure to believe, and the willful rejection of him" (his plan and his work) (Vriezen, 135).

This plan cannot be turned aside (14:27). The prophet and his audience, both in Act 2 and in the entire drama, live in the middle of the accomplishment of it. Thus, in Act 2 the coming of the Assyrian is accomplished history (14:25a) while the judgment of the Assyrian still remains to be accomplished (14:25b). For the reader of the Vision this, too, has become accomplished history.

The Vision confronts the events of history with the reality of the living God whose acts and whose plan are becoming visible in the events of the day. In that light the times reveal "an old world perishing" and a "new about to be born" (Vriezen, 146). Most recent writers have worked within the limits of their discipline in interpreting what the historical prophet saw and said on these issues. To look at the same issues from the vantage point of the complete Vision of the Book of Isaiah only strengthens and completes the picture. In this, Yahweh's plan/strategy is consistently related to his work. Together they build the basis for a theology of history. "History is the work of Yahweh of Hosts, who is enthroned on Zion. It unfolds according to a plan which he has determined" (Wildberger, VTSup 9 [1963] 89).

Episode E: *Burden over the Philistines (14:28–32)*

Bibliography

Beck, B. L. The International Roles of the Philistines During the Biblical Period. Diss., Southern Baptist Theo. Seminary, 1980. 146–50. **Begrich, J.** "Jesaja 14, 28–32. Ein Beitrag zur Chronologie der israelitisch-judäischen Königszeit." *ZDMG* 86 (1932) 66–79 and *ThB* 21 (1964) 121–31. **Brunet, G.** *Essai,* 154–57. **Childs, B. S.** *Isaiah and the Assyrian Crisis.* SBT 2/3. Naperville, IL: Allenson, 1967. 59–61. **Donner, H.** *Israel unter den Völkern.* VTSup 11. Leiden: E. J. Brill, 1964. 110–13. **Fullerton, K.** "Isaiah 14:28–32." *AJSL* 42 (1925) 86–109. **Irwin, W. A.** "The Exposition of Isaiah 14:28–32." *AJSL* 44 (1927–28) 73–87. **Kedar-Kopfstein, B. A.** "A note on Isaiah 14:31." *Textus* 2 (1962) 143–45. **Savignac, J. de** "Les 'Seraphim'." *VT* 22 (1972) 320–25. **Tadmor, H.** "Philistia under Assyrian Rule." *BA* 9 (1966) 86–102. **Wiseman, D. J.** "Flying serpents?" *TynBul* 23 (1972) 108–10.

Translation

First Speaker: 28 [a] *In the death year of King Ahaz* [b] — 4+3
this burden came to be:
Yahweh: 29 *Do not rejoice, you Philistines, all of you* [a] — 4+4
that the rod that struck you [b] *is broken.*
For, from the root of a snake — 3+2+3
a viper will emerge,
and his fruit (will be) a darting adder.
30 *And the first-born* [a] *of poor people will find pasture.* — 3+3
the needy will lie down in safety.
But I [b] *shall destroy your root by famine* — 3+2
and your remnant someone [b] *will kill.*
Chorus: 31 *Wail,* [a] *oh gate!* — 2+2+3
Howl, oh city!
Melting away, [b] *O Philistia, all of you.*
For a cloud comes from the north — 4+3
and (there is) no straggler [c] *in its ranks.* [d]
First Speaker: 32 *What can one answer a nation's* [a] *ambassadors?* — 4
Second Speaker: *That Yahweh has secured Zion* — 4+4
and in her [b] *the afflicted of his people find refuge!*

Notes

28.a. Syr *mškl' dplšt* = משא פלשת "burden of Philistia" is placed before the section. It is an obvious editorial addition intended to add clarity of organization like the headings that follow.

28.b. MT אחז היה "Ahaz, there came." J. A. Bewer ("Critical Notes," *OT and Semitic Studies.* W. R. Harper Memorial Volume 2 [Chicago: U.P., 1908], 224–26; *AJSL* 54 [1937] 62; *FS A. Bertholet* [Tübingen: Mohr 1950], 65) emended to read וָאֶחֱזֶה "then I envisioned" (cf. 6:1). Wildberger has aptly noted that this would not make sense without the name of the king to date the passage. It was apparently inspired by Bewer's conviction that the passage could not possibly date from this time. MT is to be kept and respected.

29.a. כֻּלֵּךְ "all of you" is a unique construction (cf. also v 31) with a slight variation כֻּלָּךְ in Cant 4:7 (GKC § 127b–c; Joüon § 94h).

29.b. MT שֵׁבֶט "the rod that struck you." LXX ὁ ζυγὸς τοῦ παίοντος ὑμᾶς "the yoke of striking you" seems to read the Heb as a constr genitive.

30.a. MT בכורי "first-born of." Some medieval MSS have בכרי, which appears to imply a pointing בְּכָרַי "my first born." But DSS[Isa] supports MT. LXX omits the word. While the phrase "first-born of poor people" may be strange, it should be kept (cf. Donner, *Israel,* 110, n. 1).

30.b. The first person of MT והמתי "I shall destroy" has been challenged. LXX ἀνελεῖ "he will kill" followed by Tg. DSS[Isa] supports first pers here but changes יהרג "one will kill" to אהרג "I will kill," harmonizing the second verb with the first, while LXX did the reverse. It is not uncommon in the dramatic style of the vision to have Yahweh speak a line that interrupts another's speech. MT should be sustained. For other suggestions cf. Wildberger and Driver ("Hebrew Scrolls." *JTS* 2 [1951] 25).

31.a. הילילי "Wail!" is fem sg while שער "gate" is masc. Apparently the word עיר "city," which is fem, dominates the grammar.

31.b. נָמוֹג is an inf abs. Brockelman (*Syntax,* 1–2) and others suggest that an inf abs may serve as an impv. But it is better to maintain its own grammatical integrity and read it as continuing the mood of the previous imperatives.

31.c. MT בודד "one separating himself." DSS[Isa] מודד "one measuring." G. R. Driver holds to the original and translates "deserter" (*JTS* 2 [1951] 26). Donner follows the variant and translates "no one counts their hosts."

31.d. מוֹעָד is also difficult. BDB (418) translates the hapax-legomena with "appointed place" like the noun מוֹעֵד. Ziegler cites a late LXX MSS with the reading ἐν τοῖς συντεταγμένοις αὐτοῦ "in his completion." B. Keder-Kopfstein ("Note on Isa 14:31," *Textus* 2 [1962] 144) suggests that this may derive from Heb בְּנוֹעָדָיו (niph ptcp pl) "in his summoned troop." He suggests with Vg's reading of *effugiet* that בודד should be emended to נודד and the whole translated "none is fleeing among his summoned troop." MT is at least as good and may be kept. The meaning is the same.

32.a. LXX ἐθνῶν "nations" (also Syr, Tg). But MT is correct in context and should be kept.

32.b. MT ובה "and in her." DSS[Isa] ובו "and in him" turns the attention back to Yahweh rather than Zion. Either reading is possible. But MT's reading is consistent with the close relation of Yahweh and Zion in Isaiah.

Form/Structure/Setting

The introduction calls vv 29–30 a "burden." Like that over Babylon and those that follow, the phrase is used with so-called "foreign prophecies." As noted in 13:1, this can be deceiving. The *genre* is that of a "foreign prophecy." But the setting is not a Zion festival where nations bow to Zion's king. It is one in which Yahweh of hosts moves the nations about to do his will, and punishes those, like Philistia, that resist him. The whole becomes a parable for Judah and Jerusalem to teach them the futility of resisting God's signals. V 31 is a choral "woe" over Philistia whose funeral is near. The avenging army is in sight. V 32 is a cryptic conclusion for Act II. It began with a question mark over Jerusalem's fate in 734 B.C. (chap. 7) at the beginning of Ahaz's reign. Now it draws to a close. The city and the throne have survived to have the question raised again. In 7:7 Isaiah answered: "It shall not happen." V 32 confirms: "Yahweh has made Zion secure!"

Comment

28 In the confused chronology of the period this could be 718 B.C. (16 years after 735–34 when Ahaz began to reign; 2 Kgs 16:1) or 715 B.C. (fourteen years before 701 B.C.; 2 Kgs 18:13) or 728 B.C. (four years before 724 B.C. when Shalmaneser marched on Samaria). The more likely date is 718 or 715 B.C. For *burden* see the comment on 13:1.

29 *The rod that struck you.* Is this King Ahaz or is this Shalmaneser? The superscription (v 28) may be construed to imply the former. But it would be strange to use serpent imagery of a Judean king. Yet the two may be related. There was a rebellion against Assyria in Palestine after the death of Shalmaneser. Ahaz followed his earlier practice and remained a loyal vassal. Philistine cities joined in the rebellion. The *rod* and the *snake* are best understood as references to Shalmaneser who laid siege to Samaria for so long and who dominated Palestine. The *viper* and *darting adder* are references to Sargon who broke the Palestinian rebellion in 718 and in 714 B.C.

30 The repression of uprisings will restore order so the common people can dwell and work in safety. Yahweh himself will put down the uprising and punish the rebels. For this Philistia will share Babylon's fate.

31 The verse returns to the call to mourning of v 29a. The coming of Assyrian armies *from the north* signals their approaching end.

32 The verse implies that an embassy sits in the antechamber of the palace awaiting an answer. What is the occasion? Have they brought an invitation for Ahaz and Judah to join the uprising? Or do they know of Ahaz's illness which has brought him to his deathbed? Either of these or both may be implied by vv 28–31. In either case the answer is clear. *Yahweh* is the foundation of Zion's security. Not Sargon, not alliances, not armed rebellion—but Yahweh! It is significant that no mention is made of the new king (or king to be), Hezekiah. The emphasis remains on Yahweh alone. The second stich repeats a basic theme of the Vision. Israel's future lies with Zion. This theme, rather than the messianic theme, dominates the book. *His people* must refer to the remnant of Israel, as well as Judean villagers. The city is and will be a secure refuge.

Explanation

The notice of Ahaz's death marks the close of an era. Philistia with Babylon symbolized the implacable rebels against Assyrian power in the ninth decade of the century. So together they are judged. The balance of power still lay with Assyria. The constant warfare was a disaster for the village people. And Yahweh's signal still summoned the Assyrian. The other side of the coin showed Yahweh's support for a neutral Zion, still following the Ahaz-doctrine of passive vassalage with Isaiah's support. Neutral Zion will provide refuge for God's people which the belligerent Samaria was unable to do.

Act III: Opportunity and Disappointment (Chaps. 15–22)

The Third Generation: King Hezekiah (ca. 715–701 b.c.)

The end of Act II was marked by reference to the death of Ahaz (14:28). The end of Act III will be marked by notice of the demission of Hezekiah's chief ministers (22:14–25). This short period marks the years when the party represented by Shebna and Eliakim controlled Judah's foreign policy. Their ill-conceived adventures spoiled any hope that the prophecies of 9:1–6 and chaps. 11–12 could be fulfilled in Hezekiah.

Three scenes comprise Act III. Scene 1 (chaps. 15–16) portrays the hopes and opportunities that existed for Judah early in Hezekiah's reign, about 715 b.c. Scene 2 (chaps. 17–19) continues the theme of optimism but ends on a shocking note of reversal (chap. 20). The time is about 715–712 b.c. Scene 3 (chaps. 21–22) portrays the results of challenging Assyria's suzerainty in 705 to 701 b.c.

Following Ahaz' death about 715 b.c. (cf. 14:28), Gilead, Samaria, and Ashdod had become Assyrian provinces. Attention then turned to the small nations to the east of Judah.

Moab's problem came, not from the Assyrians, but from someone out of the desert, or from a revolt of the poor in their own land (chaps. 15–16). She turned to Jerusalem for help, thereby rousing the city to hope for a renewal of David's old authority (16:5) over Moab.

The ruin of Damascus and the fate of Israel are balanced by a hint of emissaries from far-off Cush who seek Jerusalem's favor (chaps. 17–18).

The center of Act III deals with the third generation (roughly the age of Hezekiah, *ca.* 715–701 b.c.) and portrays an Egypt that is weak and in disarray. Her condition provides an opportunity for the Lord to picture hope for an age of blessing in which Assyria, Egypt (under Ethiopian rule), and Israel will play leading roles. Isaiah's prophecy at the time of the Ashdod rebellion (713–712 b.c.) is directed against any idea in Jerusalem that help against Assyria could be expected from the Egyptian. Judah apparently did support the Philistine rebels initially, but then sent tribute to Sargon II before he arrived at the theater of war. Hezekiah's essential tendency toward seeking independence by force presages the tenor and events of his reign. The tendency precluded the fulfillment of the beautiful vision of 19:25.

The destruction of Babylon, the site of the only major rebellion against Sargon to succeed for any length of time, came in 710 b.c. and is noted in chap. 21 with the emotional disappointment of Jerusalem. The uneasiness of the region is reflected in the burden on Edom and the picture of the Dedanites from Arabia, which matches the depiction of Moab in chaps. 15–16.

Act III closes with a bitter scene of Jerusalem in confusion, poorly armed, and poorly prepared for battle. Two high officials are charged with neglect of duty.

Astonishingly, the chapters of this act avoid the name of Hezekiah altogether. He is not mentioned in the hints of hope, in the warnings concerning royal policy, or in the blame for disaster in 701 B.C. (See the following *Excursus*). Instead, senior officials of his administration are introduced by name (22:15–24): Shebna and Eliakim, who are also known from 2 Kgs 18:18. Throughout Act III a speaker using the first person represents the attitudes of the government (15:5–9; 16:9, 11; 21:2–4, 6–7, 10, 16; 22:4, 14). Shebna is not identified until the end, but he is probably this spokesman.

Excursus: Silence about Hezekiah

Hezekiah is not mentioned by name in the section that obviously portrays a part of his reign. Why not?

2 Kings and 2 Chronicles make much of Hezekiah's religious reforms. The Vision of Isaiah ignores them. Instead it points to his political policies and military ambitions. The unfortunate way in which religious zeal is often equated with "hawkish" and chauvinistic political and military policies is a major problem that receives too little attention. The Vision faces up to the issues involved.

Hezekiah and Josiah are two cases in point. Both are praised in the histories of Kings and Chronicles for monotheistic reforms in conformity with the old confederacy and with the authority of Moses (2 Kgs 18:4–6 and 2 Chr 30:14–15). They are also recognized for their conformity to David's ways (2 Kgs 18:3 and 2 Chr 29:2). They, more than any others, strove to reestablish the power and greatness of David's era. Like David, they blended commitment to cultic renewal and glory with efforts to expand their borders and press their military advantages to the limit. This entire program won the approval of the historians in 2 Kings and 2 Chronicles. Both of them succeeded briefly (Hezekiah for about four years; Josiah for some twenty-five to thirty years) but the historians uncritically attribute to them total success (2 Kgs 18:7a; 22:2; 23:25; 2 Chr 29:2; 31:20–21; 2 Chr 34:2).

Did they whip up religious enthusiasm and zeal to unify and strengthen the state in its political aims? Or did they see political independence and military strength as necessary for religious loyalty and faithfulness? Or did they see them as two sides of the same coin: prosperous independence and power as rewards for reform and faithfulness to God's law?

The Deuteronomic History (2 Kings) and 2 Chronicles lean to the last of these possibilities. Isa 22 points to the first. It argues that Judah under Shebna and Eliakim, Hezekiah's ministers, presumed upon God's intentions. They presumed that Yahweh wanted independence and power for Judah, that God's will and their policies were identical. On this basis they whipped up support for the war (22:13) and made desperate efforts to arm the city (22:9–11a) without asking about Yahweh's specific intentions for that moment (22:11b).

The Vision has contended that political independence did not necessarily lead to fidelity to Yahweh. Political power had not brought justice to the poor. Success was more likely to create hubris than to breed spirituality. (Cf. G. Brunet, *Essai,* 157–58.)

Therefore, Yahweh was not necessarily committed to a policy of independence and power for Israel or Judah. He looked for more. The Deuteronomic History, in attributing total "success" to Hezekiah, failed to see that. The Chronicler also missed that point, as many churchmen since that time have done. Both the Chronicler and the Deuteronomist thought of Hezekiah and Josiah as "bright spots" in Judah's history. The Vision sees them rather as two more steps to ultimate doom. God has had enough of blood sacrifices and rituals, which cultic reform proliferated (1:11–17). There is no emphasis in 2 Kings or 2 Chronicles on justice for the poor in the land. God wanted political decisions that were realistic in view of his support of the Assyrians (chaps. 8–10). He wanted recognition that only in repentance and turning to Yahweh could salvation be found (30:15). Neither Shebna nor Eliakim was capable of this. They both lost God's support and favor.

The Vision refuses to see hope for Judah in cultic reform or in religious revival, as 2 Kings and 2 Chronicles apparently do. It calls instead for a consistent political and religious policy that accepts God's decisions about Israel's and Judah's roles in history. These had been revealed through Isaiah (chaps. 7–10) and are viewed as still valid in 705–701 B.C., in 640–609 B.C., and indeed in 435 B.C. Nationalistic revival is not a part of God's plan for Israel or Judah in that time. Cultic reform that is seen as a means to nationalistic revival is flawed from the start.

The potential for progress toward peace and prosperity that was open to Hezekiah is pictured in chap. 19. It lay in cooperation with Assyria and Ethiopia. His government, in 715 B.C. presumably under Shebna, chose instead to depend on Egypt's illusory promises, i.e., those of the Delta kings whose days were numbered anyway. Judah entered briefly into the Ashdod conspiracy. Fourteen years later, their policies unchanged, they came under the condemnation of God and the retribution of Assyria.

The Vision names Shebna and Eliakim, but not Hezekiah, although the Act certainly applies to his reign. It does so in order that full judgment may fall upon the policies involved, rather than be diverted by personal attacks on the popular king.

HISTORICAL BACKGROUND: SCENES 1 AND 2

Bibliography

Donner, H. "The Separate States of Israel and Judah." *IJH,* 415–21. **Hall, H. R.** "The Ethiopians and Assyrians in Egypt." *CAH* 3 (1925) 270–88. **Kitchen, K. A.** *The Third Intermediate Period in Egypt (1100 to 650 B.C.).* Warminster: Aris and Phillips, 1973. 362–80. **Randles, R. J.** *The Interaction of Israel, Judah, and Egypt from Solomon to Josiah.* Diss. Southern Baptist Theological Seminary. Louisville, Ky.: 1980. 168–95. **Spalinger, A.** "The Year 712 B.C. and Its Implications for Egyptian History." *Journal of the American Research Center in Egypt* 10 (1973) 95–101.

The years that followed Ahaz' death (14:28) offered unparalleled opportunity to fulfill the glorious vision of 9:1–6 and chaps. 11–12. Assyria had established a line of political and military control along the southern borders of old Israel, Aram, and the coastal area of Philistia. This left to Judah the opportunity to extend her influence in the Transjordan states (chaps. 15–16).

Judah's loyal tribute to Assyria over almost two decades, as well as the elimination of rival powers on her northern border, had removed any threats from that direction (chap. 17).

Changes in Egypt offered promising opportunities. A major shift of influence and power occurred in the last quarter of the eighth century B.C. Libyan sovereignty, the twenty-second dynasty, was drawing to a close. Nubian (Ethiopian) power was rising under a king called Pianchi. Between 730 and 720 B.C. Pianchi invaded and established his rule as the twenty-fifth dynasty as far north as Memphis. But he did not go on to establish his rule over all Egypt. Until 715 B.C. the major cities of the delta were ruled by minor kings under what has been called "the Kingdom of the West" with a capital in Sais (the twenty-third dynasty). Pianchi died in 716 B.C. and was succeeded by his brother, Shabaka (716–702 B.C.). Shabaka's determination to force all Egypt to recognize his rule, as well as his willingness to cooperate with Assyria, offered an unparalleled opportunity for Judah's participation (chaps. 18–19).

Scene 1: *Burden: Moab (15:1—16:14)*

Bibliography

Alonso-Schökel, L. *Estudios de poética Hebrea.* Barcelona: J. Flors, 1963. ———. "Traducción de textos poéticos, III. Isa 15–16." *CB* 18 (1961) 336–46. **Rudolph, W.** "Jesaja XV–XVI." *Hebrew and Semitic Studies Presented to G. R. Driver.* Oxford: Clarenden Press, 1963. 130–43. **Schottroff, W.** "Honoraim, Nimrim, Luhith, und der Westrand des 'Landes Astoreth' (Jes. 15 . . .)." *ZDPV* 82 (1966) 163–208.

Translation

Herald: 15:1 *Burden: Moab.* 2
Messenger: (to Jerusalem's court)
Indeed! In a night[a] *it was destroyed* 3+3
Ar (in) Moab[b] *was silenced.*
Indeed! In a night it was destroyed 3+3
Kir of Moab was silenced.[c]
2 [a]*The daughter of Dibon has gone up*[a] 3+2
(to) the High Places to weep.
Over[b] *Nebo and over*[b] *Medeba* 4+2
Moab wails.[c]
On all its heads[d] *(is) baldness:* 3+3
[e]*every chin shaved bare.*[f]
3 *In its*[a] *streets they dress in sackcloth.* 3+2
On their rooftops[b] *and in their open areas*[b]
all of them wail 2+2
collapsing[c] *with weeping.*
4 *Then Heshbon and Elealeh cried out.* 3+4
Their sound was heard as far away as Yahaz.
Therefore the loins[a] *of Moab tremble.*[b] 4+3
His soul is faint within him.

Shebna: (see *Form Structure/Setting*)

5 *My* [a] *heart cries out for Moab!* 3+2+2
Its refugees [b]*—as far as Zoar,*
Eglath Shelishiyah!

Messenger:

Indeed, (on) the ascent of Luhith 3+3
they climb upon it with weeping.
Indeed, (on) the way of Horonaim 3+3
they raise a cry of destruction. [c]
6 *Indeed, the waters of Nimrim* 3+2
are dried up.
Indeed, the grass is withered. 3+2+3
The shoots are used up.
Greenness does not exist.
7 *Because of this the savings* [a] *(which) one had made* 4+4
and their reserve [b] *funds*
they carry over the valley of the poplars.
8 *Indeed, the outcry pervades* 2+2
the border of Moab.
As far as Eglayim her howling (is heard) 3+3
To [a] *Beer Elim—her howling.*
9 *Indeed, the waters of Dimon* [a] 3+2
are full of blood.

Yahweh: (from heaven)

Indeed, I shall put additional things upon Dimon: 3+3+2
for the remnant of Moab—a lion [b]
and for the remainder—terror [b].

Moab's spokesman: (to Moabites)

16:1 *Send* [a] *the lamb* [b] *of the land's ruler* 4+2+4
from the rock in the desert [c]
to the mountain of daughter Zion.
2 *And it shall be:* 1+2+2
like a fluttering bird
pushed from the nest,
the women of Moab will be 3+2
(at) [a] *the fords of the Arnon.*

Moab's spokesman: (to Jerusalem)

3 *Give* [a] *advice!* 2+2
Make a decision!
Establish your shadow like the night 3+2
between the noons. [b]
Hide refugees! 2+2
Do not expose a fugitive!
4 *Let them sojourn with you:* 2+2
Moab's banished ones. [a]
Become a hiding place for him 3+2
from a destroyer!

Herald:

When [b] *the oppressor* [c] *shall have come to an end,* 3+2+3
destruction shall have ceased,
trampling [d] *shall be finished from the land,*
5 *a throne shall be established in integrity* 3+3+2
and one shall sit on it with truth
in the tent of David,

judging and seeking justice 3+2
and expediting [a] *righteousness.*

Chorus: (Judah) [6] *We have heard of Moab's pride:* 3+2
proud [a] *Moab!*
Its pride and its exaltation and its arrogance! 3+3
Its strength [b] *was not so.*
[7] *Therefore it wails:* 2+2+2
Moab for Moab.
The whole of it [a] *wails.*
For raisin-cakes [b] *of Kir-Haresheth* 3+3
only the stricken moan. [c]
[8] [a] *Like the fields of Heshbon* [a] 2+3+4
the vine of Sibmah languishes.
[b] *The lords of nations have broken down her choice vines* [b]
(which) touched Jazer 2+2
(which) spread out (to the) desert.
Her shoots spread out 2+2
and passed over (to) the sea.

Shebna: [9] *Because of this, I weep,* 2+2+2
with Jazer's weeping,
(for) the vine of Sibmah.
I cover you [a] *(with) my tears,* 2+2
Heshbon and Elealeh.
because over your ripe fruit and over your harvest 3+2
a shout [b] *(of conquest) has fallen.*

Yahweh: [10] *Joy and gladness are removed from the fruitful land.* 4+3
No one sings in the vineyards. No one cheers. [a]
No one treads [b] *wine in the presses.* 4+2
I [c] *have caused shouting to cease.*

Shebna: [11] *Because of this* 1+4+3
my stomach murmurs for Moab like a lyre
and my inward being for Kir Haresheth.

Heavens: [12] *And it shall be* 1
When he appears, [a] 2+2+3
when he wearies himself,
Moab, on the high place,
when he comes to his sanctuary to pray, 4+2
he will not be able.

Herald: [13] *This is the word which Yahweh has spoken to Moab in time past.*
[14] *But now Yahweh says:*

Yahweh: *In three years* 2+2
like the years of a bond-slave, [a]
the glory of Moab will be reduced 3+3
in all the great murmur.
The tiny miniscule remnant [b] 3+2
will not be much. [c]

Notes

1.a. בְּלֵיל as a constr form before a relative clause (cf. Wildberger and Joüon § 129*q*, 158*d*) would mean "In the night (in which) Ar was destroyed." DSS^Isa^ בלילה and LXX *νυκτός* (followed by Syr Tg Vg) read it as an abs "by night" or "in a night." The latter reading preserves the parallelism and is preferred. Other ways to the same result are to read לֵיל as לֵיל or simply to understand לֵיל as an abs form, as König did (§ 337*y*).

1.b. LXX read ער מואב as *ἡ Μωαβῖτις* "Moab" and קיר־מואב as *τὸ τεῖχος τῆς Μωαβίτιδος* "the wall of Moab." In both cases LXX has failed to see the names of towns or cities, trying instead to understand them as other Heb words.

1.c. The second נדמה "silenced" is omitted by LXX and Tg but translated by ʾA and Θ as *εσιωπησεν* (aorist) "was silenced," by Σ as *εσιωπηθη* (aorist pass) "became silent" and by Vg as *conticuit* "silenced." KB and L. Köhler (*Kleine Lichter* [1945] 32–34) suggested that one should follow the versions. But the stark repetition appears to be intended as emphasis. We follow MT and the Greek versions.

2.a-a. Syr and Tg read עָלְתָה בַּת דִּיבֹן "the daughter of Dibon has gone up" like Jer 48:18.

2.b. עַל usually means "upon" and has been so translated by most commentaries. It may also mean "concerning" and was so understood by Kissane, J. A. Bewer (*The Book of Isaiah,* vol. 1, chaps. 1–39 [New York: Harper & Bros., 1950]), and Hertzberg. This would imply that the two cities in the north were already destroyed. But Wildberger notes that the actual invasion occured in the south.

2.c. יְיֵלִיל (also in v 3 and 16:7) is different from the "normal" יֵילִיל. *BHS* suggests changing it. However, the special form must have been preserved for a reason (cf. אֲיֵלִיל in Jer 48:31; יְיֵלִילוּ in Hos 7:14; and תְּיֵלִילוּ in Isa 65:14; GKC § 70 *d*). They preserve the letter of the preformative from assimilation into the first letter of the root.

2.d. MT ראשיו "its heads." DSS^Isa^ ראושו. Some MSS read simply ראש "every head." (Cf. Jer 48:37.) LXX *ἐπὶ πάσης κεφαλῆς* "on every head." However, MT makes sense. The pronoun refers to the country, not the cities.

2.e. DSS^Isa^ and many versions and manuscripts add וְ "and." MT may be kept.

2.f. MT גרועה appears in several MSS as גדועה, which is a more usual word for "hacked off" or "cut off." MT is an unusual form but certainly not impossible (cf. Driver, *WO* 1 [1947] 29). Cf. Ezek 5:11.

3.a. The suffixes in the verse vary from masc to fem. Masc probably refers to Moab as a people. Fem refers to it as a country or to its cities.

3.b. Ancient and modern scribes have sensed a verb lacking here. LXX supplies *καὶ κόπτεσθε* "and beat their breasts in mourning." Driver (*JTS* 41 [1940] 163) suggests קָעוּ meaning "they cry." Rudolph (in *Hebrew and Semitic Studies*) suggests יְנֻהוּ or נָהוּ "they oppress" and is followed by Kaiser. A better course is to keep MT and divide the verse differently. See the translation.

3.c. ירד. KB suggests "moving up and down in weeping." Wildberger sees only a metaphor "they flow down in tears."

4.a. חֲלֻצֵי "prepared for military service." LXX reads *ἡ ὀσφὺς* "the loins," which renders חַלְצֵי. The parallelism to the second stich supports LXX.

4.b. יָרִיעוּ "raise a war cry" fits MT's reading of חֲלֻצֵי "warriors." But it does not fit a setting of dismay. LXX *γνώσεται* "knows" suggests Heb ידע as Gray recognized. A. Guillaume disagrees (293–95). Others (Marti, Duhm, Kissane, Ziegler) suggest יָרְעוּ "they trembled." Kaiser suggests רָעֲדוּ with the same meaning.

5.a. LXX *ἡ καρδία* "the heart." Tg בליבהון "their heart." But first person should be kept with MT. Cf. 16:9, 11.

5.b. DSS^Isa^ ברוחה, Syr *brwḥh* "in his spirit." Cf. LXX *ἐν ἑαυτῇ* "in herself." Driver (*JSS* 13 [1968] 44) suggests that MT בריחה "her refugees" should be read as בריחו "his refugees." The word is usually an adjective (cf. BDB, 138), but here it is used as a noun.

5.c. יְעֹעֵרוּ is a unique word. BDB (735) explains it as a pilp form from עוּר = יערערו "raise a cry of destruction." The word occurs nowhere else and remains obscure.

7.a. יתרה occurs only here. BDB (452) reads it as a constr fem noun related to יתר "remain over."

7.b. פְּקֻדָּתָם is used only here and in Ps 109:81 in this sense. See BDB, 824. It means that for which one is responsible.

8.a. LXX *ἕως τοῦ φρέατος* "even to the well." Also Vg *usque* and Syr *wlbʾrʾ* presume an implied עַד "unto."

9.a. MT דִּימוֹן "Dimon," DSS[Isa] דיבון "Dibon," Vg *Dibon,* LXX Ρεμμων, Syr *rjbwn.* No Moabite city called Ribon or Dimon is known. So it would be easy to follow DSS[Isa] to substitute the well-known town Dibon. But MSS of G read δειμων or δεμμων or δημων while Tg 'A Σ Θ all support MT's דימון. (Cf. H. M. Orlinsky, "Studies in the St. Mark's Scroll-V," *IEJ* 4 [1954] 5–8 and *The Bible and the Ancient Near East,* ed. G. E. Wright [Garden City, NY: Doubleday, 1961], 117–18.) Wildberger (592) suggests that Dimon may still be identical to Dibon, noting the identification of Dimona in Judah (Josh 15:22) with Dibon in Neh 11:25.

9.b. LXX καὶ Αριηλ . . . Αδαμα transliterates the Heb words as names rather than translating them as "lion" and "earth." The text of this half verse has raised many questions. J. Reider ("Contributions to the Scriptural Text," *HUCA* 24 [1952/53] 87) suggests emending שארית to שחל to parallel אריה with a second word for "lion." G. Hoffman ("Versuche zu Amos," *ZAW* 3 [1883] 104) emends אריה "lion" to אראה "I have a vision" and אֲדָמָה "ground" to אֲדַמֶּה "I speak a parable." Kissane, Rudolph (in *Hebrew and Semitic Studies*), Eichrodt, and Wildberger keep the MT but change אדמה "ground" to אֵימָה "terror" or "dread," which appears to be a good solution to a difficult text.

16:1.a. MT points שִׁלְחוּ as an impv. Some MSS point it שָׁלְחוּ pf "They have sent." LXX ἀποστελῶ first pers fut ind "I will send." Also Syr *ʾšdr* and Tg יהון מסקי מסין למשיחא דישראל. Modern interpreters have tried many emendations like שֶׁלְחוּ, אֶשְׁלַח, (וְ)שָׁלְחוּ, אֶשְׁלָחָה, but none improves MT.

1.b. MT כר משל־ארץ becomes in LXX ὡς ἑρπετὰ ἐπὶ τὴν γῆν "like a reptile on the land," which apparently read the Hebrew consonants as כְּרֶמֶשׂ לָאָרֶץ. Other emendations do not improve on MT. The Moabite ruler was traditionally known to possess great herds of sheep (2 Kgs 3:4).

1.c. מדברה "in or toward the desert" is a problem since Sela is not in the desert. LXX πέτρα ἔρημος, Syr *kʾfʾdmdbrʾ,* Vg *de Petra deserti* are translations which have suggested the emendation סלע הַמִּדְבָּר "rock of the wilderness." GKC (§ 90*d*) suggests that MT may be translated "from the rock in the wilderness."

2.a. One would expect a preposition before מעברת "fords." The ancient versions have usually supplied one, as have modern translations.

3.a. K הביאו m pl. Q הביאי f sg. Versions and some MSS have followed Q. DSS[Isa] הביו (from the root יהב) suggests the reading הבי "give." Wildberger (593) notes that the use of הביא עצה is unknown in OT. But יהב עצה appears in Judg 20:7 and 2 Sam 16:20.

3.b. צָהֳרָיִם is a dual form. Perhaps a colloquial emphatic emphasis like "high noon."

4.a. MT נִדָּחַי is pointed as "my banished" niph ptcp & first pers suffix. The word is familiar in Isaiah. Cf. 11:12; 27:13; 56:8. The question turns on the suffix "my." LXX οἱ φυγάδες Μωαβ and Syr *mbdrʾ dmwʾb* seem to read נִדְּחֵי "banished one of Moab," as do two Heb MSS. Kaiser suggests the pronoun results from an "eschatological interpretation" of the passage.

4.b. כִּי introduces a dependent clause. The question is whether it relates backward to v 4a–b or forward to v 5. Dillmann suggests the former and adds עַד "until." But Wildberger is surely right in choosing the latter, as the *waw* which begins v 5 indicates.

4.c. הַמֵּץ is a *hapax legomenon.* BDB (568) relates it to a late Heb word meaning "to press" or "to suck." Hence "extortioner" or "oppressor." DSS[Isa] המוץ "the chaff" (cf. 17:13), or חָמוֹץ (E. R. Rowlands, "Mistranscriptions in the Isaiah Scroll," *VT* 1 [1951] 228) "a ruthless one" BDB (330).

4.d. תַּמּוּ is pl while רֹמֵס is sg. DSS[Isa] תַּם is sg. LXX, Syr, and Vg also read a sg.

5.a. מְהִר inf constr from מהר "to hasten." (Cf. E. Ullendorff, "The Contribution of South Semitics to Hebrew Lexicography," *VT* 6 [1956] 195.)

6.a. גֵּא is probably an error for גאה (cf. BDB, 144). DSS[Isa] has גאה "proud" as do two Heb MSS (cf. Jer 48:29).

6.b. בַּדָּיו is usually translated "idle talk" (BDB, 95). It could mean "isolation" (BDB, 96). Vg translates here and in Jer 48:30 with *fortitudo* and *virtus* "strength" or "might." C. Rabin suggests a similar meaning for the Hebrew ("Hebrew *baddim* 'Power,' " *JSS* 18 [1937] 57–58). לֹא־כֵן "not so" suggests a contrast.

7.a. כֻּלֹּה is a strange but frequent form indicating entirety (BDB, 481–82).

7.b. לאשישי (BDB, 84) "pressed raisin cakes." Jer 48:31 אַנְשֵׁי and Tg אנש = "men of." Driver (BZAW 77 [Giessen: Töpelmann, 1958], 43) suggests comparing אשישי with Arab *ʾaṯṯa* "live comfortably." Thus "you shall moan for the luxurious dwellers of Kir-Hareshetti." However, the traditional meaning of MT is sufficient.

7.c. The pl תהגו "they mourn" breaks the chain of sg verbs. Many change to a sg with

Tg and one MS. However, if נבאים is the subject, the pl is correct. The word order is emphatic.

8.a-a. The pl subject with sg verb is a problem. GKC § 145u explains the pl as collective. But commentators still try emendations. Cf. G. R. Driver (*JTS* 38 [1937] 40) who suggests reading כי שדמות as כשדמות "as the fields of Heshbon, (so) does the vine of Sibmah languish." Tg has a text which reads, "Behold the armies of Heshbon are plundered, the districts of Sibmah beaten." Driver's suggestion provides a smoother text with a minimum of change, in spite of the Masoretic accentuation (contra Wildberger).

8.b-b. What is the subject of this stich? Some have thought בעלי גוים the subject and translated "the lords of the nations have broken down her choicest vines." (So NIV, RSV, following Fohrer, Kaiser, Bewer, and Gesenius.) But others read שרוקיה as subject and translate "the choice grapes overcame (even) the lords of nations." (So Wildberger, Eichrodt, Steinmann, Duhm, Marti, Dillmann, Delitzsch, Hitzig.) Yet the prominent position of בעלי גוים favors the former reading.

9.a. אריוך has been judged an impossible form (cf. GKC § 75*dd*, Bauer-Leander § 57*t*″). DSS[Isa] reads ארזיך. But this in itself is no help. Emendation may deal with the troublesome middle letters to read ארויך from רוה "to saturate" meaning "drench you" (so NIV, Wildberger, and others).

9.b. NIV translates "been stilled," but see RSV "battle shout."

10.a. Many MSS, DSS[Isa], Tg, Vg (perhaps LXX & Syr) seem to read ולא adding "and."

10.b. הדרך is missing in LXX. It is difficult to achieve in any other language the effect of the Heb repetition.

10.c. The first pers appears for the only time in this verse. LXX reads *πέπαυται*, a passive which might indicate reading a hoph הָשְׁבַּת. But this is not reason enough to change MT.

12.a. Wildberger and others suggest omitting "when he appears" as dittography, especially since the use of the verb in this sense is unique. However, it makes sense, providing a rising intensity of meaning and may be kept.

14.a. May also be "a mercenary" (cf. Jer 46:21).

14.b. LXX *καὶ καταλειφθήσεται* reads ושאר as a verb like וְנִשְׁאַר "will be left over." Syr and Vg support this. MT makes sense as it is and should be kept.

14.c. DSS[Isa] reads כבוד "glory." LXX *ἔντιμος* "honored." Both may be influenced by כבוד in the previous line.

Form/Structure/Setting

The set includes Jerusalem's court where a messenger brings distressing news from neighboring Moab to Shebna the principal government figure; Yahweh's heavenly court from which Yahweh, Heavens, and a herald speak; and room for Moab's spokesman and Judah's chorus. The time is the beginning of Hezekiah's reign (about 718 B.C.).

Two chapters, 15 and 16, together fall under the title: משא מואב "Burden of Moab." They are unified around the single theme of Moab's plight and together they form the first scene of the third act of the Vision.

Six speeches provide a setting for the central speech in 16:3–4a in which Moab makes her plea for aid. A final announcement brings an up-to-date word from Yahweh concerning Moab.

Title: The Burden of Moab (15:1a)

A Announcement of Moab's desperate situation (15:1b–4)
B Yahweh's sympathy, but determined judgment (15:5–9)
C Moab's decision to flee to Judah (16:1–2)
KEYSTONE Moab's appeal for refugees and its meaning (16:3–5)

C′ Judah's choral recognition of Moab's collapse (16:6–8)
B′ Shebna's lament over Yahweh's judgment on Moab (16:9–12)
A′ A tiny, weakened remnant will survive (16:13–14)

The reference in 14:28 to the death of Ahaz is a signal that these chapters are to be placed in the following reign, that of Hezekiah. The invasion that befalls Moab is not documented historically. An incursion of groups from the desert which drives the refugees toward the border of Judah fits the description given here.

16:13–14 may be a sign that Moab's new-found allegiance to Judah was short-lived, as indeed the references to her participation with Assyria in the events of 701 B.C. imply.

The form of the speeches varies. 15:1b–4 relate a straightforward account of the disaster, though told in a very emotional way. Vv 5–9 are a lament, although it becomes a threat in v 9. In 16:4b–5 is found a hopeful oracle that sees in the appeal from Moab the possibility of a restoration of the Davidic empire.

Note that the משא "burden" here is not a prediction of disaster, not "an oracle." It is a scene noting the invasion and its results as a sign that imperial influence and authority of the Davidic dynasty begin to reassert themselves at this time.

An almost verbally identical parallel to Jer 48:29–37 may be found in 15:2c–7a and 16:6–11. (Cf. Wildberger 605–11 for a full treatment and bibliography.) Jer 48 is clearly based on quotations from many texts, including Isa 15–16 and Num 21 and 24. The two passages have other parallels in Jer 11, 23, and 46.

The Isaiah parallels occur in the corresponding elements of the chiastic structure B–C and C′–B′ noted above. The composition is clean and straightforward. Whatever may have been their relation to the Jeremiah texts, their use in Isaiah is pristine and meaningful. If dependency exists, it is Jeremiah that is dependent on the Isaiah text as Schwally ("Die Reden des Buches Jeremia gegen die Heiden," *ZAW* 8 [1888] 177–217), Duhm, Rudolph (in *Hebrew and Semitic Studies*), Schottroff (*ZDPV* 82 [1966] 163–208), Kaiser, and Alonso-Schökel (*Estudios,* 420) have noted.

Excursus: Moab

Bibliography

Bartlett, J. R. "The Moabites and Edomites." *POTT,* 229–58. **Molin, G.** "Moab." *BHH* II, cols. 1229–32. **Van Zyl, A. H.** *The Moabites.* POS 3. Leiden: E. J. Brill, 1960.

Moab is mentioned by name in 15:2, 4, 8, 9 and 16:2, 4, 6, 11, 12, 13, 14. All of the place names in the passage are to be found in the strip of land east of the Dead Sea which extends just north of the sea's north end, eastward to the edge of the wilderness, and southward just beyond the sea's southern tip. This is the territory that Moab inhabited during its thousand-year history.

Moab, like Israel, came to its land from elsewhere (Deut 2:9). That earlier home is unknown. The language of Moab is preserved on the Moabite Stone which was discovered in 1868 and is now in the Louvre in Paris (cf. *ANET,* 320–21). The language is west-semitic, like Hebrew (cf. F. Cross, D. N. Freedman, *Early Hebrew Orthography* [New Haven, CN: American Oriental Society, 1952], 35–42; van Zyl, *Moabites,* 161–92). They apparently occupied their land before the Israelites arrived (Num 21:25; 22; 23).

Interaction between Moab and Israel is attested by biblical references. Balaam's story in Num 22–24 documents a rivalry for territory at an early time. Apparently Benjamin paid tribute to King Eglon of Moab until Ehud delivered it. 1 Sam 14:47 mentions Saul's war with Moab. 1 Sam 22:3–5 tells of David's seeking refuge in Moab. He later subjugated Moab (2 Sam 8:2–12; 1 Chr 18:11).

The Moabite Stone reports that Omri and Ahab ruled the northern part of Moab for forty years. King Mesha brought tribute to the King of Israel (2 Kgs 3:4). Later he stopped the tribute, leading to an expedition by Joram of Judah and Jehoshaphat (2 Kgs 3:4–27). Amos refers to a continued break between Moab and Edom (Amos 2:1–3). But not much else is known of her history during the following century.

Then it was touched, like its neighbors, by Assyrian expansion. In 728 B.C. its name appears along with Ammon, Ashkelon, Judah, Edom, and Gaza in the list of those bringing tribute to Tiglath-Pileser III (*AOT* 348, Text II R 77, line 10). Another text, a letter found in Nimrud (cf. H. Donner, "Neue Quellen zur Geschichte des Staates Moab," *MIO* 5 [1957] 159 and H. W. F. Saggs, "The Nimrud Letters, Part II," *Iraq* 17 [1955] 134), says that Moab, Mushur, Gaza, Judah, and Ammon brought tribute. It would seem that Moab like Ahaz bought the Assyrians off from an invasion of their land. However, during this time Moab was threatened by nomadic elements from the desert, as a letter from that time relates (cf. Donner, 156 and Saggs, 131). The invaders are reported to have come from the land of Gidir. But nothing more is known of this.

Moab participated in the Ashdod rebellion against Sargon in 713–711 B.C., but like Judah and Edom changed their minds and paid tribute (cf. *ANET* 287 [c]). In 701 B.C. Sennacherib reports that Kammusunabdi of Moab brought tribute and kissed his feet (*ANET,* 287, ii.37–iii.49).

Other references to Moab continue in the following century. They withstood an attack by Arabs in the reign of Ashurbanipal. Later they fought in Nebuchadnezzar's armies (2 Kgs 24:1). Jeremiah (27:3 and 40:11) speaks of Moab, while Ezekiel records a threat against Moab (25:8–11). Later references refer to Moabites as persons, but never more as a country.

Comment

The majority of comments refer to the remarkable number of geographical locations. For location of these, Wildberger's map (610), Simons' study (*GTTOT* § 1245–66 and Map IIIa), and van Zyl (*The Moabites*) have been of the most help. The number and precision of place names in these two chapters require comment. But not all can be precisely located now.

15:1 ער מואב "ʿAr (in) Moab" is taken by Simons to refer to a district in Moab which may also stand for the entire country. Its capital is קיר "Kir" which is located "in the center of the district of the same name" near the middle of Moab in the upper *wadi el-kerak,* as it is known today. (Cf. also 16:7, 11; 2 Kgs 3:25; Jer 48:3, 13.) Both ער and קיר may be related to Hebrew words meaning "city" and thus could be understood here as synonyms (cf. Wildberger, 611).

15:2 דיבן "Dibon" is a town some twenty miles north of Kir. נבו "Nebo" and מידבא "Medeba" are villages east of the northern end of the Dead Sea another fifteen to twenty miles north of Dibon.

15:4 חשבון "Heshbon" and אלעלה "Elealeh" are villages northeast of Nebo and Medeba. יהץ "Yahaṣ" is a village back near Dibon. (Cf. 16:8, 9.) The disaster seems to have devastated the northern villages of Nebo and Medeba, Heshbon and Elealeh. Towns further south, like Yahaṣ and Dibon, mourn and tremble.

15:5 צער "Zoar" (Jer 48:4, 34; *GTTOT* § 1254 and 404) is one of the five "cities of the plain" (Gen 14). The location of these cities near the Dead Sea is disputed. Deut 34:1–3 seems to locate Zoar near the foot of "Mount Nebo, the top of Pisgah (now located as *gebel en-neba* near the end of the Dead Sea), opposite Jericho" (cf. *GTTOT* § 404–14). Another theory places all the "cities of the plain" near the south end of the sea with Zoar at the tip (cf. *MBA,* 26). עגלת שלשיה "Eglath Shelishyeh" is not identifiable. *GTTOT* § 1255 calls it "wholly unintelligible." לוחית "Luhith" (Jer 48:5), חורנים "Horonaim" (Jer 48:3, 5, 34), and נמרים "Nimrim" (Jer 48:34) cannot be positively identified. They seem to describe a route for flight south to Edom.

15:8 אגלים "Eglayim" is modern *rugm el-gilimeh* southeast of *el-kerak.* באר אילים "Beer-Elim" (cf. Num 21:16) may be located in the *wadi et-temed* northeast of Dibon.

15:9 דימון "Dimon" lies some 15 miles north of *el-kerak.* (Cf. Jer 48:2 מדמן means "waters of Dimon.")

16:1 סלע (cf. 42:11) may be a proper name. If so, it is the forerunner of Petra at *wadi Musa.* But it is far more likely to be a reference to flight to the rocky heights.

16:2 מעברת לארנון "Fords of Arnon" must refer to the point where the highway crosses the Arnon river south of Dibon.

16:7 קיר־חרשת "Kir-Haresheth" is equivalent of Kir (15:1).

16:8–9 שבמה "Sibmah" is located by *GTTOT* § 298 near Heshbon. יעזר "Jazer" is probably modern *hirbet gazzir* just northeast of the northern tip of the Dead Sea.

Explanation

What happened in Moab to occasion this outcry? Dibon's mourning (15:2) concerns the devastation of, first, the villages of Nebo and Medeba and, soon after, their neighboring villages, Heshbon and Elealeh (15:4). It is a national disaster (15:2). People flee the countryside around the southern end of the Dead Sea (15:5) and around the northern tip toward the Jordan. Jerusalem is to be entreated by gifts to accept the refugees (16:1–2). Moab asks for advice and support (16:3–4a). An announcement is heard that aggression will cease when the Davidic dynasty holds sway over the territory again (16:4b–5).

A chorus of Judeans proclaims Moab's pride to be the cause of her calamity (16:6–8). Yahweh laments Moab's destruction, although he had occasioned it himself as judgment on her false worship (16:9–12). He acknowledges that this is judgment upon Edom (16:13) but relents to grant her a tiny and weak surviving remnant (16:14).

No evidence exists to suggest that Assyria invaded the country at this time or that a large army moved down the Jordan toward Moab or approached her from the south. The transjordanian states were threatened repeatedly in their history by tribes from the desert. A recent discovery tells of such an attack on Edom at about this time by the Gidiraya who are presumed to be a tribe from the east (H. Donner, "Neue Quellen zur Geschichte des Staates Moab in der zweiten Hälfte des 8. Jahrhundert v. Chr.," *MIO* 5 [1957] 173). Van Zyl (*Moabites* 20) regards 15:1–9a and 16:6–11 as originally parts of a taunt song composed by the Bedouin tribesmen to celebrate their victory. Wildberger (597) also points to the Gidiraya as the likely villains of the piece. A recent suggestion that a revolt of slaves within the kingdom accounts for the destruction raises another possible explanation.

Moab's rulers appeal to Jerusalem to receive their refugees. A symbolic lamb is to be sent, reminiscent of the thousands which Mesha once sent in tribute (2 Kgs 3:4) to the king of Israel. Judah's authorities and people are sympathetic to the appeal. Even Yahweh is sympathetic.

The implication is that Moab becomes Judah's vassal again. The Lord's judgment drives Moab back into the arms of the Davidic king in Jerusalem (16:5). It may well be that Moab joined Jerusalem and Ashdod in the rebellion against Assyria that was suppressed by 710 through Sargon II in his campaign against the Philistine states. Moab and Jerusalem withdrew from the coalition soon enough to avoid Assyrian wrath by paying tribute.

The scene portrays the beginning of that process as Jerusalem is beginning to dream of restored glory. The first step is acceptance of Moab's invitation to Jerusalem to "establish her shadow" (16:3), that is, to cast the cloak of her protection over Moab.

Scene 2
Burdens: Damascus and Egypt, 716–714 B.C. (17:1—20:6)

The setting for the scene is Jerusalem, who is seen as one that still has a choice about her future. Aram and Israel do not. So Judah is the central factor from D to D′ of the outline. It begins with the accusation that Jerusalem failed to respond to the effects of the judgment meted out to Aram and

Israel which spilled over onto it (17:1–3 and chap. 7). This is then focused on the confused and violent international scene (17:12–14), on the arrival and dispatch of Ethiopian messengers (18:1–2), and the note that Assyria sends gifts to Zion (18:7).

Yahweh's action against Egypt (19:1–15) has an immediate effect relating to Judah (19:16–17), but other results spread out and are no longer identified with Judah or Jerusalem. The language of Canaan (19:18) and the altar in Egypt (19:19–22) complete this part of the cycle. Jerusalem's apostasy (17:10–11) in forgetting Yahweh has, in this scene at least, forced the abandonment of the view that she is the center of Yahweh's world. Cult and worshiping congregation are now pictured in Egypt.

The outer frame of the scene uses a broader setting. The desolate cities of Damascus and Ephraim are a witness to God's accomplished judgment (17:1–3). Israel is compared to what is left in a field after the harvesters are gone (17:4–6). But when someone "looks to his Maker" (17:7–8) in such a time, the experience can be productive. So Israel's situation, though apparently hopeless, could be changed by God's creative power if the tiny remnant turns to him.

The corresponding paragraphs that close the scene with the marvelous view of Egyptian and Assyrian cooperation (19:23) bring Israel, not Judah or Jerusalem, back into the scene as their partner in the triad (19:24–25). "Man looks to his Maker" (17:7–8) corresponds to Egyptian and Assyrian worship of Yahweh (19:23). Recognition of Israel's miniscule possibility of destiny (17:4–6) contrasts with her position as third in the triad of superpowers (19:24–25).

But the scene closes (20:1–6) as it began (17:1–3) with recognition of gloomy reality. In the last two decades of the eighth century, Israel's ruined cities are no more than a monument to her apostasy and God's retribution. Jerusalem is prevented from serving God's purpose by her perverse political leadership and policies which reduced the vision of chaps. 18–19 to a vision of "what might have been," like the magnificent vision of what Hezekiah's reign might have been (chaps. 11–12), which was negated by his admiration of Babylon's rebellion (chaps. 13–14).

Scene 2 marks the turning point for this generation in the Vision. The spark of hope that appeared in chap. 11 was fanned into flame by the response of Moab in chaps. 15–16, by the Ethiopian messengers in chap. 18, and the vision of political accommodation in chap. 19. But after 712 B.C. it died. Hezekiah's Judah was committed to policies that inevitably led to the disaster of 701 B.C., as the next scene will show.

The four chapters comprising Scene 2 (17–20) form one symmetrical whole which climaxes with the bringing of gifts to Yahweh in Zion (18:7). Characteristic of the section are the "in that day" passages, with the variations "in that time" (18:7) and "in the year" (20:1). The thematic pattern is again an arch:

A *Behold* Damascus and Ephraim, ruined cities! (17:1–3)
#B *In such a day* the glory of Jacob will be like tiny leftovers (17:4–6)
C *In such a day* man looks to his Maker (17:7–8)

#D *In that day* you (fem sg) forgot God your Savior (17:9–11)
E *Woe!* Raging of the nations (17:12–14)
F *Woe!* Go, swift messengers (18:1–2)
#*G Peoples see: Yahweh is silent (18:3–6)
KEYSTONE *At that time:* Gifts to Yahweh in Zion (18:7)
#*G′ *Behold!* Yahweh coming to Egypt (19:1–15)
F′ *In that day* Judah will be a terror to Egypt (19:16–17)
E′ *In that day* five cities in Egypt to speak the language of Canaan (19:18)
D′ *In that day,* an altar to Yahweh in Egypt (19:19–22)
C′ *In that day,* a highway; Egypt and Assyria worship together (19:23)
B′ *In that day* Israel will be third to Egypt and Assyria (19:24–25)
A′ *In the year* Sargon came to Ashdod, Yahweh spoke through Isaiah: those who trust in Egypt will be put to shame (20:1–6).

Twice the sections are introduced with הנה "behold." 17:1 points to the devastation in Aram and Israel from the Assyrian invasions from 733 to 718 B.C. The second (19:1) points to Yahweh's intervention against Egypt which makes it unwise to expect help for rebel causes from that quarter.

Jerusalem is addressed, especially in 17:9–11 and in the final prophecy (20:1–6). The announcement of Assyria's gifts for Yahweh in Zion (18:7) is the centerpiece of the broad vision. Yet, amazingly, the subject matter is about Israel (B 17:4–6 and B′ 19:24–25). Jerusalem is mentioned only in the capstone of the arch (18:7).

The vision is the second of the book (after chaps. 11–12) which portrays what God had in store for his people. But the hopes are frustrated by political decisions which drew Jerusalem away from the plan Yahweh had for them.

The two speeches of Yahweh are key elements in the arch (*). The first (18:4) announces his inaction while the messengers carry out their mission. After the gifts are brought to Jerusalem, signaling Assyria and Ethiopia's invitation for Judah to join their coalition, Yahweh's second speech announces his active re-entry into history to bring a turning point in Egyptian history (19:1).

Planting and harvest imagery is used at key points (#). 17:4–5 interpret the situation of Israel after the fall of Samaria like that of a field after the harvesters have finished their work, leaving only "leftovers" for the poor to gather. 17:10–11 picture Jerusalem's pagan worship that uses little artificial gardens. 18:4–6 picture Yahweh's work in terms of a farmer's methods. 19:5–10 and 15 portray the distress of Egyptian farmers and those who depend on agriculture when the waters of the Nile dry up.

Religious issues dominate other passages. The usually human reaction which turns to God after a disaster (17:7–8) is contrasted with Jerusalem's "forgetting" God (17:9). God's goal of bringing Egypt and Assyria to worship him dominates four of the "in that day" sections (19:18–25).

The outer frame is firmly set in historical realities. Damascus and Ephraim are monumental ruins, lessons from the past (17:1–3). Hezekiah's determination to join the Ashdod rebellion with Egypt's (twenty-third dynasty of delta cities) encouragement (20:1–6) renders moot the vision that precedes.

Episode A: Reflections on Israel's Position (17:1–8)

Bibliography

Donner, H. *Israel unter den Völkern.* VTSup 11. Leiden: E. J. Brill, 1964. 38–42. **Vogt, E.** "Jesaja und die drohende Eroberung Palästinas durch Tiglatpilesar." *Wort, Lied, und Gottesspruch.* FS. J. Ziegler. Würzburg Echter Verlag: Katholisches Bibelwerk, 1972. II. 249–55.

Translation

Herald:	1 *A burden:* [a] *Damascus.*	
Yahweh:	*See Damascus! Changed* [b] *from (being) a city,*	2+2
	it has become [c] *a twisted* [d] *ruin:* [e]	3+3
	2 *her cities, abandoned forever.* [a]	
Chorus:	*They are become (a place) for flocks*	3+3
(echo)	*that lie down with no one terrorizing (them).*	
Yahweh:	3 *Fortification has ceased in* [a] *Ephraim*	3+2
	and royal rule in Damascus. [b]	
	Aram is a remnant [c]	2+4
	like the "glory" (which) the Israelites have become. [d]	
Herald:	*Expression of Yahweh of Hosts.*	
Yahweh:	4 *And it is* [a] *in such* [b] *a day*	3
	that the glory of Jacob is faded.	3+3
	The fat of his flesh is wasted away.	
	5 *It is*	1+3+3
	like harvesting standing grain, [a]	
	one harvests sheaves with his arm.	
	It is	1+3+2+3
	like gleaning sheaves	
	in the Valley of Raphaim	
	6 *when some gleanings are left in it.* [a]	
	Like [b] *beating an olive tree:* [b]	2+3+2
	two or three olives	
	in the topmost branches;	
	four or five	2+2
	in the fruitbearing branches. [c]	
Herald:	*Expression of Yahweh,*	2+2
	God of Israel.	
Yahweh:	7 *In such a day*	2+3+4
	a man should heed his Maker!	
	His eyes should look to the Holy One of Israel.	
	8 *He should no longer heed* [a] *(the sanctuaries)* [a]	4+2
	made by his hands.	
	What his fingers have fashioned	3+2+2
	he should no longer see:	
	[b] *(the asherim and the incense altars.)* [b]	

Notes

1.a. On משׂא see *Note* on 13:1.

1.b. מוּסָר hoph pass ptcp from סור "turn," therefore "changed." The masc form is a problem, since Damascus and the following verb are fem. *BHK* with Duhm, Donner (*Israel* . . . , 39), Kaiser, and Vogt (*Wort, Lied, und Gottesspruch,* 255) read מוסרה. Donner identifies the form as a hoph of יסר meaning "chastized." But Wildberger and Clements correctly reject this for the traditional reading.

1.c. וְהָיְתָה pf with *waw* of the verb "to be." The form is unquestioned. The problem lies in the time viewpoint. RSV and NIV translate as fut with most commentaries making the passage a prediction which must be dated prior to the fall of Damascus in 732 B.C. The time viewpoint of a pf with *waw* is dependent on its antecendent (Watts, *Syntax,* 114) which in this case is a ptcp with no hint of time. This is translated here in a "timeless" or neutral way. The contextual setting in a scene of Hezekiah's reign calls for a past time, which the grammar does not forbid. (Cf. *Form/Structure/Setting* for further discussion.)

1.d. מְעִי from מעה means "internal organs," "guts." It is a hapax, appearing only here. Some have emended to read מעיר "from a city" (Schmidt; A. B. Ehrlich, *Randglossen zur hebräischen Bibel* [Leipzig: 1908], IV, 64; Procksch). Others follow the LXX and see it as dittography for מעיר, thus eliminating it altogether (de Lagarde, *Semitica* I [Göttingen: Dieterich, 1878], 29; Gray; Duhm; Marti; *BHS;* and Kaiser). Wildberger is undoubtedly correct in following Delitzsch, C. W. E. Nägelsbach (*Der Prophet Jesaja,* [Leipzig: Klasing, 1877]), A. Knobel (*Der Prophet Jesaja* [Leipzig: Weidmann, 1843]), and Young in considering it an alternative form of עִי a noun from עוה "bend or twist" (BDB, 730).

1.e. מַפָּלָה appears in 23:13 and 25:2 as מַפֵּלָה a noun built on נפל "fall," hence "what has fallen," a ruin.

2.a. עֲזֻבוֹת עָרֵי עֲרֹעֵר "the cities of Aroer are abandoned." LXX καταλελειμμένη εἰς τὸν αἰῶνα "abandoned to the (end of the) age" (cf. 26:4 and 65:18). Tg renders עֲרֹעֵר as עָרֶיהָ "her cities." Aroer is the name of three places mentioned in the OT. One is a Moabite town south of Dibon on the Arnon river mentioned in Num 32:34, Deut 2:36, and Jer 48:19 (see Simons, *GTTOT* III b XI/F) which leads Wildberger (635) to suggest these verses belong in chap. 15. But none of the towns is near Damascus, which has led most recent commentaries including Steinmann, Mauchline, Fohrer, Donner (*Israel*. . .), Eichrodt, Alonso-Schökel, Kaiser, and Clements to follow the emendation עֲזֻבוֹת עָרֶיהָ עֲדֵי עַד "its cities abandoned forever," which draws upon the LXX & Tg readings. RSV follows this emendation. NIV renders MT literally. There is an unusual proliferation of combinations of the Heb letters (ר) ד ע in this verse—five times forms with ע, three times with ר, the last with both ר and ד. DSS [Isa] adds ו "his" to ערער to pronounce it עֲרֹעָרוֹ, thus different from MT. LXX has changed the ר to ד. The verb עדר (BDB, 727) has uses meaning "help" (1 Chr 12:34 [33]), "hoe" (Isa 5:6; 7:25), and "be lacking" (1 Sam 30:19; Isa 34:16; 40:26; 59:15; Zeph 3:5, and others). As a noun it seems to mean"flock or herd." The alliteration has become too subtle for the scribes and interpreters.

3.a. A number of interpreters, including Marti, Duhm, Procksch, Eichrodt, and Vogt (*Wort* . . . , 250) translate "a fortress *for* Ephraim." Wildberger correctly rejects this as a possibility for מִן which must be translated "from."

3.b. DSS[Isa] מדרמשק adds ר to MT's "from Damascus." The expanded name appears in 1 Chr 18:5 and often in the Chronicler's history. (Further see R. Ruzecka, *Konsonantische Dissimilation* [1909], 78; F. Rosenthal, *Die aramaistische Forschung* [Leiden: E. J. Brill, 1939], 15–18).

3.c. LXX adds ἀπολεῖται "be destroyed" which has led Duhm, Marti, F. Feldmann (*Das Buch Isaias* [Münster: Aschendorff, 1925]), and Donner (*Israel*. . .) to insert יֹאבַד to the text. Wildberger suggests moving the accent *athnah* to the next word. MT has the better reading.

3.d. DSS[Isa] יהיה instead of MT יִהְיוּ. Wildberger correctly supports MT. The subject of the verb is בני־ישראל.

4.a. והיה here and twice in v 5 is often translated a fut as outdated grammar thought all converted perfects to be futures. However, the context should decide the issue of time (cf. Watts, *Syntax,* 30, 114). The time of vv 1–3, dominated by participles, was present. That viewpoint is continued in this translation.

4.b. The demonstrative pronoun is definite referring to the conditions already mentioned (GKC § 136*b*), but the context is less specific. Therefore the translation "such a."

5.a. קָצִיר is a noun (BDB, 894) meaning "harvest." It is seen as a problem because the following word קָמָה is a noun meaning "standing grain" (BDB, 879) making קציר superfluous.

It also appears to overburden the stich with four words. Luzzato, Nägelsbach, and Cheyne read it as showing the time of harvest, which Wildberger includes in parentheses. But he prefers to eliminate it as a gloss. Others suggest emending it to קָצֵר (*BHS*, Duhm, Buhl, Procksch, Kissane, Steinmann, Donner [*Israel* . . . , 39], Vogt [*Wort* . . . , 255, n 11], Kaiser, Clements). Still others suggest seeing קָצִיר as an abstract sg representing a group (Gesenius, *Lehrgebäude* § 163³ 164²). In this case it designates the agent (Knobel, C. von Orelli [*The Prophecies of Isaiah*, tr. J. S. Banks, Edinburgh: T. & T. Clark, 1887], Dillmann, and, earlier, Kimchi). We follow Wildberger in omitting it.

6.a. The antecedent for בוֹ "in it" needs to be clear. Wildberger correctly relates it to "Jacob" in v 4.

6.b-b. The concern for the antecedent in (a) leads some to relate it to זית "olive tree" and to suggest that this be placed at the end of v 5 (Gray and Procksch) while others (*BHS*) suggest adding אוֹ "or," following LXX ἤ. None of this is necessary if the suggestion in (a) is followed.

6.c. סְעִפֶיהָ פֹּרִיָּה "her fruitbearing limbs" (BDB, 703, 826). פֹּרִיָּה is a fem act ptcp (cf. Ezek 19:10) "bearing fruit." The fem suffix is difficult to explain. זית "olive tree" is masc. Hitzig and Driver (*JTS* 2 [1951] 25) have suggested dividing the words to make ה the article for פריה. They would read סְעִפֵי הַפֹּרִיָּה "the limbs of the fruit tree." DSS^Isa reads סעפי but omits the ה altogether. Wildberger notes that the lack of an article is not unusual in poetry.

8.a-a. MT המזבחות "the altars." Wildberger states the objections to this word well: "works of his hand" is never used of altars in the OT but of idols.

8.b-b. The same applies to "the asherim and the incense altars" at the end of the verse. (So Wildberger, Kaiser, Fohrer, Kissane, Donner, etc.) However, it must be noted that DSS^Isa and the Versions uniformly include these words. Whether in the original writing or in the glossator's version, the idols and their sanctuaries have come to be identified. Clements considers this to be a late addition, in a sense extending the gloss to the entire paragraph.

Form/Structure/Setting

The section is called "a burden." The attempts to define the literary form and intentions of a "burden" and of so-called "foreign prophecies" are nowhere so thoroughly confused as in dealing with sections like this in Isaiah. The name of Damascus is called, but the content of the pericope as well as the following paragraphs which depend on it turns unmistakably to deal with Israel. So the "Burden: Damascus" is primarily concerned with Israel, and both are probably intended to communicate a truth to Jerusalem. It calls attention to a condition that is lamentable.

The first element (vv 1–3) is introduced by הנה "See!" It is continued by a participle "changed" and three verbs (perfect with *wāw*) "it has become," "abandoned forever," and "they lie down." The verb "to be" occurs in each of the three verses. Such a frequent recital of "to be" in a language where it can be implied without being written requires attention. It seems intended to stress the resultant condition that has come to exist, a condition that is present in the setting or context.

The other major signal in the passage is "Expression of Yahweh of Hosts" (vv 3 and 6) which indicates that God himself is speaking. His speech serves here to interpret Israel's position and status in that time, a continuing point in the Vision.

Vv 5–6 are parabolic in nature, comparing Israel's situation to a field that has been harvested, or an olive tree from which most of the fruit has already been taken. The implication is that some will survive and be sustained, if only the very poor.

Vv 7–8 take the form of an admonition to repentence. It is one of the "mankind" passages in the Vision like that in 2:9 and 20. Note the parallel to 6:11–13 where the cluster of motifs (destroyed cities, mankind, and "hope" for a remnant) is parallel, and to 2:9–22 where the motifs of mankind, destroyed cities, looking to God, and abandoning idol worship are common. But, whereas the "day of Yahweh" was central in chap. 2 and implied in chap. 6, the reference here is to events that have already taken place.

Comment

1–3 The burden laments the devastation of Syria and its capital. Its continued ruin has removed the threat to Ephraim and the need for fortification on either side of that border. One way to stop an armaments race is to have both territories reduced to rubble. Thus the rivalry on the border between Syria and Israel which had raged for more than a century was ended in 732 B.C. by the Assyrian invasions. Now peace reigns because there is nothing more to destroy. Royal rule with its pride and ambition has ceased to be. That situation continues in Hezekiah's reign, to which this passage refers. Both Aram and Israel are *remnants* of their former *glory.* God himself notes and describes the situation.

A series of words with *mēm* preformative, participles, and nouns with occasional parallel formations shape the passage: *changed, fallen, abandoned* (participle but no *mēm*), *terrifying, fortification, royal rule.* The key phrase is *changed from being a city.* Her external physical structure is changed. She is a ruin, a pasture for peaceful flocks. But also the concept and dynamic are changed: fortification and kingly ambition have ceased.

The phrase אין מחריד "no one terrorizing" is a common phrase in Scripture to picture a peaceful promised land (Lev 26:6), after the exile (Jer 30:10 = 46:27). See also Ezek 34:28; 39:26; Mic 4:4; Zeph 3:13; and Job 11:19 (BDB, 353). The irony is that ignominious defeat and destruction brought the peace (cf. 11:6–9) that royal might promised, but could never deliver. Syria and Israel shared a common demotion, from *glory* to the role of a *remnant.*

So far as is known, Damascus did not rise again after 732 B.C. and Samaria's fate was sealed by its destruction in 721 B.C. and the subsequent crushing of the Philistine-led rebellion in 720 B.C. The scene pictured in vv 1–3 fits their status during the last two decades of the century.

The parallel position of Syria and Ephraim in v 3 convinces Clements that the reference must be to 734–32 B.C. That is correct, but it is seen here as past history which has led both of them to a common fate as Assyrian vassals. This obviated Ephraim's intense efforts to fortify the border and removed Damascus' ability to exert royal power over its weaker neighbors.

7–8 אדם "a man." A proper attitude is contrasted with reactions to such a devastating catastrophe. He should turn from false worship which has proved ineffective, from his self-made idols and false sanctuaries. (The *asherim* are pillars used in the sanctuaries which were often objects of worship.) He should look for the true God. He should respect the fact that Yahweh's prophets had foretold and correctly interpreted the Assyrians' coming and would therefore *look to the Holy one of Israel.*

Explanation

Devastation and destruction, horrible as they are, do achieve certain desirable goals and present some useful possibilities. Damascus can no longer be either a nation or a city. But it is a place of peace and tranquility, which is more than could be said of it before. Now the feverish activity of "fortification" and the pride of "royal rule" are gone from both Damascus and Ephraim. Neither is necessary any longer.

Israel is likened in a parable (vv 5–6) to a field of grain and to a tree of ripe olives. The field is harvested and the tree is beaten to make the olives fall down. These are pictures of the Assyrian invasions and the resultant destructions. The field and the tree look desolate, stripped of the grain or olives. But if one looks carefully, it is seen that some grain remains at the corners, or in stalks lying on the ground. On the tree some olives remain in the highest branches. The poor in Israel were accustomed to existing on such leftovers (Deut 24:19–22). Israel as a whole now shares their lot.

Idolatry is often a temptation to the rich and ambitious. It bolsters pride and self-esteem. It feeds the dreams of wealth and power. But conditions of humiliation and bare survival should lead a people to search for the true God who can save, for the Maker and Savior of Israel (cf. 2:9, 11, 17–18).

Episode B: Jerusalem Admonished (17:9–14)

Bibliography

Alonso-Schökel, L. "Textos poéticos: analisis y traducción. IV." *CB* 19 (1962) 282–94. **Fohrer, G.** "Σιων." *TDNT* 7 (1964) 291–319. **Hayes, J.** "The Tradition of Zion's Inviolability." *JBL* 82 (1963) 419–26. **Jirku, A.** "Jes. 17:10c." *VT* 7 (1957) 201. **Lutz, M.-H.** *Jahwe, Jerusalem und die Völker.* WMANT 27. Neukirchen-Vluyn: Neukirchener Verlag, 1968. 47–51. **Schmidt, H.** *Israel, Zion und die Völker.* Diss., Zürich, 1966. **Schreiner, J.** *Sion-Jerusalem Jahwes Königssitz.* Munich: Kösel Verlag, 1963. 261–63, 278. **Stolz, F.** *Strukturen und Figuren im Kult von Jerusalem.* BZAW 118. Berlin: Töpelmann, 1970. **Vaux, R. de** "Jerusalem et les prophètes." *RB* 73 (1966) 481–509. **Wanke, G.** *Die Zionstheologie der Korachiten.* BZAW 97. Berlin: Töpelmann, 1966. 113–17.

Translation

Earth: 9 *In such a day* 2+3+3
(to Jerusalem) *his* [a] *fortified cities became*
[b] *like abandoned cities of the Hivites and the Amorites* [b]
which they abandoned before Israel. 5+2
And they are a desolation.

10 *But you (fem sg) have forgotten the God of your salvation!* 4+4
You have not remembered Rock, your fortress.
Because of this, you planted gardens of "the Beloved" [a] 4+3
and set them out: a twig for a foreign (god)!
11 *In the day you plant it, you fence in* [a] *carefully.* 3+3
In the morning that you sow it, you make it bud.
A harvest heaped high [b]*—* 2+2+2
a share [c] *in a day—*
like green shoots [d] *that are wilted.*
Chorus: (people of Jerusalem) 12 *Woe* [a]*—like the raging of many peoples,* 4+3
they rage like the raging of the sea.
And roaring of people, [b] *like the roaring* 3+3
(which) mighty waters roar.
13 [a]*(To peoples who roar like the roar of many waters:)* [a] 5+2+2
when one rebukes [b] *them,* [c]
they [c] *must flee afar off.* [d]
And they [c] *are driven* 1+2+2
[e]*like chaff of the hills* [e]
before the wind,
or like a tumble-weed before a storm wind. 3
14 *Toward the time of evening,* 2+2
see: sudden terror!
Before morning—no one is there. [a] 3
This is the way of those who loot us, 3+2
[b]*the habit of those who plunder us."* [b]

Notes

9.a. LXX *αἱ πόλεις σου* "which (were) your cities" implies מַעֻזֵּךְ as in v 10. The emendation in *Note* 9.b-b. should be adopted, making the entire passage an address to Jerusalem with a contrast between dependence on "fortified cities" and failure to look to God, "Rock, your fortress" (v 10).

9.b-b. MT means something like "thickets and underbrush." LXX *οἱ Αμορραῖοι και οἱ Ευαῖοι* "the Amorites and the Hivites." *BHK* suggests adoption of LXX reading though Wildberger follows MT, Cheyne, and DSS[Isa] in keeping the rest of the line. Thus the emended Heb line is עָרֵי מָעֻזּוֹ כַּעֲזוּבוֹת הַחִוִּי וְהָאֱמֹרִי. (See *Translation*).

10.a. נעמן "the beloved" is generally believed to be the name of a fertility god. It is pl to agree with the preceding word in a constr state (GKC § 124*q;* Joüon § 1360). Jirku (*VT* 7 [1957] 210) suggests that this is a false vocalization of an original נַעֲמָנְמָה which is mimicry of endearing sounds as in Ugaritic (cf. Aistleitner, *WB,* 1494).

11.a. תשגשגי may derive from שגג (שגא, שגה), "grow," "grow large" (BDB, 960) as Gray, Duhm, Marti, Fohrer, Kaiser, Clements, Wildberger think; or from שוג "fence in" (סוג BDB, II, 962/691) as in Cant 7:3 [2] (similar to שׂוּךְ BDB, 962) as Hitzig, Procksch, Leslie, Ziegler, and others have thought. Both the meaning of quick growth and fencing in would apply. This is the only use of either root in a pilp form. The second meaning appears to be most likely.

11.b. נֵד (BDB, 622 "a heap") is found only in Exod 15:8; Josh 3:13, 16; Ps 33:7, and Ps 78:13, all of the piling up of waters in miraculous crossings of the Reed Sea or Jordan. LXX and Tg apparently read עד "until." Vg *ablata est messis* "harvest has retreated" implies נָד (from נדד) "retreat or flee." The word remains unclear.

11.c. נַחֲלָה might ordinarily mean "inheritance" as Vg translates *hereditas* and LXX *κληρώσῃ* "obtain a portion." Or it may be a niph ptcp from חלה "be weak," "sick" (BDB, 317) as Ibn Ezra had already shown.

11.d. LXX read כאב "as a father," and אֱנוּשׁ as אֱנוֹשׁ "a man." *BHS* records Duhm's unlikely suggestion that LXX τοῖς υἱοῖς σου misread an original לפניך "before you" as לבניך "to your sons." A basic question remains: does the second line of verse 11 (a) continue the reference to the "gardens of the beloved" or (b) return to application to Israel. If (a), it may be translated "harvest piles up in a day—a share (of the harvest), like fresh greenness, (becomes) wilted." If (b), the translation will read: "harvest is past in a day of sickness like incurable pain." Or is it possible that the double meaning is intentional? This possibility should not be ruled out. The translation follows the context and (a) above.

12.a. הוי "woe, alas" See *Note* on 5:8.

12.b. "A roaring of peoples" is set apart in MT by an accent mark, creating an uneven line. LXX adds a word, πολλῶν "many" or "great," which led Schmidt, Procksch, and others to suggest a rearranged word order with כבירים "great" or "mighty" after לאמים. Wildberger properly rejects the change, suggesting instead that the division in the line be moved over to provide a balanced line.

13.a-a. A word-for-word repetition of five words of the previous line (with רבים "many" for כבירים "mighty"). This is an echo or repetition, probably for effect. It falls out of the metric pattern and is omitted from some MSS and Syr.

13.b. וְגָעַר pf 3 m sg "and he will rebuke" is rendered ויגער impf in DSS[Isa]. But problems remain. A subject is missing in the entire section. To supply this Duhm inserted וְהוּא, Marti ויהוה הוא, and Procksch ויהוה. Wildberger suggests that יהוה may have been abbreviated to י and then been lost in DSS[Isa's] form יגער, becoming the ו. The subject is understood to be Yahweh in any case.

13.c. All these are sg in Heb. Reference to the preceding pl suggests they be translated as collectives.

13.d. מִן "from" is used with ideas of flight to mean "away" (GKC § 119v).

13.e-e. I. Eitan's suggestion ("A Contribution to Isaiah Exegesis," *HUCA* 12/13 [1937–38] 65) to read כַּמֹּץ instead of כְּמֹץ "like the chaff" and הרים like the Arab *harra* meaning "refuse" is not necessary. Wildberger (665) has correctly noted the MT's figure is fitting and strong as it is.

14.a. Many MSS and versions have added a *wāw*.

14.b-b. Syr reads *wmntʾ dbzwzn*. See also LXX[A], MSS of the Lucianic transmission, Vg, and Arab. These suggest the reading וגורל בוזינו, omitting ל from the second word as dittography for the ל before it. The change affects syntax, but not meaning.

Form/Structure/Setting

This section relates to Jerusalem, as the pronouns in second feminine singular indicate. She is accused of blatant idolatry (vv 10–11). The section first notes in an "in such a day" passage (v 9) that Jerusalem has shared some of Israel's and Damascus' destruction. Her outer ring of fortress cities, apparently those along the upper border with Israel, have been abandoned. It goes on to accuse Jerusalem of having forgotten her God and of pagan practices in contrast to the kind of behavior one expects of humans in disaster (vv 7–8). Ironically, the motif of harvest is cited, in contrast with the pitiful little "Adonis gardens" of the devotees.

A chorus of Jerusalemites bewail their condition with a "woe" passage (vv 12–14). They see themselves as the victims of their times, helpless to defend themselves from looters. Recent studies by Schmidt and Lutz have isolated a genre of speeches in which the peoples gather against Jerusalem. Wanke places the genre in the temple theology and service of the Korahites. This theme can and should be traced in the prophetic books.

However, there is also a clear direction shown within the Vision of Isaiah. The theme of nations marching at Yahweh's signal begins in 5:26–30. 8:9–10 echo the sentiments of super-patriots whose bravado challenges the nations to do their worst. 14:27 speaks of Yahweh's hand outstretched over the nations. 17:12–14 echo again the fears of the people. 29:5 repeats the motif with a word of hope. 34:2–3 depict Yahweh's destruction of the nations, but there is no hint that this relates to Jerusalem. Only in 34:8 is Zion's cause credited with the motif.

The theme is complex. Some texts in Isaiah and in other prophets have the nations (or peoples) assembling against Jerusalem, but Yahweh saves them. Some have Yahweh fighting against the nations with little relation to Jerusalem, while in a few texts Yahweh fights against the city. The chorus here (17:12–14) seems to repeat a familiar theme which illustrates the anxieties and fears of the city in a time when they have little reason to be so anxious.

Comment

9 Jerusalem's *fortified cities* were probably those abandoned during the invasion of Israel and Aram and never reoccupied after the march of the Assyrians to Judah's borders in 734–732 B.C..

The *Hivites* and the *Amorites* were some of those who populated Canaan before the entrance of the Israelites. Their *abandoned cities* were ruins that all Israel would know.

The implication of this is that not only Aram and Israel had suffered in the years of Assyrian invasions (cf. 8:7–8). Judah also bore its scars.

10 But Jerusalem did not have a healthy response of renewed concern with the worship of Yahweh who had given her salvation in the past, who was the foundation of her hope for defense. Instead she increased her devotion to pagan worship.

The Beloved is probably the name of a fertility god. The *gardens* described here fit the picture given by Plato (*Phaedrus,* 276*b*) and other Greek and Latin authors. H. Ewald (*Commentary on the Prophets of the Old Testament,* vol. 2, tr. J. F. Smith [London: Williams & Morgate, 1875–81] 116) was apparently the first to suggest a connection. Greek vases dated about 400 B.C. portray the scene. (Cf. H. Haas, *Bilderatlas zur Religionsgeschichte* [Leipzig: W. Scholl, 1926]; pictures are on 105.) Others have suggested a relation to the worship of Osiris in Egypt or to Tammuz in Mesopotamia (see Wildberger, 658). However this may be, the nearer and more likely relation of *the Beloved* was with the Canaanite Ba'al (*IDB* 1:48). The custom apparently was for grain to be planted in shallow pots or potsherds, watered, and placed in the sun. The plants grew very rapidly, but wilted equally rapidly. This represented the rise and the death of the god, who was then mourned with great passion (cf. Ezek 8:14) until the coming of the natural rains caused all the fields to turn green, a sign of his rebirth.

The term נעמן "the Beloved" is apparently an epithet and does little to identify the "foreign (god)" worshiped in these rites (cf. L. A. Snijders, *OTS* 10 [1954] 1–21; R. Martin-Achard, *THAT,* I, 520–22). The worship of heathen gods in Jerusalem is denounced by Jeremiah and Ezekiel. This passage attests to its presence a century earlier.

12 These people who engross themselves in idolatry's fantasies reflect here their hysteria in fear of anyone who might approach their city. When darkness descends (v 14) they are terrified. Daylight reveals no one is there. It is ironic that the genre of poetry which was once used by the Temple singers to portray Yahweh's unceasing care for his city would be cited by those whose pagan imaginations have been overcome with nightmarish fears.

Explanation

Attention turns from Israel and mankind to Jerusalem. She, too, has been humiliated by the wars. But no salutory effect followed, no awakening of precious memories of faith. Rather, Jerusalem forgot Yahweh God who had saved her. She cultivated her pagan passions and wailed her hysterical fears to the world.

Episode C: Messengers from Ethiopia (18:1–7)

Bibliography

There is a remarkable *lacuna* in the literature on this passage. Notes on words or expressions may be found below.

Translation

Chorus:	1 *Woe! The land of winged boats* [a]	4+4
(People of Jerusalem)	*which is* [b] *in the region of* [b] *the rivers of Cush*	
	2 *is sending envoys by sea* [a]	3+4
	with vessels of papyrus over the surface of the water.	
(To the messengers)	*Go, swift messengers,*	3+4
	to a nation tall and smooth-skinned, [b]	
	to a people feared near and far,	4+3+4
	a very strong nation [c]	
	whose land is divided [d] *by rivers.*	
(To the world)	3 *All you inhabitants of the world,*	3+2
	and you dwellers in the earth,	
	like a banner raised on the mountains, you will see (*it*).	4+3
	Like a trumpet, you will hear (*it*).	
Shebna:	4 *But Yahweh said to me, thus:*	5
	"I will remain still [a] *and observe in my place."*	3
Heavens:	*Like heat shimmering* [b] *over the light.*	4+4
	Like a cloud of dew in the heat [c] *of harvest.*	
	5 *For at wheat-harvest* [a] *-time, when the blossoms are gone,*	4+4
	when the bud becomes a ripening grape,	
	one cuts off the shoots with a knife	3+3
	and removes the branches. He cuts (*them*) *off.*	

6 *They are left, all of them,* 2+2+2
to mountain eagles
and to the beasts of the land
who will spend the summer on them, 3+3+2
and all the beasts of the land
will spend harvest-time on them.
Earth: 7 *In such a time* 2+4+3
a gift may be brought to Yahweh of Hosts
from [a] *a people tall and smooth-skinned,*
from a people feared near and far, 4+3+4
a nation of great might [b] *and subjugation,*
whose land is divided by rivers,
to the place of the Name, 3+2+2
Yahweh of Hosts,
(to) Mount Zion."

Notes

1.a. צלצל is a word with various meanings and kindred words (BDB, 852–53). Wildberger's exhaustive description (679) sums up the possibilities. "Whirring," "buzzing" in comparison with Deut 28:42, and with Akk and Arab parallels, leads to the translation "land of whirring wings." Most modern translations follow this. Jerome translated *umbra* relating it to צֵל "darkness." He was followed by Luther, Dillmann, Buhl and others. The Vg translates *cymbalum* following the Heb צלצלים "cymbals." Tg translates ספינן "ships." Jerome cites Θ as *naves.* LXX in Job 40:31 translates בצלצל דגים ἐν πλοίοις ἁλιέων "in ships of fishermen." Wildberger cites parallels in Eth *ṣalala* "swim" and Aram צלצל "ship," and admits that Arab *ẓulẓul* is different (cf. Driver, FS T. H. Robinson [1950] 56; *JSS* 13 [1968] 45; and Gesenius, *Thesaurus* [Leipzig: G. Vogel, 1829–53], 1167*f*). Wildberger's presentation is convincing.

1.b-b. מעבר ל means, literally, "beyond," "on the other side of." Most translations and commentaries follow this without question. Some (Duhm; Marti; Donner, *Israel unter den Völkern,* VTSup 11 [1964] 122) have treated it as a gloss. Wildberger says the obvious: The reference is to Cush (Ethiopia or Nubia), and it does not lie "beyond the rivers." Procksch points it מַעֲבָר ל "access to," "corridor to" with reference to 16:2 and Gen 32:23 and translates "an access to the rivers of Cush." E. Vogt ("*ʿeber hayyarden* = REGIO FINITIMA IORDANI," *BZ* 34 [1953] 118–19) shows that (מ)עבר הירדן often means "in the region of Jordan." In the same way מעבר לנהרי־כוש means "in regions adjacent to the rivers of Cush."

2.a. Many commentators (including Wildberger, 680) would change this to mean "river" on the grounds that such ships were not seaworthy. But Clements (164) is surely right that it is not impossible that "the sea" means the Mediterranean coast.

2.b. DSS^{Isa} has an additional letter וממורט as well as the superimposed *waw.* This is the normal form of a pual ptcp but the shorter form may also be used (cf. G. R. Driver, *JTS* 2 [1951] 25 and GKC § 525).

2.c. קַו means a measuring line. The reduplicated form appears only here (and v 7) in Heb. In 28:10 and 13 it seems to be used as a meaningless sound which leads Donner (122) and others to see in it a designation for a foreign language. J. Fischer (*Das Buch Isaias, 1–39* [Bonn: Hanstein, 1937]) thinks of the sound of marching feet. Driver (*JSS* 13 [1968] 46) supports BDB in rendering it as a reduplicated adjective "very strong." K^{Or} and DSS^{Isa} have קוקו (one word) which, following the Arab *ḳuwwatun* "strength," "power," and *ḳawija* "tense," "be strong," would mean "tensile strength."

2.d. בזא occurs only here and v 7. BDB (102) translates "divide," "cut through" in dependence on Syr *bzʾ* "tear," "cut." The Versions had trouble with the word, but offer no good solution. L. Köhler ("*Bāzāʾ* = fortschwemmen," *ThZ* 6 [1950] 316–17) looks to Arab *bazza* "forcefully carry away" and suggested the translation "swim away." But the meaning "divided" is better.

4.a. K offers a different vocalization. But the received text is stronger (Wildberger, 680).

4.b. For different suggestions on צת cf. Wildberger (680).

4.c. בחם means "in the heat of." LXX, Syr, and Vg have apparently read ביום "in the day of." The orthographic variation is slight. Wildberger follows the Versions.

5.a. קציר means "grain harvest" which comes in early summer. לִפְנֵי does not mean "before" in a time sense, but "in view of" or "facing" (cf. Wildberger, 681). The harvest of grain occurs at the same time that the work in the vineyards must be done.

7.a. עם "a people." LXX ἐκ λαοῦ, Vg *a populo,* DSS[Isa] מעם "from a people." Following DSS[Isa] is supported by the parallel phrase three words later.

7.b. See note on 2.c.

Form/Structure/Setting

The chapter presents three movements: the approach of a delegation from "the land of winged boats" brings dismay to Jerusalem (vv 1–2a); the delegation is sent to "a nation tall and smooth-skinned" (v 2b–c); and it is anticipated that "the nation tall and smooth-skinned" will bring gifts to Yahweh in Zion (v 7). In between, all the world is called to take notice of the delegation's trip (v 3). Yahweh intends to sit back and observe developments (v 4a). An enigmatic explanation is offered which uses the parabolic language of the farmer trimming the grain of shoots before actual harvest time (vv 4a–6).

The "woe" (v 1) is not formally an indication of mourning or a curse on Cush. It is simply a cry of dismay at the thought of more military activity in the region. The parable (vv 4a–6) continues the series begun in 17:5–9.

Comment

1 *Woe* does not introduce a curse on Cush (Ethiopia). It is a cry of dismay by Jerusalemites at the news that the delegation is approaching. They assume that military operations in their land will bring renewed disasters. "Whirring wings" (see *Notes*) may refer to insects in the upper Nile valley. Or it may be a reference to sail boats.

Cush is the land of Ethiopia or Nubia which at this time had its capital at Napata above the fourth cataract. A strong new dynasty (the twenty-fifth of Egypt) was building. Pianchi in 728 B.C. had handed the Libyan ruler, Tefnakht, a defeat and extended his control as far down river as Memphis. But he had not followed up on that advantage. Kitchen (*The Third Intermediate Period,* 369) has called the period 728 to 715 B.C. a lull between storms in Egypt. In 716 B.C., Shabaka succeeded his brother to the Ethiopian throne and began immediately to consolidate Ethiopian control of lower Egypt. An initial success was achieved by 715 B.C. This period, 716–15 B.C., was one of feverish political activity as he sought allies for his attempt to gain control of the Nile delta. This activity apparently reached as far as Jerusalem.

2 The *messengers* are sent on their way again. But commentators are not agreed to whom they are sent. The description is not definitive. ממשך is an obscure word which probably means "lean" or "tall." מוֹרט is equally obscure relating to something cut off, perhaps implying something shaved: hence "smooth-skinned." The lines *a nation feared, a very strong nation,* and *divided by rivers* also leave open several possibilities.

Wildberger (with others) assumes that this describes the Ethiopians themselves and sees this as a rejection of the envoys. W. Janzen (*Mourning Cry and Woe Oracle,* BZAW 125 [Berlin/New York: De Gruyter, 1972], 60–61) and Barth (*Israel und das Assyrerreich,* 13) understand this to be a summons to other messengers, perhaps divine messengers, to go to Assyria with news of these developments. The key point is that the country referred to is Assyria. This is correct. Clements (165) assumes that the envoys are conspiring against Assyria. But is this true? If the envoys come from Shabaka in 716 B.C., then their mission relates to his attempt to control Egypt. Can it be that he is enlisting aid against the delta kings, not against Assyria? And can it be that Jerusalem here is simply referring them to its overlord, Assyria, as the only one who can make such a decision?

At this time (716 B.C.) Cush (Ethiopia) and Egypt are not one and the same. After the Ethiopian dynasty gains control, there is evidence that they were on friendly terms with the Assyrians. When in 712 B.C. Sargon attacked Ashdod, its ruler Iamani fled to Egypt, now under Ethiopian rule. There Shabaka, "the Pharaoh of Egypt," "which land now belongs to Cush," obligingly extradited the fugitive Iamani to the Assyrian's satisfaction (Kitchen, *The Third Intermediate Period,* 380). If this is true, the vision of friendly relations between Egypt under an Ethiopian ruler and Assyria (Isa 19:23–25) finds its basis in historical fact. So the best interpretation appears to be that the envoys from Shabaka are sent on to Assyria to try to arrange for support or at least a promise not to interfere, as he presses his claims to authority over all Egypt.

4 The solo voice that speaks in first person requires identification. Similar passages occur in 21:2–4, 6, 10 and in 22:14. The last instance is identified by the succeeding verse to be Shebna, Hezekiah's prime minister who is undoubtedly the designer of Judah's foreign policy throughout this period. The solo passages in first person, not otherwise identified from 18:4 through chap. 22, are assigned to Shebna.

7 *In such a time* most appropriately refers to the events envisioned in vv 3–6 and planned for in vv 1–2 to take place, that is, when Ethiopia and Assyria begin their campaign against lower Egypt.

The gifts to be brought to Yahweh of Hosts come from the Assyrians (cf. *Comment* on v 2). They relate to their activities in conjunction with Ethiopia. They may be seen as recognition of Jerusalem's loyalty in referring the messengers to Assyria. Or they may be intended to secure Jerusalem's commitment to protect Assyria's flanks as they invade Egypt. In either case, Zion, Yahweh (and the royal house in Jerusalem) are accorded a high status and privilege. This continues the tendency of chap. 16 to document a considerable recovery of influence and power for Jerusalem even within its vassal status.

Explanation

Against the background of a glance at the ruins of Damascus and her former fortress towns on the border of Israel, Judah is reminded that despair has led them to forget Yahweh and turn to idolatrous practices (17:10–11). Their anxiety about political disturbances (vv 12–13) leads to a notice that in the midst of terrors, a limit is set. The terror vanishes before dawn (v 14).

18:1 presents another anxious moment as messengers arrive from the new Ethiopian ruler Shabaka, to whom the answer is given correctly that they should seek out the Assyrian overlord.

At that point (18:3) a picture of the potential inherent in that moment is spread over the next chapter. The Lord promises to "remain quiet," i.e., approving, as the coalition between Ethiopia and Assyria is forged with the ostensible purpose of putting the Egyptian delta under firm Ethiopian rule.

At that time, Assyria will bring gifts to Zion (18:7) to obtain their support in the campaign against Egypt (the delta) and to recognize its loyalty in sending the delegation on to Nineveh (18:2). At this point Yahweh abandons his spectator position to enter the conflict, ensuring victory over Egypt by creating internal dissension (19:2–4), by drying up the vitally important river (vv 5–10), and by confusing the vaunted wisdom of the Egyptian counselors (vv 12–15).

The result would be: demoralization of Egyptians so that even tiny Judah's forces bring terror to them (19:16–17); colonization of five cities in Egypt by Palestinians, probably as garrison cities (v 18); recognition of Yahweh in Egypt, leading to worship and dependence on him (vv 19–22); an open highway for diplomatic and commercial activity between Egypt and Assyria, with relations so cordial that the two worship together (v 23); and finally, Israel, whose position lies astride the highway just mentioned, occupying a position exceeded only by Egypt and Assyria with her influence being *a blessing* for all the land. This beneficent result is possible because Yahweh would call Egypt "my people" (cf. vv 19–22) and Assyria "my handwork" (cf. 10:5–6) and Israel "my inheritance," her historic title.

One must keep in mind that all this is predicated on Judah's having learned her lesson from Damascus (chap. 17) and on her having acted as a loyal vassal (18:3, 7; 19:17). This would apply if Hezekiah had followed policies of peace and servitude like his father Ahaz.

These chapters suggest a theology of history in which Yahweh is seen as the prime mover in Assyrian expansion in Palestine and in which his hand may be seen in the rise of the twenty-fifth Dynasty in Egypt, whose openness to Assyrian alliance could have presaged a period of peace and prosperity for the entire region.

As a matter of historical fact, this dream or vision was not fulfilled. Hezekiah did not follow his father's policies, but succumbed to the hawkish ideas of his advisors who never gave up their false hope that Judah's salvation lay in Egypt's reassuming sovereignty over the region. It was an unrealistic hope since the Egyptian delta was torn by dissension. These advisors led Israel to participate in the abortive attempt by Ashdod to be free of Assyria that is reflected in chap. 20. Despite Isaiah's warnings, they joined Ashdod. They were so emotionally tied to the success of Merodach-Baladan's rule in Babylon that they became hysterical at the report of his defeat. And finally they are shown to be what they are under the condemning eyes of God in chap. 21.

But the hopes for Hezekiah, which seemed so great in the pictures of 7:1—9:6 and in chap. 11 and which were so well prepared by his father's carefully cultivated ties to Assyria, were shattered by the willful, nationalistic ambitions and pride of the period and by the dangerously wrong assessment of the relative strength of the other nations. Most of all, they failed because of their inability to be led by the Lord in seeing and doing what he wanted, in joining with him in bringing blessing, peace, and prosperity to that generation and region.

Episode D:
Yahweh against Egypt (19:1–17)

Bibliography

Calderone, P. J. "The Rivers of Masor." *Bib* 42 (1961) 423–32. **Gottwald, N. K.** *All the Kingdoms of the Earth.* New York: Harper & Row, 1964. 222–28. **Randles, R. J.** "The Interaction of Israel, Judah and Egypt: From Solomon to Josiah." Diss., Southern Baptist Theological Seminary 1980. 155–208.

Translation

Herald:	1 *Burden:* [a] *Egypt.*	2
	See Yahweh,	2+3+2
	riding [b] *on a light cloud*	
	and coming (to) Egypt.	
Earth:	*The nonentities* [c] *of Egypt tremble before him*	4+4
	and Egypt's heart melts within it.	
Yahweh:	2 *I incite* [a] *Egypt* [b] *against Egypt.*	3+3
	A man fights against his brother,	
	a man against his neighbor,	2+2+2
	[c] *city against city,*	
	[d] *kingdom against kingdom.* [d]	
	3 *The spirit of the Egyptians is poured out* [a] *within them*	4+2
	and its strategy I swallow up.	
	They seek out the nonentities [b] *and the spiritualists,* [c]	3+2
	the mediums [d] *and familiar spirits.* [e]	
	4 *I confine Egypt in the hand of cruel masters* [a]	2+4
	and a powerful king [b] *who will rule over them.*	
Herald:	*Expression of the Lord,* [c] *Yahweh of Hosts.*	4
Heavens:	5 *The water from the river* [a] *dries up*	3+3
	and the river-bed is desolate and dry.	
	6 *The canals* [a] *stink.* [b]	2+4+3
	They diminish and the streams of Mazur [c] *dry up.*	
	The reeds and rushes decay. [d]	
	7 *Plants* [a] *(are)* [b] *upon the Nile* [b]	2+2
	upon the mouth of the Nile—	
	every sown place along the Nile	3+3
	is dried up, [c] *blown away, nothing left.* [d]	
	8 *The fishermen* [a] *mourn and lament—*	3+4
	all who cast [b] *a hook in the Nile.*	

Those who spread a net on the surface of the water
languish. 4
9 *Those who work with combed*[a] *flax*[b] *are embarrassed,* 4+2
as are the weavers of linen.[c]
10 *Her weavers*[a] *are crushed.* 3+3
All wage[b]*-earners are sick*[c] *at heart.*
Earth: 11 *Yet surely the princes of Zoan (are) fools.* 4+3+2
The [a]*wisest of Pharaoh's counselors*[a]
(gives) stupid advice.
(To the Egyptian Wisemen) *How can you say to Pharoah:* 3+2+2
"I am one of the wise men,
one of the kings of old."[b]
(To Egypt) 12 *Where are they? Where are your (m) wise ones?* 3+3+1
Let them declare to you (f) now
that they know[a]
what Yahweh of Hosts 2+2+2
has planned
against Egypt.
Heavens: 13 *The princes of Zoan act foolishly.*[a] 3+3+4
The princes of Noph are deceived.[b]
The chiefs[c] *of her tribes cause Egypt to err.*
14 *Yahweh has mixed within her*[a] *a spirit of* 5+4+3
dizziness,[b]
which causes Egypt to stagger in all[c] *its doings*
like the staggering of a drunkard in his vomit.
15 *Egypt has nothing* 3+2
it can use
(which has) head or tail 2+2
[a]*sprout or stalk.*[a]
Earth: 16 *In such a day* 2
Egypt[a] *is like (the) women.* 3+2
It[b] *trembles and is in dread*
in the face of the waving hand of Yahweh of Hosts 4+3
which he is waving[c] *against it.*[b]
Heavens: 17 *(As)*[a] *the soil of Judah becomes* 3+2
for Egypt a festival,[b]
everyone who[c] *remembers* 3+3
her sign[d] *toward it trembles*
in the face of the plan of Yahweh of Hosts 4+4
which he is planning against it.

Notes

1.a. Concerning משא see the note on 13:1.

1.b. Cf. S. Mowinckel, *VT* 12 (1962) 299.

1.c. אלילי "worthless things, idols." BDB, 47. LXX τὰ χειροποίητα "things made by hand"; Vg *simulacra* "images."

2.a. סכסך is identified as an obscure pilp form. Wildberger derives it from סוך I related to a "thorn" Arab *šawkun* and meaning to "prick" or "needle." BDB (697, 968) relates to שכך IV, a root derived from Semitic parallels relating to "thorns."

2.b. LXX and Θ Αἰγύπτιοι "Egyptians." However, the collective meaning would fit. Also the implication that more than one authority claims to be "Egypt" in that time is true. See *Historical Background* above.

2.c. DSS[Isa] ועיר "and a city." The ו is missing in the Versions.

2.d-d. LXX καὶ νομὸς ἐπὶ νομόν "and district against district" (cf. the use of νομός for Egypt's provinces in Herodotus, II, 4). The rulers of cities were also called "kings" thus also justifying the Heb term.

3.a. נבקה is niph pf 3 f sg from בקק "empty" (BDB, 132) "be emptied," "be poured out." *BHS* suggests ונבקה, but see GKC § 67*dd.* Marti and others follow LXX ταραχθήσεται "agitated," "troubled" to read נָבֹכָה niph pf from בוך (Esth 3:15) "be perplexed," "confused" (BDB, 100). However, MT may be kept.

3.b. LXX τοὺς θεοὺς αὐτῶν "their gods."

3.c. LXX καὶ τὰ ἀγάλματα αὐτῶν "and their images," Vg *divinos suos* "his gods." Heb אִטִּים is a *hapax.* BDB (31) translates "mutterer." Wildberger (700) thinks it a loan-word from Akk relating to spirits of the dead.

3.d. אֹבוֹת "mediums" (cf. 8:19; 29:4). LXX τοὺς ἐκ τῆς γῆς φωνοῦντας "ones who speak from the ground" (see note on 8:19). M. Dietrich relates Ug *ilib* to Heb אוֹב meaning "spirit of the dead" (*UF* 6 [1974] 450–51).

3.e. ידענים "fortune-tellers," or "familiar spirits," is usually paired with אוב.

4.a. The pl noun and sg adjective requires explanation. Br. *Synt* § 19c calls it an emphatic pl to recognize a higher power. Joüon § 148a explains the sg adjective as a frequent occurrence. Hummel ("Enclitic *Mem* in Early NW Semitic," *JBL* 76 [1957] 101) thinks the final *mem* in אדנים was originally a *mem* enclitic on a sg form. The pl may well describe local tyrants who are forced, in turn, to render allegiance to a higher ruler.

4.b. LXX βασιλεῖς σκληροὶ "fierce kings."

4.c. האדון "*the* Lord" has no counterpart in either LXX or Syr.

5.a. יָם as in 18:2 means here not "sea" but the Nile river. Cf. Herodotos, II, 97 and Pliny, Nat. Hist. XXXVII *in Nilo cuius est aqua maris similis* "in the Nile whose waters are like the sea," Seneca, *Nat. Quaest.* IVa, 2: *continuatis aquis in faciem lati ac turbidi maris stagnat* "an expanse of water, broad in shape, indeed which overflows into a troubled sea." (Both cited by Wildberger.)

6.a. נהרות may refer to the branches of the Nile or to its network of canals.

6.b. האזניחו. DSS[Isa] omits א. GKC § 19*m* and 53*g* explains it as *Aleph prostheticum.* The *hapax* probably means "they stink."

6.c. מָצוֹר is sg whereas Egypt is usually a dual מצרים. Delitzsch, Dillmann, and Kittel thought it referred only to lower Egypt. None of the Versions understood it to mean Egypt. Wildberger (701) suggests it is deliberately chosen because it has a double meaning (also siege) so that its name would also indicate its fate.

6.d. קָמֵל "decay" BDB (888). The word occurs only here and in 33:9. Other meanings ("become black" Wildberger; "he afflicted with lice" *KB*) have been suggested, but are no improvement.

7.a. ערות: a *hapax.* BDB (788) "bare places." LXX καὶ τὸ ἄχι "swamp-grass." Vg *nudabitur* "be stripped." Wildberger (701) traces its meaning to an Egyptian word for the stalk or stem of a plant. He also finds LXX καὶ correct, a *waw* lost through haplography, which puts ערות "stalks" with קנה "a reed" and סוף "a rush."

7.b-b. Missing in LXX. But it may be seen as emphatic repetition.

7.c. DSS[Isa] יבש (for MT יִיבַשׁ) is a pf form instead of impf (BDB, 386). Both mean "be dried up, withered."

7.d. ואיננו "nothing of it" is missing in LXX. DSS[Isa] ואין בו has a meaning similar to MT.

8.a. DSS[Isa] הדגים "the fish." Wildberger notes the MT maintains the parallel meaning to the second half of the verse.

8.b. The constr state before a preposition is unusual. Cf. Br. *Synt.* § 70.

9.a. שריקות a *hapax* may be related to a later Heb root and a Syr word meaning "combed." Wildberger (701) suggests moving the athnah back one word and reading שׂרקוֹת, an act ptcp following Vg *pectentes* and Syr *dsrḳjn* "the combers," thus giving a balanced verse:

The flax workers are dismayed: 3+3
the combers and weavers of linen.

9.b. This pl of a fem word פִּשְׁתָּה speaks of the stems of flax which must be worked to obtain the hemp fiber needed for spinning.

9.c. DSS[Isa] חוורו "they bleach." However, MT makes sense as it is.

10.a. שתתיה appears to be a pl of שֵׁת "foundation," but this is meaningless and does not fit the masc מדכאים that follows. LXX οἱ διαζόμενοι αὐτὰ ἐν ὀδύνῃ "which draws the chair of the weaver's loom." This leads to a word שְׁתִי "woven goods," or "warp" (BDB, 1059–60). This led Zimmern to compare it to Akk *šatū* and Heb שתה "weave," the Aram שְׁתָא "weave" and שְׁתְיָא "warp" (Wildberger, 702). I. Eitan ("An Egyptian Loan Word in Isa 19," *JQR* 15 [1924/25] 419–22) added Copt *štit* "weaver." These lead to שְׁתִיתֶיהָ "her weavers" (cf. *BHS*, KB, Wildberger [702], and NIV).

10.b. LXX ζῦτον "beer," Syr *škr*ʾ = שֵׁכָר "drink." These have led to many emendations. But שכר in Prov 11:18 clearly means "wages."

10.c. אגמי usually "pools of." Vg *lacunas ad capiendos pisces* "places for taking fish" (followed by Ibn Ezra) has led some MSS to read אגמי מים "pools of water." But cf. T. Nöldeke (*ZDMG* 40 [1886] 727) and M. D. Goldman (*AusBR* 2 [1952] 50) identified אגמי with עגמי "ones grieved," which in Job 30:25 is also used with נפש "soul" (BDB, 723).

11.a-a. The five words in this half-verse lead commentators (Wildberger and others) to suspect it is too full and suggest that עצה "counsel" should be eliminated. The unusual double constr form led G. R. Driver (*JTS* 38 [1937] 40) to emend יֹעֲצֵי "counselors of" to יַעֲצוּ "they give counsel." But the double constr is possible and Masoretic accentuation suggests a three-part line.

11.b. קדם may mean "former times" or "the East." The wisdom of Edom and of Teman (cf. 1 Kgs 5:10 and Jer 49:7) was famous. But in Egypt the wisdom of the past, especially of past kings, was highly favored.

12.a. וידעו qal impf "and they know" or "that they know." LXX εἰπάτωσαν "let them say" and Vg *et indicent* "and saying" or "and let them say" (ptcp as impv) has led Gray, Duhm, Kissane, Kaiser, and Wildberger to read וְיֹדִעוּ hiph juss "and make them to know." This parallels וְיַגִּדוּ "let them declare." The Masoretes abandon metrical balance to point it as they do. MT should be sustained.

13.a,b. DSS[Isa] נאולו and נשואו. Wildberger follows KB in suggesting the existence of so-far unknown verb roots אול beside יאל and שוא beside נשא.

13.c. פִּנַּת "chief of." Following Syr and Tg and in view of Judg 20:2 and 1 Sam 14:38, many (including Duhm, Marti, Ehrlich [*Randglossen*], and Kaiser) read a pl פִּנֹּת "chiefs of." Wildberger (702) suggests that the sg is to be understood as collective (cf. Gray; GKC § 145*bc*).

14.a. LXX has a plural αὐτοῖς.

14.b. עועים pl "a spirit of distortings," BDB, 730, "warped judgments." DSS[Isa] עועיים strengthens the view that this is a reduplicated form of עוה.

14.c. A masc suffix beside a fem in 13*c* parallels the use of masc and fem for Egypt in v 12.

15.a-a. LXX translates freely ἀρχὴν καὶ τέλος "beginning and end."

16.a. LXX οἱ Αἰγύπτιοι "the Egyptians" pl has caught the evident sense. The Heb uses a collective sense and a sg verb.

16.b. DSS[Isa] has pl forms for MT's sg.

16.c. DSS[Isa] adds ידו "his hand." But MT's meaning is clear as it is.

17.a. The expansive prose style raises questions of relation to v 16. והיתה "and it (fem) will be" has "the soil of Judah" for its subject and this is not a continuation of the verbs "tremble" and "be in dread." It is better understood as an expansion of the controlling clause "Egypt becomes like the women." Judah's festival is another comparison.

17.b. חָגָּא is a *hapax.* LXX φόβητρον "a terrifying object." Vg *erit in festivitatem* "will be in festival mood" has read it as חגג "to celebrate a festival." The more usual meaning follows LXX. G. R. Driver (*JTS* 34 [1933] 378) is followed by KB with the meaning "shamed," but (in *JSS* 13 [1968] 46) he added "to be struck" as a possible meaning. We follow Vg, *BDB*, 290. See *Comment.*

17.c. כל אשר: Wildberger (728) translates "everytime when" and suggests different subjects for the two verbs. The time reference is not impossible, referring to the festival. But the common subject for both verbs is surely present. Both refer to the celebrant of the festival.

17.d. אֹתָהּ may be the sign of direct object with the third fem sg pronoun "her." But את may also be read as the "defective" form of אות "a sign" BDB, 16. It appears thus frequently (cf. Exod 4:8, etc.) and is regularly written without ו in pl and with suffixes, and, hence, "her sign." As such it is a strong reminder of the festival of Yahweh's "signs and wonders," Passover.

Form/Structure/Setting

The chapter consists of a vision of Yahweh's intervention in Egypt (vv 1–15) that reverses his stance in 18:4 and foresees the fine results which could develop from that move (vv 16–25).

The vision portrays: (1) Yahweh's approach and Egyptian dismay (v 1); (2) Yahweh's speech (2–4) announcing internal conflict and deliverance to a fierce king, the Ethiopian Sabaka; (3) a drought that brings economic disaster (vv 5–10); (4) a taunt against the counselors of Pharaoh (vv 11–15).

The results are pictured with five "in that day" announcements: (1) Judah will terrorize the Egyptians (16–17); (2) five cities will speak a Canaanite language (18); (3) an altar to Yahweh will be set up in Egypt; Egyptians will worship Yahweh and he will respond to them (19–22); (4) a highway between Egypt and Assyria; they will cooperate even in worship (23); (5) Israel, Egypt, and Assyria under Yahweh's rule (24–25).

Vv 5–10 pick up the theme of Yahweh's control of weather and nature, including planting and harvest, which appeared in 17:4–6 about Israel, in 17:10–11 about Jerusalem, and in 18:4–6 about impending developments.

References to Yahweh's "plan" or "strategy" appear in 19:12 and 17. This theme which figured prominently in Yahweh's bringing of the Assyrian (chaps. 7–10) is now invoked in relation to the rise of the Ethiopian (twenty-fifth) dynasty in Egypt. It was suggested in 17:7–8 that the time was ripe for mankind to turn to the worship of Yahweh after the judgment on Aram and Israel. Egyptian and Assyrian participation in such worship with Israel is portrayed in 19:18–25.

In 17:10–11 Jerusalem is accused of "forgetting God" and of pagan practices. Chap. 20 will show that the governmental policies of Jerusalem have heeded neither the burden of Damascus nor that of Egypt. It marches to the rhythm of a different drummer, Merodach-Baladan's Babylon (chap. 21), which will lead to its downfall (chap. 22).

Vv 1–4 are a threat introduced by הנה "see." Calling attention to God's own action in such a form is typical for Isaiah (cf. 3:1; 8:7; 10:33; 22:17; 24:1; 26:21; 30:27; 35:4; 40:9, 10; 51:22; 54:11; 60:2; 62:11). In chap. 3 the introduction leads to Yahweh's own speech in v 4. It is the same here in chap. 19. Yahweh's speech begins in v 2. Wildberger (708) notes the parallel between the chapters. In chap. 3 God turns Judah over to its own self-destruction. The same thing occurs in chap. 19 where Egypt is victimized by its own paranoia and by indecisive leaders. It is usual in Isaiah to close such a threat with the formula "expression of the Lord Yahweh of Hosts."

In vv 11–15 the passage begins like a speech of judgment (see Wildberger, 717) but is quickly changed by the recognition (vv 14–15) that Yahweh is responsible.

Comment

1 The burden of Egypt stands as a counter-weight to that of Damascus. Both call attention (*see*) to developments. Damascus and Israel stood desolate as monuments to Yahweh's completed judgment, which Jerusalem chose to ignore (17:10–11). Now Egyptian developments are seen as Yahweh's work, suggesting new opportunity, if Judah will only see it and act upon it.

The figure of Yahweh *riding on a cloud* fits the background of OT celestial imagery which was taken over from Canaanite pictures of Baal, the weather god (cf. Wildberger's summary, 710). Yahweh is pictured as riding the heavens (Deut 33:26), the cherubim and the wings of the wind (2 Sam 22:11/Ps 18:11), and riding the skies (Pss 68:5 [4]; 104:3). His freedom of movement, universal scope of action, as well as his control of nature, are recalled. No wonder the idols and Egyptians tremble.

Heart melts: cf. 7:2, where similar language speaks of Judah's lack of moral strength before Aram and Syria and urges the king not to weaken in his resolve. The words and ideas come from the formal language of Holy War (cf. Deut 20:3). They imply that collapse of morale ensures victory.

2 *I will incite Egypt against Egypt* (cf. Judg 7:22; 2 Kgs 3:23; Isa 3:5; Zech 14:13; Ezek 38:21; 1 Sam 14:20), *city against city, kingdom against kingdom* are apt descriptions of the situation in Egypt of the twenty-fifth Dynasty. Breasted (*History of Egypt* [New York: Scribner's, 1905], 536) wrote "The power of the dominant house rapidly waned until there was at last an independent lord or petty king in every city of the Delta and up the river as far as Hermopolis. We are acquainted with the names of eighteen of these dynasties, whose struggles among themselves now led to the total dissolution of the Egyptian state."

3 Internal chaos leads to Egypt's impotence as it had to Judah's (cf. chap. 3). God turns them over to a strong tyrant ruler from outside the realm. For Judah this was Assyria (7:17). For Egypt it is Ethiopia's new ruler, Shabaka. Their panic leads them to useless necromancy (cf. 8:19–22).

4 Wildberger (712) notes a return to the language of Holy War. The usual term is נתן ביד "put into the hand of" (cf. von Rad, *Der Heilige Krieg im Alten Israel,* ATANT 20, 3rd ed. [Zürich: Zwingli Verlag, 1958] 7). The phrase here is stronger: סכר ביד "shut up in the hand of."

The identity of the *cruel masters* and *powerful king* has been debated. Bright (*HI,* 281) suggests the Ethiopian Pianchi who took over upper Egypt in 730 B.C. Kitchen (*The Third Intermediate Period,* 125) suggests that it is Shabaka who first established the authority of the Ethiopian dynasty over the cities of the Delta in 716–12 B.C. This suggestion fits the polarity of Egypt–Ethiopia in chaps. 18–19 and the basic time frame of this section of Isaiah. Shabaka clearly fits the context best as Procksch and Eichrodt have agreed. There has been no lack of other suggestions, depending on the particular fragmentation of the book which the commentator preferred. Wildberger favors Sargon since, in his opinion, this refers to a foreign domination. And Ethiopia is not foreign enough. If one breaks away from the contextual setting, almost any king that ever conquered Egypt will do. And there have been many.

5–10 The failure of the Nile to provide sufficient water is the ultimate nightmare for an Egyptian. "The Prophecy of Nefer-Rohu" (sometimes called Nefertiti) pictures such a scene (*ANET,* 445): "The rivers of Egypt are empty, (so that) the water is crossed on foot. Men seek for water for the ships to sail on. Its course is (become) a sandbank. . . . [D]amaged indeed are those good things, those fish ponds (where there were) those who clean fish, overflowing with fish and fowl." The text is much earlier than Isaiah's time, but illustrates Egypt's dependence on the Nile's rise and fall.

The Egyptians believed the Nile's timely rise and fall was a gift of the gods (see Wildberger, 714). Herodotus (II, 9) could not explain the regular annual ebb and flow of the Nile. Of course, it is now known that the winter rains over central African plateaus which drain through the Nile and the summer rains over the Ethiopian highlands which drain through from the Blue Nile together account for the phenomena (cf. A. Moret, *The Nile and Egyptian Civilization,* tr. M. R. Dobie [New York: A. A. Knopf, 1927]; W. S. LaSor, "Egypt," *ISBE,* II, 31).

The drought affects farmers, fishermen, and the secondary enterprises that depend upon them, in this case the textile workers. The speech is a remarkable description of economic distress that follows the failure of the annual Nile floods. The context draws upon the picture of Yahweh's reign over the weather and over nature (19:1) to account for the conditions. Egypt's troubles are cumulative and interrelated. The external political pressures (19:4) combine with internal ones (19:2–3) and natural economic disasters (19:5–10) to bring Egypt to its knees.

11–15 The passage begins like an accusation. The speech asks the counselors of the court to defend themselves (v 11). When they are silent, the speech turns to the Egyptians with the challenge that they make the wise men talk (v 12). It closes by recognizing that Yahweh has caused the counsel of the wise to err (vv 14–15).

11 *Zoan* is usually identified as Tanis, the Egyptian delta city nearest Palestine. The *counsel* that is required is political advice. The wise men of Egypt claimed a direct descent from the most ancient kings, who were also the most wise.

12 But the content of wisdom according to this speech lies in knowing *what Yahweh of Hosts has planned against Egypt.* This the wise men never claimed to know. But the message, actually addressed to Jerusalem and its leaders rather than Egyptians, insists that this is the only basis for true wisdom and political counsel. Chaps. 18–19 are intended to elucidate exactly this *plan* for that period.

13 *Noph* is Memphis (or On or Heliopolis), at the head of the Delta, which often served as Egypt's northern capital. Pianchi conquered Memphis in 728 B.C. But then he withdrew to Napata. It remained for his brother Shabaka to control it effectively from 715 B.C. onward. *The chiefs of her tribes* emphasizes the splintered nature of Egypt in this time—a far cry from the proud and powerful unity of other days.

Kitchen's descriptions (*The Third Intermediate Period,* 348–77) of the twenty-second, twenty-third, twenty-fourth, and twenty-fifth dynasties shows that in 715 B.C. there were four pharaohs in Egypt claiming the throne. (See chart in Wildberger, 720–21.) Osorkon IV ruled in Tanis (the eastern delta), the last of the Bubastide or twenty-second Dynasty. Shoshenk VI was presumably in Leontopolis (the central delta), the last of the twenty-third Dynasty. Bokchoris ruled in Sais (the western delta) as the last of the twenty-fourth Dynasty. Breasted writes of knowing the names of at least eighteen kings or princes who ruled delta cities in that time (*History of Egypt* [New York: Scribner's, 1905], 536). Shabaka was just assuming the throne in Napata (upper Nile). He would take control of Egypt within the year.

14–15 Egypt (the delta kings) seems to have no discernible policy to meet the Assyrian threat and seems to be blind to the rising power of Ethiopia. The Vision suggests that even "the folly of man may serve the purposes of God" (Clements, 169). God has waited for things to develop ("for the harvest to ripen": 17:5). Now he moves toward his goals. Kitchen (*The Third Intermediate Period,* 333, n 75) believes chap. 19 belongs in this period (716 B.C.) just before Shabaka has assumed control.

16–17 Against the divided princedoms even Judah's force was a threat. But this is only true as Yahweh acts through Judah. And that depends on Judah's cooperation with God's plan, i.e., being willing to work with Assyria and Ethiopia (19:2). *In such a day* (lit., "in that day") points back to 19:1 when Yahweh rides the clouds in Egypt, the day when his plan matures (18:4–6). The general comparison to women *trembling* is unique in the OT. Often a woman in childbirth is so pictured.

תנופת יד "The waving hand" recalls the cultic waving of sacrifices "before Yahweh" to dedicate them to him (cf. Exod 29:24). (See R. J. Thompson, *Penitence and Sacrifice in Early Israel Outside the Levitical Law* [Leiden: E. J. Brill, 1963], 206, n 4.)Wildberger (732) interprets this to mean that he brings judgment, but also that he claims the land as his own. The waving hand also is a reminder of the plagues against Egypt and of the open way through the Sea of Reeds. The verses picture Egypt's dread when they recognize that Yahweh is directing the battle ("waving his hand"; cf. 5:25; 9:12, 17, 21; 10:4) against them. *The women* are not identified. They seem to be civilian nonparticipants who can only tremble at the thought of the developing battle.

אדמת יהודה "the soil of Judah" is unique. It calls to mind the promised land inherited by Yahweh's chosen people. Some would translate חגא as "shamed" or "be struck" (see *Notes*). The Vg directs its thought to חג "festival," which fits the context, parallel to "remember" or "makes mention" in the next line. The festival must be Passover. The thought that the event celebrated in Passover might repeat itself in Yahweh's plan was awful to Egypt. One remembers the plagues on Egypt (Exod 7–10), especially the death of the first-born (chaps. 11–12).

The reason for fear was the recognition of God's plan. The cognate reduplication (*planning* and *a plan*) also occurs in 14:26 and 8:10. It suggests that the *plan* of Yahweh will be fulfilled by events in Egypt. The idea that plans proclaimed long ago may be signs of God's later work is found in 40:21; 41:26; 44:8. The news that Yahweh, of Passover fame, has plans for Egypt is reason enough for fear.

It is worth passing notice that Randles in commenting on v 17 writes: "Manasseh of Judah . . . was compelled to participate in the invasion of Egypt led by Ashurbanipal in 667 B.C." (*The Interaction of Israel, Judah and Egypt,* 232; cf. *ANET,* 294).

Explanation

See under 19:18–25.

Episode E: Worship of Yahweh in Egypt (19:18–25)

Bibliography

Abel, F. M. "Les confins de la Palestine et de l'Egypte." *RB* 49 (1940) 224–39. **Beek, M. A.** "Relations entre Jerusalem et la diaspora egyptienne au 2e siecle avant J.-C." *OTS* 2 (1943) 119–43. **Causse, A.** "Les origines de la diaspora juive." *RHPR* 7 (1927) 97–128. **Feuillet, A.** "Un sommet religieux de l'Ancien Testament. L'oracle d'Isa 19:19–25 sur la conversion de l' Egypte." *RSR* 39 (1951) 65–87. **Harmatta, J.** "Zur Geschichte des frühhellenistischen Judentums in Ägypten." *Acta Antiqua Academiae Scientiarum Hungaricae* 7 (1959) 337–409. **Hengel, M.** *Judaism and Hellenism.* Tr. J. Bowden. London: SCM Press, 1974. **Jirku, A.** "Die fünf Städte bei Jes 19:18 und die fünf Tore des Jahu-Tempels zu Elephantine." *OLZ* 15 (1912) 247–48. **Schürer, E.** *Geschichte des jüdischen Volkes* III. Leipzig: J. C. Heinrichs, 1909. **Steuernagel, C.** "Bemerkungen über die neuentdeckten jüdischen Papyrusurkunden aus Elephantine und ihre Bedeutung für das Alte Testament." *TSK* 22 (1909) 1–12. **Vogels, W.** "Egypte mon Peuple: L'Universalisme d'Isa 19:16–25." *Bib* 57 (1976) 494–515. **Wilson, I.** "In that day. From text to sermon on Isaiah 19:23–25." *Int* 22 (1967) 66–86.

Translation

Earth: 18 *In such a day, there would be* 3+3
five cities in the land of Egypt
speaking the language of Canaan 3+3
and swearing[a] *(allegiance) to Yahweh of Hosts.*
One would be called the city of destruction.[b] 4
Heavens: 19 *In such a day, there would be* 3+2+3
an altar to Yahweh
in the middle of the land of Egypt
and a pillar dedicated to Yahweh at its border 4
20 *which would become a sign, a witness*[a] *to Yahweh of*
Hosts in the land of Egypt. When they cry out to
Yahweh in the face of oppressors, he will send[b] *a savior*
and judge[c] *who will deliver them.*
21 *And Yahweh will make himself known to Egypt* 3+3+2
and Egypt will know Yahweh
in such a day.
They will worship (him with) sacrifices and offerings. 3+3+1
They will vow a vow to Yahweh.
And they will fulfill (it).
22 *And (if) Yahweh strike Egypt with a plague* 3+2
striking and healing,[a]
(if) they turn to Yahweh 2+3
he will respond to them and heal them.
Earth: 23 *In such a day there would be* 3+3
a highway from Egypt to Assyria.

Assyria would come to Egypt. 3+2
And Egypt to Assyria.
And they would worship,[a] *Egypt with Assyria.* 3
Heavens: 24 *In such a day* 3+2+2
Israel would be third
to Egypt[a] *and Assyria*[a]*:*
a blessing in the midst of the land, 3
25 *with which Yahweh of Hosts is blessing them,* 5
"Blessed[a] *(be) my people, Egypt,*[b] 3+3+2
the work of my hands, Assyria,
and my inheritance, Israel."

Notes

18.a. Wildberger notes that "to swear by" someone in Heb. is נשבע ב. Syr does read *wjmjn bmrjh.* However, the reading with ל appears in 45:23 and 2 Chr 15:14 with the meaning "to enter a relationship by an oath" BDB, 989 (cf. also Josh 6:22; 9:20).

18.b. הֶהֶרֶס a *hapax* appears to be intended to mean "destruction": City of Destruction. DSS[Isa], supported by many MSS, and several versions have החרס "the Sun," Vg *civitas Solis.* LXX πόλις ασεδεκ "city of righteousness" (cf. 1:26). 'A and Θ simply transcribe it as αρες, confirming MT. Syr also confirms MT. Tg combines the two meanings קרתא בית שמש דעתידא למחרב "the city Beth-Shemesh (House of the Sun), which is to be destroyed because of that." Wildberger traces the translation on to Jerome who identifies this with Heliopolis. The consensus of interpreters is that it does refer to Heliopolis in Egypt which is often called און or אן in the OT but which in Jer 43:13 is called Beth Shemesh.

20.a. לְעֵד "a testimony." LXX εἰς τὸν αἰῶνα = לָעַד reading the same consonants, but pronouncing them differently.

20.b. DSS[Isa] has ושלח for MT's וישלח "he will send." It is a change of tense only.

20.c. וָרָב "and ruler." *Kametz* under *waw* is apparently to strengthen pronunciation (GKC § 104*g*). DSS[Isa] וירד impf "and he will rule." LXX reads a ptcp κρίνων "judge." Vg *propugnatorem* "defender." *BHS* וְרָב changes it to pf with וְ "and he will rule" (also Kissane, Feldmann, Wildberger). The question is whether it will pair with "savior" before it with MT or with "and he will deliver" after it. There seems to be no reason to abandon MT's reading.

22.a. Two inf absolutes. Cf. Joüon § 123*m.* The second action grows out of the first.

23.a. עבד in v 21 had a cultic meaning "to serve," "worship." LXX translates δουλεύσουσιν giving it a political meaning: Egypt will serve Assyria. If it has the cultic meaning one must translate "Egyptians will worship with Assyria(ns)." Cf. Gray and Wildberger. The issue is not easy. The verb ועבדו is pl. Egypt and Assyria are sg, joined not by "and" but by אֶת־ "with" or a sign of direct object. "Worship" certainly fits the context best, but "serve," "be a vassal" fits the historical situation more realistically. The context calls for a cultic meaning (cf. Wildberger, 744).

24.a,a. LXX reverses the order.

25.a. LXX ἣν εὐλόγησε 3 sg aorist "which (fem) he praises," i.e., a verb. *BHS* suggests reading בֵּרְכָהּ, a fem suffix, because the antecedent must refer to "blessing" or "land," both of which are fem. This is not reflected in translation because the personal pronoun is absorbed in the English relative pronoun (cf. G. Wehmeier, *Der Segen im Alten Testament* [Basel: Reinhardt, 1970], 87).

25.b. LXX ὁ λαός μου ὁ ἐν Αἰγύπτῳ "my people who are in Egypt" loses the force of the concluding statement.

Form/Structure/Setting

See under 19:1–17.

Comment

18 *Speaking the language of Canaan* means Hebrew, or possibly Aramaic. *Swearing allegiance to Yahweh of Hosts* apparently means that a ruling majority of Jews or proselytes existed.

Five cities. Jer 44:1 knows of four cities in Egypt where Jews are living some 130 years later: Migdol (apparently near the Palestinian border), Tahpanhes (probably also near the border), the land of Pathos, and Noph (Memphis). One is to be called *city of destruction* (see *Notes*). Nothing further is known of such cities.

Jews were in Egypt from early times, probably from Solomon's time on (cf. 1 Kgs 14:25–28 and 2 Chr 12:1–9 which may imply taking prisoners). Lists of Jews/Israelites to be returned to Israel regularly mention Egypt (cf. 11:11 "lower Egypt, upper Egypt, and Cush"; Obad 20 "Sepharad" is probably located in Libya: see J. D. W. Watts, *Obadiah;* and J. Gray, "The Diaspora of Israel and Judah in Obadiah v 20," *ZAW* 65 [1953] 53–59).

The letters found in Elephantine (modern Aswan) witness to a strong Jewish community of mercenaries (A. E. Cowley, *Aramaic Papyri of the Fifth Century BC* [Oxford: Clarendon, 1932]; *ANET,* 222; *DOTT,* 256–69; R. K. Harrison, "Elephantine Papyri," *ISBE,* II, 58–61). They also testify to the presence of Aramaic in Egypt in the fifth century B.C. It is clear that readers of the Vision would find familiar data in such a reference to the five cities. They would be told that Yahweh planned this as early as the reign of Hezekiah.

19–22 *An altar to Yahweh.* The usual movement in God's future is directed toward a return to Palestine or Jerusalem (10:21; 11:11–16; 14:1–2, etc). But here in chap. 19 the movement is away toward Egypt. The political influence movement from Judah to Egypt (vv 16–17), the cultural influence through language (v 18), and now the religious effect of submission to Yahweh are unmistakable. This is the most positive interpretation of the outward flow of population from Israel in the OT (comparable only to the NT's commissions in Matt 28:19–20 and Acts 1:8).

Note the alliteration in מִזְבֵּחַ *mizbe^a^h* "altar" and מַצֵּבָה *maṣṣebah* "pillar." An altar implies sacrifice and a priesthood (perhaps, though not necessarily, even a temple). It is a public symbol. A pillar or *maṣṣebah* is a usual sign beside a "high place" in Canaan. Both are to be clearly dedicated *to Yahweh.* This is the point: the worship of Yahweh in Egypt will be open and official. They are both to be a *sign* and a *witness* to Yahweh in Egypt (v 20). Yahweh will reveal himself to Egypt and Egypt will *know Yahweh* (v 21). A more complete statement of the full mutual relation of Yahweh and Egypt cannot be imagined. That relation includes answered prayers (vv 20–22) and a whole range of worship (v 21). Yahweh will do saving acts for them. He will send a savior in times of oppression, as he did for Israel in the judges (v 20). He will respond to repentance and prayers in times of distress (v 22).

Most comment on these verses has sought a historical correspondence (see *Excursus* below). But that misses the point. Historical fulfillment here, like historical fulfillment in each of the five "in that day" passages, *did not occur.* The political decisions taken by Jerusalem's government in the years between 716 and 714 B.C. prevented that (see chaps. 20–22). This Vision, like that of chaps. 11–12, shows God's view of the potential. The Vision puts God's view side by side with man's failure to see, hear, or understand and his determination to have his own way—even when that brought disaster.

The thought of an altar and a pillar to Yahweh in Egypt runs directly counter to the movement to concentrate worship, even in Palestine, to Jerusalem (or one place) only (cf. Deuteronomy). Hezekiah participated in such a reform (2 Kgs 18:4; 2 Chr 31:1) to which the Rabshakeh makes reference (2 Kgs 18:22/Isa 36:7). This culminated in Josiah's reform and destruction of high places throughout the land (2 Kgs 22:4–20; 2 Chr 34:33) almost a century later. Ezra brought the process of concentrating sacrifice and worship in Jerusalem exclusively to completion (Ezra-Nehemiah). Other tendencies did exist (see *Excursus* below), although Deut 7:5; 12:3 and Exod 23:24 and 34:13 prohibit the raising of a *maṣṣebah.*

Excursus: Jewish Colonies and Temples in Egypt

The outward flow of population from Israel probably existed from Solomon's time onward and Egypt was a prime recipient of such movement. Even earlier, Genesis reports movements in that direction by Abraham, Jacob, and Joseph. Jacob's descendants are reported to have lived there for four centuries. But there are no reports of altars or temples being built. Patriarchal worship did not require such, at least not in permanent form.

Solomon is reported to have had extensive commercial (1 Kgs 10:28–29) and diplomatic relations with Egypt (1 Kgs 3:1). These may well have called for exchange of personnel. Refugees from Solomon's kingdom were welcome in Egypt. Hadad of Edom (1 Kgs 11:18–22) and Jeroboam (1 Kgs 11:40) spent their years of exile there. Egypt campaigned against Judah and Israel in Rehoboam's day (1 Kgs 14:25–28; 2 Chr 12:2–12; see *MBA,* 120) and in Asa's time (2 Chr 14:8–14; 16:8; see *MBA,* 122). Such campaigns usually took prisoners for slaves or mercenaries.

At the other end of the kingdom period, Jeremiah records a significant number of Judeans who fled to Egypt (Jer 42–45; 2 Kgs 25:26; see *MBA,* 164). Evidence of a strong community of Jewish mercenaries in Aswan (Elephantine) is provided through the discovery of papyri there from the fifth century B.C. (cf. R. K. Harrison, "Elephantine Papyri," *ISBE,* II, 59–61; *ANET,* 222, 491). It contained a temple, cultus, and a priesthood.

J. Harmatta (*AAASH* 7 [1959] 337–409) names ten places between Migdol and Syene where Jews settled. The names of two priests are mentioned, one of whom lived at Thmuis. In the Hellenistic period Jewish settlements are known in many locations in Egypt (see *MBA,* 182). Josephus (*Wars of the Jews,* III, 10[2]) tells of a temple at Leontopolis built by Onias, a deposed High Priest (cf. Wildberger, 737–39, for a detailed presentation). Alexander used Jewish mercenaries (Josephus, *Contra Apionem,* I, 192). Ptolemy I brought 100,000 Jews to Egypt to colonize military settlements (*The Letter of Aristeas,* 12–14). M. Hengel (*Judaism and Hellenism,* 27) suggests that Ptolemy is continuing a policy which the Persians and even the last Pharaohs of the twenty-sixth Dynasty had practiced.

There were Israelites and Jews in Egypt from early times onward. But that should not obscure the fact that Isa 19 is not speaking of Jews, but of Egyptians who worship Yahweh. Statistics on Egyptian proselytes are much more difficult to document.

23 *A highway from Egypt to Assyria.* Roads serve many purposes. They bear the traffic of trade. Soldiers and chariots march on them and send their caravans of supply on them. Pilgrims use them (cf. 11:16; 40:3; 62:10). International routes that connected Mesopotamia and Egypt already existed (*MBA*, 9). Various kinds of roads existed, from trodden paths that could accommodate caravans of camels from Abraham's time to built-up roads to handle chariots from Solomon's time (cf. I. Mendelsohn, "Travel, etc., in the OT," *IDB* 4:688–90).

What is meant here goes beyond the physical existence of a road. It speaks of its various uses and functions. Communication of all kinds will be made possible. That included trade and political interaction. But the context here draws one to a cultic meaning for עבד "serve" and to the meaning "with" for אֵת. The highway facilitates a common worship. An illustration of this in modern terms is seen in common participation in worship by representatives from Muslim countries during diplomatic negotiations. Cf. 18:7 where Assyria (a people tall and fierce) sends gifts to Yahweh in Jerusalem, implying recognition of Yahweh, to say the least. However, one misses the concrete ליהוה "to Yahweh" that was emphasized in vv 19–20.

A political interpretation would translate "the Egyptians will serve (i.e., be vassals of) Assyria." This would imply that Egypt bows to the Assyrian hegemony which Yahweh sponsors (according to 10:5–7). It would fit the announcement in 19:4 if the "fierce king" is Sargon. However, it was shown above that this must refer to Ethiopia and Shabaka. The Egypt mentioned here is that of the twenty-fifth Dynasty under Shabaka who maintained a formal and generally peaceful understanding with Sargon's Assyria.

24 This verse is the climax of the scene. Israel stands with Egypt and Assyria as a means of blessing in the midst of the earth. The highway runs through Palestine. Worship has its highest expression in Jerusalem.

Blessing in the land is a reminder of Gen 12:3 (G. Wehmeier, *Der Segen im AT* [Basel: Reinhardt, 1970], 87). Abraham's call promises that he and his descendants will be a blessing and that those who bless him (and his descendants) will be blessed. Worship of Yahweh by Assyria and Egypt implies that they "bless themselves" by the God of Abraham. He owns the entire world and is worshiped accordingly in Jerusalem's temple.

25 Yahweh's blessing uses phrases usually reserved for Israel. *Egypt—my people.* If Egypt recognizes Yahweh as "its God," then they are his people (Wildberger, 795). This is the corollary of v 21 above (cf. Ps 47:9–10 [8–9], where reference is made to "the people of the God of Abraham"). *My people* has strong covenant meaning in the OT where Israel is understood to receive and maintain that relation to God through covenant. The vowing of vows to Yahweh (v 11) may have a similar connotation. But the theme is not developed. The LXX translation (see *Note*) "My people who are in Egypt and Assyria" limits the application to Jews there. Wildberger (745) notes that MT is nearer to the thought of Isa 40–66 than to Hellenistic Judaism.

Assyria—the work of my hands. In 64:8 the claim is made that Israel is "God's people" and "the work of his hand." Israel is seen as God's creation in 43:1, 15 בָּרָא "creating"; 44:2 עֹשֶׂה "making"; 44:2, 24 and 45:11 יֹצֵר "forming." Other references are found in Deut 32:6; Isa 41:20; Ps 100:3. Yahweh has also created the peoples of the earth (Ps 86:9). His relation to Assyria is already clear from his commands to her (7:17, 18, 20) and the term "rod of my anger" (10:5). Assyria as a world power in Palestine is a creature of Yahweh's plan, according to this passage. But this verse goes beyond that to assure Assyria of Yahweh's blessing and to claim Assyria as a means of blessing (a la Abraham) to others.

Israel—my inheritance. Deut 32:9 reads "Yahweh's portion is his people: Jacob his alloted inheritance" (Deut 4:20; Ps 28:9; 47:5; 94:5; Mic 7:14). Some commentators (Duhm, most recently Fohrer) suggest that Israel's title is the highest and best. It is certainly not less than the others. But that is to miss the significance of the passage. All three titles traditionally belong to Israel. Here they are shared with Assyria and Egypt. Yahweh's divine *imperium* is seen to draw within its scope and purpose the entire known world.

Explanation

Chap. 19 pictures the latent possibilities in the moves described in chaps. 15–18, as God would see them. The chapter paints a "scenario," a visionary image. The time is 716–15 B.C. Shabaka has just ascended the throne of his brother in Ethiopian upper Egypt (Nubia, i.e., modern Sudan). He is preparing to assert his rule over lower Egypt as well. To that end he seeks allies in Assyria and Judah (18:2). Yahweh gives tacit approval and apparently Assyria is willing.

In 18:5 the pruning of the shoots before the harvest is mentioned. What Yahweh announces in 19:2–11 is exactly that. Egypt (the delta or lower Egypt) is condemned (a "burden"). Yahweh himself assures the outcome of the internal struggle by instigating civil wars among the city-rulers of the delta (vv 2–4) and by causing drought in the land (vv 5–10) which brings economic ruin. The leaders are confused and helpless (vv 11–15).

Five passages beginning with "in such a day" portray the potential results. The Egyptians will be terrified at what Yahweh is doing (vv 16–17). Hebrew presence and influence (including religious influence) will be felt in five cities (v 18). Worship of Yahweh will be practiced in Egypt and recognized by Yahweh (vv 19–22). Cooperation between Egypt and Assyria will open routes to peace, trade, and pilgrimage (v 23; cf. 18:7). Israel will have an important place beside Assyria and Egypt and will account for Yahweh's blessings for the whole land. Yahweh will claim and bless each of the troika: Egypt, Assyria, and Israel (vv 23–25). This is one of the most universal statements of Yahweh's intentions to be found in Scripture. It builds on Isaiah's view of Assyria as Yahweh's tool (chap. 10) and points toward the picture of Cyrus as Yahweh's servant (chaps. 45–46).

The chapter speaks of God's will. The language of the Vision is "God's plan" or "God's strategy." Suppose, at any juncture in time, God were to make the world do exactly what he wanted it to do. What would happen? (Short years ago Camp David accords opened communications between Egypt and Israel for the first time in three decades. If God had people in the Middle East in our time do exactly as he wants them to, what would happen?)

Isa 18–19 asks and answers just such a question. Sargon is hard at work about 716 B.C. to consolidate a fractured empire. Judah has a new king. Egypt nears the end of a period of chaos as a strong new Pharaoh is crowned in the Ethiopian capital, Napata.

Shabaka seeks aid, or at least neutrality, on Egypt's northern border while he subjugates the errant cities of the delta (18:1–2). His messengers are referred by Jerusalem to Assyria, which holds genuine authority in the region. Yahweh awaits developments (18:4a), but is understood to be prepared to act before the harvest (4b–6).

The Vision dramatically portrays two basic developments. Gifts are brought to Yahweh in Mount Zion by the Assyrians (18:7). This shows their agreement and commitment to his plan. Then Yahweh, himself, moves against the Egyptians of the delta to put them under the suzerainty of a cruel, powerful king, Shabaka of the Ethiopian twenty-fifth Dynasty, in 716 B.C. (19:1–15).

Such developments would pave the way for five specific results of God's plan: (1) Judah's prestige and influence over Egypt increases dramatically (vv 16–17); (2) five cities in Egypt speak a Canaanite tongue and swear by Yahweh (v 18); (3) an altar to Yahweh is established in Egypt and a memorial monument to him set up on its border; he is worshiped and he will respond to the worshipers (vv 19–22); (4) a highway is completed from Egypt to Assyria (of course, by way of Judah) which will serve commerce and mutual worship of Yahweh (v 23); (5) Israel, Egypt, and Assyria are proclaimed a triad of blessing under Yahweh (vv 24–25).

Can one imagine? Modern Egypt, Israel, and Syria-Iraq becoming a triad of blessing and peace today? Open borders, flowing commerce, mutual worship? Even the possibility that Muslim, Christian, and Jew would worship together in Jerusalem? The dream has too many hindrances for it to become reality for our day. It seems that this was also true in 716 B.C., as chaps. 20–22 testify.

But God's dreams! Worth thinking about!

Episode F: Isaiah Demonstrates against an Alliance with Egypt (20:1–6)

Bibliography

Beck, B. L. *The International Roles of the Philistines During the Biblical Period.* Diss., Southern Baptist Theological Seminary, 1980. 151–53. **Bright, J.** *HI,* 281–80. **Brunet, G.** *Essai.* 145–53. **Gottwald, N.** *All the Kingdoms of the Earth.* 167–68. **Tadmor, H.** "Philistia under Assyrian Rule." *BA* 24 (1966) 86–102. **Spalinger, A.** "The Year 712 B.C. and its Implications for Egyptian History." *Journal of the American Research Center in Egypt* 10 (1973) 95–101.

Translation

Narrator: (reading from a scroll) [1] *In the year that the Tartan* [a] *came to Ashdod, when Sargon* [b] *King of Assyria sent him, he fought against Ashdod and took* [c] *it.* [2] *In that period, Yahweh spoke*

through [a] *Isaiah,* [b] *son of Amoz: "Go and take off*
the sackcloth from your body and your sandals [c] *from*
your feet." He proceeded to do so, walking stripped
and barefoot.

3 *Then Yahweh said:*
"Just as my servant has walked 4+2
stripped and barefoot, [a]
three years, 2+2+2
a sign and a portent
against Egypt and against Ethiopia,
4 *so the king of Assyria will drive away* 4
the captivity of Egypt 2+2
and the exiled group [a] *of Ethiopia,*
youths and elderly 2+2
naked and barefoot
with stripped buttocks [b] 2+2
and the nakedness of Egypt."

Heavens: 5 *They will be dismayed and ashamed* 2+2+2
of Ethiopia, their hope, [a]
and of Egypt, their boast.

Earth: 6 *The inhabitants of this coast will say* 4+2
[a]*in that day*[a]*:*
"See! Thus (it has happened to) our hope 3+3
whither we had fled [b] *for help,*
for deliverance [c] *from before the king of Assyria.* 4
How shall we ourselves escape?" 3

Notes

1.a. תרתן "tartan" is an Akk title for the military leader, the king, or crown-prince. Cf. 2 Kgs 18:17. For the Akk meanings, see Wildberger, 748. DSS[Isa] תורתן "turtan." (Cf. D. M. Beegle, "Proper Names in the Isaiah Scroll," *BASOR* 123 [1951] 28).

1.b. The exact pronounciation varies: MT סַ֫רְגוֹן "Saregon." 'A Θ *σαραγων*. B סַרְגוֹן "Sargon." Σ *σαργων* (also LXX[Q]), LXX *αρνα* or *σαρνα* (Ziegler reads *Σαρναν*). Chrysostom quotes 'A Σ as *σαργουν*. Akk *šarru-kīnu* means "the king is steadfast" or later *šarru-ukīn* "he (a god) has elected the king" (cf. P-W 1 A, 2 Col 2498).

1.c. DSS[Isa] וילכודה indicates an older pronunciation. The form is undoubtedly the same.

2.a. LXX *πρὸς* "by" for MT ביד "by the hand of."

2.b. DSS[Isa] ישעיה "Isaiah" (like v 3) instead of MT ישעיהו "Isaiahu." Syr adds *nbjʾ* "the prophet."

2.c. DSS[Isa] and the Versions are pl. The same variation in sg and pl for sandals occurs in Exod 3:5 and Josh 5:15.

3.a. *BHS* moves the *athnaḥ* forward two words. It judges that this is the logical center of the verse. MT has chosen the metrical center.

4.a. DSS[Isa] גולת for MT גלות. Meaning is the same.

4.b. חֲשׂוּפַי is an unusual form. Many emendations and explanations have been proposed. *BHS* (with Gray and Wildberger) is most likely with חֲשׂוּפֵי, "bare of," a constr pl.

5.a. DSS[Isa] מבטחם "their trust" from בטח for MT מבטם (BDB, 613) from נבט "their hope," "expectation" (cf. v 6 and Zech 9:5).

6.a-a. LXX omits "in that day."

6.b. MT נסנו from נוס. Wildberger "we fled." DSS[Isa] נסמך "on whom one reckoned," niph from סמך which is usually followed by על "upon."

6.c. MT has heavy accents (*zaqeph-katon*) on successive words: a very unusual accentuation.

Form/Structure/Setting

The chapter is a sober narrative. The opening phrase sets the historical frame (v 1). The second verse narrates a command for a symbolic act by his prophet, Isaiah. Vv 3–6 are a Yahweh word with its echo explaining the symbolic action.

7:1–17 are of the same genre: narrative related to an historical incident. However, the narrower classification of recognizable symbolic action occurs only here, unless Isaiah's withdrawal with his children in chap. 8 should be so classified.

On symbolic actions see G. Fohrer, "Die Gattung der Bericht über symbolische Handlungen der Propheten," *ZAW* 64 (1952) 101–20; and *Die Symbolischen Handlungen der Propheten,* ATANT 25 (Zürich: Zwingli-Verlag, 1953).

Comment

1 *The year* is apparently 712 or 711 B.C. Sargon has not been active in Palestine since one year after Samaria's destruction, 721 B.C., when a residual rebellion of Israelites and Philistines was put down. Assyrian texts report that Azuri, king of Ashdod, withheld tribute and tried to organize a coalition of states to rebel (*ANET,* 286/249–62). This could well have taken place over several years and may have included contacts with Hezekiah. This brought Sargon's forces back into the area.

The Assyrian military action was thorough. Ashdod and its allies, including Gath, were defeated. A new king, approved by the Assyrians, was soon deposed by a Greek, Iamani. The Assyrians intervened again, reorganized the government, and deported some of their people, bringing in others from the east. The same report mentions friendly notes from the king of Ethiopia.

Sargon's accounts claim personal credit for the victory. This account, probably more accurately, speaks of an officer sent to represent the king, i.e., the Tartan. Not since chap. 7 has the Vision presented an event with such precise dating. Sargon ruled from 722–705 B.C. He was a strong and effective king.

2 *In that period* broadens the time span of "in that year" in v 1 to make room for the "three years" of v 3. It is intentionally locating the following events in the period immediately before the invasion in 711 B.C.

The words from God order Isaiah to act out a prophetic sign, like Hosea's marriage (Hos 1–3) and Jeremiah's yoke (Jer 27). The literal translation "spoke by the hand of Isaiah" is most fitting. Yahweh's message is delivered by Isaiah's actions: taking off his clothes and sandals. *The sackcloth* is probably the basic undergarment worn by the men. The text reports that Isaiah obeyed.

3–4 A word from God interprets the sign which had now been acted out for some three years (i.e., 714–11 B.C.). It is a prediction that Assyria will conquer the peoples Egypt and Ethiopia, leading many of them captive back to Assyria along the highways of Palestine.

Political changes had occurred in Egypt during this period. Shabaka, the Ethiopian king, consolidated his hold on Egypt's delta. The scheming kings of the delta cities who conspired to keep the Palestinians in revolt against Assyria were gone. No effective help would be forthcoming from Egypt in that period.

4 There is no record of an Assyrian invasion of Egypt until the reign of Esarhaddon. In 671 B.C. he defeated Tirhakah, occupied Memphis, and installed Assyrian governors over local Egyptian princes. A second rebellion was crushed by Ashurbanipal in 667 B.C. with Manasseh's participation. On this occasion the rebel princes *were* marched to Nineveh, much in the way this verse pictures the march of captives.

5 *They* refers to Palestinian rebels who had counted on the new Ethiopian dynasty to continue the policies of the kings of the lower Egyptian cities. Shabaka apparently sought a diplomatic accommodation with Assyria to replace the confrontation that had existed (cf. 18:2 and Sargon's report of a message from the Ethiopian king). During this period a refugee ruler from Ashdod who sought political asylum in Egypt was extradited at Assyria's request. This policy effectively stripped Ashdod and Jerusalem of substantial support from that side in 712 B.C. During Shabaka's lifetime Egypt kept peace with Assyria. However, when his successor Shebtako came to the throne in 702 B.C., he promptly sent his brother Taharqa to aid Hezekiah against Assyria. He was decisively defeated at Eltekeh in 701 B.C. (K. A. Kitchen, *The Third Intermediate Period in Egypt,* 383–86). The policy of confrontation was again in force and it was only a matter of time before Assyria undertook a serious invasion of Egypt.

6 The chorus of the Philistines says it all. If the Egyptian might can be so stripped away, the might that had fed their own hopes and dreams, what hope do they have?

Explanation

The grim narrative of chap. 20 with its disturbing acted sign brings the beautiful vision back to stark reality. Jerusalem's leaders have agreed to join the so-called Ashdod rebellion of 714–12 B.C. This means that they have cast their lot with the delta kings of Egypt (twenty-second, twenty-third, and twenty-fourth dynasties) against Ethiopia and Assyria. The prophet's protest underscores a fact well-known to the readers of the Vision: this flies in the face of the expressed plan of Yahweh. The rebellion by the Philistine cities with Hezekiah's support prevented the prompt implementation of Shabaka's search for support on that northern border or, in a way, made it unnecessary.

Isaiah's sign is intended to counter what is perceived to be an actual or potential royal policy which depends on Egyptian support, that is from the delta kings, against Assyria. Ashdod's messengers had visited Jerusalem and Hezekiah was tempted to join the revolt.

Isaiah's protest is thoroughly consistent with his counsel to Ahaz (7:4) and his evaluation of the Assyrian's destiny (7:17; 10:5–6). This is no private advice to the kings and his counselors, but a public demonstration intended to catch the attention of the nation. It is not a prediction of a specific event, but an evaluation of Egypt's long-term inability and lack of will to counter Assyrian pressure.

But Judah stubbornly leaned toward an anti-Assyrian and pro-Egyptian (i.e., the cities of the delta, not the Ethiopian dynasty) stance which was short-sighted and unrealistic. It involved a fateful miscalculation of Assyria's power and will. Hezekiah's ministers had involved Judah in the Ashdod rebellion from the very beginning of his reign. It broke out fully by 714 B.C. and was suppressed by Sargon's forces in 712 B.C. (cf. *MBA,* 149). Judah apparently lent its support in the early stages but sought Assyria's amnesty before the fighting started. Of course, hopes for Egyptian support were fruitless. Egypt was being overrun by Ethiopian forces friendly to Assyria.

Through the following years Shabaka (716–702 B.C.) maintained correct, almost friendly relations with Assyria, thus gaining external peace for Egypt during his reign (Kitchen, *Third Intermediate Period in Egypt,* 380).

Scene 3: Four Ambiguous Burdens (21:1—22:25)

Episode A: Burden: A Swampland (21:1–10)
Episode B: Burden: Silence (21:11–12)
Episode C: Burden: In the Wasteland (21:13–17)
Episode D: Burden: The Valley of Vision (22:1–14)
Episode E: Shebna Is Dismissed (22:15–25)

A Summary of the Action

The warning against Babylonian influence (chaps. 13–14) had gone unheeded in the circles that controlled Judah's foreign policy under Hezekiah. Their admiration for Merodach-Baladan's success in holding power in Babylon from 721 to 710 B.C. had undoubtedly influenced their decision to participate in Ashdod's rebellion in 714 to 712 B.C. When Sargon took Babylon in 710 B.C. Merodach-Baladan escaped. At Sargon's death in 705 B.C. he took Babylon a second time, only to be ousted in 703 B.C. by Shalmaneser. Either of the periods when Babylon was retaken by Assyria could be the occasion for the scene in chap. 21, but the latter period (703 B.C.) fits the relation to chap. 22.

Hezekiah's activistic tendencies led him to plan his own rebellion against Assyria on the death of Sargon in 705 B.C. (cf. *Historical Background* below and *MBA,* 152). By 701 B.C. Babylon had been subdued for a second time and the approach of Sennacherib's forces revealed how pitifully inadequate Judah's military preparations had been (chap. 22). Responsibility is placed squarely on the shoulders of Hezekiah's advisors, who were undoubtedly leaders in the activist faction.

Scene 2 portrayed Hezekiah's unparalleled opportunity (chap. 19) which was missed because of opportunistic attempts to play power politics. Scene 3 portrays the situation some decades later. The government's commitment to independence and power has not changed and it must face the debacle of that policy. A historian would lay the blame on miscalculation. The Vision blames the unwillingness of Judah's leaders to heed God's direction revealed through Isaiah, the prophet.

Chapters 21 and 22 form a single scene. The uncharacteristic headings ("burden" followed, not by a people or country, but by a mysterious descriptive word) and the first person speaker who is in such anguish about the reports and vision tie the chapters together into one scene. Not since Isaiah reported in the first person (chap. 8) have so many first person passages by others than Yahweh been strung together.

The speaker has authority to order a lookout (21:6), can speak of "my threshed ones" (v 10) in apparent reference to his suffering people, can speak of "my people" (22:4), and can apparently be addressed in the plural (22:9–14). The most likely person to be presented in such an anonymous way is Shebna, Judah's highest appointed official, or Hezekiah himself. The Lord addresses the king's most trusted advisors in 22:15–25.

The two chapters pursue a common theme: a series of military disasters involving troops from Elam, Media, and Kir that overcome Babylon (21:9) and Arabian strong-holds (21:13–17) and threaten Jerusalem (22:1–8). A setting in the years 703–01 B.C. as Sennacherib reasserted Assyrian sovereignty in Babylon (against Merodach-Baladan) and in Palestine (against Hezekiah) provides a credible background.

The speaker reacts to a fearful vision (21:2–5) which was anticipated by the interlocutor's announcement (v 1). He is instructed to post a watch (vv 6–8) and then reacts to the messenger's words (vv 9–10). An enigmatic burden intervenes (vv 11–12), but is followed by an ominous word about Arabia's fate (vv 13–16; cf. a similar form and language in chap. 16) sealed with an oracle from Yahweh.

The speaker responds to the interlocutor's questions to a troubled Jerusalem (22:1–3) with an anguished plea to be left alone (v 4). The interlocutor continues to describe the scene and address Jerusalem (second feminine singular; vv 5–8) before he turns to address the king, royal house, or the chorus (in second masculine plural) with a scathing accusation that they concentrated attention on armament while ignoring Yahweh, his plan, and will (vv 9–13). The speaker concludes by recognizing that their guilt cannot be expunged (v 14).

The prophetic charge to Shebna is in second masculine singular (vv 15–19), supported by two "in that day" passages (vv 20–25). The connection of the scene with events about 701 B.C. is confirmed by parallel references to Shebna and Hilkiah in 2 Kings 18–19.

HISTORICAL BACKGROUND: SCENE 3
HEZEKIAH'S REBELLION (705–701 B.C.) AND SENNACHERIB'S CAMPAIGN (701 B.C.)

Bibliography

Bright, J. *HI,* 298–309. **Clements, R. E.** *Isaiah and the Deliverance of Jerusalem.* JSOTSup 13. Sheffield: U. of Sheffield, 1980. 9–27. **Donner, H.** *IJH,* 446–51. **Luckenbill,**

D. D. *The Annals of Sennacherib.* Oriental Institute Publications, II. Chicago: 1924. *ANET*³, 287–88.

Sennacherib's reign began (705 B.C.) with turmoil among the vassal states of Babylon (cf. chap. 21) and Palestine. After restoring his authority in Babylon (703 B.C.), he turned to Palestine. Records of the campaign are to be found in the so-called Taylor prism (*ANET*³, 287–88) and in 2 Kgs 13–16 and 2 Chr 32:1–8. See *MBA,* maps 153 and 154. (The problems raised by trying to reconcile these accounts with the longer accounts in 2 Kgs 18:18—19:37 = Isa 36–37 and 2 Chr 32:9–21 will be discussed in the commentary on chaps. 36–37).

Hezekiah, King of Judah, apparently led the rebel states in Palestine. Ashdod and Ekron joined the rebellion, the latter only after deposing Padi, its king, and sending him in chains to Hezekiah for safe-keeping. Hezekiah's government then worked intensively to strengthen its defenses. He encouraged Simeonite tribesmen in their occupation of adjacent territories of Gaza and Edom who did not join the rebellious states (2 Kgs 18:8; 1 Chr 4:42–43). He established the borders of Judah by building fortress cities (2 Chr 32:28). Hezekiah also built new aqueducts (including a tunnel) to supply water for Jerusalem even during a siege (see *Excursus* below), and he strengthened diplomatic and religious relations with the provinces of former Israel (2 Chr 30:1–5).

Archeologists have found special seals on storage jars from that period which are marked with the royal stamp "belonging to the king" and the names of four cities: Hebron, Socoh, Ziph, and Mimshe(le)th. The last apparently means "government" referring to Jerusalem itself. Jehoshaphat had divided Judah into twelve administrative districts (*MBA,* 130). These seem to refer to administrative centers of Hezekiah's day (*MBA,* 152).

Sennacherib first marched through Phoenicia, reinstating his authority (*MBA,* 153). He collected tribute from many kings including those of Ammon, Ashdod, Moab, and Edom (*ANET,* 287). He continued southward into Philistia. He banished the king of Ashkelon (*MBA,* 154) and reconquered cities subject to Ashkelon. He defeated an Egyptian army at Eltekeh. He fought against Ekron and restored Padi, their king, to the throne, presumably after arranging with Hezekiah for his release.

Sennacherib writes in more detail about his campaign against Judah. He claims to have taken forty-six of Judah's fortress cities and driven out two hundred thousand inhabitants with their livestock. 2 Kgs 18:13 confirms the capture of "all the fortified cities of Judah." Isa 22:7–8a speaks in the same way: "The defenses of Judah are stripped." Sennacherib claims to have shut up Hezekiah in Jerusalem "like a bird in a cage" (*ANET,* 288). He gave some of Judah's territory and towns to Ashdod, Ekron, and Gaza. He harassed Jerusalem and forced many of Hezekiah's troops to desert him (*ANET,* 288; cf. Isa 22:2a–3). He reports Hezekiah's payment of heavy tribute (cf. also 2 Kgs 18:14–15) including sending Sennacherib his own daughters, among others, as concubines and a personal messenger as a slave.

Assyria had incorporated units of soldiers from conquered regions into its forces in Sargon's times (cf. *ANET,* 284–85; H. Tadmor, "The Campaigns of Sargon II of Assur," *JCS* 12 [1958] 34). They may be presumed to be present with Sennacherib, (cf. 22:6) although he makes no specific reference to them.

Sennacherib did not depose Hezekiah or punish him personally beyond the reduction of territory and the demand for additional tribute. Clements (*The Deliverance of Jerusalem,* 20) suggests that the proven stability of the Davidic dynasty led the Assyrians to value its continuation. Isa 22:19–24 suggests that the dismissal of Hezekiah's prime minister may have prompted the Assyrian action.

Episode A: Burden: A Swampland (21:1–10)

Bibliography

Barnes, W. E. "A Fresh Interpretation of Isaiah XXI 1–10." *JTS* 1 (1900) 583–92. **Boutflower, C.** "Isaiah XXI in the Light of Assyrian History." *JTS* 14 (1913) 501–15. **Buhl, F.** "Jesaja 21:6–10." *ZAW* 8 (1888) 157–64. **Carmignac, J.** "Six passages d'Isaie eclaires par Qumran." *Bibel und Qumran.* FS H. Bardtke. Ed. S. Wagner. Berlin: Evangelische Haupt-Bibelgesellschaft, 1968. 37–46, especially 43. **Cobb, W. H.** "Isaiah XXI 1–10 Reexamined." *JBL* 17 (1898) 40–61. **Dhorme, P.** "Le desert de la mer (Isaïe, XXI)." *RB* 31 (1922) 403–6. **Galling, K.** "Jes. 21 im Lichte der neuen Nabonidtexte." *Tradition und Situation.* FS A. Weiser. Göttingen: Vandenhoeck & Ruprecht, 1963. 49–62. **Kleinert, P.** "Bemerkungen zu Jes. 20–22." *TSK* 1 (1877) 174–79. **Lohmann, P.** *Die anonymen Prophetien gegen Babel aus der Zeit des Exils.* Diss., Rostock, 1910. 61. ———. "Zur Strophischen Gliederung von Jes. 21:1–10." *ZAW* 33 (1913) 262–64. **Macintosh, A. A.** *Isaiah XXI: A Palimpsest.* Cambridge: University Press, 1980. **Scott, R. B. Y.** "Inside of a prophet's mind." *VT* 2 (1952) 278–82. **Sievers, E.** "Zu Jesaja 21:1–10." *Vom Alten Testament.* FS K. Marti. BZAW 41. Giessen: Töpelmann, 1925. 262–65.

Translation

Herald:	1 *Burden: A Swampland.* [a]	3
	Like storm-winds to sweep [b] *into the south country*	3+2+2
	he comes [c] *from a wilderness*	
	from a land that is to be feared.	
Shebna:	2 *A hard vision*	2+2
	has been declared to me:	
Heavens:	*The traitor betrays!*	2+2
	The violent work violence!	
Earth:	*Go up, Elam!*	2+2
	Lay siege, Media!	
Yahweh:	*I shall stop all her groaning!* [a]	3
Shebna:	3 *At this my body is full of pain.*	4

	Pangs seize me	2+2
	like pangs of childbirth!	
	I am overcome by [a] *what I hear,*	2+2
	I am dismayed by [a] *what I see.*	
	4 [a]*My heart skips a beat.* [a]	2+2
	A shudder overwhelms me.	
	For me it makes the twilight of my love [b]	3+3
	to become a time of anxiety.	
Herald:	5 *Setting the table—*	2+2+2
	spreading the rug [a]*—*	
	eating—drinking.	
	The officers rise.	2+2
	They anoint [b] *a shield.*	
Shebna:	6 *For thus my Lord says to me:*	5
Yahweh, or king:	*Go. Have a lookout stand guard.*	3+3
	Have him report what he sees.	
	7 *If he sees a rider,*	2+2
	a team of horses,	
	a rider [a] *(on) a donkey,*	2+2
	a rider [a] *(on) a camel,*	
	have him pay attention,	2+2
	very close attention.	
Herald:	8 *Then, the watchman* [a] *cried out:*	2
Watchman:	*Upon a watchtower, my lord,*	3+2+2
	I am standing	
	continually, by day.	
	At my post	2+2+2
	I am keeping my station	
	all night.	
	9 *Look! There! Someone is coming!*	3+2+2
	A chariot with a man!	
	A team of horses!	
	He answers and says:	2+3
	"She has fallen! Babylon has fallen! [a]	
	All the images of her gods	3+2
	have been shattered [b] *on the ground!"*	
Shebna:	10 *My threshed ones,* [a]	1+1
	and my [a] *threshing-floor son,*	
	what I have heard	2+3
	from Yahweh of Hosts,	
	God of Israel,	2+2
	I announce to you (pl)!	

Notes

1.a. MT "a sea wilderness" or "swampland." The title is apparently taken from the word מִמִּדְבָּר in line 3. The style of titles that listed nations in 13:1; 15:1; 17:1 and 19:1 changes here. In 21:1, 11, 13 and 22:1 obscure words sometimes taken up from the first lines are used. Wildberger (763) and Macintosh (*Isaiah XXI,* 407) have full reviews of the suggestions of versions and commentators. The translation "desert" is wrong. מדבר is a wilderness, not a desert (BDB, 184).

1.b. Inf constr defining more precisely (GKC § 114*o*).

1.c. The subject is indefinite "he" or "it." In v 3 the subject is personal 3rd m sg.

2.a. MT אנחתה suffix without *Raphe* "her groanings." An unusual but possible form. The fem pronoun must refer to the one under attack. The "groaning" may be from pain or from strenuous effort.

3.a. MT מִשְּׁמֹעַ "from hearing." LXX *τὸ μὴ ἀκοῦσαι*, Tg מלמשמע, Syr *dl*ʾ ʾ*šm*ʿ. All these translate מן in a negative or a privative sense, followed by Marti, Kaiser, and others. But a causative sense fits the context better, as Duhm, Fohrer, Eichrodt, and Wildberger have noted.

4.a-a. DSS^Isa^ תועה ולבבי. Wildberger calls it "not understandable."

4.b. LXX *ἡ ψυχή μου* "my soul," Syr *šwpr*ʾ. G. R. Driver (BZAW 77 [Giessen: Töpelman, 1958], 44), related it to Arab *nasafa* and translated "my faintest (i.e., scarcely-breathed) wish has been turned into anxiety for me." The usual is better.

5.a. צפה הצפית "spreading the rug" has given the Versions and commentators trouble. See Wildberger (765) and Macintosh (24–25). The meaning of II צפה (BDB, 860) suggests preparation of a meal which fits the context.

5.b. MT משחו "they anoint" or "they oil." LXX *ἑτοιμάσατε θυρεούς* "prepare weapons," Tg מריקו וצחצחו זינא "polish and shine the weapons."

7.a. DSS^Isa^ רוכב in the second instance and a superimposed *waw* in the first suggests reading as a ptcp "riding" instead of MT רֶכֶב a noun "rider." LXX *ἀναβάτην* supports reading as a ptcp as do the Tg and Syr. Wildberger correctly chooses to sustain MT.

8.a. MT אריה "then the lion called out" makes no sense. LXX *Οὐρίαν* reads it as a proper noun. Ibn Ezra, followed by Delitzsch, read כאריה "like a lion" "with a lion's voice." R. Lowth, as early as 1778 (*Isaiah,* London: Nichols), suggested הָרֹאֶה "the seer," "the watchman" which is now supported by DSS^Isa^ and accepted by Fohrer, Eichrodt, Young, Auvray, A. Schoors (*Jesaja,* Roermond, 1972), Kaiser, Wildberger, and Macintosh.

9.a. LXX, Eth and Arab versions omit the second נפלה "she has fallen." MT's emphatic usage should be kept.

9.b. DSS^Isa^ שברו is pl allowing the pl subject that precedes. LXX *συνετρίβησαν* suggests a pass parallel with the previous line. Both support Procksch's suggestion to read שֻׁבְּרוּ "they have been shattered." Wildberger and *BHS* agree.

10.a. The pual ptcp "my threshed" (one or things) does seem to need a noun. Sievers (*BZAW* 41, 263) suggested עם־מדשתי "people of my threshing"; Procksch בן־מדשתי "son of my threshing" (*BHS*). With Wildberger it is better to let MT stand.

10.b. The possessive pronoun relates to the controlling noun בן in the construct form. Cf. J. Weingreen and G. Weinberg (*VT* 4 [1954] 50–59) and Wildberger (767).

Form/Structure/Setting

The episode shifts back and forth from a vision (vv 2, 5) to a cry of personal anguish (vv 3–4) to a dramatic confirmation of the vision (vv 6–9) to a closing address to the audience (v 10).

It can be read as a monologue by an unidentified speaker who is distressed at the news of Babylon's defeat. It was decided to recognize this person who carries the scene (vv 2, 3–4, 6–8a, and 10), but to reflect the very dynamic lines between by having speakers speak for themselves, rather than be cited by the primary speaker. By implication, this must be someone in Jerusalem who is deeply involved in the party that supports Babylon's policies. Thus Babylon's overthrow brings distress to this speaker and his political stance.

Ibn Ezra argued that this speaker could not be the prophet Isaiah "since the prophet's views are known to be joy—not sorrow" (cf. Macintosh, *Isaiah XXI,* 15). Ibn Ezra thought they must come from the King of Babylon. It is in fact not Isaiah who speaks here. Nothing in the context identifies him as the speaker.

When we recognize that chaps. 21 and 22 form one larger whole as we have done by placing them in the same scene (see Introduction to Scene 3), it is evident that the speaker is identified by name at the end of the scene. He is Shebna, the palace steward and chief minister (22:15). He with his deputy, Eliakim (22:20), had probably shared more responsiblity for Hezekiah's anti-Assyrian policies than any others. It is appropriate that he be recognized as the speaker in the first person speeches of this chapter.

Comment

1 *Swampland* is identified as Babylonia by v 9. That which *comes* is either an invading army or the news of such an invasion.

2 Commentators who have expected Isaiah to be the speaker here have been troubled at the prophet's reaction. Why should Isaiah agonize over the fulfillment of his own prophecies, the confirmation of his teaching? But the text makes no mention of Isaiah. The speaker who sees the vision and shows such emotion throughout the scene is probably Shebna (cf. 22:15–24). 2 Kgs 18:18–19:7 and Isa 36:3–37:7 recount Shebna's role in diplomatic negotiations. He was apparently Hezekiah's palace governor, perhaps the most influential officer in the country. His views may well be reflected in Hezekiah's departure from his father's neutral policies to become a participant in the anti-Assyrian rebellion in 714–711 B.C. and a leader of that opposition in Palestine in 704–701 B.C. (J. M. Ward, "Shebna," *IDB* 4:312).

The content of the vision is condensed into three cries. The first simply recognizes a violent scene. The second exhorts Elam and Media (or their soldiers) to attack. The object of the attack is not named. The third, in first person, promises to bring a quick end to the victim's (her) groaning. The victim is identified as Babylon later in the scene (v 9b).

The last speech may well be understood to be spoken by the enemy commander or, better, by Yahweh himself. If the enemy commander, this could be the Assyrian general. Šargon forced Merodach-Baladan (cf. commentary to chap. 13–14) to abandon the city in 710 B.C. Sennacherib repeated the maneuver in 703 B.C. The close connection of chaps. 21 and 22 favors the latter occasion.

Elam and *Media* were peoples from the Iranian highlands who were becoming active in Mesopotamian affairs near the end of the eighth century (see *Excursus,* "Elam"). Elamite collaboration had made possible Merodach-Baladan's capture of Babylon in 720. Commentators have been very occupied with determining their roles here and in 22:6. (Cf. Macintosh, 63–75). The outcry of the vision does not define their role, whether for or against Babylon, but it does establish their participation in the struggle.

3–4 The emotional reaction to the vision, a premonition of news announced in v 8, is the most prominent feature of the entire scene. The same kind of anxiety or dismay is observed in 22:4 and condemned by the speeches of that chapter. Shebna's despairing response shows that Babylon's collapse is the first sign that the foundations of his foreign policy for Judah are crumbling.

Merodach-Baladan's successful campaign that captured Babylon and held it for a decade (720–710 B.C.) had been the signal to other peoples that Assyria might be resisted. It sustained the hopes of Judah's resistance party and led Hezekiah to move away from his father's policies of loyal vassalage. It encouraged Ashdod in its rebellion of 714–711 B.C.

Merodach-Baladan's reassertion of his claim to Babylon after Sargon's death (705 B.C.) sparked an attempted general uprising throughout the Empire (chap. 39). It led to Hezekiah's decisions to arm himself and to build a coalition of Palestinian states for such an uprising (see commentary on chap. 22).

The collapse of Babylon in 703 B.C. to which this vision refers presaged the collapse of all opposition to Sennacherib and disaster for those who advised it (as Shebna had) or who led it (as Hezekiah had).

4 *The twilight of my love* (cf. the parallel figure in v 12) seems to picture the longed-for future which is now put in jeopardy by the vision: Shebna's dream of an independent and prosperous country, free from imperial oppression and taxation.

5 The verse pictures the beginning of a military campaign in the field. The cryptic presentation does not show clearly whether this takes place in far-away Babylon or in Judah. The next orders for placing a guard suggest that the verse pictures Judean preparations for the inevitable Assyrian reprisal, when or if their Babylonian campaign is successful.

8 The MT's "the lion called out" makes no sense (cf. note). An emended text reads "the seer." The term lends the account an added dimension; *the watchman* is more than a military guard on watch. And the account is parallel to the vision of v 2.

9c The shattering of images may be intended to depict the physical destruction of temples. But it also reflects the loss of prestige and respect resulting from their inability to protect the city. The recognition that neither Sargon nor Sennacherib destroyed the city, but only reoccupied it, would support the latter meaning.

10 *Threshed ones* and *threshing-floor son* are literal renderings of words apparently intended to show sympathy for the Judean people who have already suffered so much. What, exactly, has been *heard from Yahweh?* Apparently this harks back to the vision of v 2, although it was not at that point attributed to God. The vision in its third statement revealed that Yahweh, himself, was directing the assault. This confirms the prophet's announcement in 7:17 and the presentation of the Assyrian in 10:5–6 as the "rod of God's anger." Shebna is forced by the vision to recognize Isaiah's position which, until now, he has refused to do. His emotional collapse is understandable.

Excursus: Elam

Bibliography

Millard A. "Elam." *ISBE* 2:49–52 and bibliography there.

Elamites were an ancient people who inhabited the plain now called Khuzistan in southwest Iran. Its capital city was Susa.

Elam emerged in the late eighth century for a period of importance that lasted from ca. 720 to ca. 645 B.C. when Ashurbanipal destroyed Susa. During this period Elamite support made possible Merodach-Baladan's successful capture and rule over Babylon in 720–710 B.C. This aid to Babylon against Assyria may well have eventually caused Elam's fall.

Elam's support for Merodach-Baladan was sporadic. In 720 its armies prevented Assyrian intervention. But in 710 it retreated, allowing Sargon to take Babylon. It even denied Merodach-Baladan asylum despite receiving an enormous gift. In 703 Merodach-Baladan persuaded Elam to send a large force with 80,000 archers (cf. Isa 22:6 and Jer 49:35). But the effort failed to stop the Assyrians. Assyria retaliated by taking back two areas on Elam's northwest border. In 700 B.C. Elam supported Merodach-Baladan's unsuccessful defense against Assyria's campaign in southern Babylonia. Merodach-Baladan apparently died in his exile on the Elamite coast of the Persian Gulf.

The half century that followed brought numerous encounters between Assyria and Elam which often involved Babylonia. A final confrontation before Susa in 646 B.C. brought defeat and devastation. Elam, as an independent nation, faded from history.

Explanation

The Burden of the Swampland (Babylon) dramatically recounts the reaction of persons (or parties) in Jerusalem to news of Merodach-Baladan's collapse before the Assyrian onslaught which involved Medes and Elamites. Either of two occasions would serve as the historical focus. Merodach-Baladan, after some ten years of ascendancy, fled Babylon before Sargon's forces in ca. 710 B.C. After he returned to power on Sargon's death (cf. Isa 39), he was again routed by Sennacherib in 703 B.C.

The scene focuses on the almost hysterical reaction in Jerusalem to news of his defeat. Why should Jerusalem have been so concerned about an event so far away? Babylon had stood for more than a decade as living proof that the Assyrians could be overcome. It was evidence that rebellion could succeed. Some in Jerusalem, probably including Hezekiah, had heeded the siren call of that example rather than the prophet's warnings (chaps. 13–14 and chap. 20). Premonitions of their own fate fueled the emotional reaction to the news about Babylon.

The shorter scenes about Dumah and Arabia reflect the anxiety and despair among neighboring peoples before the anticipated reaction of Sennacherib to Hezekiah's challenge, now that he is relieved of concern about Merodach-Baladan's threat to his southern flank.

The final verses announce that they (and presumably Judah) have not long to wait.

Episode B: Burden: Silence (21:11–12)

Bibliography

Lohmann, P. "Das Wächterlied Jes. 21:11–12." *ZAW* 33 (1913) 20–29.

Translation

Herald:	[11] *Burden: Silence* [a] *(Dumah).*	2+3
Watchman:	*Someone is calling* [b] *to me from Seir:*	
	"Keeper, what (is left) of the night? [c]	3+3
	Keeper, what (is left) of the night?"	
Herald:	[12] *The keeper* [a] *said.*	2+2+2
Watchman:	*Morning is come,*	
	but also [b] *night.*	
	If you (m pl) must ask, ask. [c]	3+2
	Turn! Come!	

Notes

11.a. 2 MSS and LXX (Ιδουμαίας) read אֱדוֹם "Edom." One LXX MSS ([534]) reads *ιουδαιας* "Judah." ʾA according to Jerome reads *duma* which is explained as meaning "silence" or "likeness." Wildberger makes a good case for keeping MT and the Arabian place names (787–91).

11.b. ʾA Σ Θ (according to Eusebius, *Die Jesajakommentar* § 80; p. 142) *προς εμε καλει τους φευγοντας* "to me he calls the men in flight." *BHS* suggests הַנּוֹדְדִים "ones fleeing" for מִשֵּׂעִיר "from Seir." The change is unnecessary.

11.c. DSS[Isa] מליל makes the first "night" identical in form to the second. לֵיל may well be a contraction for the abs form (cf. Joüon § 96*Am*).

12.a. Note the change from 1st (v 11) to 3rd pers. But note the relation in vv 6 and 8.

12.b. The text is clear. But several have sought clarity of meaning through emendation (see Wildberger, 788). The ambiguity is apparently intentional.

12.c. For explanation of the Hebrew forms cf. GKC § 75*h*.

Comment

11 A second *Burden* has an even more ambiguous and mysterious title: *Silence.* The Hebrew sound is similar to "Edom" and the reference to Seir in the next line leads the LXX to insert that name here. Wildberger thinks it refers to a place name. Cf. *MBA,* 115; LaSor, *ISBE* 2:995. However, the parallel to other ambiguous titles (21:1, 13; 22:1) suggests that it be allowed its mysterious character, especially in view of the ambiguity in the *keeper's* response (v 12). The theme of a lookout or watchman is continued from vv 6 and 8. The question is broad and common.

12 The answer says nothing specific, only recognizing that it is proper to ask, even when nothing can be given in reply. It reflects the times when people want to know what is happening, anxiously anticipating great and fearful events, yet recognizing that those events have not come into sight.

Episode C:
Burden: In the Wasteland (21:13–17)

Translation

Herald: [13] *Burden: In the wasteland.* [a] 2
Earth: *In the thicket in the wasteland* [b] *they lodge,* 3+2
the Dedanite wanderers.
[14] *To meet a thirsty one* 2+2
they bring [a] *water.*
Inhabitants of the land of Tema 3+3
meet [b] *a refugee with his bread.*
[15] *For they have fled in the face of swords* 3+3
before a drawn sword,
before a bent bow 3+3
and before the weight [a] *of battle.*
Shebna: [16] *For thus my Lord* [a] *has said to me:* 4
"In just a year, [b] *like a bond-servant's year,* 4+4
all the glory of Kedar will be finished,
[17] *and the remnant of the number of bowmen, heroes*
of the Kedarites, [a] *will be small."* 7
For Yahweh, God of Israel, has spoken. 5

Notes

13.a. LXX omits both words of the heading. Cf. possible renderings "in the waste place," "against Arabia," "in the evening." See also the same word in the next line.

13.b. LXX (followed by Syr Tg Vg) ἑσπέρας "of evening." MT "in the wilderness" is more fitting.

14.a. DSS[Isa] האתיו is the full form to which BDB (87) pointed. On the pointing of verbs "doubly weak" cf. GKC § 76*d* and Bauer-Leander § 59*g*.

14.b. LXX (supported by Syr Tg Vg) *συναντᾶτε*, an impv "meet, encounter," leads many to vocalize Heb קִדְּמוּ also an impv in place of MT's pf ind. Apparently the verb is intended to parallel הֵתָיוּ "bring" in the previous line. MT has both in pf tense and they should be kept.

15.a. DSS[Isa] כבוד "glory." MT "weight" or BDB "vehemence" is better.

16.a. DSS[Isa] and many MSS and Tg יהוה "Yahweh."

16.b. DSS[Isa] שלוש שנים "three years" (cf. 16:4).

17.a. DSS[Isa] has בני inserted above the line, apparently to correct an omission in copying. This brings it in line with MT (cf. S. Talmon 119).

Comment

13 The third ambiguous title may mean "against Arabia," "in the evening," or "in the wasteland." A tendency to expect the name of a country in such a title, connected with the names Dedon and Tema in vv 13 and 14, supports the first. Parallels to "Swampland" (v 1), "the wasteland" (13b), and "Valley of Vision" (22:1) support the last. Parallels to "night" (v 11) and "twilight" (v 4) might suggest the second. The overwhelming impression again is mystery and ambiguity. *Dedanites* are a people of Arabia (Cohen, *IDB* 1:812; LaSor, *ISBE* 1:909). In Jer 49:8 and Ezek 25:13 they appear in connection with Edom as they do here to the parallel burden (v 11 "Seir" and "Dumah").

14 *Tema,* modern Teima in Arabia, is an oasis (Cohen, *IDB* 4:533; *MBA,* 115). The scene is one of devastation and privation, of hungry and thirsty refugees.

15 An explanation cites military invasion as the cause. There are no specific data on which to attempt historical identification as to time or event.

16–17 *Kedar* (J. A. Thompson, *IDB* 3:3–4) appears again in 42:11 and 60:7 (cf. Jer 49:28–32; Ezek 27:21). It is a place east of Palestine, apparently in north-Arabia. Assyrian records speak of Kedarites and Arabs in the same breath. They were a considerable force that pre-occupied the Assyrians under Sennacherib, Asshurbanipal, and Esarhaddon. Sennacherib writes of defeating Hazail, king of the Arabs/Kedarites.

The announced destruction of Kedar is an explicit and specific word from Yahweh. If Dumah (v 11) implies a place name (along with Dedan and Tema, cities in Arabia), the question of that verse is answered by the word from Yahweh in vv 16–17. For Shebna the vision/news of Babylon's fall and the vision of Arabian refugees (vv 13–14) interpreted by the prophecy of vv 16–17 prepare for a very negative evaluation of Judah's position, as Assyria advances.

Episode D: *Burden: The Valley of Vision (22:1–14)*

Bibliography

Box, G. H. "Some Textual Suggestions on Two Passages in Isaiah." *ExpTim* 19 (1908) 563–64. **Dahood, M.** "בֵּין הַחֹמֹתַיִם. (Isa 22:11 etc. Nota discussionem sensus accurati.)" *Bib* 42 (1961) 474–75. **Gottwald, N.** *All the Kingdoms of the Earth,* 193–96. **Guillaume, A.** "A Note on the Meaning of Isa 22:5." *JTS* 14 (1963) 383–85. **Torczynor, H.** "Dunkle Biblestellen." *Vom Alten Testament.* FS K. Marti. BZAW 41. Giessen: Töpelmann, 1925. 276. **Weippert, M.** "Mitteilungen zum Text von Ps 19:5 und Jes 22:5." *ZAW* 73 (1961) 97–99.

Translation

Herald: 1 *Burden:* [a] *Valley of Vision.* [a] 3+2+2
Heavens: [b] *What is the matter with you,* [b] *then,*
(to Jerusalem) *That you have gone up,* [c]
all of you, [c] *to the housetops?*
Earth: 2 *Noise! A city full of roaring!* 1+3+2
A city jubilant!

Heavens:	*Your profaned are not those profaned by the sword*	4+3
	and not those dead in battle.	
Earth:	3 *All your chiefs*	2+2+2
	who fled together	
	without bowmen were taken prisoner. [a]	
Heavens:	[b] *All who were found in you* [b]	2+2+2
	have been taken prisoner together	
	even when they had fled far away.	
Shebna:	4 *Because of this I have said*	2+2+2
(to Heaven & Earth)	[a] *Look away from me!* [a]	
	I am bitter in my weeping!	
	Do not hurry to comfort me	2+2
	because of the destruction of the daughter of my people.	
Earth:	5 *Yea, there is a day of roaring and trampling and terror*	5+3+2
	belonging to my Lord, Yahweh of Hosts,	
	in the Valley of Vision.	
	[a] *(A day of) digging a ditch* [a]	2+2
	and crying out toward [b] *the mountain,*	
	6 *for Elam has lifted a quiver*	3+3+3
	with manned [a] *chariot, horsemen,*	
	and Kir uncovered a shield.	
(to Jerusalem)	7 *So it came about that your (fem sg) choice* [a] *valleys*	3+2
	are filled with chariotry.	
	And the horsemen [b] *are powerfully arrayed at the gates.*	4+4
	8 *So he* [a] *stripped away Judah's screen.*	
	So [b] *you (fem sg) looked in that day*	3+4
	toward the armory of the House of the Forest. [c]	
Heavens:	9 *The breaches* [a] *in the City of David—*	3+2
(to the royal government)	*you (m pl) saw* [b] *that they were many.*	
	Then you collected water in the Lower Pool.	4
	10 *You (m pl) counted* [a] *the houses of Jerusalem.*	3+4
	Then you (m pl) demolished [b] *the houses to make*	
	the wall inaccessible. [c]	
	11 *You built a reservoir between the walls* [a]	4+3
	for the water of the old pool.	
	But you (m pl) did not look [b] *to her Maker.*	3+4
	The one shaping it long ago, [c] *you (m pl)*	
	did not see. [d]	
Earth:	12 *Then my Lord,* [a] *Yahweh of Hosts,*	1+3+2
	called in that day	
	for weeping and for wailing	2+3
	for shaved heads and for wearing sackcloth.	
	13 *But see!*	1
	Joy and revelry, slaughtering cattle and killing sheep.	2+2+2
A Reveler:	*Eating and drinking—for tomorrow we die.*	2+3

Shebna: [14] *But Yahweh of Hosts has revealed in my ears* 2+2
"I swear this guilt will not be atoned for you (m pl)[a] 5
before you die," [b]*said my Lord Yahweh of Hosts.*[b]

Notes

1.a-a. LXX *τῆς φάραγγος Σιων* "about the Zion ravine." This interprets the Hebrew to refer to the Hinnom Valley west of Jerusalem, which leads Schmidt to emend חזיון to הִנֹּם, which Wildberger (805) properly calls "too simple." Guillaume suggests (*JTS* 14 [1963] 383–85) that one follow Arab *ḥadwa* to read "the valley opposite."

1.b-b. מה־לך "what to you (fem sg)?" DSS[Isa] מלכי "my king." Tg מא לכון "what to you." MT's fem pronoun refers to Jerusalem. The prose may ask "What's the matter with you?" or "What do you want?" etc.

1.c. MT עָלִית "that you (fem) have gone up" is rendered by DSS[Isa] עליתי "I have gone up," by LXX *ἀνέβητε* "you (pl) go up," by Tg סליקתון "you (pl) go up." The different persons in the Versions have led them to variations on כלך "all of you" in LXX *πάντες* "all" and Tg כולכון "all of you."

3.a. MT אֻסָּרוּ "they were taken prisoner" is the only occurrence of אסר in pu'al. DSS[Isa] אסורה seems to be a qal pass ptcp fem "bound" or "imprisoned." Tg גלו "reveal" or "exile" suggests the reading ס(א)רו "they turned aside" (BDB, 693) as followed by Procksch, Bruno "depart," and *BHS, or* הֻסָרוּ hoph pf (BDB, 694) "they were removed or taken away" (Wildberger and *BHS*).

3.b-b. LXX *οἱ ἰσχύοντες ἐν σοὶ* "the healthy among you (pl)." Driver (*JTS* 41 [1940] 164) and *BHS* accordingly emend to נֶאֱמָצַיִךְ "your bold ones," a niph pf of אמץ which does not otherwise appear in niph. Others (Duhm, Guthe, Feldmann, Procksch, Kissane, and *BHS*) emend to אַמִּיצַיִךְ "your mighty ones" (BDB, 55). Wildberger defends MT, treating מרחוק ברחו as a concessive clause "although they had fled far off."

4.a-a. DSS[Isa] שועו ממני "cry for help from me" from שוע "cry for help" (BDB, 1002) rather than MT שעו "look away" (BDB, 1043). MT is better.

5.a-a. מקרקר קר is a term occurring only here. BDB (903) relates it to קיר "wall" and later Heb קִרְקֵר "tear down a wall." GKC and KB could find no meaning for it. LXX and Syr were also mystified by it. But new attempts have been made. Aram, Syr, Arab, and latter Heb have the root meaning "growl," "roar," "crow," or "cackle." And now *ḳr* in Ugaritic suggests the possible meaning "a spring" (*Ras Shamra Parallels,* ed. L. R. Fisher, vol. 1. [Rome: Pont. Bib. Inst., 1972] § II, 495; *ḳrt* 120, 222; cf. Wildberger). However, the possibility that מקרקר may be a pilp form from קוּר I "bore or dig" (cf. BDB, 881) and קָר a shortened form of מקור "a spring, fountain" has hardly been explored. The references to the building of the reservoirs (vv 9b–11a) suggest this possibility. DSS[Isa] קדשו "his holy one" (for MT קָר וְשׁוֹעַ) "his holiness growling against the mountain."

5.b. DSS[Isa] על "against" for MT אל "toward."

6.a. MT אדם "man or mankind." The parallels before and after name nations. A natural suggestion is ארם "Aram" or "Syria" (C. F. Houbigant, *Biblica Hebraica* [Paris: Briasson, 1753]; Lowth; *BHK*). Others suggest it is a gloss (Duhm, Marti, Gray, Fohrer, Wildberger). Yet the horses and chariots are the very center of attention in v 7. The intention seems to be something like "with chariots manned by riders" (without regard to nationality).

7.a. B. E. Shafer ("מבחר|מבחור = 'Fortress,'" *CBQ* 33 [1971] 389–94) translates מבחר "fortress": "Your valley fortresses were full of chariots." But if the reference continues the thoughts of v 6, the allusion must be to enemy chariots, not Judean (cf. Wildberger, 807).

7.b. The verse is divided after "chariotry" and before "the horsemen" by the *athnaḥ* in MT (followed by LXX and Tg). Wildberger (806) suggests putting the *athnaḥ* under פרשים and eliminating the article since chariots and horses are usually mentioned together. MT makes sense as it is and should be kept.

8.a. LXX reads a plural. However, the MT reference is to the subject in v 5, Yahweh or his emissary.

8.b. Note a change of subject, returning to the form of address of vv 1–3. LXX missed the change and translated with a plural.

8.c. LXX τοὺς ἐκλεκτοὺς οἴκους τῆς πόλεως "the choice houses of the city." But MT is to be sustained. Wildberger thinks the longer phrase בית יער הלבנון "house of the forest of Lebanon" is understood (cf. 1 Kgs 7:2).

9.a. Ehrlich (*Randglossen,* III, 136) notes that בקע as a verb usually refers to "digging wells" (Judg 15:19) and that בקיע means "a natural spring" (IV, 77). However, to make sense here he had to assume that a לא "not" had been lost. His suggestion had the advantage of making vv 9–11a have a single topic.

9.b. DSS[Isa] ראית(מ)ה presents an unusual form (cf. Meyer, *Grammatik* § 64:2b) but does not improve the text.

10.a. ספרתם has no counterpart in LXX.

10.b. DSS[Isa] ותתוצו notes an alternate form of the verb (cf. Deut 7:5 and Exod 34:13). וַתִּתְצוּ is generally held to derive from נתץ "pull down" or "break down" (BDB, 683). The *dagesh forte* has been dropped in תְ (cf. GKC § 20 *m*), but is marked by *raphe* (cf. Meyer § 14:6).

10.c. DSS[Isa] לבצור is a qal inf for MT's piel inf. Wildberger (823) has objected with reason to the usual rendering "fortify" or "strengthen." The verb should mean "make them inaccessible."

11.a. DSS[Isa] is pl. MT is dual.

11.b. DSS[Isa] adds a final ה as in v 9b.

11.c. מרחוק "from far off" is missing in Σ Θ. Donner has suggested omitting it. LXX ἀπ' ἀρχῆς "from of old" takes it to refer to time instead of space.

11.d. A. Sperber (*Historical Grammar* [Leiden: E. J. Brill, 1966] 647) suggests that ראיתם "you see" should be read as יראתם "you fear." Wildberger (808) correctly rejects the change.

12.a. Missing in LXX, Eth, and Arab.

14.a. DSS[Isa] changes the word order, placing לכם "to you" immediately after יכפר "be attoned." But this is unnecessary.

14.b-b. The closing formula has frequently been thought to be a later addition (Duhm, Gray, Fisher, Procksch, Donner, and Wildberger).

Form/Structure/Setting

This moving and turbulent episode does not fit normal molds. It contains: (1) an accusing question about turbulent behavior (vv 1–3); (2) a defensive rejoinder (v 4); (3) a portrayal of war in Judah as "day of Yahweh" (vv 5–8); (4) an accusation of government for inadequate preparation, but especially for lack of spiritual sensitivity (vv 9–11); (5) an accusation of disobedience to Yahweh's instructions (vv 12–13); and (6) a confession that Yahweh has withheld absolution (v 14).

The scene builds the tension steadily with probing, accusing questions (v 1) and observations (vv 2–3, 5–8, 9–11, 12–13) before it has the city's leadership confess God's unyielding disapproval. The dismissals that are obviously required will follow.

The entire episode involves Jerusalem, which is addressed directly in vv 1 and 7–8. It is Jerusalem's misguided leadership that pleads so plaintively in v 4, receives such a direct rebuke in vv 9–11, and confesses to having been discredited in v 14. The leadership is named as Shebna and Eliakim in the next episode.

The accusers are like the speakers in chap. 1 and may well be represented as the covenant witnesses, Heavens and Earth.

Comment

1 *Valley of Vision* is vague, deliberately so. It is taken from v 5 below.

2–3 The contrast between consternation at the threat and jubilation at the "macho" feeling of preparation for heroic struggle surfaces here and in vv 12–13. The commentaries generally place parts of this chapter in differing times. When seen as drama, this is unnecessary. The date is 701 B.C. The Assyrians, with an international contingent of mercenaries, occupy Judah and threaten Jerusalem. The government calls for unusual military measures for defense. The inhabitants vacillate between attempting to flee (v 3) and displaying nationalistic fervor (vv 2, 13).

Profaned in the sense that a dead body is thought of as "profaned." But there are no dead—yet! Rather, the behavior of the city's leadership (or army officers, as Clements suggested) is contemptible. They are responsible for the policies that brought the Assyrians. Some try to flee but are caught.

4 Shebna recognizes the total failure of the policy. Hezekiah could speak in this way, too, but he is not addressed in the chapter. Shebna is named in v 15.

5 The crisis is related to Yahweh's *day. The valley of vision* is applied to Jerusalem, but the implications remain obscure. *Digging a ditch* picks up a theme which will be developed in vv 9–11: the extension of the city's water system in view of the siege to come. *Crying out toward the mountain* may refer to prayers directed toward Zion.

6 *Elam's* presence before Jerusalem is a surprise. At Babylon (chap. 21) it was natural, the only question being "On whose side?" The best explanation seems to be that the entire verse is stressing the international make-up of the attacking troops: bowmen from Elam, chariots with drivers from various nations, and foot-soldiers from Kir.

Kir is a land or a city, mentioned by Amos 9:7 as the origin of the Arameans. Amos 1:5 and 2 Kgs 16:9 report this as the place to which residents of Damascus will be exiled. No place by this name exists in early records of Mesopotamia. M. C. Astour ("Kir," *IDBSup,* 524) points to its meaning "wall" and thinks it is a translation of Der which also means "wall." Der was a city east of the lower Tigris basin (modern Babrah) between Elam and Babylon.

The chariotry is only identified by אדם "man" or "mankind." The phrase could be emended to read Aram or Edom. But that is too easy and does not really fit. *Mankind* may well be intended as a contrast to the ethnic units in Sennacherib's army: an international troop of chariot drivers representing mankind.

7 The status of the invasion is portrayed. The valley-roads approaching Jerusalem are held by chariot-riding brigades. The cavalry has taken up positions opposite the city's gates. The Rabshakeh's force approached from the south, which made the fortress towns on the north and west useless. *The valleys* are the access roads to Jerusalem near Timnah (see *MBA,* 154) or those that led from Lachish into the highlands between Hebron and Jerusalem.

8 The enemy (or Yahweh?) has penetrated the line of fortress-towns which protected the city from invasion along the ridge roads in the north or from the valley roads to the west (2 Kgs 18:13).

The House of the Forest (cf. Notes) was a storehouse for arms (1 Kgs 7:2–5), a part of the palace complex. Having lost a major part of the army by desertion (v 3) and abandoning the hope that the ring of armed towns could protect the city (v 8a), the citizenry of the city called for arms from the royal armory to protect themselves from the anticipated invaders (cf. W. S. LaSor, "Jerusalem," *ISBE* 2:1008).

Vv 1–3 and 7–8 are all addressed in second feminine singular to the city. Vv 9–11 and 14 are addressed in second masculine plural to the ruling house, the government.

9 The government belatedly recognized the many lacks in the city's defenses. Hezekiah's strategy had been to expand his borders and strengthen his perimeter of fortress towns (cf. 2 Chr 32:29; *MBA,* 152). These verses suggest that the efforts to fortify Jerusalem (2 Chr 32:2–8) came only after Sennacherib's campaign in 701 B.C., which did not bring an attack from the north (cf. Commentary on 10:32, which is seen to picture Yahweh's approach, not the Assyrian's). Instead he drove down the coast, regaining control of Philistia (see *MBA,* 154, and comment on v 7).

Excursus: Hezekiah's Pools and Waterworks

Bibliography

Amiran, R. "The Water Supply of Israelite Jerusalem." *Jerusalem Revealed: Archaeology in the Holy City 1968–1974.* Ed. Y. Yadin. New Haven and London: Yale University Press and the Israel Exploration Society, 1976. 75–78. **Avi-Yonah, M.** *EAEHL,* 597. **Brunet, G.** *Essai sur l'Isaie de l'Histoire.* Paris: Picard, 1975. 293–95 (includes a summary of the work of Lods, Simons, and Vincent). **Burrows, M.** "The Conduit of the Upper Pool." *ZAW* 70 (1958) 221–27. **Kenyon, K. M.** *Jerusalem: Excavating 3000 Years of History.* New York: McGraw-Hill, 1967. 69–77. ———. *Digging Up Jerusalem.* London: Ernest Benn, 1974. 144–60. (Cf. the excellent summary by W. LaSor, "Jerusalem," *ISBE* 2.)

From earliest times Jerusalem's water came from the Gihon Spring, located in the Kidron Valley just east of the northern part of the City of David. R. Amiran ("Water Supply," 75) describes the spring as "a typical karst spring, and its waters gush intermittently (this may be the origin of the Hebrew name: *giha,* 'a gushing forth'). Each gush lasts about 40 minutes, with a break of about 6–8 hours between, according to the season. The discharge is about 1200 cubic meters per day, though in summer it drops considerably."

At about the time of David, cisterns lined with lime began to be built to catch and keep rain water. Pools and aqueducts were also built to use the water of the spring efficiently. Access to water was also a prime military consideration in the defense of the city.

Jebusite Jerusalem had an access shaft cut through the rock which archeologists call "Warren's shaft" (cf. Kenyon, *Jerusalem,* 19–22) to which reference is apparently made in 2 Sam 5:8. They also built the first aqueduct down to the Kidron Valley.

A small reservoir to hold the waters of the spring had existed from the early Israelite Monarchy (2 Kgs 18:17). This is probably the "upper pool" of Isa 7:3/36:2. Two aqueducts have been found which lead from this pool down the valley. One is short, extending only some fifty-four yards. The second (II) was used for irrigation of terraced gardens extending to the foot of the Kidron Valley. It drained into the Pool of Shelah (or Sheloah), literally "the aqueduct." This is the modern Birket el-Hamra and is probably to be identified with "the lower pool" of Isa 22:9.

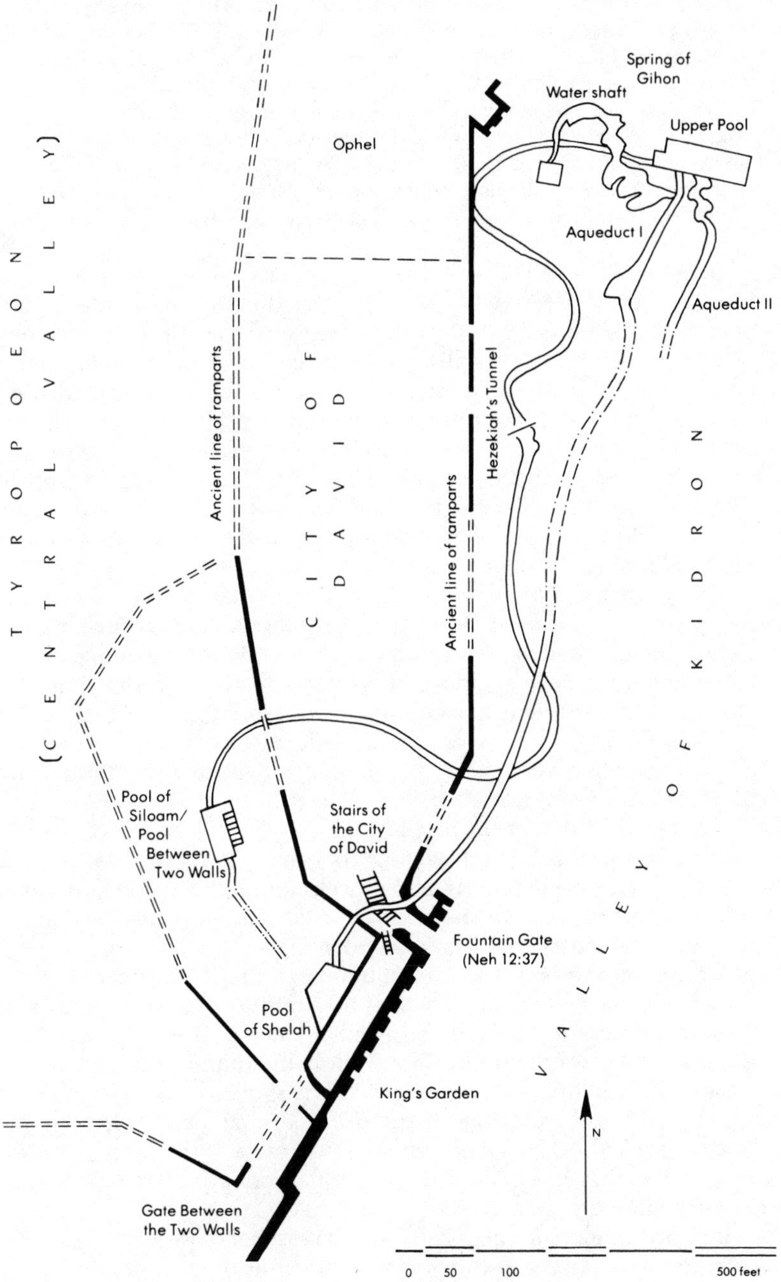

TYROPOEON
(CENTRAL VALLEY)
Ophel
Spring of Gihon
Water shaft
Upper Pool
Aqueduct I
Aqueduct II
Ancient line of ramparts
CITY OF DAVID
Ancient line of ramparts
Hezekiah's Tunnel
VALLEY OF KIDRON
Pool of Siloam/ Pool Between Two Walls
Stairs of the City of David
Fountain Gate (Neh 12:37)
Pool of Shelah
King's Garden
N
Gate Between the Two Walls
0
50
100
500 feet

Repeated references in the Bible (2 Kgs 20:20; Isa 22:11; 2 Chr 32:2–4, 30; Ben Sirach 48:17) report monumental work related to springs, aqueducts, pools, and tunnels, which brought water into the city walls. The discovery of this tunnel in 1880 with an inscription carved into its rock wall (*ANET,* 321) shows how Hezekiah brought water from Gihon to the pool of Siloam. Avigad's discovery of an eighth-century wall to the west leads to the assumption that it joined the old wall of David's City on the south "encompassing the pool of Siloam" (Avi-Yonah, *EAEHL,* 597). This was, then, "the pool between the walls" (Isa 22:11).

The Assyrian was virtually at the door. A major part of that effort involved assuring the city of an adequate water supply. An aqueduct begun by Ahaz (7:3) was rushed to completion along with other projects (2 Chr 32:3, 30).

9b *The Lower Pool* בְּקִיעֵי was filled to capacity.

10–11a A survey of Jerusalem's houses was done both to arrange housing for those villagers who sought safety in the city and to meet needs for defense. Walled cities usually had two walls with a space between, allowing defenders the open space needed to overcome attackers who had penetrated the outer wall. In peace-time that space tended to be built up by squatters with temporary shacks which soon became permanent dwellings. The government apparently took two steps to meet this problem. The houses were demolished to regain the open space between the walls and parts of it were flooded with water from the old pool. This latter created a flooded moat and also ensured water reserves for the besieged city.

11b The government (including the unnamed king) is accused of failure to look to God in its time of peril. It failed to recognize Yahweh's stake in the city which he had made and formed long before Israel existed. The Vision's view of Zion emerges here again—a city whose destiny is older than Canaan, the promised land, and which will survive the collapse of Israel and Judah (2:1–4; 65:17—66:24). The government's failure to reckon with that destiny, even to endanger that destiny as it pursued adventurous nationalistic and personal ambition, is the thrust of this accusation.

The description of this event in 2 Kgs 18:17—19:37/Isa 36–37 contradicts this view. It shows Hezekiah appealing to Isaiah (2 Kgs 19:1–8). In 2 Kgs 19:15–19 Hezekiah prays directly to Yahweh about the second threat to the city. He is supported in each instance by divine assurances through Isaiah. How are these two views to be reconciled?

Chap. 22 appears to be set in a time before the final denouement pictured in 2 Kgs 18–19/Isa 36–37. A comparison suggests that Hezekiah's appeal to Isaiah and prayer to Yahweh followed a long period in which no such advice or assurance was sought. The Vision maintains that the policies of Shebna and Eliakim during Hezekiah's reign ignored prophetic directions to Ahaz (chap. 7) and warnings to themselves (chap. 20). There is no hint of a mood to seek the Lord's direction now—even with Assyria's cavalry at the gates. Their policy has been one of national independence without regard to God's strategies for them.

12 The Lord (and prudence) called for a reversal of policy, abject humiliation before Sennacherib's authority, penance for their rebellion, promises to rebel no more, payment of tribute due, and penalties for the armies' trouble. Hezekiah did exactly this during the 712 B.C. Ashdod rebellion. The city was spared, but it cost virtually everything in the royal treasury.

13 But this time, a nationalistic celebration raises the city's feelings to a fever-pitch of bravado—feasting on animals driven into the city, with no thought of needing them to rebuild the country afterward, drinking an excess of wine, with no thought of saving strength and wit to defend the city. So Jerusalem's rulers had kindled the nationalistic fires in the people's hearts with celebration and feasting (vv 13 and 2a), although they were quite well aware of the city's vulnerability (vv 9–11a).

14 Such callous and irresponsible conduct in officials is unforgivable, as Yahweh's bitter oath confirms.

The address in vv 9–14 has been consistently in second masculine plural. No names are used. The application would fit the entire government or royal house with its appointed officers, which in this case would be identical. This includes Hezekiah and the officials Eliakim, Shebna, and Joah (2 Kgs 18:18). It is interesting to note that this chapter continues the convention of the Vision and does not mention Hezekiah's name. Only in the superscription (1:1) and in material quoted from 2 Kgs does it appear. This obviously intentional slight, in contrast to the treatment accorded Uzziah (6:1) and Ahaz (7:1–17 and 14:28), is significant. The Vision's negative attitude toward Hezekiah's era, as seen in chap. 22, contrasts with the positive views of 2 Kgs and 2 Chr. Perhaps for this very reason it avoids naming the popular king by name; or, by naming his officials, Shebna and Eliakim, it implies that they must bear responsibility for the policies which they had persuaded the king to follow (cf. prophecies in 3:4, 12).

In any case the scene does not picture the conclusion of the military confrontation. That was patently known to every Judean who heard (or read) the Vision. Instead, it turns to God's word to Shebna and Eliakim.

Explanation

The time approaches when the Assyrian armies will be at the gates (cf. chap. 36). Hezekiah's government had been arming to prepare this bid for liberty for some three to four years. But then news came of Babylon's fall in 703 B.C. (chap. 21) and the perceptive in Jerusalem simply "waited for the other shoe to drop."

Now the Assyrians with their polyglot armies of mercenaries and impressed troops were in the area. Jerusalem was in an uproar (v 2), but it is difficult to tell whether it was from panic or jubilation. The naive bravado of pumped-up nationalism covered the nervous fears of the city. But the city had no reason to cheer. The first military encounters showed Judean soldiers unwilling to fight (v 2b). They were captured in ignominous flight and made prisoner.

The Assyrians made a show of force which promptly stripped Jerusalem of its forward defenses in the armed towns and villages near the border. They all surrendered (vv 5–8a). This left the city to fend for itself. The intensive military preparations of the past years had prepared for a very different kind of war with the enemy kept at a distance from the city by strong outposts of armed towns. Now, feverish preparations were required for the city to withstand a siege, as Jerusalem looked to its internal armaments (v 8b).

Whatever the populace may have expected, government ministers were well aware of the weaknesses which their foolish bravado had now laid bare.

Jerusalem was in no shape to withstand a siege. The population was undoubtedly swollen with refugees from the countryside. The major concern was for water (vv 9–11a). Jerusalem's water supply had always been a problem (see *Excursus:* "Hezekiah's Pools and Waterworks"). The source for water lay outside the walls, vulnerable to any siege force. So now the government undertook heroic measures to improve the situation. But they showed no sign of understanding how wrong-headed their entire policy had been over some fifteen and more years. They still did not look to God who made the city and its people long before (v 11b).

God was calling for repentance (v 12) as he had through Isaiah (chap. 20) more than a decade before. Nineveh knew what to do when Jonah preached. They wept and wailed, shaved their heads, wore sackcloth, and sat in ashes. That is what God wanted here. This would indicate that the city, beginning with its leaders, had seen the error of its policies and its ways—that it was prepared for radical change. On such a basis they could sue for peace from Sennacherib, pay tribute, and render faithful vassalage as they had in 712 B.C.

But just the opposite occurred. There was celebration of the temporary liberty—all the more precious because it was unlikely to last (v 13). The drunken show in the streets reflected the irresponsibility of the leaders. They, especially Shebna the prime minister, knew how deep their guilt was. They were aware of the precarious nature of their venture. But, once again they had counted on Egypt. A new and nationalistic Pharaoh promised support. But what came was too little and too late. For the moment Sennacherib's forces could concentrate on Jerusalem. Shebna felt an unforgivable guilt because of the matter (v 14).

Episode E:
Shebna Is Dismissed (22:15–25)

Bibliography

Jenni, E. *Die Politischen Voraussagen der Propheten.* ATANT 29. Zürich: Zwingli-Verlag, 1956. 42. **Martin-Achard, R.** "L'oracle contre Shebna et le pouvoir des clefs." *TZ* 24 (1968) 241–54.

Translation

Prophet: 15 *My Lord*[a] *Yahweh of Hosts said this:* 5
"Get up and go to this steward 3+3
[b]*against Shebna who is over the house.*[bcd]
16 *What are you doing*[a] *here,* 3+3
and who gave you permission to be here,
that you (m sg) have hewed out for yourself a grave here?" 5

Echo Chorus: *Hewing out*[b] *his grave*[c] *on the height* 3+4
cutting out[b] *a resting place for himself in the rock.*
Prophet: [17] *See! Yahweh is hurling you*[a] *(m sg)* 3+2+2
a hurling,[b] *O mighty man,*[c]
and grasping you[d] *(with) a grasp.*
[18] *Winding up, he will throw*[a] *you (m sg) a throw like a ball* 3+1+3
to a land wide on both sides.[b]
There you shall die. 2+3+3
There the chariots[c] *of your glory*
(will be) a disgrace (to) the house of your master.
King: [19] *I shall dismiss you (m sg) from your position!* 2+2
Echo, the Courtiers: *He will*[a] *throw you (m sg) out of your office!*
King: [20] *And it will be in that day* 3+2+2
that I shall call to my servant,
to Eliakim, son of Hilkiah.
[21] *I shall clothe him in your robe,* 2+2+3
I shall fasten on him your sash,
and I shall place your authority in his hand.
He will become a father 2+2+2
to (every) inhabitant of Jerusalem
(and) to the house of Judah.
[22] *I shall place the key of David's house on his shoulder* 4
When he opens, no one will close. 3+3
When he closes, no one will open.
[23] *I shall drive him—a peg*[a] *in a firm place.* 4
It will become a seat of honor for his father's house. 5
[24] *All the weight*[a] *of his father's house will hang on him, the offspring and the offshoot; all the small vessels from the bowls to all the jars.*
Prophet: [25] *In that day,* 2+3
expression[a] *of Yahweh of Hosts,*
the peg will be removed 2+3
which was driven in a firm place.
It will be hewn down and will fall 2+3
and the burden which (hung) on it will be cut off.
For Yahweh has spoken. 3

Notes

15.a. Missing in 2 MSS LXX, Θ, and Syr, probably because יהוה is also rendered by κύριος.

15.b-b. MT עַל "upon" or "against" Shebna is parallel to אֶל "to" or "toward" the steward which precedes. Wildberger (831–32) transposes the entire stich to make it a heading over the paragraph. Others (N. J. Schlögl, *Die heiligen Schriften des Alten Bundes* [Wien: Burg Verlag, 1922]; *BHK*) suggest emending to אֶל. But the changes are unnecessary. "Against" defines the nature of the mission "to" the steward.

15.c. Vg *praepositus templi qui habitat in tabernaculo* "the one placed over the temple who dwells in the tabernacle," is explained by Wildberger (840) as mistakenly reading "the house of your master" (v 18) as a reference to the Temple of the Lord. But the matter is secular and refers to the royal palace and probably the government.

15.d. Gesenius says 2 MSS add ואמרת אליו "and you shall say to him" (v 22) at the end of the verse. LXX Tg Vg contain the addition. Wildberger (832) considers it original, but it is unnecessary when the arrangement of MT is followed.

16.a. DSS^Isa combines the two words to מהלך, presumably a piel ptcp from הלך "coming here." This is a possible meaning, as the question posed by the second stich shows. However, MT makes the same point with more emphasis.

16.b. Archaic case endings for genitive (cf. GKC § 90*m*). Cf. Br. *Synt* § 70*f*.

16.c. LXX *σεαυτῷ* "for yourself." This smooths out the change of persons. But MT poses the more difficult text that must be kept and explained (cf. *Form*).

17.a. MT טלטל a pilp form is unique (BDB, 376), usually translated "throw far away" like the hiph. I. Eitan ("A Contribution to Isaiah Exegesis," *HUCA* 12/13 [1937–38] 68) suggests that it has an iterative sense "shake back and forth." Ehrlich (*Randglossen,* IV, 79) says טלטל can mean "stretch out long."

17.b. טלטלה, as a noun or an adjective, has been challenged. Duhm expected inf abs and suggested removing ה and placing it with גבר as a vocative. Kaiser (148) follows Ginsberg ("Some Emendations in Isaiah," *JBL* 69 [1950] 51–60) כְּטַלְטֵל הַבֶּגֶר and Driver (*JSS* 13 [1968] 48) בְּטַלְטֵלָה בֶּגֶר in translating "as one shakes out a garment." Wildberger (832) is right in rejecting the need for emendation.

17.c. Fohrer, followed by Wildberger, sees this as intended ironically: "du Kerl" ("you fine fellow").

17.d. עטה is also a *hapax* (cf. BDB, II, 742). KB suggests that in Jer 43:12 the root means "rid oneself of lice" (following von Gall). Kaiser (148) uses that meaning here after emending to "garment" in the previous line. However, the basic meaning of "grasp" or "seize hold of" for this text is supported by BDB, KB, Wildberger, and others.

18.a. צנף is usually translated "wind up" which led Galling (*BRL,* 239) to think of Egyptian mummies. LXX *καὶ ῥίψει σε* "and he will throw you" and Eitan's suggestion that it be understood like Arab *ḍafana* "to kick" provide Wildberger's meaning "throw him with a powerful kick."

18.b. Lit. "wide of both hands," i.e., to the left hand and to the right hand.

18.c. "Chariots" were used as vehicles for persons of rank. Kissane emends to read וּשְׁמָמָה קִבְרַב כְּבוֹדֶךָ "and thy splendid tomb shall be desolate." LXX reads a singular *τὸ ἅρμα*. Duhm agreed that "one vehicle is enough." But these emendations are unnecessary; with Wildberger, MT may be sustained.

19.a. Tg, Syr, Vg have 1st pers followed by many interpreters who point out that י and א were very similar in old Hebrew (cf. *BHK* and *BHS*). It is better to take the change of person as a signal of a change in speaker.

23.a. "a tent-peg."

24.a. כבוד in v 23 meant "honor." But here the original meaning of "weight" is called for.

25.a. MT נאם "expression" is rendered by DSS^Isa נואם, merely a change of form (cf. E. Y. Kutscher, *Isaiah Scroll,* 498.

Form/Structure/Setting

This highly dramatic chapter consists of five parts. Vv 1b–8 address Jerusalem and its inhabitants in second feminine singular. It chides the city for its ambiguous excitement, mixing despair and revelry (v 2a), and for the cowardly behavior of its officers in the field (vv 2b–3). It records an official's (is this Shebna?) plea to be left alone with his grief (v 4). A somber reminder that Yahweh plans such a day (v 5) is coupled with the military report of troops having overrun Judah's outer defense perimeter (vv 6–8a). The final word is a transition to the following section: Jerusalem is forced to look to the royal armory and the defenses of the walled city itself (v 8b).

The second part (vv 9–14) addresses the royal house and its ministers in second masculine plural. Vv 9–11 accuse them of following policies of military preparation with no regard to the Lord's intentions in the matter. Vv 12–13 record what the Lord required at such a time: repentance and reversal of policy; and what actually happened: celebration and bravado. V 14 continues this address with Yahweh's vow to hold them responsible for this situation.

The third part (vv 15–19) focuses attention on Shebna, the responsible high official with accusation, threat, and announcement of judgment.

15–18 The paragraph is clearly marked out from its surroundings and exhibits the characteristics of the "speech of a messenger" (Westermann, *Basic Forms,* 98–102). The Versions were aware of this, as the additions in LXX and Tg show, filling in what they perceive as gaps in the form (cf. Wildberger, 834).

Note that the first line of the speech parallels that in 22:1.

22:1	מה־לך אפוה כי עלית . . . תשאות מלאה עיר הומיה
22:16	מה־לך פה . . . כי חצבה לך . . . חצבי מרום קברו

The same shock with which the question is asked in v 1 reappears in this question to Shebna.

The outline:

15b A kind of superscription: "Against Shebna"
15a Introductory formula "Thus says the Lord"
15ba Instruction to the prophet: "Go to," like instruction to a messenger
16 Accusation: "What are you doing here?"
17–18 Announcement of Yahweh's judgment

V 19 has the king's measured words that demote Shebna. They, like 8a, are transitional, opening the way for the announcement that comes in vv 20–24 of Eliakim's appointment in Shebna's place.

20–24 The king's speech continues, but no longer addresses Shebna directly, as he speaks of his successor, Eliakim. What follows is the fullest description of this position of honor and authority that exists in Scripture.

25 A prophetic word in heavy prose style closes the chapter in a dark tone of gloomy judgment. The king's change of leadership is seen as more cosmetic than real: the policies remain. God's judgment cuts deeper—Eliakim will also fall.

The chapter is one woven whole of many colors and styles. It presumes the growing tensions of the Assyrian advance on the city (vv 6–7) and the political demotion of Shebna, the chief architect of Hezekiah's policy of national independence and rebellion (v 19). It sees through the hypocrisy and unrealistic views of the city (v 2), of the government (vv 9–11 and 12–13), of the prime-minister (v 16), and of the change of prime-ministers (v 25). Judah's ruin is manifest: "the destruction of the people" (v 4). Hers is a sin that cannot be atoned for (v 14). She, with the government, will collapse (v 25).

The chapter avoids Hezekiah's name, in line with the entire section. But his involvement in every stage is transparent.

Comment

15 This is the first genuinely prophetic word in the chapter. The form is classic (see *Form*). As Elijah was sent to Ahab (1 Kgs 21:17–23), so now one is sent to Shebna. The messenger (prophet) is unnamed. It may as well be Isaiah as anyone else, but the text does not specify.

שֶׁבְנָא "Shebna" is written in 2 Kgs 18:18, 26 with ה. LXX Σομναν, Vg *Sobnas.* Brockelmann (*VG,* I, 75*a*) suggests that the variations of vowels o/u d of consonants b/m is a very understandable phenomenon in the language. The name is interesting. R. de Vaux, ("Titres et fonctionnaires égyptiens a la cour de David et de Salomon," *RB* 48 [1939] 400) thought it was an Egyptian name, and the idea that Shebna was a foreigner has been carried on by Kaiser (153). But the name appears frequently in its longer form שבניה|שבניהו "Shebniah" (1 Chr 15:24; Neh 9:4; 10:11, 13[10,12]) and must be seen as one indigenous to Judah (M. Noth, *Personennamen,* 258). Inscriptions also bear the name (see Wildberger, 836–37). Shebna's name, along with Hilkiah's, appears in the account of the Rabshakeh's visit in 701 B.C. (cf. 2 Kgs 18:18/Isa 36:3; J. M. Ward, "Shebna," *IDB* 4:312).

הסכן הזה "this steward" (*IDB* 4:443). The term appears in the OT otherwise only as a feminine סֹכֶנֶת "maidservant, nurse" (1 Kgs 1:2, 4). M. J. Mulder ("Versuch zur Deutung von *sokenet* in I. Kön. I 2, 4," *VT* 22 [1972] 43–54) pleads for the meaning "representative" or "substitute" and thinks of the old queen. Such a meaning in the masculine is supported by inscriptions in several languages (E. Lipinski, "SKN et SGN dans le semtique occidental du nord," *UF* 5 [1973] 191–207). Thus the term apparently means the one who represents the king. However, these instructions depreciate the title by adding "this." The tone is unmistakable.

Who is over the house is the title of a ranking member of government under the king (cf. R. de Vaux, *Ancient Israel,* 129–31). It is used first in Solomon's list of officials (1 Kgs 4:6) where it has an unimportant position. Ahishar was apparently the *major domo* only. The title is mentioned several times (1 Kgs 16:9; 18:3; 2 Kgs 15:5). By Hezekiah's time the position had grown in importance in much the same way that Joseph's grew under Pharaoh (Gen 40–44; 45:8). Shebna's position must have been very much like that of a vizier in Egypt. "All affairs of the land passed through his hands, all important documents received his seal, all the officials were under his orders. He really governed in Pharaoh's name . . . ." (R. de Vaux, *Ancient Israel,* 130). 2 Kgs 15:5 uses the title for Jotham, the heir of the stricken Azariah: "He was over the household, governing the people of the land." (Cf. H. J. Katzenstein, "The Royal Steward [Asher ʿal ha-Bayith]," *IEJ* 10 [1960] 149–54; T. N. D. Mettinger, *Solomonic State Officials* [Lund: Gleerup, 1971] 70–110.)

Eliakim will succeed Shebna in that office. In 2 Kgs 18:18/Isa 36:3 Eliakim leads the delegation and bears the title "who is over the palace." At this time, presumably shortly before the meeting with the Rabshakeh, Shebna bears the greater title and the major responsibility.

16 That the instructions say "against Shebna" foretells a message of judgment. The confrontation opens with a challenging question (cf. 1 Kgs 21:19).

The word פֹּה "here" occurs three times in the first half of the verse. The meeting takes place in the royal mausoleum. It is macabre in the extreme. In this episode (a scene which deserves to be remembered beside "Nero fiddled while Rome burned") the prime minister chooses the moment when Jerusalem's citizens are frantically arming for a last-ditch stand against the invaders to visit the elaborate mausoleum he was preparing for himself in the royal cemetery. The question conveys the horror at his presumption, along with the irony of this action at this time by this official. Such is the character of the chief administrator of Hezekiah's regime.

The place where the kings from David to Ahaz were buried was inside the walls, in the old city of David (de Vaux, *Ancient Israel,* 58; 1 Kgs 2:10; 2 Kgs 16:20). Israelite funeral practices of the period preferred crypts cut into rocky hillside (cf. *IDBSup,* 119 and *ISBE* 2:558). Perhaps Hezekiah's renovations for the city included plans for a new necropolis outside the city "on the height," since the record in Kings omits listing his burial in the city of David. An inscription on a tomb in Siloam contains the title, but with the name incomplete. De Vaux (*Ancient Israel,* 129) asks, "Could it be the tomb of Shebna?"

But the bizarre question remains: What is Shebna, Jerusalem's ranking official, doing out there at this time? This may compare with the most scandalous revelations of investigative reporting in another age. Why should he be preoccupied with dignity in death, while most people in Jerusalem were still hoping to live?

17–18 Yahweh's personal fury exhausts the prophet's language potential as Isaiah portrays him seizing Shebna and throwing him out, like a ball, into open country (i.e., away from capital city), to die with his chariot, useless, alone, meaningless without the rank it symbolized—a disgrace to the royal house he served.

What exactly was Shebna's crime? Kaiser relates it to Isaiah's concern for justice and thinks of exploiting the poor (153–54), but looks to pride in office beyond that. Clements emphasizes "the pretensions of a prominent tomb for himself" (187). J. M. Ward (IDB 4:312) stresses Shebna's identification with anti-Assyrian policies. Wildberger (841) combines the shock at his pride with recognition of *eine Politik des öffentlichen Ruins,* literally, "a political stand of public ruin."

The context sets the stage: v 4, the recognition of the result of destructive policies, vv 9–11, emphasis on armament and military preparation rather than God's purposes, v 13, failure to repent and insistence on futile heroics in the face of an overwhelming enemy. These were the faults of the government. Now Shebna's callous attention to preparation of his elaborate mausoleum adds the last straw. Had he been influenced by the Egyptians whom he courted?

Mighty man translates גבר *geber* a man according to his power (Wildberger). But that is as nothing when God takes hold of him. Ps 52:3, 9[1, 7] describe such a hero who is snatched and torn from his tent. M. Klopfenstein (*Die Lüge nach dem Alten Testament* [Zürich: Gotthelf-Verlag, 1964] n. 319) suggests that Ps 101:7 and Ps 52:4–6[2–4] were directed at officials of the court who misused their offices. Ps 52:7[5] is similar to vv 17–18.

A land wide on both sides has been taken to refer to Mesopotamia. Fohrer thinks of the Philistine coast. The term is not specific enough for the interpretations laid on it.

19 The tone shifts from having Shebna exiled from the city (perhaps the country) to having him lose his position, standing or office. This is more in line with his appearance in 2 Kgs 18:18/Isa 36:3 where his title is "the secretary" and he is listed after Hilkiah who now holds the first position and the title which formerly belonged to Shebna. The indirect speech through the prophet changes to the king's direct speech. In more restrained tones he announces demotion from his high position. A spokesman echoes the decree.

20–22 The king's speech continues: Eliakim will be put into Shebna's place with all the symbols of rank. These include a tunic, sash, and the key to the royal house. His roles, which presumably Shebna had before him, include being *father* for Jerusalemites and Judeans. This probably means being available to help in all affairs—a role somewhere between the Saudi monarch's availability to his subjects and a Chicago ward-boss' service to his constituents. He also served as chief of ministers in the royal government. He made decisions which carried royal authority and could not be appealed.

23 The king will establish him in office. The metaphors here appear to be mixed. *A peg in a firm place* seems to picture a tent peg driven in firm ground, while v 24 pictures a fixture to hold pots and pans on a kitchen wall, strong enough to support his broader family (*his father's house*), including direct descendants (*offspring*) and related members (*offshoot*). Such an appointment provided economic support and safety for the whole family, as it still does in many countries such as India.

The scene in 2 Kgs 18:18/Isa 36:3, which names both men, appears to reflect the situation after these changes have taken place. Eliakim is the leader over the palace. Shebna has been demoted to a secondary role. But the fact that Shebna is still there is an indication that this was a cosmetic change. Policy remained the same. There is no sign that either of them recognized the error of his ways.

25 *In that day* looks beyond the setting of vv 15–24 dealing with Shebna's demotion to announce Yahweh's reversal of the announcement that Eliakim will take Shebna's place. He is no better and must now be removed.

Explanation

The overwhelming accusation of vv 1–14 has its effect. A prophet who is sent to denounce Shebna in Yahweh's name (v 15) finds him preparing his own mausoleum (v 16). The prophet passionately announces God's decree of his downfall (vv 17–18). This leads the king to mandate his dismissal (v 19).

But this is not a real change of direction, as the new appointment shows. Eliakim, who has held second position in the government, simply exchanges positions with Shebna (v 20). Eliakim becomes the administrator of the palace, while Shebna is "demoted" to secretary. This game of musical chairs is played out with pomp and circumstance as the new prime minister is installed with all the formality and confidence that the office deserves (vv 21–24).

But all this has an empty ring. Eliakim's policies are identical with those of Shebna. The change will not mislead Sennacherib's representative. The policies that have long characterized Hezekiah's Jerusalem will continue. (See 2 Kgs 18:19–25/Isa 36:4–10.) Nor has the Rabshakeh missed the rift that exists between the prophets and the court (2 Kgs 18:26/Isa 36:11).

It is no wonder that the prophet returns to disassociate Yahweh from promises of permanence for Eliakim that were spoken in the installation ceremony (v 23–24). On the contrary, Yahweh declares that Eliakim must also be removed (v 25) so that no part of that wrong policy and wrong administration may remain.

The remainder of Hezekiah's life was apparently a very different one. Manasseh may well have joined him as coregent shortly after this. It was Manasseh's mark of loyal vassalage, like that of Ahaz his grandfather, that lay over the first half of the following century. That shows the required change of policy and direction which Shebna's dismissal and Eliakim's appointment did *not* demonstrate.

Act IV: The Impact of Tyre's Fall (Chaps. 23–27)

THE FOURTH GENERATION:
THE VASSAL YEARS OF HEZEKIAH AND MANASSEH (*ca.* 700–640 B.C.)

Bibliography

Elat, M. "The Political Status of the Kingdom of Judah within the Assyrian Empire in the 7th Century BCE." *Lachish V* (1975) 61–70 (esp. 64). **Ehrlich, E. L.** "Der Aufenthalt des Königs Manasse in Babylon." *TZ* 21 (1965) 281–86. **Ginsburg, H. L.** "Judah and the Transjordan States from 734 to 582 BCE." *Alexander Marx Jubilee Volume.* Philadelphia: Jewish Publication Society of America, 1950. 347–68. **Randles, R. J.** *The Interaction of Israel, Judah, and Egypt from Solomon to Josiah.* Diss. Southern Baptist Theological Seminary, Louisville, KY, 1980. 210–38.

In chapters 23–27 two concepts are intertwined. One speaks of Yahweh planning the course of events (23:9, יעצה) and then deciding the fate (יפקד) of Tyre (23:17), the kings (24:21), the land (26:21a) and Leviathan (27:1).

But another concept describes processes much less personal by which the land is defiled by the broken covenant (24:5), by a curse that consumes the earth because of blood-guilt (24:6). This concept speaks of the floodgates of heaven opening and the foundation of the earth being shaken (24:18b–20) because of the guilt. It pictures the royal banquet for all peoples where it is announced that Yahweh of Hosts will swallow up (בלע) the cursed shroud of permanent death—a shroud that has covered all the peoples and nations because of the reproach that lay heavy on the land (25:6–8). It speaks of the land revealing the blood-guilt that it had hidden until that time (26:21). This second concept is like that of Gen 4:10–12 where the ground (אדמה) was under a curse because human blood had been spilled on it. The same view is found in Num 35:33–34: "Bloodshed pollutes the land. . . . Do not pollute the land." 2 Sam 2:21 speaks of land cursed because of a violent crime.

The two concepts are united by the picture of Yahweh of Hosts reigning on Mt. Zion (24:23). Only under the reigning glory of the Divine King can the two views be reconciled. It is imperative that the entire passage be interpreted as a unit with the two concepts dependent upon each other. In the OT, the consequences of the curse are often pictured, but not the way in which a curse can be lifted or ended. Once unleashed and operative, the damning power of a curse, like that brought on the land by repeated killings, seemed to have a demonic life of its own, which no ordinary mortal could stop. Yahweh of Hosts on Zion could and did! He decided the fate and swallowed up the curse! Only through such judgment and amnesty could the ominous and pervasive effects of the curse and guilt be counteracted.

Thus Act V has a strong element (marked below by "A") relating to that mysterious sphere of blessing/curse or holy/profane. It also has another element (marked below by "B") relating to history. The two are intertwined. In 23:9 Yahweh of Hosts planned trouble for Tyre (B). He is also said to defile or pollute (חלל) the pride of their glory (A). In 23:17 Yahweh will decide Tyre's fate (B). In 24:5 the land is polluted/profaned (A) by its inhabitants. The eternal covenant is broken (B). A curse consumes the land while the people must bear their contamination (A). In 24:21 Yahweh will decide the fate of kings and armies (B). Throughout 25:6–8 the feast of Yahweh of Hosts functions in terms of element A, but in 26:21a Yahweh will settle the fate of the land (B) while 26:21b tells of the land's being forced to reveal its blood-guilt (A). In 27:1 Yahweh settles the fate of Leviathan, symbol for Tyre (B). In 27:13 Israel will be gathered from far places (B). She will again be sanctified to worship God on the holy mountain in Jerusalem (A).

Just as the specific crime of dumping dangerous chemicals may result in a festering condition that requires a remedy far beyond punishment of the offender, so here the crimes of pride (23:9) and the breaking of laws and covenant (24:5) had brought about a condition in which the curse prevails (24:6) like a shroud over the whole land (25:7) causing destruction, ruin, and death (25:8). The violent crimes have led to blood-guilt and its results so that the entire land is cursed because of the sins of its people. (Cf. J. Pedersen, *Israel* III-IV [Copenhagen: Paul Branner, 1940] 270–76.)

This Act is a virtual catalog of the vocabulary of curse: אלה "curse" (24:6) and חרפה "disgrace" (25:8) which אכל "consume" (24:6), חלל "profane" (23:9), חנף "resist the sacred" (24:5). The people involved are דמם "silenced" (23:2), בוש "shamed" (23:4), קלל "humbled" (23:9), אשם "contaminated" (24:6), חור "pale in weakness" (24:6). The causes of this are עבר "disregarding instruction" (24:5), חלף "violating a statute" (24:5), הפר "making the eternal covenant meaningless" (24:5) and, as summaries, דמים "blood-guilt" and הרוגים "slain" (26:21). The cumulative effect of murders, assassinations, and wars are seen in the curse and its debilitating loss of all vitality. This condition could very properly bear the label המות לנצח "the death forever" (25:8).

As the curse was all-consuming, אכלה (24:6), so the remedy had to be able to swallow totally, בלע (25:7, 8), the evil contaminant. The two words share a semantic field. The second often carries the sense of "making to disappear" (*TWAT* I, 660).

The wonder of Yahweh's decree of salvation in 25:8 and his act of salvation in 26:21 can be seen in 27:13 as "those who were perishing will come and worship on the holy mountain in Jerusalem." The mountain's holiness had been secured or restored, and the people of Israel had been sanctified so that they could enter its sacred walls again.

While the curse that resulted from the breach of covenant had a kind of automatic and autonomous character, the scenes never allow Yahweh's judgment to be seen in totally impersonal terms. His sovereign decisions on the throne control the course of events. He planned it (23:9). He determined the fates of the parties involved. He "swallowed up the cursed plague of everlasting death" (25:8), thus taking the control of events away from the continuing power of blood-guilt and curse. And he would thresh and gather Israelites from greater Palestine to join those from Assyria and Egypt to worship in Jerusalem.

The list of scenes and their contents is as follows:

Scene 1: Burden: Tyre (23:1–18)
Scene 2: The Devastated Land (24:1–13)
Scene 3: Yahweh and the Kings (24:14–22)
Scene 4: Yahweh of Hosts Reigns on Mount Zion (24:23–25:8)
Scene 5: Response from a Yahwist (25:9–12)
Scene 6: Judeans on Pilgrimage to Jerusalem (26:1–21)
Scene 7: "That Day" for Tyre and for Israel (27:1–13)

HISTORICAL BACKGROUND

The half century that followed the siege of Jerusalem (700–640 B.C.) saw the Assyrian Empire reach the apogee of its power. Sennacherib had even defeated an Egyptian army under Taharqa at Eltekeh (Kitchen, *The Third Intermediate Period,* 383–85). Judah had no choice other than to submit itself to Assyrian vassalage during the rest of Hezekiah's reign and that of Manasseh, his son.

As in the reign of Ahaz, this put Judah in the spectator's position through most of that period. Twenty years passed quietly. But the accession of Esarhaddon to Assyria's throne (680–669 B.C.) brought a more aggressive policy to affairs in West Asia. Between 677 and 663 B.C. the Assyrian storm broke over the area with unparalleled fury. Until this time the principal battles had been fought between the superpower Assyria and local coalitions of kingdoms. Egypt, potentially the other superpower, had usually avoided major confrontation. But in this decade and a half the great powers clashed repeatedly.

The shock waves must have been felt throughout the Near East with apocalyptic intensity. Manasseh had the wisdom to keep to the sidelines as much as possible. Egypt's Phoenician allies caught the brunt of the first assaults. Sidon was attacked in 677 B.C. Esarhaddon invaded Egypt in 674 and again in 671 B.C. Ashurbanipal (669–627 B.C.) drove into Egypt in 667–666 B.C. and again with a terrible sack of Thebes in 663 B.C. These blows were finally too much for the 25th dynasty, which withdrew to its Ethiopian home.

Esarhaddon's destruction of Sidon and subjugation of Tyre in 677 B.C. was a step toward his invasion of Egypt in 674 and 671. Ashurbanipal followed the same procedure in 667. Manasseh was forced to supply forces and participate with Assyria in the invasion of Egypt in that year (*ANET,* 294).

Baal I of Tyre apparently supported Tantamani in Egypt's ill-advised rebellion of 664 B.C. Ashurbanipal repaid him by capturing Tyre on his return trip and turning the entire Phoenician area into Assyrian provinces with severe restrictions on her ability to profit from the sea trade which had traditionally been her exclusive province.

Perhaps it was at this time that Manasseh, suspected of belonging to the rebellion, was taken to Nineveh, only to be released and returned home (2 Chr 33:9–11; H. J. Katzenstein, *The History of Tyre* [Jerusalem: Schocken Institute, 1973] 292; Randles, *Interaction,* 221).

The Vision's Interpretation of the Period

Act IV portrays the nadir of Palestine's fortunes in the abstract colors and sounds of cataclysmic ultimacy, marking the end of an age. Only Tyre's fate at the hands of Esarhaddon (or is it Ashurbanipal?) is described specifically (chap. 23). Assyria and Egypt are rarely mentioned in the act. But the clash of the Titans is portrayed with an appropriate sense of "ultimate" doom—although always within Yahweh's range of control.

The mood for this generation, like that of Ahaz (Act II, chaps. 7–14), is one of submission and acceptance. Manasseh submitted to Assyria. He sent labor gangs to build Kar Esarhaddon and Nineveh (*ANET,* 291). This was branded "apostasy" and "idolatry" by 2 Kgs 21 and 2 Chr 33, but the Vision sees it as acceptance of Yahweh's "plan" that ordained Assyria for just such a mission.

"The Rod of Yahweh's Anger" had broken through the northern ring of protective states, the Hittite and Amorite cities west of the Euphrates which had been rebuilt by David. Assyrian pressure in Uzziah's reign broke through this ring (Act I, chaps. 1–6). Tiglath-Pileser had continued to chip away at it until Aram collapsed, and Sargon II had applied the pressure that destroyed Israel (Act II, chaps. 7–10). Babylon's counterweight had slowed Assyria's western expansion until Babylon was overcome in 711 B.C. (chap. 13) and 703 B.C. (chap. 21). Philistine resistance collapsed about the same time (14:28–32), and with the fall of Babylon and Philistia, Judah's opposition was put down (Act III, chaps. 15–22).

Now the Phoenician cities that guarded the approaches to Egypt and that had played such a vital role in Palestine's political, cultural, and economic life for well over half a millennium were vulnerable. Esarhaddon subdued them in 677 B.C. on his way to overcoming Egypt in 671 B.C. Ashurbanipal repeated the occupations in 667/66 B.C. and again in 663. After a brief resurgence in 620–605 B.C., Egypt's subjugation was confirmed by Nebuchadnezzar in 572 B.C. and was continued by the Persian Empire.

With this, collapsed the last pillar that supported the political, social, and economic system within which Israel had existed. The Mesopotamian and Egyptian anchors to the east and to the south, which had sheltered and enriched Canaanite civilization and culture, disappeared in the stormy Assyrian tide that broke over the land. Lacking these, the possibilities of another *pax Davidica* also vanished. Judah had no chance to survive as a sovereign state. These chapters, with those that follow (28–39), mark the end of an age and the civilization it nurtured.

The Vision insists that all this was from God. His judgment over that civilization had deep roots. That judgment had prepared Canaan to receive Israel in the first place, and now Israel is taken into the depths with it. Yahweh's larger strategy looked to a different basis for political stability. He was preparing Israel for a better matrix for her mission than Canaan could provide, a better civilization than Canaan's could possibly be. He calls Israel and Judah to see and believe this (chaps. 40–66). He offers them privileged and handcrafted roles in that new age. The future lies not in their old cities and political structures, but in a new "planting" (27:2–6). This replanting will be the theme of the last six acts.

In the midst of devastation there is hope, because it is God who is acting. *On this mountain* he who controls life and death sentences tyrants to death (26:14) but promises that the dead of the faithful will rise (26:19). He will punish and slay Leviathan, the dragon (27:1). Israel's new planting will fill all the civilized world (not just Canaan) with fruit (27:6). God will harvest it from the Euphrates to the River of Egypt, David's old boundaries (27:12). Even those beyond, in Assyria and Egypt, can be part of the pilgrim congregation at Zion's festivals (27:13).

The chapters fit exactly into the entire Vision's view of God's relation to history. The view is optimistic: the best is yet to be. It is forward-looking and sees God's goals staked out in the future. It can relate those to ultimate ends (overcoming death; killing the dragon). But they are not pushed to an ultimate future beyond history. They are drawn into a future that is in God's hands, determined and executed on God's mountain. That mountain is Zion, not heaven, and the means of worship on that golden day is pilgrimage, like that which was possible throughout the Persian and Graeco-Roman period to the time of the Destruction of Jerusalem in A.D. 70.

These chapters have much more to do with the Vision's perspectives than they do with those of Daniel or Enoch. To pull them out of their context and treat them from the latter perspective is to do violence to their nature and intention.

THE ANNOUNCEMENT OF YAHWEH'S ROYAL REIGN

The usual division of these chapters has relegated chap. 23 to the collection of "foreign prophecies" that precede it and has treated chaps. 24–27 as a self-contained unit. However, chap. 22, with its description of Jerusalem in 701 B.C., was found to be a natural closing scene for Act III. Tyre's fall will be seen to have its natural historical setting in the seventh century. All of chaps. 23–27 will be shown to present repeated responses to the fall of Tyre, so the chapters are grouped here together. A natural break occurs after chap. 27, which is universally recognized.

The internal structure of chaps. 23–27 supports this division. The climactic declaration in 25:6 that Yahweh prepares a banquet on Zion is the keystone in a grand arch of announcements in the style of Yahweh's royal reign on Zion that begin in 23:1 and continue through 27:13.

Tyre is ordered to respond (23:1–7)
- A Yahweh planned this against Tyre (23:8–9)
  Response from sailors (23:10)
  - B Yahweh stretched his hand over the sea (23:11–12a)
    Responses from the sailors and prophets (23:12b–18)
    - C See Yahweh devastating the land (24:1–3)
      Responses (24:4–20)
      - D Yahweh judges armies and kings (24:21)
        Responses (24:22)
        - E Yahweh of Hosts reigns (24:23)
          Individual responses (25:1–5)

KEYSTONE On Mount Zion, Yahweh of Hosts prepares a banquet (25:6)

E′ He destroys death forever (25:7–8)
Response of Jerusalem (25:9)
D′ The hand of Yahweh on this mountain: Moab judged (25:10–12)
Response of Judah (26:1–20)
C′ Yahweh coming to judge the inhabitants of the land (26:21)
B′ Yahweh to judge Leviathan, monster of the sea (27:1)
Response of Israel (27:2–11)
A′ Yahweh will thresh and gather Israel (27:12–13)

On the rising steps of the chiastic ladder, Tyre and the land are called to respond. On the descending steps, Jerusalem, Judah, and Israel are called to respond. Note the span of seventy years provided for the Act. This skeletal theme of Yahweh's royal day is fleshed out in terms that fit the context of the Vision as responses to the fall of Tyre. This destruction (chap. 23) is seen as a symbol of the generation in which the last resistance to imperial tyranny collapses. The entire land, all the cities (city-states), and even the sea, with its channels of commerce and power, come under the rule of Assyria, "the rod of Yahweh's anger."

The land and its cities provide evidence of Yahweh's devastation (24:1–13). Response to the devastation varies from jubilation to despair (24:14–16).

The scene is brought under the "kingship" theme by the announcement that the terror has solid basis, for the ultimates of cosmic judgment are involved (vv 17–20). Through these Yahweh will judge the powers and will reign gloriously on Zion (vv 21–24). A psalm rejoices in this recognition (25:1–5) before the kingship theme is developed through announcement of the banquet for the peoples when Yahweh will "swallow up death forever" (vv 6–8). A confessional hymn (v 9) precedes the further kingship theme of victory over the nations (Moab) (vv 10–12). Chap. 26 celebrates and develops the theme's significance for Jerusalem and its people who are then warned to prepare for a continuation of wrath (v 20).

The closing themes announce Yahweh's "coming from his dwelling" to punish the earth/land for its sins (26:21) and his punishment of Leviathan, "the monster of the sea" (27:1). The rest of chap. 27 deals with the consequences for Israel.

Thus the act in its artistry communicates on more than one level: The dramatic portrayal of Tyre's historical fall before Assyrian pressure (687 B.C.) is used to typify the final subjugation of all "the land" (see *Excursus*); it is the last of the great "cities" (see *Excursus*) to fall before the empire. This fall in turn is set in the context of Yahweh's rule on Zion which humbles the proud of the nations and which "visits/punishes" (see *Excursus*) any dissenting power in heaven or on earth until his rule is complete and acknowledged.

This is not apocalyptic (see *Excursus*) of the type that characterized the Judaism of the second century B.C. onward. It is the application of Kingship-of-Yahweh themes from Solomon's temple on Zion, reborn to new life and meaning in fifth century Jerusalem, paralleling the development of the themes in Zech 9–14 and in Malachi. A significant difference from the pre-exilic forms lies in the absence of a role for the Davidic king. Hope lies in the direct intervention of God who provides a strong city and protects it (26:1) and who preserves his vineyard (27:2–5) in contrast to the ruined land and empty cities all about. The application to the era of Manasseh, when the king was powerless, is obvious.

Scene 1: Burden: Tyre (23:1–18)

Bibliography

Dahood, M. "Textual Problems in Isaiah." *CBQ* 22 (1960) 400–409. ———. "The Value of Ugaritic for Textual Criticism, Isa 23:9." *Bib* 40 (1959) 160–64. **Grünberg, S.** "Exegetische Beiträge, Jesajah 23:15." *Jeshurun* 13 (1926) 50–56. **Katzenstein, H. Y.** "משא עור—היסטוריה, גיאורגרפיה ארכיאולוגיה Onus Tyri—historia, geographia, archaeologia." *HaMikra' weToledot Yisrael.* Tel Aviv: University of Tel Aviv, 1972. **Lindblom, J.** "Der Ausspruch über Tyrus in Jes. 23." *ASTI* 4 (1965) 56–73. **Linder, J.** "Weissaġung über Tẏrus, Isaias Kap. 23." *ZKT* 65 (1941) 217–21. **Rudolph, W.** "Jesaja 23:1–14." *FS F. Baumgärtel.* Erlanger Forschungen A 10. Erlangen: Universitätsbund, 1959. 166–74. **Watson, W. G. E.** "Tribute to Tyre (Isa XXIII 7)." *VT* 26 (1976) 371–74.

Translation

Herald: 1 *Burden: Tyre* 2
First Mourner: *Howl,* [a] *O ships of Tarshish,* [b] 3+3
for (it) is destroyed without a house [c] *to come home* [b] *to.*
From the land of Cyprus 2+2
it was made known to them.
Second Mourner: 2 *Mourn,* [a] *inhabitants of the coast,* 3+2
merchants [b] *of Sidon,* [c]
who send [d] *your messengers* [e] 2+2
3 *on many waters.* [a]
The seed of Shihor, 2+3+3
the harvest of the Nile [b] *(was) her* [c] *revenue.*
Thus she became the merchant of nations.
Third Mourner: 4 *Shame on you, Sidon!* 2+3+3
For the sea has spoken,
the sea's stronghold, saying, [a]
"I have not been in labor. 2+2
I have not given birth.
I have not raised boys 3+2
(nor) brought up girls."
First Mourner: 5 *As soon as a report* [a] *(is made) to Egypt,* 3+3
they will writhe in pain at the news about Tyre.

Second Mourner: [6] *Cross over* [a] *to Tarshish!* 2+3
Howl, O [b] *inhabitants of the coast!* [b]
Third Mourner: [7] *Has this been a city of revelry* [a] *for you?* 3+3
One whose origin [b] *(was) from days of old?*
One whose feet took her 2+2
to sojourn [c] *far away?*
Heavens: [8] *Who planned this* 3+3
against Tyre, the giver of crowns, [a]
whose merchants [b] *(are) princes,* 3+3
whose traders [c] *(are) the honored of the land?* [d]
Earth: [9] *Yahweh of Hosts planned it* 3+4+4
to defile [a] *the pride of all glory,* [a]
to dishonor all the honored of the land.
First Mourner: [10] *Till* [a] *your land,* 2+3+3
for ships [b] *of Tarshish* [c]
no longer have a wharf! [d]
Earth: [11] *When he stretched out his hand over the sea,* 3+2
he caused kingdoms to tremble!
Yahweh had issued a command concerning Canaan 3+2
to destroy her fortresses. [a]
[12] *Then he said:* [a] 1+3+3
"Do not continue your revels,
oppressed [b] *virgin-daughter Sidon!"*
Second Mourner: *Rise! Cross over (to) Cyprus!* [c] 3+3
Even there you cannot find rest for yourself!
Third Mourner: [13] *See the land of the Chaldeans!* [a] 3+4+3
This was the people who no longer exist!
Assyria assigned her to wild beasts. [b]
They raised their siege towers. [c] 2+2+2
They stripped her citadels,
making her a ruin.
First Mourner: [14] *Howl, O ships of Tarshish,* 3+3
for your stronghold is destroyed.
First Prophet: [15] *And it will be in that* [a] *day* 3
[b] *that Tyre will be forgotten* [c] *for seventy years,* 4+3
like the days of one king.
At the end of seventy years [b] 3+4
(you will be) like the song of the harlot:
[16] *Take a harp,* 2+2+2
go about the city,
forgotten harlot.
Make a good melody! 2+2+2
Repeat a song,
so that you will be remembered!
Second Prophet: [17] *And it will be* 1+3
at the end of seventy [a] *years*
Yahweh may decide Tyre's fate 3+2
and it will return to its hire. [b]

It will entice [c] *all the kingdoms of the land* 3+2
upon the face of the ground.
Third Prophet: 18 *And it will be that her merchandise and her profit* 3+2
(will be) dedicated to Yahweh.
It will not be hoarded or stored 4
But to those dwelling before Yahweh 4+2+4
will its merchandise belong,
for eating, for satisfaction, and for choice [a]
clothing.

Notes

1.a. DSS[Isa] אילילו has exchanged א for ה which occurs frequently in that text.

1.b. LXX Καρχηδόνος (also in vv 6, 10, 14) and OL *Carthago* have "Carthage"; Vg *naves maris* "ships of the sea."

1.c. Note parallel in v 14 where מָעֻזְּכֶן "your refuge" stands for מבית "house" here.

1.d. MT מִבּוֹא "from coming" or "when one comes (home)." But see מְבוֹאֹת יָם "gate of the sea" in Ezek 27:3. If it reads מִמָּבוֹא it could mean "without a harbor." Wildberger (with *BHS*) suggests simply reading מָבוֹא "coming home" and an adverbial usage.

2.a. MT דֹּמּוּ "be silent," an impv. LXX τίνι ὅμοιοι γεγόνασιν "what have you become like?" has apparently read it as pf from דמה I "be similar." Interpreters have made numerous suggestions (cf. Wildberger). F. Delitzsch (*Prolegomena eines neuen hebräisch-aramäischen Wörterbuch zum Alten Testament* [Leipzig: J. C. Heinrichs, 1886] 64, n. 2) suggested a parallel to Akk *damāmu* "mourn" and M. Dahood (*CBQ* 22[1960] 400) has found Ug *dmm* to mean "mourn." This makes a good parallel to "howl" in v 1.

2.b. MT is sing. LXX Tg Vg are plural suggesting they read סחרי (cf. *BHS, Kaiser, Wildberger*).

2.c. LXX Φοινίκης "Phoenicia."

2.d. Probably a wrong word division of עברים (cf. Procksch, *BHS,* Wildberger).

2.e-3.a. A comparison with Ps 107:23 מְלָאכָה בְּמַיִם רַבִּים "business on many seas" suggests a different verse division and a similar reading here. DSS[Isa] מלאכיך "your messengers" adds support to this understanding. So Duhm, Marti, Procksch, Ehrlich, Rudolph (FS Baumgärtel, 168), Auvray, and Wildberger suggest: עברים מלאכיו (or ה) במים רבים "who send his/her messengers on many waters." They are probably correct.

3.b. Omitted in LXX.

3.c. LXX "your."

4.a. Omitted in Syr.

5.a. LXX ἀκουστον γένηται "began to be heard" implies "it is heard," as do Syr (*d*)*ʾštmʿ* = נִשְׁמַע and Vg *cum auditum fuerit.* Wildberger follows the LXX, like Marti, H. Guthe (*Jesaja,* Tübingen: J. C. B. Mohr, 1907), Feldmann, Procksch, and Ziegler. However, MT makes sense and may be kept.

6.a. DSS[Isa] עוברי "(those of Tarshish) passing over." Follow MT.

6.b-b. LXX οἱ ἐνοικοῦντες ἐν τῇ νήσῳ ταύτῃ "the inhabitants in that island" apparently refers to Tyre itself. אי may mean "island" but is usually "coast" referring to Phoenicia or Philistia.

7.a. DSS[Isa] העליזה adds the article.

7.b. DSS[Isa] has a plural like Ezek 36:11.

7.c. Vg *ad peregrinandum* "to a stranger." Watson (*VT* 26 [1976] 372) has another translation: "Can this be your joyful city, to whom, since ancient times, her tribute they brought to her feet, obliged to reverence at a respectful distance?" But the plain reference is to successful trade rather than tribute.

8.a. MT is hiph ptcp (see BDB 743). DSS[Isa] המעטרה appears to be piel or pual ptcp. Vg *coronata* "crowned." Wildberger correctly supports MT.

8.b. The reading of the Leningrad codex lacks a vowel at the end. With other Heb MSS read ־הָ "her," combined with אשר "whose."

8.c. MT כִּנְעָנֶיהָ "her traders" is unusual. But see Bauer-Leander 564.

8.d. DSS[Isa] adds the article. Wildberger calls it the "Prosaisierung" which occurs often in that text.

9.a-a. DSS[Isa] כול גאון צבי "all the pride of glory" for MT גאון כל צבי "pride of all glory."

BHS would make further changes on this example, but MT may be used as it stands including the tristich accentuation which *BHS* has ignored (Wildberger, 857).

10.a. MT עִבְרִי "pass over." DSS^{Isa} עבדי "serve, till" is supported by LXX *ἐργάζου* "work."

10.b. MT כַּיְאֹר "like the Nile" is supported by DSS^{Isa}, but LXX has no equivalent for it.

10.c. MT בת־תרשיש has been challenged by Kissane, Procksch and others. Wildberger (857) notes the problems for the first five words of the verse and solves them by following LXX, reading עבדי first; then dividing כיאר בת following LXX to read כי אניות, the letters כי א_ת from MT, reading רב as a corruption of ניו to get LXX's *πλοῖα* "ships": עִבְדִי אַרְצֵךְ כִּי אֳנִיּוֹת תַּרְשִׁישׁ "Till your land, for ships of Tarshish" have no wharf any more.

10.d. MT מֵזַח BDB "girdle" makes no sense. Procksch suggested emending to מַלָּח "sailors." *BHK* and *BHS* suggest מָחוֹז "harbor," Kissane מָנֹחַ "harbor." But KB draws on Egy *mḏḥ* "build ships" and *mḏḥ.t* "carpenter shop" and suggests that מזח means "wharf" or "dock." Cf. also *CHAL* and מחוז in Ps 107:30.

11. *BHS* follows Procksch, Rudolf (FS Baumgärtel, 169), Steinmann, Eichrodt, Kaiser, and Wildberger (857) in reversing the order of the verse-halves. They argue that Yahweh is presumed as subject in a-b while he is only mentioned in c. But such anticipation is not infrequent in Hebrew and MT may be sustained.

11.a. MT מעזניה is difficult to understand. DSS^{Isa} מעזיה omits the *nun* and makes good sense: "her fortresses."

12.a. ויאמר "then he said" falls outside the metrical order.

12.b. DSS^{Isa} omits the article of MT and is probably right. (See Wildberger, 858.)

12.c. כֹּתִיים lacks a vowel. K and DSS^{Isa} supply it as כִּתִּיִּים. Q reads כִּתִּים. There is no difference in meaning.

13.a. The reference to far away Chaldea has struck many commentators as irrelevant. Ewald, followed by von Orelli and Cheyne suggested reading כנענים "Canaanites" for כשׂדים "Chaldeans." Procksch, Kissane, Rudolf, and *BHS* suggest eliminating "land of the Chaldeans." Others suggest reading כתיים "Cyprus" like the previous line (Meier [cited by Duhm], Marti, Guthe, Kaiser). Wildberger (858) sees the verse as a gloss on "Cyprus" in the previous verse. But the destruction of Babylon is a major theme in the Vision (chaps. 13 and 21) and may properly be the comparison drawn for Tyre. MT should be kept.

13.b. צִי "wild beast" or "demon." Cf. 13:21.

13.c. DSS^{Isa} בחיניה reads "her" for MT "his." KB calls the meaning of בחין or בחון uncertain. LXX is no help. But Tg translates "their watchtowers" followed by Syr. *CHAL* suggests "siege-towers" following BDB 103.

15.a. DSS^{Isa} הוא leaves out the article of MT which the phrase requires. Probably haplography.

15.b-b. Omitted in DSS^{Isa}. Wildberger attributes it to the copyist returning to the second צר, a common copyist's error.

15.c. נִשְׁכַּחַת has an old fem ending for נשכחה (cf. Joüon §42*f*).

17.a. DSS^{Isa} (שׂ)בעין for MT שׂבעים "seventy." This (like ציין in v 13) is probably an old Aramaic pl ending.

17.b. MT לְאֶתְנַנָּה "to a prostitute's hire." LXX *καὶ πάλιν ἀποκατασταθήσεται εἰς τὸ ἀρχαῖον* "and again be appointed to its former state." Tg לאתרה "to its place." Wildberger (859) notes that they may have objected to the term "a prostitute's price." He also notes the probable need to add a *mappik* in the suffix "its."

17.c. Here also LXX refuses to translate the offending words related to prostitution: *καὶ ἔσται ἐμπόριον πάσαις ταῖς βασιλείαις τῆς οἰκουμένης* "and will be a traveling merchant to all the kingdoms of the world."

18.a. עָתִיק is a *hapax legomenon.* BDB (801) "choice, eminent." But עַתִּיק "old" is found in 1 Chr 4:22. Vg *usque ad vetustatem* "all the way to old age." Arab *ʿtjḳ* "noble" suggests that עתיק may also mean "choice" or "eminent" (see Wildberger, 859).

Form/Structure/Setting

The scene is divided in three parts. Vv 1–7 present mourners regaling Tyre, Sidon, and their dependencies with cries of grief concerning their losses. Vv 8–13 shift to a different setting to reflect on Yahweh's involvement and intention in doing this. Vv 14–18 return to the first setting but present three prophecies of Tyre's return to power and influence after an appropriate interval of time.

The chapter stands under the title משא צר "Burden: Tyre." Its form is clearly a call to lament (Wildberger, 861). "Howl!" occurs in vv 1, 6, 14. But there is a very different tone here from that addressed to Moab (chaps. 15–16). There was a marked sympathy for Moab, but Wildberger (861) correctly detects a kind of sarcasm in this poem. Sidon is called to shame (v 4) and counseled to emigrate to Tarshish (v 6).

The call to lament (vv 1–7) is composed of imperatives: "howl" (v 1), "mourn" (v 2), "be ashamed" (v 4), "cross over" (v 6), and "howl" (v 6), with the resumption of the theme in "howl" (v 14). Yet this is not a lament because of cruel fate, but a testimony to Yahweh's plan (vv 8–9). He has good grounds for these events, which are brought out in the central reflection in vv 8–13, the heart of the chapter. Moreover, Yahweh's action is in accordance with other actions against ambitious, proud countries like Babylon (v 13). See also chap. 2:12–21.

The final portion (vv 14–18) presents three prophecies. Two speak of the length of Tyre's sentence—seventy years. A long generation will pass before she returns to her prosperous trade. The last suggests that her return to power and prosperity is predicated on the dedication of her profits to maintaining Yahweh's Temple and its staff. This prophecy of her return to prosperity stands in contrast to Babylon's permanent destruction (chaps. 14, 21) and Edom's final end (chap. 34).

The prophets deal with Tyre (Phoenicia) in three other periods. It is listed with other surrounding peoples as scheduled for judgment by Amos (1:9–10). This relates to the eighth century. It is also listed by Jeremiah as among the nations made to drink Yahweh's cup of wrath (25:22) and is one of those to hear Yahweh's announcement that he has decided to turn the region over to Babylonian rule (27:3). Ezekiel's great prophecy against Tyre and her king (26:2–29:18) falls in the same early sixth century period. Zech 9:2–4 and Joel 3:4–8 testify to prophecies against Tyre in the Persian period. Thus the prophets have been concerned with the role of Tyre throughout the period with which the Vision is concerned and continue that interest in the very time in which the Vision is composed.

But the Vision's author has chosen to deal with Tyre's fate in his fourth act (the reign of Manasseh and the Assyrian kings Esarhaddon and Ashurbanipal). It could have fallen in Act I (parallel to Amos 1:9–10), or Act VI (parallel to Jeremiah and Ezekiel) or in one of his last two acts (parallel to Joel and Zechariah). The decision to place it here is obviously deliberate. The fall of Tyre (Phoenicia) before Assyrian might marks the climax of her rise to power over the prostrate bodies of Aram/Israel (chap. 10), of Babylon (chaps. 13–14, and 21), of Philistia, Moab, Egypt (in spite of the hopeful signs of chap. 19), and of Jerusalem under Hezekiah (chap. 22; though spared the destruction of the city and the execution of the king). The depiction of Tyre's fall introduces the period when Palestine lies in abject submission to Assyria's imperial will. Manasseh has no choice but to do his liege-lord's will. All chance of resistance or expression of national autonomy is gone.

Comment

1 *Tyre* was an important city throughout antiquity (cf. Kapelrud, *IDB* 4:721–23). It was closely related to its neighboring Phoenician cities and hinterland, although its position on an island often made it possible to escape degradations that befell its land-based neighbors. Interpreters have had difficulty with the identification of Tyre in the chapter. Cf. S. Erlandsson (*Babylon,* 97–98) for a summary of the varying interpretations. Kaiser (159–68) follows Duhm and Marti in thinking that vv 1–14 refer primarily to Sidon with references to Tyre being glosses. Fohrer (258–60) and others make a threefold division of the chapter with separate oracles referring to Tyre, Sidon, and/or Phoenicia as a whole. A better approach relates the whole chapter to Phoenicia while its cities, Tyre and Sidon, are mentioned by name (cf. Erlandsson, *Babylon,* 98; Hayes, *Oracles against the nations* [Diss. Princeton. 1964] 209; Scott, 294). Rudolf (*FS* Baumgärtel, 166–74) represents a combination of these views. The chapter is related to Phoenicia under the rich variety of terms which represented the whole area and its principal parts (Kelley, *BBC* 5:257).

Interpretation of the chapter has also been complicated by trying to distinguish whether this is a prophecy of future destruction or a taunt song recalling a recent destruction. (Cf. Erlandsson, *Babylon,* 97 and Kaiser, 162.) Lindblom (*ASTI* 4 [1965] 56–73) makes a strong plea for the latter approach. From the perspective of drama, that viewpoint has much more contemporaneity with the event, which has just taken place and has all Tyre's allies attempting to adjust to the news.

A third problem for interpretation lies in fixing the historical occasion to which it refers. Assyrian kings attacked the region at least four times, each with devastating results—Shalmaneser V (722 B.C.) and Sennacherib (705–681 B.C.) in the eighth century, and Esarhaddon (677 B.C.) and Ashurbanipal (668 B.C.). Nebuchadnezzar besieged Tyre for thirteen years before defeating it in 572 B.C. Artaxerxes III put down a rebellion there in 351 B.C. But none of these actually destroyed Tyre until Alexander built a causeway to the island in 332 B.C.

There are a number of factors in the chapter which help to determine the particular invasion that is pictured. The description of Tyre's political influence (v 8), of its "ships of Tarshish" (v 14), of its control of Cyprus (v 12), and of its commanding commercial position (vv 2–3, 8b) do not fit all of these. Although Tarshish is mentioned in a number of biblical texts, it only existed as a colony of Phoenician (or Tyrian) power into the seventh century B.C. when it was lost to Phocaean Greeks (cf. Herodotus I, 163 and IV, 152), as Wildberger (864) has noted.

Cyprus had been colonized by Tyre about 800 B.C. or earlier (cf. S. Moscati, *The World of the Phoenicians,* tr. A. Hamilton [London: Weidenfeld and Nicolson, 1968] 103). Later the island became independent before finally falling under Greek dominance.

Arguments for dating the text have often concentrated on the picture of Tyre's destruction (v 1) but have ignored the other considerations. Wildberger (864–65) insists that the chapter pictures the breakdown of Tyrian dominance of the Mediterranean area. This fits the time of Esarhaddon (677 B.C.). Such a date also fits the chronological sequence of the parts of the Vision, placing the destruction in the reign of Manasseh.

The sequence of events is described in the Assyrian annals (cf. *ANET,* 291). A rebellion by Tirhaka of Egypt was the occasion for a Phoenician uprising which was brutally put down in 677 B.C. (cf. *MBA,* 156). The Assyrian inscriptions go on to speak of a new port city being founded, called Esarhaddon's Port, and of Assyrian reorganization of the region into three provinces (Moscati, *The Phoenicians,* 20–21). At this time Esarhaddon claimed sovereignty over Cyprus and Greece, as far as Tarshish (R. Borger, *AfO* 9 [1956] 86). This action effectively ended Phoenicia's independence, her control of shipping in the eastern Mediterranean, and her control of Cyprus. Having conquered Egypt and taken over Phoenicia's commercial power, Esarhaddon and Ashurbanipal had brought Assyria to the peak of her power and the Palestinian area to the lowest point in its history.

Tyre was certainly an ancient city (v 7), known throughout the ancient world. It was built on a rocky island some six hundred yards offshore and some twenty-five miles south of Sidon. The name appropriately means "rock." The name may have a Semitic origin, referring to wanderers from the East who broke through the Lebanese mountain range to establish their homes on the Mediterranean coast.

But the Phoenicians did not find the sea to be a limit or a barrier. They turned it into a highway and an opening to trade, commerce, and colonization. Their mighty *ships of Tarshish* were apparently capable of carrying the mineral ores mined in northern Greece, Spain (?), or even on the shores of the Black Sea. They put in at ports in Egypt, Cyprus, Rhodes, Sicily, and north Africa. They were certainly skilled at transporting the purple cloth, timber, and glassware for which the Phoenicians were famous, as well as the grain of Egypt (v 3).

Phoenicia's earliest ties were with Egypt, at least from the sixteenth century B.C. Carthage was founded as a colony in north Africa in the ninth century. Tyre's great King Hiram supplied David and Solomon with timber and craftsmen in the tenth century.

7 Phoenicia's mainland *merchants* in *Sidon* served as middlemen for caravans from all Palestine (v 2), helping them trade their products for the exotic imports from overseas. These ports of commerce undoubtedly provided unrestrained recreation for boisterous sailors and caravan drivers in ways known to seaports of all times (v 7). Tyre was indeed *the merchant of the nations* of this period (v 3), *one whose feet took her to sojourn far away* (v 7).

8 Phoenicia's strategic importance to all the nations of the region gave pause to any power that threatened to destroy her altogether. Many would have liked to control her power or share her revenues. But all were too dependent upon the network of commercial contacts that she knew and controlled to risk destroying her. She was in fact *the giver of crowns, whose merchants are princes, whose traders are honored of the land.*

So the shocked question is justified: *Who planned this against Tyre?* Whose interests are served by this action? The question prepares one for the central, most significant section of the chapter.

9 The question is answered directly: "*Yahweh of Hosts.*" He has no commercial interests to be served. On the other hand he has two basic reasons for the judgment. The first picks up the Vision's motif concerning judgment against pride and arrogance in the words *pride of all glory* גאון כל־צבי. The very thing that makes humankind admire Tyre (they are *the honored of the land* נכבדי ארץ) makes Yahweh determined to *dishonor the honored of the land* . . . להקל. In 2:12–21 Yahweh announced his intention of bringing judgment on all pride and honor in the land. This verse documents his completion of that announced goal. With the fall of Tyre the last of *the honored of the land* have fallen.

The word *the land* הארץ which is brought to prominence in these verses is a key to the interpretation of all the chapters in Act IV. (See *Excursus,* "The Land.") The reference is to Palestine-Lebanon, extending to the Euphrates in the northeast and to the "River of Eygpt" and beyond to Egypt in the south. All this "land" was served by Tyre's commerce and, accordingly, it treated Tyre with deference. All the "land" envied Tyre's wealth and imitated her styles.

11 The second reason for Yahweh's judgment of Tyre is contained in the term *Canaan* in v 11b. *Yahweh issued a command concerning Canaan to destroy her fortresses.* This picks up the purposes of Yahweh that have deep roots in the OT (cf. Zobel, *TWAT* 4:236–43). Israel's relation to Canaanite culture has the same ambiguity that Yahweh has. Israel adopted Canaan's language, many aspects of its economy and cult, and even its structures of government through David. They took over the Canaanites' fields and their walled cities. Yet there also runs a negative attitude, from the destruction of Sodom and Gomorrah (Gen 18–19) to the warnings in Deuteronomy and Leviticus against adopting Canaanite customs.

The Vision sees the Assyrian invasions as determined destruction of a political and economic way of life which the Canaanites exemplified, a feudalism that centered in its walled cities and small kingdoms. Yahweh had determined the end of this entire system. Thus the command to dismantle one of the last remnants of that system and that power in the *fortresses of Canaan* is the basis for Tyre's collapse.

To accomplish this, Yahweh *stretched out his hand over the sea* (11a). The sea, with its synonyms "floods," "streams," is often pictured as Yahweh's original archenemy. It is also seen as the one who first fell to Yahweh's expression of his cosmic dominion of all things (Pss 93:3–4; 95:5). When Yahweh signals to the sea, the kingdoms which depend upon sea power and commerce tremble.

12b Even a retreat to *Cyprus* cannot cure the problem. Phoenicia's strategic position as a mainland port where land and sea merchants and traders could meet has been the basis of her power. Without that she has no foundation; her ships have no homeport (v 10).

13–14 Babylonia, *land of the Chaldeans,* is held up to Tyre as an example of a country which had defied Assyria and felt its wrath. Tyre's fate will be similar. The *ships* who hear the news when they make port anywhere in the Mediterranean world will have good reason to mourn.

15–18 Three prophecies speak of Tyre's future, for she will have a future.

The term *seventy years* is worth comment. It is used to speak of the extent of the exile (Jer 25:12; 29:10; Zech 1:12; Dan 9:2; 2 Chr 36:21). It may also be used of a person's full life span (Ps 90:10). The term was discussed at length some years ago (C. F. Whitley, "The Term Seventy Years Captivity," *VT* 4 [1954] 60–72; A. Orr, "The Seventy Years of Babylon," *VT* 6 [1956] 304–6; O. Plöger, FS F. Baumgärtel [Erlangen: Universitätsbund, 1959] 124–30; P. R. Ackroyd, "Two OT Historical Problems," *JNES* 17 [1958] 23–27; R. Borger, "An Additional Remark," *JNES* 18 [1959] 74). The round number is intended to indicate an extended period of time. Tyre did, in fact, recover enough to withstand Nebuchadnezzar's siege for thirteen years—from 585 to 572 B.C. Although subject to the Persians, Tyre continued active, resisting Alexander for seven months before falling to him in 332 B.C.

The prophecies proclaim that Tyre's seductive influence on international trade will again be felt in the Levant before long. The distinctive thrust of the prophecy is the claim that her profits will be *dedicated to Yahweh,* that they will support the Temple personnel, presumably in Jerusalem. Tyre's restoration is motivated by the will to make her a contributor to the worship of Yahweh in Jerusalem as she was under Hiram in the days of David (1 Kgs 5–7; 1 Chr 14:1). No such contribution is recorded for the rebuilding or maintenance of the second Temple.

Explanation

The fall of Tyre with the attendant collapse of the other Phoenician cities of the coast and across the waters had widespread implications. These are noted by the references in the chapter to Egypt, Canaan, the Chaldeans, and Assyria, as well as to the cities themselves: Tyre, Sidon, Tarshish, and Cyprus. The fall of Tyre marked the completion of the Assyrian conquest of all West Asia. The Vision has recorded the stages by which Assyria has pursued its goal for some eighty years. With the fall of Tyre it has reached its pinnacle. All the land and the trade routes of the sea are in its hands.

On another level the chapter marks the completion of Yahweh's plan to use Assyria as the "rod of his anger" not only against Israel but also, on Yahweh's day, against "all the proud and lofty, all that is exalted, all the cedars of Lebanon . . . every ship of Tarshish" (2:12–16). With the fall of Phoenician power, this part of God's goal has been achieved.

V 11 implies the achievement of a goal announced much earlier. The verse is reminiscent of the Song of Sea (Exod 15:12–16a) where Yahweh "stretched out his right hand . . . the people of Canaan will melt away." It picks up the memory of the promise of the land of the "kings of Canaan" to Israel (Ps 135:11) and of Israel's early struggles with them (Judg 4:2, 23, 24; 5:19). It echoes the reminder in Judg 3:1–3 that among the nations left in Canaan to test the Israelites were "the Sidonians and the Hivites living in the Lebanese mountains."

The potential for theological associations with the fall of Tyre is fully exploited here. To summarize, they include seeing the defeat and occupation of Phoenicia as the completion of God's conquest of Canaan begun with

Joshua, of his use of the Assyrian to bring an end to the era of city-states, and of his judgment against all human pride and arrogance which Tyre and Lebanon symbolized so well.

The Vision suggests that the fall of Tyre was another sign to Israel's leaders, in this case Manasseh in Jerusalem, to guide them in their political decisions regarding Assyria. (Cf. chaps. 7 and 20.) Seen religiously, the recognition of Yahweh's role in the disaster should have led to humble faith in him, to dependence upon him as protector and guide rather than upon any human power. In the larger context the Vision suggests that, although Manasseh did make his policies conform to God's new order by submitting to the Empire (chaps. 24–27), succeeding generations did not heed the sign by adjusting their goals politically or religiously. They were still blind and deaf, thus preparing the way for Jerusalem's final collapse before the Babylonians (chaps. 28–33).

Excursus: Chapters 24–27 as Apocalypse

Bibliography

Anderson, G. A. "Isaiah 24–27 Reconsidered." *Congress Volume: Bonn.* VTSup 9. Leiden: E. J. Brill (1963) 118–26. **Aubert, L.** "Une primière apocalypse (Esaïe 24–27). *ETR* (1936) 280–96. **Beek, M. A.** "Ein Erdbeben wird zum prophetischen Erleben." *ArOr* 17 (1949) 31–40. **Brockhaus, G.** "Untersuchungen zu Stil und Form der sogenannten Jesaja-Apokalypse." Master's Thesis, Bonn (1972). Typescript. **Coggins, R. J.** "The Problem of Isaiah 24–27." *ExpTim* 90 (1979) 328–33. **Dominguez, N.** "Vaticinios sobre el fin del mundo." *CTom* 51 (1935) 125–46. **Elder, W.** *A Theological-Historical Study of Isaiah 24–27.* Diss., Baylor University, 1974. **Fohrer, G.** "Der Aufbau der Apokalypse der Jesayabuchs. Jesaja 24–27." *CBQ* 25 (1963) 34–45/BZAW 99 (1967) 170–81. **Gilse, J.** "Jesaja XXIV—XXVII." *NedTTs* 3 (1914) 167–93. **Henry, M. L.** *Glaubenskrise und Glaubensbewährung in den Dichtungen der Jesajaapokalypse.* BWANT 86. Stuttgart: Kohlhammer Verlag, 1967. **Hilgenfeld, A.** "Das Judentum in dem persischen Zeitalter." *ZWT* 9 (1866) 398–488. **Hylmö, G.** *De s. k. profetishka liturgiernas rytm, stil och komposition.* Lunds Universitets Arsskrift N.F. Avd. 1. Bd. 25. Nr. 5 (1929). **Lagrange, M. J.** "L'apocalypse d'Isaie (24–27)." *RB* 3 (1894) 200–231. **Liebmann, E.** "Der Text zu Jesaja 24–27." *ZAW* 22 (1902) 285–304; and *ZAW* 23 (1903) 209–86. **Lindblom, J.** *Die Jesaja–Apokalypse: Jesaja 24–27.* Lunds Universitets Arsskrift, N.F. 1, 34, 3. Lund: C. W. K. Gleerup, 1938. ———. "Die Jesaja–Apokalypse (Jes 24–27) in der neuen Jesaja–Handschrift." K. Humaniska Vetenskapssamsfundets i Lund Arsberattelse 2 (1950–51) 79–144. **Lohmann, P.** "Die selbständigen lyrischen Abschnitte in Jes 24–27." *ZAW* 37 (1917/18) 1–58. **Ludwig, O.** *Die Stadt in der Jesaja–Apokalypse.* Diss., Bonn. Köln: W. Kleikamp, 1961. **March, W.** *A Study of Two Prophetic Compositions in Isaiah 24:1–27:1.* Diss., Union Theological Seminary, New York, 1966. Typescript. **Millar, W. R.** *Isaiah 24–27 and the Origin of Apocalyptic.* HSMS 11. Missoula, MT: Scholars Press, 1976. **Mulder, E. S.** *Die Teologie von die Jesaja–Apokalypse, Jesaja 24–27.* Djarkarta: J. B. Wolters, 1954. **Otzen, B.** "Traditions and Structures of Isaiah 24–27." *VT* 24 (1974) 196–206. **Plöger, O.** *Theocracy and Eschatology.* Tr. S. Rudman. Richmond, VA: John Knox Press, 1968. **Redditt, P.** *Isaiah 24–27: A Form Critical Analysis.* Diss., Vanderbilt University, 1972. **Ringgren, H.** "Some Observations on Style and Structure in the Isaiah Apocalypse." *ASTI* 9 (1973) 107–15. **Rochais, G.** "Les origines de l'apocalyptique." *ScEs* 25 (1973) 36–40. **Rudolph, W.** *Jesaja 24–27.* BWANT iv, 10. Stuttgart: Kohlhammer Verlag, 1933. **Sievers, E.** *Jesaja 24–27.* Verhandlungen der königl. Sächs. Ges. d. Wiss. zu Leipzig, phil.-hist. Kl. B 56 (1904) 151ff. **Smend, R.** "Anmerkungen zu Jes 24–27." *ZAW* 4 (1884) 161–224. **Vermeylen, J.** "La composition littéraire de l'apocalypse d'Isaie." *ETL* 50 (1974) 5–38. **Vriezen, T. C.** "Prophecy and Eschatology." *Congress Volume: Copenhagen.* VTSup 1. Leiden: E. J. Brill, 1953. 199–229. **van Zyl, A. H.** "Isaiah 24–27: Their Date of Origin." *OTWSAP* 5 (1962) 44–57.

APOCALYPTIC AND PROPHECY

Bauckham, R. J. "The Rise of Apocalyptic." *Themelios* 3/2 (1977–78) 10–23. **Fichtner, J.** *Prophetismus und Apokalyptik in Protojesaja.* Inaug. Diss., Breslau, 1929. **Hanson, P. D.** *The Dawn of Apocalyptic.* Philadelphia: Fortress Press, 1975. ———. "Jewish Apocalyptic Against Its Near Eastern Environment." *RB* 78 (1971) 31–58. ———. "Old Testament Apocalyptic Reexamined." *Int* 25 (1971) 454–79. **Koch, K.** *The Rediscovery of Apocalyptic.* Tr. M. Kohl. SBT 2d ser. 22. London: SCM, 1972. **Schmidt, J. M.** *Die jüdische Apokalyptik. Die Geschichte ihrer Erforschung von den Anfangen bis zu den Textfunden von Qumran.* Neukirchen-Vluyn: Neukirchener Verlag, 1969.

In accord with the general interpretation of this commentary, this section is interpreted as a literary portrayal of a period (viz., the reign of Manasseh) within the era of judgment which coincides with Mesopotamian oppression of Palestine (Assyrian and Babylonian).

This act portrays a depth of oppression unmatched in other eras. The area (הארץ) is totally under the heel of the tyrant. No city (after Tyre) can resist his demands. With the exception of Moab, no nations are mentioned because no organized nation worthy of the name existed. The other nations, including Egypt, had been subdued and kept under Assyria's discipline.

The characteristics of this section that correspond to the rest of the Vision show that it is intended as a part of the great era of Assyrian power that ended the age of small states and cities in Palestine. Those characteristics that are unique are used to demonstrate the extreme helplessness of the peoples in that era. This description fits the reign of Manasseh. In terms of sustained humiliation, Judah had never experienced anything like it before, nor would she again until the days of Antiochus Epiphanes. So the comparison to Maccabean times is apt. But the literature is prophetic and liturgical in style. Only by stretching the definition and the dating of "apocalyptic" can it be called that.

With the fall of Tyre, the last of the great city-states had fallen. After Damascus, Babylon, and Thebes, no city could be found that was strong enough to withstand the imperial invader. Jerusalem was still there, but only because it had capitulated in 701 B.C. and continued to render tribute.

The Vision uses the act to pose the question: If national existence for Israel/Judah is no longer possible and if the power of being a fortified city-state is denied Jerusalem, what can the future hold for the people called Israel and for the cult center called Zion? The act establishes a foundation and a direction in answering that question. The foundation that is reiterated is God himself—Yahweh of Hosts and his strategy and purpose. The direction looks to the exercise of his great power: The enemy will die, but Yahweh will "raise the dead" of Israel; Yahweh will kill the dragon, regaining control from the chaotic forces loosed on the region through Assyria. Death poses an ultimate end for the tyrant (as in chap. 14). But it holds no such meaning for Israel, for God reaches beyond death to renewed life. Israel's hope is that ultimately even all that the dragon, Leviathan, symbolizes is under the control of God. The key factor in Israel's hope does not really deal with Assyria at all, but with the will and strategy (עצה) of God. When the day of his "wrath" is over, all good things are possible again for those who trust and love him.

Unity

Critical studies of chaps. 24–27 have wrestled with the question of unity. A group of scholars from Duhm on (including Rudolph, Kaiser, Vermeylen, and Wildberger) have found that the chapters are best understood as having been formed gradually over a long period of time with frequent additions along the way.

However, a significant counter view has developed with Lindblom, Anderson, Ringgren, and Redditt. They see the material as being disparate in genre and style, but intentionally put together as a cantata or liturgy. In his summary even Wildberger speaks of the finished work as a "symphony."

The second view is much closer to the approach of this commentary: these chapters, like the entire Vision, comprise a dramatic literary structure. Although Wildberger (904–5) has proposed an analysis in which three or four layers of material are distinguished, he treats the section as a unified prophecy of the eschatological turn of events.

Forms

An announcement, introduced by הנה "behold," opens the section, supported by descriptions of results (24:1–13). This is parallel to such passages as 3:1, 8:7, 10:33, 13:9, and 22:17. It will be continued in 26:21 by a similar announcement. The entire section builds on this announcement.

Contrasting responses follow. A chorus records joyful celebration from afar (24:14–16a), while a solo voice cries out in distress and supports this with a picture of the scope of the judgment (24:16b–20).

The familiar formula ביום ההוא "in such a day" or "in that day" introduces the first of several such passages (24:21–23; 26:1; 27:1, 2, 12, 13). This manner by which pictures of the results of Yahweh's acts are presented is familiar throughout chaps. 2–31, but appears after that only in 52:6. The seven appearances of the phrase as a compositional device in this section are parallel to its use in chaps. 2–4 (7x), 7 (4x), 10–12 (6x), 17 (3x), 19 (6x), 22 (4x), and 28–31 (4x). Whether these are understood to be eschatological in nature and intent (with Wildberger and others) depends upon the understanding of the announcement (24:1–13) on which they are based. See *Commentary.*

As in other parts of the Vision, (5:1–7; 12:1–6), songs and hymns are important elements of the section. The song in 27:2–4 forms a counterpart to 5:1–7. The hymns in 25:1–5 and 26:1–6 are very important structural elements of the section. 25:9 is another such poetic piece, a thanksgiving song fragment.

The announcement of the Lord's banquet for the peoples on Zion's mount (25:6–8) stresses the positive results of Yahweh's awful acts. 25:10–12 contrasts Yahweh's acts "on this mountain" with the destruction of Moab in much the same style that prophecies in chaps. 13–22 have done.

26:7–21 interacts with events and the announcement in a complex form which consists of "we" sections (vv 8, 12, 18), one "I" response in psalm form (v 9), addresses to Yahweh in 2nd person (vv 11–18) and a response to the people in vv 19–20. The passage is begun with an impersonal observation in v 7 and an announcement of God coming to punish (v 21).

The whole is an artistic and complex work of response and interpretation based on the announcement in 24:1–13 which is repeated in 26:21.

STRUCTURE

Reddit has proposed a four-part division of the materials (319, 395).
1. The Present World Order is dissolved: 24:1–20.
2. The Place of Jerusalem in the coming order: 24:21–26:6.
3. The necessity of Yahweh's judgment: 26:7–21.
4. Conditions for Israel's deliverance: 27:1–13.

Wildberger (904) has followed his own analysis of layers and forms to treat the chapters in the following outline:

I. The basic layer which is the point of crystallization for all with the theme: world judgment.
   A. 24:1–6 Announcement of the devastation of the whole earth, with additions:
      24:7–9 The drying up of the vines.
      24:10–12 The destruction of the city of Chaos.
      24:13 The harvest among the peoples.
   B. 24:14–20 The premature rejoicing of Israel and the shock of the one seeing the vision.
   C. 26:7–21 Yahweh's people in the crisis of the End.
      26:7–18 The lament of the people unable to find salvation.
      26:19 The oracle of salvation: resurrection from the dead.
      26:20–21 Israel during Yahweh's approach for world judgment.
II. Eschatological pictures:
   A. 24:21–23 The end of the world's kingdoms and beginning of God's rule.
   B. 25:6–8 The joyous feast on Zion.
   C. 25:9–10a An eschatological song of thanksgiving, with additions:
      25:10b–11 Moab in the manure pile.
      25:12 Destruction of its fortifications.
III. The City-songs
   A. 25:1–5 A hymn: the destruction of the strong city (1–3) and protection of the faithful (4–5).
   B. 26:1–6 A hymn: Yahweh, the protector of Jerusalem (1–4) and the destroyer of the proud city (5–6).
IV. Additions: eschatological impressions.
   A. 27:1 The victory over the dragon of Chaos.
   B. 27:2–5 The new vineyard.
   C. 27:6–11 Israel will bloom as the secure city lies in ruins.
   D. 27:12 The gathering of the faithful.
   E. 27:13 The return to Zion.

Wildberger's outline is based throughout on the assumption that the section is to be understood in an eschatological sense. Redditt's outline is a much more sober and restrained presentation. This commentary suggests an even more restrained interpretation (see *Comment*) and an arrangement in accord with the dramatic or cantata-like form which so many have perceived in it.

Scene 2: The Devastated Land (24:1–13)

Bibliography

de Groot, J. "Alternatieflezingen in Jesaja 24." *NThSt* 22 (1939) 153–58. **Nevas, J. C. M.** *A Teologia da Traducao Grega dos Setenta no Libro de Isias.* Diss., Lisbon, 1973. **Niehaus, J.** "*raz-pešar* in Isaiah XXIV." *VT* 31 (1981) 376–78.

Translation

Heavens:	1 *See Yahweh*	2+3
	destroying[a] *the land*[b] *and laying it waste*[a]*!*	
	He twists its surface	2+2
	and scatters its inhabitants!	
Earth:	2 *And this happens as much*	1
	to the priest as to the people	2
	to the master[a] *as to his servant,*	2
	to the mistress as to her maid,	2
	to the seller as to the buyer,	2
	to the lender as to the borrower,	2
	to the creditor as to the debtor.	4
First Mourner:	3 *The land is totally emptied*[a]—	3+2
	totally plundered.	
	For Yahweh	2+3
	has spoken this word.	
Second Mourner:	4 *The land dries up.*[a] *It withers.*	3+3
	The world languishes. It withers.	
	The height of the people of the land languishes.[b]	4
Third Mourner:	5 *The land itself is contaminated under*[a] *its inhabitants.*	4
	For they pass over laws.	2
	They change a statute.	2
	They break a permanent covenant.	3
First Mourner:	6 *Therefore a curse devours land*	4+3
	and inhabitants in her are held guilty.	
Second Mourner:	*Therefore inhabitants of a land disappear*[a]	4+3
	and humankind is left (only) a few.	
Third Mourner:	7 *New wine dries up!*	2+2+2
	A vine withers!	
	All who would be light-hearted[a] *groan!*	
First Mourner:	8 *Rejoicing with a tamborine is ended!*	3+3+3
	The tumult of revelers has ceased!	
	Rejoicing with a lyre is ended!	
	9 *No one drinks wine with a song!*	3+3
	Beer is bitter to its drinkers!	

Second Mourner: [10]*A desolate city* [a] *is broken!* 3+3
Every house is barricaded preventing entry!
[11]*A cry for wine (is) in the streets!* 3+3+3
All joy drys up. [a]
Revelry is banished (from) the land. [b]
Third Mourner: [12]*Only horror is left in the city!* 3+3
Only ruin (at) a battered gate!
First Mourner: [13]*For this is how it is inside the land,* [a] 5+2
among the peoples: [a]
like an olive tree that has been beaten, 2+3
like gleanings [b] *when the grape harvest is finished.*

Notes

1.a. The verbs בקק and בלק have similar meanings (see Wildberger's survey p. 913). LXX translates בוקק as *καταφθείρει* "destroying" and בולקה as *ἐρημώσει αὐτὴν* "will make it desolate." Delitzsch followed Ibn Ezra and Gesenius in interpreting בקק as "emptying." But this is now generally rejected. G. R. Driver (*JTS* 38 [1937] 41–42) posits a bi-radical root בק from which both verbs derive and translates "crack" and "cleave."

1.b. DSS^Isa^ האדמה "the ground" for MT הארץ "the land" (cf. Kutscher, *Isaiah Scroll,* 216). ארץ appears twenty-four times in this chapter (see *Excursus*). It may be translated "land" or "earth." The narrower meaning has been used here as more consistent with its use elsewhere in the Vision.

2.a. MT כאדניו "so his masters" is a plural where parallels are singular, cf. 19:4 and 1:3. However, this may simply be a "plural of majesty" (cf. GKC § 124*i;* Br. *Synt.* § 19*c*).

3.a. תִּבּוֹק is a unique form of the verb in v 1. It is apparently a niph impf form in analogy to the *ayin waw* group (cf. Bauer-Leander § 58*p*ʾ; followed by Duhm, Marti, and Wildberger). This allows the form to parallel closely the following verbs.

4.a. MT נבלה is missing in LXX. Because it is repeated in the second stich, some commentators (Procksch) suggest leaving it out. De Groot (*NThSt* 22 [1939] 156) thinks it is one of the "alternative readings" in the chapter. But Wildberger (914) correctly notes that the style of the chapter is marked by the piling up of synonymous words like בקק/בלק in v 1. Here נבלה supports אבלה in a similar fashion.

4.b. MT אמללו "languish" is pl. מרום "height" is sg. DSS^Isa^ אמלל is sg. LXX *οἱ ὑψηλοὶ τῆς γῆς* "the heights of the land" and Syr *dlʾ rwmh dʾr*ᶜ lead Talmon ("Aspects of the Textual Transmission," *Textus* 4 [1964] 118–19) to see עם "people" as a parallel reading to מרום "height." DSS^Isa^ has עם written in above the line—an apparent correction added after the text was copied. Wildberger prefers to read עִם "with" and put an article in המרום to read "it has fallen apart—that which is above with the earth." None of these is conclusive and MT, with a simple correction to sg following DSS^Isa^ LXX etc., may be kept.

5.a. LXX *διὰ* "through" or "by means of"; Σ *ὑπὸ* "by" but also with an acc may be "under." However, MT תחת "under" is correct. Wildberger (914) notes that the earth has to bear the burden of its inhabitants. Notice the alliteration חרו/חפרו/חלפו/עברו/חנפה and compare them with חרפה in 25:8.

6.a. MT חרו "burned" (BDB, 359) from חרר. DSS^Isa^ חורו (BDB, 301) from חור "become white, are bleached white." Σ *ἐκτρυχωθησονται* (Eus.) "are used up"; G. R. Driver ("Notes on Isaiah," *Von Ugarit nach Qumran,* BZAW 77 [Berlin: Töpelmann, 1958] 44) suggested behind the Gr. a Heb. root חור like Arab *ḫāra*(*w*) "be weak" or "be limited." KB suggests a second root חרה comparable to Arab *ḥarā*(*j*) "reduce" and *HALAT* agrees. Cf. also G. R. Driver, *JTS* 2 (1951) 26. This suggests the translation "they disappear," a good parallel to the following stich.

7.a. MT שְׂמֵחֵי "merry ones." DSS^Isa^ שומחי reads this as an act ptc (cf. Kutscher, *Isaiah Scroll,* 340).

10.a. MT קרית־תהו "city of chaos." LXX *πᾶσα πόλις* "every city" reflects a tendency to generalize the judgment.

11.a. MT ערבה. BDB, 787, posits a root ערב IV "be arid, sterile" and another V "become evening" (788). It sees ערבה here meaning "has grown dark," followed by Wildberger. LXX *πέπαυται* "be restrained, prohibited." Tg שלימת "is finished, ended." Syr *bṭlt* "has ceased." Vg *deserta est* "be forsaken." Houbigant suggests emending to עברה "pass away" following the Versions. BDB's choice between IV "dries up" and V "grows dark" is more colorful than the bland translation of the Versions and emendations.

11.b. הארץ "the land" is missing in LXX[B].

13.a. De Groot (*NThSt* 22 [1939] 157) thinks "in the midst of the land" and "among the peoples" are alternative readings. Wildberger correctly calls them "parallel concepts."

13.b. *BHS* refers to Jer 6:9 in suggesting that MT כעוללת be doubled to כעולל עוללות "glean the gleanings." Wildberger (915) agrees, noting the tendency in the chapter to such reduplication and the reformation of 11b to a three-stich line, 2+2+2. However, the change is not pressing, since MT makes good sense and meter as it stands and is supported by DSS[Isa].

Form/Structure/Setting

Attention is drawn from Tyre to the hinterland. Yahweh is devastating the land. The witnesses converse about the destruction of "the land" and "the city." Tyre's fall has lent a measure of completeness and finality that previous judgment had not had.

The scene concentrates attention on one theme: the devastated land. While always being related to that theme, the dialogue allows variations:

Yahweh is the active agent in the devastation (vv 1, 3).
All elements of the population are involved (v 2).
The land is withered because of the people's sin (vv 4–6).
Social life is at a standstill (vv 7–9).
The cities lie abandoned in ruins (vv 10–12).
The land is abandoned and bare (v 13).

The witnesses describe the scene to the audience with animation, with astonishment that it is Yahweh who is doing this, and with horror at the thoroughness of what has been done. The narrow attention which the first scene had given to Tyre itself and its clients beyond the sea is now broadened. This survey of the Phoenician hinterland and the Ante-Lebanese mountains to the Syrian Plateau and Palestine to the south reveals devastation, nothing but devastation.

Comment

1 The recognition that *Yahweh* himself is *laying waste the land* makes the statement take on a measure of horror. What is to be understood as הארץ "the land"? The answer one gives determines one's attitude to the entire section. When one translates it "the earth," that very act predisposes the reader to see this as referring to all the world and thus as apocalyptic in scope and meaning.

However, the Hebrew word is common enough. It is used regularly in Isaiah in the ordinary sense of a defined territory, political unit, or land. It is sometimes defined precisely "land of Egypt," "land of Judah." (It is interesting to note that "land of Israel" does not occur in Isaiah.) There seems to be no reason to understand it differently here. It refers to a defined territory.

The land occurs a large number of times in this chapter and deserves special treatment. Its natural scope would include the Phoenician hinterland along the coast from the mountains to sea. But in a broader sense, which is appropriate here, it takes in the Palestinian-Syrian area, fanning out from the Phoenician coast to include what, from an Israelite point of view, was embraced in David's kingdom. The Assyrian campaigns have been taking one after another of its constituent elements. With the fall of Tyre the whole *land* is under their control.

Excursus: The Land

Bibliography

Brueggemann, W. *The Land.* Philadelphia: Fortress Press, 1977. **Ottoson, M.** "ארץ." *TDOT* I (1973) cols. 418–36. **Plöger, J. G.** *Literarische, Formgeschichtliche und Stilkritische Untersuchungen zum Deuteronomium.* BBB 26. Bonn: Peter Hanstein Verlag (1967) 60–129. **von Rad, G.** "Verheissenes Land und Jahwes Land im Hexateuch." *ZDPV* 66 (1943) 191–204 = *Gesammelte Studien zum Alten Testament* 87–100. **Rost, L.** "Bezeichnungen für Land und Volk im AT." FS O. Procksch. Leipzig: Deichert, 1934. 125–48 = *Das kleine Credo* (1965) 76–101. **Stadelmann, L. I. J.** *The Hebrew Conception of the World.* AnBib 39. Rome: Biblical Institute Press, 1970.

הארץ may be paired with "the heavens" and thus properly be translated "the earth" in Isa 1:2. Even this is still in terms of "the land," from horizon to horizon, which is spanned by the sky. The more usual designation is that of a particular territory or space in which someone lives or over which someone reigns.

The synonyms of אדמה "ground" and תבל "world" are helpful but do not change the basic sense. The land is inhabitable like the ground and unlike the sea. The land, like the world, is unlike תהו "chaos." It has order and organization. "Land" is the recognizable territory that one inhabits, visits, knows about. In the Near East, for Israel, "the land" was essentially the territory that faced the eastern Mediterranean Sea. This included Palestine/Syria and the wings in Mesopotamia in the Northeast and Egypt/Ethiopia in the South. The edges of Arabia come into view occasionally, as does Libya and distant Tarshish. This was הארץ "the civilized land," האדמה "the cultivatable land," or תבל "the world" to Israel. Its horizons marked the world of their day. Their heavens spanned this land. Their sea, the Mediterranean and perhaps the Red Sea, was its contrasting member.

In that setting "the land," "the world," and "civilization" were terms that were much nearer to each other than the three terms would be today. They all meant in that time the area of Palestine-Syria and Mesopotamia and Egypt. Therefore for translations (RSV, NIV, etc.) to render הארץ as "the earth" in chaps. 24–27 when they had rendered it "the land" in previous chapters confuses the issue. Brueggemann does not even discuss these instances in his book, presuming that they do not apply. In all these instances the prior judgment that the chapters are apocalyptic in nature and must be treated differently accounts for the change.

This commentary has found reason to doubt that there is a substantial difference in the literary nature of these chapters. הארץ has, therefore, continued to be translated "the land." This means that the devastation, destruction, and shaking described in these chapters involves Palestine, Syria, Mesopotamia, and Egypt. This was the world from Jerusalem's perspective. These are the same territories which have felt the power of Assyrian armies in the previous acts of the Vision.

Yet one should not overlook the deep emotion and meaning that "the land" had for the Israelite. Brueggemann writes (*The Land,* 2) "The land is never simply physical dirt but is always physical dirt freighted with social meaning derived from historical experience." As Brueggemann uses it, this meaning in Exodus and Deuteronomy relates to the promises made to Abraham, the occupation under Joshua, and the consolidation under David. In this sense "the land" was particularly Israel's land. This sense has meaning here.

But the Vision reaches back to a deeper level of meaning like that in Gen 1–11 in its concern with the relation of mankind אדם to the land and the issues of the age of Noah. It sees a closer parallel between the issues of the eighth to the fifth centuries and the age of Noah than to the age of Moses and David.

Thus the problem of the ground האדמה and of the land הארץ lies in the curse upon them because of the blood spilled there. Compare Gen 3:17 in which the ground האדמה is cursed because of Adam. In Gen 4:10–12 Cain, who had been so closely related to the ground האדמה, must flee to the land ארץ and the city (4:17).

In Gen 6:1–8, although there is repeated reference to the relation of mankind and ground, there is no mention of blood-guilt. But from 6:11 on, the terms change to הארץ "the land" with constant reference to violent sins. In the story of Noah, God announces the destruction of mankind and the land because of the high level of blood-guilt. But after the flood, God promises that he will never again curse the ground because of mankind.

There is a distinct change in the new age. One might say that the Age of Adam-Ground has become the Age of the Land, of nations, peoples, national boundaries, and wars. Gen 9:6 announces man's responsibility for his own crime: "Whoever sheds blood of mankind, by man shall his blood be shed."

But the blight of curse is not entirely absent. In Gen 9:25 we read of the curse upon Canaan. In chap. 11 men build a city but are cursed because of overweening ambition. So they are scattered over all the land כל־הארץ. The chapter uses ארץ only.

In Gen 12:1–3 Abraham is called to go from his land ארץ to the land which God would show him. He was destined to be the decisive reason for blessing or curse.

In the Vision of Isaiah, chap. 2 had emphasized the role of mankind אדם relating to Yahweh's day. The Vision reaches its climax (65:17) with Yahweh creating a "new land" and a new heaven just as he did through and after the flood. There is a conscious parallel drawn throughout the Vision to the era of the flood with the intention of emphasizing the idea that in the eighth to the fifth centuries B.C. Yahweh was bringing one age to an end and opening the door to another.

2 The devastation has touched all classes of people.

3 The completeness of the waste and plunder is achieved in Assyria's campaigns into Palestine and Egypt in 677 and 668 B.C.

5–6 The discussion turns to the reasons for the destruction. It is clearly blamed on lawlessness and a breach of covenant by its inhabitants. These are not necessarily Israelite laws which would have no validity here, but obedience to law, the maintenance of a common morality, and fidelity to contractual agreement in perpetuity, which have a universal base. Such a moral breakdown lies at the core of the problems. Countries do not have sins, but people do. And countries suffer as a consequence of the guilt of their peoples. So the curse which is normally a part of every covenant obligation (cf. Deut 28:15–68) falls across the land because the covenant was broken.

5 *Contaminated.* The verse describes the result for the land on which blood is spilled (cf. Num 35:33). The violent murders, wars, and executions on this land have brought down the reproach foreseen in the law (see 25:8 for a very similar word).

Break a covenant. Laws are contained in the covenants, and both the laws and covenant contain provisions that curses shall fall on those who break them. Israel's covenants were typical (cf. Deut 28:15–68).

A permanent covenant. This is more than a political agreement. A comparison with Gen 8:21/9:8–17 is instructive. This also deals with the curse on the land/ground because of man's violence. The obvious reference is to the everlasting covenant of Gen 9:12.

6 *A curse.* This is the result of a broken covenant and a blood-drenched land (cf. Num 35:33) as v 5 has indicated. The concepts related to the terrible curse, the land, and its inhabitants will be one of the major themes of the next two chapters. The curse is understood to have an evil dynamic of its own which, once unleashed, continues without limit. The problem of releasing the land and its people, including Israel and Jerusalem, from this awful ban will occupy the rest of the act.

Held guilty. The word אשם does not speak so much of personal responsibility as of being smeared or branded with the dreadful contamination.

God's people (Israel) are responsible for a share, at least, of the whole land's guilt, shame, and disgrace. Their violence had spilled blood upon it. Their idolatries contributed to its shame. Their infidelities were a part of its disgrace. Theirs was a part of the shroud of death that had covered the land for centuries.

Yahweh's actions make reparation to the land for his people's disgrace and blood-guilt. This is the first step in reversing the curse of the land in 24:6, 17–18.

7–9 Signs of life die out across the country.

10 קרית־תהו "a desolate city" has occasioned discussion and deserves thorough examination.

Excursus: The City

Bibliography

Frick, F. S. *The City in Ancient Israel.* SBL Diss. Series, No. 36. Chico, CA: Scholars Press, 1977. **Gill, D. W.** "Biblical Theology of the City." *ISBE* 1:713–15. **Ludwig, O.** *Die Stadt in der Jesaja–Apokalypse.* Diss., Bonn, 1961. **McCown, C. C.** "City." *IDB* 1:632–38. **Myers, A. C.** "City." *ISBE* 1:705–13. **von Rad, G.** "Die Stadt auf dem Berge." *EvT* 8 (1948/49) 439–47; *Gesammelte Studien,* 214–24.

Studies of the city in the four passages in this act (24:10–12; 25:2–5; 26:1–6; 27:10–11) have usually been carried out under the presupposition that the literature is apocalyptic, giving particular significance to the meaning of the city. Ludwig's dissertation is a case in point. His primary concern is to date the apocalypse by use of the city imagery.

The significance of "the city" is important for the entire Vision. It struggles to uncover the role of Jerusalem from chap. 1 through chap. 66, and the song in

25:1–5 is a part of that development which stands in dialogue with the views of Psalms and Chronicles.

Other cities are emphasized in the Vision. These include Damascus and Samaria (7:8–9; chap. 17), Babylon (chaps. 13 and 21), and Tyre (chap. 23). It is not the cities themselves that are important here, but what they stand for. They have represented an era in which cities dominated the political scene. They were the seats of influence and of wealth, and they were often the real power within the small nations. Sometimes foreigners simply seized the city and were thereby able to control the larger countryside for generations.

Such were the "walled cities" of the Canaanites that faced Joshua, the cities of the Philistines, the Phoenician cities, Damascus, Haran, Carchemesh, and even Babylon. Such also was Jerusalem. Each of these was stronger and more important than the territory it dominated—territories which fluctuated in size depending upon the particular strength of the reigning "king" of the city.

The biblical story recognizes this. The growing importance of the cities in the area can be sensed in the story of Abraham. What is not noted in the text is the reason why this is happening. Egypt's previous control of the area has been weakened. Various peoples are beginning to assert their claims by building fortress cities which can control trade routes and the surrounding countryside with its villages.

The placement in the biblical story of the narrative of the Tower of Babel (Gen 11) immediately after the genealogies of the sons of Noah indicates its evaluation of the importance of both for the age after the flood. Presumably, in the period that the Vision pictures, this is the age that is coming to an end.

Babylon played the decisive role in Mesopotamia. The Arameans moved into Haran and Damascus. The Canaanites controlled the Phoenician plain from their strongholds in Byblos, Ebla, Tyre and Sidon, but they also spread south into the cities of Palestine. The Israelites infiltrated Palestine and conquered the walled cities wherever they could. Edomites, Moabites, and Ammonites took over the cities in cis-Jordan. And the Philistines seized the seven cities of the lower coast. For well over a thousand years cities had been the most stable and persistent elements in a political picture that was otherwise very turbulent and changing.

This scene of the Vision presents a picture of a scarred and empty landscape in the area which is dotted with the ruins of these cities—empty and lifeless. The stark reality of the scene conveys a deeper reality. Like the bleached bones of animals of another time, these ruins signify that an age has passed never to return. For the following era (many centuries) cities would not play that role again. In an age of empires they could not.

This is one of the bitter lessons the Vision attempts to convey to post-exilic Jerusalem. Jerusalem cannot return to the role she played under David. The Jews, however, did not give up that idea very easily. Jerusalem remained a hotbed of conspiracy and revolt, through the Persian, the Greek, and even the Roman periods. The Vision teaches that such is a lost and false hope. That role for Jerusalem, as also for Babylon, Tyre, Damascus, and Ashdod, is gone forever. That is the desolate and empty city of 24:10.

Of course urban life would continue under imperial rule. Indeed it would flourish with new vigor and meaning in the Persian period, while the Hellenistic city would come to be the measure of a cultured lifestyle unknown to earlier times. Similarly, the Vision foresees a new role for Jerusalem within the providence of God. It is to be a Temple city, drawing pilgrims from the entire Empire and beyond (cf. 2:1–4 passim to 66:19–21). The beautiful song in 26:1–4 fits into that strand of the Vision's theme.

13 The common comparison with the barren field stripped of its fruit after harvest, or the bare tree after the olives have been beaten off the trees (for that is the way it is still done), was fitting for the lands and cities that had been plundered of everything of value.

Explanation

The scene surveys the devastation which the Assyrian campaigns have brought about in the whole country, from the Euphrates to the River of Egypt. Yahweh is the prime cause. The effects are universal on all the land's peoples and on all its parts. The fields are barren and unplanted. The cities are ruined and are without life. A curse has bound the land. It looks like a tree after its fruit and leaves have been stripped off.

The terrible effects of God's campaign of judgment through the Assyrian "rod of his anger" are surveyed. God's judgment is both horrible and thorough. Canaanite civilization had dominated Palestine/Syria for well over a millennium. Now it is about to disappear.

Noah's curse had been on it for a long time (Gen 9:25–27). Israel's entry into Canaan assumed this curse and capitalized on it. But Israel had not been able to transform the land. It came to share the Canaanite characteristics that God abhorred. And now she shares in the suffering of the land.

Gen 6–9 presents the problem of man's (אדם) relation to the land (ארץ) in its classic form, just as Gen 2–3 present man's (אדם) relation to the ground (אדמה). Gen 6–9 suggests that man's first encounters with the larger problems (social, economic, political) involved in his relation to territorial questions ארץ were disastrous, leading to judgment and a new beginning with Noah and his family.

The Vision of Isaiah picks up a similar theme dealing with man (אדם) and the land (ארץ). The treatment is more focused than in Genesis because it is pursued parallel to a treatment of Israel/Jerusalem in terms that involve both territory and people. It is also more focused because it is treated parallel to God's dealing with the nations, i.e., in history.

Three instances are particularly important to the Vision. In chap. 2 אדם occurs seven times while ארץ "land" occurs two times. God will come on his day to "shake the land" in such a way that the pride of "humankind" will be humbled.

In chap. 6 Yahweh is praised because "his glory fills the whole *land.*" But a judgment is foretold through which "the *land* will be utterly forsaken," and even if a tenth remain in the land it will be wasted again. The buildings will stand with no man (אדם) in them, and humankind (אדם) will be banished from the *land.*

In chap. 13 the announcement that armies from distant lands will come to "destroy the entire land" fulfills the prediction of 10:23 of a decreed destruction upon the whole *land.* The sun, moon, and stars join the battle to make the land desolate (v 10). Man (אדם) will be more scarce than gold (v 12) and the land (ארץ) will be shaken from its place (v 13). The burden then comes to focus upon Babylon (v 19) and upon the King of Babylon (chap. 14). At his death witnesses will ask: "Is this the individual who shook the *land?*" Then the account brings in a synonymous term: "who caused the world (תבל) to become a desert." It goes on to speak about the destruction of *cities.*

This is enough to show how the uses of ארץ have changed to a broad use of the meaning "land." Even תבל "world" is used in this extended meaning. The prophecy of the destruction of the whole land occurred in 10:23 and 13:5. There is no reason to see the meaning in chaps. 24–27 in any other way.

The terms ארץ and הארץ occur in chap. 24 thirteen times. The word תבל occurs once, and the word לעולם "to the age, forever," which occurred first in 14:20, is repeated here. ארץ appears in chap. 26 six times, תבל twice and לעולם once. The questions are: What kind of literature is this? With its descriptions of judgment on the Day of the Lord, is it of a different genre than the rest of the Vision? And what does ארץ mean in these chapters?

The complete destruction of the land has been anticipated in chaps. 10 and 13. So *that* is nothing to set it apart. The participation of the cosmic bodies was anticipated in 13:10. Therefore, these chapters should be seen as a climax and culmination of the previous sections and of a piece with them, and it is misleading to give them a distinctively different genre—a position that would lead to a fragmentation of the book that is unnecessary and wrong. Issues raised in and by chaps. 24–27 should be understood in the light of the book itself and as a part of the larger message and meaning of the book. The basic characteristics of apocalyptic *cannot* be demonstrated in this section.

Moreover, the meaning of הארץ "the land" has been carefully developed by the Vision so far. Its narrow meaning has been the Land of Israel as it existed for the northern kingdom and for Judah. But its broader territorial meaning has included all "the land" of the greatest reach of David's reign, its wings on both ends of "the fertile crescent," Babylonia and Egypt, including the Phoenician territory of Tyre and Sidon on the coast.

The reference to the "cities" being destroyed picks up the descriptions of such devastation visited upon Samaria and Damascus, upon Babylon and Tyre, as on many others.

The appearance of the word לעולם "to the age, forever" in 14:20, 24:5, and 26:4 gives a permanence to the message that it might not otherwise have. The parallel to the uses of אדם and ארץ in Gen 6–9 as well as the appearance of לעולם in Gen 9:12–16 provide a hint of the direction interpretation should go.

Just as Gen 6–9 describes the end of an age and the beginning of another, so the Vision of Isaiah is doing the same thing. The old order is that into which Abraham came, in which Moses worked, in which Israel occupied Canaan, and in which David built his kingdom. Palestine with its adjacent lands in that age was a territory of tribes and cities, of city-states and small kingdoms. In that age Israel had found its existence as twelve tribes occupying the sparsely settled land alongside others who had migrated thither from other places (Moab, Edom, Philistia). They conquered walled cities and built their own. David and Solomon brought the period to a climax by making the area a mini-empire. But their successors allowed it to disintegrate. In the ninth and early eighth centuries the fragmented peoples and cities were in constant warfare with each other.

The Vision of Isaiah takes up the course of events in the reign of Uzziah at mid-eighth century. It announces that Yahweh is bringing about drastic changes, not only for Israel and Judah, but also for all their neighbors. He is sponsoring the rise of Assyria to establish imperial rule over the entire Near East. Assyria's conquests will destroy, not just Israel and Judah, but the entire "world" within which they existed: its economy, its political framework, and its social structures.

This destructive goal is reached when Assyria subjugates Phoenicia in 655 B.C. (Isa 23). Thus Yahweh has indeed devastated *the whole land* from Israel and Damascus (chap. 10), to Babylon (chaps. 13–14 and 21) on one end and Egypt (chaps. 18 and 19) on the other, including Edom, Moab, Philistia in between. The whole land lies devastated (chap. 24). The cities which had represented the best of that civilization—Babylon, Damascus, Tyre, and Memphis (eventually Jerusalem as well)—have fallen. This is not simply a military tragedy. The economy which had made their prosperity possible has been changed drastically. They would never again have the same power and riches. Truly *an age had come to an end!*

Isaiah's Vision sees this as the work and will of God. It calls upon those who survive the destruction to be alert to God's will for them, to God's new structures and God's new ways of life within the imperial structures that now dominate the scene. These were destined to exist for a long time. After Assyria came Babylon, Persia, the Hellenistic kingdoms, and the Romans. God was calling for a people to serve him in the new age, just as he had called Abraham, Moses, and David in the old age. Israel and Judah in the old age had been blind, deaf, uncomprehending, and rebellious toward God. The Vision implies that the people of God in the new age tended to be just the same. For them, then, there could be no hope (chap. 65)—only those who yield to God and seek to serve him in his new way will share his life and his city.

Scene 3: Yahweh and the Kings (24:14–22)

Bibliography

Ben David, Y. "Ugaritic Parallels to Isa 24:18–19." (Heb.) *Leš* 45 (1980) 56–59. **Niehaus, J.** "*raz-pešar in Isaiah XXIV.*" *VT* 31 (1981) 376–78.

Translation

Heavens: 14 *They raise their voices!* 3+1
(turning) *They shout joyously!*
On account of Yahweh's majesty 2+2
[a] *they cry out from the west!* [ab]

Earth: 15 *Because of this they glorify Yahweh in the east,* [a] 4+2
in the coastlands of the sea,
the name of Yahweh, 2+2
God of Israel!
First Chorus: 16 *From the extremities of the land* 2+2+2
we hear songs: [a]
"Honor to the Righteous One!"
Solo Voice: *But then I say:* 1+2+2
"I am ruined! [b] *I am ruined!* [b]
Woe to me!"
Second Chorus: [c] *Traitors betray!* 2+3
With treachery traitors betray! [c]
Heavens: 17 *Terror, tomb,* [a] *and trap* 3+3
(be) upon you, inhabitant of the land!
Earth: 18 *May it be that* 1
whoever flees from the sound [a] *of dread* 3+3
will fall toward the pit,
and whoever climbs from inside the pit 3+2
will be caught in the snare!
Heavens: *For sluices from a height* [b] *have been opened.* 3+3
So land's foundations quake.
19 *The land is thoroughly* [a] *broken up.* 3+3
[c] *Land* [b] *is split apart.*
Land is badly eroded. [c] 3+4
20 *Land* [a] *trembles much, like the drunkard.*
Earth: *May it wander* [b] *like* [c] *the shack!* 2+2+3
May its guilt be heavy on it!
May it fall [d] *and not rise again!*
Heavens: 21 [a] *In such a day* [a] 3
when Yahweh decides the fate [b] 2+3+3
of the army of the highlands in the height
and of the kings of the lowlands in the lowlands,
22 *may they be gathered like a herd* [a] *in a pit,* 3+2+3
shut up in a locked place,
and after sufficient days have their fate decided.

Notes

14.a-a. LXX *ταραχθήσεται τὸ ὕδωρ τῆς θαλάσσης* "the water of the sea will be troubled" seems to have read a reduplicated לים.

14.b. מִיָּם "from a sea." Kaiser translates "the shout (louder) than on the sea" referring to GKC § 133*e*. Wildberger (932) notes that מים is apparently parallel to בארים "in the east" (v 15a; cf. below). Therefore it probably also indicates a direction "from the west" (cf. Br. *Synt.* § 111*a;* and M. Dahood, "Hebrew-Ugaritic Lexicography V," *Bib* 48 [1967] 427).

15.a. בארים occurs only here in the plural. אור (BDB, 21) means to "become light, shine." Wildberger (932) traces the struggle to ascertain its meaning from Kimchi and Ibn Ezra's "valley" and many others to Procksch (באיים) "on the islands" and on to *BHS* באיי הים "on the islands of the sea." Kaiser refers to a second meaning for אור "dawn" in M. Jastrow, *Dictionary of the Targum* I (New York: Pardes, 1950), and returns to a suggestion made by Ewald to translate it "the east."

16.a. LXX τέρατα "miracles" leads G. R. Driver (*JSS* 13 [1968] 50) to the Syr word *dmjr* "astounding, wonderful." He suggests that there was a Heb word זְמִירוֹת "strange things." This could be a parallel idea to צבי "honor." But Wildberger (932) notes that the words are not syntactically parallel.

16.b. רזי has not been definitely identified. KB writes "meaning unknown." BDB (931) tentatively notes that it is an opposite to צבי "honor" from רזה "grow lean." LXX καὶ ἐροῦσιν Οὐαὶ "and they will say, 'Alas' " seems to have passed over both רזי־לי s altogether. Σ το μυστηριον μου εμοι το μυστηριον μου εμοι (Eus.) "my secret to myself, my secret to myself." Σ Θ το μυστηριον μου εμοι (Syh.) "my secret to myself." Θ *mysterium meum mihi* (Jerome) "my secret to myself." Vg *secretum meum* "my secret." Wildberger (932) notes that all these have apparently thought of the Aram רז "secret." However, the following "woe" points, like BDB, to רזה with the meaning "disappear, be overcome." He translates *Aus mit mir!* "Away with me!"

16.c-c. LXX shortens the lines to τοῖς ἀθετοῦσιν "they condemn them."

17.a. Literally "pit." To reproduce the alliteration of the Hebrew translate "tomb."

18.a. Omitted in LXX.

18.b. ממרום means "from a height." It is not necessary to spell out "in the heavens" (cf. *BHS* and Wildberger's comment [933]).

19.a. MT רעה is missing in DSS^Isa but 1QIsa^b has רוע leaving out ה. Delitzsch, Duhm, Marti, and Gray (see BDB, 949) had already guessed that ה was a dittograph for the following letter. רֹעַ is a cognate inf abs.

19.b. The article occurs on only the first use of ארץ. Wildberger (933) follows Gray and Feldmann in calling it a dittograph to be eliminated. For the uses of ארץ in this chapter see the Excursus: "The Land."

19.c-c. LXX ἀπορίᾳ ἀπορηθήσεται "totally perplexed" shortens and imitates the Heb form but is a very free rendering.

20.a. DSS^Isa הארץ "the land" (cf. Kutscher, *Isaiah Scroll,* 411).

20.b. DSS^Isa substitutes a final א for ה (cf. Kutscher, 163).

20.c. DSS^Isa inserts a conjunction "and (is) like a shack."

20.d. DSS^Isa lacks the fem ending. MT is sustained by noting that this is a quotation of Amos 5:2 and by the consistent fem subjects in the verse.

21.a-a. Missing in LXX.

21.b. On פקד see G. André, *Determining the Destiny: PQD in the OT* (Lund: Gleerup, 1980). Review in *JBL* 101 (1982) 430–31.

22.a. *BHS* suggests that ה belongs to the following word אסף האסיר "a gathering of prisoners (col.)." However, אסיר is missing in DSS^Isa LXX and Tg which leads S. Talmon ("Aspects of the Textual Transmission," *Textus* 4 [1964] 123), *HALAT,* and Wildberger to think that אסיר is a later addition, not original. The verse reads well without it.

Form/Structure/Setting

The dark mood of the last scene is broken by the sound of excited cheers for Yahweh from far edges of the land (vv 14–16). But the cheering is not unanimous. A single voice speaks its woe and a chorus supports him with cries of "Foul!" (v 16). The response of the witnesses is a sharp reprimand, reminding one of the nature of the curse recalled in v 6 and of the solemnity of the judgments that mark the end of the age (v 18c–20a). The renewed curse falls on people (v 18), on the land (v 20b–d) and on the kings (vv 21–22).

This scene like scene 1 creates space for a delayed reaction in later scenes ("after sufficient days" v 22).

Comment

14–16 *They raise their voices.* Who are these who shout encouragement to Yahweh from the outer edges of the land which forms this stage of action? Are they the Israelites who have been exiled to far places? Are they members of Yahweh's heavenly court? Are they admirers from among the nations? They remain unidentified. It is sufficient to note that Yahweh's work is known and appreciated. He is recognized as *majestic,* as *God of Israel,* and as *the Righteous One.* The last designation may describe his victories as much as his ethic.

16 *But then.* There is dissent, both individual and group, from those who would insist that there is no justice in this, only treachery. This cry would come from some who have felt the loss personally, but admit no personal guilt to account for it. They think they have been cheated.

17 *Terror . . . upon you.* The verse implies that the *inhabitant of the land* deserves everything that happens to him (cf. Jer 48). It reacts to the complaints of v 16 with the first of four curses spoken against the land and its inhabitants. Note the alliteration of פחד "terror," פחת "pit or tomb," and פח "snare or trap."

18ab The second curse. The response supports the inevitability of disaster. The words are a quotation from Amos 5:19 (cf. Ps 139:7–12). When the Lord's judgment lies over the land, there is no escape.

18c *Sluices from a height.* This reminder of Gen 7:11 and 8:2 joins the picture of land quaking and moving (v 19) to evoke a sense of a time like that of the flood. As in 2 Kgs 7:2, 19 and Mal 3:10, the picture is of a sky-firmament that keeps out the cosmic ocean beyond. The third curse (v 20b–c) affirms the quaking disaster and calls for it to be terminal.

21 *In such a day.* The scene of Yahweh's day of judgment over all the powers of the earth (cf. 2:12–17) is recalled to set the stage for the final curse. פקד has sometimes been translated "visit" or "punish" but is probably more accurately understood as "decide the fate of" (see below).

The army in the highlands (v 21) may also be translated "the power in the heights." When the entire section is thought to be apocalyptic, this has been understood to refer to Yahweh's overcoming a divine force in heaven; but when the passage is understood to be of the same character as the rest of the Vision, there is no reason to break out of the framework set by the context. In this sense it is far more fitting to understand this to be a reference to armies in the high plateaus and hill-country of Syria/Palestine. The antithesis refers to the coastal lands of Phoenicia/Philistia and the lower Jordan Valley. Together they include the entire territory under discussion.

22 *After sufficient days.* Like the "seventy years" that Tyre will need to wait for its final verdict, the final judgment on the kings will come later. In the meantime they will be imprisoned. *Pit* is sometimes used as a synonym of *Sheol.* If that were true here, it would be the first hint of the theme of "death" which becomes prominent in the following scenes. It would also be the first indication in Scripture of a final judgment after death. But the term is also an indication of a stockade or dungeon, and it should probably not be pressed further.

Excursus: Decide One's Fate

פקד has defied satisfactory definition. Gesenius and *BDB* suggest meanings like "visit" and "punish." But the variety of translations in the Versions reflect their uncertainty about it.

Gunnel André (*Determining the Destiny: PQD in the Old Testament.* ConBot 16. Lund: Gleerup, 1980) has demonstrated that its basic meaning is "to determine the destiny, to destine, to assign." This meaning is cogent, especially for its use in the prophetic literature.

פקד and its derivatives occur 18 times in the Vision. Eight of these occur in chaps. 23–27. It is the most meaningful word Hebrew possesses to define God's function in determining what will happen to a person or group in a given situation, whether they are under blessing or curse, or placed in battle or rescued from danger. God is pictured as the sovereign making decisions and carrying them out.

The idea is central in the prophets. Jeremiah employs the word repeatedly. The Vision of Isaiah makes use of it in key chapters. In chap. 10 Israel's fate is determined: destruction by the Assyrians. The world's destiny is fixed because of its evil and sin (13:11). Yahweh's decision will be accompanied by thunder and earthquake (29:6). In 60:17 the decision is positive to Israel, establishing peace for her. In 62:6 Yahweh destines keepers for Jerusalem.

The central and climactic position of chaps. 23–27 is emphasized by the repeated use of פקד. Yahweh will determine Tyre's destiny after seventy years (23:17). The armies of the highlands and the kings of the lowlands will have their fate decided after many days (24:22). The climax is reached in chap. 26. Yahweh's decisions had ruined the tyrants (v 14), and he had been determining Israel's destiny even in her distress (v 16). The great day of destiny is at hand when he will settle the fate of the inhabitants of the land in terms of their sins (v 21). In that day Yahweh will determine the destiny of Leviathan (27:1).

פקד does mean to make a decision, to determine the fate of, the future of someone or something. This includes judgment. It also includes providence. It fits God's sovereign activity of moment-by-moment decision making, his control over life and death, blessing and curse, success and failure, his disposition of individuals, peoples, and nations, as well as the heavenly host and the divine powers. It is also appropriate to describe his great judgment over the land and its peoples, including Israel and Jerusalem.

The word is parallel to God's work in establishing (שים) a course of action or a fate. That, too, is a sovereign activity of Yahweh-King. In this Act this sense occurs in 23:13; 25:2; and 27:9. The principal uses of שים are found in chaps. 28 (3x), 41–42 (10x), 50–51 (7x) and 57 (4x).

Explanation

This scene returns to Yahweh, acclaiming his majesty and giving glory to Him as God of Israel—glory to the Righteous One. Complaints from inhabitants are met with dire curses which emphasize the judgment on the land, its inhabitants, and armies. The scene ends with the notation that Yahweh uses such a time to set the course of kingdoms and determine the limits to royal power. This is God's time for major changes.

All this hints at much more than historical meanings. The Assyrian devastation, complete over the entire Near East, is understood as Yahweh's work. It marked the end of an age, just as the devastation of the Great Flood had done. Through it Yahweh should be recognized and glorified. All this marks the justified condemnation of kings and armies (political entities) even beyond the grave. The culmination of all this will be presented in the next scene in the revealed presence of the sovereign, reigning Yahweh in Zion. The Vision portrays Yahweh's mighty acts relating to the whole land, the sea, and their peoples. It also keeps firmly in view his intentions and acts on behalf of Israel and Jerusalem. Chaps. 23–24 have done the former. Chaps. 25–27 will do the latter.

Scene 4: Yahweh of Hosts Reigns on Mount Zion (24:23—25:8)

Bibliography

Coste, J. "Le text grec d'Isaïe xxv 1–5." *RB* 61 (1954) 67–86. **Emerton, J.A.** "A Textual Problem in Isaiah 25:2." *ZAW* 89 (1977) 64–73. **Gray, B.** "Critical Discussions. Isaiah 26; 25:1–5; 34:12–14." *ZAW* 31 (1911) 111–27. **Lohmann, P.** "Zu Text und Metrum einiger Stellen aus Jesaja. II. Das Lied 25:1–5." *ZAW* 33 (1913) 256–62. **Welton, P.** "Die Vernichtung des Todes und ihr traditiongeschichtlicher Ort. Studie zu Jes. 25:6–8, 21–23 und Exod 24:9–11." *TZ* 38 (1982) 129–46.

Translation

Herald: 23 *May even the moon* [a] *be ashamed* 2+2
and the sun [b] *be abashed!*
For Yahweh of Hosts reigns 3+3+3
on Mount Zion and in Jerusalem
before his elders in glory! [c]
A Worshiper: 1 *Yahweh, you are my God!* 3+3
I exalt you! I adore your name!
For you have done a wonder— 3+2+2
things planned [a] *long ago—*[b]
being faithful (in your) faithfulness!
2 *For you have transformed* [a] *a city* [b] *to a heap of rubble!* [c] 4+3
A fortified city to a ruin!
A foreigners' [d] *stronghold (is) no longer a city!* 3+3
(It will) never be rebuilt!
Second Worshiper: 3 *Because of this a strong people honor you!* 4+4
A city of ruthless nations fear you!
Third Worshiper: 4 *But you continue to be a refuge for the poor,* 4+4
a refuge for the needy in his distress,
a shelter from a storm, 2+2
a shade from the heat.
Fourth Worshiper: *When (there is) a spirit of ruthless persons* 3+2+2
like a wall of falling rain
5 *like heat in a drought,*

you subdue an uproar of strangers. [a] 3+3+3
[b] *(Like) heat (subdued) by the shade of a cloud* [b]
a triumph song of ruthless persons becomes
subdued. [c]
Herald: [6] *Yahweh of Hosts will make* 3+2+2
for all peoples
on this mountain
[a] *a feast of rich foods* 2+2
a feast of treasures [a]
rich foods of marrow 2+2
of refined treasures.
[7] *He will swallow up on this mountain* 3+3+3
the shroud which enshrouds [a] *all the peoples*
the shadow which overshadows all nations. [b]
First Elder: [8a] *He will swallow up the death* [a] *(which) endures*
forever. [b] 3
Second Elder: *My Lord Yahweh will wipe a tear* 4+2
from every face.
Third Elder: *The disgrace of its* [c] *people he will remove* 3+3
from all the land.
Herald: *For Yahweh has spoken.* 3

Notes

23.a. LXX ἡ πλίνθος "tile, limestone." *BHS* suggests it vocalized Heb הַלְּבֵנָה for this meaning.

23.b. LXX τὸ τεῖχος "the wall." Read Heb as הַחֹמָה. But cf. 13:10 where different words for sun and moon are found. Wildberger is correct that they are also to be so understood here.

23.c. LXX δοξασθήσεται "is glorified" assumes יִכָּבֵד a verb (see *BHS*). Although translation is difficult, MT should be sustained.

1.a. DSS[Isa] עצית (cf. Kutscher, *Isaiah Scroll,* 221), meaning unknown. *BHS* and Wildberger would move the *athnaḥ* to this word, but this is unnecessary.

1.b. MT מרחוק "from afar" is probably to be understood as temporal.

2.a. שמת מן means literally "constitute from," thus "transform."

2.b. מעיר "from a city." LXX πόλεις "cities." Tg קרוי is also plural. Syr *ḳrjt'*, sg. Vg *civitas,* sg. With Wildberger and *BHK* keep the sg.

2.c. LXX εἰς χῶμα, Tg לגלין both imply an indefinite form which leads *BHS* to suggest לְגַל. The difference is minimal.

2.d. LXX τὰ θεμέλια τῶν ἀσεβῶν "the foundation of the ungodly." Two Greek MSS read זדים "insolent ones." But the change is unnecessary.

5.a. LXX ὀλιγόψυχοι "fainthearted."

5.b-b. Lacking in LXX.

5.c. Tg ימאכון "they will be defeated," Syr *ntmkk. BHS* emends the vowels יַעֲנֶה to read a passive form. But the range of meaning in the active form is sufficient without change.

6.a-a. Missing in LXX.

7.a. MT לוט is identified in BDB (532) both as a noun meaning "covering" and as an act ptcp of לוט "to cover." There is nothing to be gained by changing the vowel with *BHK.* Wildberger (956) reports in detail the attempts at emendation and reordering. The old versions are confused about it. The parallel of לוט with מסכה "shadow" is the most stabilizing element in the picture. The use of פני "face" before it raises questions. Long ago Houbigant and Lowth suggested moving it before כל־העמים: "the shroud that covers the face of all the peoples." Delitzsch thought Job 41:5[41:13] פְּנֵי לְבוּשׁוֹ "his outer garment" offered a parallel to mean here "the upper (outer) side of the veil." Nägelsbach describes it as an identical genitive, i.e., that לוט and פנים mean the same thing, "the front side." Wildberger judges them all to be signs that no one knows with any certainty.

The form of the second הָלוֹט has been debated (Wildberger, 959). Kimchi emends to הָלוּט, a pass ptcp. GKC § 72*p* views it as an act ptcp instead of the usual לָט (supported by Delitzsch, von Orelli, Duhm, BDB, etc.). Many contemporaries prefer the passive (cf. *BHS*) in light of 1 Sam 21:10. The translation follows Nägelsbach's suggestion.

7.b. DSS[Isa] הגואים (Kutscher, *Isaiah Scroll,* 511), which is explained as the insertion of א to distinguish the similar letters on both sides.

8.a-a. LXX translates *κατέπιεν ὁ θάνατος* "the death swallow up." 'A *καταποντισει τον θανατον* "he will plunge death into the sea"; Σ *καταποθηναι ποιησει τον θανατον* "will make the death be swallowed up"; Θ *κατεποθη ο θανατος* "death is swallowed up" (cf. 1 Cor 15:54); Syr is also passive. Wildberger (960) finds it unlikely that in parallel to ובלע (v 7) a passive should be read. The Greek Versions have great difficulty with the passage. However, several (with Syr) suggest reading ובלע, i.e., adding a conjunction.

8.b. לנצח "(which) endures forever." Σ (acc. to Eus.) correctly translates *εις τελος*. But 'A (acc. to Marchalianus) and Θ (acc. to Marchalianus and Syh.) as well as 1 Cor 15:54 translate *εις νικος* "to victory." נצח means "victory" in Aramaic and Syriac. Jews speaking Aramaic have carried the meaning back for Hebrew (cf. Wildberger, 960). But this leaves the question open concerning the word's relation. Does it modify "he will swallow," or does it modify "the death"? Most translations have chosen the former. Its position in the sentence as well as the parallels suggest the latter.

8.c. LXX *τοῦ λαοῦ* "the people." MT is to be confirmed here. But note that the antecedent of the Heb pronoun is not defined. Most translations have "his" implying Yahweh. However the parallelism makes it more likely to be "it" for "all the land."

Form/Structure/Setting

The scene implied in the last lines of Scene 3 takes shape before our eyes. Attention turns to Jerusalem. The vision of chap. 6 is recalled. The dire prediction of an empty and desolate land has been fulfilled. We return to the throneroom for matters of great moment.

The throne room of Yahweh is portrayed on Mount Zion. It is the second of three such scenes in the Vision. Chap. 6 features the giving of Yahweh's word to his messenger. This scene presents a banquet to announce Yahweh's great deed. Chap. 66 portrays a tour of his new city, the new heavens and the new earth.

The throne scene has three elements: Yahweh's appearance on his throne in glory before his elders (24:23), the announcement of a banquet for all peoples (25:6), at which a heroic deed will be announced (25:7–8). The mighty deed will effect an end to the long chain of vengeance and curse that has plagued the land and all its peoples—an end to the reign of "the death" in the land.

A song of praise and thanks (25:1–5) adorns the throne scene. It is sung by individuals. Its outline is clear:

Address to Yahweh (v 1a).
Adoration of Yahweh (v 1b).
His wonderful acts—the reason for praise (v 1cd).
  Detail: Destruction of a city (v 2).
Citation of praise from others (v 3; cf. 24:14–16).
Thanks for refuge (v 4ab).
Especially, a refuge from violence (v 4c–5).

This has been called a "city-song" because it cites a city's destruction and because it is thought to be a link in a chain of such city-songs (24:10–

12; 26:5; 27:10). But the worship element of praise is more important here than the incidental reference to "the city." The latter places the song in context; the former demonstrates its form and function in the throne scene.

Comment

23 *May the moon be ashamed.* M. Klopfenstein (*Scham und Schande nach dem Alten Testament,* ATANT 62 [Zürich: Zwingli-Verlag, 1962] 82) suggests that when something is revealed to have no meaning, its pride is badly damaged and thus "is shamed." In comparison with the glory of Yahweh, the sun and moon must recognize their meaninglessness. The phrase may be a formality used in announcing the throne appearance.

Yahweh of Hosts. In this act, the full throne title appears only in this enthronement scene.

Reigns means that he is holding court. This is a sign that he is in full charge of events (cf. Pss 29:10; 93:2; *Comment* on 6:1).

On Mount Zion and in Jerusalem. The Vision has maintained throughout that Yahweh's judgments on Israel and the land would preserve the integrity of Jerusalem as his "dwelling" and as the seat of his temple.

Before his elders. In each of the heavenly throne scenes there are other beings surrounding Yahweh's throne. 6:2 calls them שרפים "seraphs." 1 Kgs 22:21 calls them רוחות "spirits." Job 1:6 calls them בני האלהים "sons of God." Here they are called זקנים "elders" (Rev 4–19 passim). They all seem to refer to the same beings who have the same functions.

In glory. In 6:3 the whole land was proclaimed to be full of his glory. The phrase means that this is a full-dress royal occasion.

25:1 *My God.* The singer confesses to being a committed devotee of Yahweh.

You have done a wonder. פלא "wonder" is the word used in Exod 15:11; Pss 77:15 [14]; 78:12 [11] for the Exodus. Ps 88:11 [10] speaks of "wonders" God does for his worshipers in judgment and redemption.

Things planned long ago. The phrase picks up the note of 23:9, accepting in faith that all of this is an act of God's faithfulness to his covenants, his people, and most of all to himself and his strategy.

2 *The city.* The Vision has described the destruction of more than one city. Babylon is outstanding in chaps. 13 and 21. This reference is probably symbolic of the end of the age of city-state culture. (See *Excursus:* "The City.")

3 *The strong* respect God's consistent use of power in judgment.

4 *The poor . . . and needy* see in God's actions concern for their plight.

5 *The uproar of strangers.* Palestine had been a prey for foreigners of all types. It was the adopted home of a long list of peoples before Moses took Israel to Canaan (Exod 3:17). The Philistines and others occupied cities in Palestine after Israel entered. More recent developments in Aram, Israel, and other states came about through the usurpation of power by foreigners.

6 *A feast.* The royal invitation is extended to all peoples. It is to be held on Zion so that they can have an audience with Yahweh of Hosts. On that occasion he will announce a great royal deed.

Royalty and feasts go together in many contexts. Mythology knows of sumptous feasts of the gods. These feasts celebrate a variety of things, and other gods are the usual guests. Yahweh's feast will be for all peoples. He moves beyond the circles of his intimates, the elders, and issues a universal invitation. (Cf. Jesus' parable of the Father's feast in Matt 22:1–14.) This is in line with the Vision's view of all nations coming to worship in the temple (2:2) and all nations gathered to see God's glory (66:18).

6–7 *On this mountain.* Identifying Yahweh's universal rule with Mount Zion is characteristic of the Vision. The phrase picks up the location from 24:23, stressing both the identical locality of the throne and the banquet, and the timing of the banquet with the throne appearance.

The great deed is announced. The action is described in three ways, all apparently referring to the one great divine-royal deed. It was customary for the king at his banquet to demonstrate his power by a heroic act. Marduk, for example, is pictured as having made a garment disappear and reappear (*Enuma Elish* IV, 28; *ANET,* 66).

Yahweh's demonstrative deed was *to swallow up* (v 7) a garment that was appropriate to his character as Lord of life and to his guest list of all peoples. It was a *shroud,* a *shadow* that lay heavy over all peoples and all nations. It was also appropriate to the time when the land lay so completely under the curse of death. The curse of the broken covenant filled the land (chap. 24) making it uninhabitable (24:6, 13, 17, etc.). בלע "swallow" is often used of the dragon, Leviathan, or Tiamat the great demoness of mythology. Note its use with Satan in the NT, "seeking whom he may devour" (1 Pet 5:8). Here the devouring entities which are customarily set against God are themselves devoured. This strange term, used also in v 8, stands in contrast to the phrase "decide the fate." In the latter Yahweh's action is highly personal, the sovereign rationally settling issues. But here the imagery belongs to the curse concept of 24:6. The OT speaks of curses often, illustrating how they were spoken and put into effect. It says little or nothing about how they may be counteracted or terminated. But this is exactly what Yahweh of Hosts' "swallowing" will do. It will bring the awful curse to an end. It will make its baleful results cease. To accomplish this, nothing will do but that the entire contamination be totally eliminated.

8 Two other verbs are used for this act. He will *wipe* and he will *remove.* The three verbs together speak of removing or abrogating something or some things. What is to be swallowed, wiped away, or removed is described with five terms (four of the five are specific with a definite article). Only *a tear* is indefinite. The other four apparently refer to the same thing, indeed the same act. *The shroud, the shadow, the death,* and *the disgrace* share their ominous and sad qualities. Each is qualified: *all the peoples, all the nations, which endures forever, from all the land.* But the first two—the shroud and the shadow—are only descriptive, not definitive.

The death is the most substantive of them all, while *the disgrace of its people* is the most relevant to this context. The thought that this refers to "death" *per se* ignores the definite article. A specific "death" is to be swallowed up. A specific "disgrace" is to be removed. This death and this disgrace comprise the shroud and the shadow over all the peoples, the very ones that had been invited to the feast. They are the peoples whose disgrace he will remove from the land.

Generations of violence had brought blood-guilt on the land. Like the land before the Flood (Gen 6), it was destined to devastation and destruction, as the Vision had already described in great detail and summarized in 24:1. Truly this was a curse of perpetual death on all the land and all its inhabitants, a curse that fed on itself as new blood-guilt was incurred for each vengeful and rebellious act.

Yahweh of Hosts decrees an end to all this, himself "swallowing" the entire matter: shroud, covering, death warrant, and disgrace. He lifts the burden of each of these from *upon* the peoples.

The disgrace (v 8) or reproach was the result of actions worthy of such blood-guilt. It is a synonym for "guilt" and "contamination" in 24:5–6. It picks up the alliteration of the series of words in 25:5. It was understood to continue to influence the life of the perpetrator. The disgrace belonged to the people, but the land had felt the brunt of its terrible ban.

The death forever (v 8). Yahweh will completely end the permanent ban of death that had lain on the land (cf. 6:11–12). The curse cannot be reinvoked. It is the counterpart of the violation of "the permanent covenant" ברית עולם (24:5 and Gen 9:12).

These verses fulfill the same role in the Vision that God's promises to Noah (Gen 8:21) play in the Flood narrative. There God promised never to curse the ground again because of mankind's sin. Rather, he will demand an accounting from man for shed blood (Gen 9:6). Then he speaks of the permanent covenant with the land. In the Vision another age has come to a disastrous end. God avoids putting blame on the land. Its inhabitants (24:5) and its people (25:7) must bear the disgrace. So now he fulfills his covenant with the land. He raises the ban of death "from off" the land, swallowing up its effects forever.

The issue of death has surfaced in the Vision before. In 14:4–20 death and the grave are pictured as appropriate endings for the career of the king of Babylon. Similarly in 26:13–14 tyrants who have ruled Israel are seen as now dead. This stands in sharp contrast to the promise to Israel that "your dead will live."

But the announcement here (v 8) is breathtaking! Surprising! Worthy of the King of Kings! The great royal edict is portrayed as final. It is not a temporary reprieve or a delay of sentence. In a section that is so filled with violence and death, the dreadful unspoken fear that the cycle of blood-guilt and vengeance can never be broken has finally been brought into the open. Yahweh of Hosts has announced that he will deal with it personally and permanently. He had taken steps to imprison the kings and their armies (24:22) to await their sentences. Now he decrees royal amnesty, removing the shrouded curse that had covered all the peoples, destroying the death-ban on the land.

My Lord Yahweh. The title changes; Yahweh becomes more personal and is directly related to his subjects. This is fitting as the meaning of the astonishing announcement is made known.

A tear from every face. What face had not felt the tear of grief? The experience of death is universal in every age. How much more in that time of violence and destruction! God's comfort was intended for those of all peoples who mourned, friend and foe alike.

Its people. This translation sees the land as the antecedent of the pronoun: the land's people. This fits the context and the meaning of all that has led up to this statement. But the antecedent has often been understood to be Yahweh himself: Yahweh's people. This would refer to Israel's sin, guilt, and disgrace. This interpretation is fitting for the passages that follow which do refer to Israel and Jerusalem. It would pick up the inferences of 6:5 "a people of unclean lips," the people with no comprehension or understanding of 1:2–3 who were capable of the acts recounted in the rest of chap. 1. The "empty land" announced in 6:12 has now become a reality and the people's disgrace is apparent. However, both meanings are fitting since Israel is also one of the peoples of the land. The people's guilt in regard to the land was also removed. Life and happiness would be possible again.

Explanation

The passage is the climax of the entire act. The cataclysmic events for Tyre and the whole land have peaked. In a throne appearance, in the full array and authority of his royal prerogative he announces that he will turn the course of events around; he will nullify the effect of the curse of death and all its implications. This puts a halt to the momentum of vengeance that has swept the land. It puts the initiative back in Yahweh's hands to deal with the outstanding issues. It also gives hope to those whose confidence is in Yahweh and who look forward to the restoration of life and hope through him. The NT picture of ultimate renewal borrows Isaiah's language (Rev 21:5).

The recognition here of a need to attack the situation on the level of the curse, as well as on the basis of God's specific decision, parallels a NT understanding that one role of blood-atonement on the Cross is to nullify the cursed effects of accrued guilt. Another role, of course, is to implement the specific acts of judgment and forgiveness by God.

Scene 5:
Response from a Yahwist (25:9–12)

Translation

Heavens: 9 *And one will say* [a] *in that day* 3
First Worshiper: *See,* [b] *our God,* 3+3
[c] *for whom* [c] *we waited and* [d] *he will save us!*
Second Worshiper: *This is Yahweh! We waited for him!* [d] 4+3
Let us rejoice, and let us be glad [e] *in his salvation!*
First Worshiper: 10 *Indeed Yahweh's hand rests on this mountain.* 4+3+4
And Moab will be trampled [a] *in its place* [b]
like a strawpile trampled [c] *in* [d] *a dungpit.* [e]

Second Worshiper: 11 *He will spread his hands in the midst of it* 3+4
as a swimmer spreads (his hands) to swim.
And he (Yahweh) will cause his (Moab's) pride to fall 2+3
along with the skill[a] *of his hands,*
First Worshiper: 12 *when the fortification*[a]*—the secure height—* 2+2
of your[b] *walls, he has laid low,*[c]
has knocked down[d] 1+3
and has made them touch the earth—even the dust.

Notes

9.a. DSS[Isa] ואמרת "you (sg) will say." Also Syr *wtʾmr.* The meaning of an impersonal 3rd person is not different.

9.b. DSS[Isa] adds יהוה "Yahweh."

9.c-c. LXX Ἰδοὺ ὁ θεὸς ἡμῶν ἐφ᾽ ᾧ ἠλπίζομεν "This is our God for whom we have waited." It has understood זֶה to be a relative pronoun. Cf. Br. *Synt.* § 105*b;* GKC § 138*g(a).*

9.d-d. Missing in LXX. However, the Hebrew form is correct and meaningful. Cf. Wildberger, 970.

9.e. DSS[Isa] נשמח "we will be glad." It lacks MT's cohortative ending which is parallel to "let us rejoice."

10.a. DSS[Isa] ונדש, a defective reading for MT's *plene* form of the niph pf "it will be trod upon." Σ *και αλοησομεν* understood it as a qal form "and we will thresh" (Wildberger, 970). 'A *και αλοηθησεται* "and it will be threshed" and LXX *καὶ καταπατηθήσεται* "and it will be trod upon" translate MT.

10.b. MT תחתיו is literally "under him." It was a problem for the Versions. LXX omits it. Tg באתרהיו. Wildberger (970) suggests a noun "in his place," thus "in the land where he lives" (cf. 2 Sam 7:10).

10.c. DSS[Isa] כחדוש (i.e., ח for ה) is apparently a scribal error. The form is unusual for a niph inf constr, הִדּוּשׁ for הִדּוֹשׁ, but see Bauer-Leander § 56*u.*

10.d. Q במו stands for the simple ב "in." K reads במי "water," but this does not fit the following word.

10.e. מדמנה is apparently derived from דמן "manure" and thus means "a manure pit." 10:31 lists a town by this name, but not in Moab. Jer 48:2 lists a place מדמן in the land of Moab. Kimchi suggested that this place is meant here, although Wildberger (971) thinks this may be a play on that name (cf. van Zyl, *POS* 3 [1960] 80).

11.a. MT ארבות is challenged by many both as to correct form and as to meaning. See discussion in Wildberger (971) who suggests "skill" as a translation.

12.a. *BHS* suggests eliminating ומבצר "fortification." Wildberger (971) defends it as part of this fulsome style. Three nouns are followed by three verbs. MT divides them that way 3+5. A different division here tries to get a better grasp of the awkward sentence. The nouns come first, a reversal of normal Hebrew order, suggesting a subordinate clause. The subject must return to Yahweh, or his hand, since the second person indicates that Moab is addressed.

12.b. Note the change of person from third to second.

12.c. Missing in LXX.

12.d. DSS[Isa] יגיע but keeps the pf form for השפיל and השח. MT apparently notes the completion of Moab's degradation, whereas DSS[Isa] expects part of it to still be fulfilled (see Wildberger, 971). However, the syntax puts the temporal factor of all the verbs under the dominant impf of v 10.

Form/Structure/Setting

The foundation of the scene is a hymn of thanksgiving (v 9). It is closely related to vv 6–8 by "in that day" as a response to the throne announcement. The announcement is greeted as the answer to prayer which justified dependence and patience and which calls for rejoicing because Yahweh's "hand," his power and his blessing, "rests on this mountain."

The hymn is expanded by application to a nearby problem: Moab. Yahweh's assertion of power in Jerusalem calls for the re-subjugation of Moab, as in the days of David.

Comment

9 *See* points to the throne scene that preceded. *Our God* claims the great king as his own. The hymn is a common one like 33:2; Pss 25:5; 40:2; Gen 49:18; Jer 14:22.

10 *Yahweh's hand rests.* The phrase is not used elsewhere but is certainly kin to the "Zion theology" of the Psalms. *On this mountain* ties the hymn to the previous passages (24:23; 25:6, 7). The verse interprets the throne scene to say that Yahweh's presence on Mt. Zion means his power will be upon Jerusalem and its government. *Moab trampled.* The speaker will claim his right to a victory over Moab.

11 The verse has a strong tone of irony or satire. The subject has changed from Yahweh to Moab. Note the way the word *hand*(*s*) is used. While Yahweh's *hand* is on Mt. Zion, Moab's *hands* will be working the manure pit. He loses his pride through the skill with which his hands "work" manure. One is reminded of the way in India that fresh cow dung is made into patties to be slapped on walls to dry.

12 The address turns in 2nd person to Moab. The figure of the dung pit is changed to realistic language.

Explanation

Jerusalem is expected to behave so piously in the day of Yahweh's throne appearance. But instead the witnesses hear it claiming a petty right of sovereignty over its small neighbor, Moab. With childish glee it is demanding, in barnyard terms, the humiliation of Judah's former vassal.

The same littleness is attributed to Jerusalem here that follows so much of her response throughout the Vision. While God is tending to weighty matters that involve the world of that day, the end of an age and the beginning of a new one, Jerusalem's attention is fixed on a spiteful provincial rivalry.

The scene pictures God's frustration and elicits the reader's disappointment.

Scene 6: Judeans on Pilgrimage to Jerusalem (26:1–21)

Bibliography

Beeston, A. F. L. "The Hebrew Verb *SPT.*" *VT* 8 (1958) 216–17. **Blenkinsopp, J.** "Fragments of Ancient Exegesis in an Isaian Poem." *ZAW* 93 (1981) 51–62. **Day, J.**

"A Case of Inner Scriptural Interpretation." *JTS* 31 (1980) 309–19. **Irwin, W. H.** "Syntax and Style in Isaiah 26." *CBQ* 41 (1979) 240–61. **Schwarz, G.** "'. . . Tau der Lichter . . .'?" *ZAW* 88 (1976) 280–81.

Translation

Narrator:	1 *In that day*	2
	this[b] *song is sung*[a]	3+2
	in the land of Judah:	
Chorus:	*We have a strong*[c] *city!*	3+2+2
	It gives structure[d] *to salvation,*	
	(with) walls and bulwarks.	
	2 *Open the gates*[a]	2+3+2
	that a righteous nation may enter	
	observing faithful deeds.	
	3 *(From) a dependent*[b] *attitude*[a]	2+3+3
	you form[c] *peace, peace,*[d]	
	when one's confidence (is) in you.[e]	
	4 *Trust in Yahweh on and on*	3+3+2
	for in Yah,[a] *Yahweh,*	
	(there is) a rock (for) ages (to come).	
Speaker:	5 *Indeed, he has humbled*[a] *those living in the height,*	4+3
First Echo:	*He makes a lofty city fall,*[b]	
Second Echo:	*He makes it fall*[b] *to earth,*	2+2
Third Echo:	*He makes it even touch the dust.*	
First Echo:	6 *A foot*[a] *tramples it—*	2+2+2
Second Echo:	*feet of one oppressed,*	
Third Echo:	*steps of poor ones.*	
Speaker:	7 *A way for the righteous (is on) level places.*	3+4
Echoes:	*You smooth*[c] *level*[a] *the path of the righteous.*[b]	
Chorus:	8 *Surely, (in) the way of your judgments*[a]	3+2
	Yahweh, we wait on you.[b]	
	For your name and your memorial[c]	2+2
	(is) [d]*the desire of (our) soul.*[d]	
Solo:	9 *My soul, I wait for you in the night.*	3+3
	Surely, (by) my spirit within me,[a] *I seek you.*	
Speaker:	[b]*Indeed when your judgments belong to the land*[b]	4+4
	they teach righteousness to the world's inhabitants.	
First Echo:	10 *A wicked one shown mercy*	2+3
	does not learn righteousness.	
Second Echo:	*In a land* [a]*of honest (persons) he does wrong.*	3+3
	He has no fear of Yahweh's majesty.	
Third Echo:	11 *Yahweh, your hand is raised,*	3+1
	but he does not envision it.	
First Echo:	[b]*Let them envision (it)!* [a]*And let them be shamed*[a]	2+2
	(by) a people's zeal.[b]	
Second Echo:	*Indeed, let fire (reserved for) your*[c] *adversaries consume them!*	4

Chorus: 12 *Yahweh, you provided* [a] *peace* [b] *for us.* 4+4+2
But also, all [c] *your works*
you have performed for us.
13 *Yahweh, our God,* 2+3
masters, other than yourself, have owned us. [a]
But even (when we were) apart from you 2+2
we memorialized your name.
First Echo: 14 *Dead do not live.* 3+3
Second Echo: *Ghosts do not rise up.*
Speaker: *Truly* [a] *you decide their fate and then you destroy them.* 3+3
Then you make all memory of them to disappear. [b]
First Echo: 15 *You have brought increase for the nation, O Yahweh.* 3+3+3
Second Echo: *You have brought increase* [a] *for the nation. You have gained (it) glory.* [b]
Third Echo: *You have extended all borders of land.*
A Tattletale: 16 *Yahweh, in the (time of) distress they (sought to) decide fate (for) you.* [a] 3+2+2
They (sought to) deter [b] *by a whispered charm*
your chastening of him.
Chorus: 17 *As a pregnant woman who draws near to birthing* 4+3+4
writhes, [a] *cries out because of her birth pangs,*
so were we before you, Yahweh.
First Group: 18 *We may have been pregnant. We may have writhed.* 2
Just the same, we will give birth to wind. 3+3+3
Second Group: *As for deliverance,* [a] *we will bring the land none.*
Third Group: *The world's population will not* [b] *fall.* [c]
Yahweh: 19 *Your dead will live!* 2+2
My corpses [a] *will rise!*
Herald: *Awake* [b] *and sing joyfully,* [c] 2+2
you that live in dust.
For [d] *the dew of lights* [d] *(will be) your dew.* 4+3
And the land will let fall (the) ghosts.
Yahweh: 20 *Go, my people!* 2+2+3
Go into your rooms
and shut your doors [a] *after you.*
Hide [b] *yourselves for a little while* 3+3
until wrath passes over.
Herald: 21 *Indeed, look!* [a] *Yahweh is going out of his place* [b] 4+4
to punish the guilt of the land's population.
The land will lay bare its violent crimes 3+3
and will no longer cover up its murder victims.

Notes

1.a. DSS[Isa] ישיר "one will sing."
1.b. DSS[Isa] הזות for MT הזה—a fem pronoun "this" for the masculine.
1.c. DSS[Isa] עוז for MT עֹז "strong." The meaning is the same.

1.d. MT יָשִׁית "it gives structure." Tg יתסם and Vg *ponetur* both presume a passive form like יוּשַׁת. Wildberger argues that the subject is Yahweh. But MT should be kept.

2.a. DSS[Isa] שעריך "your gates."

3.a. Origen's Hexapla transliterated יצר "shape" as ιεσρο which apparently implied a reading of יִצְרוֹ(וֹ) "his mind" or "form." Ibn Ezra reads מי שיצרו סמוך עליך אתה השם תצרנו בשלום "the one whose mind is founded on thee, you will keep the name (of that one) in peace."

3.b. סמוך imples dependence, leaning, being supported, and is passive.

3.c. MT points תִּצֹּר, i.e., from the root נצר "keep." The same consonants can be pointed תִּצֹר from יצר "shape" or "form" like the first word of the line. These words call to mind the potter shaping his clay.

3.d. LXX Syr omit one "peace." Such repetition is common in these chapters. Both should be kept.

3.e. MT בָּטוּחַ "being trusted" is a pass ptcp. The same root in different form begins the next verse. LXX translates only the second of the two with ἤλπισαν "they trusted," suggesting the first was lost to haplography. Vg *quia in te speravimus* "because we have trusted in you." Hexapla χι βακ βατιου transliterates MT כי בך בטוח. 'A οτι επ αυτω πεποιθασι "that in him they have trusted." Tg ארי במימרך אתרחיצו "for we set our trust in your word." *BHK* suggests emending to בָּטוֹחַ "trusting," an inf abs. But Wildberger (976) notes that Ps 112:7 uses בָּטֻחַ to mean "confident" (*CHAL*, 37) and supports Marti's observation that בָּטוּחַ follows סָמוּךְ in emphasizing the firmness of trust, the fixed attitude of confidence.

4.a. The presence of both ביה and יהוה raises questions. LXX translates ὁ θεὸς ὁ μέγας ὁ αἰώνιος "God, the great, the eternal." This appears to be paraphrase rather than translation. 'A οτι εν τω κυριω κυριος ο στερεωσας τους αιωνας "for in the Lord, the Lord who has established the eons." *BHS/BHK* suggest deleting ביה. Wildberger (976) proposes trading places between כי and ביה and taking the latter into the first half of the verse. But that simply adds to an already full stich. A. Guillaume ("Psalm LXVIII.5," *JTS* 13 [1962] 322–23) suggests pointing according to an Arabic verb *bāha* as בָּיהּ meaning "he remembered, he was mindful of." But that is neither likely nor helpful. This, like "peace" in v 3, is an example of the tendency to repeat words in this section.

5.a. DSS[Isa] השת is apparently a scribal error.

5.b-b. The virtual repetition of words again raises questions. The first is missing in LXX Syr and DSS[Isa]. Tg translates the first with מאך "lower, humble" and the second with רמה "high, be high." So *BHK* suggests emending the first to read יַפִּילָהּ "he makes it fall." Gray, Ehrlich *(Randglossen)*, Fohrer, Kaiser, Wildberger and others would shift the *athnaḥ* drawing the first back into the first half of the verse. This is much more helpful and is adopted here.

6.a. רגל "foot" has no translation in LXX, Syr, Tg, or equivalent in DSS[Isa]. Wildberger (976) defends it as necessary for the style of the passage.

7.a. ישר "level" is missing in LXX. With Wildberger (982) it is to be kept. NIV has taken it as a vocative address to God "O upright One." But the repetition of the previous word makes this unlikely.

7.b. DSS[Isa] צדק for MT צדיק "righteous" but there is no change in meaning.

7.c. תפלס is understood (by Fohrer, Kaiser, Wildberger) to be a relative clause "straight is the path, which you smooth for the righteous." This can only be done by ignoring the Masoretic accents that relate מעגל צדיק to each other. DSS[Isa] תפלט "you deliver," perhaps because the scribe did not know the infrequently used word פלס (so Wildberger).

8.a. Wildberger (983) correctly takes ארח משפטיך as an adverbial accusative "in the way of your judgments."

8.b. DSS[Isa] קוינו leaves out the suffix "on you."

8.c. DSS[Isa] לתורתך "for your law."

8.d-d. LXX omits. Syr and some MSS of Tg appear to have read נַפְשֵׁנוּ "our souls." The translation of נפש with "soul" is done with reluctance since it means something very different from the Greek ψυχή.

9.a. *BHK*, following Guthe, emends to בַּבֹּקֶר "in the morning" to balance "in the night" of the first stich. However, MT makes sense and is fitting.

9.b-b. LXX διότι φῶς προστάγματά σου ἐπὶ τῆς γῆς "because your appointments are light upon the earth." This has led Procksch and Rudolph to suggest emending כי כאשר to read כָּאֹר "when it lights up." The translation follows MT.

10.a. LXX Tg Syr add the definite article. But for a reading in constr state this is unnecessary.

11.a-a. *BHS* suggests deletion. Wildberger (983) complains of such lack of understanding for the text's style.

11.b-b. LXX expands to read γνόντες δὲ αἰσχυνθήσονται · ζῆλος λήμψεται λαὸν ἀπαίδευτον "but, knowing, they will be ashamed: zeal will seize an ignorant people." Wildberger characterizes it as "full of fantasy but hardly an accurate translation."

11.c. The suffix is missing in LXX, but necessary here.

12.a. The meaning of שפת is agreed. See Wildberger's discussion (984).

12.b. Bruno suggests emending to שָׁלוּם "revenge" (cf. *BHS*).

12.c. Bruno suggests emending to כְּגְמֻל "like recompense" by referring to Syr. But apparently Syr does not support the changes (cf. Wildberger, 983). Neither is needed.

13.a. LXX adds οὐκ οἴδαμεν "we did not know." So *BHS* suggests inserting בַּל נֵדַע. The translation follows MT.

14.a. לָכֵן in the sense of "therefore" does not fit well here. Perhaps the meaning of "indeed, surely" is better (*CHAL*, 177 #3).

14.b. DSS[Isa] ותאסר "you imprison." But MT is supported by LXX καὶ ἦρας "and you remove, destroy," Tg ותוביד, and Syr *wʾwbdt.* Wildberger (984) notes that אבד "destroy" is related to זכר "memory" in Ps 9:7 and to שם "name" in Ps 41:6.

15.a. The second יספת לגוי "you have brought increase for the nation" is missing in one MS. Wildberger (984) properly recognizes this as haplography in that MS and notes that the repetition fits the style here.

15.b. LXX has apparently read נִכְבָּדֹת "glory" for the sense "you have brought increase of glory for the nation." A similar reading occurs in Ps 87:3. Procksch and *BHS* recommend emendation. The change is not necessary.

16.a. Two MSS offer פקדנוך "we decide your fate." Often the translation "visit" for פקד is given as in Judg 15:1 and Ezek 23:21.

16.b. צָקוּן "they deter" has been a problem for the translations. LXX ἐν θλίψει "in affliction," Vg *in tribulatione,* and Syr *bḥbwšjʾ* seem all to have read it as a noun. It can be pointed צֹקוֹן in constr meaning "magic power" as Dillmann, Duhm, and Ehrlich *(Randglossen)* have done. Wildberger (984) is correct in looking for a verb form here. Gesenius and Delitzsch consider it 3 c pl pf from צוק + *nun* (cf. Deut 8:3, 16). Such a root exists (BDB, 848): I in hiph "constrain, press upon," II "pour out, melt." BDB assumes II but emends to צֹקוֹן "constraint of magic." Translation here reads צָקוּן with Gesenius as pf 3 c pl "they constrained, deterred."

17.a. LXX lacks the word.

18.a. DSS[Isa] ישעתך "your deliverance." Maintain MT.

18.b. C. F. Whitley ("The Positive Force of בל," *ZAW* 84 [1972] 215–16) suggests that בל has a positive meaning here. Wildberger correctly rejects the idea of opposite meanings for בל in the same verse.

18.c. DSS[Isa] יפולו for MT יפלו. Kutscher *(Isaiah Scroll,* 331) calls it a pausal form, but Wildberger (985) insists it is an accented penultima form. It is often assumed that this can be an idiom for birth or even for miscarriage because of the context. The meaning is obscure.

19.a. *BHS* follows Syr *wšldjhwn* in emending to נִבְלֹתָם "their corpses." Wildberger (985) thinks MT contains a gloss—a note by a reader who wants his own body included in the resurrection. But if the speaker is God himself, the 1st person suffix lays claim to all the corpses of the righteous as his own.

19.b. DSS[Isa] יקיצו "let them awake." LXX translates a ind fut ἐγερθήσονται "they will awake."

19.c. DSS[Isa] וירננו "and they shall sing" (pf). 'A αινεσουσιν "they will praise." LXX εὐφρανθήσονται "they will rejoice." Yet MT is consistent in its address to those "who dwell in the dust." The imperative should be maintained.

19.d-d. "The dew of lights." Schwarz (*ZAW* 88 [1976] 280–81) suggests the translation "dew of the spirits of the dead." But this has little to commend it. Cf. Ps 139:12 with "light" in the sg. P. Humbert ("La rosée tombe en Israel," *TZ* 13 [1957] 491) suggests the special meaning "luminous particles."

20.a. Q דלתך, a sg. But K with dual "doors" is correct.

20.b. חבי is generally described as an Aramaism. Wildberger notes that Hebrew uses חבא in the niph. (Cf. G. Bergstrasser, *Hebraeische Grammatik* II [Hildesheim: Georg Olsm, 1962] § 29*c.*)

21.a. DSS[Isa] lacks חנה. MT is to be sustained.

21.b. LXX ἀπὸ τοῦ ἁγίου "from the sanctuary." A good paraphrase, but not a witness to a different text.

Form/Structure/Setting

Pilgrims from the land of Judah approach the Holy City during the uneasy calm that has settled over the land after the fall of Tyre. Jerusalem has remained relatively untouched by the war that has ravaged the land and other cities. The pilgrims try to make this a normal festival occasion such as had been the custom in Jerusalem before the bad times. But the pall of war still hangs heavy in the air.

The chorus is strong in this scene. Solo voices represent a teacher as well as other pilgrims with different moods. Then Yahweh appears with his herald. His announcement picks up the theme of his reaction to the death of his people (25:7–8) and of further judgments (23:17; 24:21).

The opening song (vv 1b–4) is a pilgrim's song. The themes of the city, the gates, the righteous, and trust in Yahweh are typical. Antiphonal statements develop the themes of their troubled times: v 5 "He humbled those on high"; v 7 "There is a level path for the righteous"; v 9 "Your judgments . . . teach righteousness." There are responses to each of these. The antiphonal exchange continues with a protest: "A wicked one does not learn" vv 10–11; "Yahweh has provided peace for us," though foreign lords reigned, vv 12–13; the assembly begins to be unruly with critical observations in vv 14–16 and a despairing chorus in vv 17–18.

This is brought to an abrupt end by an epiphany (vv 19–21). Yahweh and his herald appear to the group with an astonishing announcement in line with that of 25:8. They are called to rejoice, but then warned to return to their homes, for Yahweh is about to emerge from Jerusalem for judgment on the land. Obviously, this is not a fitting time for entertaining pilgrims.

Thus the chapter consists of three formal structures. The pilgrim song (vv 1b–4) opens the scene. The dialogue of the pilgrims (5–18) is the body of the scene. The epiphany (vv 19–21) brings it to a close.

Comment

1. *In that day* refers to the time of the great throne appearance in 24:23–25:8. *A strong city* is Jerusalem, the goal of the pilgrimage. It stands in contrast to "the ruined city" of 24:10, 12 and 25:2.

2 The *gates* are those of Jerusalem (cf. Ps 24:7). The *righteous* and those *observing faithful deeds* are the pilgrims fulfilling their vows.

3 *A dependent shape* refers to the willing and malleable spirit of the worshiper, not willful or rebellious. The other requirement is that God *be trusted.* Of such God does indeed form *peace.*

5–6 The processional dialogue resumes the theme of the destroyed city (24:10, 12; 25:2). The *lofty city* recalls the picture of the high and mighty ones who will be brought low (2:11–18) and of the mighty king who would be brought down to Sheol (14:11). The verse implies that the city was guilty of oppressing the poor.

7 A theme from the pilgrim psalms stresses that the path of the *righteous* (the pilgrim) will be *smooth* and *level* (cf. 40:3).

8 The chorus confesses that *the way of God's judgments* requires patient hope, which a solo voice fervently repeats (v 9).

9 The teacher reflects that God's judgments are necessary in order for the *world's inhabitants* to learn *righteousness.* The implication is that they need something which the faithful pilgrims already know. It also implies that God's judgments are intended for other peoples, not Israel. At this point the discussion begins to get out of hand as they turn their attention to the *world's inhabitants.*

10–11 The pilgrims see little chance that the *wicked* can be changed, much less *learn righteousness.* They are blamed because they do not recognize God's uplifted hand. This is exactly the criticism that the Vision has leveled against Israel/Judah from the beginning. They are "blind, deaf, and without understanding." Here the pilgrims can see that in the *wicked,* but not in themselves.

12 The pilgrims get back on track with a confession that Yahweh has in fact provided *peace for them.* In the midst of violence and turmoil they have survived.

13 A second verse notes that it has not been easy under foreign domination, but they had continued to worship him.

14 The reference to other *masters* undoubtedly refers to the Assyrian emperors. The ones who brought this up are rebuked for having stirred up the *ghosts* which had been laid to rest. It is not necessary to mention them, for *ghosts do not rise up.* The teacher picks up the point and directs the thought to God, implying praise for his control of them: *You decide their fate and then you destroy them.* The teaching recalls 24:21–22 where the kings and armies are imprisoned against the day of their judgment. The teacher then admonishes the speakers that God has made all memory of them to disappear. It is not necessary to mention them, especially not in God's presence.

15 An objection is raised. *The nation* would normally be used for someone other than Israel. Here it would properly be related to the other *masters* and must be the Assyrian Empire which in this period grew to its greatest proportions. Yahweh did allow *the nation* to grow, *gain glory,* and *extend all borders of its land.* Note the protests on the same subject in 10:7–11. It is hard to see and understand the workings of God in history from the perspective of only a few years. The Vision calls for us to trace it through the centuries, three centuries.

16 The literal translation "they judged you," addressed to God, does not fit the context. The references here seem to be to the practice of magic and sorcery. In a time of distress someone tried to take God's place and assume responsibility for determining *fate* by the use of spells. It is not clear who is accused, whether the foreign masters or some of the Israelites. It is probably the latter.

17 The distress and confusion of the times are compared to a woman in childbirth.

18 Cynical rejoinders indicate the despair of the times. *Fall* has sometimes been understood to mean "be born." At this point the mood of the pilgrimage has been turned away from the pious thoughts with which it began.

19 The pilgrims are interrupted by the appearance of Yahweh and his herald. One may imagine a scene like that in Acts 9:3. As the pilgrims fall back because of the bright epiphany, God speaks: *Your dead will live! My corpses will rise!* He reasserts the announcement made at the banquet on his mountain (25:7–8). It is significant that the dead are recognized as belonging to Israel *and* to Yahweh. This does not contradict the statement of v 14 that *dead do not live.* That was said of foreign masters whom God had condemned to be forgotten. A distinction is made between them and these that belong to Israel and to God. God has decided their fate, too. They will live!

The herald addresses the dead, calling for them to *awake and sing. Dew* is a very important element in Palestine's ecosystem. During the long dry months it is the only moisture the vegetation receives. It became a symbol for life. Light is also an important symbol of life and well-being (cf. 9:1[2]; 42:6, 16; 58:8, 10; J. Hempel, *Die Lichtsymbolik im Alten Testament,* StG 13 [Heidelberg, 1960] 352–68). Egyptian texts claim a heavenly origin for dew. It is the tears of Horus and Thot and bears the power of resurrection in itself (J. de Savignac, "La rosée solaire de l'ancienne Egypte," *NC* 6 [1954] 345–53). Wildberger (998) suggests the meaning of *dew of lights* to be the "dew that brings life, salvation, and happiness."

20 But the next word of the epiphany turns the pilgrims back from Jerusalem to their homes. They are to go inside and close the doors behind them, to *hide until wrath passes over.* The horrors of the judgment are not yet finished. For the third time in this act notice is given that these events stand between the times (cf. 23:17; 24:22).

21 The herald points to Yahweh leaving *his place* in Zion to punish (פקד) the guilt of *the land's population.* The guilt of the people began to be separated from that of the land itself in 24:5 (cf. 24:6b, 17; 25:8c). *The land* will apparently be called as a witness. It will no longer serve to *cover up* for the people's guilt in all the murders and acts of violence that have transpired. This essential step in moving toward justice is about to take place (cf. 24:5–6, 20).

Explanation

By using the device of a pilgrimage scene, the Vision has presented the dilemma of Judean faithful worshipers. They want to go to Jerusalem and worship Yahweh. They want to believe and repeat the usual rituals of faith in Yahweh to bring peace and safety. But they have also experienced the heel of the invader and the tyrant. They have seen what happened to their neighbors and their friends over a long time. They have lived with the constant fact of death all around them for three-quarters of a century. It is not surprising that pious songs are mixed with cynical observations and that despair lies not far beneath the surface of their thoughts.

The epiphany is dramatic and powerful. Once more they are asked to wait a little while. The *wrath* is not quite finished. But they are assured that God's terrible acts are effectively dealing with the curse of death which has hung over the land so long.

Excursus: Yahweh and Death

Bibliography

Bailey, L. R., Sr. *Biblical Perspectives on Death.* Philadelphia: Fortress, 1979. **Birkeland, H.** "The Beliefs in Resurrection of the Dead in the Old Testament." *ST* 3 (1950/51) 60–78. **Botterweck, G. B.** "Marginalien zum alt. Auferstehungsglauben." *WZKM* 54 (1957) 1–8. **Fohrer, G.** "Das Geschick des Menschen nach dem Tode in Alten Testament." *KD* 12 (1968) 249–62. **Haenchen, E.** "Auferstehung im Alten Testament." *Die Bibel und wir.* Tübingen: Mohr, 1968. 73–90. **König, F.** *Zarathustras Jenseitsvorstellungen und das Alte Testament.* Wien: Herder, 1964. 214–40. **Martin-Achard, R.** *De la mort à la résurrection.* Neuchâtel: Delachaux & Niestlé, 1956. 101–12. **Nötscher, F.** *Altorientalischer und alttestamentlicher Auferstehungsglauben.* Würzburg: C. J. Becker, 1926. 154–59. **Preuss, H. D.** " 'Auferstehung' in Texten alttestamentlicher Apokalyptik (Jes 26:7–19, Dan 12:1–4)." *Linguistische Theologie* 3 (1972) 101–72. **Rost, L.** "Alttestamentliche Wurzeln der ersten Auferstehung." *In memoriam E. Lohmeyer* (1951) 67–72. **Savignac, J. de.** "La rosée solaire de l'ancienne Égypte." *NC* 6 (1954) 345–53. **Sawyer, J. F. A.** "Hebrew Words for the Resurrection of the Dead." *VT* 13 (1973) 218–34. **Stemberger, G.** "Das Problem der Auferstehung im Alten Testament." *Kairos* 14 (1972) 273–90. **Virgulin, S.** "La risurrezione dei morti in Isa 26:14–19." *BeO* 14 (1972) 49–60. **Zolli, E.** "Il canto dei morti risorti e il ms. DSI[a] in Isa 26:18." *Sef* 12 (1952) 375–78.

The size of the bibliography is a sign of the interest which a discussion of the resurrection in the OT awakens. But is the interest due to the content of the OT? Or is it a carry-back of interest from later times, especially the NT?

The issue in this act has more to do with the question of whether Yahweh can be trusted with the fate of Israel and the welfare of its people than it does with the doctrine of life after death. The topic of death and the assurance that all matters of life and death are firmly in Yahweh's hands is clearly central here.

In a book that is so filled with violence and destruction it is not surprising that the theme of death would have considerable attention. Words using the roots מות "die" and הרג "kill" are spotted at various places in the book to provide a very serious reflection on God's relation to death. Tracing these words will certainly not be a complete study but they will give us an entrance into it.

Time divisions in the early acts are marked by the death-year of kings (6:1; 14:28) while 38:1–20 is concerned with Hezekiah's mortal illness. The temptation in times of distress to resort to necromancy and spiritualism is noted in 8:19 and in 26:16.

Serious treatment of the subject begins in chap. 14. Death is here seen as the great leveler of men. The taunting song is directed to the king of Babylon who considered himself the greatest of all, perhaps even a god. Now he has been cut down and is dead just like any man. All Sheol prepares to meet him, saying with glee, "You have become weak, as we are" (v 10). The king's ambition is contrasted with his helplessness in death; he does not even get a proper burial (vv 19–20).

This reminder that death sets limits on the power and ambition of even the most awesome of tyrants recurs in 26:14. The limit to the length of life is part of God's control of events (cf. also Gen 6:3). The Lord reminds the people that the tyrants of which they complain are already dead. Funeral preparations have already been made for Assyria's king (30:33).

In chap. 22 Jerusalem is in crisis. There are dead, but not from battle (v 2). There is a crisis of leadership. Shebna, the prime minister, is found working on his mausoleum in the royal cemetary rather than on the critical problems of the country (v 16). He will have no chance for atonement (v 14) before death finds him in a far country (v 18). Instead of the honored memorial among the royalty he had served so long, he will die alone and unmourned.

In chap. 25 Yahweh's throne appearance announces a banquet in which he will totally dissolve the ubiquitous hold of death over all in the land (vv 6–8). Here death is seen as the curse which repeated blood-guilt has brought upon the land and all its inhabitants (24:6). God, and only God, can break the grip of that curse and remove the "reproach" of the people from the land (v 8).

In chap. 26 the people are not comforted by the reference to the death of the tyrants (v 14). They complain of their own unsuccessful efforts even to repopulate the land (v 18). To which Yahweh answers that their dead will live, will rise, and will rejoice when the land gives birth to her "ghosts" (v 19). V 20 picks up the theme again. When God judges the people of the land, the dark secrets of previous murders will be secret no longer. "The land will conceal her slain no longer."

A further reference occurs in chap. 27. The exiles in Assyria and in Egypt are said to have been perishing. But they will be gathered by God to come and worship him on his holy mountain in Jerusalem (v 13). Separation from the temple is equivalent to death. Being allowed to participate again in Jerusalem is like coming back to life.

Rulers in Jerusalem who have made a covenant with death are spoken of in 28:15. A lie and falsehood are synonyms. It is as though these are idols, or national deities of foreign powers. God promises that the ruse will not work. The covenant with death will be annulled and they will be overcome by the scourge that sweeps the land (v 18).

Hezekiah's view of his coming death is presented in detail in 38:1–20. Salvation is seen as preservation of life. And the meaning of life is essentially the ability to participate in Jerusalem's worship.

In chaps. 40–48, the problems are those of life in exile, and death does not play a prominent part. However, the question of whether life is meaningful or has permanent significance is broached.

In chaps. 49–54, the call for Jerusalem to find meaning in her life even through suffering and humiliation leads to the great proclamation that suffering even to death can be vicarious, can be God's will, can have atoning and healing power, justifying many (53:7–12). The people recognized that this was done for them (vv 4–6).

Attention returns to death in 65:15. Death will be the recompense of those who are rejected from a place where long life will be the norm, rather than the exception (v 20). But even in that place to which believers from all peoples may come to worship God, the death of the rebels from among his people will continue to be a bitter memory that cannot be forgotten (66:24).

The Vision is keenly aware of the issues that death brings when the people are called to review ten generations of the most turbulent and disastrous history that Israel ever knew. The major points made are that life and death are clearly in the control of God. Death for the tyrants and for the rebels in Israel is a just retribution for their sins.

Death can become a curse resulting from unbridled violence in the land. But God can and will control that as well. His goal for his people, in fact for all peoples, is life and peace. He is the source of both. Life at its best and most vibrant is that which is lived in his temple, in his presence, and in accord with his teaching. This is his promise for his people, but particularly for the "humble, the contrite, who tremble at his word." These shall have life.

But this survey makes it equally clear that the Vision has no doctrine of a general resurrection. There is no great new hope for life after death which goes beyond the basic Israelite trust in God for all the promises of life. For that, one must wait until the Christian gospel is preached.

Scene 7: *"That Day" for Tyre and Israel* (*27:1–13*)

Bibliography

Alonso-Schökel, L. "La Canción de la viña. Isa 27:2–5." *EstEcl* 34 (1960) 767–74. **Herrman, J.** "סאסא Jes 27:8 und שאשא Hes 39:2." *ZAW* 36 (1916) 243. **Jacob, E.** "Du primier au deuxième chant de la vigne du prophète Esaïe. Réflexions zur Esaïe 27:2–5." FS W. Eichrodt. *Wort, Gebot, Glaube.* Zürich: Zwingli Verlag, 1970. 325–30. **Robertson, E.** "Isaiah XXVII 2–6." *ZAW* 47 (1929) 197–206.

Translation

Heavens: 1 *In that day* 2
Yahweh with his sword will decide the fate of 3+3
the hard, great, and strong one,
of Leviathan,[a] *a fleeing serpent,*[b] 4+4
Leviathan, a twisting snake.
Earth: *And he will kill the monster* [c]*which is in the sea.*[c] 4
Herald: 2 *In that day*[a] 2+2+2
a fruitful[b] *vineyard (there will be)—*
sing to her.[c]
Yahweh: 3 *I, Yahweh, am her keeper!* 3+2
Moment by moment, I watch her!
Lest one put her in judgment[a] 3+3
night and day I guard her!
4 *Wrath*[a]*—I have none.* 3+4
If one would give me[b] *thorns,*[c] *briers*[d] *in the battle*[e]
I would set out against them. 2+2
I would burn[f] *them altogether.*[f]
5 *Rather let one lay hold on my protection.* 3+3+3
[a]*Let one make peace with me.*[a]
Peace let one make with me.
Heavens: 6 *In the coming times*[a] 1
Jacob will take root.[b] 2+3+3
He will blossom, and Israel will send out shoots.
They will fill the world's surface with fruit.
First Israelite: 7 *Has he struck them (with a blow) like the blow of*
those striking him?[a] 3+3
Or has he been killed like the killing of those killing him?[b]

Second Israelite: 8 *By driving her away,*[a] *by sending her (away),*[b] *do*
you contend with her? 3+5
Or has he removed her[c] *by his fierce wind*
in a day of east winds?
Third Israelite: 9 *Therefore, by this will the guilt of Jacob be expiated?* 4+4
And (is) this all the fruit of removing this sin?[a]
Heavens: *When he made all the stones of an altar* 3+3+3
(to be) crushed like stones of chalk,
Asherim and incense altars no longer stand
upright.
Earth: 10 *Indeed, a fortified city stands abandoned by itself alone,* 4+4
a habitation deserted and forsaken like a wilderness.
Heavens: *There a calf grazes.* 3+2+2
There he lies down
and strips away[a] *its branches.*
Earth: 11 *When its twig*[a] *is dry, it is broken.*[b] 3+4
Women come, making a fire of them.
Heavens: *For it was not a discerning people.* 4+3+3
Therefore he had no compassion on them.
His maker did not show him favor.
Earth: 12 *But it will be in that day* 3
Yahweh will thresh out grain[a] 3+3
from the River [b]*to the Wadi of Egypt.*[b]
Heavens: *And you, yourselves, will be gathered* 2+2+2
one to another,[c]
O Israelites.
Earth: 13 *And it will be in that day:* 3
A great trumpet will be blown 3+4+3
and those perishing in the land of Assyria will come,
and those driven away in the land of Egypt.
Heavens: *And they will bow down*[a] *to Yahweh* 2+3
in the holy mountain in Jerusalem.

Notes

1.a. J. A. Emerton, "Leviathan and *ltn:* the vocalization of the Ugaritic word for the dragon," *VT* 32 (1982) 327–33: "The commonly accepted theory that Ugaritic *ltn* was pronounced *lōtān* raises difficulties. It is better to try to relate the word more closely to Hebrew *liwyātān* and I have suggested the following development: *liwyatānū* > *līyitānu* > *lītānu* (spelled *ltn*)."

1.b. בָּרִחַ is a unique form in the OT. An adjective from "to flee" would be written בריח which is apparently what Q intends. DSS[Isa] בורח is a ptcp "fleeing," LXX *φεύγοντα* "fleeing." 'A *μοχλον* "bar, bolt," Vg *vectis* "a lever, a bolt" seem to think of בְּרִיחַ II "bar" (BDB, 138) but this has no meaning here. Albright (*BASOR* 83 [1941] 39 n. 5) suggested "pre-historic serpent." The Ugaritic texts include the same word. The descriptions are clearly very old.

1.c-c. Missing in LXX.

2.a. *BHS* with Duhm and *BHK* suggest that ביום ההוא is dittography for אשר בים which has been written twice, covering the word ואמר "and one said" or "and I said." The opening is abrupt, but not enough to justify this change.

2.b. The Leningradensis text reads חֶמֶר "wine," which is one of the very few consonantal variants from other texts of the Ben Asher group (see *BHK*). Also DSS[Isa] reads חומר (Kutscher, *Isaiah Scroll,* 375). Most other MSS, *BHS,* LXX *καλός*, Tg and Syr read חמד "delight." Cf. Amos 5:11.

2.c. לָהּ "to her." The antecedent must be כרם "vineyard" which is usually masc. However, in Lev 25:3 it is fem as it is here.

3.a. Vg and LXX ἁλώσεται read a passive יִפָּקֵד (cf. Num 16:29; Prov 19:23). The same sense is achieved by using an indeterminate subject.

4.a. LXX τεῖχος and Syr *šwrʾ* apparently read חֹמָה "wall" instead of MT חֵמָה "wrath." Robertson (*ZAW* 47 [1929] 200) looks to an Arabic cognate for the meaning "tent" (for a night watchman), while G. R. Driver suggests the meaning "fiery wine" (*TZ* 14 [1958] 133–35). MT should be supported.

4.b. Wildberger (1008) correctly notes that the suffix on נתן often stands for the dative. Kimchi remarked that מי־יתנני stood for מי יתן לי.

4.c. DSS[Isa] שומיר. Kutscher (*Isaiah Scroll,* 385) says this should be read שימיר. BDB (1036–39) suggests three roots שמר: I (v) "to keep, guard"; II (n) "dregs"; III (n) "thorns." DSS[Isa] apparently wants to read it as "a keeper, guardian" from I. MT places it under III "thorns."

4.d. DSS[Isa] Syr Tg Vg add the conjunction ושית.

4.e. במלחמה "in the battle" is placed in the first line by MT. Many interpreters like Wildberger and *BHS* find the meaning difficult and want to eliminate it altogether or draw it into the second line.

4.f. DSS[Isa] adds a *waw* at both ends of the phrase. *BHS* suggests adding a *daghesh.* The change is of no consequence. It is better to stay with MT "I burn it altogether" (BDB, 428).

5.a.-a. LXX ποιήσωμεν εἰρήνην αὐτῷ "let us make peace with him," Syr *wʾbd lh šlmʾ* "and I will make peace for her." MT has the speaker continue to be Yahweh and the subject indeterminate.

6.a. הבאים "the coming ones" has given the commentators and translators trouble. For a survey of suggestions see Wildberger (1013). The word is a short form for "the coming days" and is used adverbally as an acc of time (Joüon § 126*i*). Cf. Eccl 2:16.

6.b. DSS[Isa] ישריש a *plene* writing of the same form. ʾA Σ Θ ῥιζώσει "he will cause to take root." 40:24 vocalizes the word שֹׁרֵשׁ a poel, i.e., passive. BDB (1057) sees this as a denominative verb "deal with roots." The meanings in hiph and poel would apparently differ little.

7.a. LXX πληγήσεται, καὶ "will he be struck, and" = הֻכָּה וְ is suggested by *BHS,* Gray and Procksch. The triple use of the same root makes translation difficult, but the LXX is no help.

7.b. DSS[Isa] הורגיו "killer" an act ptcp for MT's pass ptcp "one being killed." This is seen as a better text by virtually all including Guthe, Gray, Duhm, Marti, Ehrlich *(Randglossen),* Procksch, Fohrer, Kaiser, Wildberger, *BHK,* and *BHS.*

8.a. MT בסאסאה was a problem even for the Masoretes, as the pointing in *BHK* and *BHS* with no vowel under the first א suggests. *BHK* notes that Q in several MSS reads בְּסַסְּאָה. ʾA, Σ, Θ, Tg, Vg (but not LXX) understood it as the measure סְאָה used in weighing grain "measure by measure." Gesenius thought the word was contracted from בסאה סאה. Dillmann follows LXX "by warfare" to suggest that it is an inf with 3rd fem sing suffix or an action noun סַאסְאָה (BDB, 685) which has been generally accepted. But the attempt to find its meaning takes another route. G. R. Driver (*JTS* 30 [1928] 371) called it a pilpel inf to be understood from the Arab *saʾsaʾ* "shooing her away," a term used in driving donkeys. F. Schulthess (*ZS* 2 [1923] 15) thought of a verb which was also derived from *ša* or *sa,* sounds used in driving goats. The parallel form שלחה "sending her" supports this (Wildberger, 1014). In this case the *mappik* in ה should be inserted and the suffix read.

8.b. *BHK* calls this a gloss, but no explanation is given (see Wildberger, 1014).

8.c. The suffix on הגה needs a *mappik.*

9.a. DSS[Isa] חטאו (cf. Kutscher, *Isaiah Scroll,* 374) "they sinned" turns the last word into a relative clause. MT, reading a noun with suffix "his sin," is to be preferred. A. C. M. Blommerde ("The Broken Construct Chain," *Bib* 55 [1974] 551) suggests that חטאתו is connected to כל פרי as an example of a "broken construct chain" to be translated "and this is: removing every fruit of his sin." Wildberger (1014) correctly judges this unlikely.

10.a. *BHK* suggests emending to qal or a plural. But the form of MT (piel pf; BDB, 478) makes good sense: "finishes" = "strips" branches.

11.a. Vg *messes illius* "its standing grain." MT means "a branch, sprout" understood as a collective.

11.b. *BHK* emends to the "energic form" following the Versions. MT makes sense and is followed here.

12.a. The positions of the prepositions מן and עד have raised questions here. *BHK* suggests moving מן from שבלת to the following word הנהר "the river." שבל may mean something that flows like a garment or a river (BDB, 987, I) or an ear of grain (BDB, 987, II). MT has apparently chosen I and understood שבלת to refer to the flowing river. This leaves no object for the verb. The emendation would supply that object "grain" while keeping the contrast "from the river." The emended form of *BHK* is used here.

12.b-b. LXX ἕως Ῥινοκορούρων "to Rinokorouron." A city of this name existed at that time where *el-ʿarīš* is today. The present name of "the river of Egypt" is *wādi el-ʿarīš.*

12.c. לאחד אחד is literally "one to one," i.e., add one more to the one already there.

13.a. DSS[Isa] והשתחו leaves out a *wāw,* a case of haplography.

Excursus: Leviathan = Tyre

Bibliography

Allen, R. B. "The Leviathan-Rahab-Dragon Motif in the Old Testament." Th.M. Thesis, Dallas Theological Seminary, 1968. **Burney, C. K.** "Old Testament Notes III. The Three Serpents of Isaiah xxvii 1." *JTS* 2 (1909–10) 443–47. **Gorden, C. H.** "Leviathan: Symbol of Evil." *Biblical Motifs,* ed. A. Altmann. Cambridge, MA: Harvard U. P., 1966. **Kaiser, O.** *Die Mythische Bedeutung des Meeres.* BZAW 78. 2d ed. Berlin: De Gruyter, 1962.

לוית֯ן "Leviathan" probably means "coiled one" from לוה like Arab *lwy* "coil," "wind" (T. H. Gaster, "Leviathan," *IDB* 3:116) and is like Ug *ltn* (see *Note* 1.a.). It also appears in Pss 74:14; 104: 26; Job 41:1 and in 2 Esdr 6:52; 2 Bar 29:3–8. Here in Isaiah, Leviathan is described as "the hard, great, strong one . . . a fleeing serpent, a twisting snake . . . the monster which is in the sea."

In another context the word might be explained by the mythical implications of the Baʿal myth in which Leviathan is killed. But Job's use transparently refers the name to a great sea creature with no mythic or supernatural overtones (cf. Gaster, *IDB* 3:116). The context here in Isaiah calls for a historical identification. On pp. 298–99 above, the arch structure of this Act was shown to balance the reference to the sea on which Tyre's sailors work (23:11–12a) with Leviathan (27:1). The name Rahab, also usually applied to a great mythological dragon, is applied to Egypt by name in 30:7. The same thing is done here. Leviathan is a symbol for Tyre. God's promise to "decide the fate" (פקד) of Tyre (23:17) is fulfilled in this passage when God "decides the fate" of Leviathan (27:1).

Form/Structure/Setting

After the delay of seventy years, attention returns to Tyre, symbolized as Leviathan the Dragon whose day of judgment has arrived. This raises the hopes of Israel's exiles. Yahweh reminds them that he is watching the vineyard and that the people will be replanted. In the meantime, the land remains desolate for the people, who still do not understand. But Israel will be gathered from the lands of her exile to worship before the Lord in Zion.

The structure of this scene returns to the form dominated by the dialogue between Heavens and Earth. It concerns things that are to occur "in that day" when Yahweh goes out from his place (26:21), "after many days" when Yahweh decides the fate of kings (24:21–22), and "at the end of seventy years" when Yahweh decides the fate of Tyre (23:17). It also includes a vine-

yard song by Yahweh and brief but spirited objections by individual Israelites.
The outline of thought carried by the dialogue is:

Leviathan is to be judged (v 1).
(Song of the Vineyard, vv 2–5).
Jacob will take root and flourish (v 6).
The desolation is a witness that this is a people without understanding (vv 10–11).
Yahweh will thresh and gather the exiled Israelites (v 12).
They will come and worship Yahweh on Zion (v 13).

It is instructive to note what is missing which might have been expected. There is no word about either an Israelite or Judean government or ruler. There is nothing about Israel's permanent return. Exile is apparently a lasting part of her existence, but Jerusalem will be there and accessible. As long as they can make pilgrimage to Zion, they are certainly not dead or nonexistent.

Yahweh is alive, at work, and in control. Israel can thrive and grow. Jerusalem gains in importance and meaning.

The song of the vineyard (vv 2–5) is the second in the Vision in which Yahweh sings of Israel as his vineyard (cf. 5:1–7). Both songs portray Israel as precious to Yahweh. In 5:1 it is laid out on "a very fertile hill." In 27:2 it is called "a fruitful vineyard." In both, the vineyard is threatened by שמיר "thorns" and שית "briers." Wildberger (1009) notes that these words are paired in 7:23–25; 9:17 [18]; 10:17, but nowhere outside Isaiah. In 27:3 Yahweh waters the vineyard "moment by moment." In 5:6 he forbids the clouds to rain on it. In 5:7 he expects justice and righteousness from his people. In 27:5 he offers peace.

The song is a conscious counterpart to the first one. It is part of the announcement that the period of judgment over his people is about to come to an end. "Of wrath—I have none" (27:4).

The questions that are asked in vv 7–9 reflect the dissatisfaction in Israel. There is still a petulant spirit reflected here which has neither recognized nor accepted the justice of Yahweh's actions. They are not ready for the new day or participation in it. They are "not a discerning people" (v 11b; and also 1:3 *passim*).

Comment

1 *In that day,* like the phrase in 25:9 and 26:1, refers to the day at the end of the seventy years (23:17) and after the many days of 24:22 when Yahweh comes from his place (26:8). *Leviathan* is a symbol for Tyre, its counterpart in this Act (chap. 23). Yahweh will decide its fate as promised in 23:17. But that decision, after the reprieve predicted in 23:15–16, will be death for the monster that is in the sea. The tension between the destruction announced here and the seeming continuance of trading activity announced in 23:17–18 is the very essence of its meaning. Tyre will no longer be "Leviathan, a twisting serpent." That existence of power and conniving intrigue will be over. She will no longer be a threat to her neighbors, especially Israel/Judah. She can return to the role she played in David's time (cf. 1 Kgs 5; 2 Chr 2:1–16) that is announced in 23:18.

2 *A fruitful vineyard* is a symbol for Israel and is a counterpart to the *vineyard on a very fruitful hill* of 5:1. But there is a substantial difference. In chap. 5 Israel was a people in its land. God's watchful care applied to both. Here Israel is a people in exile (cf. v 12). God extols his watchcare over her, and his protection and peace are emphasized (vv 3b–5). He promises to plant and cultivate his vineyard but there is no reference to the land. A return to live in the land of Canaan is not included here. The omission is not an oversight. Rather, they will *fill the world's surface* (v 6). Israel's destiny, still under God's watchcare, has changed.

3 *Lest one put her in judgment.* The position of the exiles as aliens in a foreign land left them undefended and often without rights before a magistrate or court. Yahweh promises his own protection.

4 *Of Wrath.* Earlier acts of the Vision have provided ample descriptions of Yahweh's wrath toward Israel in judgment for her sins. But by this time his attitude toward Israel will have "turned the corner": *I have none.*

Briers and *thorns* are the symbols of the void in the land left by Israel's evacuation (5:6; 7:23–25; 9:17 [18]; 10:17). Their place and function are now finished. God himself will *burn them altogether.*

5 *Rather* is an emphatic conjunction expressing an alternative. "On the other hand," Yahweh is saying, let one seek my *protection, make peace with me.* Yahweh understands that Israel, as a rebellious people, has in fact been at war with him. He is offering them a peace treaty. He is offering them protection under his sovereignty.

6 *Jacob will take root.* Earlier chapters have spoken of being uprooted, a figure of displacement and exile, but also a figure that implies a wilting and dying plant. The figure here is of being transplanted and beginning to prosper in the new ground.

7 *Has he struck them?* This raises the first of the skeptical questions. They are not addressed to God himself, but to the speaker of v 6. They want to know whether their adversaries have been dealt a hard retribution similar to their own, or whether they have suffered the brutalities which Israel has suffered.

8 *Do you contend with her?* The question is addressed to Yahweh. It asks whether *driving her away,* i.e., the Exile, was in fact a form of judicial process. The speaker is skeptical. He thinks it is more likely that God has simply lost patience and let his wrath overflow like a *fierce wind.* The implication is that justice and a reasoned process had nothing to do with it.

9 *Will the guilt of Jacob be expiated?* The question asks whether this will, in fact, remove the accumulated guilt of Israel's sins. Is it possible that all of this, i.e., the century and more of constant foreign harassment and invasion from the time of Uzziah through that of Manasseh, is due to God's removal of the sins of Israel? In answer the witnesses point to the stark evidence left by the desolation. *Altars crushed* at least means that idolatry has ceased.

10 Ruins testify to a commercial and militaristic civilization that has now become quietly pastoral.

11 This happened because *Israel was not a discerning people.* The Vision has been making this point from 1:2–3 on. It has used the figures of blindness and deafness. The questions show that the condition lingers on. God did not show the favor that he has now announced for his people because of that lack of discernment. But now he has come to announce that he will take personal responsibility for his vineyard.

12 *In that day,* like that in vv 1 and 2, refers to Yahweh's actions after the seventy years (23:17) and after the "many days" (24:22) when Yahweh goes out of his place (26:21). The other decisions and actions which are entailed, like the judgment of the kings and the destruction of Leviathan, the restoration of a chastened Tyre and the expiation of the guilt of the land, will include *gathering* the exiled Israelites from Mesopotamia and Egypt. God's nurture of his vineyard, to mix the metaphor, includes *threshing* and *gathering,* harvesting like grain, in the dispersion of the Israelites. The election through Abraham of those who seek him and yearn for him is still valid and will be rewarded.

13 *Those perishing.* This act has had a great deal to say about Yahweh's acts in regard to the dead in the land. The reference here is to those for whom existence in exile, cut off from contact and relation to the worship of God in Israel, is like a living death. Life for them is unthinkable without a sense of the presence of Yahweh and an opportunity to worship him. This was the spiritual "hell" of exile (cf. Ps 137).

The land of Assyria and *the land of Egypt.* These two areas continued to be the major concentrations of Israelites and Jews in the dispersion, although a heavy addition in southern Mesopotamia in 598 and 586 B.C. would shift the emphasis to Babylon.

The purpose and the goal of the *gathering* may come as a surprise or disappointment to many. There is no reference to the reestablishment of the people in Canaan (*à la* Joshua). Nor are they promised the reestablishment of the kingdom even under a son of David. Instead they are promised the opportunity to make pilgrimage to Jerusalem, to *bow down to Yahweh.* This should be no surprise to the reader of the Vision. From 2:1–4 on, the future has been promised to a demilitarized *holy mountain in Jerusalem.* It will be the place of Yahweh's dwelling and the peoples can come there to worship him and learn of his *torah.* Yahweh here promises exiled Israel that privilege. The people who have the hope of seeing Yahweh in his glory in his holy mountain need not consider themselves "dead" or "perishing." To be able to be in his presence is life of the highest order.

Explanation

The scene picks up the beginning theme of the act—the destruction of Tyre—affirms it, and then deals with the consequences for Israel. God affirms his care and protection for Israel, now in exile. But his words are met with skeptical questions. The lessons of the devastation of Israel have not yet been learned. Yet the scene closes with the affirmation that God will make it possible for exiled Israelites to overcome the disabilities of distance and separation and thus be among the worshipers on his holy mountain in Jerusalem. The reference to the exiles as "perishing" picks up the theme of "death" earlier in the act. It assures the exiles of meaningful "life" through faithful continuation of their relationship to Yahweh, who offers the hope of worship in Jerusalem.

Act V
Requiem for the Kingdom of Judah (Chaps. 28–33)

THE FIFTH GENERATION:
KINGS JOSIAH AND JEHOIAKIM (CA. 640–605 B.C.)

Bibliography

Barth, H. *Israel und das Assyrerreich in den nichtjesajanischen Texten des Protojesajabuches.* Diss., Hamburg, 1974. **Dietrich, W.** *Jesaja und die Politik.* BEvT 74. Munich: Kaiser, 1976. **Donner, H.** *Israel unter den Völkern.* VTSup 11. Leiden: E. J. Brill, 1964. **Hoffmann, W. H.** *Die Intention der Verkündigung Jesajas.* BZAW 136. Berlin: De Gruyter, 1974. **Huber, F.** *Jahwe, Juda und die andern Völker beim Propheten Jesaja.* BZAW 137. Berlin: De Gruyter, 1976. **Irwin, W. H.** *Isaiah 28–33: Translation with Philological Notes.* Diss. Pontifical Biblical Institute, Rome, 1973. **Janzen, W.** *Mourning Cry and Woe Oracle.* BZAW 125. Berlin: De Gruyter, 1972. 49–62. **Jensen, J.** *The Use of tôrâ by Isaiah: His Debate with the Wisdom Tradition.* CBQMS 3. Washington: Cath. Bib. Assoc., 1973. **Kraus, H.-J.** "*hôj* als prophetische Leichenklage über das eigene Volk im 8. Jahrhundert." *ZAW* 85 (1973) 15–46. **Laberge, L.** *Isaïe 28–33: Étude de tradition textuelle.* Diss. Pontifical Biblical Commission, Rome/Ottawa, 1968. Microfilm-Mary Wash Informational Services, Ottawa, 1977. **Lutz, H.-M.** *Jahwe, Jerusalem und die Völker.* WMANT 27. Neukirchen-Vluyn: Neukirchener Verlag, 1968. **Schmidt, H.** *Israel, Zion, und die Völker. Eine motivgeschichtliche Untersuchung zum Verständnis des Universalismus im Alten Testament.* Diss. Zürich, 1966. **Vollmer, J.** *Geschichtliche Rückblicke und Motive in der Prophetie des Amos, Hosea, and Jesaja.* BZAW 119. Berlin: De Gruyter, 1971.

Act V is set in the final half-century of Judah's existence (*ca.* 640–605 B.C.) in the reigns of Josiah and Jehoiakim. The disintegration of the Assyrian Empire with the concurrent rise of Egypt and Babylon occupied world attention while Judah was acting out the final scenes of the judgment pronounced on her a century earlier.

Each of the five scenes begins with "woe," a monotonous funeral chant. The "woes" of these scenes forbid seeing renewal, new life, or hope of return to the glory of Judah's past in the extension of Davidic boundaries under Josiah; the renewed importance of the Holy City, Jerusalem; the promise of Egyptian patronage; or even in God's promise to judge the tyrant. Clearly, the message is that Judah has no political future. Instead, the act continues to portray true hope as centered in Yahweh's support of Zion as a city of worship, Yahweh's promise of grace, and the outpouring of his spirit, as previous acts of the Vision have done.

Comparison will reveal that these five "woe" scenes are parallel to the "woes" for Israel in chaps. 5 and 10, while the Jerusalem scenes are parallel to chaps. 2, 4, and 66. But note the contrast to chap. 11. There is no Davidic heir apparent in these scenes.

Scene 1: Disaster from Expansion (28:1–29)
  Episode A: Woe, Ephraim's Drunkards (28:1–13)
  Episode B: Scoffers in Jerusalem (28:14–22)
  Episode C: Yahweh's Strategy: A Parable (28:23–29)
Scene 2: Disaster in Jerusalem's Political Involvement (29:1–24)
  Episode A: Woe, Ariel (29:1–6)
  Episode B: Like a Dream (29:7–14)
  Episode C: Woe, You Schemers (29:15–24)
Scene 3: Disaster from Self-Help in Rebellion (30:1–33)
  Episode A: Woe, Rebellious Children (30:1–18)
  Episode B: Hope from the Teachers (30:19–26)
  Episode C: A Cultic Theophany (30:27–33)
Scene 4: Disaster from False Faith in Egypt (31:1–32:20)
  Episode A: Woe to Those Who Depend on Egypt (31:1–9)
  Episode B: Suppose a King . . . (32:1–8)
  Episode C: Until Spirit Is Poured Out (32:9–20)
Scene 5: God's Promise to Judge the Tyrant (33:1–24)
  Episode A: Woe, You Destroyer (33:1–6)
  Episode B: See! Their Valiant One (33:7–12)
  Episode C: Who Can Survive the Fire? (33:13–24)

Historical Background (ca. 640–587 b.c.)

Bibliography

Breasted, J. H. *A History of Egypt.* New York: Charles Scribner's Sons, 1946. 565–81. **Bright, J.** *A History of Israel.* 3rd ed. Philadelphia: Westminster, 1981. 313–17. **Kitchen, K. A.** *The Third Intermediate Period in Egypt.* Warminster: Aris & Phillips, 1973. 339–408. **Oded, B.** "Judah and the Exile." *IJH,* 456–69.

Specific references to Assyria and to Egypt occur in the central chapters of this section. The references to Assyria are preoccupied with its imminent fall (30:31; 31:8). References to Egypt deal with the eagerness of certain parties in Jerusalem to make contacts and alliances with Egypt (30:2; 31:1). These references fit the conditions of the second half of the seventh century b.c. and are thoroughly credible historical innuendos of that time.

It is clearly an age in which Egypt is active and gaining strength while Assyria is weakening and fading away. Psamtik I (Psammetichus I) had first fled to Assyria. Then under the patronage of the Assyrians he returned to rule Sais and Memphis by the order of Ashurbanipal in 665 b.c. Assyria's preoccupation with wars in Mesopotamia left him largely to his own resources, which he used extremely well. By 640 b.c. when Ashurbanipal had reestablished his rule over Babylon and Elam and had brought major elements in eastern Palestine to order, Psamtik was firmly in control of all Egypt. He had first seized control of Thebes, over a period of time placing his own men over the major cities. He had shrewdly gained mastery of the priesthood there and brought the mercenary lords under firm control. Egypt was united as it had not been for centuries. He had made an alliance with Gyges of Lydia by 654 B.C. and had apparently positioned himself as an ally to Assyria in its final struggles to keep its empire alive. He reestablished close relations to the port cities of the western Mediterranean. His strength may partially have come from his use of Greek mercenaries.

This new-found strength undoubtedly led to renewed claims to Egypt's traditional position of power and privilege in Syria-Palestine, especially along the coast. He invaded Philistia and laid lengthy siege to Ashdod.

Meantime, Assyria had all kinds of troubles of its own. In 652 B.C. Babylon rebelled. There was conflict in Palestine, perhaps fomented by Psamtik (cf. 2 Chr 33:11), and Arab tribesmen raided Assyrian garrisons on the eastern edges of Palestine. By 640 B.C. Ashurbanipal had brought order to that part of his empire and settled down to spend his last years in more peaceful pursuits. He made no effort to reconquer Egypt.

Manasseh died in 642 B.C. and was succeeded by his son Amon. But it was apparently a sign of those troubled times that he was assassinated two years later by persons in the palace who were in turn killed by outraged citizens (2 Kgs 21:23–24). The violent acts reflected Judah's position as a vulnerable buffer state in the international power struggles of the period. Josiah was crowned king before his eighth birthday. The account in 2 Kings is primarily concerned with his great reforms (22:1–23:29) and only the cryptic news of his death fighting the Egyptians at Megiddo hints at the political tightrope that he walked in keeping his nation out of trouble in those unsettled times. In some sense he kept both the weakening Assyrian rulers and Psamtik I satisfied with his relations to them for thirty years before that fateful battle.

At exactly the time that Josiah was reforming worship in Judah and consolidating his political hold on a wider territory, Assyria was facing a coalition of forces that would destroy it over a fifteen-year period. In 626 B.C. the Assyrians were defeated at the very gates of Babylon.

At this time apparently a horde of foreigners that Herodotus calls Scythians swept down through Palestine to the very borders of Egypt. They were finally stopped and the force of their march halted. They retreated from the territory. Their presence may well account for a decade's delay in further developments in Mesopotamia.

By 616 B.C. the issues in the struggle were clear. Assyria's fate was sealed. The major contest for succession to its imperial power was joined. The principal claimants were Media, Babylonia, and Egypt. Media apparently agreed to support Nabopolassar's claim to Babylonian ascendancy. But Egypt contested his claims. In 616 B.C. an Egyptian army fought a battle with Babylonian forces north of Babylon. The result was indecisive. The Egyptians withdrew. Cyaxares led Median forces in the successful assault on Asshur in 614 B.C. United Babylonian and Median forces destroyed Nineveh in 612 B.C. Assyrian armies retreated to Haran in Syria, which was also captured in 610 B.C.

In 609 B.C. Neco, who had just succeeded to the Egyptian throne, pressed north to stop the Babylonian armies before they could occupy Palestine. (On this campaign Josiah tried to stop him at Megiddo and died in the process.) Neco apparently intended to help the last Assyrian king retake Haran. This failed. But he did establish the Euphrates as the boundary between Egypt and Babylonia. This meant that all Palestine including Judah came under his direct control for a brief period (609–604 B.C.). He placed Jehoiakim on the throne and thus made Jerusalem a pawn in the struggle for sovereign power over the Near East.

The tone of the references in chaps. 30–31 reflects a time well before Assyria's fall but with the prospect of that fall already "in the air." It is a time when Egypt's ambitions are known and there are eager supporters in Judah. Almost any point between *ca.* 650 and 620 B.C. might fit. Perhaps a point early in the boy-king Josiah's reign (*ca.* 640–633 B.C.) may serve best.

But the respite from Babylonian pressure was brief. In 605 B.C. Nebuchadnezzer, as a general, was pressing a campaign in northern Syria. He defeated Egyptian forces at Carchemesh and again near Hamath, apparently gaining Neco's recognition that West Asia belonged to the Babylonian sphere of influence (cf. 2 Kgs 24:7). When Nabopolassar died, Nebuchadnezzer returned to Babylon to assume the throne. He required only a short time to consolidate the empire before resuming his campaigns in the West. In 604 B.C. he asserted sovereignty over Palestine. His armies took Ashkelon and deported its leaders. Jer 36:9 reports a great assembly held in Jerusalem to meet the crisis. Jehoiakim became a Babylonian vassal (2 Kgs 24:1), though apparently an unwilling one.

Meanwhile, Pharaoh Neco turned his attention to domestic issues. With or without royal permission, some from his court continued to encourage border states like Judah to keep Babylon occupied. Nebuchadnezzer was not able to move into Egypt after an indecisive battle at the border in 601 B.C. But this failure apparently encouraged Jehoiakim to rebel against him in 598 B.C. The Judean rebellion received no Egyptian support. Jehoiakim died and Jehoiachin was taken off as a hostage. Zedekiah ascended the throne, apparently under Babylonian patronage. But continued patriotic agitation under the mirage of Egyptian favor characterized his ten-year reign.

Psamtik II succeeded Neco in 593 B.C. and was in turn succeeded by his son, Apries (Hophra in Hebrew usage), in 588 B.C. Apparently under the active encouragement of Apries, Tyre, Sidon, Moab, and Ammon pressed Zedekiah to join in revolt. The Egyptian lobby in Jerusalem won out. But Apries used the occasion for his own ends, attacking Tyre and Sidon in naval and land battles, and occupying the Phoenician plain. He may also have gained control of Lebanon. These successes meant little to Jerusalem, for Egypt showed neither will nor ability to penetrate inland from the coast. The Babylonian forces worked unhindered throughout the siege and destruction of Jerusalem (cf. the account in 2 Kgs 25).

The politics of Judah's last half-century were overshadowed by its position as a miniature border state between empires in Mesopotamia and Egypt. When Assyrian power ebbed at mid-seventh century, a great Egyptian wave swept across Palestine to the Euphrates. But when Babylonian power prevailed in 605 B.C., the Egyptian tide ebbed. And Judah was drowned in the undertow.

During this period there were those in Jerusalem who saw the extension

HISTORICAL DATA PARALLEL TO ISAIAH 28–33

Year	*Egypt*	*Judah*	*Assyria*	*Babylon*
660	Psamtik I (663–609)	Manasseh (697–642)	Ashurbanipal (669–633)	
650				
640	Psamtik I controls all Egypt (640)	Amon (642–640) assassinated; Josiah begins rule (640–609)	Ashurbanipal reestablishes rule over Babylon (640)	
				Nabopolassar (633–605)
630			Assyrians defeated at the gates of Babylon (626)	
		(Scythians drive to the border of Egypt)		
		[Isa 28–29]		
620			Egyptians fight Babylon north of Babylon; no decision (616)	
			Cyaxares takes Ashur (614)	
			Nineveh falls (612)	
610		[Isa 30–33]	Haran falls (610)	
	Neco (609–593) marches through Judah (609)			
		Josiah dies (609)		
	Egypt rules west of the Euphrates (609–604)		Babylon rules east of the Euphrates (609–604)	
		Jehoiakim (609–598); under Egypt (609–604)		Nebuchadnezzer (605–562)
	Neco defeated at Carchemesh; withdraws from Palestine (605)			
		Nebuchadnezzer reestablishes control of Palestine to the River of Egypt (604)		
	Neco withstands Babylonian invasion, holding his border (601)			
600				
		Jehoiakim tests Babylon's rule (598)		
		Nebuchadnezzer lays siege to Jerusalem, deports leaders to Babylon		
		Zedekiah (598–587)		
	Psamtik II (593–588)	Babylonian vassal		
	Apries (Hophra) (588–526)	Nebuchadnezzer puts down Judaean revolt (587)		
	Apries marches to help Jerusalem but backs off without a fight			
		Destruction of Jerusalem and Temple		
		Wholesale deportations begin		

of Egyptian influence as Judah's opportunity to reassert itself. And well they might, for the great period of Israel's beginnings from Moses to Solomon was made possible by Egypt's benign nominal control of Palestine.

But others in Jerusalem, like Jeremiah, were not impressed. They correctly saw that Egypt's real interests lay in Africa and the Mediterranean basin. This meant only marginal interest in Palestine which hardly reached beyond the coastal areas. Egypt's interest simply lay in using states like Israel as a buffer against Mesopotamian invasion.

The pro-Egyptian party was undoubtedly active in Josiah's reign, but not dominant. Josiah's policy welcomed Egypt's pressure on Assyria and Babylon, but kept them at arm's length. That he should have died fighting an Egyptian army that was only passing through remains an enigma perhaps only explainable by the impossibly complex politics of that day.

The pro-Egyptian party was naturally dominant during the early part of Jehoiakim's reign and continued to be influential until the very end in 587 B.C., with tragic results.

Scene 1: Disaster from Expansion (28:1–29)

Three episodes comprise this scene. The first, "The Drunkards of Ephraim" (vv 1–13), casts a sad backward look at Ephraim's closing years (as in Acts I and II) and at the intervening years in that region. (Josiah was apparently able to reincorporate a substantial part of the area into his kingdom and, presumably, Jehoiakim continued to have control there until the Babylonian invasions.) The second, "Foundation Stone in Zion" (vv 14–22), is addressed to the leaders in Jerusalem who claim to be bound by a "covenant with death." The third, "Yahweh's Strategy" (vv 23–29), uses a lesson from a farmer's experience to illustrate God's work for Israel.

Episode A: Woe, Ephraim's Drunkards (28:1–13)

Bibliography

Betz, O. "Zungenreden und süsser Wein. Zur eschatologischen Exegese von Jesaja 28 in Qumran und im Neuen Testament." *Bibel und Qumran.* FS H. Bardtke, ed. S. Wagner. Berlin: Evangelische-Haupt-Bibelgesellschaft, 1968. 20–36. **Childs, B. S.** *Isaiah and the Assyrian Crisis.* Naperville, IL: Allenson, 1967. 28–31. **Driver, G. R.** " 'Another Little Drink'—Isaiah 28:1–22." *Words and Meanings.* FS D. W. Thomas. Cambridge: U.P., 1968. 47–67. **Exum, C.** "A Literary Approach to Isaiah 28." *SBL 1979*

Seminar Papers, vol. 2. Ed. P. Achtemeier. Missoula: Scholar's Press, 1979. 123–51. Reprinted in *Art and Meaning: Rhetoric in Biblical Literature,* ed. D. J. A. Clines, D. M. Gunn, A. J. Hauser. JSOTSup 19. Sheffield: U. of Sheffield, 1982. **Hallo, W. H.** "Isaiah 28:9–13 and the Ugaritic Abecedaries." *JBL* 77 (1958) 324–38. **Köhler, L.** "Zu Jes 28:15a und 18b." *ZAW* 48 (1930) 227–28. **Loretz, O.** "Das Prophetenwort über das Ende der Königstadt Samaria (Jes. 28:1–4)." *UF* 9 (1977) 361–63. **Melugin, R. F.** "The Conventional and the Creative in Isaiah's Judgment Oracles." *CBQ* 36 (1974) 305–6. **Oudenrijn, M. A. van den.** "Priesters en profeten by Isaias (Is XXVIII 7–13)." *Studia Catholica* 14 (1938) 299–311. **Peterson, D. L.** "Isaiah 28, a Redaction Critical Study." *SBL 1979 Seminar Papers.* Vol 2; ed. by P. Achtemeier. Missoula: Scholars Press, 1979. 101–22. **Pfeiffer, G.** "Entwöhnung und Entwöhnungsfest im Alten Testament: der Schlüssel zu Jesaja 28:7–13?" *ZAW* 84 (1972) 341–47. **Roberts, J. J. M.** "A Note on Isaiah 28:12." *HTR* 73 (1980) 49–51. **Rost, L.** "Zu Jesaja 28:1ff." *ZAW* 53 (1935) 292. **Selms, A. V.** "Isaiah 28:9–13: An Attempt to give a New Interpretation." *ZAW* 85 (1973) 332–39. **Stolz, F.** "Der Streit um die Wirklichkeit in der Südreichsprophetie des 8. Jahrhunderts." *WuD* 12 (1973) 9–30. **Vogt, E.** "Das Prophetenwort Jes 28:1–4 und das Ende der Königsstadt Samaria." *Homenaje a Juan Prado.* Madrid: Instituto Benito Aries Montano, 1975.

Translation

Heavens: 1 *Woe!* — 1
Crown [a] *of the pride* [b] *of the drunkards* [c] *of Ephraim,* — 4+4
[d] *the beauty of its glory,* [a] *now a drooping blossom* [d]
who (were) [e] *at the head* [f] *of a fertile valley,* [g] — 3+2
(are now) those struck down by wine.

Earth: 2 *See! The Lord* [b] *had one, mighty* [a] *and strong.* [a] — 4+4
Like a hailstorm, a destructive storm, [c]
like a storm of [d] *mighty, overflowing* [d] *water,* — 4+3
he threw [e] *(them) to the land by hand.* [f]

Heavens: 3 *They (fem) were trampled* [a] *by feet,* — 2+4
crown of the pride of Ephraim's drunkards.
4 *And she became* [a] *a drooping flower,* [b] — 3+2+4
the beauty of its glory,
which (was) at the head of a fertile valley.
Like a first-born [c] *(fig?) before summer,* — 3+4+3
which when one sees it,
no sooner [d] *is it in his hand than he swallows it.*

Chorus: 5 *In that day* — 2+3
[a] *Yahweh of Hosts became*
a crown of glory — 2+2+2
and a diadem [b] *of beauty*
for a remnant of his people
6 *and a spirit of justice* [a] — 2+2
for the one who sat on the (seat of) judgment [a]
and strength — 1+3
for those who were turning back the battle (at the) gate. [b]

Heavens: 7 *But these too* 2+2+2
reeled[a] *with wine*
and staggered[b] *with strong drink.*
[c]*Priest and prophet*[c] 2+2+2
reeled[a] *with liquor,*
were swallowed up[d] *from wine.*[e]
They staggered[b] *from liquor.* 2+2+2
They reeled[a] *with drink.*[f]
They overflowed[g] *(with) booze.*[h]
8 *For*[a] *all the tables* 2+2+3
were full of vomit,[b]
filth,[c] *with no clean place.*
Earth: 9 *To whom could such a one have taught knowledge?*[a] 3+3
And to whom could he have explained a message?
Ones weaned from milk? 2+2
Or ones just taken from the breast?
10 *That*[a] *(it should be)* 1
"Tsaw[b] *for* tsaw.[b] 2+2
Tsaw[b] *for* tsaw.[b]
Qaw[c] *for* qaw.[c] 2+2
Qaw[c] *for* qaw.[c]
Little one,[d] *here!* 2+2
Little one,[d] *here!*"
Heavens: 11 *Yet even*[a] 1
by such a stammering[b] *lip* 2+2+3
and with another tongue
he spoke to this people,
12 *he who had said to them:* 3
"This (is) your[a] *(place of) rest.* 2
Give rest to the weary. 2
This is your (place of) repose." 2
But (there was) no willingness to listen.[b] 3
Earth: 13 *The word of Yahweh*[a] *for them was:* 4
"Precept[b] *for precept.*[b] 2+2
Precept[b] *for precept.*[b]
Line[c] *for line.*[c] 2+2
Line[c] *for line.*[c]
A little here. 2+2
A little there."
In order that they would walk and stumble back 4+3
and be broken, be snared, and be captured.

Notes

1.a-a. Irwin (4–5) notes that עטרת . . . תפארתו "crown . . . drooping blossom" forms a stereotyped phrase (cf. 62:3; Jer 13:18; Ezek 16:12; 23:42; Prov 4:9; 16:31) which is here deliberately broken up.

1.b. DSS[Isa] גאון is the more usual form for MT גאות "pride," which also occurs in 9:17.

1.c. LXX *μισθωτοὶ* "hirelings" reads the Heb as שְׂכִיר; 'A Σ Θ translate MT correctly *μεθυοντες* "drunkards." (Cf. F. Wutz, *BZ* 21 [1933] 12; G. Rinaldi, "Οἱ μισθωτοὶ Ἐφραὶμ bei Is 28,1," *BeO* 9 [1967] 164.)

1.d-d. Two pairs in genitive relation form a substantive sentence. Cf. M. Gilula, "צְבִי in Isaiah 28:1—A Head Ornament," *Tel Aviv* (1974) 128.

1.e. The past time viewpoint (cf. Watts, *Syntax,* 30–31) is chosen for vv 1–13. The passage looks back on conditions in Ephraim a century earlier.

1.f. ראש "head" may describe the hill of Samaria above a fertile valley (cf. Mic 1:5; É. Dhorme, *L'emploi métaphorique des noms de parties du corps en hébreu et en akkadien* [1923; reprinted Paris: P. Geuthner, 1963], 22). But "head" may also refer to its status as capital of the country.

1.g. DSS^Isa גאי "proud ones of" for MT גֵּיא "valley" (BDB, 161). G. Driver (in *Words and Meanings,* 48) and NEB favor the change. Irwin (6) argues that the parallelism supports MT.

2.a. Syr *ḥjlʾ wʿwšnʾ* "strength and might"; Vg *ecce validus et fortis Dominus* "behold powerful and strong (is) the Lord"; LXX ἰδοὺ ἰσχυρὸν καὶ σκληρὸν ὁ θυμὸς κυρίου "behold robust and fierce (is) the anger of the Lord." All these take חזק ואמץ to be nouns refering to Yahweh (cf. *BHS*). Irwin (8) suggests making לְ emphatic which comes to the same thing. However, MT makes sense as it is and refers to the Assyrian. See the comparison with other usage made by Laberge (*Isaïe 28–33,* 266–70).

2.b. DSS^Isa ליהוה "to Yahweh" for MT "to the Lord." But cf. 6:11 and 7:20.

2.c. קטב "destructive." Jews at a later date knew a demon by this name (M. Jastrow, *Dictionary* II, 1346). Irwin (8) sees it as the name of a god "Qeteb" who was a companion of Reshep or Deber as agents of Death (cf. A. Caquot, "Sur quelques demons de l'Ancien Testament: *Reshep, Qeṭeb, Deber,*" *Sem* 6 [1956] 53–68) and translates "tempest hell-sent." The intention is to indicate a superlative (cf. 13:6). Irwin cites full literature.

2.d-d. DSS^Isa כברים שוטפים does not change the meaning of MT.

2.e. הֵנִיחַ is the same root as "Noah" and has two families of meaning: I "to give rest to"; II "to lay or set down." This pointing relates it to II (cf. BDB, 628). The figure of a powerful rainstorm (cf. 8:6–8; 14:3) adds to the symbolic implication. Donner is concerned that an object for the verb is missing. Wildberger suggests that the "crown of the pride" (v 1) is intended.

2.f. ביד "by hand" is often understood as "power" or "force." But note the parallel position to ברגלים "by feet" that follows.

3.a. The fem pl form is followed by a sg עֲטֶרֶת "crown." *BHS* suggests a change in pointing to make it sg with an "energetic" ending. *BHK* suggests changing "crown" to עֲטְרוֹת "crowns." Other emendations abound. Of these, the singular energic is preferable (cf. Irwin 10). However, the mixture of pl and sg has continued from v 1 and the sg "crown" may also be read as a collective.

4.a. DSS^Isa והייתה, but no change in meaning.

4.b. ציצת is a fem form of ציץ in v 1.

4.c. MT כְּבִכּוּרָהּ "its first-born." The Versions have with ʾA ὡς πρωτογενημα "the first-born (pl)" suggesting that one drop the *mappik* in ה.

4.d. DSS^Isa בעודנה adds a seemingly meaningless *nun* epenthetic before the suffix.

5.a. Tg inserts משיחא "Messiah." Wildberger (1043) comments that they could not conceive that the change announced here could happen except by the appearance of the Messiah.

5.b. צפירה, according to Wildberger and BDB, 862, is like the Arab *ṣafara* "to braid." It means here "a braided crown" (cf. Ezek 7:7, 10).

6.a. The *athnaḥ* needs to be moved to the second משפט "judgment" (cf. Delitzsch and Wildberger, 1044).

6.b. Dahood, following Syr and Θ, translates "from the gate." But this requires elaborate explanations of why the מן "from" is missing and the *he*-directive has lost its force (cf. Irwin 13–14; GKC § 90e). DSS^Isa שער eliminates the *he*-directive.

7.a. שגו "reeled" (BDB, 993) has a basic meaning "go astray, err." But a use for drunkenness occurs in Prov 20:1 and for love in Prov 5:19–20. Driver has challenged this meaning (*Words and Meanings,* 51) preferring "was wrapped up in, addicted to." Irwin (14) defends the translation "reel."

7.b. תעו "staggered" (BDB, 1073) has also been challenged by Driver who prefers meanings like "cackled, croaked, guffawed" (*Words and Meanings,* 52). I. Eitan ("Isaiah Exegesis," *HUCA* 12/13 [1937/38] 71) derives the word from תעע and translates in accordance with an Arabic root meaning "be faint, languid." Irwin (15) defends the meaning "stagger."

7.c-c. DSS[Isa] כוהן ונבי shows the variant spellings for the same words used at Qumran. Tg has ספר "scribe" in place of "prophet."

7.d. בלע "befuddled" (BDB, 118) has as its basic meaning "are swallowed up." G. R. Driver (*ZAW* 52 [1934] 52) points to a Syriac parallel root "was struck down." Wildberger (1053) notes that the meaning "were struck down by wine" is not impossible but prefers "confused." Irwin (16) cites J. Barth's *Beiträge zur Erklärung des Jesaias* (Karlsruhe-Leipzig, 1885), 4, and *CHAL*, 41, for "confused" but then makes a strong case with parallels in Isaiah for the meaning "are swallowed up." Both meanings are possible.

7.e. LXX and 'A omit "with wine."

7.f. רֹאֶה is pointed in MT as a ptcp, "seeing," i.e., a vision." But its parallels suggest an alcoholic drink. It is the only occurrence of this form (BDB, 906). G. R. Driver (*JTS* 36 [1935] 151–53; *Words and Meanings* 52) supported by C. S. Rodd ("Rediscovered Hebrew Meanings," *ExpTim* 71 [1959] 131–34), D. W. Thomas ("Isaiah LIII," *ETL* 44 [1968] 85), and M. Dahood (*Proverbs and Northwest Semitic Philology* [Rome: Pont. Bib. Inst. 1963] 206; *Psalms* II, AB 17 [Garden City, NY: Doubleday, 1968] 78), makes רֹאֶה a noun from ראה "drink one's fill," a by-root of רוה (cf. Irwin 18). M. Pope (*The Use of the Old Testament in the New, and Other Essays*, FS W. F. Stinespring, ed. J. M. Efird [Durham, NC: Duke U.P., 1972], 196) thinks the word has been altered to conceal an offensive word. From Ugaritic he suggests an original חרא meaning "excrement" (see Irwin's comment, p. 18).

7.g. פקו "they stumble" (BDB, I, 807). Driver (*Words and Meanings*, 53; and NEB) translates "collapse" or "hiccup." Irwin (18–19) suggests reading the root פוק as cognate with פוץ (BDB, II, 807) "flow, overflow" and supports his view with parallels. He reads it in parallel to נבלעו "were swallowed up." The meaning continues in the next verse.

7.h. פליליה "making decisions" (BDB, 813; GKC § 118g). But Irwin (19) suggests "soddenness, moisture" reading פלל = בלל "mix, confuse" (BDB, 117). Hence the meaning "booze." There is no preposition here as in the other statements. *BHK* and *BHS* supply ב which Wildberger notes is required in fact or as understood. Irwin (20) deals with the issue by treating the noun as "accusative of material," citing Dahood ("Ugaritic-Hebrew Syntax and Style," *UF* 1 [1969] 19; *Psalms* III, AB 17A, 397–98).

8.a. כי may also be read as an emphatic particle "indeed" (cf. Irwin, 20).

8.b. DSS[Isa] קיה for MT קיא is probably a careless transcription (cf. Wildberger, 1053).

8.c. צאה "filth" is put in the second stich by MT. Recent interpreters are virtually unanimous in changing the *athnaḥ* back one word and putting it into the third line.

9.a. דעה "knowledge" is rendered *κακα* "evil" in LXX (apparently reading רעה; cf. Wildberger, 1053) and אוריתא "law" by Tg. Irwin (21) draws on Ugaritic parallels to translate "the message" as a parallel to שמועה "a report." This is helpful, but does not adequately deal with the root meaning.

10. The verse is made up of repeated sounds: צו "tsaw" four times, קו "qaw" four times, and a pair of words repeated once. Wildberger (1053) understands these to be names of letters of the alphabet: צ Tsade and ק Qoph. LXX has paraphrased the verse: *θλῖψιν ἐπὶ θλῖψιν προσδέχου, ἐλπίδα ἐπ' ἐλπίδι, ἔτι μικρὸν ἔτι μικρὸν* "Accept trial upon trial, hope upon hope: yet a little, yet a little." It has found a single repetition sufficient and supplied a verb for the first two stichs. Only the third corresponds to MT.

10.a. כי is a particle of result following a question (BDB, 472b).

10.b. צו "precept" is understood to be from צוה "command" (BDB, 846). LXX *θλῖψιν* "pressure, affliction, trial" apparently read צר "straits, distress" (BDB, 865).

10.c. קו "line" is understood to be קוה's second root meaning (BDB, 876). LXX follows the first meaning "hope, wait for" (BDB, 875). Some interpreters have thought these are intended as nonsense sounds repeated endlessly, i.e., in the same sense as v 11. This translation follows the nonsense explication for v 10 and contrasts the meaningful explanation in the repetition in v 13 (see *Form* and *Comment*).

10.d. LXX understands this to be "a little." Wildberger (1053) points to the suggestions of Wellhausen, followed by Procksch, that this pictures a drunken schoolteacher who orders his pupils to repeat the alphabet and has come to the letters *tsaw* and *qaw.* They then understand זעיר "little" to refer to a child being called upon to recite. G. R. Driver (*Semitic Writing* [London: G. Cumberlege, 1944; Oxford U.P., 1954], 90) suggests emending שם "there" to שִׂים which could be understood as "pay attention" (cf. Kaiser's "Boy, be careful!"). The main question is whether "little" applies to what is taught or who is being taught. Driver (in *Words and Meanings,* 104) thinks it refers to "another little drink."

11.a. See 10.a above.

11.b. לעג comes from a root meaning "mock, deride, stammer." It is sometimes used of foreigners (33:19; 37:22). BDB (541) suggests the noun, used only here in this sense, means "stammerings." KB thinks this refers to the people of stammering lips. *CHAL* refers it to the stammering itself, "by stammering lips."

12.a. המנוחה, lit., "the rest." The definite article is used to imply the possessive pronoun. Cf. Irwin (24), Joüon § 137f (I2), and Dahood (*Psalms* III, AB 17A, 379).

12.b. Irwin's suggestion (24) to divide MT's אבוא שמוע "willingness to listen" as אבו אשמוע "they would not listen" creates more problems than it solves.

13.a. LXX κυρίου τοῦ θεοῦ "the Lord, God." MT should be kept.

13.b,c. See notes on v 10 above.

Form/Structure/Setting

The episode is composed of three parts: Vv 1–4 are a mourning cry over Ephraim, using the metaphor of drunkards to recall the confused last years of the Northern Kingdom almost a century before (cf. chaps. 5 and 10). Vv 5–8 recount Yahweh's presence with the remnant, and their potential for renewed social health, but a series of disasters followed because the leaders continued in a state typified by drunkenness. Vv 9–13 use a parable of teaching children their letters to show how God used even drunken priests and prophets to speak his message to a people doomed to repeated disaster.

The episode's unity lies in the consistent metaphor of drunkenness for Ephraim. It contrasts the bumbling and repulsive ineptness of people, priest, and prophet (vv 1, 3–4, 7–8) with the decision (v 2), determined compassion (vv 5–6) and patience (vv 9–10) of Yahweh as he worked with them. The episode fits the beginning of Josiah's reign when he apparently extended his sovereignty over the territory formerly occupied by Northern Israel and thereby may well have aroused dreams in Jerusalem of renewing the days of David's glory.

Comment

1 *Woe.* The Lament continues that of Act II (chap. 10) recalling the dreadful fall of the Kingdom of Israel.

עטרת "crown" may be of gold or silver for a king, of flowers for a party, or refer to the crownlike figure of a walled city on a hill. *Pride* and *glory* (cf. 13:19 of Babylon) are contrasted with ציץ נבל "a drooping blossom" (cf. 40:7–8) which pictures its present state. A similar contrast is made between being *head of a fertile valley* and *those struck down with wine.*

The metaphor of drunkenness dominates the episode. It is a figure of Israel's stumbling, bumbling life during the last decades of its existence (*ca.* 740–21 B.C.). Its relevance a century later lies in Josiah's regained control over that territory. Now one mourns again the circumstances that led to that earlier disaster.

2 חזק ואמץ "one mighty and strong" is a fixed pair of words (cf. Laberge, 266–70, for a study of its appearance in the OT). Here it refers to the Assyrian emperor Shalmaneser who laid siege to Samaria (cf. 10:3 and 2 Kgs 17:3–

6) or to Sargon II who actually captured the city and took its people into exile (2 Kgs 17:6). He was the Lord's agent in destruction (10:5–6).

3–4 The Assyrian attack is seen as an explanation of the faded crown. *Like a first-born fig* refers to the first figs to appear on the tree and is used as a figure of the ease with which the mighty Assyrians swallowed up the city.

5–6 The chorus chants its faith that Yahweh used the catastrophe in order that he become a *crown of glory* for the *remnant* who were left (cf. 10:20–23). Although the king and his court were gone, Yahweh remained. Through his spirit, *justice* could again be found in the courts and genuine *strength* for its defenders.

7–8 The remaining representatives of God, the *priests* and the *prophets,* are accused of being drunkards. The disgusting picture is portrayed in detail.

9–10 One scoffs at what such teachers could possibly teach, even to the youngest children. Like a bumbling schoolmaster, they repeat letters of the alphabet, צ *tsade* and ק *qoph,* using their earlier names "tsaw" and "qaw," for the children to learn (Wildberger, 1053). Interpreters have understood this to mean everything from speaking in tongues to being code-words for great thoughts. (Cf. *Notes.*) But the picture of the drunken teacher is most simple and appropriate. זעיר "little," in this context, seems most likely to refer to the children of v 9b. Both verses deal with the issue of *teaching knowledge* (9a) and the incompetency of the drunken teachers, the prophets, and the priests (7b).

11 The respondent insists that God continued to speak to his people even through such a *stammering lip. With another tongue* is understood (Wildberger, 1060) to refer to the Assyrians. 33:19 speaks of "the people of a speech too obscure to hear, a stammering tongue," while 36:11 tells of the Assyrians being asked to use their usual tongue, Aramaic. God spoke to that age even if it had to be through drunken prophets/priests and through the Assyrian invaders.

העם הזה "this people" is a specific, but impersonal, designation which contrasts with the personal "my people" or "your people" in other places. Wildberger (1061) notes the deep disappointment inherent in its tone (cf. 6:9). Laberge (271–79) has an extended excursus on the phrase, noting its usage fifty times in the Pentateuch and Deuteronomic History and thirty-one times in Jeremiah. He concludes that it is not specifically deuteronomic. It is used in two ways, one with a good, positive sense and the other a shifting, changing sense. The phrase occurs ten times in Isaiah, always (according to Laberge) concerning the population of Jerusalem and always, like Jeremiah, in a bad sense. Laberge's identification of the people with Jerusalem must be questioned. In 6:9–10 the reference is ambiguous, but the commentary has found its likely reference to the doom pronounced on northern Israel. In 8:6, 11, 12 the references again point to northern Israel following the prophecy in v 4. The reference here (in 28:11) is to Ephraim. In 29:13–14 for the first time the context favors an identification with Jerusalem. Laberge is right in sensing a consistent negative implication in the use.

12 Note the close association of these verses with Exod 33:13–14 where a discussion between Moses and God over which of them should own "this people" leads to God' promise "I will give you rest." Von Rad (*Der Heilige Krieg im alten Israel,* ATANT 20 [Zürich: Zwingli Verlag, 3rd ed., 1958]) and C. H. Keller ("Das quietistische Element in der Botschaft Jesajas," *TZ* 11 [1955] 81–97) have both stressed the relation of this vocabulary to the theme of Holy War in Deut 12:10; 25:19; 1 Kgs 5:8 (4); 8:56. Note how Mic 2:10 negates this promise for his own time.

המנוחה "the rest" carries connotations of dwelling and of the secure condition of that residence. It could refer here to Yahweh's *rest* in Zion (e.g., Ps 132:8, 14; 1 Kgs 8:56), but the context refers to Ephraim, not to Yahweh or Zion. Hence, the implication *your rest* (cf. *Notes*). The words are much closer to Deut 12:9; 28:65; and Ps 95:11, referring to Israel's rest (contra Wildberger; see *Notes*). The verse builds a beautiful chiasmus of five lines which portray Yahweh's original offer to Israel of *rest* in Canaan and her responsibility to *give rest to the weary* there. The same sovereign Lord spoke through priest, prophet, and foreigner to interpret his action in the days of Assyria's rise to power. The original offer was conditioned upon Israel's willingness to listen, according to the emphasis in Deuteronomy. That condition was understood still to apply in the eighth century. But Israel failed to fulfill that one condition.

ולא אבוא שמוע "but (there was) no willingness to listen." Like the condition of God's offer to Jerusalem in 1:19, those in Deuteronomy and here were not fulfilled (cf. 30:9, 15). Laberge (280) notes a close relation to the Pentateuch (esp. Deut 13:8; 23:5; Lev 26:21). The verse contrasts God's original good news for Israel with the garbled instruction given through drunken prophet and priest.

13 But even the basic lesson by a drunken teacher, teaching the alphabet (v 10), was turned by Yahweh into an authentic word to Israel. When צו "tsaw" is understood to derive from צוה "command," the name of a letter can mean *precept* or *command* (cf. *Notes,* 10.b.). The name of the second letter קו "qaw" is understood as a noun from קוה meaning *line* (cf. *Notes,* 10.c.). In the same vein the reference to "little ones" becomes impersonal *a little.*

What began in v 10 as mumbling incompetence is turned by the Lord in v 13 to be an instrument of judgment leading to their destruction. The four verbs in the last two lines, *stumble, be broken, be snared,* and *be captured,* are repeated from 8:15, reinforcing the understanding that this section points back to the events of 734–21 B.C. that are pictured in Act II (chaps. 7–10).

Explanation

The low ebb of circumstances recalls the sorry last days of northern Israel. They had become alcoholics, or like alcoholics. The Lord sent a strong power to destroy them (v 2). Even the reminder that Yahweh will turn things around in the day of his triumph (vv 5–6) does not prevent the continued description of those sorry days when even priests and prophets in drunken stupor could only repeat nonsense syllables (vv 7–11). Even efforts to get his message through by foreigners brought no better response. So "the word of Yahweh" to that generation, which appeared to be only monosyllabic nonsense spoken by drunken prophets and priests (vv 11–13), turns out to have been deliberate reminders of the inexorable processes of judgment that fulfilled the predictions of 8:15.

The passage is not so much a sign of Isaiah's struggle with priests and prophets as Wildberger (1061) and others have thought. Both priests and prophets, indeed all the leaders of Israel, had been caught up in the alcoholic stupor. The passage specifies the result of Israel's failure to recognize Assyria's rise to power (cf. 7:17; 10:5–6) and the ambivalence inherent in the covenantal doctrine of election. For an earlier scene of Israel's drunkenness, cf. Am 6:6–7.

In the first failure, Israel's leadership continued the petty rivalries and politics of intrigue when it needed to recognize that the extent of Assyria's power marked a fundamental shift in world political balance that demanded corresponding changes in their political philosophy and in their religious understanding of what Yahweh was about. Isaiah understood that Yahweh had caused the change and thus that their very allegiance to him demanded a changed attitude toward Assyria. He who had promised Israel "rest" in Canaan now called for this recognition. But they were not "willing to listen."

The second failure lay in their deafness to the "ifs" and "if nots" in the covenant formulations (cf. Deut 28:1, 15). Election through Abraham was no guarantee of protection under all circumstances. It promised that God would address them. This address demanded an answer. When they were unwilling to listen, much less to answer, Israel had forfeited her special relation to Yahweh (cf. Wildberger, 1062).

Episode B: Scoffers in Jerusalem (28:14–22)

Bibliography

Hooke, S. H. "The Corner-Stone of Scripture." *The Siege Perilous.* London: SCM Press, 1956. 235–49. **Köhler, L.** "Zwei Fachwörter der Bausprache in Jesaja 28:16." *TZ* 3 (1947) 390–93. **Lindblom, J.** "Der Eckstein in Jes 28:16." *NorTT* 56 (1955) 123–32. **Quiring, H.** "Der Probierstein." *FuF* 25 (1949) 238–39. **Szlaga, J.** "Symbolika kamienia i fundamentu w Ks. Izajasza 28:16–17." *Studia Peplinskie* 2 (1971) 149–57. **Virgulin, S.** "Il significato della pietra di fondazione in Isa 28:16." *RivB* 7 (1959) 208–20.

Translation

Heavens: 14 *Therefore, hear* [a] *the word of Yahweh,* 4+2
you scoffers,
you speech-makers [b] *of this people* 3+2
who (are) in Jerusalem.
15 *For you have said:* 2+3
"We have made a covenant with Death [a]
and with Sheol [a] 2+2
we have made an agreement. [b]

An overwhelming scourge, [c] 2+2+2
when (it) passes over, [d]
will not come upon us.
For we are established. 2+2+2
A Lie (is) our refuge.
We have hidden ourselves in the Falsehood."
Herald: 16 *Therefore, thus says my Lord Yahweh:* 5
Yahweh: *See me laying* [a] *a stone in Zion.* [b] 4
First Courtier: *A tested* [c] *stone.* 2
Second Courtier: *A corner (stone)* [d] *of value.* [e] 2
Third Courtier: *A foundation (well) founded.* [f] 2
Herald: *He who believes* [g] *will not be in haste.* [h] 3
Yahweh: 17 *And I establish justice as a line* [a] 3+2
and righteousness as a plummet.
Herald: *Hail will sweep away* [b] *refuge Lie,* 4+3
and waters will overflow (any) shelter.
18 *Your covenant with Death will be annulled.* [a] 3+4
and your agreement [b] *with Sheol will be invalidated.*
When an overwhelming scourge passes over 4+3
you shall become a victim of its devastation.
19 *As often as it passes over* 2+2
it will strike you.
Indeed morning by morning it will pass over, 3+2
by day and by night.
Earth: *The understanding of this message* 3+2
will be sheer terror!
20 *For the bed is too short to stretch out* [a] 3+3
and the covering (too) narrow to wrap oneself in. [b]
Heavens: 21 *But* [a] *Yahweh will rise as* [b] *(at) Mount Perazim* [c] 4+3[d]
as (in) a valley in Gibeon, he will quiver
to do his work. 2+2
Chorus: *Strange* [e] *(is) his work!*
Heavens: *And to serve his service.* 2+2
Chorus: *Alien (is) his service!*
Earth: 22 *And now, do not scoff (pl),* 3+3
lest your bonds [a] *be made strong(er)!*
For I have heard annihilation strictly determined 3+4+3
from my Lord, [b] *Yahweh of Hosts,*
upon the whole land.

Notes

14.a. DSS[Isa] reads a sg for MT's pl.

14.b. משלים may be understood as LXX ἀρχοντες "rulers" or, from another use of the root, to mean "speak in parables or proverbs." Wildberger (1064) notes that the other references to politics seem to favor the former, while the parallel to אנשי לצון "scoffers" favors the latter. He suggests the passage is directed not to the politicians themselves, but to the counselors and theoreticians of Jerusalem's policies (cf. Kaiser). Irwin's (25) "reigning wits" keeps one foot in each camp.

15.a. Note that neither מות "death" nor שאול "Sheol" has an article. The Canaanite concepts are explained by N. J. Tromp, *Primitive Conceptions of Death and the Nether World in the Old Testament* (Rome: Pont. Bib. Inst., 1969), 99.

15.b. חֹזֶה "agreement" (BDB, 302, n.) appears again in the pl in v 18. LXX has *συνθήκας* "agreement, common deposit" to parallel *διαθήκην* for ברית "covenant." However, Syr *ḥzw*ʾ "vision" takes up another meaning of the Heb root. Vg *pactum* agrees with LXX, having its synonym *foedus* for ברית. The issue is being widely discussed (cf. Wildberger, 1065 and Irwin, 27) and is not yet settled. Until it is, the translation can hold to something like "agreement."

15.c. DSS[Isa] and Q read שוט (cf. v 18; BDB, 1002) "scourge, whip." K has שיט "oar." LXX *καταιγὶς* "hurricane" and Syr *šwwt*ʾ *dgrwpj*ʾ "flood plain" seem to have understood שֶׁטֶף "flood" as the next word. But MT reads שׁוֹטֵף, an active ptcp "overwhelming, overflowing" (BDB, 1009). J. Barth ("שׁוֹט שֹׁטֵף," *ZAW* 33 [1913] 306–7) referred to the Koran (89:12) "God poured out on them the *sawṭ* (the watery flood) of punishment." S. Poznanski ("Zu שׁוֹט שֹׁטֵף," *ZAW* 36 [1916] 119–20) noted that Jewish traditions used this meaning of the phrase. Irwin (27–28) translates "the flood lash" and cites H. Gese ("Die strömmende Geissel des Haddad und Jes. 28:15 u. 18," *Archäologie und Altes Testament,* FS K. Galling [Tübingen: Mohr (Siebeck), 1970] 127–34) who refers to coins and statues of the rain-god Haddad with a lash in his hand.

15.d. K עָבַר pf, Q יַעֲבֹר impf, "it passes over." Wildberger (1065) chooses Q. Irwin (27) discusses the grammatical issue in light of Ugaritic and favors K.

16.a. יִסַּד "laying" is apparently a 3 m sg piel pf (cf. BDB, 413; GKC § 155f). Irwin (30) correctly notes that in this form it must be considered a relative clause without a relative particle to account for the change of person. DSS[Isa] מיסד is a piel ptcp. 1QIsa[b] יוסד is a qal ptcp. The Versions support the latter reading, suggesting the pointing יֹסֵד (*BHK*). Irwin (31) keeps the *lectio difficilior* of MT. Most other interpreters follow Qumran and the Versions.

16.b. בציון "in Zion" is the natural rendering. Irwin (31) understands בְּ as *beth essentiae* (GKC § 119i) and translates "I have founded Zion as a stone." Thus Zion is the stone. He then draws parallels to 29:1–8 and 31:4–9. But one may ask whether it should not also parallel 8:14b.

16.c. בחן "tested, testing" (BDB, 103). The word's meaning has not been clearly established (cf. Wildberger's review of research 1066–67). L. Koehler ("Zwei Fachwörter der Bausprache in Jesaja 28:16." *TZ* 3 [1947] 390–93) compares it with the Egyptian *bekhen*-stone. Driver (NEB) calls it granite. *CHAL* (37) offers "schist gneiss" as the technical term. With all the confusion it is best to stay with the traditional meaning.

16.d. פנת "corner of" is a constr form (BDB, 819).

16.e. יקרת "preciousness of, weight of" (BDB, 429; GKC § 130f[4]). Wildberger (1067) prefers the sense of value. Irwin (31) insists on the sense of weight.

16.f. מוּסָד מוּסָּד (BDB, 414; GKC § 71). MT places the *zakeph qaton* above the second word causing them to be read together, the first a noun and the second a hoph ptcp "a founded foundation." Irwin (30–31) moves the accent to the first word, dividing them and making the second govern the remaining words of the stich: "a weighty corner foundation, founded by . . ." Irwin must then find a new meaning for the following word (see note 16.g below). *BHK* and Wildberger (1067) take the second word to be dittography and recommend deletion with some LXX MSS. MT's arrangement and understanding seem to have the best of it.

16.g. המאמין "he who believes" (BDB, 52). The root means "to support" and could in the niph be understood as the one who builds a sure or supported structure. But the form is a hiph ptcp and hiph is consistently used in the OT for faith (cf. 7:9). There is a noun אָמָּן which means "builder, artist," but it occurs only in Cant 7:2. Irwin (30–32) translates "the Master Builder" and thus makes the entire verse conform to the imagery of building the wall. But the result is too contrived to be credible. In Deut 1:32 the form (hiph ptcp) means "none of you (was) a believer in Yahweh your God."

16.h. יחיש has several possible identities. If it is derived from חוש I (BDB, 301) it means "will be in haste." A second meaning of this root is found in Eccl 2:25 (BDB, 302; G. R. Driver, *JTS* OS 32 [1930–31] 253–54; F. Ellermeier, "Das Verbum חוש in Koh 2:25," *ZAW* 75 [1963] 197–217; W. von Soden, "Akkadisch *ḫâšum* I 'sich sorgen' und hebräisch *ḥûš* II," *UF* 1 [1969] 197) "will worry." LXX *οὐ μὴ καταισχυνθῇ* "never be put to shame" apparently read יבוש. Syr *l*ʾ *ndḥl* "not be afraid" followed the second meaning of the root חוש. Vg *non festinet* "not be hasty" follows the first meaning. Or the word may be derived from נחש (BDB, 638) "practice divination." But the root with that meaning occurs only in piel. Another root חשה (BDB, 364) may be considered. It means "be silent, unresponsive, still." Tsevat (*TWAT* I 591) considers this a hiph form and translates "he who trusts, does not press." While the meaning nearest MT is maintained, the interpreter does well to hear the overtones of other meanings.

17.a. קו "line" (BDB, 876, II). Cf. v 13.

17.b. יעה (BDB, 418) is a *hap. leg.* יָע is a small shovel used to clean the altar. Hence the meaning "sweep away."

18.a. כֻּפַּר would normally mean "be atoned" (BDB, 497; GKC § 145o). Tg ויבטיל "will cause to cease"; LXX *μὴ καὶ ἀφέλῃ ὑμῶν τὴν διαθήκην τοῦ θανάτου* "no and he will take away your covenant of death." Driver (in *Words and Meanings,* 60–61) defends MT. Irwin (33) thinks the word should be הפר "break" since this is the usual word with "covenant." But Wildberger (1068) joins Delitzsch (who points to Gen 6:14) and M. Weinfeld ("Covenant Terminology in the ANE and Its Influence on the West," *JAOS* 93 [1973] 197 n. 101) in defending MT's reading and calling for a broader meaning of כפר in the sense of "annul, cancel." Perhaps it also means to compensate for any guilt left over from breaking the covenant oath.

18.b. See note 15.b. LXX ἐλπὶς "hope," OL *spes* "hope"; but Vg correctly *pactum* "pact, agreement."

20.a. DSS[Isa] משתריים (cf. Kutscher, *Isaiah Scroll,* 289). Read MT.

20.b. DSS[Isa] uses ב as the preposition of comparison rather than MT's כ. DSS[Isa] is probably right. Cf. Irwin (35) and Dahood's list of the uses of מן and ב in comparison (*Psalms* III, AB 17A, 397–98).

21.a. כִּי "but." In v 20 the particle was used in explanation of the previous verse. Here it is in contrast (cf. Irwin, 34).

21.b. MT כ "like." DSS[Isa] ב "on." LXX *ὥσπερ ὄρος* "just as a vision." DSS[Isa] also reads ב in the second half of the verse and is supported by LXX. The changes from MT bring very different understandings of the verse (cf. Irwin 35). Keep MT but note the significance of the others.

21.c. LXX *ἀσεβῶν* "ungodly." Laberge (284) suggests that it represents Heb רפאים "Rephaim." Note the appearance of both words in 2 Sam 5:18, 20.

21.d. This meter follows MT. Irwin (35) suggests 3+1+3 with *Yahweh* "suspended between parallel cola" and serving as subject of both (cf. M. Dahood, "A New Metrical Pattern in Biblical Hebrew," *CBQ* 19 [1967] 574–79; *Psalms* III, AB 17A, 439–44).

21.e. MT זר "strange." LXX *πικρίας* "of bitterness." Wildberger notes that LXX apparently read מר for זר.

22.a. DSS[Isa] uses a fem form. Both genders are possible.

22.b. אדני "Lord" is missing in some MSS, in LXX Syr and DSS[Isa]. יהוה "Yahweh" and אדני appear together frequently in Isaiah and should be kept.

Form/Structure/Setting

The episode begins with "therefore," joining it to the preceding episode. But the setting has changed.

The words are addressed to leaders in Jerusalem (vv 14, 18, 22). They are to turn their attention from old Ephraim to current events in Jerusalem where Yahweh's crucial actions are about to take place (vv 16, 21). The leaders put forward their "covenant with Death" (v 15) as their reason for recalcitrance. Yahweh announces his own initiative, continuing his commitment of a "stone" laid in Zion (v 16) to accomplish his continued goals of "justice" and "righteousness." He will insist on breaking the offending treaty (covenant) (vv 18–19). The very idea brings terror (vv 19c–20). Yahweh's new initiative is formally announced (v 21). The leaders are warned of the decree of full annihilation which had been divinely determined for the whole land (v 22 as in chap. 24 and 6:11–13). The polemical dialogue turns on "the covenant with Death" and "the stone" which Yahweh has placed in Zion. The strategic position of this episode in Act V is clear. It states the terms of tension which will dominate the act as they had the history of Judah during its final decades of existence.

Comment

14 *Therefore* relates the entire episode to the previous review of the attitudes of Northern Israel prior to 721 B.C. (vv 1–13). God speaks and acts in light of previous experience, and Jerusalem, probably under Jehoiakim, bears a haunting resemblance to those last years of the Northern Kingdom.

Scoffers and *speech-makers* are degrading terms applied to the political leaders of Jerusalem. אנשי לצון "scoffers," lit. "men of scorning," may mean "men worthy of scorn" or "men whose attitude is scornful," i.e., "scoffers." The latter is a better parallel to משלי "speech-makers" or "makers of proverbs." A second meaning of משל could result in "rulers of this people" but that does not fit here. Ehrlich (*Randglossen* IV 100) translates "wits, epigrammatists, sloganeers." Irwin (25) combines the two meanings in translating "ruler, wit."

This people. See *Comment* v 11. Here the reference is clearly to the people of the enlarged Judean kingdom of the Josiah/Jehoiakim era.

15 The verse presents the leaders' statement of Jerusalem's foreign policy and thus of their faith. ברית "covenant" is to be understood in the sense of "treaty" or "firm agreement." *Death* and *Sheol* are used metaphorically to excuse an action which might otherwise be deemed unacceptable or which jeopardizes their lives. It may imply that they felt they had no choice in the matter. If the setting is in Josiah's reign, this could refer to Judah's long-standing vassal-treaty with Assyria and its new relation to Egypt which under Psamtik I had become Assyria's ally. The *overwhelming scourge* in this setting must refer to the Scythian invaders who swept down through the weakening Assyrian defences.

כזב "Lie" and השקר "the Falsehood" round out the names attributed to the treaty-partner, probably Egypt. The speech has parodied the kind of thing that Jehoiakim's ministers might actually have said. But why should the terms *Death, Sheol, Lie,* and *Falsehood* be used? Duhm (200) and Schmidt (93) suggested that these refer to the Egyptian God of death, Osiris. This does not mean that they pray to that god, but that they have signed a treaty guaranteed by that god. Thus Osiris would have served as the divine guarantor of this treaty with Egypt. *Death* and *Sheol* come directly from such an identification. *Lie* and *Falsehood* are derisive prophetic characterizations of the idol and its mythical representation. מות "Moth" or "Death" was also a Canaanite god. It was easy to draw the comparison to the Egyptian Osiris. But overtones of meaning spill over the literal speech. A pact with death had dire connotations, even if it were made under extreme pressure (cf. 2 Kgs 23:33–34). That anyone in Jerusalem could realistically have expected good to come from it, much less genuine security, is hard to believe. The speech implies such incredulity. (But compare Jeremiah's encounters with the supporters of Egypt.) Jehoiakim probably had no choice in the matter.

שׁיט שׁוטף "an overwhelming scourge" is used to describe great foreign invasions. The Vision has pictured these as the work of God in chaps. 10, 13, and other places. This speech interprets Jerusalem's foreign policy in light of the conviction that these invasions (i.e., the Assyrian and the Babylonian) are actually inspired by Yahweh. This makes the term "covenant with Death" take on massive ironic meaning.

שמנו "we are established," מחסנו "our refuge," and נסתרנו "we have hidden ourselves" are all phrases with religious meaning and were common to temple usage (Wildberger, 1073). שׂים "establish" is regularly used of God's assurance concerning the temple and the throne. The others appear in the Psalms (cf. Ps 27:5). The leaders undoubtedly mixed pious religious language (cf. Ps 46:6a, 12[5a, 11]) with their political assurances that Jerusalem was secure under their policies. This speech derides their policy as a treaty with *Lie* and *the Falsehood,* both referring to idolatrous Egypt or its Pharaoh.

16 Yahweh responds to the implication that these policies were necessary for their time. He repudiates the implication that the old values could no longer be held. He affirms again that what he has done and is determined to do in Zion deserves trust and faith.

See me laying a stone in Zion. He calls attention to his choice and commitment to Zion. What God has done and is doing in Zion is the key to all this history. Such a cornerstone of Zion could be understood in terms of the Davidic House or of the Temple. (Cf. Wildberger, 1076, for a survey of the many meanings which interpreters have found in this verse.) In the Vision, from 2:1–3 through 65:17–66:24, the future of Zion is secure in its role as a place of worship. The Temple, its function and its witness, is the abiding element in Zion. It continued as the symbol of God's presence, his work, and his will. This stone is acclaimed as a *tested stone,* a *cornerstone,* and a *foundation well founded.* The believer is affirmed in his patience, as he waits for God to complete his work.

17 God commits himself again to *justice* and *righteousness* as the only fitting standards by which to measure right and wrong. The implication is that the fluctuating reasonings of practical politics or personal advancement (as in Jehoiakim's case) are not to be trusted in that time any more than in the time of Ahaz (7:4–9). The very thing that Jerusalem's rulers had hoped to avoid will sweep over them (v 15b), but the military scourge will be aided by cosmic forces of *hail* and *flood waters.*

18–19a Their self-serving *covenant* will be swept away and repeated waves of the *scourge* will devastate the land again. The regular incursions by Nebuchadnezzar in 603, 598, and 587 B.C., as well as other unrecorded military pressures, are clearly in view.

19b This message could do no other than bring *terror,* for it shows Jerusalem's policies to be totally and disastrously wrong. They have failed to assess what God is doing in their time. They have misjudged the relative strength and will of the great powers.

20 The figure of *bed* and *covering* being *too short* and *too narrow* applies to the inadequacies of the treaty alignment that had been made with Egypt. It left Judah no room to accommodate itself to Babylon's resurgence in Palestine or to Yahweh's new initiatives.

21 *Yahweh will rise as at Mount Perazim.* Mount Perazim is not further identified in the OT. But a place called Baal Perazim turns up in a story (2 Sam 5) in which David routs the Philistines in a battle that also moves past *Gibeon.* (Some interpreters have seen the latter as a reference to Josh 10.) The Philistines moved to try to crush David's new kingdom and its capital, Jerusalem, but were beaten back in decisive battles (*MBA,* 100). Wildberger (1079) notes that the account in 2 Sam 5 is formulated as a "holy war" in which Yahweh himself enters the battle. It is also interesting to note the reference to floods of water (2 Sam 5:20).

In the Isaiah text the "holy war" concept that Yahweh fights for Israel is turned around. Here the reference, *his work,* is to the Assyrian and Babylonian invasions begun in the days of Tiglath-Pileser and continued by Nebuchadnezzar. The implications were clear, though neither name is called. That Jerusalemites should cry out in disbelief: זר מעשהו "His work is strange!" and נכריה עבדתו "His service is alien!" is understandable. They believed that Yahweh's proper work lay in calling, saving, and leading Israel to fulfill his promises to Abraham to establish his people in Canaan and to David to establish Zion in safety and security. The Vision has argued repeatedly that they were blind, uncomprehending, and unbelieving to his "other work" which the prophets had announced, that through the Assyrians and the Babylonians he was bringing total devastation to the land and exile to its peoples. Thus, in their eyes, this message contradicted their understanding of what they considered to be his real "work" in and through Israel. It is no wonder they called it *strange* and *alien.* They may well have found that God himself had become *strange* and *alien* to Israel.

22 The last speech exhorts Jerusalemites not to *scoff* at this announcement and not to ignore it.

Your bonds are those which political alliances had placed upon them. Prudence and restraint were needed to keep a bad situation from getting worse, because the ban, announced in 6:13 and continued at various points in the Vision since that time, is understood still to be in force upon *the whole land* (see the discussion in *Excursus: "The Land"*).

Explanation

Judah's current leadership found itself in a hopeless situation. (Was this Jehoiakim's position under Egypt?) The irony of a covenant with death, Sheol, a lie which was supposed to provide refuge and safety from the overwhelming scourge, is not lost on the hearers. That was not the first, nor the last, time that politicians lamely portrayed hopeless policies as full of assurance and promise.

But Yahweh will not allow himself to be identified with their defeatist and misguided policies. His work in Zion was begun long before and continued through this time. His foundation stone was a standard for judging righteousness and justice. These policies could not survive that test. Not the shifting political treaties, but the recognition and acceptance of Yahweh's affirmed foundation in Zion, deserve faith.

That "stone" could be construed to refer to the Davidic dynasty. But this does not conform to the usual line of the Vision's assurance. The place of

Zion as God's chosen meeting-ground with Israel and the peoples, that is the temple, is what is promised throughout the Vision as that to which God is committed for the future. It is the place of the word (*Torah* in 2:3) and of his presence.

Parallel to that is the recognition of the "work" of Yahweh which is identified with the "overwhelming scourge." This is consistent with the Vision's picture of God's instigation and involvement in the Assyrian invasions from the time of Tiglath-Pileser and in the Babylonian invasions and devastations under Nebuchadnezzar. This message, from that of Isaiah in 734 B.C. (7:17) through the intervening century to this time, had lost none of its shocking quality. It defied understanding for most Israelites. Thus it was accurately called "his strange work," "his alien task." (See *Comment.*) The prophetic faith, which holds that God works not only in the comfortable ways of election, salvation, and protection for his people, but also through the great movements of history for the accomplishments of his purposes for his people and the world, is mind-boggling. Few indeed are those who hold such a faith. The *Vision of Isaiah* does hold it.

The political machinations by which Judean kings tried to put off the inevitable were doomed from the start, partly because their age already lay under the ban announced in 6:11–13, and repeated since then, that "the whole land" would be completely devastated, but also because they could not find the spiritual insight and humility to come to terms with God's work in their time.

The reference to the "stone" (v 16) must be compared to that in 8:14. The language is different. There Yahweh "becomes" the stone, the offense, the test. Here he lays it in Zion. In both instances the stone which provides assurance (8:14 "sanctuary"; 28:16 "a foundation well founded") is also a standard by which leaders and their policies are to be tested (of both kingdoms in 8:14; of those who proclaim a "covenant with death" in 28:18).

The NT sees this as a reference to Christ. The LXX has already added ἐπ' αὐτῷ making the last line of v 16 read "one believing on him." So Christians interpreted the verse Christologically. 1 Pet 2:6 quotes the verse to support the view that Jesus Christ is the cornerstone of the church into which believers are built as living stones (vv 4–5). The passage goes on to use stone imagery from Ps 118:22 and Isa 8:14–15. The distinction between believers and unbelievers is determined by God's laying the cornerstone. Rom 9:33 mixes references to 8:14 and 28:16 to describe Israel's attempt to gain righteousness through the law. All the NT references follow LXX readings, "not be put to shame" (cf. *Notes*).

This same work, the laying of the foundation stone, is part of the action deemed so "strange" and "alien" (v 21). That God could at one and the same time affirm the durability and value of Zion with its temple (v 16) and also rise against its government through foreign invaders was incomprehensible to most Israelites. The Vision proclaims that this was in fact God's strategy. The kingdom was doomed. But the values inherent in Zion and the temple, symbols of Yahweh's presence and purpose, would remain the foundations of faith (cf. 2:1–3 and 65:17–66:24).

Christians have seen in Christ the successor to that symbol of God's presence and saving work which the temple on Zion represents here. The threat to the continuity of the symbol when the Romans besiege Jerusalem is met in the NT with the meaning of Christ's resurrection (John 2:19–22; Mark 13:2; 14:58; 15:29; Matt 26:61).

There is an ancient and continuing tradition of a rock on Zion. The Psalms echo it (Ps 28:1; 61:3[2]). Isa 30:29 calls it "The Rock of Israel." H-J. Kraus (*Psalmen,* BKAT XV/1 [Neukirchen-Vluyn: Neukirchener Verlag, 1978] 225) speaks of it as "that mythical, weathered bed-rock which the fires of chaos cannot reach." (Cf. also H. Schmidt, *Der heilige Fels in Jerusalem,* Tübingen: Mohr, 1933.)

The Muslim Dome of the Rock is built over the stone which tradition says was the surface of Araunah's threshing floor (2 Sam 24) which David bought to be the site of the new temple. The site is also identified as Mt. Moriah (2 Chr 3:1) relating it to the place of Isaac's sacrifice (Gen 22:2). These traditions were accepted by Josephus (*Antiquities* I.xiii.224, 226; VI.xiii.333), the Book of Jubilees (18:13), ancient rabbis, and Jerome. It is continued in Muslim tradition by the name *maqam el-Khalil* "Abraham's place" applied to the Dome of the Rock.

Episode C:
Yahweh's Strategy: A Parable (28:23–29)

Bibliography

Amsler, S. and Mury, O. "Yahweh et la sagesse du paysan. Quelques remarques sur Esaïe 28:23–29." *RHPR* 53 (1973) 1–5. **Guthe, H.** "Eggen und Furchen im Alten Testament." FS K. Budde. Ed. K. Marti. BZAW 34. Giessen: Töpelmann, 1920. 75–82. **Liebreich, L. J.** "The Parable Taken from the Farmer's Labors in Isaiah 28:23–29." *Tarbiz* 24 (1954/55) 126–28. I-II (Heb. with an English resumé). **Schuman, N. H.** "Jesaja 28:23–29: Een Boerengelijkenis als politieke profetie. Ook een manier van exegetiseren." *Segmenten* 2 (1981) 83–141. **Thexton, S. C.** "A Note on Isaiah XXVIII 25 and 28." *VT* 2 (1952) 81–83. **Vriezen, T. C.** "Essentials of the Theology of Isaiah." *Israel's Prophetic Heritage.* FS J. Muilenburg. Ed. B. Anderson and W. Harrelson. New York: Harper & Bros., 1962. 128–46. **Whedbee, W. J.** *Isaiah and Wisdom.* 51–68. **Wilbers, H.** "Étude sur trois textes relatifs à l'agriculture: Is. 28:27,28; Amos 2:13 et 9:9." *Melanges de l'Université St. Joseph.* Beyrouth: 1911–12. 269–83.

Translation

Heavens: 23 *Pay attention and heed my voice!* 3+3
Hearken and hear (what) I say!
24 *(Is it) all day* 2+3+3[a]
(that) the plowman plows for sowing?[b]
(That) he breaks and harrows his ground?
25 *Does he not, when he has leveled its surface,* 3+2+2
scatter dill[a]
and sow cummin?

(*Does he not*) *set* [b] *wheat in rows,* [c] 3+2+2
and barley in its place, [d]
and emmer (*on*) *its border?* [e]
Earth: [26] *For he instructs one concerning good order.* [a] 2+2
His God [b] *teaches him.*
Heavens: [27] *For dill is not threshed with a threshing-sled.* 5+4
Nor [a] *is a cart-wheel rolled over* [b] *cummin.*
With a stick dill is beaten out, 4+2
and cummin with a rod.
[28] *Grain* [a] *is crushed* 2+3+2
but not forever [b]
does it continue to be threshed. [c]
If [d] *one drive the wheel of his cart* (*over it*), 3+3
he does not crush it with his horses. [e]
Earth: [29] *Also this* (*is*) *from Yahweh of Hosts* 4+1+4[a]
(*from whom*) *goes out*
wonderful strategy, excellent success. [b]

Notes

24.a. MT's meter is 2+3+3. Kissane and Irwin (38) divide after החרש for 4+4.

24.b. לזרע "for sowing." *BHS* considers it redundant, and suggests deletion. The question concerns the meaning of ל "for" (cf. Irwin, 38). If it is understood as privative "without sowing" (cf. A. Blommerde, *Northwest Semitic Grammar and Job* [Rome: Pont. Bib. Inst., 1969] 21) the meaning parallels v 25. Or it can be understood as emphatic: "Indeed the sower breaks and harrows his soil." In Heb. the word falls in the middle of the verse. All three meanings are fitting.

25.a. קצח "dill" is *nigella satina* or black cummin (cf. H. N. and A. L. Moldenke, *Plants of the Bible* [Waltham, MA: Chronica Botanica Co., 1952] 152–53).

25.b. שָׂם "put, set" (BDB, 962). Irwin (39) notes that it means "plant" in 41:19 and Ezek 17:5. For another meaning, cf. S. C. Thexton, "A Note on Isaiah XXVIII 25 and 28," *VT* 2 (1952) 81–83.

25.c. שורה "in rows" from its root שור "to saw." Irwin (39) suggests "millet" following BDB's (965) hint that it should be some grain and other suggestions depending on Arab *ḏurratun* which refers to a kind of grain. LXX omits it.

25.d. נסמן "in its proper place" (BDB, 702), a *hapax,* is missing in LXX. *CHAL's* "unexplained" sums it up.

25.e. DSS[Isa] and LXX make it pl "its borders." This word (sg or pl) is clear. If שורה and נסמן are parallels, they fit the customary meanings "in rows" and "in its place."

26.a. משפט is generally understood here in this way. Cf. Wildberger (1084) and Irwin (40).

26.b. "His God." Irwin (40) calls this "an example of delayed explication."

27.a. The first לא "not" applies to both verbs.

27.b. יוסב "rolled over" hoph impf 3 m sg from סבב (BDB, 686). DSS[Isa] יסוב is qal impf.

28.a. לחם "grain." For this meaning Wildberger (1084) cites 30:23 and Ps 104:14 while Irwin (42) turns to Ugaritic.

28.b. לנצח "forever" (BDB, 664). D. W. Thomas ("Further Remarks on Unusual Ways of Expressing the Superlative in Hebrew," *VT* 18 [1968] 124) considers this a superlative as does NEB "to the uttermost," LLS "*hasta lo ultimo.*" Irwin (42) pleads for the meaning "forever."

28.c. אדוש "threshing" qal inf abs "as if from אדש" (BDB, 190; GKC § 113w[3]), but this verb does not otherwise exist. J. Barth (*Die Nominalbildung in den semitischen Sprachen* [2nd ed. 1894; reprinted Hildesheim, 1967] § 49b) suggests that it is like Aram *Aphel,* a causative form. DSS[Isa] הדש niph inf "being trampled, threshed" is a reasonable substitute.

28.d. Read the parallel clauses as an implied condition with Irwin (42).

28.e. The reference to horses has caused extended discussion. Irwin (43) cites Jerome's comment that "horses" is used here parallel to "wheel" as "sled" is used in v 27.

29.a. With Irwin (43), who reads יצאה "goes out" as related to both parts of the verse (cf. vv 20–21). He then reads the second as a relative clause.

29.b. תושיה "wisdom" (BDB, 444), "success" (*CHAL*, 388b) cannot be clearly analyzed. Its meaning is largely drawn from being parallel to עצה "counsel," "strategy" (cf. Job 5:12).

Form/Structure/Setting

The opening formula, "Pay attention and heed my voice!" marks the beginning of the episode and its nature. This is the kind of thing a teacher would say. It is a wisdom formula (cf. Prov 4:1; 7:24; Job 33:1, 31; 34:2; Ps 49:2[1]). The closing phrase (v 29) has been appropriately called a "summary-appraisal form" (B. S. Childs, *Isaiah and the Assyrian Crisis,* 128).

The parable of the farmer who must work differently in different seasons and who is careful not to destroy the results of one season's work while doing that of another is applied to Yahweh's plans and work. To whom is this spoken? (Cf. Wildberger, 1088–89.) The "scoffers" and "speech-makers" of this people (v 14) are likely candidates, especially if some of "the wise" are among them (cf. Amsler and Mury, *RHPR* 53 [1973] 1–5). They would claim that God's ways are consistent and fixed. The parable in wisdom style defends the prophetic understanding that God acts in history in accordance with the times and conditions as he moves to achieve his goals. This is God's עצה "strategy" (v 29).

The genre of this passage is called תורה "instruction" (v 26) and אמרה "saying" (v 23). These stand in clear contrast to the ordinary prophetic genres, but are at home in wisdom literature. אמרה appears repeatedly in Isaiah (5:24; 29:4; 32:9). In the last two instances it is paralleled by קול "voice." Wildberger (1090–91) notes that the only other occurrence of these together is in Gen 4:23. The comparison with Lamech's speech in Gen 4:23 leads to the recognition of how the parable of God's instruction to the farmer parallels the tradition that God introduced agriculture to mankind (Gen 3:23; 4:1–16). While this is merely implied in Genesis, it is stated in considerable detail in the literature of the ANE. An ancient Sumerian myth describes the process by which Enlil and Enka taught the farmer (S. N. Kramer, *History Begins at Sumer* [Garden City, NY: Doubleday, 1959] 104–12; "Sumer," *IDB* 4:460). Diodorus of Sicily reports Egyptian teachings that Osiris was interested in agriculture among other arts and crafts (*Diodorus of Sicily,* tr. C. H. Oldfeather, vol. I [New York: G. P. Putnam's Sons, 1933] § 15, p. 51). Isis was credited with the discovery of wheat and barley culture (*Diodorus* § 14, p. 49). Virgil, the Latin poet (70–19 B.C.) wrote a beautiful passage of how Ceres instructed farmers in their craft (Virgil, *Georgics* I, 287–310, with tr. H. R. Fairclough [New York: G. P. Putnam, 1922] 102–3). Ovid, another Latin poet (43 B.C.–A.D. 17) wrote a similar passage (Ovid *Metamorphoses* V, 341–45; tr. E. J. Miller, vol. I [Cambridge, Mass.: Harvard U.P., 1939] 263).

However, the genre of each of these passages is different from the one here in Isaiah. They tell of the god's instruction with no intention to project meaning beyond the telling. Here, the material becomes a "parable" because it is told as an analogy for another truth: that God's strategy for history, like his strategy for agriculture, is wonderful and achieves success. Thus his instruction should be sought by political leaders, as it is sought and followed by farmers. And his strategy is to be trusted with patient faith by the king's counselors as it is by simple farmers.

Comment

23 The call for *attention* implies an intimate group of listeners in the style of the wisdom teachers.

24 A *plow* in OT times consisted of a wooden beam to which the yoke of oxen or asses (1 Kgs 19:19) was attached to pull the plow. At the other end, a second piece of wood was fixed vertically at an angle with the handle on the upper end and a metal point on the lower (1 Sam 13:20) to break the ground. The farmer guided the plow with one hand and goaded the oxen with the other (Luke 9:62; Judg 3:31; 1 Sam 13:31).

All day translates the Hebrew literally. In parallel to v 28 *forever,* it apparently means "all the time," "continually." Other tasks need to be interspersed with plowing in the process of agriculture.

25 The farmer's work is diverse in what he does and what he plants. His seeds include spices (*dill* and *cummin*) as well as a variety of grains. One should note how different this is from the culture of the vineyard in chap. 5.

26 It was commonly believed in the ancient world that God (or the gods) taught the farmer how and when to do the complex things involved in agriculture (see *Form/Structure/Setting*). Undoubtedly the Canaanites taught the same thing. The content of this *instruction* is therefore generally acknowledged. God teaches the farmer how to do his work in *good order* משפט. This word is usually translated "justice." Its use in this setting demonstrates a facet of its meaning which is not immediately obvious when used in law.

27 The verse returns to the *good order* of the farmer which has different work for each season and which is careful that one kind of work does not destroy the work of another kind. חרוץ "a threshing sled" (*IDB* 4:636) is a device, probably using iron, to be drawn by oxen or an ass. It was dragged over the grain to separate kernels of grain from the husks. Then the mass is thrown into the air to allow the wind to separate the heavy kernels which fall back on the floor from the husks which are blown away (i.e., winnowed). עגלה "a cartwheel" was a frame with rollers for the same work. But it would be nonsense to use such massive equipment for the delicate spices of *dill* and *cummin.*

28 Even *threshing* can be overdone. The farmer is careful not to let the cartwheel damage the kernels of grain on the threshing floor.

29 The general observations of the parable and its implications from the culture-myths are now brought to focus. *Yahweh of Hosts* is identified as the one who is behind all of this. Every Israelite and Judean knows that. The parable is not told to teach this obvious truth. By analogy, the parable ascribes to Yahweh the same skills, knowledge, and strategy in managing political and historical matters. From him *goes out* the design of the times. הפליא עצה "wonderful strategy" picks up that strand of the Vision which teaches that Yahweh's עצה "strategy" controls the events and movements of the centuries (8:10; 11:12; 16:3; 30:1; 36:5) and that he advises a strategy to meet such times (יעץ in 7:5; 14:27; 19:12; 23:8; 32:7; 32:8). Cf. G. von Rad, *OTT,* 163, n. 21. It is used here to counter the argument of pragmatic political strategy defended by the "scoffers" and "speech-makers" of v 14.

פלא "wonder" is used in the OT to describe God's wonderful acts of deliverance. The telling of God's deeds includes man's astonishment and surprise (R. Albertz, *THAT,* II, 418). The Psalms praise God for these acts in extravagant terms.

עצה "strategy" in the Vision refers to God's decision in the specific historical situation. It is not an ideal plan fixed in eternity (Wildberger, 1095). The royal heir is titled פלא יועץ "Wonder of a Counselor" (9:5) and the king to come is promised רוח עצה "the spirit of counsel" (11:2). Both foresee the ability to master a situation, to plan a way out of or through the problem. Wildberger (1095) notes that the Divine King, Yahweh of Hosts, is seen to act the same way. תושיה "success" is a word with several facets. It implies "prudence" which results in "success" and "salvation."

Explanation

The episode uses a description of how God instructs the farmer in the complex tasks of agriculture. In this, one recognizes that every season demands different tasks and every crop must be treated individually. This example is an analogy for God's "strategy" for the nation and his willingness to teach the leaders how to guide their people through the intricate pressures and problems of their times. The politician needs instruction in "good order" or "justice" just as much as the farmer does. The "scoffers" and "speech-makers" of v 14 had made their "covenant with Death" without seeking such instruction.

The episode ends by recommending Yahweh of Hosts to the political leaders as one who had proved his "wonderful strategy" in the work of the farmer. This "strategy" sometimes employed miraculous happenings which evoked wonder, as it did for Hezekiah in 701 B.C. (37:36–37). God's strategy is geared to fit the circumstances, but it is not limited or controlled by them.

This is a strategy with "excellent (or great) success." This must be measured by God's own standards, not limited to human expectations. The "speech-makers" were wrong in assuming that God had no plan for the changed circumstances (Egypt's seizure of power over Palestine) which they thought forced them to accept "the covenant with Death." God continued to confirm his "cornerstone" in Zion. This was his firm commitment (v 16). To recognize this was a base for firm faith and the patience which grows from such faith (v 16b).

The analogy of the farmer who follows God's instructions very carefully, but still has to wait in patient faith for the harvest, is applicable to the leader and the people. God has a strategy for their times which will achieve the "justice and righteousness" which are always his goals. The analogy pleads for patience and understanding of the ways of God. He had taught the farmer to pace his work to the changing seasons. God seeks to teach Judah's leaders to recognize how he paces himself to the course of history in directing the rise and fall of nations. The three episodes in this scene plead for Judah not to make the mistakes that Israel made in a similar situation a century earlier.

Scene 2: Disaster in Jerusalem's Political Involvement (29:1–24)

The first of Scene 2's three episodes, "Woe, Ariel" (29:1–8), mourns Jerusalem (or the founding patron deity of the city) which will now be attacked and humbled by Yahweh himself. The second, "Like a Dream" (29:9–14), portrays the fulfillment of the task assigned in 6:11–13 as a horrible nightmare that will be seen as no more than a dream after it has passed. The third, "Woe, You Schemers" (29:15–24), speaks against those who plot in Jerusalem. It foresees a new opportunity for Jacob.

Episode A: Woe, Ariel (29:1–8)

Bibliography

Albright, W. F. "The Babylonian Temple-Tower and the Altar of Burnt-Offering." *JBL* 39 (1920) 137–42. **Feigin, S.** "The Meaning of Ariel." *JBL* 39 (1920) 131–37. **Godbey, A. H.** "Ariel, or David-Cultus." *AJSL* 41 (1924) 253–66.

Translation

Herald: 1 *Woe!* 1

Ariel,[a] *Ariel,*[a] 2+3

City [b]*where David camped.*[b]

Yahweh: *Add*[c] *year to year.* 3+2

(to Jerusalem) *Let festivals take place on schedule,*

2 *when I shall bring distress to Ariel* 2+3+3

and there will be moaning[a] *and lamentation.*[a]

She will be[b] *for me like an ariel.*[c]

3 *And I shall encamp encircled*[a] *against you.* 3+3+3

I shall lay siege against you (with) a tower.[b]

I shall raise siegeworks[c] *against you.*

Heavens: 4a *You will be humbled. From a land you will speak.*[a] 3+3

(to Jerusalem) *From dust your sayings will mumble.*[b]

Earth: *And it shall be:* 1
(to Jerusalem) *Your voice will be like a ghost from a land.* 3+3
From dust your sayings will whisper.
Heavens: 5 *And it shall be:* 1
(to Jerusalem) *Your insolent horde*[a] *(will be) like fine dust,* 4+4
the horde of ruthless ones like chaff blowing away.
Herald: *And it will happen with sudden suddenness:* 3+4
6 *By Yahweh of Hosts her fate will be decided!*[a]
With thunder, earthquake, and great sound, 4+5
whirlwind and storm, and flame of devouring fire.
Earth: 7 *And it shall be:* 1
Like a dream, a night vision, (will be) 3+4+4
the horde of all the nations mustered[a] *against Ariel,*
and all the army[b] *(against) her, and the siegeworks*[c] *(against) her, and those causing her distress.*
Heavens: 8 *And it shall be:* 1
just as a hungry person dreams he is eating 5+3
but wakes (to find) his stomach[a] *empty,*
or just as a thirsty one dreams he is drinking 5+5
but wakes to find he is faint,[b] *his stomach dry,*
so will be the horde of all nations 4+3
mustered around Mount Zion.

Notes

1.a. DSS^{Isa} ארואל "Aruel" for MT's אריאל "Ariel." D. M. Beegle (*BASOR* 123 [1951] 29) and Kutscher (*Isaiah Scroll,* 97) doubt the transcription of *waw* where the difference between *waw* and *yodh* is often so tenuous. LXX interprets in support of MT πόλις Αριηλ "City Ariel." Tg has מדבחא "altar" (Jastrow, *Dictionary,* 731). Wildberger notes parallels to the personal name in Ezra 8:16 and to an altar in Ezek 43:15–16 (cf. also Gen 46:16; Num 26:17; 2 Sam 23:20; Isa 33:7). See *Comment.*

1.b-b. The sentence follows a noun in construct (cf. GKC § 130d). Wildberger observes that this construction tends to follow nouns designating time (Gen 1:1) or place (Ezek 39:11). Irwin (47) notes that "camped" can imply both "dwell" and "besiege," and that the latter sense becomes clear in v 3.

1.c. DSS^{Isa} ספי (fem sg for MT's masc pl) addresses the command to the city, MT to its inhabitants.

2.a-a. A repetition of virtually the same word. E. König (*Stilistik, Rhetorik, Poetik* [Leipzig: T. Weicher, 1900] 157) considered the duplication deliberate for effect.

2.b. DSS^{Isa} והייתה "and you shall be" for MT's "she shall be."

2.c. כאריאל "like Ariel" is the same as the proper name in v 1. But the setting leads many to translate as "hearth of God" (Wildberger), "an altar hearth" NIV (cf. 31:9). NEB translates "my Ariel indeed," and Irwin (47) suggests changing MT's כַּאֲרִיאֵל to כִּי אֲרִיאֵל and parsing כִּי as emphatic: "Ariel indeed." A further possibility is to read here "as a lioness of God" (Irwin, 48). The potential for double entendre would surely not have been lost on the author.

3.a. MT כדור "like the circle." LXX ὡς Δαυιδ "like David" reads *daleth* in place of *resh.* However, Syr and Vg support MT.

3.b. MT מצב "tower" is a *hapax.* BDB (663) "palisade, entrenchment." LXX χάρακα "a rampart."

3.c. MT מצרת "siegeworks" (BDB, 849). Some MSS read מצדת, but this has few possibilities (BDB, 841). For a full discussion, see Wildberger, 1098.

4.a-a. LXX reads "your words shall be made to fall to the ground." Wildberger (1099) properly calls it a free translation.

4.b. MT תשח "shall mumble" (BDB, 1005, "shall come low"). G. R. Driver (*JSS* 13 [1968] 51; *Von Ugarit nach Qumran,* FS O. Eissfeldt, BZAW 77 [Berlin: A. Töpelmann, 1958], 45) suggests "pour out."

5.a. DSS[Isa] זדיך "your insolent ones" (BDB, 267) for MT זריך "your strangers" (BDB, 266). LXX has missed it altogether in ὁ πλοῦτος τῶν ἀσεβῶν "the riches of the ungodly." DSS[Isa] has the best reading.

6.a. LXX translates ἐπισκοπὴ γὰρ ἔσται "for there shall be a visitation," i.e., changing the verb to a noun. Note that MT has returned to a 3 fem sg. *BHS* (and others) suggests emending to 2nd person. But variation seems to be consistent with the nature of Isaiah's text.

7.a. DSS[Isa] הצובאים writes it fully (*plene*), but suggests no different word.

7.b. צביה "her host" (BDB, 838, suggests "all that fight against her"). The genitive is objective: "the host (against) her."

7.c. DSS[Isa] מצרתה "her siegeworks" as in v 3 above. But MT makes sense and should be kept.

8.a. נפשו "his stomach" usually means "soul" (BDB, 659). Irwin (55) translates "throat," citing Dahood, "Hebrew-Ugaritic Lexicography," *Bib* 49 (1968) 368.

8.b. Two MSS leave out הנה עיף "behold faint" (BDB, 746). Wildberger, Procksch, Kaiser, and *BHS* suggest omitting them, but the rhythm and sense fit. We have kept MT.

Form/Structure/Setting

The episode begins with "Woe" and ends with a kind of concluding "thus it will be" which mark its limits. It is compactly and carefully crafted. The "woe" cry (v 1a) is followed by an imperative, functioning as a protasis in a conditional construction: "Add year to year. Let festivals take place" with the meaning "if" or "when" you hold festival. This is followed by twelve sentences beginning with *waw* with perfect tenses (so-called converted perfects). The first eight (vv 2–4) extend the protasis by describing the festival's drama of divine testing for Zion which leads to her humiliation as unto death. The last four provide the apodosis of the construction which applies the figure to the besieging "hordes of nations" which surround Jerusalem. Four (vv 2–3) are in the first person with Yahweh as speaker. They dominate the first section. Two are in the third feminine singular of היה "to be" (v 2bc) and expand the first of the group. Two are second feminine singular (v 4ab) to expound the emphasis of the three first person verbs. Five occurrences of והיה "and it shall be" (vv 4b–8) introduce ten similes, six of them headed by כְּ "like" with others implied. This list of similes is capped by a concluding line (v 8c) beginning with כֵּן "so" or "thus" and a repetition of the verb יהיה "it will be."

The whole is in the form of an arch which relates the imagery of the royal Zion festival to the realistic siege at the walls of Jerusalem by "the horde of nations." It is further supported by the theme "Ariel" (vv 1, 2, 7), the theme of "siege" (vv 2, 7, 8), and "the horde" (vv 5, 7, 8).

The outline of the arch:

A Let festivals take place (v 1)
 B I shall bring distress to Ariel (vv 2–3)
  C You shall be humbled (v 4)

KEYSTONE Your hordes shall be like fine dust (v 5)
C′ Yahweh will decide her fate (v 6)
B′ The horde of nations against Ariel will be like a dream (v 7)
A′ Thus will be the horde of nations (v 8)

The episode deals with the critical siege of Jerusalem by interpreting it in the context of the Zion festival in which Yahweh tests the city by ordeal in order to humble her, after the fashion of the king's ordeal. The great drama demonstrates the helplessness of the city in itself; indeed, it is as good as dead. She exists by the decree and power of Yahweh God. If that is understood to be true in the festal drama, it is equally true of the historical reality. Once Yahweh has decided Zion's fate the oppressing nations will no longer be a factor. They will appear like a dream, a memory of the festal drama's terrible moment of humiliation. (Note the parallel experience in chaps. 36–37 in which the prophetic oracle serves the same purpose which the reference to the festal drama does here.)

On the place of ritual humiliation in the Jerusalem royal festival cf. J. D. W. Watts, *Basic Patterns in Old Testament Religion* (Louisville, KY: Jameson Press, 1971) 134; A. R. Johnson, *Sacral Kingship in Ancient Israel* (Cardiff: University of Wales Press, 1955) 93–126; J. H. Eaton, *Kingship and the Psalms,* SBT 32 (London: SCM, 1976) 199–201; and *Festal Drama in Deutero-Isaiah* (London: SPCK, 1979) 24–26.

If the "horde of nations" around Jerusalem is found to be the central theme, a different focus is brought to view. This is a common theme in Isaiah (5:26–30; 8:9–10; 13:1–5; 31:4–5 to name a few). It has historical roots in the siege of Jerusalem in Ahaz's day (734 B.C.; chap. 7), Sennacherib's siege in Hezekiah's day (701 B.C.; chaps. 22 and 36–37), and Nebuchadnezzar's sieges in 598 and 587 B.C. The theme is picked up in Jeremiah, Ezekiel, and Zechariah. (Cf. R. de Vaux, "Jerusalem et les prophètes," *RB* 73 [1966] 481–509; J. H. Hayes, "The Tradition of Zion's Inviolability," *JBL* 82 [1963] 424; H. J. Hermisson, "Zukunftserwartung und Gegenwartskritik in der Verkündigung Jesajas," *EvT* 33 [1973] 56, n. 8.)

The usual form has the nations gathered around the city with Yahweh defending it. But here the situation is reversed. Yahweh lays siege to the city and is identified with the besieging peoples. This is a literary inversion of the *Völkerkampf* pattern which derives its meaning as a parallel to the humiliation of the king in ancient festal ritual. In this case it portrays a ritual humiliation of the city which is carried to the very point of death.

Comment

1a *Woe* picks up the feeling of death in Jerusalem that was introduced by the mood of chap. 28, especially by "the covenant with death" (28:15). *Ariel* has various possible meanings (cf. notes 1.a, 2.c, and BDB, 72). These include "lioness of God," "God's champion or hero," and "altar-hearth of El." The name identifies Jerusalem. If the reference is to an ancient epithet related to the city, as is probable, it refers to El as the founding patron deity of the city. The meaning is that although Jerusalem is a city founded by God in Jebusite, pre-Israelite times, and although David himself claims the city, Yahweh must fight against it. Cf. v. 8 below.

City where David camped. The phrase refers to David's troops kept there. It establishes the relation to David, but avoids associating "David's city" with the divine promises about the city.

1b *Add year to year* is probably a reference to the celebration of New Year's festivals in which Yahweh's beneficent patronage for another year is sought. This view is reinforced by the references to *festivals.* The Vision has noted the emptiness of ritual observance (1:11–15) when it fails to reflect God's attitude and intention. Although the ritual stresses Jerusalem's ties to God and is intended to ensure her safety and prosperity, the verse implies that the celebration will not deter God from his determined path.

2 The first two lines clearly indicate that Yahweh will be an enemy to Ariel with predictable results (cf. Lam 2:5). The third line is cryptic. Does *like an ariel* mean something like the use of the word in 2 Sam 23:20, "a heroic champion?" If so, this is a deliberate play on the word which reflects the ambivalence of the message. Yahweh's usual stance is that of staunch defender against all enemies, but now his strange or alien stance (cf. 28:21) makes him Jerusalem's enemy.

3 God is laying siege to the city. Two words from the root צרר/צור are used: צרתי "I shall lay siege" and מצרת "siegeworks." G. Gerlemann ("Contributions to the Old Testament Terminology of the Chase," *Miscella Veteris Testamenti* 4 [Lund, 1946] 89) found this a word used of hunting when a wild animal is surrounded. Irwin (48) thinks this makes the meaning of Ariel "Lion of God" much more plausible. The Lion of God is surrounded by the Divine Hunter. This is the artistic metaphor which interprets the siege of Jerusalem.

4 *A land* must here refer to the world of the dead (cf. N. J. Tromp, *Primitive Conceptions of Death,* 23–46, 85–91, 98; M. Ottoson, "ארץ," *TWAT* I, 430–31). Ariel, after being besieged, descends into the land of the dead, becoming like a ghost.

5 The alternative readings of DSS[Isa] *your insolent population* and MT *your foreign horde* (Irwin's translation, 52) state the issue. Does this refer to Jerusalem's population or to the besieging enemy? המון "horde" recurs in v 7 with a clear reference to the enemy. Here, however, the context makes it parallel *the dust* (v 4) of the land of the dead. The *hordes* are the nations who represent Yahweh (vv 2–3) before Jerusalem. They belong to Jerusalem (*your . . . horde*) in the sense that they are her problem.

The humiliation (v 4) has five parallel observations:

Jerusalem's *voice* will be like that of a ghost (v 4b).
Her *hordes* will be like fine dust (v 5).
Yahweh will *decide her fate* (vv 5c–6).
These *hordes* of nations will seem like a dream (v 7).
The experience will prove ephemeral (v 8).

If the experience humbles Jerusalem to the point of deathly helplessness, then the nations around the city are a part of that deathlike unreal experience, *like dust.*

6 Yahweh is the only reality. He alone has power and can make a decision. After he has acted (vv 7–8) all the threats of the nations will seem as unreal as a dream only partly remembered.

Explanation

The meaning of this passage is similar to that of chap. 7. Attention is called away from the threatening military situation to the underlying reality of God's purpose and action. By referring to the ancient ritual of humiliation through ordeal which preceded the "deciding of fate," the passage interprets Jerusalem's military difficulty as God's humiliation of the city which must precede his decision about her fate. When the decision has been made, everything else will seem unreal, like a dream. Yahweh, his sovereign decisions and his salvation—these are the only realities to consider, the only decisive factors.

Paul refers to life's trials in a similar vein when they are seen from the perspective of participation in Christ's resurrection (Rom 8:18; Phil 3:7–11).

Episode B: Like a Dream (29:9–14)

Bibliography

Schmidt, J. M. "Gedanken zum Verstockungsauftrag Jesajas (Is. VI)." *VT* 21 (1971) 68–90. **Schmidt, K. L.** "Die Verstockung des Menschen durch Gott." *TZ* 1 (1945) 1–17.

Translation

Earth: (to Jerusalemites)
9 *Tarry* [a] *and be astounded!* [b] — 2+2
Delight yourselves [c] *and gaze intently!* [c]
You, who are drunk [d]*—but not from wine,* — 2+2
you, who stagger [e]*—but not from liquor!*
10 *For Yahweh has poured out* [a] *over you* [b] — 3+2
a spirit of deep sleep.

Heavens:
So he closed your eyes, the prophets, [c] — 3+3
and your heads, the seers, [c] *he has covered.*

Earth:
11 *So the whole vision became for you* — 4+3
like the words of the sealed book,
which when they give it to one who knows the Scripture, [a] — 4+3
saying, "Read this, please,"
he says, "I cannot, — 3+3
for it is sealed."
12 *But if one had given* [a] *the book to* [a] *one who does not know how to read saying "Read this please," he would have said, "I do not know how to read."*

Herald: 13 *So my Lord* [a] *proceeded to say:* 2
Yahweh: *Because this people approaches with its mouth* [b] 6
and with their lips they [c] *honor me* 2+3
while its heart is far from me,
so that their fear of me is (*only*) [d] 3+3
a human command [e] (*that is*) *memorized,*
14 *therefore, see me* [a] *again* [b] 3+3+2
doing wonders [c] *for this people,* [d]
the wonder [c] *and a wonder!* [c]
Heavens: *But the wisdom of the wise shall perish* 3+3
and the discernment of the discerning ones will be hidden. [e]

Notes

9.a. התמהמהו ותמהו "tarry and be astounded" are usually considered a hithpalpel impv from מהה (BDB, 554; GKC § 55g) and a qal impv from תמה (BDB, 1069). LXX ἐκλύθητε καὶ ἔκστητε and Vg *obstupescite et admiramini* support this distinction, contra *BHK, BHS,* and Wildberger who emend in order to derive both from תמה.

9.b. Delitzsch, followed by Irwin, suggests that the use of two forms of the same root here and in the second stich should be understood as hendiadys, "the expression of an idea by the use of two independent words connected by 'and' " (*Webster's New Collegiate Dictionary*). But cf. notes 9.a and 9.c.

9.c. LXX omits. The Versions give varying translations. השתעשעו is usually seen as a hithpalpel impv from שעע "blind yourselves" (BDB, 1044). As such it is the only occurrence with that sense in that stem (cf. 32:9 in qal). A second use of this root means "make sport, take delight in" and occurs in hithpalpel twice in Ps 119 (vv 16, 47) and several times in pilp including Isa 11:8 and 66:12. Another possibility is the root שעה "gaze at" (BDB, 1043) which is also known in Isa 17:7; 22:4; 31:1; and 41:10. This translation uses BDB's second root meaning for השתעשעו and reads וְשֹׁעוּ from שעה (with J. M. Schmidt, "Gedanken zum Verstockungsauftrag Jesajas (Is. VI)," *VT* 21 [1971] 68–90) for the second word.

9.d. MT שָׁכְרוּ "they are drunk" (BDB, 1016). DSS[Isa] שכרון is apparently a noun "drunkenness" (but Irwin [56] sees the form as qal pf plus *nun paragogicum* [cf. GKC § 44*l*] and parallel to the form of the next verb) occurring otherwise in Jer 13:13; Ezek 23:33; 39:19. LXX κραιπαλήσατε "debauch yourselves," supported by Tg and Vg, suggests the impv שִׁכְרוּ (cf. *BHK* and *BHS*). MT may be kept and read as a relative clause.

9.e. MT נעו "they stagger" qal pf from נוע (BDB, 631). Tg טעו "go astray" (Jastrow, *Dictionary,* 542) and Vg *movemini* "move about" again suggest that an impv is indicated (cf. *BHK, BHS,* and Wildberger). However, DSS[Isa] נעוו raises the same question of tense as in note 9.d. It also suggests a different root from MT, a niph pf 3 m sg from עוה "be bowed down, twisted." Irwin (56) translates "they are agitated" (cf. Isa 21:3; 24:1). With Irwin MT should be sustained and read as a relative clause.

10.a. Vg *miscuit* "he mixed" or "he confused." There is no other witness to this meaning.

10.b. DSS[Isa] עליכמה. The additional *heh* is common in DSS. Cf. Kutscher, *Isaiah Scroll,* 442.

10.c. "The prophets" and "the seers" are often dubbed glosses. There is no textual evidence for this.

11.a. Q סֵפֶר (BDB, 708). K הַסֵּפֶר "the book, the Scripture" (BDB, 706–7). The usual reading today follows Q (*BHK, BHS*) "to read." Wildberger (1112–13) follows K translating "the Scripture" as in Dan 1:4, 17. But note that the article is missing in Daniel. The translation follows K. See *Comment.*

12.a-a. DSS[Isa] has a number of insignificant variations.

13.a. Many MSS have יהוה "Yahweh." Wildberger thinks it is original. MT may be kept.

13.b. LXX omits. LXX[B] OL Vg include "his mouth" with the previous phrase, i.e., move the *zakeph qaton* to בְּפִיו.

13.c. MT כבדוני "they honor me" has concerned interpreters and translators because of the sg possessive pronouns on "mouth" and "lips." DSS^Isa^ כבדתי "I honor" does not make sense, but see Irwin's note (58) that *BHS* misreads נו for ת. Syr OL Vg read a sg כבדני "it honors me" to correct the problem. But note the return to pl in יראתם "their fear." Such changes are frequent in Heb. Keep MT and read sg as collectives for "this people."

13.d. LXX μάτην δὲ "but in vain" (cf. Matt 15:8–9) which *BHS* retranslates to וְתֹהוּ: "Their fear of me is in vain." However, MT makes sense and should be kept.

13.e. DSS^Isa^ כמצות "like a command"; Tg concurs. Syr uses the preposition *b* "by commands of." But MT has "command" as the predicate nominative and should be sustained.

14.a. MT's short form הנני is written fully in DSS^Isa^ הנה אנוכי "see me!"

14.b. K יוֹסֵף ptcp "adding"; Q יסיף hiph impf 3 m sg "(who) will multiply." K fits the context; Q strains it through a shift of person. LXX προσθήσω "I shall add"; Syr *mwsp* "adding"; Vg *addam* "add." Irwin (59) follows K: "I am he who will again."

14.c. DSS^Isa^ reads פלה "be separate, distinct" in all three instances for MT's פלא "be wonderful." The ideas are related, but MT's is better.

14.d. את־העם־הזה "this people" is often thought to be superfluous because it breaks up the metrical form. That is not reason enough to delete it here. If the line is read as a tristich, even that argument is not valid.

14.e. Irwin (59) argues that the verb is denominative, from סתר "the secret place" which refers to Sheol in 28:18; 45:19; Ps 139:15 as Tromp (*Primitive Conceptions of Death,* 46–47, 97) has shown. If this is true, it adds to the imagery of life after death in this section. The verb is a contrast to "will perish" in the previous line.

Form/Structure/Setting

This episode turns from the political emergency to address the people. It begins, like v 1b, with an imperative addressed to the citizens of Jerusalem. The setting continues to be that of festival. But the episode is not concerned with the festival drama, as vv 1–8 were, but with the people and their reactions.

The syntactical structure is this:

Imperatives: "Tarry!" "Gaze intently!" "Be drunk!" (v 9).
כִּי with perfect tense: "For Yahweh has poured sleep" (v 10).
Three clauses begun with *waw* consecutive and imperfects:
"So he closed the eyes of the prophets" (v 10b).
"So it became like words of a sealed book" (v 11a).
"So my Lord said:
Because this people approaches me—
so that their fear of me is only—" (v 13).
A verb-less clause using הִנֵּה with a participle:
"Therefore, behold me doing wonders—" (v 14a).
Perfect with *waw* followed by inverted order with imperfect:
"But the wisdom of the wise shall perish" (v 14b).

The episode picks up the theme of drunken stupor from chap. 28 and that of God-caused blindness from 6:9–10. It also resumes the theme of insincere worship from chap. 1.

Comment

9 The commands are still addressed to the festal throng, moving through Jerusalem to the throbbing carnival sounds. They move in a kind of stupor.

10 But the stupor is from God, as he had predicted in 6:9–11. The *prophets,* leaders, and *seers* are affected alike.

11–12 *The whole vision.* This book is called The Vision. But every act has complained that the people of that generation did not "see" and did not respond. Having a sacred tradition, a Holy Scripture, or divine vision is of no use if it is *sealed.*

13 The Lord's speech specifies his analysis. *This people* is a term that has appeared before (6:10; 8:11) when God wants to distance himself from the people's attitudes and decisions. Their religion is found to be only verbal. It lacks heart, mind, and will. This affects the character of their worship. *Their fear* means their attitude in worship. It should be founded on a divinely inspired awe, deep respect of the Holy One. But it has become מצות אנשים "a human command" which can be taught and recited without involving the will.

14a For this reason God must intervene with *wondrous acts* to restore the sense of his holy and awesome presence.

14b Because God is going to intervene, the ordinary prognoses of wise and discerning persons cannot correctly advise concerning the course of coming events.

Explanation

God does not reveal himself the same way in all seasons. The Vision reveals God's strategy and intentions to its readers. But the generations portrayed in The Vision were blind to the implications just as 6:9–11 predicted that they would be. Even the Scriptures were meaningless to them.

God recognizes the sorry state of religion which is only lip worship, the repetition of learned phrases. Truly "the fear of Yahweh" is not only the beginning of wisdom, but also the foundation of worship which involves the heart. Holy awe leads to genuine devotion. Yet God in his grace determines to do more "wonders" for this people, miracles which defy prediction or explanation. The ways of God can neither be confined nor limited.

Episode C:
Woe, You Schemers (29:15–24)

Bibliography

Payne, J. B. "The Effect of Sennacherib's Anticipated Destruction in Isaianic Prophecy." *WTJ* 34 (1971/72) 22–38. **Whedbee, W. H.** *Isaiah and Wisdom.* Nashville: Abingdon, 1971. 73–75, 130–31. **Ziegler, J.** "Zum literarischen Aufbau im Buch des Propheten Isaias." *BZ* 21 (1933) 138–41.

Translation

Heavens: 15 *Woe to those who (try to) dig too deep for Yahweh* [a] 3+2
to hide a strategy.
Whose deeds are in the dark. 3

Earth: *Who say:* 1
"Who sees us? 2+2
Who knows (about) us?"
Heavens: [16] *Oh, your perversity!* [a] 1+3
As if the potter be regarded like clay!
As if the thing made should say to its maker, 3+2
"He did not make me!"
Or a thing formed of clay [b] *to the one who forms it,* 3+2
"He does not understand!"
Earth: [17] *Will not* [a] *very soon now* 3+3+3
Lebanon turn into the orchard [b]
and Carmel be reckoned a forest?
[18] *The deaf hear in that day* 4+2
words (read from) a scroll.
After [a] *gloom and darkness* 2+3
blind eyes will see.
[19] *The meek shall increase joy in Yahweh.* [a] 4+2+3
The humble of humanity [b]
will exult in the Holy One of Israel. [a]
[20] *When the terrorist* [a] *shall come to nought,* 2+2+3
the scoffer [b] *shall be finished,*
all who are intent on evil shall be cut off:
[21] *those who by a word make a person to be an offender,* 3+3+3
who lay a trap [a] *for one who reproves* [b] *in the gate*
and so turn aside a just case with an empty argument. [c]
Herald: [22] *Therefore, thus says Yahweh, God* [a] *of the House of Jacob, Who redeemed Abraham:* 5+3
Yahweh: *Not now will Jacob be shamed!* 4+4
Not now will their faces grow pale!
[23] *For when they see their children,* [a] 3+3
the works of my hands, in their midst,
they will sanctify my name. 2
Heavens: *And they will sanctify the Holy One of Jacob.* 3+3
They will be in awe of the God of Israel.
Earth: [24] *Those errant of spirit will know understanding,* 3+3
and the murmurers [a] *will learn (their) lessons.*

Notes

15.a. מיהוה "from Yahweh." LXX *οὐ διὰ κυρίου* "not through the Lord" has interpreted this as a privative מן building on the basic idea of "separation, apart from, not from." Tg מן קדם יהוה translates "before Yahweh's face," building on another sense of מן. Vg *a Domino* "away from the Lord" is a more literal translation of the Heb. The idea of "hiding" suggests that "from" means to keep away from his knowledge and sight. Irwin (61) would combine with the previous word to translate "too deep for Yahweh." His argument is cogent.

16.a. MT הפככם appears to be a noun (BDB, 246; GKC § 147c) with a pronominal suffix "your perversity." DSS[Isa] הפך מכם "he overturns from you." LXX and Syr omit the term. Vg *perversa est haec vestra cogitatio* "wrongheaded is this idea of yours" Wildberger (1125) correctly calls a free translation. T. H. Robinson ("The Text of Isaiah 29:16," *ZAW* 49 [1931] 322) suggests reversing two letters to read הַכְּפָכִים "as flasks" (cf. *BHS*). Wildberger (1126) suggests reading MT as a vocative and points to a parallel meaning in Ezek 16:34.

16.b. DSS[Isa] חמר "clay" for MT's אמר "says." The reading is aesthetic and makes better sense. For an opposing view see M. Held, "The YQTL-QTL (QTL-YQTL) sequence of identical verbs in Biblical Hebrew and Ugaritic," *Studies and Essays in Honor of Abraham A. Neumann* (Leiden: E. J. Brill, 1962) 281–90.

17.a. הלוא is a particle for a negative question. But many interpreters translate in the same sense as הנה "see, indeed, look." This fails to reflect the aesthetic change in Hebrew.

17.b. הכרמל is a "cultivated garden" or "orchard" (BDB, 502, I). It is also the name of a mountain in Israel (BDB, 502, II). Wildberger (1133) and Irwin (62–63) translate the first usage in the generic sense and the second as the proper name.

18.a. מן in מאפל and מחשך is literally "from gloom" and "from darkness." The meaning may be "in contrast to gloom" or "away from the time of gloom," i.e., "after."

19.a. Wildberger (1134) joins Procksch in deleting ביהוה and בקדוש ישראל as being pious glosses. There is no textual ground, nor does the irregular meter justify it.

19.b. Irwin (64) follows *CHAL* (14) in translating אדם as "land (cf. M. Dahood, "Hebrew-Ugaritic Lexicography," *Bib* 44 [1963] 292; *Psalms* III, AB 17A, 39–40). Both meanings are fitting. Wildberger (1134) sees superlative meaning in it: "the poorest of mankind."

20.a. MT עריץ "terrifying" is sg as is LXX *ἄνομος* "lawless." Both are adjectives used in place of nouns. Perhaps "the terrorist" will fill the place.

20.b. MT לֵץ "scorner" (BDB, 539); LXX *ὑπερήφανος* "one who appears great"; Tg בזוזא "plunderer."

21.a. יקשון is usually understood as qal impf from קוש and thus a *hapax* (BDB, 881) "lay a snare." Some propose reading it as יָקֹשׁוּ qal pf from יקש or as יְיַקְשׁוּן qal impf from יקש or נקש (*BHK, BHS*). Neither changes the meaning. It refers to legal traps, parallel to the "by a word," i.e., slander, of the parallel stich.

21.b. Cf. Amos 5:10. V. Maag, *Text, Wortschatz und Begriffswelt des Buches Amos* (Leiden: Brill, 1951) 153: "the resident lawyer who sees to it that the great scoundrels are publicly called to order."

21.c. תהו "emptiness" also means "wasteland" (BDB, 1062). Wildberger (1134) thinks of "empty arguments," parallel to "words" of the previous stich. Irwin (65) translates "thrust the innocent into the wasteland" and points to Amos 5:12. The preposition ב favors Wildberger's point. It is used three times here, but never as "into."

22.a. The relative particle obviously has "Yahweh" as its antecedent, yet it is followed directly by "to the House of Jacob." *BHK* and *BHS* suggest changing אֶל "to" to אֵל "God" reading "God of the House of Jacob" to eliminate the problem. LXX translates *ἐπὶ τὸν οἶκον Ιακωβ ὃν ἀφώρισεν ἐξ Αβρααμ* "upon the house of Jacob, whom he selected from Abraham." But Wildberger (1135) curtly notes that פדה does not mean *ἀφορίζειν* and את does not mean *ἐξ*. The emendation to read אֵל "God" is the simplest. The fact that Yahweh's speech is 3rd person, i.e., not addressed to Israel, strengthens the suggestion.

23.a. ילדיו "their children" is often thought to be a gloss. The thinking goes: not children, but Yahweh's great deeds are "the works of his hand." There is no textual evidence for this. Irwin (66) brings metrical data to support MT.

24.a. רוגנים "murmurers" (BDB, 920). But Ehrlich (*Randglossen* IV, 105) insists that it means "persons who speak falsehood." G. R. Driver (in *Von Ugarit Nach Qumran,* FS O. Eissfeldt, BZAW 77 [Berlin: A. Töpelmann, 1958] 45) uses Syr and Arab to derive the meaning "muddled." Wildberger (1135) finds a reference to the wilderness journey of ancient Israel and pleads for the traditional meaning.

Form/Structure/Setting

The episode has three parts and a conclusion (cf. J. Ziegler, *BZ* 21 [1933] 138–41):

Vv 15–16 Woe to planners who exclude God (v 15)
who presume to be able to hide (v 15)
as if—a three-fold simile of clay and potter (v 16).

Vv 17–21 God's reversal is near (v 17)
when blind and meek will be advantaged (vv 18–19)
when violent cunning will fail (vv 20–21).
Vv 22–23 Yahweh announces a new opportunity for Israel.
V 24 Conclusion—Then even the "errant in spirit" can understand.

Comment

15–16 *Too deep.* Strategists who think they can elude Yahweh's sight or knowledge are ridiculed (cf. Ps 139).

17 In Yahweh's plan things will soon be reversed: the forest turned into an orchard, the orchard into a forest. *Carmel* appears also in 16:10; 33:9; 35:2. The word may be a proper noun for a mountain or a common noun for an orchard. *Lebanon* is famed for its forests and great trees (cf. S. Virgulin, "Il Libana nel libro di Isaia," *RivB* 7 (1959) 343–53).

18–19 The *deaf,* the *blind,* the *meek,* and the *humble* have suffered much in a world that honors power and cunning. But their day will come when God changes all the rules to work to their advantage.

20 Then the cunning and the evil-doers will no longer be able to do their work.

22 Note the identification *God of the house of Jacob, who redeemed Abraham.* The message is about Israel who will have her chance again. *Not now* may carry the meaning "no longer." Israel has not had an identifiable existence for well over a century. *Redeemed:* Laberge (300) has a study of the uses of פדה "redeem" in Isaiah. It occurs in 1:27, 35:10, 51:11, as well as in this verse. It is frequent in the Psalms, a total of fifty-seven times in the OT. One group of uses refers to redemption from slavery. Only once is it used of a חרם "banned thing" related to sacrifice. Isa 51:11 has the positive sense of liberation like that in Deuteronomy. Some uses identify God as the one who liberates. But only this verse speaks thus of Abraham. The name Abraham appears in 41:8; 51:2; and 63:16. *The Holy One of Jacob* is unique. It usually reads "The Holy One of Israel."

23 God expects the sight of surviving *children* after all the terrible and uncertain times to lead Israel to view them as the *works of God's hands,* as products of his miraculous preservation. This should prompt genuine worship and commitment in contrast to that in v 13. *The works of his hands* may be found in Deuteronomy to mean the people's conduct. In other places it refers to their sins, idols, or the work of an artisan (cf. Laberge, 312). It occurs of God's work especially in the Psalms and in Isaiah (5:12; 19:25; 60:21; 64:8).

24 This, in turn, will reverse the conditions of v 14b. *Understanding* will return to the leaders.

Explanation

The reversal of fortunes takes a strange turn. Judgment on those who seek to elude Yahweh's scrutiny is understandable. The turn of fate that makes the deaf, blind, meek, and humble have their day is to be expected in the Vision, as is the end of shrewd conniving. But the word about Jacob comes as a surprise. God's continued love for Israel and his undying hope of genuine response is a symbol of his unending grace.

Scene 3:
Disaster from Self-Help in Rebellion (30:1–33)

The scene builds upon the real struggle between God and the Judean leaders, who are determined to follow their own plans. The first episode, "Woe, Rebellious Children" (30:1–18), draws a contrast between what God is doing and the policies of Judah's leaders, while the second and third episodes portray religious teachers and prophets teaching a blind, euphoric hope which ignores the real rebellion of their leaders. Episode B, "Hope from the Teachers" (30:19–26), calmly repeats the doctrine of hope in God. The teachers, blind to the real issues on which the fate of the nation hung, went on teaching "peace, peace, when there was no peace" (Jer 6:14, 8:11). Episode C, "A Cultic Theophany" (30:27–33), presents the religious exercise of cultic prophecy. Judah's leaders cultivated the shallow hope that Yahweh would appear in a miraculous way to effect their salvation without their having to be concerned about the policies of the nation.

Episode A:
Woe, Rebellious Children (30:1–18)

Bibliography

Dahood, M. "Accusative ʿ*esah* 'Wood' in Isaiah 30:1b. *Bib* 50 (1969) 57–58. **Emerton, J. A.** "A Textual Problem in Isaiah XXX.5" *JTS* 32 (1981) 125–28. ———. "A Further Note on Isaiah XXX." *JTS* 33 (1982) 16. **Gray, A. H.** "The Beatitude of 'Them that wait'." *ExpTim* 48 (1936) 264–67. **Hertlein, E.** "Rahab." *ZAW* 38 (1919/20) 113–54. **Huber, F.** "Semantische Analyse der Wörter *bitha* and *suba* in Jes 30:15." *Jahwe, Juda und die andern Völker beim Propheten Jesaja.* BZAW 137. Berlin: De Gruyter, 1976. 140–47. **Jenni, E.** *Die Politischen Voraussagen der Propheten.* ATANT 29. Zurich: Zwingli Verlag, 1956. 83. **Kuschke, A.** "Zu Jes 30:1–5." *ZAW* 64 (1952) 194–95. **Melugin, R. F.** "Isa 30:15–17." *CBQ* 36 (1974) 303–4. **Murison, R. G.** "Rahab." *ExpTim* 16 (1904) 190. **Reymond, P.** "Un tesson pour 'ramasser' de l'eau à la mare (Esaie xxx, 14)." *VT* 7 (1957) 203–7. **Schunck, K-D.** "Jesaja 30:6–8 und die Deutung der Rahab im Alten Testament." *ZAW* 78 (1966) 48–56. **Ziegler, J.** "Zum literarischen Aufbau im Buch des Propheten Isaias." *BZ* 21 (1933) 131–49.

Translation

Yahweh: 1 *Woe, rebellious children!* 3+2
Herald: *Expression* [a] *of Yahweh.*

Yahweh:	*To those executing a plan,* *but not one from me!*	2+2
	To one making an alliance, [b] *but not (by) my spirit!*	2+2
	With the result: adding [c] *sin upon sin.*	2+2
	2 *Those hurrying* [a] *to descend to Egypt* *but who did not ask my advice,*	3+3
	to take refuge [b] *in Pharaoh's protection* *and to seek shelter in the shadow of Egypt.*	3+3
Heavens:	3 *Pharaoh's protection shall become a shame for you* *and shelter in the shadow of Egypt a humiliation!*	5+4
Earth:	4 *Although his* [a] *princes are in Zoan* *and his* [a] *envoys reach Hanes,*	3+3
	5 *everyone will be made odious* [a] *by (this) people that are useless to them.* [b]	2+3
	Not for help, [c]*not for profit,*[c] *(do they live),* *but for shame and also disgrace.*	4+4
Court Jester:	6 [a]*Burden: animals of the Negeb.*[a]	3
	In a land of trouble [b] *and anguish,* *of lioness and growling* [c] *lion,* *of viper and flying serpent,*	3+3+3
	they carry [d] *their riches on the backs of asses,* *on the hump of camels their treasures,* *on behalf of* [e] *a people that are useless.*	4+3+3
Yahweh:	7 *Egypt* [a] *(is) worthless!* *They provide empty help!*	2+2
	Therefore, I call this one [b] *"Rahab:* [c]*Roaring (while) Sitting Still.*[c]*"*	3+3
Heavens:	8 *Now come!* *Write it on a tablet near them.* [a] *Upon a scroll inscribe it,*	2+3+2
	that it may become for a later day *a witness* [b] *forever.*	3+2
Earth:	9 *For it is a rebellious people,* *lying sons!*	4+2
	As sons, they are not willing to heed [a] *Yahweh's instruction,*	3+2
	10 *who say to the seers* *"Do not see!"* [a]	3+2
	and to the visionaries *"Do not envision for us what is right!*	1+3
	Speak to us flattering things! *Envision praiseworthy things!* [b]	3+2
	11 *Turn* [a] *from* [b] *the way!* *Turn aside from* [b] *the path.*	2+2
	Stop bringing up before us *the Holy One of Israel!"*	2+2

Herald: 12 *Therefore,* [a] [b] *thus says the Holy One of Israel:* [b] 5
Yahweh: *Because of your rejecting this word* 4+3+2
so that you trust in a perverse [c] *tyrant* [d]
and so that you rely on him,
13 *Therefore may this guilt* 3+2
be for you
like a break collapsing, 2+3
bulging out in a high wall,
which suddenly, with suddenness, 3+2
comes (to) its breakup.
14 *It shall break up* [a] 1+3+3
like a clay vessel breaking up,
smashed—not spared. [b]
No shard will be found among its fragments 4+3+3
(big enough) to take fire from the hearth
or to scoop up [bc] *water from a pool.* [bc]
Herald: 15 *For* [a] *thus said my Lord,* 3+3
Yahweh, [b] *the Holy One of Israel:*
Yahweh: *In returning* [c] *and rest you could be saved.* 3+2+2
In quietness and in trust [d]
could your heroism consist.
[e] *But you are not willing!* [e]
Heavens: 16 [a] *Then you say: "No!* [b] 2+2+2
But on a horse [c] *let us flee!"*
So you proceed to flee.
And "On a speedster let us ride!" 2+3
So your pursuers were speed(ier).
Earth: 17 *One thousand,* 2+3+4
facing the threat [a] *of one,*
facing the threat [a] *of five, you flee,*
until you are left 2+3+2
like a flagstaff on top of the [b] *mountain,*
or like a banner on the [b] *hill.*
Heavens: 18 *Surely,* [a] *Yahweh waits to be gracious* [b] *to you.* 4+3+3
Surely, he rises up [c] *to show you mercy,*
for Yahweh is a God of justice.
Earth: *Blessed are* [d] *all who wait for him!* [d] 3

Notes

1.a. DSS^{Isa} נואם. Cf. Kutscher, *Isaiah Scroll,* 178, 498.

1.b. MT לנסך מסכה is a cognate usage which has four possible meanings (BDB, 650–51): (1) "pour out a libation" (as in 48:5); (2) "cast a molten image" (30:22; 42:17); (3) "weave a web" (25:7); (4) "negotiate an alliance." The latter fits the parallel with "doing a plan." M. Dahood (*Bib* 50 [1969] 57–58) suggests that עצה means "wood" or "idols of wood" and Irwin (71) translates "making a wooden idol without my consent, and casting a molten image without my spirit." But the passage calls for political acts, and the idea that Yahweh might have at some other time given consent for idolatry is unimaginable. The usual understanding fits the

LXX translation συνθήκας "understandings, agreements," and the normal meaning of עשות עצה "execute a plan" (cf. 2 Sam 17:23; Isa 25:1).

1.c. ספות should be understood as qal inf constr from יסף "to add." So LXX προσθεῖναι "to add, join," with similar meanings in Syr Tg Vg. Then the change which *BHS* recommends is superfluous.

2.a. Cf. NEB; Irwin 71; Gen 37:25.

2.b. לָעוֹז "to take refuge" would usually be written לָעוּז. But the form as written does occur (cf. GKC § 72q; Joüon § 80k).

4.a. LXX omits the pronouns. Vg includes them.

5.a. K הִבְאִישׁ hiph pf 3 m sg from באשׁ "be odious, stink" (BDB, 93); Q הֹבִישׁ hiph pf 3 m sg from בושׁ "come to shame" (BDB, 101; GKC § 78b). Q seems to be the first of numerous emendations (cf. *BHS,* following Procksch). DSS^{Isa} כלה באש has divided the words differently and omitted *yodh.* If this is pointed כָּלָה בָאֵשׁ it means "destroyed by fire" (cf. Irwin, 75; Zeph 1:18; and *Anath,* III, 42–43, in C. H. Gordon, *Ugaritic Handbook,* AnOr 25 [Rome: Pont. Bib. Inst., 1947] 188). If it is pointed כָּלָה בֹאשׁ it means "be utterly shamed" (cf. Ps 71:13 and Irwin, 75). K offers the most interesting variant on the theme of humiliation and deserves acceptance as the "difficult reading."

5.b. This is MT's division of the verse. *BHS,* supported by Wildberger, would move the *athnaḥ* back, making למו a part of the second line. But MT's division makes sense and is metrically sound with the uses of *makeph.* The change makes all kinds of emendations seem necessary (cf. Wildberger, 1149).

5.c-c. LXX omits; *BHK* and Wildberger (1149), following Duhm, Marti, and Fohrer, accept. Wildberger's metrical reasoning only applies if the *athnaḥ* is moved. As it stands, MT is sound.

6.a-a. LXX ἡ ὅρασις τῶν τετραπόδων τῶν ἐν τῇ ἐρήμῳ "the vision of the four-footed ones of the wilderness." Note the word plays and ambiguity of the passage (see *Comment*).

6.b. DSS^{Isa} adds a third term between MT's two, וציה "drought" (BDB, 851), although S. Talmon ("Aspects of the Textual Transmission," *Textus* 4 [1964] 113) thinks that it is simply a variant of one of the other two.

6.c. MT מֵהֶם "from them." The meaning is not clear, which has led to numerous attempts at emendation (cf. Wildberger, 1158; Irwin, 76–77). DSS^{Isa} reads ואין מים "and no water." In view of the parallel, the emendation נֹהֵם "growling" (BDB, 625) seems to be the best solution.

6.d. DSS^{Isa} reads a sg "one carries."

6.e. MT על usually means "upon, over." Here the meaning "on behalf of" (BDB, 754) is more fitting.

7.a. *BHS* suggests omitting מצרים "Egypt" (see Wildberger, 1158), but the metrical reasons are not valid. Irwin (77) calls this "a good example of delayed explication."

7.b. Irwin (75) ignores the *athnaḥ* to read "this Rabah." But the order should be reversed for that.

7.c-c. MT הֵם שָׁבֶת seems to be the pl pronoun "they" and a pausal form of a seldom used noun "a sitting still" (BDB, 992). The phrase is strange and has naturally led to many attempts at emendation (cf. *BHS* and Wildberger, 1158–59). Irwin (77) reads הם as a noun, a shortened form of המון "a roar" (BDB, 242). This is coupled in this "double-barrelled name" with שבת which may come from the root שבת "cease" or from שבב "burn." As such it may be a deliberate pun. The best possibilities in context would be for שבת to be from שבת "resting" or an inf constr from ישב "sitting down." This translation follows Irwin on הם and the derivation from ישב.

8.a. *BHS* advises deletion. See explanation in Wildberger (1166). No textual evidence supports it.

8.b. MT לָעַד, i.e., the prepositions ל "to" and עד "unto." Since a second עד follows, it makes no sense. Tg לסהדו קדמי "for a testimony before me" or "a previous covenant"; Vg *in testimonium* "in witness"; 'A Σ Θ εις μαρτυριον "for a witness." They all suggest reading לְעֵד "for a witness" (cf. *BHS*).

9.a. MT שמוע inf constr "to hear." DSS^{Isa} לשמוע inf constr plus preposition "to hear." Both forms are grammatically possible with no difference in meaning.

10.a. LXX adds ἡμῖν = לָנוּ "to us, at us" (cf. *BHS*). The addition is unnecessary. The prohibition is against exercise of their clairvoyant gift. The parallel forms that follow do not require the addition even if they explain the LXX's insertion.

10.b. DSS[Isa] מתלות (cf. F. Nötscher, "Entbehrliche Hapaxlegomena in Jesaia," *VT* 1 [1951] 302) for MT מהתלות "deceptions" (BDB, 251 and corrective note on 1122), a *hapax* related to התל or תלל "mock, deceive." Both terms remain obscure. Irwin (81) reports a suggestion from M. Dahood that the parallel to חלקות "smooth or flattering words" indicates a derivation from הלל "praise." He translates "give visions of glory."

11.a. DSS[Isa] תסורו impf for MT's impv. But the impv form in parallel הטו supports MT.

11.b. מִנֵּי is not "from me" but an older form of מן "from" (BDB, 577; GKC § 102b).

12.a. Wildberger (1174) correctly distinguishes between לכן here, which joins related sections to each other, and in v 13 in which it follows a complaint with a judgment.

12.b-b. The entire formula is missing in some LXX MSS, making this a part of the previous section. MT is right. The formula introduces a new form.

12.c. DSS[Isa] ותעלוז "and you will rejoice" for MT ונלוז "perversity." Irwin (84) joins the two words to read "perverse tyrant," lit., "tyranny most perverse."

12.d. Many commentators, including Wildberger, have trouble with עֹשֶׁק "oppression" and emend to עִקֵּשׁ (transposing two letters) "a crooked way" (BDB, 786).

14.a. *BHS* suggests omitting as dittography. See Irwin's defense (84) of the repetition on the grounds of style.

14.b. DSS[Isa] records variant spellings. But they seem to be of no textual significance.

14.c. גבא "cistern" (BDB, 146) is a *hapax* in this meaning. Ezek 47:11 and the Damascus Scroll 10:12 suggest that this is an open pool used to get salt through evaporation. P. Reymond (*VT* 7 [1957] 203–7) has shown that the word originally meant "collect, gather." That could lead to either of these meanings. He suggests that חשף means "scrape, to lift up"; *CHAL* "scoop, skim." So Wildberger (1175) suggests that גבא means something like "puddle" or "pool."

15.a. Missing in LXX.

15.b. Missing in LXX because אדני is also translated *κύριος* "Lord."

15.c. The usual translation sees שובה as a noun from שוב "returning" (BDB, 1000). As such it may mean returning from war or from a war-like diplomacy (Fohrer, Duhm). Wildberger (1181) uses this derivation but translates "conversion." Irwin (86) follows DSS[Isa] שיבה "sitting" from ישב. M. Dahood ("Some Ambiguous Texts in Isaiah," *CBQ* 20 [1958] 41–45) defended MT but understood שוב to also mean "sit" as a by-root of ישב. G. R. Driver (*JSS* 13 [1968] 51) points to Arab *raǧaʿa* and its development in meaning ("returned, came home, rested, stayed quiet, was reconciled") to suggest that שובה be translated "staying quiet."

15.d. 4QpIsa[c] ובטח "security" (cf. J. M. Allegro, *Qumran Cave 4* [4Q158–4Q186], Oxford: Clarendon [1968], 24), although DSS[Isa] agrees with MT בבטחה "in trust." Irwin (86) sees the 4QpIsa[c] reading as making the parallel phrase conform exactly, the four words serving as synonyms.

15.e-e. LXX *καὶ οὐκ ἐβούλεσθε ἀκούειν* "but you were not willing to hear." Wildberger (1182) notes that this fits 28:12 and 30:9, as well as 1:19, but does not fit here. The point here is not "hearing" but "turning."

16.a. *BHS* put this on the same line with the preceding stich.

16.b. לא־כי is a strange construction. Irwin (86) suggests dropping *makkeph* and joining כי with the following line. Donner (*Israel,* 161) among others suggests reading לא־כן as an emphatic "No!" Wildberger (1182) notes that MT's combination also occurs in Gen 18:15b; 19:2; 42:12; etc., meaning "no, but" or simply "no." MT may be kept.

16.c. This may mean in horse-drawn carts or chariots (cf. S. Mowinckel, "Drive and/or Ride in OT," *VT* 12 [1962] 286).

17.a. גערת "threat" (BDB, 172). Irwin (87) translates "roar" following the suggestion of H. G. May ("Some Cosmic Connotations of *Mayim Rabbîm,*" *JBL* 74 [1955] 17) about its use in other passages.

17.b. The definite article may indicate a particular mountain, Mt. Zion (cf. Irwin, 87).

18.a. לכן usually means "therefore" (BDB, 485). Blommerde has collected a bibliography on לכן as an emphatic particle (*Northwest Semitic Grammar and Job,* BibOr 22 [Rome: Pont. Bib. Inst., 1969] 31–32) which Irwin (88) uses to translate here "surely." The distinction changes the entire meaning of the verse (see *Comment*).

18.b. חֲנַן "be gracious" is a unique form of a qal inf constr (BDB, 335; GKC § 67cc). DSS[Isa] חונכם is apparently an inf of חון (cf. F. Nötscher, *VT* 1 [1951] 299, #4). But Leslie Allen in a private conversation suggests that DSS[Isa] is simply a plene form corresponding to MT-type orthography חָנכם. Wildberger (1190) recommends MT as the "difficult reading" and refers to Bauer-Leander § 58p on Amos 5:15.

18.c. Some MSS read ידום "stands still" for MT ירום "raises himself." G. R. Driver (*JTS* 38 [1937] 44) follows D. Yellin (*Israel Abrahams Memorial Volume* [1927] 456) in rendering רום "desire eagerly, wait, tarry" as the Arab *rāma.* All these serve to gain parallelism with חכם "waits" in the first stich. However, MT makes good sense as it stands.

18.d-d. The construction כל־חוכי לו "all who wait for him" has a constr ptcp followed by a preposition when it would ordinarily require a noun. But cf. GKC § 130a or Joüon § 129m.

Form/Structure/Setting

The episode displays a succession of genres to contrast the leaders' policies with Yahweh's revealed strategies. These genres are arranged in a structure that places Yahweh's curse at the crown of an arch.

A A lament over rebellious children who depend on Egypt (vv 1–7)
B An indictment of a rebellious people who are unwilling to heed Yahweh's instruction (vv 8–11)
KEYSTONE Because you reject this word and trust in a tyrant, your guilt becomes a curse (vv 12–14)
B′ Yahweh's word rejected (vv 15–16)
A′ Therefore you are abandoned, helpless; Yahweh's grace waits on justice: "blessed be all who wait on him" (vv 17–18)

The historical setting must be placed before the fall of Assyria (cf. 30:31 and 31:8) but after Egypt had begun to conspire in Palestinian politics. This was a situation that prevailed through most of Josiah's reign.

Comment

1 The complaint about *rebellious children* picks up a theme begun in 1:2. The following sections define the nature of the rebellion. *A plan:* The Vision has consistently avowed that Yahweh has a strategy, a plan, for Israel. The political leaders have one, too. But the strategies differ.

2 The leaders plan an alliance with Egypt. In Ashurbanipal's late reign and in those of his successors, Assyria had become less aggressive. But Psamtik I, Pharaoh of Egypt, increased in power and ambition. Jerusalem's leaders were determined to play the game of power politics, pitting one superpower against the one they thought would be its successor.

3–4 This prediction is seen as false. In solid fact, it was a misjudgment. Egypt's power in Palestine was short-lived. Babylon, not Egypt, was destined to succeed Assyria—and that for just over a half-century.

5 Thus, reliance on Egyptian suzerainty by princes in Egypt as well as by leaders in Jerusalem was *useless, no help,* destined to be *a shame,* and *a disgrace* (note the repetition from v 3). Those who are not willing to be humble will be humiliated by their willful folly.

6 A derisive *burden* or prophecy of judgment pictures the poor *animals* of burden, camels or donkeys, which make up Egypt's caravans in the south of Palestine. They are made to travel through the terrors of wild animals in *the land of trouble and anguish.* The *Negeb* was wilderness and part desert, a wild and rugged terrain. אפעה is a snake. J. J. Hess ("Beduinisches zum Alten und Neuen Testament," *ZAW* 35 [1915] 126) suggested that this is the Uraeus serpent representing Egyptian royalty. Y. Aharoni (*Osiris* 5 [1938] 474) understood it to be a poisonous snake of that region. Wildberger (1162) remarks that the writer could hardly have cared about the exact definition. As for שרף מעופף "flying serpent," שרפים with wings appear in 6:2 around the throne of God. Wildberger (1163) cites Num 21:4–9 which took place in the Negeb. Esarhaddon reported seeing yellow serpents that could fly on his campaign to Egypt (R. Borger, *Die inschriften Asarhaddons, AfO Beiheft* 9 [Graz: Ernst Weidner, 1956], 112). Herodotus (II 75; III 109) reports similar occurrences. J. Feliks (*The Animal World of the Bible* [Tel Aviv: Sinai, 1962], 107) thinks of the cobra which often climbs trees. But there are very few trees in the Negeb. Cf. also O. Keel, *Jahweh-Visionen und Siegelkunst,* SBS 84/85 (Stuttgart: Verlag Katholisches Bibelwerk, 1977), 71.

7 *Rahab* was the name of the mythical monster that ruled chaos (cf. Ps 89:11 [10]). Egypt is called Rahab in Ps 87:4 where she stands beside Babylon (cf. H. J. Kraus, *Psalmen,* BKAT 15/2 [Neukirchen-Vluyn: Neukirchener Verlag, 1978], 604 and Wildberger, 1164). But here Egypt is called by the monster's name only to be doomed to inactivity. Yahweh's word makes her a harmless monster, a dragon who breathes fire and roars, but is in fact innocuous Ps 89:11 [10] tells of Yahweh's victory over Rahab at Creation. She is his opponent now in appearance only.

8–9 Yahweh calls for his accusation against the people to be written down for a *later day.* In a sense, this is exactly what the Vision of Isaiah does. It bears witness to Israel's and Jerusalem's *unwillingness to heed Yahweh's instruction* through all those twelve generations. The call to write fits the larger genre of covenant judgment against Israel based on Yahweh's complaint (1:2). That complaint is repeated for Josiah's generation.

10–11 They tried to still the voices of the prophets so that the will of God would not be presented. Even in Jesus' day he could say: "O Jerusalem, you who kill the prophets" (Matt 23:37).

12 Yahweh's judgment condemns them for rejecting his word. *A perverse tyrant* must refer to the Pharaoh of Egypt.

13–14 The judgment curse is pronounced in a metaphor of a high masonry wall which has begun to bulge in the middle. This guilt will be like that wall. When it collapses, as collapse it must, it will leave behind nothing large enough to be useful. The curse is spoken in masculine plural to the people, or more likely, to the ruling party.

15 The judgment is supported by a repetition of God's word and plan. He had called for retreat and quiet patience, for a heroic restraint and waiting. But the activists in the palace could not wait. They saw in the crumbling decadence of Assyria's imperial power an unparalleled opportunity, especially since Egypt was prepared to encourage them. But their plans were shortsighted, fixed on the immediate goal of relative autonomy for a brief generation (Josiah's reign, 640–609 B.C.). That slight glory would be bought with the price of Jerusalem's complete destruction by the Babylonians in 598 and 587 B.C..

16 The activists refused Yahweh's call to patience and acquiescence. So they tried to flee (presumably to Egypt). But their pursuers were faster.

17 After all their bravado, they broke and ran before the first show of authority appeared. Thus they became a hollow and lonely symbol without meaning or following.

18 So now, Yahweh's mercy for them must wait on justice. The phrase, *rise up to show you mercy,* contains an inner tension. *Rise up* usually refers to Yahweh's rousing himself for war on his enemies. Here it is paired with *to show you mercy.* Yahweh is forced to a violent course of action because Israel refused the quiet course which he had planned, for he is *a God of justice.* The final line is a sigh over what might have been: *Blessed are all who wait for him!* Israel under Josiah had not been willing to do this.

Explanation

This episode in vv 15 and 18 contains two of the clearest expressions of the Vision's message: Yahweh has been calling upon Israel/Judah since the days of Uzziah to accept a passive role in international politics in order to assume a new part as God's spiritual representative, his servant, to the world. This role will be defined in later chapters. He called for a willingness on the nation's part to turn inward to its faith and to rest on God's grace and promises. It would require quietness in the midst of turmoil and trust that God would control the great forces that were devastating the region. That would be a heroism of a very different sort. The final blessing of this episode (v 18) is dedicated to such who wait.

God waits in expectation for Israel (5:2, 4, 7). The prophet Isaiah waited in hope (8:17). In the day of God's salvation, the redeemed will say, "We waited for him and he saved us" (25:9). The righteous say, "We wait for you" (33:2). "Those who wait for the Lord will renew strength" (40:31). "You will know . . . those who wait for me will not be disappointed" (49:23). "Islands wait in hope for (God's) arm" (51:5). Sometimes God does fearful things that are not expected ("waited for") (64:2, [3]). The Vision's presentation of a people who live in hope, waiting for Yahweh, often surprised by Yahweh, comes to a poignant focus in this passage. There is much more here than a reflection of the forward thrust in faith toward a future goal. (Cf. D. A. Hubbard, "Hope in the Old Testament," *TynBul* 34 [1983] 33–59; J. van der Ploeg, "L'esperance dans L'Ancien Testament," *RB* 61 [1954] 481–507; H. W. Wolff, *Anthropology of the Old Testament,* ed. M. Kohl [Philadelphia: Fortress Press, 1974] 149–55; W. Zimmerli, *Man and His Hope in the Old Testament,* SBT, 2nd series, 20 [Naperville, IL: Allenson, 1971] 1–11.) The emphasis in the Vision lies on those who were willing in faith to listen to God and to leave the fulfillment of his vision to him. Israel and Jerusalem were not willing. They insisted on fashioning their own salvation. In this they failed repeatedly, for God's power and God's plan were not part of their actions. In doing this, they confirmed their "rebellion" against God which is documented in this episode.

Episode B: *Hope from the Teachers (30:19–26)*

Bibliography

Bacher, W. "Isaïe, xxx, 21." *REJ* 40 (1900) 248–49. **Laberge, L.** "Is 30:19–26: A Deuteronomic Text?" *EglT* 2 (1971) 35–54.

Translation

First Teacher:	19 *Indeed,*[a] *O people in Zion,*	2+2
	you dweller[b] *in Jerusalem,*	
	you will surely not weep!	2+2
	He will certainly be gracious to you![c]	
	(Responding) to the sound of your cry,	2+2
	as soon as he hears it,[d] *he will answer you.*	
Second Teacher:	20 *Although*[a] *my Lord has given you*	3+2+2
	bread of adversity	
	and water of affliction,	
	your Guide[b] *will no longer hide himself.*[c]	3+4
	Your eyes will be seeing your Guide.[b]	
First Teacher:	21 *And your ears will hear a word*	3+2
	from behind you saying,	
	"This is the way!	2+2
	Walk in it!"	
	when you turn to the right	2+2
	or when you turn to the left.	
Second Teacher:	22 *You shall defile*[a] *your silver-plated images*	4+3
	and your gold-plated idols.	
	You will scatter them like[b] *a contaminated thing.*	3+3
	"Filth!"[c] *you will say of it.*	
First Teacher:	23 *He will give the rain for your seed*	3+2
	(with) which you seed the ground.	
	Bread will come (from) the ground,	3+3
	rich and nutritious.	
	Your sheep will graze	2+2+2
	in that day	
	(in) enlarged pasturage.	
Second Teacher:	24 *The oxen and the asses,*	2+2+3
	that work the ground,	
	will eat prepared fodder	
	which is a winnowing[a]	2+2
	of shovel and pitchfork.	
First Teacher:	25 *On every high mountain*	3+3+3
	and on every raised hill	
	there shall be streams of running water,	

in the day [a] *of great slaughter* 3+2
when towers are falling.
Second Teacher: [26] *The light of the moon shall be like the sun.* 4+4+3
And the light of the sun will be sevenfold
[a] *like the light of the seven days,* [a]
in the day of Yahweh's binding up 3+2+3
the fracture of his people,
when he heals the wound (from) his blow.

Notes

19.a. כי is emphatic. Irwin (88) takes it as a sign of the vocative.

19.b. יֵשֵׁב "he dwells" qal impf (BDB, 442). The word must be a relative clause (Irwin, 88) or be repointed יֹשֵׁב as a ptcp "dweller" as apparently Syr *jāteb* and Tg יתיב have done (cf. *BHS* and Wildberger). The ptcp fits best.

19.c. MT יָחְנְךָ "be gracious to you" is a remarkable form of the impf (cf. GKC § 67n). DSS[Isa] supplies the more usual form יחונך.

19.d. MT כשמעתו "according to his hearing" is a fem inf constr (GKC § 45d). DSS[Isa] שמועה is the more usual noun form.

20.a. The relation to the previous verse suggests that the clause be read conditionally or as a concession (cf. RSV).

20.b. מוריך "your Guide" (BDB, 435) comes from ירה "throw, cast, direct, instruct." Irwin (90) draws on the context and the use in Hos 10:12 "rain down" to translate "Rain-giver." Perhaps it is a double entendre with a play on both meanings. The following lines support the translation "Guide."

20.c. יכנף "hide himself" (BDB, 489) is a *hapax legomenon* derived from a noun meaning "wing." Irwin (91) draws on a Ugaritic text to translate "lift wing." But his interpretation stretches the entire text beyond reason.

22.a. LXX[BS*] *καὶ μιανεῖς* "you will defile" (as well as LXX[AQS^c] *καὶ ἐξαρεῖς* "you will drive out") is sg, as are OL and Vg. But the entire passage moves from a collective sg back to pl. There is no reason to change MT in spite of the following sg pronouns.

22.b. LXX *ὡς ὕδωρ* "like water" reads כמי for MT כמו. If one takes the LXX reading then תזרם should be understood from זרם "pour in a flood" (BDB, 281). The stich would read "you will pour forth filth like water." But MT makes sense and may be kept.

22.c. צֵא is frequently understood (Fohrer, Kaiser) as qal impv from יצא "go out" (BDB, 422). The parallel calls for it to be like דוה "contaminated thing." *BHK* suggests צואה "excrement" to keep the fem parallel. *BHS* repoints as צֹוא which probably has the same meaning. G. R. Driver (*ZAW* 77 [1958] 45) agrees with *BHK* and derives צא from צוא "filth" or "excrement" (BDB, 844; *CHAL*, 301). This meaning fits the text and context (cf. LXX *κόπρον* "dung, manure," and the Versions).

24.a. זֹרֶה is a qal act ptcp (BDB, 279; GKC, p. 525). If it is kept, it may be understood as a constr and one must translate "which is a winnowing of." DSS[Isa] יזרה turns it into an impf, also active. Most translators point it זֹרָה as a pual pf "is winnowed."

25.a. LXX *ἐν τῇ ἡμέρᾳ ἐκείνῃ* "in that day" for MT ביום "in the day." Wildberger (1192) remarks that this emphasizes the eschatological understanding of it.

26.a-a. LXX omits. Commentators have generally viewed it as a gloss (cf. *BHS*). It is a kind of comment. But there is no hint as to when it was inserted. It may well have been original. Irwin (96) defends it on metrical grounds.

Form/Structure/Setting

The setting of the episode is a place where teachers are to be found, perhaps a corner of the temple court or a schoolroom. It does not deal with the issues of the previous episode, nor are the teachers aware of the matters which dominated the confrontation between Yahweh and the political leaders.

This little homily on assurance and hope is presented in a style not unlike the teaching of the Wise or the admonitions of the Deuteronomists. It addresses the pilgrims in Jerusalem. It recognizes that past times have been difficult (v 20), but assures that better times are coming.

The entire mood and tone are mild and calm. The sermon is built in an arch capped by a version of the second commandment (v 22):

A Good news for Jerusalem: your gracious Guide responds to you (vv 19–20)
B Your Guide teaches: This is the way! Walk in it! (v 21)
KEYSTONE Defile and get rid of your idols (v 22)
B′ Your Guide provides rain and blessing even through crisis (vv 23–25)
A′ In that beautiful day Yahweh heals his people (v 26)

Comment

19 The repeated addresses *people in Zion* and *in Jerusalem* are to be distinguished from "people of Jerusalem." They are those who are gathered in Jerusalem for the festival, not those who live there. *Not weep* directs the episode away from lament. *Your cry* is a cry for help such as would come from a people in distress (Wildberger, 1196). In 15:8 it was Moab's cry for help. Ps 22:6 (5) cites the patriarch's cry which God answered (cf. also Pss 107:13 and 142:2, 6). A lament pleads with God to answer. This verse assures the plaintiff of his response.

20a Like Ps 107, this verse recalls the trials of Israel in the wilderness when hunger and thirst were major problems. God sent manna to eat (Exod 16:12, 15, etc.) and water from the rock. Wildberger (1189) supplies the word "without" to make the lines conform to this sense of assurance. This is unnecessary and wrong. The verse acknowledges the distress that has been the people's lot (see *Note* 20.a.). *Bread of adversity* and *water of affliction* are provisions for prisoners (cf. 1 Kgs 22:27). The bad times are seen to have been like a prison sentence from God.

20b מוֹרֶיךָ "your Guide" is unique as a name for Yahweh (cf. Wildberger, 1197). In Gen 12:6 and Deut 11:30 "the oak(s) of Moreh" uses the term. But the meaning there is obscure. The verb ירה in hiphil is used of God teaching his people in 2:3 and 28:26. His teaching can be called תורה "torah" or "instruction" (Pss 25:8; 94:12).

לא־יכנף עוד "no longer hide himself" recognizes periods when God's guiding, instructing presence has not been sensed. It promises that this will no longer be true. The idea of God's withdrawal appears in Exod 19:21; 20:21–23. This is explained in some places by the brilliance of his glory which a person could not survive (cf. Isa 6:5). But it is also understood in terms of deliberate withdrawal. Yahweh is called "A God who hides himself" (45:15), and psalmists plead for him not to hide his face from them (Pss 27:9; 102:3 [2]; 143:7). Ps 44:25 [24] asks why he hides his face from his people. Job acutely experienced God's absence and silence. The OT understands that God's presence is not simply a fact of existence, presumed to be universal and constant. It is a gracious and deliberate gift offered by God which is to be welcomed and recognized as such.

In Judaism from Ezra on, the Torah functioned to teach the people. But in the Vision this is done by the instructing, guiding presence of Yahweh with his people (cf. 2:3). *Seeing* God and hearing his voice in instruction are understood to be ways of knowing and experiencing his presence.

21 God's words are like those a shepherd speaks *from behind,* keeping his flock on the path.

22 The anticipated presence of the Guide makes urgent the need to rid the place of *idols.* Such were often plated with *silver* or *gold.* The role of idols to represent God's presence is understood here. The true presence of God among his people removes the need for artificial symbols.

23 Palestinian agriculture is totally dependent on *rain.* Yahweh claims to be able to give and to withhold rain (Amos 4:7; Isa 5:6; 2 Kgs 8:1; Deut 11:13; 28:12).

24 בליל חמיץ "prepared fodder" is a unique and obscure phrase. *BDB* (330) translates "seasoned." L. Köhler ("בליל חמיץ Jes 30,24," *ZAW* 40 [1922] 15–17) identified חמיץ as "sorrel," a plant with a sharp taste. The text implies a favored food for cattle. בליל implies a treatment of some kind.

25 *Streams* on the heights suggests abundance of water. *Great slaughter* and *towers . . . falling* set the scene in a time of war when destruction is commonplace and expected.

26 The effect of the *sun* and the *moon* is felt for the great day. Moderns would be appalled at the thought of a seven-fold increase in the sun's heat and light. The intention here is symbolic of participation by the cosmos which is also a part of Yahweh's realm. 24:23 had pictured an opposite reaction where the sun and moon were ashamed (became pale) before the Lord's glory.

Yahweh's healing work will be applied to his people's wounds, even to those which his punishment had caused. The idea that God punishes but also heals is found in Deut 32:39; Job 5:18; and Hos 6:1.

Explanation

The implied hearers within the Vision are despondent pilgrims in Jerusalem. With heightened political tensions, the threat of war, and prophetic teachings that Yahweh has sent the wars against them, they tended to despair of Yahweh's help and goodness.

The passage is a classic example of an assuring homily in the wisdom/deuteronomic style. The gracious, healing, guiding nature of God is certain and dominant. The name for God which is most prominent is "your Guide" (v 20). Because God is responsive, his people need not weep (v 19). Past afflictions and trials should not cloud the hope that God will again appear to guide his people (v 20). God's presence is a gentle reminder of "the way" whenever they are tempted to stray (v 21) and is a strong admonition against idolatry (v 22). God provides what is needed for the farmer and the herder (vv 24). The basic understanding of Yahweh's role in bringing rain to Palestine is dominant here, as it is in Deuteronomy. The blessing of rain will be abundant enough to provide streams on the mountaintops (v 25a).

Only v 25b gives a hint that the episode is set in a time of turmoil and war. This stressful factor is otherwise ignored. But the distress and wounds are recognized in v 20a and in 26b. In both instances Yahweh's responsibility for the people's hurt is recognized. Yet the positive message of God's grace, his providential guidance, the gift of rain, and the healing of his people's hurt dominate all else. One strong demand is clear: Get rid of the idols! (v 22; cf. John's final plea to his fledgling church, 1 John 5:21).

Episode C: A Cultic Theophany (30:27–33)

Bibliography

Ginsberg, H. L. "An Obscure Hebrew Word." *JQR* 22 (1931) 143–45. **Gordis, R.** "Midrash in the Prophets." *JBL* 49 (1930) 421–22. **Guillaume, A.** "Isaiah's Oracle against Assyria (Isaiah 30:27–33) in the Light of Archaeology." *BSO(A)S* 17 (1956) 413–15. **Milgrom, J.** "An Alleged Wave-Offering in Israel and in the Ancient Near East." *IEJ* 22 (1972) 33–38. **Sabottka, L.** "Is. 30, 27–33: Ein Übersetzungsvorschlag." *BZ* 12 (1968) 241–45.

Translation

First Prophet: 27 *See the Name of Yahweh,* 2+2
coming from a distance,
his anger burning, 2+2
[a] *his liver raging,* [a]
his lips are full of indignation 3+3+3
and his tongue devouring like fire,
28 *and his breath* [a] *like an overflowing stream,* [b]
(which) reaches [c] *to the neck* 2+2+2
to signal [d] *nations*
with a signal for destruction [e]
and a restricting bridle 2+3
on [f] *the jaws of* [g] *peoples.*

Second Prophet: 29 *This song will be yours* 3+2
like a night (when) one celebrates a festival,
when the heart's gladness starts when a flute (plays), 4+4
in approaching the mountain of Yahweh, to the Rock [a] *of Israel.*

First Prophet: 30 *When Yahweh makes the majesty of his voice heard* 4+3
and his descending [a] *arm seen*

with raging anger 2+3
and a flame of devouring fire,
a cloudburst, a storm, 2+2
and hailstones.
Second Prophet: 31 *For at* [a] *the sound of Yahweh* 2+2+2
Assyria will be broken—
the very rod (with which) he strikes.
First Prophet: 32 *When it shall be:* 1
every stroke of the appointed [a] *staff* 4+4
which Yahweh lays on it (will be)
(accompanied) by timbrels and by lyres 2+2+2
and a battle-wave-offering, [b]
(the kind) with which [c] *he sets out to battle.*
Second Prophet: 33 *For a funeral pyre* [a] *(was) being prepared days ago.* [b] 3+3
This particular one has been made ready for the king. [c]
Deep he made (it). Wide he made (it). 2+2+2
Its pyre (for) fire,
and wood aplenty.
First Prophet: *Yahweh's breath,* 2+2+2
like a stream of lava,
(will be) kindling it.

Notes

27.a-a. משאה may have a range of meanings from "burden" to "utterance" to "smoke" which might relate to נשא "lift up." Θ Syr Tg Vg related it to the basic meaning of כבד to translate "burdensome is his oracle." Wildberger (1208) recommends staying with "burden." Hummel ("Enclitic *Mem* in Early Northwest Semitic," *JBL* 76 [1957] 100) proposed emending וּכְבֵדוֹ־ם שֹׁאָה (adding a *waw* parallel to אפו "his anger," separating enclitic *mem,* and reading *sin* שׂ as *shin* שׁ) "his liver raging" which is followed by Irwin (97) saying "27–28 read like an anatomy handbook." The emendation is very attractive, since no other form fits the context.

28.a. This entire verse is deliberately ambiguous beginning with רוחו: "his breath" if seen as a third of the parts of Yahweh, "his spirit" if seen as a contrasting picture of God.

28.b. נחל is the second ambiguous term: "stream" (BDB, 636) or "portion, inheritance" (BDB, 635, usually fem).

28.c. יחצה (BDB, 345) is the third ambiguity: "reaches to" if the former is "stream," "apportioned" if it is "inheritance."

28.d. נפה (BDB, 631) means "wave, swing back and forth," which may refer to water's action or to the liturgical "wave-offering."

28.e. שוא may mean "destruction" (BDB, 996, usually fem) or "emptiness" (BDB, 996).

28.f. עַל is usually seen as the preposition "upon" (BDB, 752). However, a change of vowel produces עֹל "yoke" (BDB, 760) parallel to "bridle."

28.g. לחיי is usually read as "jaws of" (BDB, 534). However, if על is read as a noun, the possibility opens for ל to be a preposition and חיי to be "lives (or life) of."

29.a. For צור "rock," LXX πρὸς τὸν θεὸν "before God"; Θ φυλακα "guard"; 'A στερεον "firm, steadfast" Σ κραταιον "strong one." But the Heb is a regular designation for Yahweh.

30.a. נחת "descending." LXX τὸν θυμὸν "the anger"; Σ την επαναπαυσιν "rest upon"; Vg *terrorem* "dread." The word is a *hapax* meaning "descend, sink down" (BDB, 639).

31.a. Cf. M. Dahood ("Ugaritic-Hebrew Syntax and Style," *UF* 1 [1969] 19) for an analysis of the syntax of which Irwin (102) has made use.

32.a. MT מוסדה "appointment" (BDB, 414); DSS[Isa] מוסדו "his appointment." Some MSS (*BHS*) read מוסרה "his chastisement" from יסר (BDB, 415–16).

32.b. תנופה may mean a "wave-offering." Irwin (104) compares this to 19:16 and Exod 20:25 to translate "the slashing stroke." The issue is whether this describes a liturgy or a realistic battle.

32.c. בה "against her." Assyria was addressed as masc before. Irwin (104) makes the pronoun refer to תנופה "wave-offering."

33.a. תָּפְתֶּה "funeral pyre" is a form unexplained. A suggestion by Procksch (cf. *BHS*) proposes to read תָּפְתֹּה which has a dative force. This Irwin (105) translates "Topheth for him."

33.b. אתמול means "yesterday." LXX *πρὸ ἡμερῶν* and Syr *mn ḳdm jwmtʾ* are something like "days ago" (cf. Wildberger, 1210).

33.c. O. Eissfeldt (*MOLK als Opferbegriff im Punischen und im Hebräischen und das Ende des Gottes Moloch* [Halle: Niemeyer, 1935] 45; cf. also M. Weinfeld, "The Worship of MOLECH and the Queen of Heaven and its background," *UF* 4 [1972] 133–54) suggested removing the article to read "to Molech," a view rejected by Wildberger (1210) and Irwin (105) but recognized by Kaiser.

Form/Structure/Setting

This episode parodies cultic ceremonies of Yahweh's coming in the Zion festival. Vv 27–28 portray the coming of the Name of Yahweh from afar, burning with anger against the nations. They employ six anthropomorphic terms:

Name of Yahweh	coming from a distance
His anger	burning
His liver	raging
His lips	full of indignation
His tongue	devouring like fire
His breath	like a stream
	a signal to the nations
	a bridle for the peoples

Vv 29–33b turn to the people's response and to the historical consequences that are promised. Yahweh's coming will occasion a song like festival songs of old when Israel climbed toward Jerusalem to worship Yahweh, "the Rock of Israel," and witnessed the drama of Yahweh acting in the storm (v 30) and the cultic punishment he meted out, portrayed in v 32 by musical accompaniment.

But the real joy of the worshiping people is occasioned by historical events which mirror the festival drama. Assyria will fall (v 31) and her king will be buried (v 33ab). V 33c returns to the theme of theophany. Yahweh's anger lights the funeral pyre of the Assyrian king.

The theophany account is a careful literary construction in two movements. The ten anthropomorphic references (six in vv 27–28, three in vv 30–31, one in v 33) center in the storm figure of vv 30–31. The "voice of Yahweh" occurs twice, while reference to "his descending arm" comes between them. This is the keystone of the arch. Yahweh's act ("his arm") has descriptions of his emotions before (vv 27–28) and after (v 33).

A second element of the structure consists of words related to fire: "burning" (vv 27, 33), "like a devouring fire" (vv 27, 30, 33), "like a stream" (vv 28, 33), and words of similar sound or letters (vv 28, 32).

The artistry of the composition lies in the choice and arrangement of words.

Comment

27 *The Name of Yahweh.* Wildberger (1216) and others have argued that the formula must read "See Yahweh coming" like Isa 26:21; 40:10; 66:15; Pss 96:13; 98:9; Deut 33:2; and Hab 3:3. *The Name of Yahweh* is usually the object of worship or veneration. This usage is unique. Apparently the *Name* here is like the "Glory" in Ezek 1:28 and passim, intended to represent Yahweh himself.

A theophany usually tells where Yahweh is coming from: Seir/Edom (Judg 5:4), Teman/Mountains of Paran (Hab 3:3), Sinai (Deut 33:2), the Heavens (Mic 1:3; Isa 26:21; 63:19; Jer 25:30; Pss 18:10, 144:5), Zion (Amos 1:2; Ps 50:2), stormwind from the north (Ezek 1:4). The phrase *from a distance* is unique. Common to all of these is the recognition that Yahweh is not bound to any place. He comes when and where he chooses.

Anger speaks of Yahweh's motivation. Wildberger (1218) notes that אף also means "nostril," which fits the list of anatomical terms used. Concerning the use of "liver" for the expression of anger, see H. W. Wolff, *Anthropology of the Old Testament* (Philadelphia: Fortress, 1974), 64.

28 The object of God's anger is the *nations/peoples.* In 17:2 and 29:7 the plural was used to describe military actions involving Assyria. Its army was composed of different ethnic units. This may be true here, as well. *Signal* is usually used with יד "hand" as in 11:15 and 13:2. Here it appears in a mixed metaphor with *bridle.* God's intervention will rein in Assyria's power and lead to its destruction (v 31).

29 The theophany is set in a *festival.* It is to be understood as the festal drama of Zion's New Year. Its purpose is clear from the name used for God: *The Rock of Israel.* It stressed assurance that Yahweh will defend and care for his people.

30 The theophany turns to the picture of the *storm* revealing God's voice and act: "his *arm descending*" for deliverance. The storm god with raised arm is a familar motif in ANE art (cf. *ANEP* 481, 484, 486, 490, 531, 532). Storm imagery is frequently used in the Psalms (Pss 18:13; 46:3; 68:3, 7–9; 77:18).

31 The name *Assyria* gives political focus to the theophany. It anticipates the break-up of the empire. In 10:5 Yahweh called Assyria "the rod of his anger." Here Assyria's destruction is announced. ב here must be construed as indicating more precisely what will be broken up (BDB, 88, I.7). יכה "he strikes" follows with no particle. Yet it must be a contact relative clause. Hence the translation *with which he strikes.* Yahweh is the implied subject. The very passage that acknowledges Assyria to be Yahweh's agent had announced that he would, in time, also determine Assyria's fate (10:12). In this episode that day has come.

32 The verse announces the identity of Yahweh, celebrated in Jerusalem's worship, with God who controls the giants of history. Every military blow against Assyria will coincide with representations in the temple's worship.

33 The reference to the king's funeral is parallel to chap. 14. The context suggests that תפתה "funeral-pyre" is related to a ceremony for the dead. Cremation was not usual in Palestine nor, as far as is known, in Mesopotamia, although it is documented for military funerals in Greece and is the usual means of dealing with bodies as far east as India. When the OT speaks of burning bodies it is taken as a sign of vengeance or degradation (cf. 1 Sam 31:12; Amos 6:10; Lev 20:14; 21:9; Josh 7:25; *ISBE* 1:812; *IDB* 1:475). The passage eloquently celebrates the fact that the king is dead. The motif of fire is continued in Yahweh's fiery breath that ignites the funeral pyre. That is reminiscent of fire from heaven devouring Elijah's altar on Carmel (1 Kgs 18:38).

Explanation

Themes from cultic drama and theophany have been blended to shape a powerful episode (Jörg Jeremias, *Theophanie. Die Geschichte einer alttestamentlichen Gattung* [Neukirchen-Vluyn: Neukirchener Verlag, 1965] 57). Within the Vision, it, like Episode B, shows religious attempts to counter the message of Episode A. Like the prophets of salvation who opposed Jeremiah, the teachers and the theophanic prophets salve the worries of the people, preventing them from facing up to the hard political decisions. This is how religious assurance can in fact be "an opiate for the people."

Scene 4: Disaster from False Faith in Egypt (31:1—32:20)

The scene centers on the criticism of those whose policy calls for dependence upon Egypt to gain independence from Assyria. Political scheming ignores God's determination of events which the drama's previous acts have portrayed. The first episode of Scene 4, "Woe to Those Depending on Egypt!" (31:1–9), is a dialogue about political leaders who prefer human dependence on alliances to dependence on an alliance with God. The second episode, "Suppose a King" (32:1–8), is a lesson in civic righteousness from the teachers. In the third episode, "Palace Forsaken—Spirit Poured Out" (32:9–20), a dialogue takes place between a speaker and a group of women that contrasts their prosperity with the devastation to come in "less than a year."

Episode A: "Woe to Those Who Depend on Egypt!" (31:1–9)

Bibliography

Geers, H. "Hebrew Textual Notes." *AJSL* 34 (1917) 133–34. **Hempel, J.** "Jahwegleichnisse der israelitischen Propheten." *Apoxysmata.* BZAW 81. Berlin: Töpelmann (1961) 1–29.

Translation

Heavens: [1] *Woe! Those going down to Egypt*[a] *for help,* 4+2
(who) rely[b] *on horses.*
They trust[c] *in a chariot that is big* 4+4
and upon horsemen[d] *that are very strong.*
They do not look to the Holy One of Israel, 4+3
nor do they seek Yahweh.
Earth: [2] *And indeed he is the Wise One.* 3+2+3
He achieves (his) purpose[a]
and does not retract his words.
He will rise up against the house of the wicked 3+3
and against those who help evil-doers.
Heavens: [3] *Egypt (is) human,* 2+2
not God![a]
Their horses (are) flesh, 2+2
not spirit![b]
When Yahweh stretches out his hand, 3+4+3
the helper will stumble, the one helped will fall.
They will all be finished off together.
Earth: [4] *For Yahweh said thus to me:* 4
"Just as the lion growls, 3+2
or the young lion, over his prey
when a band of shepherds 3+2
is called out against him,
he is not terrified by their voice 3+3
nor is he daunted by their noises."
So Yahweh of Hosts will descend 4+4+2
to fight upon Mt. Zion
and on its hill.
Heavens: [5] *Like birds hovering,* 2+4+2
so [a]*Yahweh of Hosts*[a] *will provide cover*
over Jerusalem.
Protecting, he will deliver![b] 2+2
Sparing, he will rescue![c]
Earth: [6] *Turn*[a] *to him,* 1+3+2
(to Jerusalem) *against whom Israel's sons*[b]
have rebelled so deeply.[c]
Heavens: [7] *For in this day* 3+4+2
they would reject, each his silver[a] *idols,*
his gold[a] *idols,*
(aside to Jerusalem) *which your sinful*[b] *hands have (also) made for yourselves.* 5
Yahweh: [8] *Assyria will fall by a sword, not by a person,*[a] 4+3
and a sword—not a human being[a] *—will devour it.*
Someone may flee to it[b] *from before a sword,* 4+3
but its choice soldiers will become slaves.[c]

[9] *Its rock* [a] *will disappear because of terror.* 3+3
Its officers will desert at sight of a battle-flag. [b]
Herald: *Expression of Yahweh* 2+3+3
whose fire (*is*) *in Zion*
and whose furnace (*is*) *in Jerusalem.*

Notes

1.a. DSS[Isa] למצרים "to Egypt" uses a preposition in place of MT's adverbial accusative.
1.b. LXX *πεποιθότες* "depending on."
1.c. LXX omits.
1.d. Or "horses" which pull the chariots.
2.a. Reading with Irwin (111) רֵעַ "purpose" (BDB, 946, III) for MT רָע "disaster."
3.a. Tg רב "noble, prince."
3.b. LXX *καὶ οὐκ ἔστι βοήθεια* "and it is no help."
5.a-a. LXX omits.
5.b. *BHS* follows Vg *liberans* to read וְהַצֵּיל hiph inf abs "delivering" for MT וְהִצִּיל hiph pf 3 m sg "he will deliver." Follow MT.
5.c. DSS[Isa] הפליט "cause to escape, make secure" for MT המליט "he will rescue." Vg again suggests inf abs. Follow MT.
6.a שובו "turn" is 2nd person while the following clause is 3rd person causing *BHS* to suggest a 3rd person jussive וישובו "and let them turn." The variation continues through the verse (cf. Joüon § 158n). This is not unusual. Sabottka (*Zephanja* [Rome: Pont. Bib. Inst., 1972], 66) cites parallels in Zeph 2:3; Mic 3:3, 9; Isa 54:1; Jer 5:21.
6.b. LXX omits. "Sons" is sometimes viewed as the one addressed by "turn." But Irwin (115) is nearer right in seeing it as the subject of the second verb.
6.c. העמיקו hiph pf 3 c pl "they made deep." The word is used for the grave in 30:33, for the plans of the government in 29:15, and for the sign to be proposed in 7:11. The figurative speech here in relation to סרה "rebellion" refers to their determination.
7.a. LXX omits the pronouns. But MT is in order when the pronouns are related to the dominant word in the constr relation: not "the idols of his silver," but "his silver idols" (cf. J. Weingreen, "The Construct-Genitive Relation in Hebrew Syntax," *VT* 4 [1954] 50–59).
7.b. LXX Ethiopic and Arabic versions omit. Various commentators have trouble fitting חֵטְא "sinful" into the sentence. Wildberger (1237) considers it a gloss. Irwin (116) follows M. Dahood ("Ugaritic-Hebrew Syntax and Style," *UF* 1 [1969] 30–31) in considering ידיכם חטא to be "a construct chain with intervening suffix." He translates "your sinful hands."
8.a. See Joüon § 160k on contrary statements.
8.b. לו "to it." DSS[Isa] ולוא, LXX *οὐκ*, Vg *non* all read it as לא "not." They have missed the contrast. Wildberger (1237) notes that "they all flee the sword, but not that of humans."
8.c. LXX *ἥττημα* "defeat." But ʼΑ Σ Θ agree on *φορον* "gift, tribute" which is an imprecise rendition of MT מס "slaves" (cf. Judg 1:30, 35; Prov 12:24; Lam 1:1) or "subject to forced labor" (BDB, 586).
9.a. The use is ironic and may refer to the Assyrian god (cf. Deut 32:2; Num 14:9).
9.b. LXX *ὁ δὲ φεύγων*, Vg *fugientes* "fleeing one(s), fugitive(s)." They have read נָס from נוס "flee." But נֵס means "standard, flag" (BDB, 651) and is quite suitable here. G. R. Driver (*JTS* 38 [1937] 45) suggests the meaning "trembling, quivering," but the usual meaning should be kept. מן may mean "because of" or it may mean "away from." The first meaning suggests "because of a flag (the enemy's)." The second "from the flag (their own)." The parallel supports the first.

Form/Structure/Setting

The fourth "woe" begins a dialogue about the fate of a city whose political leaders continue to make political decisions without reference to Yahweh's decisions concerning the direction history is to take. The speakers can't believe that they prefer human political alliances when an alliance with Yahweh is possible. A parable (or simile) is used in v 4 to describe Yahweh's protection of Jerusalem with a parallel simile in v 5. The challenge to repent (v 6) is set against Israel's previous apostasy which had taken place under very different circumstances (v 7). The climax is reached in Yahweh's announcement of the fall of Assyria (vv 8–9).

The setting of the episode is the familiar "balcony of Heaven" from which Yahweh and his aides view and discuss Israel and the world.

Comment

1 *Woe* expresses distress over the situation in Jerusalem. In Assyria's declining years, Jerusalem's leaders cast about for political alliances that will help them profit from that collapse. Egypt seems to be the best support for their aims. They have not looked for God's goals, yet only he is dependable and sure. They fail to appreciate the advantage of divine assistance over human promises.

2–3 Note the contrast between divine and human plans and powers:

Egypt is human—not God!
Their horses are flesh—not spirit!

Egypt is not reliable. It must often break its promises and fail to reach its goals. Beyond that Egypt has not been chosen to play the key role in this period of history. But God! He is רוח "spirit," not בשר "flesh." The words do not define God's essence. But in *flesh* they do summarize the totality of human finitude. God is beyond that. He is constant. He achieves his רָע "purpose," and his strategy. Yet humankind, like Jerusalem here, prefers its own crutches to dependence upon God. It seals its own doom, for

When Yahweh stretches out his hand
the helper will stumble, the one helped will fall.
They will all be finished together!

4 The *lion's* self-assured and undeterred attention to his purpose is a parable of Yahweh's intention to protect Zion. The *noise* and disturbance of international upheavals will not deter him.

5 The figure is changed but the assurance of Yahweh's protection is even stronger. This promise fits the period and holds for the immediate future. Yet the reader is aware that Jerusalem is destroyed in the next generation.

6–7 Sentences in second person plural are apparently addressed to seventh-century Jerusalem. The rest of the verses are in third person plural form referring to eighth-century Israelites. The comparison is intentional. Israel's apostasy in the eighth-century (1:2–7; 2:6–8; 5:8–25; 9:8–10:4) had occurred during Assyria's rise to power. Even then their attitude had been inexcusable. But now, Assyria is weak and near collapse. The day which 10:20–21 had foretold is near at hand when Israel will be forced to recognize how useless their idols are. Instead Jerusalem's leaders are determined to adopt an idolatrous political course. They are challenged to repudiate it.

8–9 Yahweh's announcement is dramatic: Assyria is about to fall. *A sword—not a person* is explained by what follows. The morale of the army is deteriorating. Its *choice troops* are its elite core, the *rock* of its military prowess. Its officers will desert and disappear. And the power that Assyria once represented will be gone. Yahweh, whose awesome seat of power is in Zion, announces this. The references to *fire* and *furnace* recall the burning anger of 30:27–33, yet the political leaders are apparently oblivious of him and his announcement.

Episode B: Suppose a King . . . (32:1–8)

Bibliography

Becker, J. *Messianic Expectation in the Old Testament.* Tr. D. E. Green. Philadelphia: Fortress, 1980. 71. **Gerleman, G.** "Der Nicht-Mensch. Erwägungen zur hebräischen Wurzel NBL." *VT* 24 (1974) 147–58. **Hermisson, H. J.** "Zunkunftserwartung und Gegenwartskritik." *EvT* 33 (1973) 54–77. **Hertzberg, H-W.** "Die Nachgeschichte alttestamentlicher Texte innerhalb des Alten Testaments." *Beiträge zur Traditionsgeschichte und Theologie des Alten Testaments.* Göttingen: Vandenhoeck & Ruprecht, 1962. 69–80. **(Hr᾽l, M.)** מנשה הראל. "נופי מדבר בנבואת ישעיהו." *BMik* 29 (1966) 79–82. **Labuschagne, C. J.** "The Particles הֵן and הִנֵּה." *OTS* 18 (1973) 1–14. **Stade, B.** "Jes. 32, 33." *ZAW* 4 (1884) 256–71. **Stansell, G.** "Isaiah 32: Creative Redaction in the Isaian Traditions." *SBL Seminar Papers.* Chico, CA: Scholars Press, 1983. 1–12.

Translation

Teacher: 1 *Suppose* [a] *a king should reign with righteousness* 4+3
and likewise [b] *princes should rule with justice.*
Student: 2 *Then each would be like a refuge from wind* 4+2
(reciting) *and a shelter* [a] *from a storm,*
like streams of water in a dry place, [b] 3+3+2
like the shade of a massive rock
in a parched land.
Teacher: 3 *And if* [a] *the eyes of those who see should look* 4+3
and the ears of those who hear should hearken
4 *and the mind of the hurried have sense to know* 4+5
and the tongue of stammerers speak fluently,
Student: 5 *then a fool would no longer be called noble* [a] 4+4
nor a knave [b] *be called honorable.*
Second Student: 6 *For a fool speaks folly* 3+3
and his mind does [a] *wickedness*
to practice ungodliness 2+3
and to speak error toward Yahweh,
leaving the hungry with an empty stomach [b] 3+3
and denying the thirsty a drink.
Third Student: 7 *The weapons of the knave* [a] *are evil.* 3+3
He plots evil plans

to ruin the poor [b] *by deceitful words* 4+3
[c] *and by slandering the needy in court.* [c]
Fourth Student: 8 *But a noble one* [a] *plans noble things* 3+3
and takes his stand upon noble things.

Notes

1.a. הֵן is usually translated "behold, see." But now Kissane and Scott, followed by Irwin (120), propose reading it as hypothetical (BDB, 243). This changes the genre to wisdom instruction and may be compared to Job 34:18–19 where a similar grouping of words occurs.

1.b. LXX *καὶ ἄρχοντες* "and rulers," and Syr Tg Vg leave out ל, which Wildberger (1250), *BHK* and *BHS* also recommend. F. Nötscher ("Zum emphatischen Lamed," *VT* 3 [1953] 380) suggested that this is an "emphatic ל." Irwin (120) seems to follow Nötscher, translating "likewise."

2.a. DSS[Isa] וסתרם "their shelter," i.e., adds *mem.* This has led to guesses that *mem* belongs before the next word to produce "from": LXX *ὡς ἀφ' ὕδατος* "as from water" and Vg *a tempestate* "from a storm" (cf. *BHK, BHS*). "From" is necessary to make English sense, as indeed Greek or Latin, but was not necessary in Hebrew.

2.b. בְּצָיוֹן "in a dry place" (BDB, 851). Another pointing produces "in Zion" as LXX *ἐν Σιων* reads it. MT is correct (cf. 25:5).

3.a. MT לא "not" is difficult to fit here, leading Σ *αμαυρωθησονται* and Vg *caligabunt* "will become dim" to think of the Heb שעע and *BHK* and *BHS* to vocalize תִּשְׁעֶינָה qal or תֻּשְׁעֶינָה hoph "they were smeared shut, blinded." However, if הֵן in v 1 is read as a conditional particle, then reading לוֹ for לא would produce a parallel hypothetical sentence here, as Irwin (121) proposes, and the problem is solved.

5.a. נדיב "noble" (BDB, 622). M. Dahood compares a similar combination of the meanings "noble" with "willing, generous" ("Hebrew-Ugaritic Lexicography," *Bib* 48 [1948] 436–37; and the discussion in Irwin, 122).

5.b. כילי "knave" (BDB, 647) appears only here (and perhaps v 7). Duhm (quoted by Wildberger, 1250) writes that the rabbis derived the word from כוּל and translated "miser." Hitzig derived it from כָּלָה and translated "waster," while most derive it (as does BDB) from נכל "a swindler, knave." Now Irwin (123) takes it as masc pl from כליות "kidneys" (BDB, 480) to get the translation "his mind" to parallel "heart" in the next line. The translation "knave, swindler" remains the best.

6.a. LXX *νοήσει* and Tg מתעשתין appear to support DSS[Isa] חושב "devise, think." But H. M. Orlinsky ("The St. Mark's Isaiah Scroll," *JBL* 69 [1950] 152–55), Kutscher (*Isaiah Scroll,* 239), and J. R. Rosenbloom (*The Dead Sea Scroll of Isaiah* [Grand Rapids, MI: Eerdmans, 1970] 40) warn that LXX usually translates חשב with *λογίζεσθαι* "to reckon." MT makes sense as it is.

6.b. נפש "stomach" as the seat of hunger (BDB, 660 § 5).

7.a. כלי כליו taking the meaning discussed in 5.b. "his kidney of kidneys," as in the phrase "heart of hearts" (cf. Irwin, 125, who translates "his inmost mind"); Wildberger (1249) "the weapons of the knave." It remains a difficult word-pair.

7.b. K ענוים is a synonym for Q עניים. Both mean "poor, humble."

7.c-c. ובדבר אביון משפט, lit., "and by a word the needy justice" is difficult. M. Dahood (*Proverbs and North-West Semitic Philology* [Rome: Pont. Bib. Inst., 1963] 39) suggests "in driving the poor from court." G. R. Driver (*ZAW* 11 [1934] 56) "by driving (out of court) the poor in judgment." Irwin (125) translates "and by slandering the needy in court" referring to BDB, 182b.

8.a. LXX *εὐσεβεῖς* "pious ones" which Wildberger (1251) discounts as one of its favorite words.

Form/Structure/Setting

The teachers are back on stage with a lesson in civics. They offer a series of definitions. Their scholarly detachment is broken only once: in v 5 with לא . . . עוד "no longer." In that phrase they imply that their clear definitions are blurred in their own society.

The episode may be analyzed in two ways. One could see the passage as an arch with v 5 as the keystone:

A King/princes = righteousness and justice (v 1)
  B Resultant security and prosperity (v 2)
    C If eyes, ears, minds, and tongues of public function (vv 3–4)
KEYSTONE Then no more confusion of fools and nobility, of knaves and persons of honor (v 5)
    C′ For a fool speaks folly (v 6)
  B′ A knave plots evil plans (v 7)
A′ Nobility plans noble things (v 8)

Or, the passage may be analyzed as a series of definitions:

1. Kings and princes should be associated with righteousness and justice. They should serve like shelters and refreshing streams (vv 1–2).

2. The public should be able to see, to hear, to know, and to speak, so that the character of public officials is known and judged accordingly (vv 3–5).

3. For the character of the fool is marked by folly, wickedness, ungodliness, and error. This feeds no one, provides water to no one (the opposite of v 2b) (v 6).

4. The character of the knave is equally transparent: evil, deceitful, and slanderous. This results in a deceitful and oppressive government (the opposite of justice and righteousness, v 1) (v 7).

5. The character of nobility is equally clear. It can be seen in the nature of the plans presented and the stands taken (v 8).

The episode belongs to the teaching of the Wise. Its setting is determined by its context. Such a teaching in the times of the deceptive politics described in chap. 31, especially in view of that telltale "no longer" in v 5, must be set in the reign of Josiah, for the destruction of Assyria is still ahead.

It may be that this is intended to be presented tongue-in-cheek. The truisms or platitudes of wisdom are presented with mock seriousness as a satirical comment on a society which has neither justice nor righteousness, in which people do not see, hear, know, or say that they have confused the folly and knavery of their political policies with nobility and honor (cf. chap. 31). At this point the Vision may well be in dialogue with the assessment of Josiah's reign given in 2 Kgs 22–23, just as Isa 22 was concerned with the evaluation of Hezekiah.

The kind of form-critical analysis that feels at liberty to restructure the book may miss these points (cf. most recently, G. Stansell, *SBL Seminar Papers* [1983] 4–7).

Comment

1–2 The lesson begins with the definition of rulers, *kings* and *princes.* They are to be identified with *justice* and *righteousness.* They are to be symbols of security and vital prosperity.

3–4 The second and perhaps key definition of the episode deals with the public. Even in a nondemocratic society, the perception and support of the public are necessary for the government. They were in Israel. The public has *eyes, ears, minds,* and *tongues.* But they are not often used, as was apparently the case in that time. If those faculties are used to *look,* to *hearken,* to *know,* and to *speak,* the public good is served, for the character and motives of public officials (implied are the king and his ministers) can be understood and judged on their merit.

5 The implication of *no longer* is that this has not been the case. *Fools* and *knaves* are being called *noble* and *honorable* without challenge. The Vision complains repeatedly that Israel and Jerusalem are blind, deaf, unperceptive, unknowing (1:3; 6:9–10; *et al*). Usually this refers to God and his plans. Here the reference is to politics and the character of the leaders. The immediate reference is to the age of Josiah, but the intention of the Vision includes the failure of later ages to correctly assess the mistakes of that earlier period, thereby making false judgments in their own times.

6–8 The remaining verses give definitions which may help to eliminate the confusion.

6 *The fool.* In the Wisdom schools the fool was regularly contrasted with "the wise" (cf. Proverbs). He is the one who has failed to master the disciplines of wisdom. But he is also the one who has a weak character, is easily tempted, and is impetuous in his decisions. The fool can be recognized by: foolish speech, a mind dedicated to wickedness, an ungodly lifestyle, and by heresy spoken against Yahweh. That should be clear enough for the public to recognize. The results of having a fool in charge of things include neglect of welfare programs and failure to take care of water resources in a dry country. That should be warning enough of the consequences of allowing a fool to rule.

7 *A knave* is different from the bumbling fool. He knows better. He deliberately chooses means that are *evil* and hatches *evil plots.* His victims are *the poor* and *the needy,* God's special wards according to the prophets and the Torah. His weapons are slander and false testimony, in the very courts that are intended to protect the rights of the people. The definition is clear. No knowledgeable public should tolerate a knave in government.

8 *A noble* (נדיב) is here only defined by reusing the same word. BDB (621–22) relates the word to meanings of motivation and voluntariness. The implication is that this is one who has no ulterior motive, who can deal objectively, thinking in ways that are not dictated by his personal interests. *Noble things* are those which such an independent and willing person would support. He would be free of the pressures of party and special interests. The arch structure suggests that nobility be related to the justice and righteousness of v 1.

Explanation

The "civics lesson" gives the hearer/reader the tools to pass judgment on the leaders and their policies described in chap. 31. Are "those who go to Egypt" to be termed fools, knaves, or noble men? Chap. 31 would probably have accepted both the designations of fool and knave as accurate. The episode also serves to place the blame on the public. Any public that fails to recognize the character of its public officials, that fails to speak out in protest and thus bring about changes in personnel and policy shares the blame for the results. The people of God are often blind, unperceptive, and uncommunicative, not only about the ways of God, but also about the ways of men in leadership and government. When they are so, they stand judged along with the fools and knaves they failed to identify and remove.

Episode C: Until Spirit Is Poured Out (32:9–20)

Bibliography

Barth, J. "Eine verkannte hebräische Imperativform." *ZDMG* 56 (1902) 247–48. **Eichrodt, W.** *Die Hoffnung des ewigen Friedens im alten Israel.* BFCT 25. Gütersloh: C. Bertelsmann, 1920. **Fensham, F. C.** "The Wild Ass in the Aramean Treaty Between Bar-Ga'ayah and Mati'el." *JNES* 22 (1963) 185–86. **Gross, H.** *Die Idee des ewigen und allgemeinen Weltfriedens im Alten Orient und im Alten Testament.* TTS 7. Trier: Paulinus-Verlag, 1967. **Humbert, P.** "פֶּרֶא: zèbre ou onagre?" *ZAW* 62 (1949/50) 202–6. **Köhler, L.** "פֶּרֶא = Equus Grevyi Oustalet." *ZAW* 44 (1926) 59–62. **Lofthouse, W. F.** "The Beatitude of Security." *ExpTim* 48 (1936) 505–9. **Schmid, H. H.** *Salôm. 'Frieden' im Alten Orient und im Alten Testament.* SBS 51. Stuttgart: Verlag Katholisches Bibelwerk, 1971. **Stansell, G.** "Isaiah 32: Creative Redaction in the Isaiah Traditions." *SBL Seminar Papers.* Chico, CA: Scholars Press, 1983. 2–4, 7–11. **Vattioni, F.** "I precedenti letterari di Isaia 32:17. Et erit opus iustitiae pax." *RivB* 6 (1958) 23–32. **Vollers, K.** "Zu Jesajas 32:11." *ZDMG* 57 (1903) 375. **Westermann, C.** "Der Frieden (Shalom) im Alten Testament." *Studien zur Friedensforschung* 1. Stuttgart: E. Klett, 1969.

Translation

First Speaker: 9 *Women* [a] *at ease,* 2+3
rise up! Heed my voice!
Complacent [b] *daughters,* [a] 2+2
give ear to my speech!
10a *(In) just days less than a year* [a] 2+2
you will shudder, complacent women.
For a grape-harvest shall fail, 3+3
a fruit-harvest will not [b] *arrive.*
11 *Tremble,* [ab] *you at ease!* 2+2
Shudder, [b] *you complacent!*
Strip, [b] *and be bare!* [b] 2+2+2
Sackcloth on loins,
12 *on mourning breasts!* [a]
Incredulous Woman: *Over pleasant fields,* 3+3
over fruitful vine,
13 *over my people's ground* 3+3
briers (and) thorns will grow up?

Second Speaker: *Indeed* [a]*—over every joyous house!* 3+2
Happy city!
14 *For a palace* [a] *shall be forsaken.* 2+3
A populous city shall be deserted.
Ophel [b] *and Bachan* [c] *shall become* [d] 3+3
caves [e] *for an age,*
a joy for zebra, [f] 2+2
pasture (for) wild asses. [g]
Chorus of Women: 15 *Until spirit is poured upon us from above,* 4+3+3
and a wilderness becomes the fruitful field,
and a fruitful field [a] *is considered the forest?*
16 *(As) justice is at home in the wilderness,* 3+3
(so) righteousness abides in the fruitful field.
Second Speaker: 17 *The result of righteousness is peace* 4+2+3
and the product of righteousness
quietness and trust for an age,
18 *so that people dwell in peaceful homes,* 4+2+2
in secure dwellings,
and in quiet resting places.
First Speaker: 19 *The forest descends* [a] *with condescension.* [b] 3+3
The city is debased [c] *in humiliation.* [d]
20 *The fortunate ones of you* 1+2+3
are those who sow beside all waters,
who send out [a] *the feet of the ox and the ass.*

Notes

9.a. Tg מדינן "provinces" for MT נשים "women" and כרכין "cities" for בנות "daughters." Wildberger (1262) commends Tg insofar as it has correctly seen that the passage addresses cities or a specific city. But this has robbed readers of arriving at that identification for themselves.

9.b. בטחות "complacent, trusting" is a rare case of Masoretes leaving a letter (ט) with no vowel sign or syllable divider on it.

10.a-a. ימים על־שנה lit. "days upon a year" is unclear. Wildberger (1262) translates "concerning year and day." Irwin (127–28) has an intensive discussion to support his view that "days" and "year" should be viewed as synonymous "in a year plus a year" and translates "next year." This is the only time reference in the passage, so there is no parallel to measure by. Perhaps Wildberger is nearer right. These do not give a measure of time, but state the subject of the warnings that deal with seasonal disasters of nature. The most natural meaning, however, seems to be "in just days less than a year."

10.b. MT בלי "without" (BDB, 115; GKC § 152t); DSS[Isa] בל. Either reading is possible. Irwin (128) explains DSS[Isa] as "the scribal practice of writing a shared consonant only once."

11.a. Syr *zwʿjn* (supported by Syh Eth Arab) suggests reading חֲרָדָה (aramaizing imperative 2 fem pl; GKC § 48i), an ancient attempt to deal with the masc imperatives (see *BHS*).

11.b. These imperatives are masc although they are addressed to women. The discussion has been intense (cf. Wildberger, 1263; Irwin, 128–29). It is best to let MT stand and translate simply.

12.a. LXX *κόπτεσθε* "beat yourself." *BHS* recommends reading impf 2 fem for MT's pl ptcp סֹפְדִים "lamentings." Irwin (128) translates as a relative clause: "at your breasts that mourn." But the על phrases should be parallel. The first two, "on loins . . . on breasts," are parallel. The next three plus one are parallel. Irwin (130) calls these על of motive referring to BDB,

745a. But if they are governed by the following "will grow up," of course they refer to place. (See note 14.d.)

13.a. כי is emphatic here.

14.a. "Palace" is singular as are "city," "Ophel/hill," and "Bachan/watchtower."

14.b. עפל "a hill" (BDB, 779) an acropolis within a city perhaps Jerusalem. Irwin (131) transliterates as a proper name "Ophel."

14.c. בחן "watchtower" (BDB, 103) is a *hapax.* Erman & Grapow (*Wörterbuch der aegyptisches Sprache,* I [Leipzig: Heinrichs, 1926] 47) call it an Egyptian loan word. See Wildberger (1264).

14.d. בְּעַד "in place of" (BDB, 126). But this does not make good sense. Irwin (131–32) would emend to בָּעַד "forever" following Fohrer. But Masoretic Hebrew has no other usage like this. Seeking a solution, most scholars omit the word. The particle should be seen as the first of a series in vv 14b–15. עד defines the end result for the series of things governed by על in vv 12–13 which are transformed. Exact translation is difficult. For על, "in place of." For עד(ב) after היה "will be," something like "ultimately" or "finally," indicating the resultant condition.

14.e. מערות may be derived from ערה to mean "bare places" (BDB, 789; *CHAL,* 208; G. R. Driver, *JSS* 13 [1968] 52) or from ערר to mean "caves" (BDB, 792).

14.f. Cf. L. Köhler, *ZAW* 44 (1926) 59; and *CHAL,* 296. But cf. also P. Humbert, *ZAW* 62 (1949/50) 202–6.

14.g. עדרים "flocks" (BDB, 727), but note the ambiguity of the root. The repetition of עד in this passage suggests reading עד רים "even for wild asses" (BDB, 910, reading רים as ראם with BDB, 937).

15.a. K וכרמל "and a fruitful field"; Q והכרמל "and the fruitful field." Wildberger (1273) thinks the Massoretes thought of the mountain near Haifa, though this cannot be the meaning here. K keeps the parallel with the previous stich: the indefinite becomes defined. The use of articles is very carefully done here.

19.a. MT וברד "it shall hail" (BDB, 136) is a *hapax.* Tg ויחות ברד "and hail will descend"; Syr similarly. *BHS* cites one MS וירד "will descend." J. Reider ("Contributions to the Scriptural Text," *HUCA* 24 [1952–53] 88) followed by G. R. Driver (*JSS* 13 [1968] 52) compares Arab *baruda* to mean "it is cool": "the forest will be cool." Irwin (133–34) derives ברד from a root that usually occurs as פרד "cut, divide" (BDB, 825) and cites E. Ullendorff ("Ugaritic Marginalia II," *JSS* 7 [1962] 345) and E. Lipiński ("Banquet en l'honneur de Baal, CTA 3 [VAB], A, 2–22," *UF* 2 [1970] 78) to support his view that ב and פ are frequently interchanged. Ugar *brd* has this meaning. *BHS* and Wildberger have the best reading, וירד "descends."

19.b. ברדת, preposition and inf constr from ירד (BDB, 432) "with descending, condescension." This repetition of the same root is an artistic device, contrasting the following pair. Irwin (134) understands this as a noun and translates "with an ax."

19.c. תשפל "become low, be abased" (BDB, 1050).

19.d. ובשפלה "humiliation" (BDB, 1050), a *hapax* related to שפל that follows.

20.a. משלחי "sending out" (BDB, 1018) may mean, as here, "driving cattle." But it also means "stretch out" a hand or a weapon against a foe. The double entendre is deliberate in contrasting the passive pastorale to the previous history of activist warfare.

Form/Structure/Setting

The episode develops as a dialogue between a speaker and a group of women. They may be pictured as gathered around a well. They are small-town housewives, economically dependent upon the vineyards and the orchards surrounding the town which witness to generations of skill and labor in planting, tending, and protecting. The dialogue contrasts developed urban and rural society with the devastation to come in "less than a year." There is nothing but the context to hint at the historical setting intended. The first-person speech and the chorus, often found in the Vision, are heard here. There is no evidence that God is the speaker. The prophet's justification for the disaster is also absent. There is only the concession that where justice and righteousness abide peace and stability can be found, which is obviously not the case here.

Commment

9 The *women at ease* would appear to be an ordinary group of Judean women, perhaps lounging around a well while the slowly flowing water fills their jars. They are at ease because the normal patterns of the agricultural year move ahead with promise of harvest; their homes are secure, their families intact.

10 Yet, the speaker warns, in less than a year disaster will strike. The *harvests will fail.* That would be a blow to the village.

11 The speaker with emotion urges them to extreme responses of mourning. Stripping off normal clothing and wearing underclothes of rough sackcloth were signs of mourning reserved for death or for an extreme disaster.

12–13 An incredulous person cannot believe that the currently fruitful and well-cared-for fields which her people had owned and cultivated for generations could be allowed to lie waste.

14 The speaker affirms his warning and extends it to the village itself, to cities, even to the palace. *Ophel* is the original core of Jerusalem which came to house the temple and the palace (cf. *MBA,* 114) or it may simply refer to a hilltop, such as was frequently the place of a walled town. *Bachan* means a watchtower. If Ophel is understood as a proper name, then Bachan would be likely to be a particular tower on the walls of Jerusalem. If Ophel is taken to be "hilltop" then it simply refers to watchtowers in general, i.e., to the defenses of the country at large. *Zebra* and *wild ass* have no significance except to illustrate that the towns are uninhabited by human society.

15 The chorus of women still do not believe the message. They ask in effect: How long will this last? as they recite the litany of hope that in a future age the spirit of God will make all the world fruitful and productive.

16 They comment that the wilderness has no monopoly on *justice. Righteousness* can live in developed culture as well as in a primitive wasteland. They seem to assume here the implied accusation of injustice and unrighteousness to account for the disastrous judgment, although the speaker had said nothing to this effect. They also seem to be reading into the announcement of disaster a theology which implied that Israel was righteous in the wilderness but had become corrupted by the culture of the developed land.

17–18 A speaker representing the women lectures the first speaker: righteousness produces *peace* and stability which her people now have every right to expect.

19 The *forest* is clearly a metaphor which must refer to the larger political or economic unit, whether the kingdom or the empire. Either could fit here. Assyria is on its last legs and the Kingdom of Judah is experiencing its last real existence or prosperity under Josiah. The *city* may refer to Jerusalem or simply to the culture that is based on city-states. The villages and their prosperity were dependent on what was happening in the surrounding world, whether they knew it or not.

20 This last verse looks almost with envy at those who have little to lose, who are not bound to houses and fields. They can move to avoid danger, can exist in almost any circumstances, and can simply drive their assets (*ox* and *ass*) to another place to start over again. That is difficult for the landowner and planter.

Explanation

The episode warns of a coming disaster that will wipe out a way of life. The women, looking about them at the homes and fields that make up their lives, see only peace, tranquility, and prosperity. They presume that this implies that justice and righteousness have brought this about and will continue to guarantee their future. They are examples of the blind, deaf, and uncomprehending people that the Vision has complained about throughout. It is hard, in the midst of plenty, to imagine hunger. It is hard, in the setting of economic and social order, to imagine chaos and disruption.

Yet the earlier episodes have pictured wrong-headed political policies and major international upheavals in the making. No interior small town, no matter how isolated, will escape the resulting problems. The relation between justice/righteousness and order/prosperity is not wrong. But the failure to see beneath the surface the things that were anything but just and righteous constituted culpable blindness.

Civilized and developed societies can be comfortable and efficient, but they are also very vulnerable. Loss of some basic services can threaten life itself. Those who had never come to depend on those services or structures survive very nicely without them. They are to be envied in the time of disaster. Although there is no "thus says the Lord" word from a prophet, the whole flow of dialogue reveals the intended meaning.

Scene 5: God's Promise to Judge the Tyrant (33:1–24)

In this final scene, Isaiah's vision approaches a major critical point as violence increases and God prepares to intervene. As the first episode opens ("Woe, You Destroyer," 33:1–6), immanent violence brings reactions from Yahweh's counselors and from a chorus in Jerusalem. In Episode B, "See Their Valiant One" (33:7–12), the situation becomes worse. In Episode C, "Who Can Survive the Fire?" (33:13–24), Yahweh intervenes. Those near and far are challenged to assess the event and recognize what the results of God's intervention will be.

Episode A: Woe, You Destroyer! (33:1–6)

Bibliography

Gerlach, M. *Die prophetischen Liturgien des Alten Testaments.* Diss. Bonn, 1967. **Gunkel, H.** "Jesaja 33, eine prophetische Liturgie." *ZAW* 42 (1924) 177–208. **Poynder, A.**

" 'Be Thou Their Arm Every Morning.' Isaiah 33:2." *ExpTim* 13 (1901/02) 94. **Schoeps, H. J.** "Ein neuer Engelname in der Bibel? (Zur Übersetzung des Symmachus von Jes 11:3)." *ZRGG* 1 (1948) 86–87. **Weiss, R.** "On Ligatures in the Hebrew Bible (נו = ם)." *JBL* 82 (1963) 188–94.

Translation

Heavens: 1 *Woe, you destroyer,* 2+3
who are not yet being destroyed!
And you traitor 1+2
whom [a] *no one betrays!*
When you finish destroying, [b] *you will be destroyed.* 3+4
As you cease [c] *treachery, someone will betray you.*
Chorus: 2 *Yahweh, have mercy on us!* 2+2
We wait for you!
Be our [a] *arm in the mornings!* 3+3
Yea! Our salvation in a time of siege. [b]
Earth: 3 *From the roaring sound* 2+2
peoples flee! [a]
From your rising up [b] 1+2
nations scatter! [a]
4 *Your* [a] *spoil is gathered* 2+2
(as) the caterpillar [b] *gathers,*
like a locust [b] *attaching,* [c] 2+2
leaping on it.
Chorus: 5 *Yahweh is exalted!* 2+3
Indeed, he dwells on high [a] *!*
He fills Zion 2+2+2
(with) justice and righteousness,
6 *and is* [a] *the* [b] *stability of her times.* [b]
The abundance of salvation, wisdom, [c] *knowledge,* 4+2+2
and fear of Yahweh—
that is his treasure.

Notes

1.a. Many MSS read בָּךְ "you" (cf. *BHS*), probably correctly; cf. note 1.c.

1.b. Irwin (137) calls attention to Zorell's (*Lexicon Hebraicum et Aramaicum* [Rome: Pont. Bib. Inst., 1947], 822b) reading of שׁוֹדֵד as poel inf instead of GKC's (§ 120b) ptcp (cf. Meyer, *Grammatik* III § 108.2b). See Irwin for further discussion.

1.c. MT כַּנְּלֹתְךָ. BDB (649) locates as hiph inf with preposition and suffix from נלה ("obtain"?) with ה prefix absorbed into the *nun.* DSS[Isa] supports the emendation suggested by Döderlein, Lowth, Knobel, and Wildberger to read כְּכַלֹּתְךָ piel inf from כלה "when you cease."

2.a. MT זרעם "their arm." Syr Tg Vg have the 1st pl suffix "our" which fits the context.

2.b. Irwin (138) translated "siege" on the basis of the description of war that follows. See J. Ziegler, "Die Hilfe Gottes am Morgan," in *Altestamentliche Studien,* FS F. Nötscher (Bonn: Hanstein, 1950), 286–88 and other references cited by Irwin.

3.a. Irwin (140) translates these verbs as precative perfects "let peoples flee, let nations scatter," citing M. Buttenwieser's and M. Dahood's use in the Psalms. Irwin overlooks the fact that the speaker has changed in v 3 so that the beginning imperatives are not so closely related to these verbs.

3.b. DSS[Isa] מדממתך "from your silencing" (BDB, 199; J. Lust, "A Gentle Breeze or a Roaring Thunderous Sound?" *VT* 25 [1975] 110–15); LXX ἀπὸ τοῦ φόβου σου "from fear of you." P. Wernburg-Møller ("Defective Spellings in the Isaiah Scroll," *JSS* 3 [1958] 262) sees DSS[Isa] meaning "be scared stiff" and thus parallel to LXX. G. R. Driver (in *Von Ugarit Nach Qumran,* FS O. Eissfeldt, BZAW 77 [Berlin: A. Töpelmann, 1958] 46) posits a noun רממה which like Akk *rimmatu* means "rumbling." Irwin (139) and Dahood divide MT into מרם מתך "at the sound of your soldiers" (M. Dahood, "Ugaritic and Phoenician or Qumran and the Versions," *Orient and Occident,* FS C. H. Gordon [Neukirchen-Vluyn: Neukirchener Verlag, 1973] 53–54). This translation stays with MT.

4.a. שללכם "your spoil." The pl suffix has raised questions. Does it address the chorus of v 2? Does it mean "the spoil you gather" or "the spoil gathered from you"? Syr *ʾjk,* Tg כמא, Vg *sicut,* followed by *BHK, BHS,* and Irwin (141), divide the word in two שלל כמו "spoil like" or כמאסף (joining two letters to the following word) with the same results. The context calls for a comparison in any case, but MT does not need to be changed.

4.b. The exact meanings of these words remain obscure. But the best suggestion is that they are different stages of locust development. Cf. Joel 2:1–11 for the figure of locusts for a military invasion.

4.c. כמשק "like a leap" (BDB, 1055; GKC §§ 67g, 85h) is a *hapax.* LXX συναγάγῃ "gathering" has drawn on the parallel stich for the meaning. H. L. Ginsburg ("Emendations in Isaiah," *JBL* 69 [1950] 57), reversing *shin* and *qoph,* reads a niph כְּמַקֵּשׁ. But the root only occurs in Heb as a polel "gather stubble" (BDB, 905). Irwin (141) reports a suggestion from M. Dahood deriving the word from נשק (BDB, 676, II) "weapons" as a noun. Irwin translated "attack." He maintains the usual meaning "jump" for the following שׁוֹקֵק. This suggestion merits attention. So מַשֵּׁק is a hiph ptcp from נשק meaning "attack."

5.a. LXX ἐν ὑψηλοῖς "in the heights" has inserted a preposition to express the locative meaning of the Heb adverbial accusative (BDB, 928–29).

6.a. MT והיה "and he is" ties the first stich closely with the preceding verse and should be considered a part of it (cf. Irwin, 142).

6.b-b. The difficulties of the phrase have led to a plethora of emendations (see Wildberger, 1284). Irwin (142–43) meets the problem of a 2nd person suffix עתיך "your times" by suggesting the *kaph* be separated and pointed כִּי to begin the next line, and that the *yodh* ending be understood as a 3rd fem pronominal suffix. See his notes for a bibliography. His suggestions are better than emending the text.

6.c. חכמת "wisdom of" is a constr form with no following abs. It is usually read as חכמה "wisdom." However, another possibility should see all four constr nouns, ישועת "salvation," חכמת "wisdom," ודעת "and knowledge," and יראת "fear," as governed by חסן "abundance of" at the beginning and "Yahweh" at the end: a case of delayed or interrupted constr relation.

Form/Structure/Setting

The division of the chapter into three parts has been recognized ever since Gunkel's article. Yet the elements within this first part do not fit a single pattern.

V 1 is a "woe" speech directed against someone accustomed to doing violence who had not yet felt the pressure of reprisal. V 2 is a plea for God's mercy in this time of crisis. Vv 3–4 address God, expecting his intervention. Vv 5–6a announce Yahweh's exaltation on Zion. V 6b–d responds with a summary confession of faith in Yahweh.

No hint of the setting is given. It assumes the "balcony of heaven" setting, so frequent in the Vision, which can accommodate Yahweh and his counselors but also provide direct sight and access to the people of Jerusalem.

Comment

1 The identity of the *destroyer/traitor* is not revealed. The context suggests a time when Assyrian power is waning and Egypt is maneuvering for a favorable position. The most likely identification is Assyria itself. The verse picks up the prediction of 10:12 in the words *when you finish destroying.* The Vision has from the beginning viewed the Assyrian role as one of destruction and judgment. In what sense *traitor/treachery* is understood is not clear, although Assyria will undoubtedly have shared in both.

2 The plea from the people is parallel to many Psalms. *Wait* is an attitude recommended throughout the Vision. Sometimes it represents God's hopes for his people (5:2, 4, 7). More often it confesses the people's hope in God (25:9; 26:8) as here. Sometimes it is contained in a promise (49:23; 51:5). Sometimes it is used in the bitterness of disappointed hope (59:9, 11; 64:3).

3 The *roaring sound* combines the possibilities of battle with indications of Yahweh's approach. They are in some sense identical (note the use of the singular *your*). The resulting flight and chaos is real enough, as peoples and nations scramble to escape the violence.

4 *Your* is plural addressing the people speaking in v 2. It is unclear whether they gain or lose by the plunder. But the chaos is everywhere, allowing the local poor to crawl like *caterpillars* and pounce like *locusts* on the undefended homes and stores.

5–6a In the midst of this chaos *Yahweh is exalted.* What can this mean? He is exalted in *Zion,* which means that he still deserves worship in the temple. Worship provides Zion with a *stability* in troubled times. Beyond that, the chaotic events are understood to serve Yahweh's purposes. He uses them (or introduces them) to promote *justice* and *righteousness* which were not being adequately served in the previous situation.

6b This justifies the confession that *salvation, wisdom, knowledge,* and the *fear of Yahweh* are the treasures that he bestows—a treasure no plunderer can touch. All four words are in construct state in Hebrew, genitives dependent on *Yahweh:* salvation acts of Yahweh, wisdom of Yahweh, knowledge of Yahweh, and the fear of Yahweh.

Explanation

This fifth "woe" moves toward completion of the requiem. It marks the last period of authentic existence for the Kingdom of Judah. Following after laments over elements of the population and over government planners, this episode turns its attention to the first of the great empires, "the rod of God's anger" (10:5), which now approaches collapse. It is time. It has served its purpose and the accumulated guilt of its excesses is about to overwhelm it (cf. Nahum).

But the episode turns from the scene of chaotic defeat and plunder to celebrate Yahweh's place in and above it all. God is in history. He determines its critical changes. There is even purpose in apparent chaos. Beyond that, God provides his most precious treasures in the sanctuary where one celebrates "the abundance of salvation, wisdom, knowledge, and fear of Yahweh," that is, the total spiritual and worship benefits which faith makes possible for those who know themselves to belong to him.

Episode B:
See! Their Valiant One! (33:7–12)

Bibliography

Hillers, D. R. "A Hebrew Cognate of *unussu/'unt* in Isa 33:8." *HTR* 64 (1971) 257–59.

Translation

Heavens: 7 *See! Their valiant one*[a] *(Ariel)!* 2+2
Outside they cry out.
Messengers of peace (Shalom) 2+2
weep bitterly.
8 *Highways are empty!* 2+3
Travelers have ceased!
A treaty has been broken! 2+2+3
One despises witnesses![a]
One has no regard (for) human beings.
Earth: 9 *One mourns!*[a] 1+2
The land languishes!
Lebanon is confounded! 2+1
It is moulded![b]
Sharon is like the desert. 3+3
Bashan and Carmel are shaking[c] *(off their leaves).*
Yahweh: 10 *Now, I will rise up!*[a] 2+2
Herald: *Says Yahweh.*
Yahweh: *Now, I lift myself up!*[b] 2+2
Now, I shall be exalted!
11 *You (pl) conceive chaff!* 2+2+3
You (pl) give birth to stubble!
Your (pl) spirit[a] *(is) a fire (that) will consume you.*
12 *Peoples*[a] *shall become burnt lime:*[b] 4+4
thorns cut down, burned by fire.

Notes

7.a. MT אראלם; a few MSS have a pl אראלים. Wildberger (1294) calls it "simply not understandable." He traces the history of attempts to explain it as from the root ירא "fear" as LXX *ἐν τῷ φόβῳ ὑμῶν* "in your fear," or from the root ראה "see" as DSS[Isa] ארא לם, Syr, Vg *videntes*, 'A *οραθησομαι* and Σ *οφθησομαι* have done with variant forms of "I shall be seen by them." Kimchi and Ibn Ezra thought it meant "messenger," parallel to מלאך in the next stich. Delitzsch divided the word ארי אל "lion of God" (cf. BDB, 72) and thus derived the meaning "their valiant one." RSV follows Delitzsch, but points it as a pl. Irwin (144) translates "the leaders." He considers also the possibility that אלם is a divine name parallel to שלום "Shalom" in the next line and that אר אלם should be translated "kinsmen of El," which would point to the patron God of David's city which appears in אריאל "Ariel" and ירושלם "Jerusalem."

8.a. MT ערים "cities"; DSS[Isa] עדים "witnesses." The context supports DSS[Isa]. Irwin (145) cites Dahood (*Psalms* I, AB 16, 56) for the suggestion that ערים are " 'Protectors' of the covenant who guarantee its existence." He points to the parallel of עיר and שלם in Job 8:6.

9.a. MT אבל "mourns" is masc. It is followed by a fem noun and verb. *BHS* suggests emending to a fem form as the Versions have done. This is superfluous if one maintains an impersonal subject as in the previous verse. Irwin (146) finds a metrical reason to support this.

9.b. MT קמל "be decayed, mouldy" (BDB, 888) is found only here and in 19:6. *CHAL* (319) translates "become infested with injurious insects." Wildberger (1295) disagrees vigorously, following GB and Zorell (*Lexicon*) to maintain "dead plants turning black."

9.c. MT נֹעֵר "shake off its leaves" (BDB, 654, II). LXX *φανερὰ ἔσται* "will be apparent, conspicuous" leads Procksch and *BHS* to read נָעֹר "are bare," an inf for MT's ptcp. Irwin (147) concurs. But the change is unnecessary (see Wildberger, 1295).

10.a. Tg אתגלי "I will reveal myself."

10.b. DSS[Isa] אתרומם makes explicit that MT ארומם "I will raise myself" is in fact a hithpoʿel form with *taw* assimilated (BDB, 927; GKC § 54c; Bauer-Leander, 405).

11.a. As in v 4 the 2nd pl suffix on רוחכם "your (pl) spirit, breath" has proved difficult. Some expect רוח to belong to Yahweh and emend with Gunkel (*ZAW* 42 [1924] 177–208), Kissane, Fohrer, and *BHK* רוחי כמו "my spirit is like fire." Procksch suggests רוח כמו "spirit-like," followed by Irwin (148). Wildberger (1295) defends MT saying that the OT sees no contradiction in "the godless digging their own grave."

12.a. Irwin (148) reads the final *mem* as enclitic and translates "my people." But the parallel "thorns" is pl. MT is to be followed.

12.b. שיד "lime" (BDB, 966). LXX omits. Tg נור "clearing, ploughed-over land" (Jastrow, *Dictionary*, 909). Wildberger (1295) notes that neither seems to have understood the Heb.

Form/Structure/Setting

Vv 7–8 portray the worsening situation. Efforts at compromise and peace have failed. The challenge for combat has been given. V 9 is the sad reaction. In v 10 Yahweh intervenes. The background situation is very near that of Episode A but lacks the narrow focus on Jerusalem.

Comment

7 *Valiant One* is a champion put forward in challenge like Goliath of the Philistines. The Hebrew word is "Ariel" (cf. the discussion in 29:1). The military figure has taken the place of the diplomats, *messengers of peace,* who lament the failure of their efforts.

8 The impending war has emptied the *highways* of commercial traffic. With a *treaty broken* and legal procedures being ignored, violent confrontation with no regard for life or limb is the order of the day.

9 The whole *land* reflects the sorry situation. Commerce, agriculture, even nature itself, stands still. Normal life and growth have ceased, as is usual in war.

10 At this point Yahweh determines to intervene.

11 He begins by telling the belligerents how foolish is their action. It is *a fire* that will consume all of them. A war begun in order to gain an advantage has become a curse of death on the very ones who initiated it. How often that is true!

12 *Burnt lime.* It is not clear whether skeletons are burned to extract lime (as in Amos 2:1) or whether lime is poured over the bodies as they are burnt up. (Cf. W. E. Staples, "Lime," *IDB* 3:134.) The ignominious deaths during such catastrophes cause people to be treated like *thorn-bushes* to be *cut down* and *burnt* up with no respect for human dignity or worth.

Explanation

This description of that ancient crisis in which negotiations gave way to military confrontation with its horrible results has a chillingly modern ring to it. Things have not changed very much. The effects of the war announcement are shown in v 8. The appalled reaction of everyone and everything is pictured in v 9, God's incensed arousal in v 10, his rebuke in v 11, and his prediction in v 12. The emotional spirit of anger in such a situation is like a spark in a powder keg.

Episode C: Who Can Survive the Fire? (33:13–24)

Bibliography

See listings above.

Translation

Yahweh: 13 *You that are far off, hear* [a] 2+2
what I have done!
You that are near, know [b] 2+1
my might!
Chorus: 14 *Sinners in Zion are afraid.* [a] 3+3
A trembling has seized [a] *the godless.*
Who among us can dwell indefinitely [b] 3+2
(with) devouring fire?
Who among us can dwell indefinitely 3+2
(with) everlasting burnings? [c]
Teacher: 15 *One walking (with) righteous acts,* 2+2
one speaking upright things,
one despising gain from acts of oppression, 3+4
one shaking his hands so as not to hold a bribe,
one stopping his ears so as not to consent to [a] *bloodshed,* 4+4
one shutting his eyes so as not to favor [b] *evil,*
16 *only that one will dwell in the heights.* 3+3
Rock fortresses [a] *(will be) his defense.*
His bread will be provided. 2+2
His water will be assured.
Heavens: 17 *Your (sg) eyes will envision a king in his beauty.* 4+3+3
They will see a land [a] *of great distances.* [b]
18 *Your (sg) mind* [a] *will muse on terror:* [b]

Where is the counter? 2+2+3
Where is the weigher?
Where is the one who counts the forts?
Earth: 19 *The barbarous* [a] *people* 2+2
you (sg) will see no more,
the people of speech too obscure to hear, 4+4
a stammering tongue which none could understand.
Heavens: 20 *Envision (sg) Zion:* 2+2
a city of festival gatherings. [a]
Your (sg) eyes will see Jerusalem: 3+2
a quiet habitation,
a tent one will never pack up, [b] 2+4+4
whose stakes one will never again pull up, [c]
none of whose cords will be broken.
Earth: 21 *But rather there* [a] 2+3
Yahweh abides [b] *in majesty!*
A place of rivers, 2+3
streams broad of span
on which no boat moves with oars, [c] 4+4
through which no majestic ship passes.
Chorus: 22 *Indeed Yahweh will be our judge.* 3+2
Yahweh, our commander.
Yahweh, our king. 2+2
He will be our savior.
Heavens: 23 *Your (f sg)* [a] *apportionments* [b] *are released.* 2+2+2
They [c] *cannot reinforce the pedestal of their* [c] *standard.* [d]
They [c] *cannot spread a flag.* [e]
Earth: *At that time it will be divided* 2+2+3
until (there is) spoil aplenty.
(Even) the lame will get their share of plunder.
Heavens: 24 *No inhabitant will complain* 3+1
"I am sick!"
The people dwelling in it (f sg) 3+2
will be forgiven (any) guilt.

Notes

13.a. *BHS* suggests DSS[Isa] has a pf instead of an impv, only a change of vowel. This only because of note 13.b. below. DSS[Isa] has no vowels. LXX ἀκούσονται "they will hear" supports the identification as pf.

13.b. DSS[Isa] ידעו "they know" for MT ודעו impv "know ye." Yet MT makes sense and should be kept in both instances (cf. Wildberger, 1295; Irwin, 148).

14.a. Irwin (149) treats both verbs as precative perfects to be translated as imperatives. But the indicative sense is fitting and has been kept.

14.b יגור "dwell indefinitely" (BDB, 157) is translated "find protection" by Wildberger (1293) while Irwin (149) falls back on the AV's "abide."

14.c. מוקדי "burnings" (BDB, 428) occurs only here and in Ps 102:4 (3). Wildberger (1295) thinks of the altar for burnt offerings in the temple. Irwin (150) translates "braziers."

15.a. Lit., "from hearing deeds of bloodshed." Irwin (151) points to BDB (1034) to note that שמע also means "consent" and should be translated here "not to consent to bloodshed."

15.b. Irwin (151) remarks that ראה ב may mean "look favorably on" (BDB, 908).

16.a. MT מצדות "fortresses." LXX σπηλαίῳ "a cave." Wildberger (1296) correctly notes that מצד is a place that is difficult to get to or attack. Irwin (152) points out Psalm parallels that picture Yahweh's abode as both a mountain and a fortress.

17.a. Irwin's translation (153) of ארץ as "city" is pushing a legitimate identification of city and city-state much too far. The Vision has made a sharp distinction between עיר "city" and ארץ "land."

17.b. Irwin (154) agrees with Gunkel ("Jes 33, eine prophetische Liturgie," *ZAW* 42 [1924] 179) on the meaning "distant" rather than "broad." He lists parallels where ארץ מרחקים always means distant city/land: Isa 13:5; 46:11; Jer 4:16; 6:20; Prov 25:25. He thinks it refers to the distant heavenly Zion.

18.a. Lit., "heart."

18.b. אימה "terror" (BDB, 33). The interpretation of this word determines that of v 19. If it is "terror," it means "the former terror" (NIV). If, however, one translates with Irwin (155) "awesome sight," it refers to the envisioned Holy City. To get this he reads אֲיֻמָּה from אָיֹם (BDB, 33) which occurs only in Hab 1:7 and Cant 6:4, 10 in this meaning. MT's more usual form אֵימָה (BDB, 33–34) apparently always means "terror." The issue turns on whether one translates v 18 to fit v 17 or v 19. Most translators have done the latter, Irwin and JPSA the former. I will do the former here, but discuss both in *Comment.*

19.a. נוֹעָז "barbarous" is a *hapax* which must be a niph ptcp. BDB (418) derives it from יעז "barbarous." Wildberger (1310) derives it from עזז "be strong" (BDB, 738) possibly meaning "insolent." Irwin (157) compares Ps 114:1 and Isa 25:3 and relates to יעז which he calls a by-root of עזז. He translates with BDB "barbarous." *BHS* לוֹעֵז follows Ewald's emendation (I, 476) referring to Ps 114:1, but this is now unnecessary.

20.a. MT מועדנו sg "our appointed festival, assembly" which Irwin (158) defends as referring to the heavenly assembly in line with his interpretation of previous verses. DSS[Isa] and the Versions read מועדינו pl "our festivals or assemblies" which fits an understanding of a restored Jerusalem with its annual pilgrimage festivals.

20.b. יצען is a *hapax.* BDB (858) translate "wander, travel"; *CHAL* (308) "pack up."

20.c. MT יִסַּע "plucked up" (BDB נסע, I, 652). Several versions read a passive like יֻסַּע. *BHS* suggests יסעו a pl to fit the subject. All are possible but MT is to be kept.

21.a. שם "there." Irwin (158) identifies it with *šumma* of the El Amarna tablets (cf. W. L. Moran, "Amarna *šumma* in Main Clauses," *JCS* 7 [1953] 78–80) and translates "look upon." For other bibliography see Irwin.

21.b. לָנוּ "for us." The word can also be a 3 m pl pf from לון (BDB, 533) "lodge, abide." This would fit the contrast to v 20. A problem lies in its pl form. But if the divine subject could be seen as sufficient to account for that, its meaning would be clear. Otherwise one could transfer *wāw* to the following word leaving לָן.

21.c. אֳנִי־שַׁיִט "a row-boat." But שיט is found only here and K of 28:15. DSS[Isa] reads שט which P. Wernburg-Møller ("Defective Spellings in the Isaiah Scroll," *JSS* 3 [1958] 262) understands to be a ptcp. The parallel to צי אדיר "stately ship" has led to the translation "galley," a big rowboat indeed, even if a bit ridiculous for an inland city like Jerusalem.

23.a. The suffix is fem sg. This usually refers to Zion, as it does here (cf. v 24b). Tg and *BHS* have missed the point.

23.b. חבל can mean "cord, band" (BDB, 286) and is often connected with the nautical picture in v 21 to read "tackle." But a second word with the same letters means "pain, pang." Another meaning of the first usage is "a measured portion, lot."

23.c. The 3 pl "they" must refer to the foreign rulers of the city.

23.d. תרן "standard" means a pole (BDB, 1076). If the nautical imagery is used it is the "mast." For the flag, it is the "flagpole."

23.e. נס "flag" has been translated "sail" in the nautical image. But it is the symbol of authority.

Form/Structure/Setting

Yahweh challenges those near and far to "hear" and "know" (v 13). The rest of the episode responds to that challenge, assessing what the results of God's intervention and rebuke will be.

Vv 14–16 reflect on the tension inherent in "dwelling with the devouring fire," that is, in depending on and worshiping Yahweh who in his holiness is understood to devour whole nations. This issue was an old one in Israel. It was first faced by Abraham on Moriah (Gen 22). Then Moses wrestled with the issue on Sinai (Exod 19–34). The liturgies used when entering the temple, where one experienced the presence of the holy God, dealt with it (Pss 15; 24:3–6). The answer given here may be compared to the Psalms.

Vv 17–19. Jerusalem is called to imagine what life will be like without the reminders of the distant liege-lord, without the terrors of secret police, tax collectors, or strangers with foreign accents, who for more than a century had ruled over them.

Vv 20–22. In a different frame of mind, Jerusalem is called to think of herself as a city preparing for a festival in honor of Yahweh.

Vv 23–24 return to the political and economic results following the withdrawal of the emperor's representatives.

The historical setting is the period which ended effective Assyrian administration of Judah. The last decades of Assyrian suzerainty were chaotic. Babylon turned back an Assyrian army in 626 B.C. Scythian invasions of Palestine during the following decade cloud the picture. Historians have had difficulty determining whose side Egypt was on in these struggles between Babylon and Assyria between 626 and 609 B.C. If this is true at this distance, how much more confusing must it have been for those living at that time? (See the introduction to Act V.)

Comment

13 Yahweh's challenge sounds like one which would be heard during the celebration of his reign in Zion's temple.

14 *Sinners/godless* point to those who have turned away from Yahweh during the times when foreign powers (and gods?) were in charge of things. They include outright idolaters who worshiped Assyrian deities, those who became indifferent to Yahweh worship, and those who took advantage of the uncertainty to ignore all laws of justice and decency. They had good reason to tremble at the thought that Yahweh and Yahwism would dominate Jerusalem. They see in Yahweh only the *devouring fire/the everlasting burnings.* For the sinner and the rebel it could not be otherwise. They cannot *dwell* or abide in the presence of Deity (cf. 66:24). That Yahweh is *a devouring fire* is understood throughout the OT as a symbol of his holiness. The essence of worship is to recognize the gift of his mercy which makes it possible and even desirable to live in near contact with the Holy One.

15 God has chosen the kind of persons he wants to dwell with him: those doing *righteous acts* and speaking *upright things,* those having nothing to do with *oppression* or a *bribe,* and those who avoid violence or *evil.* What separates a person from God is not finite vulnerability to his holy fire, but incompatibility in terms of character and commitment. It is the *sinner* and the *godless* who cannot abide God's presence, not the human penitent and worshiper who follows God's principles in life.

16 One so committed and of such character is welcome to *the heights,* be they of Zion or of what it represents as God's dwelling place. God will be that person's *defense* and provide for his or her needs.

17 *Your* is masculine singular, apparently addressing the individual worshiper. The vision set before him deals with anticipated realities in government and society. *A king in his beauty* means one in his official royal regalia. It does not define what (or what kind of) king. It brings to mind a Judean king who can in his own dignity and worth appear before the people as his own person—not simply a vassal puppet of some other power. Judah achieved such a status for a brief period under Josiah. *A land of great distances* describes an enlarged area under the control of the crown. This, too, was Judah's experience under Josiah.

18 The *terror* will only be a memory, defined by experiences with *the counter and the weigher* in the humiliating routine of collecting taxes and with the military supervisor of *forts,* who kept a watchful eye to see that Judah's forces were able to join Assyrian expeditions when ordered to do so but were not so strong as to encourage dreams of rebellion.

19 The vision of the new time makes the presence of foreigners, military and civilian officials and observers, with their strange accents and obscure speech, only a memory.

20 The worshiper is challenged to *envision Zion* after the withdrawal of the Assyrians: a city of stability and permanence where the quiet is interrupted only by its festivals.

21 It will be a city known by Yahweh's presence celebrated in *majesty. A place of rivers* is a metaphor with no real counterpart in Jerusalem. *Rivers* are symbols of prosperity, smooth in contrast to the ocean's waves. The absence of *boats with oars* and *majestic ships* contrasts it to the Nile and the Euphrates where imperial naval ships and royal barges are found. Their absence symbolizes the return of Jerusalem to the status of a small, landlocked country with no need of such.

22 Not the emperor but Yahweh will be *judge, commander, king,* and *savior.* The city apparently returns to the status of Israel before Saul was made king when Samuel could protest "Yahweh was your king" (1 Sam 12:12b).

23 *Your* is feminine singular referring to the city. "Lot" or *apportionment* is the normal Hebrew reading of this word. Wildberger (1318) follows others in other meanings to fit a presumed Egyptian setting for the previous verse. But *boats/ships* are not the dominating motif here. Recognizing Yahweh as *king, judge, commander,* and *savior* in place of the emperor called for a new political and economic order. With tax collectors gone (v 18) new economic arrangements had to be made at all levels. *Apportionments* applies to the fields that are assigned peasants to work for a period. It applies to the assignment of lands that belong to the crown and to permits to do business in the cities. Now that the Assyrian overlord is no longer present many changes are called for. The Assyrians can no longer enforce their authority or defend their *flag.* The fact that the military and police officials are already gone means that the civilian apparatus must soon follow. When they are gone *it* (the *apportionments*) will be divided up again. There will be jobs and privileges and land, *spoil aplenty* to be divided by the new ruler. Obviously, hometown people will get their share of things which foreigners and their lackeys had enjoyed before. *Even the lame will get their share.*

24 None will be *sick* on that day, or disadvantaged in the division of spoils. There will be a general amnesty for past crimes to celebrate the return of freedom.

Explanation

The episode is an illustration of the close relation between religion and politics in ancient Judah. The event described is political. Assyria must relinquish sovereignty over the city, along with all the privileges that this entailed. But the result is described in terms of Yahweh's reoccupation of the city, its defense, and its economic structure.

The episode is also consistent with the Vision's position. The future for Jerusalem and for Israel will not include the reconstitution of the Davidic kingdom. It will bring recognition that Yahweh is present in Jerusalem and may be worshiped there.

"Indeed Yahweh will be our king . . . our savior!" (v 22).

Index of Authors Cited

Index of Principal Subjects

Index of Biblical Texts

A. The Old Testament

B. Old Testament Apocrypha and Pseudepigrapha

C. New Testament

D. Dead Sea Scrolls

Index of Key Hebrew Words